# PNEUMATIC DISCERNMENT IN THE APOCALYPSE
## AN INTERTEXTUAL AND PENTECOSTAL EXPLORATION

# PNEUMATIC DISCERNMENT IN THE APOCALYPSE

## AN INTERTEXTUAL AND PENTECOSTAL EXPLORATION

### DAVID R. JOHNSON

CPT Press
Cleveland, Tennessee

Pneumatic Discernment in the Apocalypse
An Intertextual and Pentecostal Exploration

Published by CPT Press
900 Walker ST NE
Cleveland, TN 37311
USA
email: cptpress@pentecostaltheology.org
website: www.cptpress.com

Library of Congress Control Number: 2018936057

ISBN: 9781935931683

To

Mom and Dad
You have put the Pentecostal in my Pentecostal context.

# TABLE OF CONTENTS

Acknowledgements ........................................................................... ix
Abbreviations ................................................................................... x

**Introduction** ................................................................................ 1
Outline and Structure of the Monograph ..................................... 1

**Chapter 1**
**Pentecostal Hermeneutics** ...................................................... 4
   Pentecostals and Intertextuality ........................................... 4
   A Pentecostal Story ................................................................ 10
   A Story of Developments in Pentecostal Hermeneutics ............ 16
   A Pentecostal (Con)textual Hermeneutic: Community,
   Scripture, and the Spirit ......................................................... 21
   Conclusion .............................................................................. 48

**Chapter 2**
**Exploring the Scholarly (Con)texts of Pneumatology and**
**Pneumatic Discernment in the Apocalypse** ........................ 50
   1907–1926 ............................................................................. 52
   1951–1975 ............................................................................. 54
   1980–2005 ............................................................................. 59
   2006–2017 ............................................................................. 77
   Conclusions ........................................................................... 99

**Chapter 3**
**Discerning the Testimonies of Wesleyan-Holiness**
**Pentecostalism** ......................................................................... 101
   The Apostolic Faith ................................................................ 102
   The Bridegroom's Messenger .................................................. 111
   The Whole Truth ..................................................................... 130
   The Church of God Evangel ..................................................... 133
   The Pentecostal Holiness Advocate and The Apostolic Faith . 146
   Summary of the Wesleyan-Holiness Stream ............................ 155

**Chapter 4**
**Discerning the Testimonies of Finished-Work**
**Pentecostalism** ........................................................................ 157
   The Pentecost ....................................................................... 157
   The Latter Rain Evangel ....................................................... 160
   Word and Witness ................................................................. 169
   The Weekly/Christian Evangel ............................................. 172
   Summary of the Finished-Work Stream ................................. 189
   Conclusions from the Early Pentecostal (Con)text(s) ............... 190

**Chapter 5**
**Discerning the Biblical Intertext: Pneumatic Discernment in**
**the Apocalypse** ........................................................................ 193
   Introduction ......................................................................... 193
   Prologue – Revelation 1.1–1.8 .............................................. 196
   ἐν πνεύματι – Revelation 1.9–3.22 ........................................ 199
   ἐν πνεύματι – Revelation 4.1–16.21 ...................................... 229
   ἐν πνεύματι – Revelation 17.1–21.8 ...................................... 308
   ἐν πνεύματι – Revelation 21.9–22.5 ...................................... 336
   Epilogue – Revelation 22.6-21 .............................................. 342

**Chapter 6**
**Pneumatic Discernment, the Apocalypse, and Pentecostal**
**Theology** .................................................................................. 347
   Pneumatic Discernment and the One on the Throne, the Seven
   Spirits, and Jesus ................................................................... 350
   Pneumatic Discernment and the Means of Discerning the Truth
   in the Apocalypse .................................................................. 356
   Pneumatic Discernment and the Church ................................ 375
   Pneumatic Discernment of the Apocalypse and Acts 15 in Inter-
   textual Dialogue .................................................................... 385
   Summary ............................................................................... 389

**Conclusions and Suggestions for Further Research**      391
   Conclusions .......................................................................... 391
   Suggestions for Further Research .......................................... 392
   Appendix 1 ........................................................................... 394
   Bibliography ......................................................................... 397
   Index of Biblical (and Other Ancient) References .................. 421
   Index of Authors ................................................................... 427

# ACKNOWLEDGEMENTS

This monograph is a slightly revised version of my PhD thesis completed at Bangor University, Wales, UK, under the supervision of John Christopher Thomas. I want to thank everyone at CPT Press who have worked tirelessly to make this publication a reality. It is a great honor for this piece to appear alongside the work of numerous remarkable scholars who have published at CPT Press, where much work has been dedicated to the study of the Apocalypse and Pentecostal theology.

I want to thank John Christopher Thomas, my *Doktorvater*, for his invaluable guidance throughout the process. You have has been a patient and kind mentor. To my fellow Bangor PhD students, a group that has become so large that space limits me from naming everyone, I wish to thank you for all the time and effort that you have dedicated over the years to read my various drafts attentively and for offering constructive and encouraging comments.

I would like to offer a word of thanks to the New Covenant community, particularly everyone who is part of our small group. Your encouragement throughout the process has been deeply appreciated. I would like to thank Morgan Waldrop for proofing a number of my drafts; your help was indispensable. Anna Spears, I appreciate all your wise counsel that you have offered throughout the writing process.

I would like to thank my family. Without your support and without the tradition that you have given me, this work would not be what it has become. Finally, I would like to thank my wife, Autumn. First of all, thank you for the graphic of the 666 as a triangular number. Your love and support throughout the process cannot be expressed with words. You have supported me throughout the lengthy and challenging process. Your encouragement is tremendous. Your patience is long-suffering. Your kindness is endless. Thank you for all you have done.

# ABBREVIATIONS

## Early Pentecostal Periodicals

| | |
|---|---|
| *AE* | *The Apostolic Evangel* |
| *AF* | *The Apostolic Faith* |
| *CE* | *The Christian Evangel* |
| *COGE* | *The Church of God Evangel* |
| *LRE* | *The Latter Rain Evangel* |
| *PE* | *The Pentecostal Evangel* |
| *PHA* | *The Pentecostal Holiness Advocate* |
| *PT* | *Pentecostal Testimony* |
| *TBM* | *The Bridegroom's Messenger* |
| *TP* | *The Pentecost* |
| *TWT* | *The Whole Truth* |
| *WE* | *Weekly Evangel* |
| *WW* | *Word and Witness* |

## Other Abbreviations

| | |
|---|---|
| ABC | Anchor Bible Commentary |
| ABYC | Anchor Bible Yale Commentary |
| ACC | Weinrich, W. (ed.), *Ancient Christian Commentary on Scripture: Revelation* (Vol. XII; Downers Grove, IL: InterVarsity Press, 2005). |
| ACT | Ancient Christian Texts |
| *AJPS* | *Asian Journal of Pentecostal Studies* |
| ANTC | Abingdon New Testament Commentaries |
| *ATR* | *Anglican Theology Review* |
| *AUSS* | *Andrews University Seminary Studies* |
| *BASOR* | *Bulletin of the American Schools of Oriental Research* |
| BBC | Blackwell Bible Commentaries |
| *BBR* | *Bullentin for Biblical Research* |

| | |
|---|---|
| BECNT | Baker Exegetical Commentary on the New Testament |
| *BLT* | *Brethren Life and Thought* |
| BNTC | Black's New Testament Commentary Series |
| BTC | Brazos Theological Commentary Series |
| BZNW | Beihefte zur Zeitschrift für die neutestamentliche Wissenschaft |
| *CBQ* | *Catholic Biblical Quarterly* |
| *CBW* | *Conversations with the Biblical World* |
| *CC* | *The Christian Century* |
| CCSS | Catholic Commentary on Sacred Scripture |
| *CTJ* | *Calvin Theological Journal* |
| CPT | Centre for Pentecostal Theology |
| *CBQ* | *Catholic Biblical Quarterly* |
| *CBR* | *Currents in Biblical Research* |
| *CTQ* | *Concordia Theological Quarterly* |
| DBCI | Porter, S.E. (ed.), *Dictionary of Biblical Criticism and Interpretation* (New York, NY: Routledge, 2007). |
| DPCM | Burgess, S.M., et al. (eds.), *Dictionary of Pentecostal and Charismatic Movements* (Grand Rapids: Zondervan, 1988). |
| EBC | Expositor's Bible Commentary |
| EDNT | Balz, H. and G. Schneider (eds.), *Exegetical Dictionary of the New Testament* (3 vols. Grand Rapids: Eerdmans, 1990-1993). |
| *EQ* | *Evangelical Quarterly* |
| FG | Fourth Gospel |
| HB | Hebrew Bible |
| *HTS* | *Harvard Theological Studies* |
| ICC | International Critical Commentary |
| *Int* | *Interpretation* |
| *IJST* | *International Journal of Systematic Theology* |
| *JATS* | *Journal of the Adventist Theological Society* |
| *JBL* | *Journal of Biblical Literature* |
| *JEPTA* | *Journal of European Pentecostal Theological Association* |
| *JETS* | *Journal of the Evangelical Theological Society* |
| *JPT* | *Journal of Pentecostal Theology* |
| JPTSup | Journal of Pentecostal Theology Supplement Series |
| *JTI* | *Journal of Theological Interpretation* |

| | |
|---|---|
| *JTS* | *Journal of Theological Study* |
| *JSNT* | *Journal for the Study of the New Testament* |
| JSNTSup | Journal for Study of New Testament Supplement Series |
| LNTS | Library of New Testament Studies |
| LXX | Septuagint |
| *MSJ* | *The Master's Seminary Journal* |
| MNTC | Moffatt New Testament Commentary |
| MT | Masoretic Text |
| NBBC | New Beacon Bible Commentary |
| NCBC | The New Century Bible Commentary |
| *Neot* | *Neotestamentica* |
| NICNT | New International Commentary on the New Testament |
| NIGTC | New International Greek New Testament Commentary |
| *NovT* | *Novum Testamentum* |
| NT | New Testament |
| NTL | New Testament Library |
| *NTS* | *New Testament Studies* |
| OEBI | Mckenzie, S.L. (ed.), *The Oxford Encyclopedia of Biblical Interpretation* (2 vols; Oxford: Oxford University Press, 2013). |
| PCS | Pentecostal Commentary Series |
| *PJT* | *Pharos Journal of Theology* |
| *Pneuma* | *Pneuma: The Journal of the Society for Pentecostal Studies* |
| *PRS* | *Perspectives in Religious Studies* |
| PTMS | Princeton Theological Monograph Series |
| *RSB* | *Religious Studies Bulletin* |
| *RTR* | *Reformed Theological Review* |
| S&HBC | Smith & Helwys Bible Commentary |
| SBL | Society of Biblical Literature |
| *SCJ* | *Stone-Campbell Journal* |
| *TDNT* | Kittel G. and G. Friedrich (eds.), *Theological Dictionary of the New Testament* (trans. G.W. Bromiley; 10 vols; Grand Rapids: Eerdmans, 1964-). |
| Th | Theodotion |
| TNTC | Tyndale New Testament Commentaries |
| TPINTC | TPI New Testament Commentaries |

| | |
|---|---|
| *TS* | *Theological Studies* |
| *TynB* | *Tyndale Bulletin* |
| WBC | Word Biblical Commentary Series |
| *WTJ* | *Westminister Theological Journal* |
| WUZNT | Wissenschaftliche Untersuchungen zum Neuen Testament |
| *ZNW* | *Zeitschrift für die neutestamentliche Wissenschaft* |

# INTRODUCTION

Being raised in the Pentecostal community suggests that the Apocalypse has been a significant part of my upbringing and formation. My magnetic attraction to the Apocalypse was polished through academic study at Pentecostal institutions, including Southeastern University and the Pentecostal Theological Seminary. With this monograph, I seek to appreciate both the formation of my people – my intertext – while also experiencing the living fire for myself. I will argue that pneumatic discernment is an essential narrative thread that appears throughout the Apocalypse. I will attempt to hear the voices of the Pentecostal community in the USA as a way to hear from my own tribe. I will then explore the thread of pneumatic discernment in the Apocalypse from an intertextual, theological, and narrative perceptive. This study seeks to provide a foundation for further theological developments in the Pentecostal communities that engage a triadic hermeneutic of Spirit, scripture, and community.

## Outline and Structure of the Monograph

Chapter one will propose a methodology that is reliant on developments in Pentecostal hermeneutics, particularly the work of R. Waddell concerning intertextuality. This methodology will first offer two brief stories, one of the early Pentecostal (con)text and a second concerning developments in Pentecostal hermeneutics in biblical studies. The chapter will explore the hermeneutical triad – Spirit, scripture, and community – from the perspective of intertextuality. The text will be approached theologically, offering a 'for us' interpretation for the Pentecostal community. The hermeneutic of this piece will employ reading approaches current in NT studies that have emerged from the Pentecostal (con)text, including intertextuality, (Reception History), and narrative criticism.

Chapter two of this work will offer a review of literature of the pneumatology in the Apocalypse. This study will examine articles, theological dictionaries, NT theologies, monographs, and sections of scholarly works that explicitly examine the pneumatology of the Apocalypse or the theme of pneumatic discernment. The review of literature seeks to uncover any convergence between pneumatology and pneumatic discernment in the scholarly literature.

Chapters three and four will offer a survey of early Pentecostal periodical literature from 1906–1918 in the USA that has explored pneumatic discernment and the pneumatology of the Apocalypse. As W. Hollenweger has suggested, the first years of the Pentecostal movement is the heart, not the infancy of the Pentecostal movement. Chapter three will investigate the publications of the Wesleyan-Holiness stream of Pentecostalism, while chapter four will explore the voices from the Finished-Work stream of Pentecostalism. The division between these two streams follows a model established by K. Alexander.

Chapter five will offer an intertextual, theological, narrative reading of the Apocalypse. The close reading of the Apocalypse will be attentive to the pneumatology of the Apocalypse, while focusing on texts that call for discernment as well as occasions that the Apocalypse directs and/or assists the churches in discerning. Significant literary markers that will be taken into consideration include: μυστήριον ('mystery'), ὁ ἔχων οὖς ἀκουσάτω τί τὸ πνεῦμα λέγει ταῖς ἐκκλησίαις ('let anyone who has an ear, hear what the Spirit is saying to the churches'), ἐν πνεύματι ('in the Spirit'), the seven Spirits, true, truth, πνευματικῶς ('Spiritually'), νοῦν ('discernment'), ὁ ἔχων ('the one having'), ψηφισάτω ('calculate'), ὧδέ ἐστιν ('here is'), σοφίαν ('wisdom'), τὸ πνεῦμα τῆς προφητείας ('the Spirit of prophecy'), τῶν πνευμάτων τῶν προφητῶν ('the Spirits of the prophets'), and characters, including the elders, angels, and fellow-servants, who offer assistance in discernment.

Chapter six will make overtures toward a Pentecostal theology of pneumatic discernment. This final chapter will be the culmination of the piece, bringing into dialogue findings and conclusions from the entire work with Pentecostal theology.

This monograph concludes by offering conclusions and implications for further research.

# 1

## AN INTERTEXTUAL APPROACH

### Pentecostals and Intertextuality

The work of R. Waddell has offered a substantial contribution to the study of Pentecostal hermeneutics in light of the literary theory of intertextuality.[1] Following the theory of intertextuality, Waddell suggests that interpretation is (con)textual and that his intertext includes the Pentecostal (con)text (along with other intertexts).[2] He writes that the Pentecostal (con)text, like '[a]ll (con)texts, whether they are literary, religious, or social, remain constructs of an interpretative community',[3] which has 'predisposed the manner in which I interpret the biblical texts'.[4] The approach of this work follows the foundation laid by Waddell concerning intertextuality and offers an intertextual reading that is (in)formed in and for the Pentecostal (con)text.

Intertextuality is a poststructural literary theory that considers the interconnectedness of texts and the impact of these textual intersections in interpretation. The term 'intertextually' finds its origins with

---

[1] See R.C. Waddell, *The Spirit of the Book of Revelation* (JPTSup 30; Dorset: Deo Publishing, 2006), pp. 39-131. Waddell surveys the works of J. Kristeva and R. Barthes, while examining the dialogue between S. Fish and J. Culler before turning to intertextuality in Revelation studies. Ultimately, in the Culler/Fish dialogue, Waddell sides with the Fishian text. Cf. S. Fish, *Is There A Text in This Class? The Authority of Interpretative Communities* (Cambridge, MA: Harvard University Press, 1980).

[2] See Waddell, *Spirit of the Book of Revelation*, pp. 97-131, for his construction of 'A Profile of a Pentecostal Reader of the Apocalypse'.

[3] Waddell, *Spirit of the Book of Revelation*, p. 58.

[4] Waddell, *Spirit of the Book of Revelation*, p. 97.

J. Kristeva who introduced the work of M. Bakhtin to the French-speaking world.[5] In relation to texts, Kristeva writes, 'any text is constructed as a mosaic of quotations, any text is absorption and transformation of another'.[6] The theory of intertextuality suggests that neither texts nor meaning are fixed entities; they are fluid and ever-changing with the exploration of new (inter)textual interactions. Hence, there is a multiplicity of meaning in the interpretation of texts because there are a variety of possible intertextual (inter)connections. In interpretation, there is not one method that would be able to answer all the questions concerning an intertext:

> Intertextuality, with its awareness of semiotics and the decentralization of meaning, can teach humility and fascination at the same time. Intertextuality promotes humility when those who study it face their own limitations, and this develops out of their fascination with the apprehension they sense in the face of the ever growing potential for the meanings of a text within that text's world.[7]

Thereby, intertextuality denotes that the interpreter is significantly involved in the process of interpretation. The interpreter chooses intertextual intersections to explore and methods for interpretation. It is concerning the role of the interpreter in the process of interpretation that the work of Waddell is significant for Pentecostal hermeneutics. Not only is the interpreter involved in the process of interpretation, intertextuality identifies the interpreter as an intertext who offers a variety of additional intertextual interconnections that can

---

[5] See J. Kristeva, 'Word, Dialogue, and Novel', in T. Moi (ed.), *The Kristeva Reader* (New York, NY: Columbia University Press, 1986), pp. 35-61, originally published as J. Kristeva, 'Bakhtine, le mot, le dialogue et le roman', *Critique* 33 (1967), pp. 438-65. See G. Allen, *Intertextuality* (London: Routledge, 2nd edn, 2000, 2011), pp. 14-59, on the influence of Bakhtin and the historical development of the theory of intertextuality.

[6] Kristeva, 'Word, Dialogue, and Novel', p. 37. G.A. Phillips, 'Poststructural Intertextuality', in B.J. Oropeza and S. Moyise (eds.), *Exploring Intertextuality: Diverse Strategies for New Testament Interpretation of Texts* (Eugene, OR: Cascade Books, 2016), p. 120, adds, 'Intertextual reading perceives a fabric made up of numerous fibers that readers *weave into text* and *produce meaning*'.

[7] S. Alkier, 'Intertextuality Based on Categorical Semiotics', in B.J. Oropeza and S. Moyise (eds.), *Exploring Intertextuality: Diverse Strategies for New Testament Interpretation of Texts* (Eugene, OR: Cascade Books, 2016), p. 134.

be considered in interpretation. In other words, the complex (in-ter)textual interactions include the intertext of the interpreter in the production of meaning. Waddell writes:

> Intertextuality does not stop with allusions or echoes but goes further into the life and community of the reader so that the 'interested perspective, ethical criteria, theoretical frameworks, re-ligious presuppositions, and sociopolitical locations' serve as (con)textual forces that converge with the literary texts.[8]

Hence, the context that is Pentecostalism becomes another (con)tex-tual force in the process of interpretation. Waddell considers that one of the 'interested perspectives' that arises from the Pentecostal (con)text includes a desire for an interpretation of scripture that is for and in the Pentecostal community.[9] Waddell writes '[a]ny reading that is explicitly *pro nobis* must concede that the context of the com-munity (in)forms the interpretation'.[10] While my (con)textual inter-text would include other (con)texts, such as a white male who lives in the USA or as an academic who has been trained in biblical studies, one of the loudest (con)textual notes that (in)forms this work is the

---

[8] Waddell, *Spirit of the Book of Revelation*, p. 39.

[9] Waddell, *Spirit of the Book of Revelation*, pp. 108-18. See K.J. Archer, *A Pentecostal Hermeneutic: Spirit, Scripture and Community* (Cleveland, TN: CPT Press, 2009), p. 225, who writes:

> Therefore, one is not a Pentecostal hermeneut because one uses a Pentecostal method; rather, one is a Pentecostal hermeneut because one is recognized as being a part of the community. The community, along with its concerns and needs, is the primary arena in which a Pentecostal hermeneut participates. The community actively participates in the Pentecostal hermeneutical strategy not passively but actively through discussion, testimony, and charismatic gifts.

For theological approaches, see S.E. Fowl, *Engaging Scripture: A Model for Theological Interpretation* (Eugene, OR: Wipf & Stock, 1998). R.W. Jenson, 'Scripture's Authority in the Church', in E.F. Davis and R.B. Hays (eds.), *The Art of Reading Scripture* (Grand Rapids, MI: Eerdmans, 2003), pp. 27-37; R.B. Hays, 'Reading the Bible with Eyes of Faith: The Practice of Theological Exegesis', *JTI* 1.1 (2007), pp. 5-21. J.B. Green, *Practicing Theological Interpretation: Engaging Biblical Texts for Faith and Formation* (Grand Rapids, MI: Baker Academic, 2011), pp. 11-12, remarks concern-ing theological interpretations, 'the tradition that has arguably examined this ques-tion most seriously is the Pentecostal tradition ... Casting aside any pretense of coming to Scripture neutrally, these scholars have sought to identify both how they are influenced and how they ought to be influenced by their theological and eccle-sial commitments in their reading of Scripture.'

[10] Waddell, *Spirit of the Book of Revelation*, p. 98.

Pentecostal (con)text because this work chooses to approach scripture in and for the Pentecostal community. This piece offers a Pentecostal reading because I am Pentecostal. I am Pentecostal because I have been shaped in a Pentecostal (con)text and read scripture for and in the Pentecostal community. This reading is for, from, and in a Pentecostal (con)text.

However, intertextuality would not suggest that the Pentecostal (con)text is a static entity that is absolutely determinative of meaning.[11] Any (con)textual interpretation remains 'a dialogue partner for a group despite the fact that the text is a product of the interpretative assumptions'.[12] In other words, whereas the Pentecostal (con)text impacts the interpretation of an intertext, the Pentecostal (con)text is another text to be interpreted. In the process of dialogue with the Pentecostal (con)text, both the Pentecostal (con)text and the intertext of the reader are (re)formed and (re)imagined. This chapter seeks to dialogue with aspects of the construct that is the Pentecostal (con)text that shapes and forms the ways that I – whose intertext intersects with the Pentecostal (con)text – interpret the Apocalypse and the theme of pneumatic discernment. I will briefly outline the intertextual approach that is employed in this monograph and then consider these aspects later in this chapter in more detail.

First, this chapter offers a story of the origins of the Pentecostal movement. In hearing a story, '[m]emory is formed intertextually by a variety of authoritative texts',[13] shaping the identities of communities. Hearing a story of the origins of the Pentecostal movement offers a description of the ethos of the Pentecostal (con)text that 'will serve as a contextual intertext for both the development of a Pentecostal hermeneutic and the application of that hermeneutic to the text of Revelation'.[14] (Re)telling the story of Pentecostalism continues the process of dialogue with the Pentecostal (con)text that (re)shapes and (re)forms the (con)textual Pentecostal identity.

---

[11] Fish, *Is There A Text in This Class? The Authority of Interpretative Communities*, pp. 314-15, suggests that one is not 'trapped forever in the categories of understanding at one's disposal (or the categories at whose disposal one is), but that the introduction of new categories or the expansion of old ones to include new (and therefore newly seen) data must always come from the outside or from what is perceived, for a time, to be the outside'.

[12] Waddell, *Spirit of the Book of Revelation*, p. 61.

[13] Waddell, *Spirit of the Book of Revelation*, p. 95.

[14] Waddell, *Spirit of the Book of Revelation*, p. 103.

Second, another story is considered in this chapter that explores recent developments in Pentecostal hermeneutics, particularly approaches in biblical studies. Hearing the story of Pentecostal hermeneutics shapes the identity of a Pentecostal hermeneutic. This story traces the progression of Pentecostal hermeneutics that forms the identity of a (con)textual Pentecostal hermeneutic.[15] The identity of the approach employed in this piece stems from this story that includes the emergence of a Pentecostal triadic approach that negotiates meaning among Spirit, scripture, and community, as well as developments in the interpretation of scripture for Pentecostals that include *Wirkungsgeschichte*, narrative criticism, and intertextuality.

Third, following the triadic paradigm that develops from these Pentecostal stories, this chapter turns to explore three elements of the Pentecostal (con)text: (1) the Pentecostal community, (2) the role of scripture in the Pentecostal (con)text, and (3) the role of the Spirit in interpretation for the Pentecostal (con)text. This chapter considers these triadic features from the perspective of intertextuality that seeks to move forward the conversation of Pentecostal hermeneutics.

(1) Community is a significant feature of the hermeneutical process because it forms the intertexts of the interpreter that impacts the reading of a text. An investigation of aspects of the Pentecostal (con)texts unveils elements that a Pentecostal reader 'brings to the text', while also functioning to (in)form the intertext of the interpreter in the Pentecostal (con)text. Four aspects of the Pentecostal (con)textual community will be considered: (i) the local worshipping Pentecostal congregation, (ii) the texts of the early Pentecostal periodical literature, (iii) the (inter)text of the *ecclesia catholic*, and (iv) the (con)text of (Pentecostal) scholarship.

(i) This chapter considers the (con)text of the 'life and community' of the interpreter by examining the Pentecostal (con)text of the local Pentecostal community. The local Pentecostal community 'is the place of formation for those who would hear the biblical text as a Pentecostal, or with Pentecostal ears'.[16] While not always overtly

---

[15] Waddell, *Spirit of the Book of Revelation*, p. 95.

[16] J.C. Thomas, '"What the Spirit is Saying to the Church" – The Testimony of a Pentecostal in New Testament Studies', in K.L. Spawn and A.T. Wright (eds.), *Spirit and Scripture: Exploring a Pneumatic Hermeneutic* (London: T&T Clark, 2012), p. 116.

quantifiable, the local Pentecostal community has a significant formative impact on the ways that a Pentecostal interprets texts. I am part
of a local worshipping Pentecostal community that forms and shapes
the 'for us' – the *pro nobis* – interpretation of this work.

(ii) A number of Pentecostals have moved toward examining the
early Pentecostal periodical literature (1906–1916) using the method
of *Wirkungsgeschichte* because the early years of Pentecostalism are
considered to be the theological heart, not the infancy, of the movement.[17] As the theological heart, the intertexts of the early Pentecostal periodical literature are significantly impactful in the formation of
theological readings and Pentecostal interpreters, while also discovering the theological ethos of the Pentecostal movement. (Re)visiting
these early Pentecostal texts also offers an opportunity for dialoguing
with the Pentecostal (con)text that (re)forms Pentecostal identity.[18]

(iii) Another aspect of the Pentecostal (con)text includes the intertext of the wider Christian tradition. While the Pentecostal
(con)text has an impact on the interpreter, the Pentecostal (con)text
is not isolated from the wider Christian (con)text. Much like the process of hearing the voices from the early Pentecostal community, dialoguing with the intertexts of the wider Christian tradition forms
and guides the intertext of Christian Pentecostal interpreters.

(iv) The final aspect of the Pentecostal (con)text to be explored
in this chapter is the (inter)text of the academy. Whereas the interpretation of this monograph is for and in the Pentecostal community,
this piece has also been formed by the academy. Chapter two will
examine the scholarly (con)texts concerning the pneumatology of
the Apocalypse and the theme of pneumatic discernment. Among
the variety of scholars who (in)form this study, chapter two will reveal a number of Pentecostal scholars who have studied the pneumatology of the Apocalypse. Hence, the academy offers methods and

---

[17] *Wirkungsgeschichte* as method and its use by Pentecostals is discussed later in
this chapter in more detail. Concerning the early years of the Pentecostal movement as the theological heart, see W.J. Hollenweger, 'Pentecostals and the
Charismatic Movement', in C. Jones, G. Wainwright, and E. Yarnold (eds.), *The
Study of Spirituality* (New York, NY: Oxford University Press, 1986), pp. 549-53; S.J.
Land, *Pentecostal Spirituality: A Passion for the Kingdom* (Cleveland, TN: CPT Press,
2010), pp. 37-44.

[18] Alkier, 'Intertextuality Based on Categorical Semiotics', p. 135, states, '*Recep-
tion-oriented intertextuality* investigates textual relationships that were produced by actual readers'.

tools that assist in the interpretation of scripture, methods that have been taken up by those who are part of the Pentecostal (con)text.

(2) In the consideration of an approach to and the function of scripture in the Pentecostal (con)text, one element that emerges is the significance of narrative approaches owing to the fact that aspects of narrative criticism are analogous with the Pentecostal intertext. In other words, the move toward narrative approaches among Pentecostal scholars has developed from a dialogue with their own (con)text. Following this intertextual construct of the Pentecostal (con)text, this chapter seeks to bring into dialogue developments in narrative criticism in biblical studies with the theory of intertextuality for the interpretation of scripture, particularly the Apocalypse.

(3) This chapter considers the role of the Spirit in the process of interpretation. For the Pentecostal (con)text, the Spirit is a significant feature of the process of interpretation of scripture. Pentecostals believe that the Spirit actively and dynamically inspires both the text and the interpreter. The final feature of this chapter explores the role of the Spirit in and for the Pentecostal (con)text.

In sum, the method of this piece follows the work of R. Waddell who has explored the theory of intertextuality for Pentecostal hermeneutics, suggesting that interpretation is (con)textual. Among a variety of intertextual convergences in the process of interpretation, a primary intertext for this monograph is the Pentecostal (con)text. The Pentecostal (con)text is be considered, first, in relation to a story of the origins of the Pentecostal movement; second, a story of recent developments in Pentecostal hermeneutics; and third, examining the Pentecostal hermeneutical triad – Spirit, scripture, and community – that emerges from the Pentecostal (con)text.

## A Pentecostal Story

I have titled this short overview of Pentecostalism 'a Pentecostal story' to emphasize that there are other Pentecostal stories beyond the North American (con)text. I tell this Pentecostal story because it describes the origins of my Pentecostal community that intertextually (re)forms and (re)shapes the identity and ethos of the Pentecostal (con)text. The Pentecostal (con)text becomes another text that converges with the intertext that is the Apocalypse in interpretation.[19]

This story begins in the early part of the twentieth century where Agnes Ozman,[20] a student at Bethel Bible College in Topeka, Kansas, was baptized in the Spirit and spoke in tongues.[21] She was following the direction of Charles Parham who instructed his students to read the Acts narratives, while identifying all the texts that described Spirit baptism.[22] From this study of Acts, each student came to the conclusion that Spirit baptism should be accompanied with speaking in tongues for the empowerment of witness. At a watch night prayer service, Ozman confirmed Parham's belief when she and her classmates sought and received Spirit baptism with the 'initial evidence' of speaking in tongues.[23] This experience of Spirit baptism as a 'definite work of grace' has become one of the distinguishing marks of

---

[19] See again Waddell, *Spirit of the Book of Revelation*, pp. 95, 103.

[20] Agnes Ozman experienced *xenolalia*, which is speaking in an unlearned known human language. This is differentiated from *glossolalia* or tongues in an unknown language. Parham proposed that *xenolalia* was for the purpose of missions – whatever language a person spoke identified his or her country for witness. This understanding ultimately failed and was rejected by many Pentecostals.

[21] A. Anderson, *An Introduction to Pentecostalism: Global Charismatic Christianity* (Cambridge: Cambridge University Press, 2004), pp. 166-70, has critiqued the western bias of most Pentecostal histories. For other stories, see V. Synan, *The Holiness-Pentecostal Movement in the United States* (Eerdmans: Grand Rapids, MI, 1971); W.J. Hollenweger, *The Pentecostals* (Peabody, MA: Hendrickson, 1988); H. Cox, *Fire From Heaven: The Rise of Pentecostal Spirituality and the Reshaping of Religion in the Twenty-First Century* (Reading, MA: Addison-Wesley, 1995); D.W. Faupel, *The Everlasting Gospel: The Significance of Eschatology in the Development of Pentecostal Thought* (JPTSup 10; Sheffield: Sheffield Academic Press, 1996); Anderson, *Introduction to Pentecostalism*; C.M. Robeck, *The Azusa Street Mission and Revival: The Birth of the Global Pentecostal Movement* (Nashville, TN: Thomas Nelson, 2006).

[22] See M.W. Mittelstadt, *Reading Luke-Acts in the Pentecostal Tradition* (Cleveland, TN: CPT Press, 2010), for the way in which Pentecostals have used Luke-Acts as their central driving narrative. See K.J. Archer, *A Pentecostal Hermeneutic for the Twenty-First Century: Spirit, Scripture, and Community* (JPTSup 28; New York, NY: T&T Clark, 2004), later published by CPT Press which will be the edition cited in this monograph; C.E.W. Green, *Sanctifying Interpretation: Vocation, Holiness, and Scripture* (Cleveland, TN: CPT Press, 2015), pp. 114-23, on an examination of early Pentecostal 'hermeneutics'.

[23] Parham is a perplexing character in Pentecostal history. Even though his impact was substantial in establishing the relationship between Spirit baptism as a 'third work of grace' with the 'initial evidence' and his role in instructing Seymour, Parham's other ideologies – *xenolalia* for missions, eschatological belief of annihilation of the wicked, Anglo-Israelism, and racial prejudices – were rejected by many

Pentecostalism.[24] Parham then moved to Houston, Texas where he continued to teach Spirit baptism. Parham met an African American minister – William Seymour. Seymour became convinced of Parham's postulation on Spirit baptism, even though Seymour was only allowed to listen to Parham's lectures from the hall because of racial prejudice and oppression. After some time under Parham's guidance, Seymour was called to become a pastor of a church in Los Angeles, California. Upon arriving in Los Angeles, Seymour immediately began preaching on Spirit baptism with the 'initial evidence' of speaking in tongues for empowerment in ministry. However after a few days of preaching, the leadership locked Seymour out of the church. Impoverished and without a place to go, Seymour sojourned with some from his congregation. He stayed in a house on North Bonny Brae Street where Seymour, along with attendants of the church, began to hold prayer meetings. Seymour continued to teach on Spirit baptism and those listening anticipated an outpouring of the Spirit. As the house meetings grew, so did the expectation for Spirit baptism. Until one day Edward Lee, a janitor, had a visionary experience while at work where he saw the apostles show him how to receive Spirit baptism. He asked Seymour to pray for him to receive Spirit baptism, and when Seymour and those attending the prayer meetings laid hands on him and prayed, Lee was baptized in the Spirit and spoke in tongues. That night, many who participated in the prayer meeting were baptized in the Spirit. The news spread quickly, and this small house prayer meeting grew so much that the house on Bonny Brae could no longer sustain the growth to the extent that the front porch of the house collapsed from the weight of the worshippers. Within a week, Seymour and his community found another place to worship

of those who were part of the Azusa Street Revival and many early 'Classical' Pentecostals. See Anderson, *Introduction to Pentecostalism*, pp. 33-35.

[24] Spirit baptism accompanied with speaking in tongues for the empowerment of witness is a distinguishing mark, but it is not the only mark; Pentecostalism is by no means monolithic. Some other distinctive features of early Pentecostals include: a premillennial eschatology accompanied by a strong emphasis upon missions, ecclesiology and a Christocentric worldview seen predominately in the 'Full Gospel' – Jesus is savior, sanctifier, healer, Spirit baptizer, and soon coming king (some Pentecostal groups hold to a 'Four-fold' instead of a 'Five-fold' Gospel removing Jesus a sanctifier). See Faupel, *The Everlasting Gospel*, pp. 28-30.

on 312 Azusa Street. Once housed on Azusa Street, the revival grew exponentially.[25]

The Azusa Street Revival broke cultural lines where worshippers from diverse ethnicities, genders, and social classes gathered under one roof to experience the Holy Spirit. The revival was filled with times of testimony where any worshipper could share their story. Seymour allowed anyone led by the Spirit to deliver a message to the community, which was often dialogical between the speaker and congregation.[26] The revival included many healings and exuberant times of worship. There were testimonies, sermons, tongues, choral hymns, songs, prayers, joyous laughter, times of silence, and sorrowful sobs. Most who came would pray for Spirit baptism. Those who attended immediately spread the word about their new experience. Azusa sent out many missionaries throughout the world to spread the news of revival. They were compelled to spread the news of God's work because they had been empowered by the Spirit and the coming of Jesus was near.[27]

As the revival spread, the Pentecostals were forced to discern new arising issues. First, issues of race became a major dividing point. Seymour – who led Azusa and was African American – created a multiracial and multi-gendered leadership community to preside over the diverse attendants of the revival. There were some who came to the revival with racial prejudices, but after being Spirit baptized, repented of their prejudices;[28] it was said at Azusa 'the color line was washed away by the blood'.[29] However, others were critical of the racial integration, especially when commenting on the Azusa altar services where men and women of diverse races would come together to cry, pray, or embrace. One such critic was Parham who, upon seeing white and non-white people together at the altar, claimed the revival to be immoral. Unfortunately, following Azusa, cultural

---

[25] Faupel, *The Everlasting Gospel*, pp. 200-27; Robeck, *Azusa Street Mission and Revival*, pp. 60-86.

[26] For more of Seymour's leadership, see Faupel, *The Everlasting Gospel*, pp. 198-200; Robeck, *Azusa Street Mission and Revival*, pp. 87-128.

[27] Faupel, *The Everlasting Gospel*; Robeck, *Azusa Street Mission and Revival*, pp. 129-86.

[28] Cox, *Fire from Heaven*, pp. 99-110, believes the racial integration of early Pentecostalism is one of its most distinguishing marks.

[29] Quoted in Anderson, *Introduction to Pentecostalism*, p. 61.

patterns of racial prejudices relapsed and many Pentecostal congregations deteriorated back to racial segregation.[30]

Second, in 1911 Pentecostalism was forced to discern a doctrinal issue concerning sanctification as a 'definite work of grace' or a definable 'crisis experience'. Seymour, along with many early Pentecostals, originated from the Wesleyan-Holiness tradition, which taught sanctification as a 'definite work of grace'.[31] They theologized that Spirit baptism was a 'third definite work' that followed sanctification and salvation. William Durham challenged this Holiness perspective and put forward the 'Finished-Work' position. The Finished-Work position claimed that the work of Christ was finished on the cross. Sanctification is provided in the atonement and received at the point of salvation. Thus, sanctification is not a 'definite work of grace', but given simultaneously with justification.[32] Whenever one sinned, it was a sign of fallen humanity. Despite their humanity, individuals should pursue sanctification in this life, but it could only be fully accomplished in the eschaton.[33] The struggle of this theological issue was so severe in the early years that Seymour (Wesleyan-Holiness) locked Durham (Finished-Work) out of Azusa for preaching the Finished-Work doctrine.[34]

end of the world

Third, the issue of Spirit baptism and 'initial evidence' came to the forefront of discussion for Pentecostals. Early on Seymour agreed with Parham's proposal that tongues alone were the 'initial evidence' of Spirit baptism for the empowerment of witness. To speak in tongues was to return to the power of the Apostles as found in Acts. Years after the revival, Seymour modified his position by stating that tongues were one of the signs of Spirit baptism, and that the

---

[30] Anderson, *Introduction to Pentecostalism*, pp. 39-51.

[31] The earliest Pentecostal US Wesleyan-Holiness denominations were Church of God in Christ, Church of God (Cleveland, TN), and Pentecostal Holiness Church.

[32] Faupel, *The Everlasting Gospel*, pp. 237-40.

[33] Some later followers of Durham would form the Assemblies of God, which is one of the largest Pentecostal denominations in the world. See Faupel, *The Everlasting Gospel*, pp. 233, 243-45.

[34] For more on this schism, see Faupel, *The Everlasting Gospel*, pp. 229-70, and Anderson, *Introduction to Pentecostalism*, pp. 45-47, who finds racial undertones between Durham (white) attempting to usurp Seymour (African American) as leader of the revival.

true, continuous evidence was a life full of the fruit of the Spirit.[35] In the end, most Pentecostals in the USA continued to adhere to the doctrine, which viewed tongues as the 'initial evidence' of Spirit baptism.[36]

Fourth, the church was forced to discern the doctrine of the trinity. A group known as the 'Oneness' or 'Jesus Only' Pentecostals believed that the baptismal formula, 'in the name of Jesus' from Acts, should supersede the trinitarian baptismal formula in Matthew.[37] This baptism modification erupted to challenge the orthodox doctrine of the trinity.[38] The Oneness Pentecostals considered that the name of Jesus was the name of the Father, of the Son, and of the Holy Spirit.[39] The issue split many Pentecostals – mostly the Assemblies of God.[40] After intense debate, the Assemblies of God ultimately rejected this doctrine, causing them to form the 'Statements of Fundamental Truths' to have definable doctrinal boundaries.[41] In response to their rejection, the Oneness Pentecostals formed their own Pentecostal communities.[42]

Despite these disputes, the Pentecostal movement continued to spread rapidly. Today, Pentecostalism is one of the largest and fastest

---

[35] In 1918, F.F. Bosworth also challenged this traditional doctrine by asking, 'do all speak in tongues?', but his proposal was rejected by the Assemblies of God General Council. See Mittelstadt, *Reading Luke-Acts in the Pentecostal Tradition*, pp. 34-37.

[36] For more on this debate, see Anderson, *Introduction to Pentecostalism*, pp. 192-98; Archer, *A Pentecostal Hermeneutic*; Mittelstadt, *Reading Luke-Acts in the Pentecostal Tradition*, pp. 34-37.

[37] For more on the history and theology of the Oneness Pentecostals, see D.A. Reed, *'In Jesus Name': The History and Beliefs of Oneness Pentecostals* (JPTSup 31; Dorset: Deo Publishing, 2008).

[38] Oneness Pentecostals rejected the terms 'trinity' and 'persons' because they were not found in scripture, see Reed, *'In Jesus Name'* pp. 179-80. Faupel, *The Everlasting Gospel*, pp. 272-306, points out that the Oneness doctrine developed in three stages: (1) attempts to harmonize the baptism formulas from Luke/Acts and Matthew, (2) a focus on the revelation of the name of God, and (3) a revelation of the nature of the godhead.

[39] On the significance of 'name' for Oneness Pentecostalism, see Reed, *'In Jesus Name'* pp. 174-78. See also Hollenweger, *The Pentecostals*, pp. 31-32.

[40] The Oneness schism hardly impacted the Wesleyan-Holiness Pentecostals.

[41] See Reed, *'In Jesus Name'* pp. 147-66.

[42] Some Pentecostals threw out the creeds and early church tradition because they believed that the corrupted ecclesial body produced corrupted dogma. Ironically, the decision for many Pentecostals to deny the creeds and ecclesial tradition caused them to create new creeds of their own.

growing Christian movements in the world. After Azusa, the impact of the revival spread beyond 'classic Pentecostal' denominations to other Christian denominations and groups often termed 'Charismatics'. In the Charismatic renewal, churches experienced Spirit baptism and speaking in tongues while remaining within their own traditions. From this and the global missionary impact, the Pentecostal/Charismatic revival has become one of the most influential Christian movements in the world.[43] The ethos of the early Pentecostal (con)text was countercultural and deemed 'premodern', 'non-modern', or 'paramodern'.[44] Elements of the Pentecostal ethos that have emerged from the Pentecostal (con)text include: (1) participation in the (Full) Gospel story, (2) their narrative character signified by the testimonies of their story, (3) their experiences of the Spirit, including Spirit baptism for the empowerment of witness, (4) their diverse worshipping community, and (5) their eschatological outlook of living in the last days.[45]

## A Story of Developments in Pentecostal Hermeneutics

This chapter turns to offer another story that describes recent developments in Pentecostal hermeneutics, especially those who have engaged biblical studies. Hearing another story continues to (re)shape the identity of the Pentecostal (con)text, impacting the method employed in this work.

---

[43] Anderson, *Introduction to Pentecostalism*, pp. 9-15.

[44] Pentecostal scholar J.D. Johns is credited with fashioning the term 'paramodern'.

[45] Pentecostals were not captive to US twentieth century models of epistemology, worldview, and hermeneutics whether modern, evangelical, fundamentalist, liberal, or dispensational. For more on the Pentecostal non-modern (or 'paramodern') worldview, see S.J. Land, *Pentecostal Spirituality: A Passion for the Kingdom* (JPTSup 1; Sheffield: Sheffield Academic Press, 1993), later published as S.J. Land, *Pentecostal Spirituality: A Passion for the Kingdom* (Cleveland, TN: CPT Press, 2010), p. 18, which will be cited in this work; Archer, *A Pentecostal Hermeneutic*, pp. 38-46, 102; Waddell, *Spirit of the Book of Revelation*, p. 112. See L.R. McQueen, *Toward a Pentecostal Eschatology: Discerning the Way Forward* (JPTSup 39; Dorset: Deo Publishing, 2012), who has demonstrated that not all early Pentecostals accepted dispensationalism. Furthermore, for a critique of the influence of Fundamental-Evangelicalism over Pentecostalism, see K.J. Archer, 'A Pentecostal Way of Doing Theology: Method and Manner', *IJST* 9.3 (2007), pp. 1-14.

The history of Pentecostal scholarship has been narrated as four generational epochs.[46] The first-generation pioneered academic study for Pentecostals but completed their graduate training in environments that did not allow integration between their faith and critical scholarship. The second-generation was able to move beyond the restrictions of the first-generation to research Pentecostal topics, but they were limited to studies in fields of history or the social sciences.[47] The third-generation of Pentecostal scholars – with help from postmodernism[48] – critically reflected upon their epistemology to deconstruct the ostensible division between 'objective' scholarship and personal faith.[49] This deconstruction allowed the third-generation to cultivate a critical theology informed by Pentecostal faith and tradition. One quintessential theological crop harvested by the third-generation was a distinctive Pentecostal hermeneutic.[50] R. Moore was a Pentecostal biblical scholar who offered a foundational Pentecostal

---

[46] R.D. Moore, J.C. Thomas, and S.J. Land, 'Editorial', *JPT* 1 (1992), pp. 3-4. See also J.C. Thomas, '1998 SPS Presidential Address: Pentecostal Theology in the Twenty-First Century', *Pneuma* 20.1 (1998), pp. 3-19.

[47] E.g. Synan, *The Holiness-Pentecostal Movement in the United States*.

[48] See J.K.A. Smith, *Thinking in Tongues: Pentecostal Contributions to Christian Philosophy* (Grand Rapids, MI: Eerdmans, 2010), pp. 50-62, for Pentecostalism's correlation with postmodernism especially concerning affective, narrative epistemology and worldview.

[49] See Land, *Pentecostal Spirituality*, pp. 23-25; Archer, 'A Pentecostal Way of Doing Theology', pp. 2-5; C.E.W. Green, *Toward a Pentecostal Theology of the Lord's Supper: Foretasting the Kingdom* (Cleveland, TN: CPT Press, 2012), p. 76.

[50] For the earliest attempts at Pentecostal hermeneutics, see G.T. Sheppard, 'Word and Spirit: Scripture in the Pentecostal Tradition – Part One', *Agora* 1.4 (1978), pp. 4-5, 17-22; G.T. Sheppard, 'Word and Spirit: Scripture in the Pentecostal Tradition – Part Two', *Agora* 2.1 (1978), pp. 14-19, G. Sheppard's articles were foundational in that he was one of the first to ask for a distinctive Pentecostal approach that is analogous to the early Pentecostal tradition. Sheppard notes that traditionally Pentecostals made use of a 'spiritual criticism' informed by their experiences for theological interpretation. H. Ervin, 'Hermeneutics: A Pentecostal Option', *Pneuma* 3.2 (1981), pp. 11-25, made another attempt at Pentecostal hermeneutics and proposed a pneumatic hermeneutic to mend the modern chasm between faith and reason. M.D. McLean, 'Toward a Pentecostal Hermeneutic', *Pneuma* 6.2 (1984), pp. 35-56, articulated a Pentecostal hermeneutic that correlates with both the way Pentecostals experience God as well as their use of scripture. He writes that if Pentecostals fail at this hermeneutical task, they will wither away. For a historical overview of the history of Pentecostal hermeneutics in biblical studies, see J.C. Thomas, 'Pentecostal Interpretation', *OEBI*, II, pp. 89-97. See also R. Waddell and P. Althouse, 'The Pentecostals and Their Scriptures', *Pneuma* 38.1-2 (2016), pp. 115-21.

approach to scripture.[51] Moore is critical of critical approaches (both liberal and conservative) that give attention to the text or reader alone, while silencing the voice of the Holy Spirit in interpretation. Moore instead offers a dynamic Pentecostal approach, which dialectically incorporates critical exegesis with the open dynamism of the Spirit.[52] He investigates Deuteronomy to reveal a dialectical tension between the charismatic word ('the God so near') and the written word ('the law so righteous').[53] Canon and charisma are partners in the continuing revelation of God to Israel; without both features being dialectically held together, a community will have either a 'Spiritless Word (rationalism)' or a 'Word-less Spirit (subjectivism)'.[54]

J. McKay contributes to the hermeneutical conversation with an autobiographical article that explores the dialectical tension within himself as an academic in biblical studies and as a charismatic.[55] He offers an analogy where biblical scholarship is like a drama: (1) the biblical text is the performance on the stage, (2) an academic is an observer or reviewer, who desires to be objective and critical, while analyzing the performance, and (3) a charismatic participates in the drama on stage as a performer. Before McKay's charismatic experience, when attempting to interpret the bible objectively, he found it full of unsolvable riddles. However after his Spirit baptism, the veil was taken away, and he discovered a whole new way of seeing the biblical performance; he became a participator. Accordingly, for McKay, a Pentecostal reading is dependent upon the removal of the veil through divine experiences, which allows one to step out of the audience and participate on stage in the biblical drama.[56]

---

[51] R.D. Moore, 'A Pentecostal Approach to Scripture', *Seminary Viewpoint* 8.1 (1987), pp. 4-5, 11, later published as R.D. Moore, 'A Pentecostal Approach to Scripture', in L.R. Martin (ed.), *Pentecostal Hermeneutics: A Reader* (Leiden, The Netherlands: Brill, 2013), pp. 11-13, which I will cite in this work; R.D. Moore, 'Canon and Charisma in the Book of Deuteronomy', *JPT* 1 (1992), pp. 75-92; R.D. Moore, 'Deuteronomy and the Fire of God: A Critical Charismatic Interpretation', *JPT* 7 (1995), pp. 11-33. See also R.D. Moore, *The Spirit of the Old Testament* (JPTSup 35; Dorset: Deo Publishing, 2011).
[52] Moore, 'Canon and Charisma', p. 75 n. 1.
[53] Moore, 'Canon and Charisma', p. 76.
[54] Moore, 'Canon and Charisma', p. 91.
[55] J. McKay, 'When the Veil is Taken Away: The Impact of Prophetic Experience on Biblical Interpretation', *JPT* 5 (1994), pp. 17-40.
[56] McKay, 'When the Veil is Taken Away', pp. 32-40.

J.C. Thomas is the first Pentecostal to postulate the hermeneutical triad – Spirit, scripture, and community – explicitly as a paradigm for Pentecostal hermeneutics. Thomas develops the triad from a narrative reading of Acts 15.[57] In Acts 15, discernment begins with the community's testimony of their experiences,[58] which leads them to the scriptures: from context to text.[59] In Acts 15, the Spirit is the source of the community's experience, who offers guidance and directs the church to certain scriptures; among a diverse selection of texts from the HB concerning the Gentiles, the Spirit guides James to a specific text.[60] Thus, Thomas proposes a triadic hermeneutical model where the Spirit is active in the community, and the community discerns their pneumatic experiences through testimony and scripture. Additionally, Thomas has been foundational in offering *Wirkungsgeschichte* as a valuable tool for Pentecostal scholarship. He deems that interpretation should not be performed in isolation from the voices of the past.[61] Thomas also anticipated the rise of the fourth-generation of Pentecostal scholarship.[62] With the continuing influence of postmodernism, Thomas believes fourth-generation Pentecostals have the opportunity to (1) sit at the wider academic table whilst utilizing a variety of postmodern critical methods akin to their worldview and ethos, (2) engage and dialogue with previous generations of Pentecostal scholarship, and (3) train in Pentecostal academic institutions.[63]

---

[57] J.C. Thomas, 'Women, Pentecostals, and the Bible: An Experiment in Pentecostal Hermeneutics', *JPT* 5 (1994), pp. 41-56. A revised version was published as J.C. Thomas, 'Reading the Bible From Within Our Tradition: A Pentecostal Hermeneutic as Test Case', in Joel Green and Max Turner (eds.), *Between Two Horizons: Spanning New Testament Studies and Systematic Theology* (Grand Rapids, MI: Eerdmans, 2000), pp. 108-22. For other works on Pentecostal hermeneutics by Thomas, see Thomas, 'Pentecostal Theology', pp. 3-19; J.C. Thomas, 'Holy Spirit and Interpretation', *DBCI*, p. 165; Thomas, 'What the Spirit is Saying to the Church', pp. 115-29; Thomas, 'Pentecostal Interpretation', pp. 89-97.

[58] In Acts 15, the council begins with the testimony of Peter, Barnabas, and Paul. Thomas, 'Reading the Bible From Within Our Tradition', pp. 112-13.

[59] Thomas, 'Reading the Bible From Within Our Tradition', p. 118.

[60] Thomas, 'Reading the Bible From Within Our Tradition', pp. 113-16.

[61] Thomas, 'Pentecostal Theology', pp. 3-19; Thomas, 'What the Spirit is Saying to the Church', pp. 115-29 (118-19).

[62] Thomas, 'Pentecostal Theology', pp. 4-7.

[63] Thomas, 'Pentecostal Theology', p. 5.

The first of the fourth-generation Pentecostal scholars to build upon the hermeneutical foundation provided by the previous generations is L. McQueen who contributes a distinctive Pentecostal theological, narrative reading of Joel for the Pentecostal community.[64] Following McQueen, K. Archer penned a monograph dedicated to describing and proposing a Pentecostal hermeneutic. Archer – following Thomas' triadic model from Acts 15 – pronounces, 'the hermeneutical strategy will be a narrative approach that embraces a tridactic negotiation for meaning between the biblical text, the Holy Spirit and the Pentecostal community'.[65] K. Archer's research indicates that the early Pentecostals read texts differently than modernistic approaches. K. Archer designates their reading strategies to be premodern or paramodern. He then offers a constructive Pentecostal approach that 'will be critical and yet remains faithful to the Pentecostal narrative tradition that shapes its identity and makes meaning possible'.[66] Archer suggests that narrative and reader-response criticisms are interpretative methods that should be utilized by Pentecostals because they correspond with the Pentecostal narrative ethos.[67] While R. Waddell's intertextual approach has been introduced earlier and will be explored later in this chapter in more detail, he advocates intertextuality 'to inquire unto the intertextual relationship between my own confessional context in a Pentecostal interpretative community and the literary references to the Spirit in the Apocalypse'.[68] He describes the profile of a Pentecostal reader as one who, while in the Spirit (ἐν πνεύματι), has a revelatory (ἀποκάλυψις) encounter with Jesus having an ear to hear, discern, and keep the prophetic Word of the Spirit in community from a fearful and humble position.[69] Waddell employs his theological and intertextual approach to explore

---

[64] L.R. McQueen, *Joel and the Spirit: The Cry of a Prophetic Hermeneutic* (JPTSup 8; Sheffield: Sheffield Academic Press, 1995), later published as L.R. McQueen, *Joel and the Spirit: The Cry of a Prophetic Hermeneutic* (Cleveland, TN: CPT Press, 2009), which will be cited in this monograph.

[65] Archer, *A Pentecostal Hermeneutic*, p. 213.

[66] Archer, *A Pentecostal Hermeneutic*, p. 212.

[67] Archer, *A Pentecostal Hermeneutic*, pp. 225-47.

[68] Waddell, *Spirit of the Book of Revelation*, p. 37. As noted above, Waddell's monograph is the first full-length monograph dedicated to pneumatology of the Apocalypse and the first to use explicitly a literary, intertextual approach from a Pentecostal perspective.

[69] Waddell, *Spirit of the Book of Revelation*, pp. 97-131.

the Spirit in the Apocalypse. L. Martin offers a Pentecostal theological narrative 'hearing' (שָׁמַע) of Judges.[70] Martin agrees that Pentecostalism must be proactive in formulating a Pentecostal hermeneutic that 'employs the hermeneutical methods that are more conducive to our ethos, theology, and view of Scripture. We [Pentecostals] cannot be precritical; we must not be anticritical; but we should be postcritical pursuing the path that Iain Provan calls "believing criticism"'.[71] Martin advocates 'hearing' as an interpretative model for Pentecostals because the biblical texts beckon to be performed orally and relationally in community, which corresponds to both the genre and history of the bible as well as the Pentecostal ethos.[72] M. Archer explores the theme of worship in the Apocalypse from a narrative critical approach and follows the triadic paradigm proposed by Thomas and K. Archer. M. Archer views the Pentecostal 'community' as including the early Pentecostal testimonies mined by the use of *Wirkungsgeschichte* as well as contributions from Pentecostal scholarship.[73] C. Green has examined the integration of vocation and sanctification in the process of reading scripture. Green explores the way that the process of interpretation sanctifies the church, even with texts that are troublesome or that lead to misunderstandings.[74]

Therefore, from the story of Pentecostal hermeneutics, a hermeneutic has emerged from the Pentecostal (con)text that aligns with the Pentecostal ethos. A Pentecostal hermeneutic that negotiates meaning among the Spirit, scripture, and community.[75] The

---

[70] L.R. Martin, *The Unheard Voice of God: A Pentecostal Hearing of the Book of Judges* (JTPSup 32; Dorset: Deo Publishing, 2008), pp. 1-2, writes, 'I am attempting to produce a *pro nobis* study that will enrich the biblical component of Pentecostal life and practice. The methodology of the study is literary-theological inasmuch as I employ synchronic literary/rhetorical methods in the critical study of Judges as a narrative theological text.'

[71] Martin, *The Unheard Voice of God*, p. 57.

[72] Martin, *The Unheard Voice of God*, pp. 66-68. See also J.D. Johns and C. Bridges Johns, 'Yielding to the Spirit: A Pentecostal Approach to Group Study', *JPT* 1 (1992), pp. 109-34, for a relational model of epistemology found in the biblical text.

[73] M. Archer, *'I Was in the Spirit on the Lord's Day': A Pentecostal Engagement with Worship in the Apocalypse* (Cleveland, TN: CPT Press, 2015), pp. 38-67.

[74] Green, *Sanctifying Interpretation*.

[75] See Moore, 'Canon and Charisma', pp. 75-92; Thomas, 'Women, Pentecostals, and the Bible', pp. 41-56; Archer, *A Pentecostal Hermeneutic*, pp. 212-60;

methodology in this piece follows the triadic formula put forth by Pentecostal scholars that stems from the Pentecostal (con)text. This chapter turns to investigate each area of the Pentecostal triad. While this monograph turns to exam each aspect of the triad, it is problematic to view any part of the triad in isolation of others because the dialogue among each aspect of the triad is where meaning can be discovered. In other words, one cannot speak of scripture without mentioning the inspiration of the Spirit or the scripture's impact in a community.

## A Pentecostal (Con)textual Hermeneutic: Community, Scripture, and Spirit

### Community
Community is a significant feature of the hermeneutical process because it forms the intertexts of the readers that impacts the reading of an (inter)text, while also implementing a defense against an individualistic outlook and offering a space for discernment.[76] I turn to explore four aspects of the Pentecostal community: (i) the local worshipping Pentecostal congregation, (ii) the texts of the early Pentecostal periodical literature, (iii) the (inter)text of *ecclesia catholic*, and (iv) the (con)text of (Pentecostal) scholarship. Each voice of the community (in)forms the discerning process by offering assistance in discovering an interpretation that is faithful.

### The (Con)text(s) of the Local Pentecostal Community
The (con)text of the local Pentecostal community has a profound impact on the formation of a Pentecostal interpreter. The local Pentecostal community is a pneumatically created space in which to encounter the Creator God and the incarnate Word through scripture, worship, prayer, testimony, sacrament, and preaching by the Spirit.[77]

---

A. Yong, *Spirit-Word-Community: Theological Hermeneutics in Trinitarian Perspective* (Burlington, VT: Ashgate Publishing Limited, 2002).

[76] See Thomas, 'What the Spirit is Saying to the Church', p. 116. See also C. Bridges Johns, *Pentecostal Formation: A Pedagogy Among the Oppressed* (JPTSup 2; Sheffield: Sheffield Academic Press, 1993), pp. 125-30; Archer, *A Pentecostal Hermeneutic*, p. 224; S.A. Ellington, 'Pentecostalism and the Authority of Scripture', *JPT* 9 (1996), pp. 28-29.

[77] F.L. Arrington, 'Hermeneutics', *DPCM*, p. 382; Thomas, 'Pentecostal Interpretation', p. 94.

Many Pentecostals perceive themselves essentially to be on a transformative soteriological journey to participate in the Full Gospel narrative of Jesus as savior, sanctifier, healer, Spirit-baptizer, and soon
coming king.[78] A number of Pentecostal scholars deem that the integration between the academy and one's faith is necessary for a faithful
interpretation.[79] R. Waddell, following Anselm, crafts this anthem for
Pentecostal hermeneutics, 'unless we believe, we shall not understand'.[80]

Experience in a local Pentecostal community is a divine encounter
of 're-creation' without which it would be nearly impossible to discern a meaningful interpretation of scriptures for the community.[81]
Experience in a local Pentecostal community creatively forms Pentecostal scholars, and their scholarship (in)forms the Pentecostal community and worship.[82] After a divine experience, a member of the
community will be asked to testify so that the whole community can
discern. Pentecostal community functions as a defense that 'can offer
balance, accountability, and support. It can guard against rampant individualism and uncontrolled subjectivism'.[83]

## The (Con)text(s) of the Early Pentecostal Community

A number of Pentecostals have moved toward hearing, discerning,
and dialoguing with the early Pentecostal literature. The first ten years
(1906–1916) is considered to be the theological heart, not the infancy,
of the Pentecostal movement.[84] As the theological heart, the

---

[78] Archer, *A Pentecostal Hermeneutic*, pp. 32, 224-25; Thomas, 'What the Spirit is
Saying to the Church', pp. 116-18.

[79] Pentecostals would affirm Jenson, 'Scripture's Authority in the Church', pp.
27-37 (29), who writes, 'the question, after all, is not whether churchly reading of
Scripture is justified; the question is, what could possibly justify any other?' See also
Hays, 'Reading the Bible with Eyes of Faith', pp. 5-21; Green, *Practicing Theological
Interpretation*.

[80] Waddell, *Spirit of the Book of Revelation*, pp. 111, 118.

[81] Ervin, 'Hermeneutics', p. 17.

[82] K.L. Spawn and A.T. Wright, 'The Emergence of a Pneumatic Hermeneutic
in the Renewal Tradition', in K.L. Spawn and A.T. Wright (eds.), *Spirit and Scripture:
Exploring a Pneumatic Hermeneutic* (T&T Clark: London, 2012), pp. 7-8. See Hays,
'Reading the Bible with Eyes of Faith', pp. 5-21.

[83] Thomas, 'Reading the Bible From Within Our Tradition', p. 119.

[84] See again Hollenweger, 'Pentecostals and the Charismatic Movement', pp.
549-53; Land, *Pentecostal Spirituality*, pp. 37-44.

intertexts of the early Pentecostal periodical literature are significantly impactful in the formation of the Pentecostal interpreter and a 'for us' interpretation.

The method employed in the process of uncovering the ethos of the early Pentecostal periodical literature by some Pentecostals is *Wirkungsgeschichte*.[85] *Wirkungsgeschichte* is a method that assists the Pentecostal community to uncover 'the effects our readings have had throughout our history and in the present-day on the Pentecostal movement'.[86] A central reason being that *Wirkungsgeschichte* is a method that is more attuned to discover premodern interpretations, aligning with the 'paramodern' worldview of the early Pentecostal communities.[87] Hearing these early Pentecostal 'testimonies' allows engagement with the Pentecostal (con)text that

> provides the Pentecostal interpreter with additional opportunities to discern and reflect upon the Pentecostal identity and ethos … such encounters with these 'ancient' testimonies have acted as a bridge between the biblical texts and me, as I have come to realize more and more that they too are part of the community in which I seek to hear what the Spirit is saying to the church.[88]

Specifically, *Wirkungsgeschichte* has been employed by Pentecostals to explore topics that include: the book of Joel,[89] 3 Jn 2,[90]

---

[85] As noted above, the initial call for Pentecostals to utilize *Wirkungsgeschichte* came from Thomas, 'Pentecostal Theology', pp. 3-19. Following Thomas, E.B. Powery, 'Ulrich Luz's Matthew in History: A Contribution to Pentecostal Hermeneutics?', *JPT* 14 (1999), pp. 3-17, engaged Luz's work concerning the use of *Wirkungsgeschichte* for Pentecostal hermeneutics. See also Luz's response: U. Luz, 'A Response to Emerson B. Powery', *JPT* 14 (1999), pp. 19-26. Pentecostals are by no means the only group that has utilized *Wirkungsgeschichte* as a method of interpretation, for example, see Blackwell Bible Commentary Series; M. Lieb, E. Mason, and J. Roberts (eds.), *The Oxford Handbook of the Reception History of the Bible* (Oxford: Oxford University Press, 2011); *Biblical Reception* (Sheffield Phoenix Press); and *Journal of the Bible and its Reception* (De Gruyter). See also footnote 139 of this chapter for significant works that explore the *Wirkungsgeschichte* of the Apocalypse.
[86] Powery, 'Ulrich Luz's Matthew in History', p. 15.
[87] Powery, 'Ulrich Luz's Matthew in History', p. 14.
[88] Thomas, 'What the Spirit is Saying to the Church', p. 119.
[89] McQueen, *Joel and the Spirit*, pp. 69-89.
[90] H.L. Landrus, 'Hearing 3 John 2 in the Voices of History', *JPT* 11.1 (2002), pp. 70-88.

Mk 16.9-20,[91] healing in the atonement,[92] eschatology,[93] the Lord's Supper,[94] soteriology and creation care,[95] worship in the Apocalypse,[96] Spirit Christology,[97] fasting,[98] the mark of the beast,[99] and Gog and Magog.[100] Pentecostals look to 'evaluate the effects of such interpretations on our Pentecostal sermons, songs and testimonies noting not only what they say (their content and understanding) but also their "fruits" seen in the Church's actions'.[101] These attempts are not purposed to salvage a fossilized epistemology, but to discern and be formed by the testimonies of the past and honor the Pentecostal tradition.[102]

*Wirkungsgeschichte*[103] is an interpretative methodology most recently put forth by NT scholar U. Luz.[104] Luz, in *Matthew in History*, begins his approach by offering a staunch critique of the historical critical method. He observes that historical scholarship tends to distance itself from the text to remain objective and thereby prevents the ability

---

[91] J.C. Thomas and K.E. Alexander, '"And the Signs are Following": Mark 16.9-20 – A Journey into Pentecostal Hermeneutics', *JPT* 11.2 (2003), pp. 147-70.

[92] J.C. Thomas, 'Healing in the Atonement: A Johannine Perspective', *JPT* 14.1 (2005), pp. 175-89; K.E. Alexander, *Pentecostal Healing: Models in Theology and Practice* (JPTSup 29; Dorset: Deo Publishing, 2006), pp. 64-194.

[93] McQueen, *Toward a Pentecostal Eschatology*, pp. 60-199.

[94] Green, *Toward a Pentecostal Theology of the Lord's Supper*, pp. 74-181.

[95] J.S. Lamp, 'New Heavens and New Earth: Early Pentecostal Soteriology as a Foundation for Creation Care in the Present', *Pneuma* 36.1 (2014), pp. 64-80.

[96] Archer, *'I Was in the Spirit on the Lord's Day'*, pp. 68-118.

[97] H.O. Bryant, *Spirit Christology in the Christian Tradition: From the Patristic Period to the Rise of Pentecostalism in the Twentieth Century* (Cleveland, TN: CPT Press, 2015), pp. 464-508.

[98] L.R. Martin, 'The Function and Practice of Fasting in Early Pentecostalism', *PJT* 96 (2015), pp. 1-19.

[99] D.R. Johnson, 'The Mark of the Beast, Reception History, and Early Pentecostal Literature', *JPT* 25.2 (2016), pp. 184-202.

[100] A.R. Jackson, 'Wesleyan Holiness and Finished Work Pentecostal Interpretations of Gog and Magog Biblical Texts', *JPT* 25.2 (2016), pp. 168-83.

[101] Powery, 'Ulrich Luz's Matthew in History', p. 16.

[102] Archer, *A Pentecostal Hermeneutic*, p. 199;

[103] *Wirkungsgeschichte* is difficult to translate, and the possibilities include reception history, effective history, history of effects, history of reception, and history of influence, see Luz, 'A Response to Emerson B. Powery', pp. 19-20 n. 2.

[104] U. Luz, *Matthew in History: Interpretation, Influence, and Effects* (Minneapolis, MN: Fortress, 1994).

to find meaning for contemporary readers.[105] Luz offers *Wirkungsges-chichte* as a way for contemporary interpreters to bridge the ditch between the contemporary context and the text. He suggests that there is no one objective, static meaning of a text; each interpretation is contextual and each new generation is given an opportunity to discern new meanings. The biblical text cannot be separated from its *Wirkungsgeschichte*: it is part of the text and 'belongs to the texts in the same way that a river flowing away from its source belongs to the source'.[106] Thus, since *Wirkungsgeschichte* brings together the text, interpreter, and interpretation, it 'shows us that we are already together and that it is an illusion to treat the texts in a position of distance and in a merely "objective" way'.[107] Texts do not have a single meaning but produce meanings again and again throughout history.[108] Luz notes that new generations cannot merely renovate antiquated interpretations, but should allow *Wirkungsgeschichte* to inform their contextual interpretation.[109]

Meaning for Luz begins with Christology in that meaning does not come from understanding a text, but to understand the one whom the text is about – Christ. Interpretation must be holistic: holding together theory and praxis.[110] Finally, Luz comments on the power of the biblical texts on account that throughout history, texts have had positive, negative, and even devastating effects.[111] Luz offers some criterion for one to determine a positive interpretation: interpretations should 'correspond with the essentials of the history of Jesus',[112] evaluate the fruit of a given text in light of the fruit of the NT canon,[113] and bring about love.[114]

Hence, in the third and fourth chapters of this work, I will utilize *Wirkungsgeschichte* as a method to hear and be (in)formed by the voices

---

[105] Luz, *Matthew in History*, p. 2.

[106] Luz, *Matthew in History*, p. 24. From this, Luz (p. 76) criticizes *sola scriptura* because no text is isolated from its rich history of interpretation.

[107] Luz, *Matthew in History*, p. 25.

[108] Luz, *Matthew in History*, p. 17.

[109] Luz, *Matthew in History*, p. 28.

[110] Luz, *Matthew in History*, pp. 13-14.

[111] Luz, *Matthew in History*, pp. 32-34.

[112] Luz, *Matthew in History*, p. 82.

[113] Luz, *Matthew in History*, p. 92.

[114] Luz, *Matthew in History*, pp. 94-96.

of the early Pentecostal literature by surveying their testimonies concerning the pneumatology of the Apocalypse and pneumatic discernment. I have split the study into two chapters, following the division put forth by K. Alexander who discovered theological distinctives among the Wesleyan-Holiness Pentecostals and the Finished-Work Pentecostals.[115] While the primary theological division stemmed from the issue of sanctification, Alexander (and subsequently others) has discovered that these theological constructs impacted the ways that the early Pentecostals approached particular issues.[116]

## The (Con)text(s) of the *Ecclesia Catholic*

The Pentecostal (con)text is a part of the larger Christian (con)text and thereby intersects with other texts that form the Christian (inter)text. While *Wirkungsgeschichte* has been used by Pentecostals to explore the voices of the early Pentecostal (con)text primarily, other Pentecostals have considered the use of *Wirkungsgeschichte* to hear the voices of the wider church tradition. Pentecostals have had diverse opinions on the way in which to incorporate church tradition within Pentecostal community, but from early on Pentecostals scholars called upon Pentecostals to embrace the testimonies of church tradition in their hermeneutical strategies.[117] Three rationales have emerged for the inclusion of church tradition in the Pentecostal community: (1) there is a historical precedent, (2) the correlation of premodern interpretations – often seen by means of *Wirkungsgeschichte* – with the Pentecostal worldview, and (3) as an interpretative guard or defense.

First, K. Archer identifies the impact of church tradition in the Oneness debate. When considering how to challenge the Oneness position, Trinitarian Pentecostals 'recognized the value of historic orthodox belief' and thereby 'searched the chronicles of church history

---

[115] Alexander, *Pentecostal Healing*. For others who follow this two stream approach, see Green, *Toward a Pentecostal Theology of the Lord's Supper*; Archer, *'I Was in the Spirit on the Lord's Day'*; Bryant, *Spirit Christology*.

[116] It is important to note that Green, *Toward a Pentecostal Theology of the Lord's Supper* and Archer, *'I Was in the Spirit on the Lord's Day'*, observe an overall continuity in the Lord's Supper (Green) and worship in the Apocalypse (Archer) among the two streams.

[117] Green, *Toward a Pentecostal Theology of the Lord's Supper*, p. 190 n. 43, is one of the first Pentecostals to reflect explicitly upon including *ecclesia catholic* in the community of the Pentecostal hermeneutical triad.

to find ecstatic gifts operating in the Church'.[118] Trinitarian Pentecostals attempted to redeem church history by finding the continuing charismatic activity of the Spirit throughout church history. Accordingly, Archer proposes, 'the community must take into consideration the wider church body and the history of doctrinal development as it assesses the validation of the meaning'.[119] C. Green, then, engages K. Archer for maintaining that Pentecostals should take into consideration church tradition without offering a way to accomplish this task. Green – who believes Pentecostals should explore church tradition – offers an approach, which petitions the early Pentecostals practice of engaging with the broader Christian tradition when reflecting on theology and spirituality.[120] Green provides an approach that remains in 'discerning conversation' with the wider church and tradition:[121]

> Contemporary Pentecostals must think and live in ways that make one story with the movement's pioneers, just as they should seek to live and think in ways that make their story one with the *apostles'* story and the story of the one, holy, catholic, and apostolic church.[122]

Second, *Wirkungsgeschichte*, as noted above, has been an interpretative method for Pentecostals to hear the voices of the early Pentecostals. But, it has also been used to hear premodern voices of the wider church, which correlate to the Pentecostal worldview:

> The emphasis which Pentecostals have placed on testimonies may provide the vehicle needed with which our churches can learn to appreciate the premodern interpretations. In a post-critical society, nonmodern and reassessed premodern interpretations will

---

[118] Archer, *A Pentecostal Hermeneutic*, p. 258. He also notes that the Trinitarian Pentecostals searched to discover the charismatic activity in church history as a way to redeem church history against the claims of the Oneness Pentecostal. Oneness Pentecostals believed that they were recovering the apostolic doctrine corrupted in the church councils.

[119] Archer, *A Pentecostal Hermeneutic*, p. 257.

[120] Green, *Toward a Pentecostal Theology of the Lord's Supper*, pp. 305-307

[121] Green, *Toward a Pentecostal Theology of the Lord's Supper*, p. 304

[122] Green, *Toward a Pentecostal Theology of the Lord's Supper*, p. 75. Green also writes (p. 303), 'I assume that one cannot faithfully tell the story of the God of Scripture without also telling the story of the *ecclesia theou*, which means that the church's story must have the same *unity* as does Christ's, for they share one history'.

determine not only the future of the church but perhaps the academy as well.[123]

J.C. Thomas, who first offered *Wirkungsgeschichte* as an interpretative method for Pentecostals, includes the wider church tradition as a voice that needs to be heard because it bridges 'ancient testimonies' with contemporary interpreters.[124] Observing church tradition allows the Pentecostal community to realize:

> We are not the first Christians to read the Bible. The Spirit has already been active in people's lives for centuries. Seeking the insight that was achieved in tradition is an act of respect for all our fathers and mothers in the faith. We should not so emphasize the authority of the Bible that we fail to see the positive significance of tradition.[125]

J.C. Thomas, H. Landrus, and L. Martin have offered significant contributions that explore voices from the wider church tradition. Thomas implements *Wirkungsgeschichte* in his commentary on the Apocalypse where he explores premodern interpretations and hears testimonies of wider church tradition.[126] Landrus hears the ecclesial voices from Tertullian to Paul Yonggi Cho to examine the interpretations of 3 John 2.[127] Martin, in a monograph on Judges, includes a section on 'precritical studies' where he reviews interpretations from

---

[123] Waddell, *Spirit of the Book of Revelation*, p. 113. However, R. Bauckham, 'Review of Robby Waddell, *The Spirit of the Book of Revelation*', *JPT* 17.1 (2008), pp. 3-8 (6), is critical of Waddell for not citing any premodern interpretations when performing his exegesis.

[124] Thomas, 'Pentecostal Theology', p. 16; Thomas, 'What the Spirit is Saying to the Church', p. 119.

[125] See C.H. Pinnock, *The Scripture Principle* (Grand Rapids, MI: Baker Publishing, 2nd edn, 2006), p. 241. See also Hays, 'Reading the Bible with Eyes of Faith', p. 15, who writes, 'We know that we have much to learn from the wisdom of the people who have reflected deeply on these texts before us. Consequently, theological exegesis will find hermeneutical aid, not hindrance, in the church's doctrinal traditions.'

[126] J.C. Thomas, *The Apocalypse: A Literary and Theological Commentary* (Cleveland, TN: CPT Press, 2012), pp. 51-86.

[127] Landrus, 'Hearing 3 John 2 in the Voices of History', pp. 70-88. Landrus examines interpretations from Tertullian, Augustine, Bede, Le Maistre De Sacy, Ambrosius, Catharinus, John Bird Sumner, Albert Barnes, Carrie Judd Montgomery, Oral Roberts, Kenneth Hagin, Raymond Brown, Frederick Prince, and Paul Yonggi Cho.

the ante-Nicene, post-Nicene, Reformation, and post-Reformation periods.[128]

Third, H. Ervin – who is one of the first scholars to offer a distinctive Pentecostal hermeneutic – suggests that the 'historical succession' of the church must be taken into account. He determines that 'a viable hermeneutic must deal responsibly with the apostolic witness of Scripture in terms of an apostolic experience, and in continuity with the Church's apostolic traditions'.[129] If church tradition is not taken seriously, there is a potentiality that an interpretation of gospel could become 'another gospel'.[130] Similarly, C. Pinnock welcomes tradition as a guard against negative or harmful interpretations. Church tradition is a defense and stabilizer in hermeneutics that acts as a fence around the text that guards against individualistic, private, or isolated (mis)interpretations. For Pinnock, a text is accompanied by centuries of Spirit inspired readings and hearings, which are the 'embodied and distilled wisdom of the ages'.[131] Consequently, with the diverse history of a text, a sect or denomination cannot contain the 'whole counsel of God'.[132]

However, Pentecostals have cautioned against constructing tradition into a static, dead entity or accepting every interpretation undiscerningly because there have been both positive and harmful interpretations throughout church history:

> Discernment is required of these testimonies no less than in testimonies offered in the context of Pentecostal worship, but the history of effects has an enormous contribution to make to a Pentecostal study of the New Testament.[133]

Pentecostals cannot aspire to absolutize tradition where interpreters uncritically accept its teachings; neither can they allow tradition to prevent new contextual interpretations.[134] Rather, Pentecostals must

---

[128] Martin, *The Unheard Voice of God*, pp. 18-30.

[129] Ervin, 'Hermeneutics', p. 23.

[130] Ervin, 'Hermeneutics', p. 23.

[131] Pinnock, *The Scripture Principle*, p. 241.

[132] Ervin, 'Hermeneutics', p. 23.

[133] Thomas, 'Pentecostal Theology', p. 16. Land, *Pentecostal Spirituality*, p. 23, adds 'Creeds must guard the faith not limit the sovereign leading of the Spirit'. See also Pinnock, *The Scripture Principle*, p. 242.

[134] Pinnock, *The Scripture Principle*, p. 242. See Hays, 'Reading the Bible with Eyes of Faith', p. 15, who writes:

hear tradition as a voice of 'counsel, not of command'.[135] Tradition is 'a life-giving complement to Scripture and cannot be set aside without harming the identity of the faith community'.[136]

In sum, the Spirit works through tradition to form a community, while participating in the process to discern these testimonies. Church tradition should be considered a living active pneumatic voice in the Pentecostal community because, first, there is a historical precedent of the early Pentecostals looking to church tradition for interpretative guidance. Emerging from the Pentecostal (con)text includes suggestions to hear (inter)texts from the wider Christian tradition. Second, tradition provides a premodern dialogue partner that correlates to the paramodern worldview of early Pentecostalism. All (inter)texts come to an interpreter in the river of history, and the waters are deep with diversity. Christian tradition is another aspect of the Pentecostal (con)text that converges with the (inter)text of scripture. Appealing to church tradition is a way for Pentecostals to acknowledge, discern, and learn from the Spirit's dynamic, diverse, and unceasing activity throughout history.[137] Because of the Spirit's activity in church history, Pentecostals should be intentional in seeing the Pentecostal story as a continuation of God's story as well as the

---

Theological exegesis, however, goes beyond repeating traditional interpretations; rather, instructed by the example of traditional readings, theological interpreters will produce fresh readings, new performances of Scripture's sense that encounter the texts anew with eyes of faith and see the ways that the Holy Spirit continues to speak to the churches through the same ancient texts that the tradition has handed on to us.

[135] Pinnock, *The Scripture Principle*, p. 242.

[136] Pinnock, *The Scripture Principle*, p. 242. R.W. Jenson, *Canon and Creed* (Interpretation; Louisville, KY: Westminster, 2010), p. 50, adds:

We cannot suppose that the Apostle's Creed, or any other actual creed, is a complete summary of the faith or is by itself an adequate guardian of the church's continuing apostolicity. Churchly declarations sometimes assert that the creed contains everything we need to believe. This is true only if we read the creed in its just-described deference to the canon. We are even more often told that the canon of Scripture contains 'all things necessary for our salvation.' This is true only if in reading Scripture we let the structure of the creed guide us to Scripture's overall trinitarian structure, and also let the teaching of the creed determine our reading of such biblical phenomena.

[137] Thomas, 'What the Spirit is Saying to the Church', p. 119, commenting on tradition writes, 'I have come to realize more and more that they too are part of the community in which I seek to hear what the Spirit is saying to the church'.

*ecclesia theou.*[138] Third, tradition offers an additional defense or guard for the Pentecostal community against creating 'another gospel' resulting from isolated, individualistic, private, and harmful interpretations from individuals or even isolated communities. Pentecostals can neither isolate themselves from the wider Christian tradition nor can they presume to hold province over the full wisdom and counsel of God. If Pentecostals are to have an ear to hear, they have a responsibility to hear the voice of the Spirit in other traditions. Accordingly, while there is not enough space in this monograph to offer a thorough *Wirkungsgeschichte* of early church voices concerning pneumatic discernment in the Apocalypse, this work seeks to hear these voices by means of edited volumes on the Apocalypse.[139]

## The (Con)text(s) of the (Pentecostal) Scholars

The final aspect of the Pentecostal (con)text to be explored is the text of the academy. Whereas a Pentecostal interpretation is for and in the Pentecostal community, this work is (in)formed by the academy.[140] Chapter two of this monograph will examine texts of the academy that form and shape this study of the Apocalypse. Beyond

---

[138] See Land, *Pentecostal Spirituality*, pp. 63-88. See also Waddell, *Spirit of the Book of Revelation*, p. 90, who adds, 'The Spirit is working universally to draw all creation back to God. The Spirit is eschatological; the Spirit is mission-focused; and the Spirit is catholic.'

[139] W.C. Weinrich (ed.) *Revelation* (ACC 12; Downers Grove, IL: InterVarsity Press, 2005); W.C. Weinrich (ed.) *Latin Commentaries on Revelation* (ACT; Downers Grove, IL: InterVarsity Press, 2011); W.C. Weinrich (ed.) *Greek Commentaries on Revelation* (ACT; Downers Grove, IL: InterVarsity Press, 2011). Some attempts at reception history for the Apocalypse include: G. Kretschmar, *Die Offenbarung des Johannes: Die Geschichte ihrer Auslegung im 1. Jahrtausend* (Stuttgart: Calwer Verlag, 1985); R.K. Emmerson and B. McGinn (eds.), *The Apocalypse in the Middle Ages* (Ithaca, NY: Cornell University Press, 1992); C. Rowland, *Revelation* (London: Epworth Press, 1993); K.G.C. Newport, *Apocalypse & Millennium* (Cambridge: Cambridge University Press, 2000); C.R. Koester, *Revelation and the End of All Things* (Grand Rapids, MI: Eerdmans, 2001), pp. 1-40; J. Kovacs and C. Rowland, *Revelation* (BBC; Malden, MA: Blackwell Publishing, 2004); Thomas, *The Apocalypse*, pp. 51-86; C.R. Koester, *Revelation: Translation with Introduction and Commentary* (ABYC 38A; New Haven, CT: Yale University Press, 2014). For a comprehensive bibliography of ancient Christian interpreters of the Apocalypse, see I. Boxall and R. Tresley (eds.), *The Book of Revelation and Its Interpreters: Short Studies and an Annotated Bibliography* (Lanham, MD: Rowman & Littlefield, 2016), pp. 125-272.

[140] It is important to note that not all scholars who identify as a Pentecostal or charismatic would follow an intentional 'Pentecostal approach' that is followed in this work, see for example C.S. Keener, *Spirit Hermeneutics: Reading Scripture in Light of Pentecost* (Grand Rapids, MI: Eerdmans, 2016).

the immense impact the wider academy will have upon this work and my formation, M. Archer has pointed out the influence Pentecostal scholarship has on a Pentecostal approach.[141] My Pentecostal (con)text has fine-tuned my ears to hear the symphony of Pentecostal scholars formed in the Pentecostal (con)text. I have been trained in the academic (con)text at Pentecostal universities and seminaries. I will include the testimonies of Pentecostal scholars in the review of literature in the second chapter of this work alongside the voices of the greater academy.[142] When interpreting the text in the fourth chapter, I will dedicate attention to hear Pentecostal scholarly works on the Apocalypse alongside the works of the wider academy.[143]

In conclusion, as an interpreter, I am influenced by the Pentecostal (con)text. As every other interpreter, I bring to the text my (con)text, experiences, and presuppositions. I have defined my Pentecostal community as (i) the local worshipping Pentecostal congregation, (ii) the texts of the early Pentecostal periodical literature, (iii) the (inter)text of *ecclesia catholic*, and (iv) the (con)text of (Pentecostal) scholarship. In the second chapter, I will examine the scholarly (con)texts of the academy that discuss pneumatic discernment and the pneumatology of the Apocalypse. In the third and fourth chapters of this study, I will utilize *Wirkungsgeschichte* as a method to hear and be informed by the voices of the early Pentecostal community by hearing their testimonies concerning pneumatic discernment in the Apocalypse. Then, in the fifth chapter, alongside engagement with the wider academy, I will offer attention to Pentecostal scholarship on the Apocalypse, while also hearing from the voices of the

---

[141] Archer, *'I Was in the Spirit on the Lord's Day'*, pp. 50-53.

[142] Waddell, *Spirit of the Book of Revelation*; Thomas, 'Pneumatic Discernment', pp. 106-24; Thomas, 'The Mystery of the Great Whore', pp. 111-36; R. Herms, 'Invoking the Spirit and Narrative Intent in John's Apocalypse', in Kevin L. Spawn and Archie T. Wright (eds.), *Spirit and Scripture: Examining a Pneumatic Hermeneutic* (London: T&T Clark, 2012), pp. 99-114; J.C. Thomas and F. Macchia, *Revelation* (THC; Grand Rapids, MI: Eerdmans, 2016). For a review of these works see the second chapter of this work.

[143] Commentaries written by Pentecostals on the Apocalypse include: R.H. Gause, *Revelation: God's Stamp of Sovereignty on History* (Cleveland, TN: Pathway Press, 1983); C.S. Keener, *Revelation* (NIVAC; Grand Rapids, MI: Zondervan, 2000); R. Skaggs and P. Benham, *Revelation* (PCS; Dorset: Deo Publishing, 2009); G.D. Fee, *Revelation* (NCCS; Eugene, OR: Cascade, 2011); Thomas, *The Apocalypse*; Thomas and Macchia, *Revelation*.

broader church tradition. Hearing these testimonies from the community assists me as an interpreter to move beyond my individualistic perspective; to be (in)formed by the Pentecostal and academic (con)text; to hear the testimonies of the wider church; and to bridge the historic ditch between my (inter)text and the (inter)text of scripture.

## The (Inter)text of Scripture

### The Nature of Scripture in the Pentecostal (Con)text

Those who are formed by the Pentecostal (con)text view themselves as 'people of the Word' and have a high view of scripture. Scripture is God's (continuing) revelation to humanity mediated through the story of Israel, the story of Jesus, and the story of the outpouring of the Spirit on the early church.[144] Scripture is a 'record of the testimonies' that tells the story of God.[145] This story is not contained statically upon the letters of a page; rather, the Spirit dynamically voices

---

[144] See Ervin, 'Hermeneutics', p. 16; Pinnock, *The Scripture Principle*, pp. 27-53. J. Goldingay, 'Authority of Scripture', *DBCI*, (New York, NY: Routledge, 2007), pp. 31-32, writes:

> In general scripture does not focus on telling us what to do, or even what to believe. Most often it is telling us stories or relating history. It is slightly odd to apply the notion of authority to stories. It can be done, though the notion of authority then has a different meaning from the usual one. If the authority of scripture denotes its capacity to tell us what to believe, then the narrative of scripture has authority insofar as it declares authoritatively what is the nature of Christian faith. It establishes that Christian faith is a gospel, a statement about things that have happened in the story of Israel and in the story of Jesus that constitute good news for readers. It is not primarily a set of statements about the being of God or about obligations that Christians have, but a story about what God has done. The authority of scripture is thus built into the nature of Christian faith as gospel.

[145] Ellington, 'Pentecostalism and the Authority of Scripture', p. 29; Smith, *Thinking in Tongues*, p. 82.

God's story to the community.[146] Scripture is a 'sanctified vessel' being 'both a human and divine document'.[147] Scripture is an occasion of theophany where 'Word, Spirit, and person(s) meet'.[148]

Hearing scripture in community is an activity where Pentecostals participate in God's story as they recite their stories as an extension of the biblical story.[149] Testimony is a 'corporate liturgy'[150] where Pentecostals share their stories.[151] In a Pentecostal community, each member is able to give testimony and each member is called to discern. In the local congregation, testimonies include stories of one's experiences as well as the story of scripture.[152] Testimony provides a defense against rampant, harmful individualism.[153] The oral nature of scripture and the oral ethos of the Pentecostal community suggest that Pentecostals are not interested in acquiring abstract knowledge when coming to a text, and hearing scripture is much more than an

---

[146] C. Bridges Johns, 'Grieving, Brooding, and Transforming: The Spirit, the Bible, and Gender', *JPT* 23 (2014), p. 147, writes, 'The same Holy Spirit who filled the Incarnate Word fills the written Word. Just as Jesus could not minister apart from the work of the Spirit, so the Bible cannot speak apart from the work of the Spirit.'

[147] Bridges Johns, 'Grieving, Brooding, and Transforming', p. 148.

[148] Bridges Johns, 'Grieving, Brooding, and Transforming', p. 149. See also Ellington, 'Pentecostalism and the Authority of Scripture', p. 21. Johns and Bridges Johns, 'Yielding to the Spirit', p. 118, comment, 'Scripture is the word of God, not word about God nor even word from God. God is always present in his word. The Spirit who breathed upon the prophets to speak forth the word continues to abide with the word. Inscripturated word is "out of" God only in the sense that it proceeds from God but never in the sense that it can be cut off from God.'

[149] See also J.D. Johns, 'Pentecostal and the Postmodern Worldview', *JPT* 7 (1995), p. 90; McQueen, *Joel and the Spirit*, p. 5; Waddell, *Spirit of the Book of Revelation*, p. 111; A. Davies, 'What Does it Mean to Read the Bible as a Pentecostal', *JPT* 18 (2009), pp. 216-29 (223).

[150] Bridges Johns, *Pentecostal Formation*, pp. 126-27.

[151] For the role of testimony in Pentecostalism, see Bridges Johns, *Pentecostal Formation*, pp. 126-27; S.A. Ellington, '"Can I Get a Witness": The Myth of Pentecostal Orality and the Process of Traditioning in the Psalms', *JPT* 20.1 (2011), pp. 1-14.

[152] J.K.A. Smith, 'The Closing of the Book: Pentecostals, Evangelicals, and the Sacred Writings', *JPT* 11 (1997), pp. 66-69, writes, 'When we arrive at a consensus on a valid reading, or accept and are inspired, blessed or encouraged by the experience of an individual who shares their story with the congregation, we put that down to his working among us'.

[153] Davies, 'What Does it Mean to Read the Bible as a Pentecostal', p. 228.

intellectual exercise.[154] Testimony undermines rationalistic approaches, which attempt to reduce the text to truth principles. Story is a way of knowing:[155] 'the truth *is* the story; the narrative *is* knowledge'.[156] The nature of scripture is communal, and scripture is not meant for private interpretation.[157] The narrative genre of scripture demands that it be heard in a community of faith in the same way in which it was formed.[158] L.R. Martin has established the oral nature of both scripture and the Pentecostal community to reveal their shared communal and narrative characteristics.[159] Martin approaches the scriptures as 'hearing':

---

[154] C.H. Pinnock, 'The Work of the Spirit in the Interpretation of the Holy Scriptures from the Perspective of a Charismatic Biblical Theologian', *JPT* 18 (2009), p. 161.

[155] Smith, *Thinking in Tongues*, p. 67, has pointed out that narrative, not propositions, is fundamental to the Pentecostal epistemology:

> Story, then, is not just an optional 'package' for propositions and facts; nor is narrative just a remedial or elementary form of knowledge that is overcome or outgrown by intellectual maturity. Rather, narrative is a fundamental and irreducible mode of understanding – and 'Pentecostal knowledge' attested in testimony bears witness not only to the Spirit's work but also to this epistemic reality. But our existing epistemological paradigms and categories are not well calibrated to deal with 'narrative knowledge'.

He adds (p. 70), 'Story makes sense of our world, our experience, and events on a register different from the deductive logic of efficient causality'. J. Goldingay, *Models for Scripture* (Grand Rapids, MI: Eerdmans, 1994), p. 62, remarks, 'A story communicates in a quite different way, less directly than is the case with a straight statement. It leaves the hearers to do more of the work, if they are to learn from it. Perhaps precisely because of that, it may communicate more powerfully than a direct statement will. Everybody responds to stories.'

[156] Goldingay, *Models for Scripture*, p. 66, adds, 'A story, however, cannot be summarized or turned into an abstract statement without losing something. The content comes through the story form and only through this form. The medium *is* the message. "A literary work *is* its own meaning, and its meaning cannot be univocally abstracted from it".' So also Smith, *Thinking in Tongues*, p. 64.

[157] C.H. Pinnock, 'The Work of the Holy Spirit in Hermeneutics', *JPT* 2 (1993), p. 16.

[158] Ellington, 'Pentecostalism and the Authority of Scripture', p. 30.

[159] As noted above, the work of Martin, *The Unheard Voice of God*, is significant in demonstrating the orality and thereby hearing (the testimony of) the biblical text instead of merely reading. See also Smith, 'The Closing of the Book', p. 64, who warns against textualization in the Pentecostal community and that 'in an oral community, texts function in a different genre, that of testimony, pointing to the experience and events of meeting God in Christ'.

Heaing the story!

(1) it is a thoroughly biblical term; (2) it accords with the orality of the biblical and Pentecostal contexts; (3) it is relational, implying the existence of a 'person' who is speaking the Word; (4) it denotes a faithful adherence to the Word, since in Scripture to hear often means to obey; (5) it implies transformation, since the hearing of the Word produces change; and (6) it demands humility because, unlike the process of 'reading' Scripture, 'hearing' entails submission to the authority of the word of God.[160]

Since a testimony cannot be adequately offered in isolation, 'it is important that individual Christians exist in a network and community of committed others, because so often truth emerges not from the struggles of the individuals but from the life of the whole community which participates in the Spirit'.[161] A hearing community is then able to discern and act as a guard against individualistic and isolated interpretations of scripture.

Finally, scripture is not just another testimony, but a unique testimony in that it is the unparalleled story of God told through the story of creation, Israel, Jesus' life, death, resurrection, and ascension, and the founding of God's church by the Spirit.[162] God's church, who formed the canon by the Spirit, confirms scripture's uniqueness. Therefore, the unique testimony of scripture and the active prophetic testimonies of the community must both be present in a community.

A Pentecostal (Con)textual Approach to Scripture

In this section, I seek to bring into dialogue developments of intertextuality and narrative criticism in biblical studies for and from the Pentecostal (con)text. Intertextuality has been employed in biblical studies to investigate scripture in scripture. While the theory of intertextuality has implications for such studies, the impact of intertextuality for the study of scripture is much broader because intertextuality suggests that the interpreter is significantly involved in

---

[160] Martin, *The Unheard Voice of God*, p. 53.

[161] Pinnock, 'The Work of the Holy Spirit in Hermeneutics', p. 17.

[162] Goldingay, 'Authority of Scripture', pp. 30-32. Waddell, *Spirit of the Book of Revelation*, p. 89, notes, 'Scripture is not simply one of many testimonies. Rather, it holds a unique position over and against the community, but not over and against the Spirit.'

the process of selecting (inter)textual explorations.[163] First, this section continues to exam aspects of intertextuality, particularly developments associated with the study of the Apocalypse. Second, this section brings into dialogue intertextuality with narrative criticism because narrative approaches have emerged from the Pentecostal (con)text.

Pentecostals have contributed significantly to the discussion concerning intertextuality especially in relation to the interpretation of the Apocalypse. This work employs the intertextual approach put forth by S. Moyise[164] and R. Waddell[165] rather than an 'intertextual'[166]

---

[163] S. Moyise, 'Intertextuality and the Study of the Old Testament in the New Testament', in S. Moyise (ed.), *The Old Testament in the New Testament: Essays in Honour of J.L. North* (JSNTSup 189; Sheffield: Sheffield Academic Press, 2000), p. 38, writes, 'I should point out that in using the word "chooses", I am not suggesting that interpretation is arbitrary and merely the product of an author's whim. Interpreters adopt certain positions because they believe the evidence "compels" them to see it that way. But the fact that equally sincere scholars feel "compelled" to see things differently suggests that this process is not ideologically neutral.' See also B.J. Oropeza, 'Intertextuality', *OEBI*, p. 453, who writes:

> In biblical studies intertextuality provides a creative way to understand thoughts, phrases, verses, or passages in relation to other texts. Biblical texts are read in light of other texts with the aim of adding new insight to their interpretation, and text relationships are not limited to canonical citations of earlier canonical references as is commonly done in studies entitled with variations of the phrase, 'New Testament Quotations of the Old Testament'.

[164] For a survey of intertextual models to Revelation, see S. Moyise, 'Models for Intertextual Interpretation of Revelation', in R.B. Hays and S. Alkier (eds.), *Revelation and the Politics of Apocalyptic Interpretation* (Waco, TX: Baylor University Press, 2012), pp. 31-45. Moyise, *The Old Testament in the Book of Revelation*; Moyise, 'Intertextuality', pp. 14-41; S. Moyise, 'Does the Lion Lie Down with the Lamb?', in S. Moyise (ed.), *Studies in the Book of Revelation* (New York, NY: T&T Clark, 2001), pp. 181-94; S. Moyise, 'Does the Author of Revelation Misappropriate the Scriptures?', *AUSS* 40.1 (2002), pp. 3-21. See also Ruiz, *Ezekiel in the Apocalypse*, which was foundational for Moyise's work and engaged by Waddell. Ruiz does not describe his approach as 'reader response' or 'intertextual' but does believe the readers to be 'active readers' who are 'active participants' in interpretation (pp. 195-225, 523).

[165] See again Waddell, *Spirit of the Book of Revelation*, pp. 39-96.

[166] I agree with Waddell, *Spirit of the Book of Revelation*, pp. 66, 83-90, who criticizes Beale's (and Aune's) approach(es) in that historical or source critical 'aims should not be coupled with intertextuality owing to ideological differences' because the 'inherent concept of texts in the theory of intertextuality is radically different from the historical-critical conception of text'.

approach which seeks to uncover the sources behind a text[167] or conjecture authorial intent.[168] To clarify this distinction between literary and historical approaches, Moyise has divided intertextuality into three sub-categories: intertextual echoes, dialogical intertextuality, and postmodern intertextuality.[169] First, with intertextual echoes, the reader/hearer investigates the potentiality that a (sub)text quotes, alludes to, or echoes an (inter)text.[170] Second, dialogical intertextuality allows an (inter)text to stand in a mutual relationship of unresolved tensions within a text rather than attempting to decode the intertext.[171] An (inter)text 'belongs to a web of texts which are (partially) present whenever it is read or studied'.[172] When coming to a text, one does not hear a single voice, but a plurality of testimonies entangled in the (inter)textual web.[173] Third, postmodern (or poststructural)[174]

---

[167] Contra Aune, *Revelation 1–5*, pp. cvi-cvii.

[168] Contra G.K. Beale, *John's Use of the Old Testament in Revelation* (JSNTSup 166; Sheffield: Sheffield Academic Press, 1998). For an overview and assessment of the Beale/Moyise debate over authorial intent, see J. Paulien, 'Dreading the Whirlwind: Intertextuality and the Use of the Old Testament in Revelation', *AUSS* 39.1 (2001), pp. 5-22.

[169] Moyise, 'Intertextuality', pp. 14-41. See also Waddell, *Spirit of the Book of Revelation*, pp. 76-83, who follows Moyise in these categories.

[170] Moyise, 'Intertextuality', p. 19, defines (1) a quotation as a break with the author's style that inserts words from another text (there are no quotations in the Apocalypse). (2) An allusion is a seemingly intentional allusion to another text. (3) An echo is considered to be an unintentional or unconscious allusion to another text. Identification of echoes presumes that an author is 'soaked in the scripture heritage of Israel' allowing an author to echo unknowingly another text. Moyise notes that although echoes have a whispered voice, this should not diminish their importance. So also Waddell, *Spirit of the Book of Revelation*, pp. 76-78.

[171] Moyise, *The Old Testament in the Book of Revelation*, pp. 127-35; Moyise, 'Does the Lion Lie Down with the Lamb?', pp. 181-94, Moyise appeals to the Lion/Lamb imagery. His evidence follows: (1) Revelation places images or titles side by side without identifying which is the 'signifier and which the signified'. (2) If Revelation intended on reinterpreting the Davidic messiah as the sacrificial lamb, the text continues to utilize Messianic language throughout the book without mentioning the lamb. (3) If Revelation intended to reinterpret the militant language in a non-militant manner, it is odd that military imagery is used profusely throughout Revelation. (4) Revelation does not offer easy answers but forces 'the reader to stop and think', which Moyise believes might be the intention of the HB language in Revelation.

[172] Moyise, 'Intertextuality', pp. 15-16.

[173] Moyise, *The Old Testament in the Book of Revelation*, p. 143.

[174] Waddell, *Spirit of the Book of Revelation*, p. 66, concludes that intertextuality 'highlights a particular poststructural characteristic'.

intertextuality finds that (1) no text is an 'island'[175] or an 'autonomous self-sufficient entity',[176] (2) the presence of other texts in an (inter)text leads to the possibility of multiple meanings because there is more than one way to recognize the interactions between (inter)texts,[177] (3) no interpretation is ideologically neutral,[178] (4) juxtaposing new (sub)texts with an intertext will reveal characteristics previously unseen,[179] and (5) it is impossible for one individual to grasp entirely the meaning of an (inter)text.[180]

Because of the seemingly limitless amount of possibilities intertwined between one's (con)text and an (inter)text, interpreters must be selective in their intertextual explorations.[181] Again, intertextuality suggests that the interpreter is significantly involved in the process of interpretation in choosing both textual intersections to explore and interpretative methods that are employed. As significant as the theory of intertextuality is in relation to the viability of a Pentecostal approach, it is disputed whether intertextuality should be categorized as an 'exegetical method' of interpretation.[182] Thus, one selection that has developed out of the narrative ethos of the Pentecostal (con)text

---

[175] Moyise, 'Intertextuality', p. 37.

[176] Waddell, *Spirit of the Book of Revelation*, p. 82.

[177] Moyise, 'Intertextuality', p. 37. S. Moyise, *Evoking Scripture: Seeing the Old Testament in the New* (New York, NY: T&T Clark, 2008), p. 139, writes, 'the likely complexity of such interactions should lead to a degree of humility in putting forward specific "solutions"'. See also Ruiz, *Ezekiel in the Apocalypse*, p. 222, who adds, 'There exists the temptation to believe that once the code is broken and the precise correspondence between symbolic expression and real significance has been established, the process of "decodification" has been completed once and for all. Not so: each interpreter, each audience is called upon to "decode" the μυστήριον anew.'

[178] Waddell, *Spirit of the Book of Revelation*, p. 82.

[179] Waddell, *Spirit of the Book of Revelation*, p. 82.

[180] Moyise, 'Intertextuality', p. 40.

[181] Waddell, *Spirit of the Book of Revelation*, p. 39, writes, 'Intertextuality reaches far beyond direct quotations to include allusions and echoes which occur when one text reminds the reader of another text'. See I. Paul, 'The Use of the Old Testament in Revelation 12', in S. Moyise (ed.), *The Old Testament in the New Testament: Essays in honour of J.L. North* (JSNTSup 189; Sheffield: Sheffield Academic Press, 2000), p. 262, who writes, 'it is important to remember that much interpretation consists in guess-work and intuition; objectivity comes to bear only in assessing the proposed interpretations'. Although I agree with Paul's initial remarks, I am suspicious of the objectivity of any assessment because ultimately whoever assesses an intertextual examination will be subjective to one's own intertext.

[182] See Paul, 'The Use of the Old Testament in Revelation 12', p. 259.

includes narrative and literary approaches to scripture.[183] In other words, the Pentecostal (con)text (in)forms a Pentecostal approach, which has included narrative critical interpretative methods.[184] I turn to exam the integration of intertextuality with narrative criticism for the Pentecostal (con)text. A few features of narrative criticism that correspond to the Pentecostal (con)text include, first, narrative criticism offers a way for Pentecostals to utilize a text-centered approach, which seeks to understand the Bible on its own terms.[185] Second, narrative applies to 'any work of literature that tells a story', aligning closing with the narrative ethos of the Pentecostal (con)text.[186] Third, a narrative approach performs a close hearing, which implies that a hearer takes into consideration 'the complexities and nuances of the text, taking note of structure, rhetoric, setting, characters, point of view, plot, and the narrator's style and his repertoire'.[187] While these technical categories of narrative criticism (in)form my reading of the

---

[183] Archer, *A Pentecostal Hermeneutic*, pp. 226-30, offers the following evidence for a Pentecostal narrative approach: (1) the genre of scripture is often narrative, (2) focus is on the world of the text and not the world behind the text, (3) scripture is read in its final form, (4) the bible is considered to be holy scripture, and (5) narrative insists on the role of the reader. Not only have literary approaches been undertaken by Pentecostals, it has also been an area of interest for Apocalypse studies as well. For narrative approaches to Revelation, see especially J.L. Resseguie, *The Revelation of John: A Narrative Commentary* (Grand Rapids, MI: Baker Academic, 2009), pp. 17-59. The terms narrative criticism and literary criticism will be used interchangeably in this monograph. See J.L. Resseguie, *Narrative Criticism of the New Testament: An Introduction* (Grand Rapids, MI: Baker Academic, 2005), p. 18 n. 4.

[184] Thomas, *The Apocalypse*, p. 17, writes, 'Discernment of these echoes and allusions is called for here'.

[185] M.A. Powell, *What is Narrative Criticism?* (Minneapolis, MN: Fortress, 1990), p. 85. Narrative criticism opposes the desire in historical criticism to be 'objective'. The aspiration to distance oneself from the text is contrary to the Pentecostal community's desire to hear and encounter God in the text. M.A. Powell, 'Narrative Criticism', in J.B. Green (ed.), *Hearing the New Testament: Strategies for Interpretation* (Grand Rapids: Eerdmans, 1995), pp. 239-55 (254), adds, 'A primary attraction has been the opportunity to study the biblical stories on their own terms – as stories, rather than simply as sources for historical or theological reflection'. This is not to disparage historical methods that focus on the world behind the text, but to observe, owing to Pentecostals' narrative ethos, that narrative approaches align with the ethos of many Pentecostals, see Archer, *A Pentecostal Hermeneutic*, pp. 192-93, 207.

[186] Powell, *What is Narrative Criticism?*, p. 23.

[187] Resseguie, *The Revelation of John*, pp. 17-18. For an extensive survey of technical narrative critical categories, see Powell, *What is Narrative Criticism?* and Resseguie, *Narrative Criticism*.

text, my reading will not be controlled by these formal categories.[188] Rather, a narrative approach aligns with the Pentecostal narrative ethos, and 'being preoccupied with story means, most of all preoccupied with plot and character'.[189] The narrative method used in this piece will primarily explore the narrative thread of pneumatic discernment, while being attentive to the character of the Spirit.

However, a dialogue between narrative and intertextuality reveals some tensions; Waddell writes:

> The epistemological stance inherent within Barthes's comment not only illustrates the tension between poststructuralism and historical criticism but also highlights a tension between poststructuralism and narrative approaches to biblical texts. Barthes announces the death of the author but he also calls into question the unity of the final form of the text, which is major premise of the narrative approaches. In theory, intertextuality calls into question the notion of the autonomous text. In other words, all texts are products of other texts (i.e. textuality).[190]

For example, while narrative criticism examines the world of the text, a world that is to be entered into, experienced, and explored,[191] intertextuality suggests that interpreters do not encounter a single voice in the world of the text, a narrator or otherwise. The (worlds of) texts are interconnected and are not viewed in isolation from other texts. Any one (inter)text offers a plurality of voices that converge in interpretation.[192] In other words, there is not one implied hearer, one implied author, or one world; rather, author and interpreter have been formed by numerous texts, shaping them to hear any one (inter)text differently. The world of a text collides with other worlds of other texts. Thus, from the perspective of intertextuality, a better analogy than the 'world of the text' might be the 'universe of the text' to emphasize the multidimensional, multiversal, ever-expanding, interconnectedness, and dynamism of texts. Furthermore, narrative

---

[188] I'm following Archer, *'I Was in the Spirit on the Lord's Day'*, pp. 62-63, on this point.

[189] S.D. Moore, *Literary Criticism and the Gospels: The Theoretical Challenge* (New Haven, CN: Yale University Press, 1992), p. 14.

[190] Waddell, *Spirit of the Book of Revelation*, p. 45.

[191] Resseguie, *Narrative Criticism*, p. 23.

[192] Moyise, *The Old Testament in the Book of Revelation*, p. 143.

criticism explores a text in its final form assuming each component of the text is part of the unified, coherent whole rather than breaking a text into sources or forms of unrelated pericopes.[193] While the theory of intertextuality would not be interested in exploring source and form critical constructs (despite some attempts to the contrary), intertextuality does create a tension concerning narrative critical approaches that consider the final form of the text.[194] Intertextuality suggests that an intertext is not a static entity; thereby, the 'final form' of a text would never be accomplished. Intertextuality indicates the possibility that (inter)texts are fluid and ever-changing, a fluidity that occurs in interactions with other (inter)texts and the (inter)text of the reader.

Therefore, this piece seeks to perform an intertextual narrative hearing/reading of the Apocalypse.[195] I will use a method of interpretation that is a narrative critical approach, emerging from the Pentecostal (con)text and that is reassessed in light of the literary theory of intertextuality.[196] While there are some tensions between narrative criticism and intertextuality, these literary approaches are also complementary in that they are text(ually) centered, propose a close reading, and take the universe of the (inter)text of scripture seriously.[197] This close narrative hearing/reading will enter into the universe of the (inter)text of scripture to offer a hearing/reading of the intertext of the Apocalypse, guided by my own intertext that is formed in and by the Pentecostal (con)text. Such a narrative approach emerges from

---

[193] Resseguie, *Narrative Criticism*, p. 39, writes, 'narrative critics are interested in narratives as complete tapestries in which the parts fit together to form an organic whole'. See also Powell, *What is Narrative Criticism?*, p. 7.

[194] See again Waddell, *Spirit of the Book of Revelation*, p. 45.

[195] A primary intertextual web entangled in the text of the Apocalypse is the HB, which has been exhibited to have more allusions than any other NT work. See Moyise, *The Old Testament in the Book of Revelation*, p. 14 and Waddell, *Spirit of the Book of Revelation*, pp. 67-68, who appeal to the index in the *United Bible Societies Greek New Testament*.

[196] For another attempt at bringing intertextuality into conversation with narrative, see J.R.D. Kirk, 'Narrative Transformation', in B.J. Oropeza and S. Moyise (eds.), *Exploring Intertextuality: Diverse Strategies for New Testament Interpretation of Texts* (Eugene, OR: Cascade Books, 2016), pp. 165-75.

[197] This seems to align closely with Archer, *A Pentecostal Hermeneutic*, pp. 223-47 (226), who proposes that a Pentecostal approach should include a reader response element, 'A narrative critical approach with a bent towards reader response would enable the Pentecostal community not only to interpret scripture critically but also to let Scripture critically interpret them'.

the Pentecostal (con)text to interpret scripture for and in the Pentecostal community.

## The Role of the Spirit in Interpretation for the Pentecostal (Con)text

'Although Pentecostals are a "people of the Book", they are foremost a "people of the Spirit", who expect the Spirit to speak an inspired message to the congregation which is relevant for the time'.[198] Those who are formed by the Pentecostal (con)text invite the Holy Spirit to guide them in interpreting a text because they regard the Spirit to be an active dynamic participator in interpretation and discernment within their community.[199] The role of the Spirit in interpretation is mysterious and thereby frequently ignored, difficult to define, and resists static dogmatization.[200] Nevertheless, Pentecostals affirm that the Spirit is active and necessary for a meaningful interpretation.[201] In the convergence of (inter)text and (con)text, the Spirit intersects between the text and community prophetically forming, inspiring, and guiding the community in interpretation.[202]

The Spirit's activity is associated with inspiration.[203] The scriptures are much more than just another (inter)text on account of the Spirit's

---

[198] Waddell, *Spirit of the Book of Revelation*, p. 126.

[199] For more on the role of the Spirit in interpretation, see Ervin, 'Hermeneutics', pp. 11-25; Arrington, 'Hermeneutics', pp. 376-89; Johns and Bridges Johns, 'Yielding to the Spirit', pp. 109-34; Pinnock, 'The Work of the Holy Spirit in Hermeneutics', pp. 3-23; Archer, *A Pentecostal Hermeneutic*, pp. 247-52; Thomas, 'Holy Spirit and Interpretation', p. 165; Pinnock, 'The Work of the Spirit in Interpretation', pp. 157-71; K.L. Spawn and A.T. Wright (eds.), *Spirit and Scripture: Exploring a Pneumatic Hermeneutic* (London: T&T Clark, 2012).

[200] Pinnock, 'The Work of the Spirit in Interpretation', p. 158, proposes that a fear of uncontrolled subjectivity from the dynamism of the Spirit is the reason that scholars have not reflected upon the role of the Spirit in interpretation.

[201] Ervin, 'Hermeneutics', p. 16, writes, 'there is no hermeneutic unless and until the divine *hermeneutes* (the Holy Spirit) mediates an understanding'.

[202] Land, *Pentecostal Spirituality*, p. 94, writes:

The Spirit who inspires and preserved the Scriptures illuminates, teaches, guides, convicts, and transforms through that Word today. The Word is alive, quick and powerful, because of the Holy Spirit's ministry. The relationship of the Spirit to Scripture is based on that of the Spirit to Christ. Even as the Spirit formed Christ in Mary, so the Spirit uses Scripture to form Christ in believers and vice-versa.

[203] Green, *Toward a Pentecostal Theology of the Lord's Supper*, p. 186.

active work of inspiration. Without the Spirit's continuous inspiration, the scriptures are not meaningful for the Pentecostal community.[204] When coming to the scriptures, Pentecostals expect to hear the words of God prophetically through the activity of the Spirit. In the Pentecostal (con)text, the bifurcation between inspiration and illumination deconstruct.[205] Pentecostals prefer the descriptions of contemporary and original inspiration rather than original inspiration and contemporary illumination.[206] The Spirit, who inspired the original text, continues to inspire the contemporary community to hear the scriptures.[207] If the Spirit is not actively inspiring the contemporary community to hear and discern the testimony of scripture, then original inspiration has no meaning to Pentecostals.[208] Pentecostals trust that the Spirit will reveal the triune God to them in either their

---

[204] Pinnock, 'The Work of the Spirit in Interpretation', pp. 160-61, notes that the authority of the bible is not greater than the authority of the Spirit. He appeals to evidence that some interpretations of scripture have been destructive. Ellington, 'Pentecostalism and the Authority of Scripture', pp. 16-38, finds that the Spirit's intimate relationship with scripture makes it meaningful for the community. See also Smith, 'The Closing of the Book', pp. 49-71.

[205] Archer, *A Pentecostal Hermeneutic*, p. 143, comments, 'Revelation, when used by these early Pentecostals, meant an experiential redemptive knowledge that one comes to comprehend through one's experience with the Holy Spirit'.

[206] Pinnock, 'The Work of the Holy Spirit in Hermeneutics', p. 5. See also Arrington, 'Hermeneutics', pp. 377, 380. Thomas, 'Reading the Bible From Within Our Tradition', p. 119, adds:

> The explicit dependence upon the Spirit in the interpretative process as witnessed to in Acts 15 clearly goes far beyond the rather tame claims regarding 'illumination' often made regarding the Spirit's role in interpretation. For Pentecostals, the Holy Spirit's role in interpretation cannot be reduced to some vague talk of illumination, for the Holy Spirit creates the context for interpretation through his actions and, as a result, guides the church in the determination of which texts are most relevant in a particular situation and clarifies how they might best be approached. This approach *does* make room for illumination in the Spirit's work, but it includes a far greater role for the work of the Spirit in the community as the context for interpretation, offering guidance in the community's dialogue about the Scripture. Although concerns about the dangers of subjectivity must be duly noted, the evidence of Acts 15 simply will not allow for a more restrained approach.

[207] M.J. Cartledge, 'Text-Community-Spirit: The Challenges Posed by Pentecostal Theological Method to Evangelical Theology', in K.L. Spawn and A.T. Wright (eds.), *Spirit and Scripture: Exploring a Pneumatic Hermeneutic* (London: T&T Clark, 2012), p. 140, adds, 'Pneumatology provides the link between text and community, since the Spirit has both inspired the original text and inspires the reading of the text today'. See also McQueen, *Joel and the Spirit*, p. 3.

[208] Pinnock, 'The Work of the Holy Spirit in Hermeneutics', p. 5.

pneumatic experiences or their encounters with scripture.[209] This
openness to the dynamic activity of the Spirit leaves room for subjectivity and a diversity of meanings for a biblical text.

Central to Pentecostal hermeneutics is the community's pneumatic experiences,[210] which opens the text to the hearers in new and
fresh ways:[211]

> Thus, in the Pentecostal narrative world, experience is not reduced
> to a flat source for the doing of theology, but experience is a dy-
> namic and thick source capable of transforming other sources uti-
> lized in the theological task; transforming sources that are them-
> selves sometimes perceived as flat into dynamic and thick ones as
> well.[212]

Pentecostals deem that the Spirit has more to say than scripture,[213]
and when gathering together, the worshiping community anticipates

---

[209] Waddell, *Spirit of the Book of Revelation*, p. 113.

[210] Smith, *Thinking in Tongues*, p. 72, reflects:

The reason why pentecostal worship is so affective, tactile, and emotive is because pentecostal spirituality rejects 'cognitivist' pictures of the human person
that would construe us as fundamentally 'thinking things.' Pentecostal worship
is 'experiential' because it assumes a holistic understanding of personhood and
agency – that the essence of the human animal cannot be reduced to reason or
the intellect. Or, to put it otherwise, rather than seeing human action and be-
havior as entirely driven by conscious, cognitive, deliberative processes, pentecostal worship implicitly appreciates that our being-in-the-world is significantly
shaped and primed by all sorts of precognitive nondeliberative 'modular' operations.

See also Yong, *Spirit-Word-Community*, pp. 245-53.

[211] McKay, 'When the Veil is Taken Away', pp. 17-40; McQueen, *Joel and the
Spirit*, p. 5, adds, 'On the one hand, my Pentecostal pre-understanding will illuminate aspects of the text of Joel left undiscovered by other interpreters. On the
other hand, a fresh critical reading of Joel will facilitate a clearer articulation of
Pentecostal eschatology and ecclesiology. The dialogical role of experience opens
up the text of Joel for questions otherwise left unanswered.'

[212] Thomas, 'What the Spirit is Saying to the Church', pp. 116-17.

[213] Land, *Pentecostal Spirituality*, p. 94, writes, 'The Spirit is the Spirit of Christ
who speaks scripturally, but also has more to say than Scripture'. While I agree with
Land that the Spirit 'speaks scripturally', I would offer an addendum that speaking
scripturally includes elements that are diverse, dissonant, and contains tensions because the meaning of Scripture is sometimes diverse, dissonant, and contains tensions. See also Archer, *A Pentecostal Hermeneutic*, p. 87, who writes, 'The Pentecostals
said yes to both the authority of Scripture and the authority of experience. This
put Scripture and lived experience into a creative dialectical tension. Pentecostalism's lived experience was coloring their understanding of Scripture and Scripture

hearing and experiencing the Spirit through testimony, preaching, sacrament, prayer, worship, songs, hymns, and pneumatic gifts.[214] An experience in the Spirit opens a new way to perceive the text: the veil is taken away.[215] After hearing the Spirit in their worshipping community, Pentecostals seek guidance to discern the Spirit's voice, and the Spirit responds by providing discernment to them.[216] As in Acts 15,[217] Pentecostals will move from (con)text to the (inter)text of scripture when discerning their experience, and therefore 'Pentecostal interpretation is an attempt at Spirit empowered prophetic reappropriation of the Scriptures that flows out of the transformative experience of Pentecost'.[218] When Pentecostals work toward discerning the meaning of their experience, 'the Holy Spirit brings into creative dialogue religious experience, the biblical text, and the discernment of the faith community'.[219]

Thus, a Pentecostal hermeneutic is dependent upon the Spirit to discern meaning in the Spirit's testimonies that are voiced in the local congregation, scripture, the early Pentecostal voices, and church tradition.[220] A Pentecostal hermeneutic exhibits trust in the Spirit –

---

was shaping their lived experiences.' Green, *Sanctifying Interpretation*, p. 134, also notes, 'While we often claim that the Spirit … will never contradict the Scripture, we often fail to see that if we hope to come into alignment with "the mind of Christ", then the Spirit *must* contradict *us* – and that includes, perhaps above all, our readings of Scripture'.

[214] Archer, *A Pentecostal Hermeneutic*, pp. 248-49.

[215] McKay, 'When the Veil is Taken Away', p. 36. See also R. Stronstad, 'Pentecostal Experience and Hermeneutics', *Paraclete* 26.1 (1992); McQueen, *Joel and the Spirit*, p. 5.

[216] Archer, *A Pentecostal Hermeneutic*, p. 248, notes that although the community will at times discern an interpretation to be invalid, the process of hearing one's testimony should always be permitted. Each testimony must continuously be discerned.

[217] Again, Thomas, 'Reading the Bible From Within Our Tradition', pp. 112-13, notes that in Acts 15, the reason for the council is to discern the Spirit's activity among the Gentiles.

[218] Martin, *The Unheard Voice of God*, p. 63. Ellington, 'Pentecostalism and the Authority of Scripture', p. 22, adds, 'It is the transformative action of the Holy Spirit which persistently intrudes on Christian experience and prevents our interpretations from becoming simply a process of reading our own needs and wants into the text and hearing only what we want to hear'.

[219] Martin, *The Unheard Voice of God*, p. 79.

[220] See Smith, 'The Closing of the Book', pp. 49-71; Ellington, 'Pentecostalism and the Authority of Scripture', pp. 16-38; Waddell, *Spirit of the Book of Revelation*, p. 89.

heard through various unique and specific mediums[221] – not to lead the churches astray.[222] Most Pentecostals agree that the Spirit is an active partner in the interpretative and discerning process, but the Spirit's activity remains a veiled mystery. For this work, the Apocalypse will be an essential model to reveal the dynamic, synergistic relationship between the hearing, discerning community and the Spirit.[223]

## Conclusion

Following the work of R. Waddell, the literary theory of intertextuality suggests that interpretation is (con)textual. Originating out of the Pentecostal (con)text and formed through the stories of the origins of Pentecostalism and Pentecostal hermeneutics, a hermeneutical approach emerged that seeks to bring into creative dialogue community, scripture, and the Spirit, an interpretative approach that is in and for the Pentecostal (con)text.

The Pentecostal (con)text was examined in four aspects: (i) the local worshipping Pentecostal congregation that significantly forms the Pentecostal interpreter; (ii) the (inter)texts of the early Pentecostal periodical literature that reveal the 'theological heart' of the Pentecostalism via *Wirkungsgeschichte*; (iii) the (inter)text of *ecclesia catholic*; and (iv) the (con)text of (Pentecostal) scholarship.

---

[221] No revelation or experience of the Spirit is unmediated. See Smith, *Thinking in Tongues*, p. 138; Waddell, *Spirit of the Book of Revelation*, pp. 51-52.

[222] See Smith, 'The Closing of the Book', pp. 69-70, for a 'hermeneutic of trust':

> The correlate for the necessity of discernment is, I think, a fundamental hermeneutics of trust, believing more in God's ability to bless us than the enemy's ability to dupe us, and trusting that if we ask the Father for bread he will not give us a stone; if we ask him for a fish, we trust that he will not hand us a serpent. While I recognize that the framework I am proposing seems risky, it should instead be understood as a model which emphasizes faith in the guidance of the Spirit.

[223] This is following the precedent of Waddell, *Spirit of the Book of Revelation*, p. 123, who finds the Apocalypse 'to be a good place to pursue the development of a Pentecostal hermeneutic owing to the apocalyptic nature of the movement's ethos. Thus, attention is now turned toward the Revelation with an expectation that not only will the text be unveiled but a hermeneutic may be unveiled as well.' See also Herms, 'Invoking the Spirit', pp. 99-114.

Scripture is the unique, dynamic testimony of the Spirit to the community, which tells the story of God through the story of Israel, Jesus, and the outpouring of the Spirit upon the church. Emerging from the Pentecostal (con)text are methods of interpretation of scripture that are narrative in orientation. Intertextuality offers tension for a narrative approach, particularly in relation to the autonomy and fluidity of texts, while also harmonizing with a narrative approach because of the close, textual, and literary aspects of narrative and intertextuality.

Pentecostals actively experience the Spirit in their communities and believe the Spirit inspires them to hear and view scripture as a dynamic testimony. Pentecostals encounter Jesus through scripture that is given by the Father through the Spirit. A Pentecostal hermeneutic expects the Spirit to guide, inspire, assist, and lead the community to discern meaning. Pentecostals anticipate a divine encounter when coming to an (inter)text.

This piece seeks to explore the narrative thread of pneumatic discernment in the Apocalypse that brings into creative dialogue the Pentecostal (con)text with the intertext of the Apocalypse. In the next chapter, I will offer an examination of the scholarly (con)texts. In chapters three and four, this work offers an examination of the early Pentecostal periodical literature using the method of *Wirkungsgeschichte* to hear the texts of the Wesleyan-Holiness Pentecostals and the Finished-Work Pentecostals concerning the pneumatology of the Apocalypse and pneumatic discernment. Such an exploration considers the 'theological heart' of the Pentecostal (con)text. Moving from (con)text to text, chapter five turns to the (inter)text of the Apocalypse to hear the narrative thread of pneumatic discernment employing a narrative critical reading method that is reimagined in light of intertextuality. The sixth chapter of this work seeks to move from text back to the Pentecostal (con)text that considers a theological construction of pneumatic discernment for the Pentecostal community.

# 2

# EXPLORING THE SCHOLARLY (CON)TEXTS OF PNEUMATOLOGY AND PNEUMATIC DISCERNMENT IN THE APOCALYPSE

Throughout the years of extensive study devoted to the Apocalypse, pneumatology has not been typically the central topic of exploration. Only recently has a full-length monograph been penned that investigates the pneumatology of the Apocalypse.[1] Few commentaries of Revelation dedicate much space to the subject.[2] The majority of the constructive research on pneumatology appears in journal articles or book chapters.[3] Chief among the scholarly debate about the pneumatology of the Apocalypse are the interpretative questions, (1) do

---

[1] Waddell, *Spirit of the Book of Revelation*. See also I.W. Sorke, *The Identity and Function of the Seven Spirits in the Book of Revelation* (Ann Arbor, MI: ProQuest LCC, 2009), who has explored the topic.

[2] For commentaries that have dedicated space to the pneumatology of the Apocalypse, see H.B. Swete, *The Apocalypse of St. John* (New York, NY: Macmillan Company, 1907); I. Beckwith, *The Apocalypse of John* (New York, NY: Macmillan Company, 1919); R.H. Charles, *A Critical and Exegetical Commentary on The Revelation of St. John* (ICC; Edinburgh: T&T Clark, 1920), I; J.M. Ford, *Revelation* (ABC 38; Garden City, NY: Doubleday & Company, 1975); D.E. Aune, *Revelation 1–5* (WBC; Dallas, TX: Word Books, 1997); Skaggs and Benham, *Revelation*; Thomas and Macchia, *Revelation*.

[3] See E. Schweizer, 'Die sieben Geister in der Apokalypse', *EvT* 6 (1951-1952), pp. 502-12; F.F. Bruce, 'The Spirit in the Apocalypse', in B. Lindars and S.S. Smalley (eds.), *Christ and Spirit in the New Testament: Studies in Honour of Charles Francis Digby Moule* (Cambridge: Cambridge Press, 1973), pp. 333-44; J.M. Ford, 'For the Testimony of Jesus is the Spirit of Prophecy', *ITQ* 42.4 (1975), pp. 285-92; R. Bauckham, 'The Role of the Spirit in the Apocalypse', *EQ* 52.2 (1980), pp. 66-83; R.L. Jeske, 'Spirit and Community in the Johannine Apocalypse', *NTS* 31 (1985),

the seven Spirits represent the one divine Spirit, or (2) do the seven Spirits represent seven archangels of Jewish angelology? The methods used to approach the pneumatology include historical approaches, source critical, as well as literary, intertextual, and theological readings. Beyond questions of pneumatology, the theme of pneumatic discernment in the Apocalypse has been largely overlooked and is treated in only a few works.[4] On account of the lack of research on pneumatic discernment, this review of literature will examine academic works that have explored Revelation's pneumatology with the prospect of uncovering some intersections of the pneumatology of the Apocalypse and discernment, examining the works in chronological order.[5]

---

pp. 452-66; K. de Smidt, 'The Holy Spirit in the Book of Revelation – Nomenclature', *NeoT* 28.1 (1994), pp. 229-44; K. de Smidt, 'Hermeneutical Perspectives on the Spirit in the Book of Revelation', *JPT* 14 (1999), pp. 27-47; M.M. Wilson, 'Revelation 19:10 and Contemporary Interpretation', in M.M. Wilson (ed.), *Spirit and Renewal: Essays in Honor of J. Rodman Williams* (JPTSup 5; Sheffield: Sheffield Academic Press, 1994), pp. 191-202; S.S. Smalley, 'The Paraclete: Pneumatology in the Johannine Gospel and Apocalypse', in R.A. Culpepper and C.C. Black (eds.), *Exploring the Gospel of John* (Louisville, KY: John Knox Press, 1996), pp. 150-73; C. Tanner, 'Climbing the Lampstand-Witness-Trees: Revelation's Use of Zechariah 4 in Light of Speech Act Theory', *JPT* 20 (2011), pp. 81-92; Herms, 'Invoking the Spirit', pp. 99-114; F. Macchia, 'The Spirit of the Lamb: A Reflection on the Pneumatology of Revelation', in C.S. Keener, C.S. Jeremy, and J.D. May (eds.), *But These are Written ... : Essays on Johannine Literature in Honor of Professor Benny C. Aker* (Eugene, OR: Wipf & Stock, 2014), pp. 214-20; J.C. Thomas, 'Revelation', in T.J. Burke and K. Warrington (eds.), *A Biblical Theology of the Holy Spirit* (Eugene, OR: Cascade Books, 2014), pp. 257-66; R. Herms, 'πνευματικῶς and Antagonists in Revelation 11 Reconsidered', in G.V. Allen, I. Paul, and S.P. Woodman (eds.), *The Book of Revelation: Currents in British Research on the Apocalypse* (WUZNT; Tübingen: Mohr Siebeck, 2015), pp. 133-46.

[4] See J.C. Thomas, 'Pneumatic Discernment: The Image of the Beast and His Number: Revelation 13.11-18', in S.J. Land, R.D. Moore, and J.C. Thomas (eds.), *Passover, Pentecost, and Parousia: Studies in Celebration of the Life and Ministry of R. Hollis Gause* (JPTSup 35; Dorset: Deo Publishing, 2010), pp. 106-24; J.C. Thomas, 'The Mystery of the Great Whore: Pneumatic Discernment in Revelation 17', in P. Althouse and R.C. Waddell (eds.), *Perspectives in Pentecostal Eschatologies* (Eugene, OR: Pickwick Publications, 2010), pp. 111-36; Thomas and Macchia, *Revelation*, pp. 485-94. See also J.-P. Ruiz, *Ezekiel in the Apocalypse: The Transformation of Prophetic Language in Revelation 16, 17-19, 10* (Frankfurt am Main: Peter Lang, 1989) who explores the 'hermeneutical imperatives' that occur in Revelation.

[5] This review of literature will limit its survey to scholarly articles, book sections, NT theologies, full-length monographs, or monograph/commentary sections or excursus that explicitly explore pneumatology or pneumatic discernment in Revelation. While J. Fekkes, *Isaiah and Prophetic Tradition in the Book of Revelation: Visionary Antecedents and their Development* (JSNTSup 93; Sheffield: Sheffield Academic Press, 1994), pp. 107-19, does not explicitly explore the pneumatology

## 1907–1926

### H.B. Swete

In 1907, a commentary on the Apocalypse, written by H.B. Swete, dedicates an introductory section to the pneumatology of the Apocalypse.[6] First, concerning ἐν πνεύματι, Swete concludes that John received a visionary experience. Second, he is critical of those who interpret the seven Spirits as the 'seven Angels of Presence'.[7] Swete identifies a trinitarian motif in the Apocalypse found in both the opening salutation (Rev. 1.4)[8] as well as the close association of the seven Spirits with the Lamb and the one on the throne (Rev. 4.5; 5.6). The plurality of the seven Spirits, Swete observes, corresponds to the seven churches (Rev. 1.4).[9] Finally, in the Apocalypse, the Spirit

---

of the Apocalypse, his examination of the seven Spirits and Isa. 11.2 has had a significant impact on the study of the pneumatology of the Apocalypse. Fekkes considers Isa. 11.2 to be an 'unlikely/doubtful' allusion of the seven Spirits on account of the textual variance between the LXX and MT. The MT has six features of the Spirit while the LXX has seven – the seventh being εὐσεβείας. Fekkes prefers the reading of the MT and locates a more likely allusion of the seven Spirits in Zechariah 4. Although Fekkes' approach and categories can be helpful, S. Moyise, *The Old Testament in the Book of Revelation* (JSNTSup 115; Sheffield: Sheffield Academic Press, 1995), pp. 17-18, criticizes Fekkes' approach for being too influenced by a historical/source critical lens that privileges the 'loudest instruments in the orchestra' and ignores the subtle nuances of some allusions. Isaiah 11.2 is at least a subtle echo and thereby should be explored as a possible intertext. See also J.K. Newton, *The Revelation Worldview: Apocalyptic Thinking in a Postmodern World* (Eugene, OR: Wipf & Stock, 2015), which will be explored in the reading and construction chapters of this monograph.

[6] Swete, *The Apocalypse of St. John*, pp. clxiv-clxvi.

[7] See G.H. Dix, 'The Seven Archangels and the Seven Spirits', *JTS* 28 (1926), pp. 233-50. Dix explains that the seven Spirits are influenced by the seven Jewish angels, which are derived from the Babylonian planetary gods. Dix traces (mainly examining Ezekiel and Daniel) from pre-exilic, exilic, and post-exilic times, influences of the Babylonian planetary gods on the seven Jewish archangels. He concludes that the Hebrew writers attempted to integrate Babylonian religious beliefs into the Jewish monotheism, and therefore the Babylonian gods were lowered to the level of angels who had mediatory functions.

[8] χάρις ὑμῖν καὶ εἰρήνη ἀπὸ ὁ ὢν καὶ ὁ ἦν καὶ ὁ ἐρχόμενος, καὶ ἀπὸ τῶν ἑπτὰ πνευμάτων ἃ ἐνώπιον τοῦ θρόνου αὐτοῦ, καὶ ἀπὸ Ἰησοῦ Χριστοῦ, ὁ μάρτυς ὁ πιστός, ὁ πρωτότοκος τῶν νεκρῶν καὶ ὁ ἄρχων τῶν βασιλέων τῆς γῆς ('Grace and peace to you from the one who is, who was, and who is coming. And from the seven Spirits who are before his throne, and from Jesus Christ, the faithful witness, the first born from the dead, and who rules over the kings of the earth').

[9] Swete, *The Apocalypse of St. John*, p. clxv.

'speaks everywhere, bearing witness to Jesus, exhorting the Churches in His Name, conveying the revelation of Jesus Christ to the Seer, and through him to the readers and hearers'.[10]

## I. Beckwith

Following Swete, I. Beckwith, in his Apocalypse commentary,[11] observes that unlike the Pauline and Johannine literatures, the Apocalypse emphasizes the operations or 'office' of the Spirit, principally as revealer and inspirer. It is unlikely that the seven Spirits refer to the sevenfold operations of the Spirit of Yahweh from Isa. 11.2 but allude to Zechariah 4.[12] Beckwith identifies the Spirit as a distinguishable person united with God and Christ. In the seven prophetic messages, Christ and the Spirit are two distinct persons, but the Spirit speaks the words of Christ. Beckwith describes Revelation as 'pretheological' because there is not the fully developed trinitarian theology which would appear in later church dogma.

## R.H. Charles

Shortly after Beckwith's commentary, R.H. Charles produces a two-volume source critical commentary, which dedicates only one paragraph to the Spirit in his lengthy introduction. Charles suggests that the original author does not conceive of a divine Spirit, and that any explicit appearance of 'spirit' is a later interpolation.[13] Charles notes an exception in the seven prophetic messages where 'spirit' is part of the original composition. While not a reference to a divine being, Charles concludes that 'spirit' is a reference to the 'Spirit of Christ'.[14]

---

[10] Swete, *The Apocalypse of St. John*, p. clxiv.

[11] Beckwith, *The Apocalypse of John*, pp. 316-17.

[12] Beckwith, *The Apocalypse of John*, pp. 426-27. Cf. Dix, 'The Seven Archangels and the Seven Spirits', p. 249.

[13] Dix, 'The Seven Archangels and the Seven Spirits', pp. 245-46, disagrees with Charles' assumption that the Spirit passages are an interpolation and a 'grotesque' attempt to fashion a trinity. See also B.W. Longenecker, 'Revelation 19,10: One Verse in Search of an Author', *ZNW* 91.3-4 (2000), pp. 230-37, who critiques Charles' proposal based on a lack of evidence.

[14] Charles, *The Revelation of St. John*, pp. cxiv-cxv.

# 1951–1975

## E. Schweizer

A few decades later, E. Schweizer begins another wave of study on Apocalypse pneumatology with an article on the seven Spirits,[15] and an article that is published in *The Theological Dictionary of the New Testament*.[16] Schweizer suggests that the Apocalypse is an early 'pre-Gnostic' document and is the most primitive example of pneumatology in the NT. He appeals to 'futuristic' or 'eschatological' elements of the pneumatology in the Apocalypse as evidence. Schweizer believes that the Spirit of prophecy is the dominant pneumatic theme in the Apocalypse that is closely related to the appearances of ἐν πνεύματι ('in the Spirit'). ἐν πνεύματι, the church – akin to John – is able to receive extraordinary power accompanied by visions and experiences from the Spirit. Schweizer emphasizes the communal aspect of the Spirit's activity to the extent that even when the Spirit moves upon an individual – such as with John – the pneumatic activity occurs on behalf of the community;[17] the Spirit 'always speaks to the community, and the one through whom [the Spirit] speaks is immaterial'.[18] Schweizer notes that πνευματικῶς ('Spiritually', Rev. 11.8) has significance beyond the translation 'allegorical' preferring 'prophetic'.[19] In the seven prophetic messages, Schweizer constructs an indistinguishable union between Christ and the Spirit: 'But this Spirit is no other than the exalted Lord Himself … He is the exalted Lord as the One who speaks to the community'.[20] Additionally, Schweizer interprets the seven Spirits as the seven Jewish archangels who 'represent the Spirit of God in His fullness and completeness. But they

---

[15] Schweizer, 'Die sieben Geister in der Apokalypse', pp. 502-12.

[16] E. Schweizer, 'πνεῦμα', *TDNT*, VI, pp. 449-51.

[17] Schweizer leaves open the possibility that every person in the community is a prophet.

[18] Schweizer, 'πνεῦμα', p. 449.

[19] Schweizer, 'πνεῦμα', p. 449.

[20] Schweizer, 'πνεῦμα', p. 510. See Schweizer, 'Die sieben Geister in der Apokalypse', p. 449, where he writes, 'Dieser Geist ist nichts anderes als der Erhöhte selbst in seinem Reden zur Gemeinde'.

also represent the throne angels, and in addition they are parallel to the angels of the churches'.[21]

## F.F. Bruce

Next, F.F. Bruce offers a reading of the Spirit in the Apocalypse where he examines four areas of pneumatology: (1) the seven Spirits, (2) the Spirit of prophecy, (3) what the Spirit says to the churches, and (4) the responsive Spirit.[22]

First, disagreeing with Charles, Bruce finds Rev. 1.4 to be an intentional semantic trinitarian phrase that places the seven Spirits between the throne and Jesus Christ. Concerning the seven Spirits, Bruce criticizes: (1) the LXX reading of Isa. 11.2 as the seven-fold operation of the Spirit,[23] (2) Swete's correlation of the seven Spirits to the seven churches, and (3) Schweizer's religio-historical reading.[24] Following Beckwith, Bruce identifies the seven Spirits as the one Holy Spirit that alludes to Zechariah 4.[25] He finds evidence of the Spirit's divinity based on the Spirit's closeness to the throne and as 'attributes or accessories' of the risen Christ, specifically the seven eyes and seven horns of the Lamb.[26] Commenting on the various symbols utilized for the Spirit, Bruce observes that the joining of several symbolic images to one reality is not unusual in Revelation.[27]

Second, Bruce identifies the Spirit of prophecy as the central pneumatological theme in the Apocalypse. The Spirit of prophecy conveys the relationship of the Spirit with the prophets as well as the testimony of Jesus. It is through the prophets that the Spirit of

---

[21] Schweizer, 'Die sieben Geister in der Apokalypse', pp. 510-11; Schweizer, 'πνεῦμα', pp. 450-51.

[22] Bruce, 'The Spirit in the Apocalypse', pp. 333-44.

[23] Even though Bruce does not see any dependence on Isa. 11.2 for the seven Spirits, he does see a possible allusion to the Davidic messiah endowed with the Spirit of Yahweh who, in Revelation, becomes the attributes – seven eyes and seven horns – of the Lamb.

[24] Bruce, 'The Spirit in the Apocalypse', p. 336, notes, 'John is never in bondage to the religio-historical roots of his symbolism; with sovereign freedom he bends and re-shapes it to serve his purpose'. Bruce observes a literary relationship between the seven trumpet angels of judgment and the chief seven angels (Rev. 5.8; 8.2-3; cf. 15.1).

[25] Bruce, 'The Spirit in the Apocalypse', p. 337. See Beckwith, *The Apocalypse of John*, pp. 426-27.

[26] Bruce, 'The Spirit in the Apocalypse', p. 335.

[27] Bruce, 'The Spirit in the Apocalypse', p. 334.

prophecy bears the testimony of Jesus.[28] Bruce notes two levels of witness: first, the whole Apocalypse witnesses to Jesus (who is the faithful witness) and second, the prophets are themselves witnesses, which would include John and Antipas. In the Apocalypse, witness is often accompanied by suffering and persecution, and the means by which the prophets overcome (Rev. 12.11). In the witness and suffering of the prophets, Jesus is 'bearing his testimony in theirs, and suffering in them';[29] therefore, 'this testimony ... is the very substance of the Spirit of prophecy'.[30] Bruce perceives a dynamic relationship between the community of prophets, the testimony of Jesus, and the Spirit of prophecy. He appeals to the two witnesses (Revelation 11) to confirm the close relationship between the prophetic ministry of the two witnesses and the Spirit of prophecy. Bruce investigates the Spirit of prophecy within the community of discernment. The genuine Spirit of prophecy is tested by whether it bears witness to Jesus. Borrowing from Pauline and Johannine thought, a true testimony affirms the lordship of Jesus (1 Cor. 12.3), his real incarnation (1 Jn 4.2), and bears the Paraclete's witness (Jn 15.26).[31] Additionally, Bruce dismisses any relationship of the Holy Spirit with πνεῦμα ζωῆς ('Spirit of life', Rev. 11.11), concluding it is an allusion to the breath of life in Gen. 2.7. Turning to ἐν πνεύματι ('in the Spirit'), Bruce finds an association between the Spirit of prophecy and John being ἐν πνεύματι, observing an allusion to Ezekiel (Ezek. 37.1 cf. Rev. 17.3; 21.10).[32]

Third, Bruce examines the role of the Spirit in the seven prophetic messages. Contrary to Schweizer, Bruce writes, 'it is not that the Spirit is identical with the exalted Lord, but that the exalted Lord speaks to the churches by the Spirit – and the Spirit can scarcely be other than the Spirit of prophecy'.[33] On the one hand, there is a clear distinction

---

[28] As opposed to the HB prophets, Bruce is careful to note that prophets in the Apocalypse refer to Christian prophets who bear witness where John is the chief example.

[29] Bruce, 'The Spirit in the Apocalypse', p. 338.

[30] Bruce, 'The Spirit in the Apocalypse', p. 338, concludes Ἰησοῦ ('Jesus') is likely an objective genitive.

[31] Bruce, 'The Spirit in the Apocalypse', pp. 338-39.

[32] Bruce, 'The Spirit in the Apocalypse', p. 343.

[33] Bruce, 'The Spirit in the Apocalypse', p. 340.

between Christ and the Spirit in Bruce's work; on the other hand, Christ and the Spirit share in a close relationship, which is extended to the community. He finds a similar relationship in Rev. 16.15 where Christ's words are recorded, but the Spirit of prophecy speaks these words.[34]

Fourth, Bruce turns to the responsive Spirit in Rev. 14.3 and Rev. 22.17, 'the Spirit is the Spirit of prophecy who takes the initiative in making the response, and is seconded by the community as a whole, so that "the Spirit and the Bride"… is an expression practically equivalent to "the Prophets and the Saints"'.[35] In other words, the Spirit's interjection 'Come!' is a call for the churches to respond accordingly, 'Come!'. Bruce, then, identifies the water of life as a symbol for the Spirit alluded to in the FG[36] and supported in Ezek. 47.1.[37]

In sum, first, Bruce finds the seven Spirits to symbolize the divine Spirit, which allude to Zechariah 4. Second, he considers the central pneumatic theme to be the Spirit of prophecy in the Apocalypse. Third, the process of discernment correlates to 1 John and 1 Corinthians. The test of discernment is whether one is bearing the Paraclete's witness and affirming the incarnation. Bruce finds a close association of the Spirit, the community, and Christ. The Spirit speaks to the community by speaking the words of Christ. Fourth, those who respond to the Spirit have discerned rightly.

### J.M. Ford

In the 1975 Anchor Bible Commentary on the Apocalypse,[38] Roman Catholic charismatic scholar, J.M. Ford, writes a section on pneumatology, while later contributing an article on Rev. 19.10.[39] Ford develops a curious source critical proposition where she identifies the

---

[34] Bruce notes even though the Gospels, Paul, and the Apocalypse have similarities, the Apocalypse – with its 'peculiar character' – cannot be generalized with other NT works.

[35] Bruce, 'The Spirit in the Apocalypse', p. 343. See Swete, *The Apocalypse of St. John*, p. 306.

[36] In fact, he obverses that only in the FG and the Apocalypse does the water of life imagery appear in the NT. In the FG, the image signifies the Spirit, which Bruce finds to be true for the Apocalypse.

[37] Bruce, 'The Spirit in the Apocalypse', p. 343, notes that if this identification is accepted, then a distinction between the Spirit of life and the Spirit of prophecy should be made.

[38] Ford, *Revelation*, pp. 19-20.

[39] Ford, 'For the Testimony of Jesus', pp. 285-92.

Apocalypse as an early Jewish or Jewish-Christian apocalypse.[40] Following Schweizer, Ford's historical approach leads her to conclude that Revelation is one of the most primitive examples of pneumatology in the NT.[41] When interpreting the seven prophetic messages, Ford concludes that the Spirit is not the distinct Holy Spirit, reasoning that πνεῦμα ('spirit') lacks the proper adjective ἅγιος ('holy') and that πνεῦμα lacks a voice that is distinct from the voice of Jesus in the Apocalypse. Ford observes that the 'seven spirits' should be understood as angels.[42] Ford is surprised to discover that even in places of persecution – such as those who do not worship the beast – the Spirit is not present. She prefers a 'binitarian' reading of Rev. 1.4 because the seven Spirits occur before the mention of Jesus and thereby cannot be on the same level as Jesus or God.

Concerning the Spirit of prophecy, Ford observes that Rev. 19.10 is a doublet of Rev. 22.8-9 where she identifies Rev. 19.10d as a gloss.[43] Prophecy is related to authority in the community where John has 'special' authority to which the community and community's prophets must submit. Following Jewish tradition and the three Pentecostal narratives in Acts, Ford proposes that the Spirit of prophecy in Revelation is a 'succinct reference to the return of prophecy as a sign of the New Covenant with Jesus as Lord'[44] and thereby a reference to a Pentecostal event, which functions analogously to spiritual gifts in Luke-Acts and 1 Corinthians. Finally, even though Ford concludes the Spirit of prophecy is a reference to the inauguration of

---

[40] Ford, *Revelation*, pp. 3-12, proposes: (1) Revelation 4–11 goes back to John the Baptist and his inner circle, (2) 12–22 is written later than 4–11 and likely originates from the disciples of John the Baptist who may have or may have not been converted to Christianity and (3) 1–3; 22.16a, 20b, 21 are later Christian additions.

[41] Ironically, although Ford is dismissive of Revelation's pneumatology, she is proactive in interpreting the pneumatology of 'Christian Apocalypses'. While Ford identifies portions of NT works (1 and 2 Thessalonians, the Gospels, Jude, 2 Peter) and post-NT works (the Didache, the Shepherd of Hermas, the Ascension of Isaiah, the Apocalypse of Peter, and the Christian Sibyllines) as Christian apocalypses, she is careful to differentiate between Christian apocalypses and Revelation. She identifies Revelation as a Jewish or a Jewish-Christian apocalypse. Her criterion for a Christian apocalypse includes: (1) concentration on the coming of messiah, (2) the Son of Man, and (3) eschatological bliss or punishment.

[42] Ford, *Revelation*, p. 19, appeals to the Shepherd of Hermas, 1 Enoch, and 2 Maccabees. Although Ford proposes Revelation 1–3 to be a later Christian addition, she does not identify the Spirit as a distinct person in these works.

[43] Ford, 'For the Testimony of Jesus', pp. 284-85.

[44] Ford, 'For the Testimony of Jesus', p. 291.

the new age and a new covenant whereby spiritual gifts are practiced, she never makes reference to the role, function, or person of the Holy Spirit in this new age. Her take on prophecy – and the Apocalypse's pneumatology – is therefore Spirit-less.

## 1980–2006

### R. Bauckham

R. Bauckham first contributes an in-depth study on the pneumatology of the Apocalypse in 1980, which is updated and published again in *The Climax of Prophecy* in 1993. Bauckham explores four areas in his study: (1) the Spirit of vision, (2) the Spirit of prophecy, (3) the seven Spirits, and (4) the Spirit and the eschatological perspective.[45]

First, ἐν πνεύματι ('in the Spirit') is a reference to the divine Spirit and should be considered 'a technical term for the visionary's experience of "rapture" by the Spirit', which includes both phenomenological and theological aspects.[46] Phenomenologically, John's visionary experience is, on the one hand, 'a suspension of normal consciousness ... his normal sensory experience was replaced by visions and auditions given him by the Spirit',[47] which signifies that the vision originates from the Spirit:[48] 'John's normal senses were overtaken by the Spirit and replaced by a visionary experience'.[49] On the other

---

[45] Bauckham, 'The Role of the Spirit in the Apocalypse', pp. 66-83, and R. Bauckham, *The Climax of Prophecy* (New York, NY: T&T Clark, 1993). This study will follow Bauckham's thought as presented in *The Climax of Prophecy*. See also R. Bauckham, *The Theology of the Book of Revelation* (Cambridge: Cambridge University Press, 1993).

[46] Bauckham, *Climax of Prophecy*, pp. 152-54 (52). Bauckham observes differences in the four ἐν πνεύματι ('in the Spirit') phrases. First, the Spirit, accenting the visionary experience, identifies Rev. 1.10 as John falling into a trance. Second, Rev. 4.2 refers to John's rapture into the heavenly court. Bauckham finds similarities between this experience and other apocalyptic works. Third, Rev. 17.3 and 21.10 are examples of geographical transportation, which are reminiscent of Ezek. 37.1 and *Bel* 36. In the Apocalypse, the language of ἐν πνεύματι ('in the Spirit') confirms that the Spirit is the agent of the visionary experience.

[47] Bauckham, *Climax of Prophecy*, p. 152.

[48] Bauckham, *Climax of Prophecy*, pp. 157-58, clarifies that the authority of John is not found in his ecstatic experience, but in the claim that the ecstatic experience occurred by the Spirit.

[49] Bauckham, *Climax of Prophecy*, pp. 152-53, compares this phenomenon to the *Ascension of Isaiah*.

hand, it is a spiritual experience – as opposed to an out of body experience – where John remains a 'free agent throughout the experience'.[50] Bauckham notes that the Apocalypse does not describe a psychological experience or the way in which his vision occurs; rather, the Apocalypse describes primarily the vision, itself. Theologically, ἐν πνεύματι ('in the Spirit') is associated with John's prophetic authority, while also serving as a literary device that guides the readers through the vision.[51] The Apocalypse is not a minimal transcript of John's experience, but a vision that is transformed into a carefully arranged literary composition. The literary medium functions to facilitate John's pneumatic vision and experience to the churches. As the Spirit inspires John's visionary experience, the Spirit inspires the medium in which it is shared.[52]

Second, Bauckham studies other pneumatic functions in the Apocalypse such as the moral or life-giving Spirit and the Spirit of prophecy. Morally, 'the Spirit brings to the churches the powerful word of Christ, rebuking, encouraging, promising and threatening, touching and drawing the hearts, minds, and consciences of its hearers, directing the lives and the prayers of the Christian communities toward the coming of Christ'.[53] Bauckham identifies the principal role of the Spirit to be the Spirit of prophecy who speaks to and through the prophets.[54] Bauckham further investigates prophecy by asking, is prophecy confined to Christian prophets or is it a function for the entire community? In response Bauckham first interprets the witness of Jesus as a subjective genitive,[55] preferring the translation

---

[50] Bauckham, *Climax of Prophecy*, pp. 152-53.

[51] Bauckham, *Climax of Prophecy*, p. 159. For example, Bauckham notes one should not read ἐν πνεύματι ('in the Spirit', esp. Rev. 17.3; 21.10) in isolation of each other because when these markers are viewed in comparison to each other, one is able to observe literary and theological significances.

[52] Bauckham, *Climax of Prophecy*, pp. 158-59.

[53] Bauckham, *Climax of Prophecy*, p. 161.

[54] Bauckham, *Climax of Prophecy*, pp. 160-62. Bauckham examines occurrences where the Spirit of prophecy speaks explicitly. First, the Spirit's words in the seven messages are the words of Christ. Second, in Rev. 14.13, he identifies the words of the Spirit as the Spirit's response, through John, to the heavenly voice. The Spirit inspires John to write and as John writes, the Spirit agrees with it. Third, in Rev. 22.17, Bauckham identifies the speaker who injects, 'Come', as the Spirit and the Bride. Thus, the Spirit of prophecy speaks through the Christian prophets who bring the word of Christ to the inhabitants of the earth.

[55] Contra Bruce, 'The Spirit in the Apocalypse', p. 338.

'the witness Jesus bore'; thereby, 'the witness that Jesus bore is the content of the Spirit-inspired prophecy'.[56] This Spirit-inspired prophecy is both the content of John's witness and the witness of Revelation. Second, citing the example of the two witnesses, he concludes prophecy and witness are equal where each person in the church is a prophet and a witness. Testimony is the verbal continuation of Jesus' testimony on earth. Therefore, the ones who bear Jesus' witness (which is Spirit-inspired prophecy) are the church.[57]

Third, Bauckham critiques those who interpret the seven Spirits as the seven archangels.[58] Bauckham notes that πνεῦμα ('Spirit') is rarely used in the early Christian literature as a reference to angels and that πνεῦμα never appears in the Apocalypse in reference to angels. Rather, Bauckham interprets the seven Spirits as the one divine Spirit evident from an intertextual reading of Zech 4.1-14.[59] For Bauckham, Zechariah 4 is the key HB passage for unlocking John's thought on the role of the Spirit in the Apocalypse. The seven lampstands in Zechariah's vision – which are the seven eyes of Yahweh – allude to the seven-branched lampstand in the holy place.[60] The seven lamps that burn before the divine throne in Revelation allude to Zechariah and Exodus.[61] In Rev. 4.5, the seven Spirits are the seven torches found before the divine throne as well as accessories of the Lamb – his seven eyes and seven horns.[62] The imagery of the eyes from Zechariah and the eyes of the Lamb from Revelation are fused together to become a vivid intertextual image of the seven Spirits. The seven

---

[56] Bauckham, *Climax of Prophecy*, p. 161.

[57] He clarifies between a vocational prophet and the church's prophetic role as witnesses: the vocational prophet speaks by the Spirit to the churches, while the churches witness by the Spirit to the world.

[58] Finding an allusion to Jewish angelology instead in Rev. 8.1.

[59] Bauckham, *The Theology of the Book of Revelation*, p. 109, notes that, concerning the seven Spirits, the number seven represents the number of completeness while it occurs four times in the Apocalypse where the number four represents the world. Thus, he concludes the seven Spirits are God's full power sent into all the earth.

[60] Bauckham, *Climax of Prophecy*, p. 163, notes the likely reason for this allusion is its central message, 'Not by might, nor by power, but by my Spirit, says the Lord of hosts' (Zech. 4.6).

[61] Cf. Exod. 25.31-40; 40.4, 24-25.

[62] Bauckham agrees with Bruce, 'The Spirit of the Apocalypse', p. 334 n. 6, that the seven Spirits identify both with the seven eyes and with the seven horns of the Lamb symbolizing the Spirit's ability to see all and to act powerfully.

Spirits are then sent out into the world to be the power of the Lamb's victory. Bauckham further explores the relationship of the Spirit, the church, and Zechariah 4 in Revelation 11. Bauckham identifies Rev. 11.3-13 as a parable for faithful prophetic witness. Bauckham interprets the two olive trees and two lampstands – an allusion to Zechariah 4 – as representing the church that is anointed with the 'oil of the Spirit'. He concludes that 'the seven Spirits are the power of the church's prophetic witness to the world, symbolized by the ministry of the two witnesses … The horns and the eyes of the Lamb are the power and discernment of their prophetic witness, which is their faithfulness to the witness Jesus bore.'[63] By the Spirit, the two witnesses are sent out into all the earth in the power and knowledge of the Lamb in order to make the Lamb's victory effective on earth. Concerning πνευματικῶς and agreeing with both Schweizer and Bruce, Bauckham prefers to translate πνευματικῶς as 'prophetic', which denotes 'Spirit-given perception'.[64] One who is able to see by the Spirit is able to discern a different reality.[65] Thus, 'prophetically' interpreted, 'the great city' is Jerusalem, Babylon, Sodom, and Egypt because when seen with 'Spirit-given perception', Jerusalem, Sodom, Egypt, Babylon, or any place that persecutes and kills the prophets are the same reality.[66]

Fourth, Bauckham deems that the eschatology of the Apocalypse is not predictive, but functions to direct believers toward the coming of the Lord in order that they might bear witness of Jesus' victory achieved through his death and resurrection. Revelation 22.17 refers to the Spirit and the bride from an eschatological perspective. The bride is the New Jerusalem or as the bride will become, not as it is. The church prays for the coming of the Lord, which is united with the voice of the Spirit. As the church prays for the Lord to 'Come' along with the Spirit, the eschatological church becomes present. Praying with the Spirit for the coming of Jesus is the heart of Christian living because it makes present the eschatological church on earth. Thus, the church is being called to pneumatic witness, inviting all of creation to taste the eschatological water of life flowing from

---

[63] Bauckham, *Climax of Prophecy*, p. 165.

[64] Bauckham, *Climax of Prophecy*, pp. 168-69.

[65] Bauckham, *Climax of Prophecy*, p. 165.

[66] Bauckham, *Climax of Prophecy*, pp. 168-73.

the new creation (Rev. 22.6). Eschatological life that is available in the present.[67]

In sum, Bauckham offers one of the most complete and comprehensive studies on the pneumatology of the Apocalypse. ἐν πνεύματι ('in the Spirit') serves (i) phenomenologically, John has an experience in the Spirit, and (ii) literarily, ἐν πνεύματι serves a narrative structural function. The Spirit brings the words of Christ to the churches, and the churches in turn bear witness. Witness in the Apocalypse is parallel to prophecy: the witness of Jesus, prophesied by the church, is empowered by the Spirit of prophecy. Bauckham identifies the seven Spirits as the Holy Spirit, which is illustrated by their closeness with both the Lamb – as his seven eyes and seven horns – and the divine throne – being located before the divine throne. Bauckham notes that the seven Spirits are the power and discernment for the churches.

## R. Jeske

R. Jeske examines the communal aspects of ἐν πνεύματι ('in the Spirit').[68] Jeske critiques every scholar who presumes that ἐν πνεύματι is a reference to an individual ecstatic experience. He asks (1) why is the experience individualistic when the Spirit acts communally throughout the Apocalypse? And (2) why are there repetitions of ἐν πνεύματι throughout the Apocalypse if Rev. 1.10 points to John's actual ecstatic experience? Jeske begins his argument by recalling various negative notions of ecstatic experiences in Christian, pre-Christian, and post-Christian literature; he concludes that prophetic acts are verbal messages rather than ecstatic experiences.[69] Jeske proposes that John receives 'inspiration' for his message apart from an ecstatic experience.[70] The purpose behind the Apocalypse, for Jeske, is John's desire for solidarity with the persecuted community in Asia Minor. John was in a crisis of exile while the community was experiencing a crisis of imperial cult pressure, possible expulsion

---

[67] Bauckham, *Climax of Prophecy*, pp. 166-73.

[68] Jeske, 'Spirit and Community', pp. 452-66.

[69] Jeske, 'Spirit and Community', p. 455, e.g. the Didache – a work dealing with prophets – regulates against 'uncontrolled prophetic activity, especially the influence of wandering charismatic missionaries, by instituting guidelines for conduct within administratively organized communities'.

[70] Jeske, 'Spirit and Community', pp. 454-55.

from the synagogue, and internal conflicts. Hence, in their shared persecution, John and the community could be brought together ἐν πνεύματι on the Lord's day for the purpose of communal worship. Jeske observes that the Apocalypse opens and closes in a liturgical worship setting and that the Apocalypse is full of liturgical elements, including doxologies, salutations, benedictions, beatitudes, prayers, and hymns.

Jeske, then, turns to explore communal discernment. Appealing primarily to the Pauline literature, Jeske proposes the community is the place for speaking and hearing. The prophet's voice should be heard in community and cannot be heard in isolation. Once the community hears the prophet, the word should be analyzed and criticized.[71] Gifts, words, and prophecies are given primarily for the edification of the community. Turning to the role of the Spirit, Jeske surmises that the primary function of the Spirit is to maintain unity: 'nowhere in the book of Rev [*sic*] is the work of the Spirit connected with the experience of an individual directly apart from the community, although we might expect that claim with regard to the prophetic office'.[72] Rather, Jeske finds ἐν πνεύματι to be a 'symbolic code for participation in the community of the Spirit, especially when particular reference is given to being in the Spirit on the Lord's day'.[73] The 'symbolic code',[74] ἐν πνεύματι, represents that the activity of the

---

[71] The prophetic words are not only subject to one's own community, but other prophets and other communities.

[72] Jeske, 'Spirit and Community', p. 462, conjectures that in Thyatira there might have been those who claimed this prophetic office and had a direct experience with the Spirit apart from a community.

[73] Jeske's work seems to create an unnecessary choice between ecstatic experience and the work of the Spirit in community going as far to say that the initial audience would 'have recourse to understanding the phrase ἐν πνεύματι ('in the Spirit') in terms other than a reference to a personal ecstatic experience of John'. Another conclusion is possible that says ἐν πνεύματι is 'more than' a reference to a personal ecstatic experience by John. See Jeske, 'Spirit and Community', p. 462.

[74] Jeske, 'Spirit and Community', pp. 463-64. Jeske gives five intentions for this symbolic code ἐν πνεύματι ('in the Spirit'). First, it is a symbol of identification in the Spirit. In order for John to overcome the physical distance from the community, he writes ἐν πνεύματι with liturgical and literary intentions. The Spirit is at work in and through the prophets in community. Second, it is a symbol of reception. John is the recipient and giver of the prophetic message, which is received by the community. Third, it is a symbol of prophetic responsibility. Jeske surmises that John's vocation as a prophet is never claimed in Revelation, but John was, by vocation, a prophet before his exile. Once exiled, it became necessary for John to

Spirit is interrelated (and indistinguishable for Jeske) to the life of the community:

> The community is to hear what the Spirits says to the churches (2.7, 11, 17, 29, 3.6, 13, 22); the Spirit of prophecy is the witness of Jesus – in which all Christians are engaged (12.17; 19.10); the Spirit is one with the community in its affirmation of its eschatological existence (14.13) and in its eager anticipation of the coming of its Lord (22.17). The connections between the seven torches (4.5), the seven lampstands which are the seven churches (1.20), the seven eyes of the Lamb (5.6 – Zech. 4.2, 11-14), and the seven spirits of God (1.20; 5.6) indicate to the present writer that the seven spirits of God (1.20) is a symbol for the various manifestations of the one Spirit of God as localized in each of the seven churches.[75]

## F.D. Mazzaferri

F.D. Mazzaferri pens a few pages investigating the Spirit of God where he explores mainly the revelatory role of the Spirit.[76] Despite being absent from the explicit chain of revelation in the Apocalypse – God to Jesus to his angel to John – Mazzaferri believes that the Spirit is active in the process of revelation because of the close relationship between the Spirit and Christ. The words of Jesus are spoken by the Spirit therefore the Spirit shares in the revelatory actions of Jesus. Mazzaferri notes that this close relationship is epitomized in the symbol of the seven eyes and seven horns of the Lamb that are the seven Spirits, which alludes to Zechariah 4.[77] Mazzaferri notices further evidence of the Spirit's role in revelation in Rev. 14.13;

---

write so that he could continue contact with his community. Thus, Jeske finds ἐν πνεύματι not to be a special claim, but an awareness and fulfillment of John's prophetic vocation and to communicate his prophetic message to the community. Fourth, ἐν πνεύματι is a symbol of participation. Participation, for Jeske, includes participation in suffering and persecution: being ἐν πνεύματι on the Lord's day is to be unified with those suffering in community. Fifth and finally, ἐν πνεύματι serves as a literary device reappearing four times throughout the narrative, which 'serves as a sign of the topical structuring of the writing' (p. 464).

[75] Jeske, 'Spirit and Community', p. 462.

[76] F.D. Mazzaferri, *The Genre of the Book of Revelation from a Source-Critical Perspective* (New York, NY: de Gruyter, 1989), pp. 300-303.

[77] Mazzaferri, *The Genre of the Book of Revelation*, p. 302. For Mazzaferri, the eyes symbolize judgment, a predominant theme in Revelation.

16.5-7; 22.20.[78] Mazzaferri considers that the Spirit of prophecy is an agent of prophetic revelation: first, because of the closeness of Rev. 19.10 and Rev. 22.6, and, second, the appearance of the plural τῶν πνευμάτων τῶν προφητῶν ('the Spirits of the prophets') likely corresponds to the plural τῶν ἑπτὰ πνευμάτων ('the seven Spirits') in the opening salutation. Critical of Jeske's proposal that ἐν πνεύματι describes only a communal experience, Mazzaferri describes ἐν πνεύματι as (1) an occurrence of revelation by the Spirit, (2) an allusion to Ezekiel's actual experiences, and (3) visionary transportation.

## J.-P. Ruiz

J.-P. Ruiz's monograph explores Ezekiel in the Apocalypse. He offers one of the most comprehensive and in-depth studies on the theme of discernment in the Apocalypse, while considering discernment to be one of the most predominate themes in the book. This work will focus on comments from Ruiz that discuss calls to active reading, reflection, and discernment, along with his brief section on the seer and the Spirit.[79]

First, Ruiz identifies 'hermeneutical imperatives' signified by the phrase: ὁ ἔχων οὖς ἀκουσάτω τί τὸ πνεῦμα λέγει ταῖς ἐκκλησίαις ('Let the one having an ear, hear what the Spirit is saying to the churches'). Ruiz puts forth three indications of the 'hermeneutical imperatives': (1) in the seven prophetic messages, the 'hermeneutical imperatives' are invitations for discernment by the Spirit:

> The messages to the churches are not immediately and automatically understandable: they are to be understood under the influence of the same Spirit who inspired their composition. The churches are summoned to be attentive to the inspired message and to apply themselves to the process of reflection which will bring them to understand it. They are invited to come thereby to an understanding of their situation and of what the risen Christ expects of them.[80]

(2) The 'hermeneutical imperatives' indicate the divine origin of the messages. (3) They assume an ecclesial setting where the Spirit speaks

---

[78] The voice is likely identified as the Spirit who gives a command to write.
[79] Ruiz, *Ezekiel in the Apocalypse*, pp. 196-214, 300-303.
[80] Ruiz, *Ezekiel in the Apocalypse*, p. 196.

actively and continuously to the churches throughout history.[81] Ruiz notes that since it is the Spirit who speaks the words of Christ to the church, the Spirit is the Spirit of prophecy.[82]

Second, another 'hermeneutical imperative' is found in Rev. 13.9 where the readers must reflect upon the proceeding description of the first beast (Rev. 13.1-8) and the following verses in Revelation 13. This reflection involves considering 'the fate which may befall those who refuse to do homage to the beast, and exhorts them to accept the consequences: ὧδέ ἐστιν ἡ ὑπομονὴ καὶ ἡ πίστις τῶν ἁγίων'.[83] Ruiz notices an allusion to Jer. 15.2 where Revelation offers an ironic twist: in Jeremiah the punishment of death will befall those who committed sin; while in Rev. 13.10, the same tragedy of death will strike the faithful who resist worshipping the beast. The 'hermeneutical imperative' invites the church to reflect upon 'their conduct and consider its consequences, and to take appropriate measures to act in conformity with "what the Spirit says to the churches"'.[84] Hence, Ruiz articulates that the church is directed to non-violence, but is also encouraged in that those who violently persecute them – such as the beast in Rev. 13.1-8 – will die by the sword.

Third, within the same context of Rev. 13.9, the readers are called to active reflection in Rev. 13.18. Ruiz discovers a correspondence between the 'hermeneutical imperative' of Rev. 13.9 and the exhortation to be attentive and calculate in 13.18.[85] He demonstrates that two of the four occurrences of wisdom in Rev. 5.12 and 7.12 are attributed to God and Christ and thus concludes that wisdom has divine qualities.[86] The other two occurrences of wisdom appear in contexts of discernment and accompany νοῦς ('discernment'). Therefore, in the Apocalypse, Ruiz suggests that every occurrence of wisdom is interrelated and likely involves divine assistance: 'the task of human wisdom is to be attentive to the unfolding of the divine

---

[81] Ruiz, *Ezekiel in the Apocalypse*, pp. 198-99.

[82] Ruiz, *Ezekiel in the Apocalypse*, p. 197.

[83] Ruiz, *Ezekiel in the Apocalypse*, p. 201.

[84] Ruiz, *Ezekiel in the Apocalypse*, p. 203.

[85] Εἴ τις ἔχει οὖς ('If anyone has an ear', Rev. 13.9) // ὁ ἔχων νοῦν ψηφισάτω ('Let the one having a mind, calculate', Rev. 13.18). ὧδέ ἐστιν ἡ ὑπομονὴ καὶ ἡ πίστις τῶν ἁγίων ('Here is the fortitude and the faithfulness of the saints', Rev. 13.10) // ὧδε ἡ σοφία ἐστίν ('Here is wisdom', Rev. 13.18).

[86] Ruiz, *Ezekiel in the Apocalypse*, p. 207.

wisdom'.[87] Turning to the calculation of the beast, Ruiz is critical of interpretations that find the Apocalypse to be a veiled criticism of Rome. Rather, 'both the number and name function as elements of a different sort of code: they reveal the true essence of their object'.[88]

Fourth, Ruiz turns to examine the occurrence of wisdom in Rev. 17.9, and notices the similarity in language between Rev. 17.9 and Rev. 13.18.[89] Ruiz suggests that wisdom and νοῦς ('discernment') are associated in the Apocalypse, and that the three 'hermeneutical imperatives' in Rev. 13.9-10, 18; 17.9 should be discerned in awareness of each other.[90] Discernment is required because the vision cannot be immediately interpreted or comprehended; rather, interpretation requires assistance from the angel along with a process of discernment by the faithful readers.[91]

Fifth, Ruiz explores the use of μυστήριον ('mystery'), which occurs four times in the Apocalypse. For Ruiz, μυστήριον ('mystery') in the Apocalypse is an enigma, which is hidden from the readers and requires revelation to be understood. The μυστήριον ('mystery') is mediated and expressed symbolically. Thus, (1) in Rev. 1.20, the risen Christ reveals the μυστήριον, (2) in Rev. 17.5, 7, an angel discloses the μυστήριον, and (3) in Rev. 10.7, the mighty angel reveals the μυστήριον of God. Ruiz, also, believes the three contexts of μυστήριον in the Apocalypse are interrelated.[92] In the Apocalypse, the μυστήριον is the transcendent, divine plan that is translated into human terms, and thereby can be only partially revealed.[93] Finally, Ruiz finds that discerning the enigmatic and bizarre images of the Apocalypse requires 'active reading'.[94] The act of reading the Apocalypse is an attempt to reveal (ἀποκάλυψις, 'reveal') the mystery (μυστήριον) of God. Ruiz deems that if the medium is the message,

---

[87] Ruiz, *Ezekiel in the Apocalypse*, p. 207.

[88] Ruiz, *Ezekiel in the Apocalypse*, p. 208.

[89] ὧδε ('here [is]'), ὁ νοῦς ('the discernment'), ὁ ἔχων ('the one having'), σοφίαν ('wisdom').

[90] Ruiz, *Ezekiel in the Apocalypse*, p. 209. Ruiz considers Daniel 7 and Ezekiel 16; 23 as examples of discernment.

[91] Ruiz, *Ezekiel in the Apocalypse*, p. 211.

[92] Ruiz, *Ezekiel in the Apocalypse*, p. 214.

[93] Ruiz, *Ezekiel in the Apocalypse*, p. 213.

[94] Ruiz, *Ezekiel in the Apocalypse*, p. 216.

then the Apocalypse is a medium of discernment: the text of the Apocalypse is filled with symbols and images that require discernment.[95] Ruiz goes as far as to say that the idiosyncratic Greek of the Apocalypse is intentionally difficult where the text consciously forces the readers to stop and reflect upon the very words of the Apocalypse.[96]

Sixth, in a section entitled the seer and the Spirit, Ruiz primarily explores the pneumatology of the Apocalypse through the intertextual lens of Ezekiel. Ezekiel's Spirit-experiences include geographical transportation and occurrences when the Spirit 'comes upon' the prophet; John, by aligning himself with Ezekiel's pneumatic experiences, places himself in the prophetic tradition.[97] The role of the Spirit in John's prophetic ministry further confirms that the Spirit is the Spirit of prophecy.[98] Ruiz notices three aspects of Ezekiel's pneumatic experience: (1) it is included in the context of Ezekiel's prophetic commissioning, (2) in the scenes to hear his mission, and (3) at the conclusion of Ezekiel's commissioning when he is returned to the exiles.[99] Similarly, John is ἐν πνεύματι ('in the Spirit') when (1) he receives his commission (Rev. 1.19), (2) when the Lamb receives the scroll from the throne (Rev. 5.7), and (3) experiences transportation (Rev. 17.3; 21.10) where John, like Ezekiel, witnesses judgment upon Babylon and sees the advent of the New Jerusalem.[100]

In sum, Ruiz offers a broad survey concerning the role discernment in the Apocalypse. Beginning with the 'hermeneutical imperatives', Ruiz finds that the Apocalypse is an exercise in active reading where one must slow down and pay close attention to the bizarre, symbolic world of the text. Specific calls for discernment occur in the contexts of: ὧδε ('here [is]'), νοῦς ('discernment'), σοφίαν ('wisdom'), μυστήριον ('mystery'), and the 'hermeneutical imperatives'. The ὧδε ('here [is]') formulas often accompany a call to have a νοῦς ('discernment') or σοφίαν ('wisdom'). Ruiz proposes that these terms are interconnected, which call the readers to a process of reflection.

---

[95] Ruiz, *Ezekiel in the Apocalypse*, pp. 219-20.

[96] Ruiz, *Ezekiel in the Apocalypse*, p. 220.

[97] Ruiz, *Ezekiel in the Apocalypse*, p. 300.

[98] Ruiz, *Ezekiel in the Apocalypse*, p. 303.

[99] Ruiz, *Ezekiel in the Apocalypse*, p. 300.

[100] Ruiz, *Ezekiel in the Apocalypse*, p. 302.

Ruiz observes the divine association of wisdom in the Apocalypse, and proposes that having wisdom is connected to divine involvement in the process of discernment. Concerning the occurrences of μυστήριον ('mystery') in the Apocalypse, Ruiz comments that the readers must stop and reflect, while receiving divine assistance from Jesus or angels. Ruiz considers that discernment is a deliberate theme in the Apocalypse to the extent that the difficult idiosyncratic Greek forces readers to stop and to reflect.

## J.C. de Smidt

J.C. de Smidt contributes two corresponding articles where he explores ἐν πνεύματι ('in the Spirit') from literary, congregational, social, and historical perspectives.[101] He begins by noting that although the term 'Holy Spirit' does not occur in the Apocalypse, any mention of 'spirit', 'spirits', or 'spirit of the Lord' in the Apocalypse is a reference to the Holy Spirit. de Smidt is critical of scholarship that denies any mention of the Spirit in the Apocalypse.[102] The Spirit is active in the life of the community and functions as mediator and originator of John's vision. Following Bauckham, de Smidt deems ἐν πνεύματι ('in the Spirit') as a phenomenological, ecstatic event where the Spirit enables John to see into heaven as 'the Spirit drew aside the thin veil between the physical and spiritual world for the seer and displayed to him, in a unique state of visionary consciousness, the spiritual world from his location in the physical world'.[103] John conveys his experience through a literary expression that is facilitated by the Spirit. Even though the Spirit plays an active role throughout the process, John maintains 'freedom of his individuality'.[104] Hence, there

---

[101] de Smidt, 'The Holy Spirit in the Book of Revelation', pp. 229-44; de Smidt, 'Hermeneutical Perspectives', pp. 27-47.

[102] de Smdit notes that the Spirit is never called the Holy Spirit but the seven Spirits are identified as 'burning lampstands', which burn with the fire of holiness and purity (Rev. 1.12; 4.5; 11.1).

[103] de Smidt is critical of the psychological proposal where John experienced a stress induced alternate consciousness; rather, John's experience was both physical and spiritual. John was able to retain his freedom of individuality. See de Smidt, 'The Holy Spirit in the Book of Revelation', p. 239; de Smidt, 'Hermeneutical Perspectives', p. 29.

[104] de Smidt, 'Hermeneutical Perspectives', p. 31. See Bauckham, 'The Role of the Spirit in the Apocalypse', p. 68.

is a synergistic relationship between John and the Spirit in his visionary experience as well as the process of writing. John creatively molds
his visionary experience into a symbolic form that is pastoral and
prophetic, while employing stylistic features such as narrative and
rhetoric. ἐν πνεύματι serves as a literary-theological expression giving legitimacy to John's vision. de Smidt prefers to translate ἐν
πνεύματι as 'in the Spirit's control'.[105] de Smidt considers that John
writes the Apocalypse to strengthen and nurture the community that
is persecuted by Rome, the Jews, and the 'heathens', as well as to address the conflict within the communities.[106] Thus, ἐν πνεύματι ('in
the Spirit') is a term of empathy between the persecuted author and
the persecuted community; being ἐν πνεύματι on the Lord's day is
to be in 'koinonia' with the Spirit who unifies the churches. Thus, the
hearing formula of the seven prophetic messages is inclusive of the
entire community and, by de Smidt's estimation, 'the whole Apocalypse could, therefore, be regarded as a "speaking in the Spirit" (Rev.
14.13)'.[107]

The Spirit is identified as the seven horns (perfect power) and
seven eyes (perfect sight) of the Lamb who is sent out into all the
earth, suggesting that the Spirit is active in the world through the
congregation. There is a union between the Spirit and the congregation that is symbolized by the burning flames in the lampstand. Thus,
on the one hand de Smidt notes, the Spirit is 'intimately connected
with the salvation, the sanctification, the worship, the discipleship,
the witness, the prayer life, and the unity of the congregations'.[108] On
the other hand, the Spirit is the empowering, prophetic witness of
the church to the world. The Spirit salvifically gives 'grace and peace'
(Rev. 1.4) to the community. The community's cry to 'Come!' is not
only directed to Jesus, but also directed to sinners. Since the Spirit is
in the second position in Rev. 1.14, it denotes for de Smidt a position
of hierarchical trinitarian importance. The second position also
serves functionally to reveal that the Spirit is interactive between the
Son and the Father. The relationship is further evident by the Spirit's

---

[105] de Smidt, 'Hermeneutical Perspectives', p. 29.
[106] de Smidt, 'The Holy Spirit in the Book of Revelation', p. 230.
[107] de Smidt, 'The Holy Spirit in the Book of Revelation', p. 242.
[108] de Smidt, 'Hermeneutical Perspectives', p. 34.

close relationship to the one on the throne as well as being the seven eyes and seven horns of the Lamb.[109]

## M. Wilson

In 1994 M. Wilson examines Rev. 19.10[110] and later offers a short section on the role of the Spirit in *The Victor Sayings in the Book of Revelation*.[111] First, Wilson begins his article by exploring the close textual relationship between the word of God and the witness to Jesus. He follows Bauckham writing 'the "witness of Jesus" is the content of the Apocalypse itself (1.2)'.[112] Wilson deems ἡ μαρτυρία 'Ιησοῦ to be an objective genitive and thereby translated, 'for the witness to Jesus'.[113] Against Ford and Charles, Wilson is unconvinced that Rev. 19.10d is a gloss.[114] However, although Wilson interprets nearly every other occurrence of πνεῦμα in the Apocalypse as referring to 'spirit', he excludes the appearance of πνεῦμα in Rev. 19.10. Rather, Wilson argues, first, that πνεῦμα in Rev. 19.10 should be not be capitalized and translated as 'essence', indicating 'the witness of Jesus is what this prophecy is all about'.[115] Second, appealing to five other textual appearances in the Apocalypse, Wilson concludes that the definite article τῆς in τὸ πνεῦμα τῆς προφητείας should be translated as 'the prophecy'. Third, 'the prophecy' should be thought as synonymous with 'the Apocalypse'. Hence, Wilson translates τὸ πνεῦμα τῆς προφητείας as the essence (or spirit) of the Prophecy (or Apocalypse).[116] Wilson suggests that the witness of Jesus is the reason for the entire Apocalypse.

Second, turning to his monograph, Wilson follows an interpretative stream that considers the seven Spirits to be an allusion to Zech.

---

[109] de Smidt, 'Hermeneutical Perspectives', pp. 42-43, later identifies the seven eyes and seven horns as the power of the Lamb to defeat the beast and the dragon. Thus, the Lamb has the ability to act powerfully through the Spirit at any time.

[110] Wilson, 'Revelation 19:10', pp. 191-202.

[111] M.M. Wilson, *The Victor Sayings in the Book of Revelation* (Eugene, OR: Wipf & Stock, 2007).

[112] Bauckham, 'The Role of the Spirit in the Apocalypse', p. 74. See Wilson, 'Revelation 19:10', p. 197.

[113] Wilson, 'Revelation 19:10', pp. 197, 201.

[114] Charles, *The Revelation of St. John*, p. 129; Ford, 'For the Testimony of Jesus', p. 291.

[115] Wilson, 'Revelation 19:10', p. 198.

[116] Wilson, 'Revelation 19:10', p. 201.

4.1-14, symbolizing completeness. In the seven prophetic messages, there is a close relationship between Christ and the Spirit. When Christ speaks to the churches, the Spirit speaks and applies the message. In fact, Wilson believes it is likely that the Spirit is the speaker throughout the Apocalypse.[117] Wilson does not find a hierarchical trinitarian relationship in the Apocalypse. Rather, Christ and the Spirit are equal. Their equal relationship is represented by the description of the seven eyes and the seven horns of the Lamb and Christ's fiery eyes in Rev. 2.18, which both are the seven Spirits – the seven burning torches.[118] The fire of the Spirit represents omniscience and purification.

## S.S. Smalley

S.S. Smalley, has offered significant contributions to the study of the Apocalypse in the form of a monograph[119] and a commentary,[120] but his most extensive consideration of the pneumatology of the Apocalypse is an article published in 1996.[121] Smalley deems that the FG, Apocalypse, and Johannine Epistles come from the same Johannine community.[122] Smalley begins his discussion of pneumatology by examining the role of the Paraclete in the FG. Smalley considers that the Paraclete in the Fourth Gospel is (1) the agent of regeneration, (2) a minister to the church, (3) an advocate, (4) a teacher, and (5) an inspirer.[123] Smalley offers a 'two-level' view of the Spirit's activities: material (earthly) and spiritual (heavenly). On the one hand, the Paraclete's activities are earthly (material), imitating Jesus' earthly

---

[117] Wilson, *The Victor Sayings in the Book of Revelation*, p. 73.

[118] Wilson, *The Victor Sayings in the Book of Revelation*, p. 73. Wilson observes that fire is a symbol of the Holy Spirit throughout the NT, citing Mt. 3.11 and Acts 2.3.

[119] S.S. Smalley, *Thunder and Love: John's Revelation and John's Community* (Waco, TX: Word, 1994).

[120] S.S. Smalley, *The Revelation to John: A Commentary on the Greek Text of the Apocalypse* (Downers Grove, IL: InterVarsity Press, 2005).

[121] Smalley, 'The Paraclete', pp. 289-300.

[122] Smalley considers that the Apocalypse has chronological priority among the Johannine literature. Smalley concludes that the Apocalypse has a more primitive (yet well-developed) pneumatology than the evolved pneumatology in the FG. Smalley considers the Apocalypse to be earlier than the FG, and he believes that pneumatic divergences between the two works are more apparent than real. See Smalley, 'The Paraclete', pp. 289-90, 296-97.

[123] Smalley, 'The Paraclete', p. 291 notes that the Paraclete's activities are too varied in the FG to be understood under a similar backdrop.

ministry. The Paraclete indwells the disciples, teaches, brings to memory, bears witness to Jesus, and leads the disciples into all truth. On the other hand, the Spirit's activity is spiritual (heavenly) since the Spirit discloses the natures of God and Christ. The Spirit is the eschatological Spirit, bringing a new age to earth and allowing the church to share in the life of God.[124]

Turning to the pneumatology of the Apocalypse, Smalley begins by noting differences between the FG and the Apocalypse concerning pneumatology. The Spirit in the Apocalypse seems to be less personal and is less defined functionally, which Smalley considers to be based on the chronological priority of the Apocalypse. The similarities between the works include: (1) the Spirit is a person distinguished from the Father and Son represented as the Spirit of God and of Christ. The Spirit and Jesus are so closely connected, which is indicated in the seven prophetic messages.[125] The words of Christ are the speech of the Spirit, and the Spirit is responsive throughout the narrative.[126] (2) Even though the theme of indwelling is not directly derived from the FG, it is found in Revelation, especially with ἐν πνεύματι ('in the Spirit'). Four times John is described as being ἐν πνεύματι where Smalley concludes each occurrence is an ecstatic experience. (3) Although the activity and function of the Spirit is not explicitly taught in Revelation, the Spirit of prophecy inspires prophetic witness seen notably in the two witnesses' prophetic ministry. The two witnesses follow in the tradition of the HB where the prophets were inspired by the Spirit and prophesied concerning Jesus.[127] (4) Concerning τῶν πνευμάτων τῶν προφητῶν ('the Spirits of the prophets'), '[John] could be referring to the witness of the Spirit of prophecy, mediated through individual prophetic spirits'.[128] Smalley

---

[124] Smalley, 'The Paraclete', p. 292.

[125] Smalley, *Thunder and Love*, p. 168 n. 67, follows Swete and observes that the seven Spirits correspond to the seven churches.

[126] As noted above, Smalley, 'The Paraclete', p. 293, proposes that Revelation's pneumatology is generally more primitive than the FG on account of Revelation preceding the FG chronologically. However, Smalley observes that the close relationship between Christ and the Spirit in the seven prophetic messages is one of the most sophisticated images of pneumatology in Johannine literature.

[127] Smalley, *Thunder and Love*, p. 154, finds ἡ μαρτυρία Ἰησοῦ ('the witness of Jesus') to be an objective genitive.

[128] Smalley, 'The Paraclete', p. 294. See Beckwith, *The Apocalypse of John*, p. 317 and Bruce, 'The Spirit in the Apocalypse', p. 339.

adds that the living water in the Apocalypse and the FG symbolizes new life of the Spirit. The Spirit's work in the Apocalypse is a balance between the earthly church and the heavenly realm.

## D. Aune

The year 1997 marks the return to the tradition of R.H. Charles with D. Aune's three-volume source critical commentary on the Apocalypse. In his commentary, Aune offers only a single-page excursus for the discussion of the Spirit,[129] and his source critical approach controls the discussion. Aune is more occupied with identifying whether certain texts are part of the early or late edition of Revelation than interpreting the pneumatological texts, themselves. Aune proposes that in the final stage of composition, the Spirit is described in personal terms and is the subject of λέγει ('saying') who mediates divine revelation to the church. The Spirit speaks (1) in the seven prophetic messages, (2) in response to the oracle in Rev. 14.13, (3) with the Bride in Rev. 22.17, and (4) as the Spirit of prophecy in Rev. 19.10, even though Aune considers all these texts to be interpolations by later editors. The Spirit is closely identified with Christ, a relationship that Aune traces to the FG. The only mention of the Spirit that might be original, for Aune, is ἐν πνεύματι, which he translates as 'in a trance' or 'in ecstasy'. He deems ἐν πνεύματι to be an apocalyptic concept of revelation, denoting 'the seer does not mediate the word of God through the inspiration of the Spirit, but the Spirit is the divine agent who mediates apocalyptic visions'.[130] Aune dismisses the conclusions of Beckwith, Bruce, and de Smidt to conclude that the seven Spirits are the seven angels of God, while conjecturing that the seven Spirits are later addition to the text.[131]

## G. Schimanowski

In a discussion exploring the worship scenes in the Revelation 4–5, G. Schimanowski dedicates a brief section to the Spirit in Revelation

---

[129] Aune, *Revelation 1–5*, p. 36.

[130] Aune, *Revelation 1–5*, p. 36.

[131] Against Beckwith, *The Apocalypse of John*, pp. 426-27; Bruce, 'The Spirit in the Apocalypse', pp. 333-37; and de Smidt, 'The Holy Spirit in the Book of Revelation', p. 241.

4.¹³² First, Schimanowski finds that the ἐν πνεύματι ('in the Spirit')
phrase in Rev. 4.2 is a reference to a temporal ecstatic experience.
Although Schimanowski leaves open the possibility that ἐν πνεύματι
suggests an actual heavenly journey, he considers a more constructive
theological conclusion to be that ἐν πνεύματι signifies an occasion
for communion with God in the heavenly world. Second, concerning
the seven torches before the thrones (Rev. 4.5), Schimanowski notes
that the present active verbs, ἐκπορεύονται ('going out') and
καιόμεναι ('burning'), represent that the seven torches are unceasing,
non-static, and constantly moving.¹³³ He also finds that the seven
Spirits are a living being who are closely associated with God and
Christ. The seven Spirits are before the throne of God and are the
seven horns and seven eyes of the Lamb.¹³⁴ Concerning the numeral
seven, Schimanowski observes that it is often symbolically interpreted as perfection, fullness, or totality. He attempts to expand this
definition to include a common, cosmic ordering principle of God's
plan.¹³⁵ Finally, he finds that the seven Spirits – as the seven
eyes/torches that go out into the world – likely allude to Zechariah
4.¹³⁶

## L.L. Thompson

In 2003, L.L. Thompson wrote an article exploring 'spirit possession'
in the Apocalypse.¹³⁷ Thompson approaches his discussion as a 'case
study', examining the description of John becoming 'spirit pos-
sessed'. Thompson observes that the four ἐν πνεύματι ('in the
Spirit') phrases express that John was under the influence of a spirit,
allowing him to see the spirit-world.¹³⁸ Even in the spirit world, John

¹³² G. Schimanowski, *Die himmlische Liturgie in der Apokalypse des Johannes: Die frühjüdischen Traditionen in Offenbarung 4–5 unter Einschluss der Hekhalotliteratur* (Tübingen: Mohr Siebeck, 2002), pp. 67-68, 114-19.

¹³³ Schimanowski, *Die himmlische Liturgie in der Apokalypse*, p. 115.

¹³⁴ Schimanowski, *Die himmlische Liturgie in der Apokalypse*, p. 115.

¹³⁵ Schimanowski, *Die himmlische Liturgie in der Apokalypse*, p. 116.

¹³⁶ Schimanowski, *Die himmlische Liturgie in der Apokalypse*, pp. 116-17.

¹³⁷ L.L. Thompson, 'Spirit Possession: Revelation in Religious Studies', in David L. Barr (ed.), *Reading the Book of Revelation: A Resource for Students* (Atlanta, GA: SBL, 2003), pp. 137-50.

¹³⁸ Thompson, 'Spirit Possession', pp. 138-40.

continued to be able to retain awareness of the human world, functioning more as a 'shaman' than a 'medium'.[139] Thompson writes, 'That spirit set the prophetic process in motion in John, inciting him to see and to hear in new ways, and then the process continued in accordance with John's natural disposition'.[140] While little detail accompanies the process of John's spirit possession, the description that John was on Patmos on the Lord's day suggests for Thompson that John was in a Christian congregation that perhaps had music and singing. Thompson considers the hymns as possible means by which spirits would become present and evoke spirit possession.[141] Thompson, then, explores John's spirit possession. Thompson observes that the spirit does not send down messages 'from above'; rather, the spirit 'opens up the human world below', working with the cultural and social context of John.[142] Thompson suggests that the spirit-language is not 'univocal' that is fixed on 'one strict meaning or reference'; rather, spirit language is 'ambiguous and multivocal', using metaphors, similes, and symbols.[143]

## 2006–2017

### Robby Waddell

In 2006, Robby Waddell's PhD thesis, published as *The Spirit of the Book of Revelation,* is the first monograph length study devoted to the pneumatology of the Apocalypse.[144] Waddell integrates intertextuality with a Pentecostal perspective to explore the pneumatology of the Apocalypse.[145]

---

[139] Thompson, 'Spirit Possession', pp. 140-41, 145.

[140] Thompson, 'Spirit Possession', p. 145.

[141] Thompson, 'Spirit Possession', pp. 143-45.

[142] Thompson, 'Spirit Possession', p. 146.

[143] Thompson, 'Spirit Possession', p. 147.

[144] Waddell, *Spirit of the Book of Revelation.*

[145] Waddell comments on the work of Pentecostal and charismatic scholars on the pneumatology of the Apocalypse that includes: S. Horton (1976), R.H. Gause (1983), and F. Martin (1988). Even though Horton does not write specifically on the Apocalypse, S.M. Horton, *What the Bible Says About the Holy Spirit* (Springfield, MO: Gospel Publishing House, 1976), p. 61, is a forerunner to Pentecostal academic study of pneumatology. He offers an overview of the Spirit throughout the bible, which includes a short section dedicated to the Apocalypse. First, Horton identifies the seven Spirits with the seven-fold Spirit in Isa. 11.2. Second, he notes the close connection between the Spirit and the work of Christ in the communities.

First, Waddell refuses to engage in the source critical discussion of Revelation; rather, he chooses to engage the text in its final form, which he deems to have a high level of literary unity where the repetitions and doublets are intentional literary devices. Waddell believes Revelation has a pneumatic structure arranged around six major structural divisions. The six divisions follow the four appearances of ἐν πνεύματι ('in the Spirit'): (1) A prologue (Rev. 1.1-8), (2) ἐν πνεύματι a vision of Christ and the seven messages (Rev. 1.9-3.22), (3) ἐν πνεύματι a lengthy drama of the Lamb and opening of the seven-sealed scroll (Rev. 4.1-16.21), (4) ἐν πνεύματι the judgment of harlot/Babylon (Rev. 17.1-21.8), (5) ἐν πνεύματι the description of the bride/New Jerusalem (Rev. 21.9-22.9), and (6) an epilogue (Rev. 22.6-21).[146]

Second, Waddell attempts to identify the little scroll held by the ἄλλον ἄγγελον ἰσχυρὸν ('another strong angel') of Rev. 10.2. Waddell suggests that the βιβλαρίδιον ('scroll') of Rev. 10.2 is the

---

Third, he finds a literary connection between the seven Spirits (Holy Spirit) with the seven lampstands (seven churches). Fourth, the seven Spirits are the seven horns (complete power) and seven eyes (complete wisdom) of the Lamb. As a result, he concludes the Spirit accomplishes the work, power, and wisdom of the Lamb on earth in the church. Gause, *Revelation*, writes one of the first Pentecostal commentaries on Revelation. Gause does not offer an introductory section on pneumatology but comments on the Spirit throughout the work. He interprets ἐν πνεύματι ('in the Spirit') as a spiritual condition where one who is ἐν πνεύματι ('in the Spirit') is in communion with God. John repeats this experience in each subsequent ἐν πνεύματι ('in the Spirit') occurrence. In the seven prophetic messages, the Spirit makes possible Jesus' relationship with the church. The Spirit is the agent of Jesus' power to the church and makes Jesus known to them. The call for the church to hear the Spirit in the seven prophetic messages transcends historical context, 'This invitation is not to one church, but to all churches of Asia and to all churches of all ages' (p. 50). Finally, the seven prophetic messages signify the divine origins of the message, i.e. what the divine Spirit says to the churches. R.F. Martin, 'Apocalypse, Book of the', *DPCM*, pp. 11-13, contributes a section on the Apocalypse that mainly deals with pneumatology. Following Jeske, Martin does not see the ἐν πνεύματι ('in the Spirit') as an actual out of body experience; rather, concluding that it illustrates prophetic authority and that the source of John's words is the Holy Spirit. Concerning the Spirit of prophecy, Martin finds a circular formula where the role of the Spirit is connected to the witness of Jesus, and the witness of Jesus is the Spirit of prophecy. The Spirit is the Spirit of life who brings the dead back to life (Rev. 11.11). Martin notices the relationship between the seven eyes and seven horns of the Lamb symbolically illustrated as the full power and wisdom of the Spirit who 'establishes the church in its unique identity as the Bride and witness of Jesus'.

[146] Waddell, *Spirit of the Book of Revelation*, p. 138.

same βιβλίον ('scroll') found in the throne room scene of Rev. 5.1. From a survey of various scholarly opinions on the interpretation/translation of βιβλαρίδιον ('scroll', Rev. 10.2), Waddell concludes that βιβλαρίδιον ('scroll') is a faded diminutive and thereby synonymous with βιβλίον ('scroll'), implying that βιβλαρίδιον should be translated 'scroll' rather than 'little scroll'.[147] Furthermore, Waddell finds an intertextual link between John's and Ezekiel's call narratives. In both accounts, the prophet receives a scroll with writing on the front and back. In Ezekiel, the prophet opens and eats the scroll immediately – which differs from the Apocalypse. Ezekiel finds the scroll sweet in his mouth, which resembles John's experience once he is able to eat the scroll.[148] Between the introduction of the scroll in Revelation 5 and the eating of the scroll in Revelation 10, Waddell observes a narrative break (Revelation 6-9) where the seven-sealed scroll must be opened.[149] Therefore, Revelation 10 is the conclusion of John's call narrative, which began in Revelation 5. John eats the scroll and 'what follows on the heels of the call narrative is the prophecy, or better put, the revelation (11.1-13)'.[150]

Third, Waddell turns to the 'hermeneutical conundrum' of ἄλλον ἄγγελον ἰσχυρὸν ('another strong angel'). Whereas Ezekiel receives a scroll from God, John receives a scroll from a ἄγγελον ἰσχυρὸν ('strong angel').[151] Waddell approaches this conundrum by exploring two interpretative options. (1) Interpreters appeal to the chain of revelation in Rev. 1.1 and observe that the ἄγγελον ἰσχυρὸν in Rev. 10.1 is the same angel of revelation (at times referred to as Jesus' angel) in Rev. 1.1 and 22.16.[152] However, Waddell is critical of this approach, suggesting that the ἄγγελον ἰσχυρὸν in Rev. 10.1 and the revelatory

---

[147] Waddell cites Mazzaferri, *The Genre of the Book of Revelation*, p. 268, to show that every other diminutive is considered to be faded in the Apocalypse.

[148] Waddell, citing Bauckham, notes that while Ezekiel does not immediately describe the scroll as bitter to his stomach, it is described as 'words of lamentation and mourning and woe' (Ezek. 2.10; 3.2). See Bauckham, *Climax of Prophecy*, p. 247.

[149] Waddell, *Spirit of the Book of Revelation*, pp. 153-55.

[150] Waddell, *Spirit of the Book of Revelation*, p. 161. He quotes Bauckham, *Climax of Prophecy*, p. 266, '11:1-13 contains the revelation of the scroll *in nuce*'.

[151] Waddell, *Spirit of the Book of Revelation*, p. 155.

[152] See Mazzaferri, *The Genre of the Book of Revelation*, pp. 264-67; Bauckham, *Climax of Prophecy*, pp. 253-57.

angels are different characters.[153] Waddell prefers interpreting the angels of Rev. 22.8-9 and 17.1 to be the revelatory angel from Rev. 1.1. (2) Taking into consideration the divine attributes ascribed to the ἄγγελον ἰσχυρὸν ('strong angel') in Rev. 10.1-11, a second stream of interpretation identifies the angel as a Christophany.[154] Appealing to HB and symbolism in the Apocalypse, the descriptive attributes of the angel – cloud transportation, rainbow, and the description of the angel's face and feet – suggest that the ἄγγελον ἰσχυρὸν is a divine character. From this, Waddell introduces a third interpretative possibility. Instead of interpreting the ἄγγελον ἰσχυρὸν as the divine Christ, he identifies another interpretative option to be that the ἄγγελον ἰσχυρὸν ('strong angel') is the divine Spirit. Waddell's evidence follows: (1) the voice of the ἄγγελον ἰσχυρὸν has divine elements (roaring like a lion and the sound of thunder). (2) The ἄγγελον ἰσχυρὸν shares characteristics with both the one on the throne and Christ, implying divinity (cloud transportation, rainbow, description of the angel's face and feet). (3) While the ἄγγελον ἰσχυρὸν ('strong angel') recalls the one on the throne and Christ, the ἄγγελον ἰσχυρὸν also differs in some respects. Waddell views these differences as evidence that the ἄγγελον ἰσχυρὸν is a character other than Christ. (4) In Ezekiel, the Spirit of God is the revelatory agent and thus John's reception of the revelation from the ἄγγελον ἰσχυρὸν parallels Ezekiel's reception of the scroll. Finally, Waddell leaves his position open, observing that even though there is sufficient evidence to interpret the ἄγγελον ἰσχυρὸν ('strong angel') of Rev. 10.1 as the Spirit, the close relationship between the Spirit and Christ in the Apocalypse makes it impossible to conclude definitively. Nevertheless, Waddell is firm on identifying the ἄγγελον ἰσχυρὸν ('strong angel') as a divine

---

[153] Waddell appeals to Bauckham, *Climax of Prophecy*, p. 256, who is also reluctant to identify these angels as the same characters, but Waddell critiques Bauckham's solution that the angels of 19.10 and 22.8-9 are different. Rather, Waddell finds clear literary parallels between 19.10 and 22.8-9. He identifies the angel of Rev. 22.8-9 as the revelatory angel.

[154] See G.K. Beale, *The Book of Revelation: A Commentary on the Greek Text* (NIGTC; Grand Rapids, MI: Eerdmans, 1999), pp. 522-26.

person based on the angel's divine attributes and the revelatory similarity to Ezekiel.[155] Waddell turns to Revelation 11 to investigate further his interpretation.

Fourth, despite the chapter division, Waddell notes that there is a narrative flow from Revelation 10 to 11, which lacks any transitional phrase (commonly καὶ εἶδον ['and I saw'] in Revelation). This literary unity supports Waddell's proposal that Rev. 11.1-13 represents John's prophecy, which naturally flows from his call narrative in Revelation 10. Revelation 11.1-2 thereby functions as a hinge for the previous and proceeding sections. Based on the literary progression of the text, Waddell suggests that the narrator in Rev. 11.1-2 is the ἄγγελον ἰσχυρὸν ('strong angel') from Revelation 10. Furthermore, while some interpreters identify two narrators in Rev. 11.1-2 and Rev. 11.3, Waddell concludes that the ἄγγελον ἰσχυρὸν identified as 'the Spirit can be seen as the narrator of the complete prophecy 11.1-13. The Spirit may even speak of the death of Christ in the third person without difficulty.'[156] Recognizing that the Spirit is the narrator throughout Rev. 11.1-13 unifies the unnamed narrator in Rev. 11.1-3 as the one who gives the scroll and the measuring rod to John with the divine speaker who uses the possessive qualifier μου ('my') to describe μάρτυσίν μου ('my witnesses') in Rev. 11.3.

Fifth, the crux of Waddell's intertextual argument is found in his discussion of the Spirit's role in the two witnesses' prophetic ministry. In Zechariah 4, the imagery of the lampstand is closely related to the Spirit of the Lord.[157] The lampstand is reinterpreted to symbolize the intimate relationship between the seven churches and the Spirit where 'the seven flames which burn before the throne also inhabit the church(es), lighting up the lampstand(s)'.[158] In other words, the seven churches (seven lampstands) shine with the light of the Spirit (seven flames) who inspires them to bear witness in the world. This intimate relationship is extended to Christ. In the seven prophetic

---

[155] Waddell responds to the interpretive difficulty, why is the divine Spirit or divine Christ depicted as an angel? In response, he argues that at times in the HB, angels (particularly 'the angel of the Lord') represented the divine.

[156] Waddell, *Spirit of the Book of Revelation*, p. 163.

[157] In Zech. 4.10, the seven lamps are the 'eyes of the Lord which range through the whole earth'.

[158] Waddell, *Spirit of the Book of Revelation*, p. 177. The imagery of the lampstand appears to describe the church in Rev. 1.12-13 and Rev. 11.1-13.

messages, 'the Spirit and Christ speak in tandem'.[159] The Spirit – symbolized as seven eyes (intertextually drawn from Zech 3.9) and the seven horns of the Lamb – is the complete knowledge and power of the Lamb. Since the Spirit is sent out into the world, the Spirit makes effective the victory of the Lamb.[160] The primary location of operation of the Spirit is the church who participates with the Spirit in accomplishing the Lamb's victory on earth.

Waddell then turns to πνευματικῶς ('Spiritually') in Rev. 11.8.[161] He understands Rev. 11.8 to be a 'grand intertextual image of the great city'.[162] Waddell follows P. Minear who understands πνευματικῶς to be a 'trans-historical' reality of an 'anti-God culture'.[163] πνευματικῶς is 'the divinely given perspective of the witnesses'.[164] The church is being called to discern 'Spiritually' (πνευματικῶς) the true divine reality. Waddell goes so far as to say that discerning the true prophetic reality is a primary purpose of the Apocalypse:

> In the center of the Apocalypse, John places the story of the two witnesses, and in the center of this brief narrative, John describes the spiritual insight of the church discerning the reality of the great city. The Apocalypse is intended to reveal to the church the true identity of Jesus as king of kings and lord of lords. Despite apparent perceptions, the beast is not the ultimate authority. If a person fears God and gives him glory then there is no longer any need to fear the beast. Like John, who was in the Spirit when he saw visions, the church must also see Spiritually.[165]

---

[159] Waddell, *Spirit of the Book of Revelation*, p. 178. Contra Schweizer, 'πνεῦμα', pp. 449-50, who does not distinguish between the Spirit and Christ.

[160] Waddell, *Spirit of the Book of Revelation*, p. 177. See Bauckham, *Climax of Prophecy*, p. 165.

[161] Waddell, *Spirit of the Book of Revelation*, pp. 181-82, translates πνευματικῶς 'Spiritually'. He notes that those who translate πνευματικῶς 'prophetically' 'capture the correct connotation but obscure the agent of the prophetic perspective, the Spirit of prophecy'.

[162] Waddell, *Spirit of the Book of Revelation*, p. 182.

[163] Waddell, *Spirit of the Book of Revelation*, p. 183. See P.S. Minear, 'Ontology and Ecclesiology in the Apocalypse', *NTS* 12 (1966), p. 96.

[164] Waddell, *Spirit of the Book of Revelation*, p. 182.

[165] Waddell, *Spirit of the Book of Revelation*, pp. 182-83.

Sixth, Waddell discusses four other occurrences of πνεῦμα ('Spirit') in the Apocalypse. (1) In Rev. 11.11, he concludes that πνεῦμα ζωῆς ('Spirit of life') is a 'double-entendre' alluding to both the breath of life in Gen. 2.7 as well as to the Spirit of life. (2) When the second beast gives πνεῦμα ('spirit') to the first beast in Rev. 13.15, it is a parody of Rev. 11.11. (3) Criticizing M. Wilson, Waddell concludes that the Spirit of prophecy in Rev. 19.10 is a reference to the Spirit by claiming πνεῦμα ('Spirit') usually refers to the Spirit throughout the Apocalypse. (4) When πνεῦμα appears in a plural form (τῶν πνευμάτων τῶν προφητῶν, 'Spirits of the prophets') in Rev. 22.6, the close parallel of language to Rev. 19.10 likely points to the plural seven Spirits.[166] Again, Waddell considers that the appearance of πνευμάτων ('Spirits') might be a 'double-entendre' where 'the hearts or minds of the prophets are thoroughly satiated with the Spirit of prophecy'.[167]

In sum, Waddell's contributions to the Pentecostal academy and the study of the pneumatology of the Apocalypse are significant. He identifies a pneumatic structure of the Apocalypse. Waddell offers a new pneumatic interpretation of the ἄγγελον ἰσχυρὸν ('strong angel') in Revelation 10. While examining the narrative of the two witnesses and Zechariah 4, Waddell concludes that the Spirit empowers the church's witness. Waddell observes that pneumatic discernment is a key theme to the entire Apocalypse. The church is called to discern 'Spiritually' (πνευματικῶς) and follow the example of John who was ἐν πνεύματι ('in the Spirit').

## P. Benham and R. Skaggs

In 2009, Priscilla Benham and Rebecca Skaggs wrote a commentary in the *Pentecostal Commentary Series*, which contains a short introductory section on the Holy Spirit.[168] First, they consider the originator of the Apocalypse to be the Spirit who is an equal person of the divine trinity. Second, following Waddell, they observe that the seven Spirits are intertextually derived from Zechariah 4, which symbolizes the complete Spirit. Third, the Spirit's closeness to the throne denotes the Spirit's divinity. The Spirit delivers the prophetic messages from

---

[166] See Mazzaferri, *The Genre of the Book of Revelation*, p. 301.

[167] Waddell, *Spirit of the Book of Revelation*, p. 190.

[168] Skaggs and Benham, *Revelation*, p. 18.

the throne to the churches, which is exemplified by the ἐν πνεύματι ('in the Spirit') phrases. Last, the Spirit is the burning lampstands before the throne, and the Spirit is the seven eyes and seven horns of the Lamb, which represent power, warmth, omniscience, and the Spirit's active role on earth.[169]

## I.W. Sorke

In 2009, I.W. Sorke published his PhD thesis on the identity and function of the seven Spirits in the Apocalypse. Sorke surveys the occurrences of πνεῦμα ('Spirit') in the Apocalypse. First, he discovers four functions of ἐν πνεύματι ('in the Spirit') in the Apocalypse: (1) a prophetic authentication derived from HB patterns, (2) a prophetic state of experience, (3) an establishment of a judicial framework for prophetic utterances, and (4) a descriptor of a transportation visionary experience.[170] Second, Sorke agrees with interpreters who identify a close relationship between Christ and the Spirit in the seven prophetic messages.[171] Third, Sorke explores the Spirit's activity in Rev. 14.13, where he notes a familiarity of language with Revelation 2–3 and Rev. 6.11. He writes, '[a]lthough the voice of the cry-ers [*sic*] is silenced in Revelation 14.13, the spirit himself extends consolation to the living by assuring these remaining believers that the works of the now silenced believers act as their surrogate voice'.[172] Fourth, Sorke examines the Spirit of prophecy in Rev. 19.10 and considers the parallel between Rev. 19.10 and 22.8-9 to be intentional.[173] He deduces that '*having* the testimony of Jesus is equaled to the *presence* of a live prophet in the midst of John's commandment-keeping community'.[174] Fifth, the Spirit's invitation, 'Come!' is a call for the return of Jesus. Finally, Sorke concludes that any other occurrence

---

[169] Skaggs and Benham, *Revelation*, p. 18.

[170] Sorke, *Identity and Function of the Seven Spirits*, p. 63.

[171] Sorke, *Identity and Function of the Seven Spirits*, pp. 64-74. Sorke finds some similarities between the hearing formula in Revelation and those that appear in the Synoptic Gospels; however, Sorke also concludes that the hearing formulas in Revelation likely recall the HB prophetic tradition.

[172] Sorke, *Identity and Function of the Seven Spirits*, p. 75.

[173] Sorke finds a subjective genitive in Rev. 19.10 because the witness of Jesus 'communicates Jesus' prophetic message through a prophet for the purpose of preparing his community for judgment' (p. 87).

[174] Sorke, *Identity and Function of the Seven Spirits*, p. 82.

of πνεῦμα ('Spirit') in Revelation is not a reference to the divine spirit.[175]

Sorke dedicates a substantial portion of his work to exploring the seven Spirits in light of Babylonian Astral-Cosmology, Second Temple literature, Greek Apostolic Fathers, Heptadic Fullness, and Dogmatic Trinitarianism,[176] concluding that these extra-biblical and historical materials are insufficient in establishing the identity or function of the seven Spirits in the Apocalypse; rather, Sorke deems that a better allusion to explore is Zech 4.1-4.[177] Briefly turning to the text, Sorke offers two 'case studies' where he examines Rev. 3.1; 4.5; 5.6.[178] In Rev. 3.1, Sorke notices the intimate relationship of Christ and the Spirit. Christ has the seven Spirits and seven stars, which reveals a close relationship among the Spirit, Christ, and the churches. Furthermore, in the seven prophetic messages, the Spirit speaks the message of Jesus to the churches. Based on the prophetic message to the church at Sardis, Sorke tentatively concludes that the Spirit functions as the giver of life. Second, Sorke investigates Rev. 4.5 and 5.6 and notices that in Rev. 4.5 the Spirit is closely associated with judgment revealed by the Spirit's vicinity to the throne.[179] In Rev. 5.6, Sorke identifies three characteristics of the Spirit: location, christological anthropomorphic identity, and mission. Since the Spirit is located before the throne and is identified as the eyes of the Lamb, the Spirit represents omniscience and omnipresence. Citing Bauckham, Sorke considers that the four appearances of the seven Spirits in the Apocalypse represent the Spirit's universal soteriological activity, which is

---

[175] Sorke, *Identity and Function of the Seven Spirits*, pp. 102-103. Cf. Revelation 11; 13.15; 16.13-14; 18.2.

[176] Sorke, *Identity and Function of the Seven Spirits*, pp. 105-89.

[177] Sorke, *Identity and Function of the Seven Spirits*, pp. 215-18. Sorke is critical of reading Isa. 11.2 as an allusion to the seven Spirits. Sorke observes that the lampstand represents the presence of God's Spirit in wholeness and completeness. The function of the Spirit in Zechariah is associated with the rebuilding of the temple for the reunion of God's people. Sorke suggests that this is the major theme echoed in Revelation. Sorke writes, 'reflected from Zechariah, the spirit in Revelation appears ontologically seven-fold, chistomorphically as the visual capacity of Christ, and globally operative by being sent "into all the earth" (Rev. 5.6)' (p. 236). The Spirit has a global function as the Spirit which goes throughout the whole earth (Rev. 5.6 cf. Zech. 4.10). The eyes gather information for the 'purpose of judicial implication and executive implementation' (p. 245).

[178] Sorke, *Identity and Function of the Seven Spirits*, pp. 256-68.

[179] Sorke, *Identity and Function of the Seven Spirits*, p. 262.

confirmed by the attribution of grace and peace to the seven Spirits in Rev. 1.4. Sorke notes that from a literary perspective, there is a conflict between the seven Spirits who go out into the world and the spirits of the unclean spirits who go out to the kings of the whole world (Rev. 16.13).[180] Following Bauckham, Sorke confirms that the Spirit is active in the church's prophetic witness. The Spirit in Revelation functions to discover universal information and judgment.[181]

Finally, in his concluding chapter, Sorke attempts to synthesize the seven Spirits of the Apocalypse with the activity of the Spirit in Acts 2. Exploring Rev. 1.4, Sorke notes that the one on the throne and Jesus are identified by their ontological nature and their functional activity, while the seven Spirits are not explicitly given a function. This leads Sorke to conclude the location of the seven Spirits defines the Spirit's function.[182] The seven Spirits are revealed as being before the throne as well as the eyes of the Lamb who are sent out into the world. Turning to Acts 2, Sorke identifies three correlations between the Spirit as described in the Apocalypse and in Acts: fire, Spirit-speech/saying, and global activity.[183] The Spirit in the Apocalypse, who is sent out into the world, correlates with the activity of the Spirit in Acts, who is given following the ascension of Jesus. Both the Apocalypse and Acts continue the gospel story following the resurrection of Jesus where the Spirit empowers the church's witness for global outreach.[184]

## T. Schreiner

While the majority of NT theologies offer only a limited amount of space to the pneumatology of the Apocalypse, T. Schreiner provides a significant examination of the subject.[185] First, Schreiner explores the four occurrences of ἐν πνεύματι ('in the Spirit'), which are associated with the Spirit's inspiration of John's message.[186] Second, in the seven prophetic messages, the words of the Spirit are the words of

---

[180] Sorke, *Identity and Function of the Seven Spirits*, p. 269.

[181] Sorke, *Identity and Function of the Seven Spirits*, p. 278.

[182] Sorke, *Identity and Function of the Seven Spirits*, p. 279.

[183] Sorke, *Identity and Function of the Seven Spirits*, p. 281.

[184] Sorke, *Identity and Function of the Seven Spirits*, p. 285.

[185] T.R. Schreiner, *Magnifying God in Christ: A Summary of New Testament Theology* (Grand Rapids, MI: Baker Academic, 2010), pp. 154-56.

[186] Schreiner, *Magnifying God in Christ*, p. 154.

Christ. The Spirit's words reach beyond the individual congregations to the entire church.[187] Third, Schreiner considers it striking that grace and peace are attributed to the seven Spirits since grace and peace are never attributed to an angel or an apostle in the NT; rather, grace and peace are the divine prerogatives of the Father and the Son. The seven Spirits are not angelic beings because they share in the divine activities of the Father and the Son.[188] Fourth, the number seven is used to symbolize the Spirit's fullness or perfection. Fifth, in Revelation 4, the seven torches are located before the throne of God, likely alluding to Zech 4.2 where the power of Zerubbabel and Joshua to rebuild the temple originates from the Spirit. Schreiner observes another HB echo of the seven torches in Isa. 4.4, which describes a 'spirit of judgment' or a 'spirit of burning', emphasizing the holiness and cleansing of the Spirit.[189] Sixth, the final reference to the seven Spirits occurs in Revelation 5 as the seven horns and seven eyes of the Lamb, which indicates that the Lamb is all-powerful and all-knowing.[190] Seventh, the Spirit is the Spirit of prophecy where John speaks to the church by the Spirit, while the Spirit is speaking directly to the church. Finally, Schreiner notes that although the theology of Revelation does not deal with the ontology of the Spirit, Revelation portrays the Spirit as a person who speaks and performs divine functions. He concludes that the Apocalypse has a striking trinitarian characteristic.[191]

## J.C. Thomas

Beginning in 2010, NT Pentecostal scholar, J.C. Thomas, offers two narrative essays on pneumatic discernment,[192] introductory sections on the Spirit in his literary-theological Apocalypse commentary,[193] and an article exploring the pneumatology of the Apocalypse.[194]

First, examining Rev. 13.11-18, Thomas unpacks the imagery of the two beasts. He finds a parody between the 'triumvirate of evil'

---

[187] Schreiner, *Magnifying God in Christ*, pp. 154-55.

[188] Schreiner, *Magnifying God in Christ*, p. 155.

[189] Schreiner, *Magnifying God in Christ*, p. 155.

[190] Schreiner, *Magnifying God in Christ*, pp. 155-56.

[191] Schreiner, *Magnifying God in Christ*, p. 156.

[192] Thomas, 'Pneumatic Discernment', pp. 106-24; Thomas, 'The Mystery of the Great Whore', pp. 111-36.

[193] Thomas, *The Apocalypse*; Thomas and Macchia, *Revelation*.

[194] Thomas, 'Revelation', pp. 257-66.

(the dragon and the two beasts) and the holy Trinity (the Spirit, the Lamb, and the one on the throne).[195] One's identity is revealed in the Apocalypse by (1) having either the seal of God or the mark of the beast and (2) whomever one worships.[196] The mark of the beast is described as a number of a man and the number of his name. Even though the beast is portrayed as being mythological and extra-human in the Apocalypse, the hearers find out the beast is a man. Thomas notes a literary link between the ὧδέ ἐστιν ('here is') formula in Rev. 13.18 and Rev. 13.10. In Rev. 13.10, wisdom is the object of the ὧδέ ἐστιν ('here is') formula where wisdom has been attributed to the Lamb (5.12) and God (7.12) leading Thomas to conclude that wisdom has divine connotations in the Apocalypse.[197] Similarly, Thomas observes that the formula that appears in 13.10 recalls the sevenfold call to hear the Spirit in the seven prophetic messages. These associations suggest that the Spirit, (divine) wisdom, and a mind are needed to calculate the number of the beast,[198] 'the hearers would know full well that the calculation to which they are called is no mere parlor game, or a calculation that may be completed owing to their own ingenuity. Rather, this calculation must take place in the Spirit!'[199] To discern the number of the beast, Thomas appeals to gematria and triangular numbers. (1) Thomas considers two interpretative options when calculating 666 via gematria: θηρίον ('beast') and Νέρων Καῖσαρ ('Caesar Nero').[200] Thomas does not consider that Nero is able to encompass the full symbolic power of the beast; and despite the atrocities of Nero, there are divergences between Nero and the beast

---

[195] Thomas, 'Pneumatic Discernment', pp. 106-12.

[196] Thomas notices economic undertones as well.

[197] Thomas, 'Pneumatic Discernment', p. 115, observes the close language of the two calls for discernment where having an ear parallels having a mind/discernment: ὁ ἔχων οὖς ἀκουσάτω τί τὸ πνεῦμα λέγει ταῖς ἐκκλησίαις // ὁ ἔχων νοῦν ψηφισάτω τὸν ἀριθμὸν τοῦ θηρίου.

[198] Thomas, 'Pneumatic Discernment', p. 115, finds a close parallel between νοῦν in Revelation and the appearance of διάνοιαν in 1 Jn 5.20. In 1 John, there is a strong link between διάνοιαν and the χρῖσμα where the χρῖσμα leads the community to know all things (οἴδατε πάντες) (1 Jn 2.10, 27).

[199] Thomas, 'Pneumatic Discernment', p. 116.

[200] The calculations are derived from the names transliterated from Greek to Hebrew.

in the Apocalypse.[201] (2) Appealing to the triangular number 153 from Jn 21.11, Thomas detects a tradition of using triangular numbers in the Johannine community. Thomas identifies 666 as not only a triangular, but also a

> doubly triangular number, as 36, the last line of numbers, is itself a triangular number ... owing to the significance of 36, which was especially honored among the ancients, and the fact that 666 is a triangular number of that triangular number, it might not be going too far to see in the number of the beast, a number that would be understood as of cosmic proportions; perhaps a king amongst numbers![202]

Second, Thomas's next essay offers an extensive narrative investigation of pneumatic discernment in Revelation 17. After commenting on the great whore and the beast, Thomas turns to discern the mystery of the name upon her forehead. Already forehead markings have appeared in the Apocalypse as either the seal of God (7.3; 9.4) or the mark of the beast (13.16; 14.9). The name upon the whore's forehead is a mystery, the third occurrence of mystery in the Apocalypse, and each takes place in the context of a call to discern pneumatically. Pneumatic discernment begins with identifying 'Babylon the Great'. (1) In Rev. 14.8 and 17.5, the hearers learn from an angel that the city is fallen, which is the city's judgment. There is likely an intertextual allusion to Babylon, the historical enemy of Israel. (2) The process of discernment continues with 'the Mother of Whores and the Abominations of the Earth', which likely alludes to the false prophetess Jezebel (Rev. 2.20-21) and contrasts the woman clothed with the sun (Rev. 12.1-6). (3) Thomas leaves open the interpretative possibility that John's 'marveling a great marvel' is an occurrence of idolatrous seduction based upon the previous appearance of 'marvel' in Rev. 13.3-4. Thomas asks, 'if John, who is "in the Spirit" at the

---

[201] Nero's death differs from the beast's death: (1) Nero's wound was not to the head, but to the body, (2) by the time of the Apocalypse, Nero would have been dead, and (3) there is no evidence of a tradition of Nero's resurrection at this time. See Thomas, 'Pneumatic Discernment', p. 120.

[202] Thomas, 'Pneumatic Discernment', pp. 121-22.

time, could be so tempted, could anyone be immune from such seduction?'[203] (4) After marveling, an angel informs John that the mystery would be revealed to him. The revelation by the angel demonstrates that the hearers will also receive divine assistance in discernment, which is affirmed by Jesus' previous assistance to the hearers
with the mystery of the seven stars.[204] The mystery portrayed in Revelation 17 is explained to be the seven hills that the woman sits upon
who are the seven kings where the beast is eighth. As in Revelation
13, the call for pneumatic discernment begins with the appearance of
the ὧδέ ἐστιν ('here is') formula as well as a call to have wisdom,
further strengthening the notion that pneumatic discernment requires divine wisdom.[205] Having wisdom begins by discerning the
symbol of the beast who is juxtaposed with the seven hills and seven
kings. Thomas considers the possibilities that the seven heads of the
beast, the seven hills, might be Rome, but as with Nero, the imagery
beckons for more than a historical equation. Attempts to determine
the seven historical kings have been futile since it is difficult to determine the identity of the first among the seven. Rather, Thomas writes
that the seven hills and seven kings would likely symbolize universal
power:

> Though the hearers might conceivably be tempted to take these
> words to mean that the seven kings have morphed into an eighth
> king, such an interpretive option is unlikely, owing to the promi-
> nence of the number seven throughout the book generally, and its
> prominence with regard to the beast in particular. Rather, this en-
> igmatic detail would likely generate more reflection on the identity
> of the beast.[206]

Thomas explores the influence of triangular numbers again when
considering that 666 is the 'eighth' doubly triangular number.[207] The
waters upon which the woman sits are a universal people. They, along

---

[203] Thomas, 'The Mystery of the Great Whore', p. 123.

[204] Thomas, 'The Mystery of the Great Whore', p. 126.

[205] Thomas, 'The Mystery of the Great Whore', p. 126.

[206] Thomas, 'The Mystery of the Great Whore', pp. 126-27.

[207] Thomas, 'The Mystery of the Great Whore', p. 129.

with the beast, bring destruction upon the whore.[208] The call to discern the whore as the 'great city' likely recalls the previous call to discern the 'great city' πνευματικῶς in Rev. 11.8.[209]

Third, in his Apocalypse commentary, Thomas writes two sections concerning the Spirit. (1) In a section entitled 'People of the Spirit',[210] Thomas proposes that the recipients of the Apocalypse are equally ἐν πνεύματι ('in the Spirit') in their hearing as the author was ἐν πνεύματι in his reception. The Spirit's activity is not limited to the prophets among their communities because 'the hearers themselves are viewed as participants in such prophetic activity'.[211] (2) Thomas explores the role of the Spirit in Revelation's composition in a section entitled 'Writing in the Spirit'.[212] Thomas attempts to hold the balance between the seemingly lengthy, intricate composition of the Apocalypse with John's pneumatic visionary experience. John is not merely a HB exegete nor is he a passive instrument controlled by the Spirit. Rather, 'the intertext that is John's life, his acquaintance with the HB, apocalyptic traditions, the Jesus tradition, his worshipping community, and the experience of the revelation itself is used "in the Spirit" to produce the text of the Apocalypse'.[213] Thomas appeals to glossolalia and its interpretation as an example 'where the Spirit speaks through an individual believer in ways that draw upon all that he or she is, while not obliterating his or her heritage or personality'.[214]

Fourth, a final work offered by Thomas is a study of the pneumatology of the Apocalypse.[215] Thomas divides his work into five areas of study. (1) Thomas begins by examining the seven Spirits, where the number seven represents completion. The seven Spirits, converging intertextually with Zech. 4.2, represent the Holy Spirit and not seven angels. Thomas notes that the appearance of the seven Spirits before the throne conveys that when the seven Spirits act, 'it is God

---

[208] Thomas, 'The Mystery of the Great Whore', pp. 133-35.

[209] Thomas, 'The Mystery of the Great Whore', p. 136.

[210] Thomas, *The Apocalypse*, p. 24.

[211] Thomas, *The Apocalypse*, p. 24.

[212] Thomas, *The Apocalypse*, p. 44.

[213] Thomas, *The Apocalypse*, p. 45.

[214] Thomas, *The Apocalypse*, p. 45. See Moyise, *The Old Testament in the Book of Revelation*, p. 40.

[215] Thomas, 'Revelation', pp. 257-66.

himself who acts'.[216] (2) Thomas explores the four appearances of ἐν πνεύματι ('in the Spirit'), which are central to the structure of the narrative, while also describing the means by which the revelation takes places.[217] (3) The next section examines the appearances of 'the one who has an ear to hear, let that one hear' that calls the churches to discern. The occurrences of these phrases suggest that the Spirit coterminously speaks with Jesus. Based on the relationship between the seven Spirits and the throne, Thomas observes that it might not be going too far to say that these words are also dynamically from the one on the throne. The relationship is further explored in Revelation 5 where the seven Spirits are the seven eyes of the Lamb. Thomas notes that (i) the appearance of the seven Spirits as the eyes of the Lamb suggests that the seven Spirits are worshipped; and (ii) the seven Spirits are sent out into the earth, representing a close connection between the prophetic witness of the church and the seven Spirits.[218] (4) Thomas turns to examine the Spirit and faithful prophetic witness. The intertextual convergence of Zechariah 4 with the description of the lampstands is closely associated with the Holy Spirit, representing the prophetic ministry of the church. The closeness of the words of the Spirit with Jesus implies that the churches convey prophetically and dynamically the words of Jesus and the Spirit. Thomas then turns to discuss Rev. 11.8 where the Spirit is the means by which the identity of the great city is revealed. Thomas prefers to transliterate the term πνευματικῶς (i.e. 'pneumatically') to convey that it is the Spirit by whom the interpretation of the great city occurs. In Rev. 11.11, it is the Spirit who raises the two witnesses from the dead. Thomas also observes that the Spirit is 'out of God', suggesting that the Spirit has her 'origin in God' (cf. Jn 14.17).[219] Thomas next turns to Rev. 19.10 observing the close relationship between the Spirit of prophecy and the witness of Jesus while concluding, 'the witness of Jesus is quintessentially pneumatic, prophetic, dynamic and active'.[220] On account of the appearance of 'living water', Thomas suggests that the Spirit is active in the offer of salvation.

---

[216] Thomas, 'Revelation', pp. 257-58.

[217] Thomas, 'Revelation', p. 258.

[218] Thomas, 'Revelation', pp. 258-61.

[219] Thomas, 'Revelation', p. 263.

[220] Thomas, 'Revelation', p. 264.

(5) Thomas concludes his article by exploring 'The Spirit and the Bride say "Come"'.[221] The call, 'Come' reveals the central role of the Spirit in the witness to the kings and the nations of the earth. The Bride offers the same witness as the Spirit; a witness that is empowered by the Spirit.[222]

In sum, Thomas has offered a helpful examination of the role of the Spirit, while also offering explicit explorations of the theme of pneumatic discernment in the Apocalypse. Revelation 13 calls the reader to discern the number of the beast. The ὧδέ ἐστιν ('here is') formulas are closely connected to the discerning process along with the call to have wisdom. Wisdom has divine associations in the Apocalypse. Thomas employs gematria and triangular numbers as well as literary interpretive approaches to discern while criticizing those who attempt to contain the symbols in historical realities.

## Cullen Tanner

Cullen Tanner offers an article exploring the Spirit, the two witnesses, and Zechariah 4 from a speech act approach.[223] He suggests the illocutionary act – the effects meant for the audience – is supposed to inspire the audience to greater dependence upon the Spirit. Tanner begins by reviewing Zechariah 4 in Rev. 1.12-13, 20; 4.5; 5.6; and 11.4, concluding any mention of the lampstands should invoke a connection to the Spirit. Whereas a lampstand represented the presence of Yahweh in the HB, the Holy Spirit is the mode of God's presence in the NT.[224] There is a convergence of symbols with the two witnesses and the two lampstands. From Zechariah, the imagery suggests that the olive trees keep the lampstand – the Spirit of the Lord – in operation by supplying it with oil. In the Apocalypse, John shifts the imagery so that the two witnesses are both the olives trees as well as the lampstand who bear the Spirit. Thus, the task of the witnesses is to

---

[221] Thomas, 'Revelation', pp. 265-66.

[222] Thomas, 'Revelation', pp. 265-66.

[223] Tanner, 'Climbing the Lampstand-Witness-Trees', pp. 81-92 (88), describes his approach: 'emphasis in speech act theory is placed on the likely effects the text had on its implied audience, rather than simply its intellectual content, with *illocution* being the intended effect on the audience and *perlocution* being the actual effects of the speech act'.

[224] Tanner, 'Climbing the Lampstand-Witness-Trees', p. 81.

'hold out the seven lamps/Spirits'.[225] Taking a look at numerology, Tanner finds that the seven Spirits are mentioned four times in the Apocalypse and correspond to the 28 occurrences of the Lamb: 'the victory that comes through the slain Lamb will come to fruition in the world as a result of the fullness of the Spirit'.[226] Finally, Tanner concludes 'an increased reliance upon the power of the Spirit will bring about the eventual victory of the Church'.[227]

## Ronald Herms

Ronald Herms explores the role of the Spirit in the Apocalypse in two article length studies.[228] In both works, Herms observes that the Apocalypse is an attractive option for pneumatic hermeneutics because of the descriptions of divine or angelic interactions that direct the churches to respond as well as the appearance of πνευματικῶς ('Spiritually').[229]

First, Herms, following Bauckham, investigates three categories of pneumatology in the Apocalypse. (1) ἐν πνεύματι ('in the Spirit') is a multivalent term in the Apocalypse: each occurrence represents an internal collection of related visions, and each vision 'telescopes' into the next, picking up on climatic themes and images from a previous collection.[230] Literarily, ἐν πνεύματι ('in the Spirit') serves both to relocate the perspective as well as to signify different heavenly figures that mediate the revelation (e.g. the exalted Christ and the mighty angel).[231] Like Bauckham, Herms observes the comparison that ἐν πνεύματι ('in the Spirit') forces between Babylon and the New Jerusalem. ἐν πνεύματι serves to give authority to John's prophecy and is a signal of his divinely inspired prophetic activity and authority.[232]

---

[225] Tanner, 'Climbing the Lampstand-Witness-Trees', p. 86. Cf. Bauckham, *The Theology of the Book of Revelation*, p. 113.

[226] Tanner, 'Climbing the Lampstand-Witness-Trees', p. 86.

[227] Tanner, 'Climbing the Lampstand-Witness-Trees', p. 91.

[228] Herms, 'Invoking the Spirit', pp. 99-114.

[229] Herms believes that a pneumatic hermeneutic is particularly significant for Pentecostal hermeneutics, see Herms, 'Invoking the Spirit', pp. 100-101.

[230] Herms, 'Invoking the Spirit', p. 101; Herms, 'πνευματικῶς', pp. 133-46.

[231] John moves from Patmos to the heavenly throne room to a desert to a mountain.

[232] Herms cites Beale who finds similar aspects in Ezekiel, see Herms, 'Invoking the Spirit', p. 107.

While Herms considers that John has an ecstatic experience, he suggests that this experience is not part of the chain of revelation in the Apocalypse;[233] rather, the Spirit 'facilitates and makes possible reception of revelation' through the vision ἐν πνεύματι.[234] Thus, ἐν πνεύματι represents a particular visionary experience of John, and reception by the churches is not contingent upon mimicking John's experience.[235] Ultimately, the occurrences of ἐν πνεύματι are not meant for the community to seek ecstatic experience but inspire prophetic faithful witness. Herms concludes:

> John's visions, at least from his perspective are critical and uncommon. The response they require is not necessarily repeatable    prophetic activity (though perhaps not out of the realm of possibility); rather, John's definition of appropriate response (demonstrated in what follows) will be a faithful witness to that prophetic message (1.3).[236]

(2) Herms turns to the hearing formulas in the seven prophetic messages and the intimate relationship between Christ and the Spirit. The seven prophetic messages are direct speech from Christ, but it is 'the Spirit as the means by which the message is brought to the churches and to whom response is urged'.[237] Christ's message is to be heard actively from the Spirit because the message is not limited to the seven prophetic messages. Throughout the Apocalypse, Christ and the Spirit are closely connected in that the Spirit enacts the message of Christ. The Spirit is active in the process of discerning and responding. 'Spirit-inspired experience' needs to be discerned by a Spirit-inspired message: 'the hearing of the message in the community of the faithful, along with the hoped-for response, constitutes what it means to "hear what the Spirit says"'.[238] Beyond the seven

---

[233] Scholars note a chain of revelation in the Apocalypse (God to Jesus to an angel to John).

[234] Beale, *The Book of Revelation*, pp. 203-204.

[235] Though Herms is cautious of requiring an ἐν πνεύματι ('in the Spirit') experience for interpreting the text, he, by way of narrative considerations, perceives John's experience as encouraging and inspiring pneumatic activity in the community because the church hears Revelation on the Lord's day – the same context John sees his vision.

[236] Herms, 'Invoking the Spirit', p. 106.

[237] Herms, 'Invoking the Spirit', p. 109.

[238] Herms, 'Invoking the Spirit', p. 109.

prophetic message, the hearing formula in Rev. 13.9-10 critiques imperial claims of power and security. (3) Herms explores the Spirit of prophecy where he identifies prophecy as (i) the book of Revelation and (ii) the faithful witness of the Church.[239] The purpose of prophecy is not the promotion of ecstatic prophetic experiences but verification of the message of Jesus. For example, John receives his prophecy from Jesus that is mediated by the Spirit and should inspire the community to be faithful witnesses. Hence, to discern pneumatically is to affirm and respond to the testimony of Jesus.

(4) Herms offers a thematic view of pneumatic discernment in the Apocalypse. ἐν πνεύματι ('in the Spirit') is a structural device as well as a specific experience for John. Although it is not necessary for the churches to mimic John's experience, the text invites them to have Spirit-inspired experiences. The Spirit and Christ are intimately connected; the Spirit mediates the prophetic messages to the churches but also invokes a response from the churches to be faithful witnesses. Herms believes that Revelation promotes a hermeneutic of pneumatic discernment where the Spirit is active in the process of reading and discerning.

Second, in 2015, Herms offers another article exploring the appearance of πνευματικῶς ('Spiritually') in Rev. 11.8.[240] Herms seeks to investigate the 'spirit-inspired interpretation' put forth in the Apocalypse by examining the 'most overt expression' of 'pneumatic hermeneutics' in the Apocalypse.[241] Herms is critical of scholarship that has limited their exploration of Rev. 11.8 to uncovering the location of the great city, whether ideologically or geographically, preferring to explore 'the interpretative freight carried by πνευματικῶς ('Spiritually') in its present literary location'.[242] Furthermore, Herms is critical of P. Minear, R. Waddell, and J.C. Thomas for not going far enough in expressing the impact of πνευματικῶς on pneumatic hermeneutics, 'the way in which John's visionary evaluations were crafted for maximum evocative force was to invoke his brand of spirit-inspired interpretation of Scripture'. Herms, following J. Levison, adds

---

[239] Herms, 'Invoking the Spirit', pp. 110-12.
[240] Herms, 'πνευματικῶς', pp. 135-46.
[241] Herms, 'πνευματικῶς', p. 136
[242] Herms, 'πνευματικῶς', p. 138.

that the work of the Spirit in interpretation reaches beyond an 'idealist' interpretation of the Apocalypse to 'reframe generalist and idealist applications for this symbolic construct toward a particular target group for the author's prophetic critique'. After offering a reading of Revelation 11, Herms provides the following observations: (1) the appearance of πνευματικῶς represents a spirit-inspired hermeneutic that is used in the Apocalypse. The Spirit is directly tied to the way in which John reads the HB. (2) The πνευματικῶς perspective extends and develops prophetic critiques of Israel and Jerusalem. (3) The πνευματικῶς perspective adds to the ongoing critique of the Jewish communities that are opposing the churches in Asia Minor. (4) The πνευματικῶς perspective 'must be more than "spirit-inspired discernment" by the readers in their "present"'. (5) Herms observes a similar prophetic 'critique' in other ancient sources, including Wis. 19.14-17; *Asc. Isa.* 3.10. (6) Herms asks to whom might John's 'rhetorical-evocative tactics' reach? (7) Herms asks further, if the rhetorical effect of the prophetic critique was intended to reach those whom the text has critiqued, is the desired outcome of John's criticism one of 'condemnation or invitation?' Herms is inclined to conclude that the prophetic critique is intended to persuade its audience to respond positively.[243]

In sum, Herms offers an exploration of the Apocalypse that takes serious a pneumatic hermeneutic that is involved in interpreting the text. While Herms does not deny the possibility that the churches have ecstatic experience, he does not find these experiences to be a requirement for a pneumatic hermeneutic. Herms attempts to build upon and move beyond the works of Minear, Waddell, and Thomas to explore the active and dynamic involvement of the Spirit in the process of reading and discernment, finding Rev. 11.8 to be the primary example of the pneumatic hermeneutic described in the Apocalypse.

### Frank Macchia

In the co-authored *Revelation* commentary in the Two Horizons New Testament Commentary Series and a book chapter, Pentecostal theologian, Frank Macchia, writes on the Spirit in the Apocalypse and

---

[243] Herms, 'πνευματικῶς', pp. 145-46.

the theme of pneumatic discernment.[244] First, Macchia begins by offering evidence for the divinity of the seven Spirits: (1) the seven Spirits appear in the opening triadic, divine greeting.[245] (2) Functionally, the seven Spirits bring about eschatological actions into fulfillment on the earth, and these actions reveal the seven Spirits' divinity. (3) The close relationship among the seven Spirits, the one on the throne, and the Lamb further illustrates a trinitarian pattern. The eyes of the Lamb symbolize the discernment or wisdom of the Lamb, 'If the Lamb is worthy to transcend the creatures to discern the scroll, so are the seven spirits. If the Lamb is worshipped for being able to discern as only God can, so are the spirits who are identified as the Lamb's eyes.'[246] Revelation 5 leads Macchia to conclude that this vision might be the only text in the NT where the Spirit receives worship.[247] Discernment, embodied as the seven Spirits, goes out into the church. The Spirit is more than Christ's speaker; the Spirit also provides wisdom to the community in order that they might discern the words of Christ. While John discerned his visionary experience ἐν πνεύματι ('in the Spirit'), the churches must discern pneumatically to understand the words of Christ spoken by the Spirit. Following Bauckham and Waddell, Macchia observes that the Spirit is the power of the church to bear prophetic witness to the world.

Second, Macchia writes on the need for discernment. He appeals to the imagery of the seven eyes of the Lamb who are the seven Spirits, which he finds to represent discernment and wisdom. Macchia suggests that there is a lack of reflection on discernment in the world that correlates to a lack of reflection on the pneumatology; theology has stressed the transcendence and mystery of the Spirit constructing a 'non-material, detached phantom'.[248] Macchia offers a solution to this lacuna from the Apocalypse, which reveals, in part, the mystery and freedom of the Spirit. The Spirit of prophecy assists in the process to discern the mysteries of God and 'the reign of God and the story of the Lamb's self-sacrificial life for the redemption of

---

[244] See Macchia, 'The Spirit of the Lamb', pp. 214-20 (215).

[245] Macchia sees the call to drink the water of life in Rev. 22.17 to be a mention of the Spirit; thus, the Spirit functions in Revelation as a participant in the good news as the water of life.

[246] Macchia, 'The Spirit of the Lamb', p. 215.

[247] Macchia, 'The Spirit of the Lamb', p. 215.

[248] Thomas and Macchia, *Revelation*, p. 485.

humanity'.[249] The Spirit discerns the words of Christ for the church today. The call for pneumatic discernment is found throughout the prophecy even within the structure (ἐν πνεύματι). The process of the discernment begins in the Apocalypse with the 'seven-fold call for discernment' in the seven prophetic messages.[250] John's experience is likely ecstatic in nature, but the vision itself is meant to subvert the world he typically sees. John's vision is not one for the sake of escape but for truth and discernment. John utilizes two interpretative lenses to understand the visionary world: (1) Hebrew scriptures and (2) the message of the Lamb. Discerners must be shaped by the story of the HB, which fill the words of the Apocalypse as well as the story of the redemptive Lamb. There is a dualism in the Apocalypse between the discerning eyes of the Lamb (i.e. seven Spirits) and the evil spirits from the beasts and the dragon. The Lamb has the eyes of the Spirit while the dragon and beast only have mouths. Hence, discernment in the Apocalypse is associated with the churches' ability to see with the Spirit and with the Lamb, to discern the way that the Lamb discerns.

In sum, the seven Spirits are identified as the divine Holy Spirit and is closely associated with the Lamb and the one on the throne. For Macchia, the seven Spirits, as the seven eyes of the Lamb, are the central image for pneumatic discernment. Discernment in the churches is connected to being able to see with the Lamb's complete wisdom and discernment, represented as the seven Spirits. John is the example: after his visionary experience, he discerns this vision through the lens of the HB and the story of the redemptive Lamb.

## Conclusions

Starting from the earliest work surveyed, two basic interpretive streams emerge when interpreting the pneumatology of the Apocalypse: historical or literary/theological approaches. Religio-historical and source critical interpreters often dismiss pneumatology as primitive or a later addition. Some seek similarities between the seven Spirits and Jewish angelology, which often leads them to conclude that Revelation's pneumatology is primitive. Conversely, those who utilize

---

[249] Thomas and Macchia, *Revelation*, p. 486.

[250] Thomas and Macchia, *Revelation*, p. 487.

theological or literary approaches tend to discover a more robust pneumatology that offers a diverse voice to NT pneumatology. The majority of research has engaged: (1) the Spirit of prophecy, which was the predominant focus of research early on. (2) Scholars have explored the trinitarian imagery in the Apocalypse where the Spirit has a close relationship with the throne and the Lamb. (3) The seven Spirits have had a varied interpretative stream, including (i) the seven Spirits parallel the seven churches; (ii) the seven Spirits are seven Jewish archangels, which some trace to the seven Babylonian planetary gods; (iii) the number seven alludes to seven-fold operation of the Spirit based on a reading of Isa. 11.2 (LXX); (iv) the number seven is intertextually derived from Zechariah 4; and (v) seven represents completeness or perfection. (4) Many interpreters viewed ἐν πνεύματι ('in the Spirit') as a reference to a phenomenological occurrence where John had an ecstatic experience. Others, while not discounting the phenomenological aspect, observed the theological and literary significance of ἐν πνεύματι ('in the Spirit'). Some even proposed a literary structure around the four appearances of ἐν πνεύματι. (5) This review has shown that some scholars have taken up the theme of pneumatic discernment in Apocalypse, even considering discernment to be a central theme of the Apocalypse. Finally, Waddell's monograph on pneumatology seems to have opened a door for Pentecostal scholarship to become active in the conversation on pneumatology and pneumatic discernment in the Apocalypse.

# 3

# Discerning the Testimonies of Wesleyan-Holiness Pentecostalism

In the next two chapters, I will explore the early Pentecostal periodical literature to discover the extent to which early Pentecostals were influenced by the Apocalypse when reflecting upon pneumatic discernment. I will accomplish this task by giving attention to pneumatological references in the Apocalypse alongside occurrences of pneumatic discernment, reflection, and interpretation. I will offer a short introduction of some of the ways that the early Pentecostals discerned. I limit the survey to the early years of the Pentecostal movement on account that the beginning years of the Pentecostal movement are considered to be the theological heart of the movement,[1] offers an investigation into early Pentecostal spirituality,[2] and provides an opportunity to hear from voices on the margins.[3] (Re)visiting these early Pentecostal texts also offers an opportunity for dialoguing with the Pentecostal (con)text that assists in identifying the Pentecostal (con)textual identity. I will follow Hollenweger's timeframe with the addition of two years to include the entire duration of World War I, covering 1906–1918. The periodical literature consists primarily of testimonies, hymns, and sermons from everyday individuals who were discerning and testifying to their Pentecostal experience. In chapter 3, I will survey the Wesleyan-Holiness publications *The Apostolic Faith*, *Bridegroom's Messenger*, *The Whole Truth*, *Church*

---

[1] Hollenweger, 'Pentecostals and the Charismatic Movement', pp. 549-53.

[2] Archer, *'I Was in the Spirit on the Lord's Day'*, p. 68.

[3] Alexander, *Pentecostal Healing*, p. 6.

*of God Evangel*, and *The Pentecostal Holiness Advocate* followed in chapter 4 by the Finished-Work publications *The Pentecost, Latter Rain Evangel, Word and Witness*, and *The Christian/Weekly Evangel*.

## The Apostolic Faith

*The Apostolic Faith* was produced out of the Azusa Street Revival and headed by W. Seymour. The paper was published on a monthly basis from 1906–1908 with a few exceptions.[4] Concerning the Apocalypse, *The Apostolic Faith* presented a diverse interpretative lens being full of allusions to Revelation, including: the Lamb, 'in the Spirit', the throne, the bride, white garments, the seal of God on their foreheads, over-comers, wisdom, mystery, tribulation, judgment, lake of fire, marriage supper of the Lamb, New Jerusalem, new heavens and new earth, and the millennial reign of Christ.[5]

### Pentecostals and Pneumatic Discernment

*The Apostolic Faith* sought guidance from the Spirit and the Word. There were many references to the Spirit speaking to them, and the Spirit was actively involved in the discernment of biblical texts, testimonies, glossolalia/xenolalia, and the testing of the spirits.[6] The Spirit assisted in interpretation by 'flashing light on the Word',[7] and put life and power into the biblical text as never before.[8] The editors of *The Apostolic Faith* believed that the Spirit accompanied the paper to the heart of the readers.[9] By the Spirit, 'the scriptures are opened to us, we understand them, and our eyes are anointed'.[10] Anyone was able to ask the Spirit for guidance:

---

[4] Alexander, *Pentecostal Healing*, p. 75.

[5] For explicit scripture references and quotes of Revelation in *The Apostolic Faith*, see *AF* 1.2 (October 1906), p. 2; *AF* 1.3 (November 1906), p. 4; *AF* 1.4 (December 1906), pp. 1, 3; *AF* 1.5 (January 1907), pp. 1-3; *AF* 1.6 (February-March 1907), pp. 4-5; *AF* 1.7 (April 1907), pp. 3-4; *AF* 1.8 (May 1907), pp. 1-4; *AF* 1.9 (June-September 1907), pp. 1-2; *AF* 1.10 (September 1907), p. 4; *AF* 1.11 (October-January 1908), pp. 1-3; *AF* 1.12 (January 1907), pp. 2, 4; *AF* 2.13 (May 1908), pp. 3-4.

[6] *AF* 1.3 (November 1906), pp. 1, 3-4.

[7] *AF* 2.13 (May 1908), p. 3. Cf. *AF* 1.11 (October-January 1908), p. 1.

[8] *AF* 1.7 (April 1907), p. 1.

[9] *AF* 1.3 (November 1906), p. 4.

[10] *AF* 1.6 (February-March 1907), p. 2.

The Holy Ghost is the Teacher of teachers. He knows the Word of God. You can talk with Him and ask Him for yourself. It is the sweetest thing to get alone with Him and let Him open the Scriptures to you. He is the interpreter of the Word, the Spirit of truth to guide you into all truth.[11]

*The Apostolic Faith* expressed that believers did not have to strain their minds to interpret a text because the Lord would assist in the process.[12] The Spirit did not speak in puzzles or allow the innocent and good to be deceived; rather, the Spirit offered wisdom and understanding and was leading the church into all truth.[13] The Spirit gave the mind of God to those who asked.[14] A central acknowledgment of pneumatic discernment was Spirit baptism because the Spirit (1) opened up everything from Genesis to Revelation,[15] (2) gave a 'clear knowledge',[16] (3) 'starts and unfolds and all you do is follow on',[17] and (4) is 'power and understanding of the Word and the glory of God upon your life'.[18] A holy quietness allowed the 'Speaker' to speak; this quietness was likened to heaven and the many waters, and mighty thunderings.[19] Pentecostals were charged to read scripture not carelessly, but prayerfully,[20] and were cautioned against looking for 'deeper things' apart from the Word.[21] Some false doctrines were metaphorically considered to be a 'dragon' that devours those who get out of the Word.[22] However, God had given to the children to recognize these spirits. A harsh spirit was not of the Spirit.[23] Divine love and recognizing the Spirit were keys to discernment. *The Apostolic Faith* added, 'Friends, if you profess to know the Spirit of God, and

---

[11] *AF* 2.13 (May 1908), p. 3.

[12] *AF* 1.5 (January 1907), p. 2.

[13] *AF* 1.1 (September 1906), p. 2; *AF* 1.5 (January 1907), p. 3; *AF* 1.7 (April 1907), p. 2; *AF* 1.9 (June 1907), p. 4; *AF* 2.13 (May 1908), p. 3.

[14] *AF* 1.7 (April 1907), p. 3; *AF* 1.12 (January 1908), p. 3.

[15] *AF* 1.3 (November 1907), p. 3.

[16] *AF* 1.5 (January 1907), p. 2.

[17] *AF* 1.10 (September 1907), p. 2.

[18] *AF* 2.13 (May 1908), p. 2.

[19] *AF* 1.6 (February-March 1907), p. 5.

[20] *AF* 1.12 (January 1908), p. 2.

[21] *AF* 1.5 (January 1907), p. 3.

[22] *AF* 1.10 (September 1907), p. 2.

[23] *AF* 2.13 (May 1908), p. 2.

do not recognize Him when He comes, there is cause for you to be anxious about your own spiritual condition'.[24] Finally, discernment was not instantaneous, and one testimony described a woman waiting three months to hear from the Spirit.[25] In discernment, the Word and the Spirit had a dynamic relationship, and it was by the Spirit opening up a woman's eyes that the scriptures had been revealed.

## The Spirit and Discernment in Revelation

'In the Spirit'

*The Apostolic Faith* attributed experiences – including testifying,[26] singing,[27] praying,[28] or playing instruments[29] – to being 'in the Spirit'.[30] W. Seymour recorded that John was 'in the Spirit' when he received the vision of the resurrected Christ. Others testified to being caught up 'in the Spirit' where their experiences correlated to John's visionary experiences,[31] and some described their Spirit baptism experience similar to John's experience:

> John also in Revelations [*sic*] says: 'I was in the Spirit on the Lord's day'. He heard Jesus speaking and says: 'When I saw Him, I fell at His feet as dead.' Just as so many in this mission have seen a vision of Jesus and have fallen at His feet as dead.[32]

*The Apostolic Faith* described trans-geographic unions with others 'in the Spirit': 'Tell the saints to love one another and keep united in love, and under the Blood every day, and humble. I am with you every day in the Spirit.'[33] In another example, G.A. Cook asked for prayer from

---

[24] *AF* 1.2 (October 1906), p. 2.

[25] *AF* 1.2 (October 1906), pp. 1-2.

[26] *AF* 1.4 (December 1906), p. 1; *AF* 1.12 (January 1908), p. 2.

[27] *AF* 1.3 (November 1906), pp. 1, 4; *AF* 1.4 (December 1906), p. 1; *AF* 1.6 (February-March 1907), p. 1; *AF* 1.7 (April 1907), p. 2; *AF* 1.11 (October-January 1908), p. 3; *AF* 1.12 (January 1908), p. 1.

[28] *AF* 1.4 (December 1906), p. 1; *AF* 1.12 (January 1908), p. 12.

[29] *AF* 1.3 (November 1906), p. 4.

[30] See also *AF* 1.9 (June 1907), p. 2; *AF* 1.10 (September 1907), p. 1; *AF* 1.12 (January 1908), pp. 2-3.

[31] E.g. *AF* 1.6 (February-March 1907), pp. 2, 8. See also *AF* 1.11 (October-January 1908), p. 3.

[32] *AF* 1.8 (May 1907), p. 3. See also *AF* 1.9 (June 1907), p. 1.

[33] *AF* 1.7 (April 1907), p. 1.

those at Azusa. He experienced a trans-geographical vision and described himself as being carried away 'in the Spirit', while seeing Seymour praying for him miles from his location. These testimonies suggest that those of *The Apostolic Faith* saw their experiences in light of John's 'in the Spirit'.[34]

Discernment in the Seven Prophetic Messages

A sermon by Seymour, titled, 'Christ's Messages to the Churches', explored the seven prophetic messages in Revelation.[35] Seymour believed that Revelation – being the final book in the Bible – was the last message from Christ given by the Holy Spirit to the church through John.[36] Seymour remarked that when offering the seven prophetic messages, the resurrected Christ was in heaven, and through the power of the Holy Spirit, Jesus walked among the churches – the seven candlesticks.[37] *The Apostolic Faith* commented:

> He [Christ] is in our midst, walking among the golden candlesticks, pruning, purging. He who moved among the golden candlesticks is moving in our midst now. We must recognize Him alone as Head over all, and know no man after the flesh. The Spirit of God will teach us if we keep low in love and humility before Him.[38]

In another case, Seymour concluded that Christ continued to walk among the churches, 'I thank God for this wonderful message to the church, a message from heaven, given by Jesus to show that He is in the church that He does walk among the golden candlesticks'.[39]

---

[34] *AF* 1.5 (January 1907), p. 1.

[35] *AF* 1.12 (January 1908), p. 3.

[36] *AF* 1.12 (January 1908), p. 3, Seymour notes that the author of Revelation, John, is the beloved disciple and that John was on Patmos suffering because of his testimony for Jesus. Seymour also describes the tradition where John was boiled in a cauldron of oil and survived to be exiled to Patmos.

[37] *AF* 1.4 (December 1906), p. 4; *AF* 1.12 (January 1908), p. 3. When exploring the cultic imagery of the lampstand, it is likely that the early Pentecostals alluded to Revelation, Exodus, and Zechariah as well as other biblical references. It is challenging to distinguish between these intertexts since they are closely associated with each other. For example, in an allegorical reading of the tabernacle (*AF* 1.4 [December 1906], p. 2), one testimony included references to the Lamb's book of life, the throne, and the sealing of the forehead.

[38] *AF* 1.5 (January 1907), p. 1.

[39] *AF* 1.11 (October-January 1908), p. 3.

Discerning the identity of the seven churches was a continuous task, but the early Pentecostals' primary desire was to hear what Revelation had to say to the church.[40] Seymour wrote:

> John was permitted to see from the beginning of the church age on down to the white throne judgment, the final winding of the world ... John saw things past, things present, and things in the future. He had witnessed the glory and power of the apostolic church, and saw the falling away of the church, and God sent him to the church with this blessed message: that she should come back to her first love.[41]

In another sermon on the message to the Ephesians, Seymour exhorted those who have received the blessing of the Holy Spirit that they should not return to apostasy and not fall from their first love. Rather, the Pentecostal church should be lights, burning and shining for God, which might allude to the candlestick imagery from Revelation. As in the seven prophetic messages, Seymour believed that the church was being called back to her first love.[42] Similarly, *The Apostolic Faith* testified of a boy providing an interpretation of tongues with the hearing formula, 'He that hath an ear hear, let him hear'. As the boy continued to speak, the Spirit spoke through him.[43] These testimonies in *The Apostolic Faith* support the assertion that these early Pentecostals observed the close relationship of the Spirit, Jesus, and the church by means of the imagery from Revelation. They discerned Revelation in a manner that desired to hear the resurrected Christ in their communities by the Spirit; a message that included coming back to their first love and not falling into apostasy.

---

[40] *AF* 1.11 (October-January 1908), p. 3.

[41] *AF* 1.11 (October-January 1908), p. 3.

[42] *AF* 1.11 (October-January 1908), p. 3.

[43] *AF* 1.8 (May 1907), p. 2.

Discerning the Mark of the Beast

*The Apostolic Faith* offers numerous references to Pentecostals having the seal of God on their foreheads, which they believed to be a symbol of Spirit baptism.[44] Being sealed corresponded to the 'full' overcomers who were differentiated from believers.[45] 'Full' overcomers: (1) followed the Lamb in the world, (2) were filled with the Holy Spirit or 'sealed with the Holy Spirit of promise',[46] (3) were ready for the marriage supper of the Lamb, (4) were washed in the blood, (5) were made holy, (6) kept 'living this salvation moment by moment',[47] and (7) would reign on the earth during the millennium. Examples of 'full' overcomers from Revelation included the 144,000 (Rev. 7.3-4, 14.1) and the 'man child' who was 'caught up unto God and to His throne' (12.5).[48] The 144,000 were sanctified;[49] they followed the Lamb to the marriage supper; and took part in the first resurrection.[50] Seymour extended the opportunity of becoming a 'full' overcomer to all because '[our Lord] will give us power to overcome if we are willing'.[51] *So is the "mark" metaphorical?*

---

[44] E.g. *AF* 1.5 (January 1907), p. 2; *AF* 1.6 (February-March 1907), p. 1; *AF* 1.8 (May 1907), pp. 2, 4; *AF* 1.9 (June 1907), p. 4; *AF* 1.10 (September 1907), p. 1; *AF* 1.11 (October-January 1908), p. 2.

[45] *AF* 1.12 (January 1908), p. 2, contains a sermon on Revelation 2–3 that is titled 'Full overcomers'. On many occasions, Pentecostals described themselves as already receiving the promises pronounced in the seven prophetic messages: the seal of God, having God's name on their heart, obtaining a stone in hand, receiving a new name, having the white stone, and being clothed in righteousness, see *AF* 1.9 (June 1907), p. 3; *AF* 1.8 (May 1907) p. 4; *AF* 1.11 (October-January 1908), p. 3.

[46] *AF* 1.9 (June 1907), p. 2, described that those baptized in the Holy Spirit have their commission written on their heads. They must work until the mighty angel from Revelation is standing with one foot on the earth and one on the sea, and declares that time will no longer be.

[47] *AF* 1.12 (January 1908), p. 2.

[48] *AF* 1.12 (January 1908), p. 2.

[49] In *AF* 1.7 (April 1907), p. 3, contains a sermon on the sanctified person typologically associated with the HB priests. The sermon is brought into conversation with those who were wearing white linen washed in the blood of the Lamb. In answering the question who are these, the preacher finds that those wearing the white linen have been sanctified by the blood of the Lamb.

[50] *AF* 1.12 (January 1908), p. 2.

[51] *AF* 1.11 (October-January 1908), p. 3.

*handwritten: historical progression - stages of God's self revelation + plan of salvation*

*The Apostolic Faith* also reflected on the mark of the beast. Some Pentecostals read the mark of the beast dispensationally[52] where the mark would appear following the rapture and during the great tribulation.[53] However, others attempted to contextualize the mark for contemporary application. In another testimony, a Pentecostal reflected, 'the baptism with the Holy Ghost is the seal of the living God in your forehead. God wants you to wear this seal, and not the badges of men and devils.'[54] Here rather than making use of the mark of the beast, this Pentecostal created an alternative opposing image: the 'badges' of the devil. *The Apostolic Faith* appealed to Revelation to generate two identifying markers: the seal of God for the saints, or the mark of the beast/badge of the devil for those who do evil deeds. This dualism is further described by Mrs. Mary Galmond who prophesied that the rich would not allow the poor to buy without the mark of the beast:

> The time is coming when the poor will be oppressed and the Christians can neither buy nor sell, unless they have 'the mark of the beast' ... the time will come when the poor man will say that he has nothing to eat and work [will] be shut down. And the rich man will go and buy up all the sugar, tea, coffee, etc., and hold it in his store, and we cannot get it unless we have the mark of the beast. 'That is going to cause the poor man to go to these places and break in to get food. This will cause the rich man to come out with his gun to make war with the laboring man. They will cause

---

[52] McQueen, *Toward a Pentecostal Eschatology*, has examined the early Pentecostal literature and found that there were various usages of 'dispensations'. Concerning dispensational thought in Pentecostalism, he comments:

> Some texts of Scripture that were acknowledged to be prophecies of a future literal situation were simultaneously understood to have contemporary spiritual applicability. The presence of such tension within a uniform script suggests that incompatible hermeneutical presuppositions were functioning simultaneously, namely (1) the presupposition of the experience of the Spirit, which resulted in contemporary applications of prophetic texts within an inaugurated eschatology, and (2) the presupposition of 'keys' (such as reading 'dispensationally') that could be applied to Scripture to 'unlock' meaning which resulted in predetermined, future applications of the texts. (pp. 140-41).

[53] Two occurrences of the three appearances of the 'mark of the beast' are in *The Apostolic Faith* (*AF* 1.5 [January 1907], p. 2; *AF* 1.12 [January 1908], p. 2), seem to be influenced by a dispensational interpretation, which included references to a pre-tribulation rapture, a tribulation, an antichrist, and the mark of the beast.

[54] *AF* 1.9 (June 1907), p. 1.

blood to be spilt in the street as it never was before.' I saw the blood ankle deep, and they were holding to the horses' bridles with the right hand and cutting and slashing right and left with their swords.[55]

Mary Galmond identified herself with the poor or laboring ones, indicated by the use of 'we' and with the second person plural pronoun usage, suggesting that she visualized herself as one who would experience this time of oppression. Contrary to the poor, she believed that the rich would take the mark of the beast, which created a dualistic outlook based upon one's economics. This criticism of wealth might originate from Revelation where the beast and the great whore have economic power by which they oppress others.

### Discerning the Mystery

*This seems like a stretch,*

The close association of Christ and the Spirit was reflected throughout *The Apostolic Faith*. In the vision of the resurrected Christ from Revelation 1, Seymour observed that the resurrected Christ was 'alive in the blessed Holy Spirit'.[56] When discerning the mystery of the seven stars in the right hand of Christ, Seymour proposed that the seven stars represented 'His Holy Ghost ministers'.[57] Being in Jesus' right hand suggests that the 'Holy Ghost ministers' had authority to preach the gospel and had power over devils. Being in Christ's hand was thereby a discerning test: anyone who was a 'live preacher' and 'Holy Ghost minister', who was saved, sanctified, and filled with the Holy Spirit and in the right hand of Jesus was authentic.[58] This exemplified the close association between the Spirit and Jesus, which included the church because the leaders of the church were in the right hand of Jesus and filled with the Spirit.

### The Spirit and the Bride

In a homily entitled, 'The Holy Ghost and the Bride', Seymour discerned that Rev. 22.17 revealed a co-working relationship between the church and the Spirit.[59] The Spirit inspired faith in God's word and empowered the church for the work of God. Those who were

---

[55] *AF* 1.2 (October 1906), p. 2.
[56] *AF* 1.12 (January 1908), p. 3.
[57] *AF* 1.12 (January 1908), p. 3.
[58] *AF* 1.12 (January 1908), p. 3.
[59] *AF* 2.13 (May 1908), p. 4.

Spirit baptized recognized the bride of Christ and heard the Spirit call the thirsty to come to Jesus. The call in 22.17 worked on multiple levels: (1) it was a call for unbelievers to come to Christ, (2) it was a call for believers to be sanctified, and (3) it was a call to those that are sanctified to be Spirit baptized. Those who were filled with the Spirit were empowered to participate in the call for sinners to be saved, sanctified, and Spirit baptized.[60]

### The Spirit in the Throne Room Vision

The Lamb, having seven horns and seven eyes, was rarely mentioned in the paper. In occurrences in which the 'Seven Horns' and 'Seven Eyes' appeared, the writer capitalized them, suggesting that these early Pentecostals believed the seven Spirits – the 'Seven Horns' and the 'Seven Eyes' – to be the divine Holy Spirit.[61]

## Summary

*The Apostolic Faith* appreciated the dynamic relationship of Christ, the Spirit, and the church as it is described in Revelation. These early Pentecostals desired to hear what the Spirit was saying to the church. They were concerned with the pneumatology of Revelation because they understood their experience as an extension of the biblical narrative. They reflected upon the way in which their experience was similar to John's 'in the Spirit' experience. *The Apostolic Faith* believed that Christ by the Spirit walked among the Pentecostal church, and continued to speak to the church through the seven prophetic messages. The paper interpreted the seven eyes and seven horns of the Lamb as the Spirit and perceived the closeness of the Spirit to the throne. *The Apostolic Faith* expounded on having wisdom and the mind of God, which was given to the church by the Holy Spirit. The seal of God was on these early Pentecostals' foreheads, against those who wore the 'badges' of the devil or had received the mark of the beast. Finally, they believed that they were co-workers in the eschatological missionary activity of the Spirit, calling unbelievers to Christ.

---

[60] *AF* 2.13 (May 1908), p. 4.
[61] *AF* 1.8 (May 1907), p. 1.

## The Bridegroom's Messenger

*The Bridegroom's Messenger* was published in Atlanta, Georgia beginning in 1907 by G.B. Cashwell who in the first year handed the editorial duties to Elizabeth Sexton. *The Bridegroom's Messenger* contained testimonies, scriptures, hymns, and prayers that were collected from a variety of people from around the world. The paper epitomized an outlook that dedicated itself to hearing from anyone in order that each believer could discern their Pentecostal experience in community. The paper permitted varying and even conflicting interpretations to stand beside each other. *The Bridegroom's Messenger* contained a variety of references, quotes, and allusions to the Apocalypse.[62]

---

[62] For explicit scripture references and quotation of Revelation in *The Bridegroom's Messenger*, see *TBM* 1.1 (October 1, 1907), p. 3; *TBM* 1.3 (December 1, 1907), p. 3; *TBM* 1.4 (December 15, 1907), p. 1; *TBM* 1.5 (January 1, 1908), pp. 1, 3; *TBM* 1.6 (January 15, 1908), pp. 2, 4; *TBM* 1.7 (February 1, 1908), p. 1; *TBM* 1.8 (February 15, 1908), p. 4; *TBM* 1.9 (March 1, 1908), pp. 1-2, 3; *TBM* 1.11 (April 1, 1908), p. 3; *TBM* 1.12 (April 15, 1908), p. 4; *TBM* 1.13 (May 1, 1908), p. 4; *TBM* 1.15 (June 1, 1908), p. 2; *TBM* 1.16 (June 15, 1908), p. 1; *TBM* 1.19 (August 1, 1908), pp. 2-3; *TBM* 2.23 (October 1, 1908), p. 1; *TBM* 2.26 (November 15, 1908), p. 2; *TBM* 2.27 (December 1, 1908), p. 2; *TBM* 2.30 (January 15, 1909), p. 2; *TBM* 2.31 (February 1, 1909), pp. 1, 4; *TBM* 2.34 (March 15, 1909), p. 1; *TBM* 2.35 (April 1, 1909), p. 3; *TBM* 2.37 (May 1, 1909), p. 1; *TBM* 2.38 (May 15, 1909), p. 3; *TBM* 2.39 (June 1, 1909), p. 3; *TBM* 2.40 (June 15, 1909), p. 4; *TBM* 2.42 (July 15, 1909), pp. 2, 4; *TBM* 2.43 (August 1, 1909), pp. 2-4; *TBM* 2.44 (August 15, 1909), pp. 3-4; *TBM* 2.45 (September 1, 1909), pp. 1-2; *TBM* 2.46 (September 15, 1909), pp. 3-4; *TBM* 3.48 (October 15, 1909), pp. 1-3; *TBM* 3.49 (November 1, 1909), p. 3; *TBM* 3.50 (November 15, 1909), pp. 1, 4; *TBM* 3.51 (December 1, 1909), pp. 2, 4; *TBM* 3.53 (January 1, 1910), p. 4; *TBM* 3.54 (January 15, 1910), p. 1; *TBM* 3.55 (February 1, 1910), p. 2; *TBM* 3.56 (February 15, 1910), pp. 3-4; *TBM* 3.58 (March 15, 1910), p. 1; *TBM* 3.59 (April 1, 1910), p. 1; *TBM* 3.60 (April 15, 1910), p. 1; *TBM* 3.61 (May 1, 1910), pp. 1, 3-4; *TBM* 3.62 (May 15, 1910), p. 2; *TBM* 3.63 (June 1, 1910), pp. 1, 3-4; *TBM* 3.64 (June 15, 1910), p. 1; *TBM* 3.66 (July 15, 1910), p. 3; *TBM* 3.68 (August 15, 1910), p. 4; *TBM* 3.69 (September 1, 1910), pp. 1, 3; *TBM* 3.71 (October 1, 1910), p. 2; *TBM* 4.72 (October 15, 1910), pp. 1-2; *TBM* 4.73 (November 1, 1910), p. 4; *TBM* 4.74 (November 15, 1910), p. 1; *TBM* 4.75 (December 1, 1910), p. 3; *TBM* 4.76 (December 15, 1910), p. 2; *TBM* 4.80 (February 15, 1911), p. 4; *TBM* 4.82 (March 1, 1911), p. 4; *TBM* 4.83 (April 1, 1911), p. 3; *TBM* 4.84 (April 15, 1911), p. 4; *TBM* 4.87 (June 1, 1911), p. 4; *TBM* 4.89 (July 1, 1911), p. 4; *TBM* 4.90 (July 15, 1911), p. 4; *TBM* 4.91 (August 1, 1911), p. 1; *TBM* 4.92 (August 15, 1911), p. 2; *TBM* 4.94 (September 15, 1911), p. 1; *TBM* 5.95 (October 1, 1911), p. 1; *TBM* 5.96 (October 15, 1911), p. 4; *TBM* 5.97 (November 1, 1911), p. 3; *TBM* 5.99 (December 1, 1911), p. 4; *TBM* 5.100 (December 15, 1911), pp. 1-3; *TBM* 5.101 (January 1, 1912), pp. 1, 4; *TBM* 5.102 (January 15, 1912), pp. 1-2; *TBM* 5.103 (February 1, 1912), p. 3; *TBM* 5.104 (February 15, 1912), pp. 1, 3; *TBM* 5.105 (March 1, 1912), pp. 3-4; *TBM* 5.106 (March 15, 1912), pp. 1-3; *TBM* 5.107 (April 1, 1912), pp. 1, 4; *TBM* 5.109 (May 1, 1912), p. 3; *TBM* 5.110 (May 15, 1912), pp.

## Pentecostals and Pneumatic Discernment

*The Bridegroom's Messenger* believed that the Spirit was directly and dynamically involved in their lives. The Spirit was described as their teacher, guide, illuminator, and a personification of truth.[63] To hear the voice of the Spirit, Pentecostals were encouraged to pray, have

---

2, 4; *TBM* 5.111 (June 1, 1912), p. 3; *TBM* 5.112 (June 15, 1912), pp. 1-3; *TBM* 5.113 (July 1, 1912), pp. 1, 4; *TBM* 5.114 (June 15, 1912), p. 1; *TBM* 5.115 (August 1, 1912), p. 4; *TBM* 5.116 (August 15, 1912), pp. 1, 3; *TBM* 5.117 (September 1, 1912), pp. 1-2; *TBM* 5.119 (October 15, 1912), p. 4; *TBM* 6.121 (November 15, 1912), pp. 1, 4; *TBM* 6.122 (December 1, 1912), p. 4; *TBM* 6.123 (December 15, 1912), p. 4; *TBM* 6.125 (January 15, 1913), pp. 2, 4; *TBM* 6.126 (February 1, 1913), pp. 2-4; *TBM* 6.127 (February 15, 1913), pp. 1, 3-4; *TBM* 6.128 (March 1, 1913), p. 4; *TBM* 6.129 (March 15, 1913), p. 1; *TBM* 6.130 (April 1, 1913), p. 1; *TBM* 6.131 (April 15, 1913), p. 3; *TBM* 6.132 (May 1, 1913), pp. 1-4; *TBM* 6.133 (May 15, 1913), p. 4; *TBM* 6.134 (June 1, 1913), p. 1; *TBM* 6.135 (June 15, 1913), p. 1; *TBM* 6.136 (July 1, 1913), pp. 2, 4; *TBM* 6.137 (August 1, 1913), p. 1; *TBM* 6.139 (September 1, 1913), p. 1; *TBM* 7.142 (October 15, 1913), pp. 1, 4; *TBM* 7.143 (November 1, 1913), p. 4; *TBM* 7.144 (November 15, 1913), p. 4; *TBM* 7.145 (December 1, 1913), pp. 1, 4; *TBM* 7.148 (January 15, 1914), p. 3; *TBM* 7.150 (February 15, 1914), p. 1; *TBM* 7.153 (April 15, 1914), pp. 2, 4; *TBM* 7.154 (May 1, 1914), pp. 1, 4; *TBM* 7.155 (May 15, 1914), p. 4; *TBM* 7.157 (July 1, 1914), p. 4; *TBM* 7.158 (July 1, 1914), p. 4; *TBM* 7.159 (August 1, 1914), pp. 2, 4; *TBM* 7.160 (August 15, 1914), pp. 3-4; *TBM* 7.161 (September 1, 1914), p. 4; *TBM* 8.163 (October 1, 1914), p. 2; *TBM* 8.164 (November 1, 1914), pp. 1, 3; *TBM* 8.166 (January 1, 1915), p. 4; *TBM* 8.167 (February 1, 1915), pp. 1-2; *TBM* 8.168 (March 1, 1915), pp. 1, 4; *TBM* 8.169 (April 1, 1915), pp. 1, 4; *TBM* 8.170 (May 1, 1915), pp. 1, 3-4; *TBM* 8.171 (June 1, 1915), pp. 2-4; *TBM* 8.172 (July 1, 1915), p. 4; *TBM* 8.173 (August 1, 1915), p. 1; *TBM* 8.174 (September 1, 1915), p. 4; *TBM* 8.175 (October 1, 1915), p. 4; *TBM* 9.176 (November 1, 1915), p. 4; *TBM* 9.177 (December 1, 1915), pp. 3-4; *TBM* 9.178 (January 1, 1916), pp. 1, 4; *TBM* 9.179 (February 1, 1916), p. 1; *TBM* 9.180 (March 1, 1916), p. 1; *TBM* 9.181 (April 1, 1916), pp. 1-2, 4; *TBM* 9.182 (May 1, 1916), pp. 1, 3; *TBM* 9.183 (June 1, 1916), p. 1; *TBM* 9.184 (July 1, 1916), pp. 1, 3-4; *TBM* 9.185 (August 1, 1916), pp. 1, 4; *TBM* 9.186 (September 1, 1916), pp. 1, 3; *TBM* 9.188 (November 1, 1916), pp. 1, 4; *TBM* 10.191 (February 1, 1917), p. 4; *TBM* 10.192 (March 1, 1917), pp. 1, 3-4; *TBM* 10.198 (April 1, 1917), pp. 1, 4; *TBM* 10.199 (May 1, 1917), pp. 1-2; *TBM* 10.200 (June 1, 1917), pp. 1-3; *TBM* 10.201 (July 1, 1917), pp. 1-2; *TBM* 10.202 (September 1, 1917), pp. 2-3; *TBM* 11.204 (1918), pp. 1, 4; *TBM* 11.205 (1918), pp. 1, 3-4; *TBM* 11.206 (October 1, 1918), pp. 1, 3-4.

[63] *TBM* 1.3 (December 1, 1907), p. 4; *TBM* 1.6 (January 15, 1908), pp. 1, 3; *TBM* 1.7 (February 1, 1908), p. 3; *TBM* 2.37 (May 1, 1909), p. 3; *TBM* 3.69 (September 1, 1910), p. 3; *TBM* 3.71 (October 1, 1910), p. 1; *TBM* 3.63 (June 1, 1910), p. 1; *TBM* 3.64 (June 15, 1910), p. 3; *TBM* 3.69 (September 1, 1910), p. 3; *TBM* 4.83 (April 1, 1911), p. 3; *TBM* 4.84 (April 15, 1911), p. 3; *TBM* 4.90 (July 15, 1911), p. 4; *TBM* 5.96 (October 15, 1911), p. 3; *TBM* 5.97 (November 1, 1911), p. 1; *TBM* 5.102 (January 15, 1912), p. 3; *TBM* 7.142 (October 15, 1913), p. 4; *TBM* 7.149 (February 1, 1914), p. 1; *TBM* 8.165 (December 1, 1914), p. 3; *TBM* 9.184 (July 1, 1916), p. 2; *TBM* 10.191 (February 1, 1917), p. 4.

pure faith, and receive the true light.[64] G.B. Cashwell exhorted the readers to pray for discernment in order to see by the 'search-light of the Holy Spirit'.[65] One hymn revealed the early Pentecostals' desire to obtain knowledge by the Spirit of God:

> O help me, Lord, these truths to grasp,
> And help me understand,
> That I am but a house of clay
> In which Thy Spirit dwells, and may
> I look to Christ from day to day,
> To strengthen me to stand.[66]

Another hymn offers an insight into the struggle of interpretation where knowledge ultimately derives from belief:

> I think if thou couldest know,
> O soul that will complain,
> What lies concealed below
> Our burden and our pain;
> How just anguish brings,
> We seek for now in vain –
> I think thou wouldest rejoice and not complain.
>
> I think if thou couldst see
> With thy dim mortal sight,
> How meaning dark to thee
> Are shadows hiding light;
> Truth's efforts cross'ed and vex'd
> Life-purpose all perplex'd –
> If thou couldst see them right,
> I think that they would seem all clear
> and wise and bright.
>
> And yet thou canst not know,
> And yet thou canst not see;
> Wisdom and sight are slow

---

[64] *TBM* 4.84 (April 15, 1911), p. 3. See also *TBM* 1.5 (January 1, 1908), p. 3; *TBM* 1.17 (July 1, 1908), p. 2; *TBM* 7.149 (February 1, 1914), p. 1.

[65] *TBM* 2.23 (October 1, 1908), p. 4. See *TBM* 9.185 (August 1, 1916), p. 4.

[66] *TBM* 7.156 (June 1, 1914), p. 1.

in poor humanity,
If thou couldst trust, poor soul,
In Him who rules the whole,
Thou wouldst find peace and rest;
Wisdom and right as well, but trust is best.[67]

Knowledge was not a merely cognitive process but included the heart and faith because 'Error does not start with the head, but with the heart';[68] trust and faith in God brought about wisdom, and was essential to the discernment process. Wisdom was provided by God and given by the Spirit,[69] the 'Spirit of wisdom and revelation in the knowledge of Christ, that the "eyes" [o]f their "spiritual understanding" might be "enlightened" to "know what is the hope of His calling and what are the riches of the glory of His inheritance"'.[70] There was a conflict between divine wisdom and wisdom of the world. The paper was critical of communities who were governed by their own wisdom rather than by the Holy Spirit:[71]

> We need wisdom. It does not follow that because good thoughts enter my mind, I must speak them out. It does not follow that because God gives me a message to some one that I should deliver it at once, or the first time we meet ... We are not granted the gift of discernment to jump on to the erring. God may want us to pray them right. Knowledge and gifts may be destructive as well as constructive in wrong directions. They must both be guided wisely.[72]

Similarly, the mind of the Spirit is required for discernment:

---

[67] *TBM* 1.15 (June 1, 1908), p. 1.

[68] *TBM* 6.121 (November 15, 1912), p. 4.

[69] See e.g. *TBM* 1.7 (February 1, 1908), p. 2; *TBM* 1.8 (February 15, 1908), p. 2; *TBM* 1.9 (March 1, 1908), p. 1; *TBM* 1.13 (May 1, 1908), p. 1; *TBM* 1.14 (May 15, 1908), p. 1; *TBM* 2.29 (January 1, 1909), pp. 1- 2; *TBM* 2.30 (January 15, 1909), p. 4; *TBM* 2.32 (February 15, 1909), p. 4; *TBM* 2.33 (March 1, 1909), p. 3; *TBM* 2.34 (March 15, 1909), p. 3; *TBM* 2.38 (May 15, 1909), p. 2; *TBM* 2.41 (July 1, 1909), p. 1; *TBM* 3.56 (February 15, 1910), p. 2; *TBM* 3.58 (March 15, 1910), p. 2; *TBM* 3.62 (May 15, 1910), p. 1; *TBM* 4.77 (January 1, 1911), p. 3; *TBM* 4.82 (March 1, 1911), p. 1; *TBM* 5.97 (November 1, 1911), p. 3; *TBM* 5.98 (November 15, 1911), p. 1; *TBM* 5.102 (January 15, 1912), p. 4; *TBM* 6.131 (April 15, 1913), p. 3; *TBM* 9.178 (January 1, 1916), p. 1.

[70] *TBM* 6.135 (June 15, 1913), p. 4. See *TBM* 3.68 (August 15, 1910), p. 4.

[71] *TBM* 4.75 (December 1, 1910), p. 3; *TBM* 4.75 (December 1, 1910), p. 3.

[72] *TBM* 2.27 (December 1, 1908), p. 4.

They have caught the mind of the Spirit and are abreast of God's thought for the human family. The Spirit is drawing the baptized ones everywhere to a deeper more definite and intelligent prayer life than ever before; and as we are melted down before Him, our vision of the needs of this world will be clearer, and our prayer-life intensified as we move on in the Spirit.[73]

The Spirit was the 'very "Comforter," illuminating the mind, warning the heart, shielding us from unseen harm, filling saintly ones with gladness, fitting laborers in Master's vineyard for effective work'.[74]

*The Bridegroom's Messenger* exhibited a belief in levels of discernment,[75] 'When we were converted, we had much light on the Bible, when we were sanctified we had more light, but when the baptism of the blessed Holy Ghost came in all His fullness we had most light'.[76] Some even proposed that believers led by the Spirit would not be deceived because, 'Spirit-touched eyes and ears and hearts … will reveal the counterfeit experiences all about us, both in and outside of the Pentecostal movement and send us back to early church-power, even though it mean [*sic*] early church persecution and their badge of honor.'[77] Refusal of the Spirit's guidance and rejection of the Spirit's teachings would lead to faulty discernment.[78] Discernment was a continual process that constantly needed to be brought to the community:

> We are so unwilling to admit our conclusions are wrong, and that there is a realm of the Spirit where we cannot live mentally except through constant supernatural illumination and revelation by the Spirit. But human wisdom is 'folly' with God. Stop this human effort of talking, reading, studying, and mental conceptions, till the power of the Spirit gets control of your mind.[79]

---

[73] *TBM* 1.11 (April 1, 1908), p. 1.

[74] *TBM* 3.47 (October 1, 1909), p. 3; *TBM* 5.109 (May 1, 1912), p. 4; *TBM* 8.165 (December 1, 1914), p. 3.

[75] *TBM* 1.7 (February 1, 1908), p. 2; *TBM* 1.11 (April 1, 1908), p. 1; *TBM* 2.26 (November 15, 1908), p. 2; *TBM* 3.63 (June 1, 1910), p. 1; *TBM* 6.136 (July 1, 1913), p. 1; *TBM* 7.144 (November 15, 1913), p. 3.

[76] *TBM* 1.14 (May 15, 1908), p. 4.

[77] *TBM* 1.18 (July 1, 1908), p. 4. See *TBM* 7.145 (December 1, 1913), p. 4.

[78] *TBM* 5.109 (May 1, 1912), p. 4.

[79] *TBM* 3.56 (February 15, 1910), p. 1.

*The Bridegroom's Messenger* also offered a robust outlook of the dynamic, dialectical relationship between the Spirit and the Word:

> The Holy Ghost is the fire, the word is the fuel. Both fuel and fire are necessary to produce heat and power. A knowledge of the word with the Spirit ends up in formalism; but aiming to follow the Spirit without the word drifts into fanaticism. Stock up with the word. Study it, asking God to open up the Scriptures and your understanding.[80]

The Word has a central feature in *The Bridegroom's Messenger*, but any attempt to discern the Word without hearing the Spirit was pointless: 'They overlooked the fact that truth by itself will never produce the effect, without the Spirit of God'.[81] It was the Spirit who presented revelation to the community through the biblical text: 'How wonderful are the deeper revelations of Jesus that the Spirit does give. As Jesus said, "He is the Spirit of Truth," the very author of all Scriptures, and the Revealer of the deep things of God.'[82] Similarly, having a greater measure of the Spirit allowed for an increased understanding of the Word.[83]

*The Bridegroom's Messenger* attempted to create boundaries against rampant or harmful interpretations. On the one hand, faulty interpretations occurred whenever an interpreter divorced the Spirit from the written word.[84] On the other hand, the Holy Spirit 'will never lead one iota outside of God's word',[85] and 'will always guide, always witness, and always work in us, and through us, and for us, in harmony with the Word'.[86] The paper endeavored to hold together the tension between the active, dynamic Spirit and the written text while being guided by both the Word and Spirit: 'May the blessed Spirit and Word give clear directions as to the very place to which He wants you to go'.[87]

[80] *TBM* 2.27 (December 1, 1908), p. 4.
[81] *TBM* 1.14 (May 15, 1908), p. 1. See *TBM* 5.109 (May 1, 1912), p. 1.
[82] *TBM* 2.25 (November 1, 1908), p. 1.
[83] *TBM* 5.103 (February 1, 1912), p. 3.
[84] *TBM* 5.109 (May 1, 1912), p. 4.
[85] *TBM* 7.145 (December 1, 1913), p. 4.
[86] *TBM* 3.51 (December 1, 1909), p. 1.
[87] *TBM* 4.94 (September 15, 1911), p. 4.

## The Spirit and Discernment in Revelation

The Throne Room Vision

Reference to 'the seven Spirits' seldom appeared in *The Bridegroom's Messenger*, but on a few occurrences, the seven Spirits were identified as the divine Holy Spirit: 'the Lamb, having seven horns and seven eyes which are the seven Spirits of God'.[88] Mrs. E.S. Hubbell offered a remarkable reading of Rev. 5.1-9 focusing upon the role of the Spirit, the Lamb, and the church in discernment:

> In the Scriptures, horns are always the emblem of power, as the eyes are of intelligence. The Pentecostal people today are praying for the gifts to be set in the church as they were of old. Many have the eyes, intelligence to perceive that the power of God in the church is far short of what it should be, but do we discern why it is so? It was as the Lamb which had been slain that to Christ were given the seven horns, symbolized of the 'all power,' and the seven eyes – the 'seven Spirits of God,' perfect wisdom and knowledge. There is such a mighty lesson here, that only the Spirit can make it plain. God grant that He indite the matter for us … We may then hope to meekly listen to the voice of the Spirit as He directs us in the use of the power of God … He will give us, one by one, the horns of power; and in meekness and humility we should accept and use what He gives us.[89]

Hubbell discerned that the imagery of the seven eyes of the Lamb represented perfect knowledge and that the seven Spirits provide knowledge, intellect, and wisdom to the churches. She observed that each person had eyes to perceive. But to receive perfect knowledge, the church needed to ask for the Spirit in meekness and humility. The seven Spirits were to be the eyes of the church in the same manner that the seven Spirits are the eyes of the Lamb. If the church desired to see, they needed the seven Spirits.

The relationship between the seven Spirits as the seven eyes of Lamb and the church is pushed further in *The Bridegroom's Messenger* when commenting on the four living creatures that were repeatedly

---

[88] *TBM* 6.125 (January 15, 1913), p. 4. See also *TBM* 6.133 (May 15, 1913), p. 4, which will be discussed below.

[89] *TBM* 6.133 (May 15, 1913), p. 4.

identified as the 'perfect' overcomers.[90] The paper observed a relationship between the eyes of the four living creatures, and the eyes of the Lamb: 'they are also identified with the Lamb, having the seven "eyes," which is the fullness of the Spirit',[91] and they 'have eyes, seeing every way, can see into the deep things of God'.[92] Hence, perfect overcomers had already received the fullness of the Spirit on account that they had received the seven eyes of the Lamb – the seven Spirits. They had perfect knowledge and were able to see the deep things of God; perfect overcomers were able to discern pneumatically.

'In the Spirit'

'In the Spirit' was a commonly utilized phrase in *The Bridegroom's Messenger* that emerged in a variety of contexts, which included: love,[93] renewed,[94] walk,[95] living,[96] move,[97] speak,[98] mysteries,[99] understand,[100]

---

[90] *TBM* 3.61 (May 1, 1910), p. 1; *TBM* 6.121 (November 15, 1912), p. 4; *TBM* 6.136 (July 1, 1913), p. 4; *TBM* 6.126 (February 1, 1913), p. 4; *TBM* 11.206 (October 1, 1918), p. 1. *TBM* 6.121 (November 15, 1912), p. 4. The four living creatures overcame by the Spirit of God, which reveals an association between the work of the overcomers on earth and the Spirit: 'the living creatures are the living expressions of the throne, or in other words the Spirit of God in the throne is worked out through them; so they have set down with Christ in His throne being perfect overcomers. Rev. 3.21'. See also Hattie Barth, *TBM* 9.188 (November 1, 1915), p. 4, who observed the participation of the four living creatures in judgment by announcing 'come' before the breaking of each of the seven seals.

[91] *TBM* 6.126 (February 1, 1913), p. 4.

[92] *TBM* 6.121 (November 15, 1912), p. 4.

[93] *TBM* 1.4 (December 15, 1907), p. 2; *TBM* 5.99 (December 1, 1911), p. 2; *TBM* 7.159 (August 1, 1914), p. 2.

[94] *TBM* 1.4 (December 15, 1907), p. 2.

[95] *TBM* 1.9 (March 1, 1908), p. 1; *TBM* 2.32 (February 15, 1909), p. 3; *TBM* 5.105 (March 1, 1912), p. 3; *TBM* 6.125 (January 15, 1913), p. 3; *TBM* 10.198 (April 1, 1917), p. 4.

[96] *TBM* 1.11 (April 1, 1908), p. 4; *TBM* 5.105 (March 1, 1912), p. 3; *TBM* 6.135 (June 15, 1913), p. 4.

[97] *TBM* 1.11 (April 1, 1908), p. 4.

[98] *TBM* 1.16 (June 15, 1908), p. 3.

[99] *TBM* 1.16 (June 15, 1908), p. 3; *TBM* 4.79 (February 1, 1911), p. 4.

[100] *TBM* 1.17 (July 1, 1908), p. 4.

read,[101] preserved,[102] singing,[103] was/being,[104] kept,[105] fellowship,[106] weeping,[107] continued,[108] 'shout, jump and play',[109] washed,[110] and submerged[111] in the Spirit. First, there was a communal aspect to 'in the Spirit'. For example, a Pentecostal missionary testified, 'many a time I feel in the Spirit when prayer is going up for me. Oh, how the clouds lift and the sunshine of God's love is shining forth, when the dear saints reach the throne in prayer.'[112] Being 'in the Spirit' created a trans-geographical Pentecostal community where believers from around the world were able to be in community and solidarity with each other. G.B. Cashwell wrote to missionaries across the world, 'I am often with you in the Spirit and will meet you when Jesus comes'.[113] Second, overcomers and the Bride must be 'in the Spirit':

> If we hinder the indwelling Holy Spirit from working in us, He cannot reveal Christ to us; and if He cannot reveal Christ to us, we shall never become conformed into His image (2 Cor. 3:17-18); and if we never become conformed to His image, we cannot become part of the Bride; and if we do not become a part of the Bride, we cannot sit on His throne with Him. We see so little 'pray-

---

[101] *TBM* 1.18 (July 1, 1908), p. 4.

[102] *TBM* 1.19 (August 1, 1908), p. 3.

[103] *TBM* 1.22 (September 15, 1908), p. 3; *TBM* 2.23 (October 1, 1908), p. 3; *TBM* 2.30 (January 15, 1909), p. 3; *TBM* 2.35 (April 1, 1909), p. 3; *TBM* 3.53 (January 1, 1910), p. 3; *TBM* 3.66 (July 15, 1910), p. 3; *TBM* 4.72 (October 15, 1910), p. 3; *TBM* 5.99 (December 1, 1911), p. 2; *TBM* 6.135 (June 15, 1913), p. 4; *TBM* 6.139 (September 1, 1913), p. 3; *TBM* 7.158 (July 1, 1914), p. 2; See also songs 'in the Spirit' in *TBM* 4.76 (December 15, 1910), p. 2.

[104] *TBM* 2.33 (March 1, 1909), p. 2; *TBM* 3.59 (April 1, 1910), p. 1; *TBM* 4.76 (December 15, 1910), p. 2; *TBM* 4.88 (June 15, 1911), p. 3; *TBM* 6.126 (February 1, 1913), p. 4.

[105] *TBM* 2.35 (April 1, 1909), p. 4; *TBM* 7.158 (July 1, 1914), p. 1.

[106] *TBM* 3.64 (June 15, 1910), p. 4.

[107] *TBM* 4.82 (March 1, 1911), p. 1; *TBM* 5.98 (November 15, 1911), p. 4.

[108] *TBM* 4.85 (May 1, 1911), p. 1.

[109] *TBM* 5.98 (November 15, 1911), p. 4.

[110] *TBM* 5.105 (March 1, 1912), p. 3.

[111] *TBM* 5.105 (March 1, 1912), p. 3.

[112] *TBM* 2.42 (July 15, 1909), p. 1.

[113] *TBM* 2.33 (March 1, 1909), p. 2.

ing in the Spirit', and 'singing in the Spirit' these days because people fail to let the indwelling Holy Spirit work in them both to will and to do of His good pleasure.[114]

To overcome 'the mists and darkness of the world ... you must be in the Spirit'.[115] Third, *The Bridegroom's Messenger* combined other images from Revelation with 'in the Spirit': 'we will be washed and be literality submerged in the Spirit, and will see the "river" of life flowing freely, and the "trees" of life bearing spontaneously, and the year round'.[116]

One testimony described a Pentecostal discerning the false testimony of someone who claimed to be the angel John saw in his vision on the Island of Patmos.[117] The paper offered a stark warning against this person, 'Search the word for yourself. Be not side-tracked or led into error, but listen to the voice of the Spirit, saying, "This is the way, walk ye in it." Do not be deceived by false teachers, but use your sanctified judgment and keep in the narrow way.'[118] The discernment process was opened to the entire community, urging: (1) search the scriptures, (2) listen to the voice of the Spirit who speaks scripturally, and (3) utilize a 'sanctified mind'. *The Bridegroom's Messenger* was observant to the role of Revelation upon the 'in the Spirit' phrases. While the paper would reference other NT passages[119] when mentioning 'in the Spirit',[120] one is able to observe that Revelation was a crucial influence.

If Anyone has an Ear

*The Seven Prophetic Messages*
In an editorial, Elizabeth Sexton explored the role of the Spirit in the seven churches and Christ walking among them:

---

[114] *TBM* 6.135 (June 15, 1913), p. 4. See also *TBM* 6.126 (February 1, 1913), p. 4.

[115] *TBM* 3.59 (April 1, 1910), p. 1.

[116] *TBM* 5.105 (March 1, 1912), p. 3.

[117] *TBM* 2.45 (September 1, 1909), p. 2.

[118] *TBM* 2.45 (September 1, 1909), p. 2.

[119] E.g. Eph. 6.18; Jude 20.

[120] See *TBM* 2.35 (April 1, 1909), p. 2; *TBM* 3.47 (October 1, 1909), p. 4. Cf. *TBM* 3.71 (October 1, 1910), p. 1; *TBM* 6.135 (June 15, 1913), p. 4.

We must acknowledge that He is in our midst, walking among the golden candlesticks, pruning, purging. He who moved among the golden candlesticks is moving in our midst now. We must recognize Him alone as head over all, and know no man after the flesh. The Spirit of God will teach us, if we keep low in love and humility before him.[121]

Much like the close relationship between the Spirit and Christ in Revelation, Sexton revealed a larger tendency in the paper to merge the actions of Christ with those of the Spirit. Another example is found in an exposition on Rev. 3.20 where the voice of the Spirit was combined with the actions of Christ: 'If the voice of the Spirit is heard, and the door opened, He will come in, just as sure as God cannot lie. If the heart has been cleansed by the blood, and the temple fully yielded to Him, there is nothing more certain in this world than the Spirit will assuredly come in (Rev. 3.20).'[122] In this testimony, it is difficult to determine if 'He' was the Spirit or Christ; in Revelation, it was Christ who promises to enter in after the door is opened and the Spirit who is speaking the words.[123] One might also wonder if this Pentecostal did not discern that hearing his voice was a reference to 'whoever has an ear, let them hear what the Spirit says to the churches', if so then discernment was the action of opening the door for the Spirit/Christ to enter. Finally, one surprising aspect of Revelation's pneumatology in *The Bridegroom's Messenger* was despite their overwhelming usage of the overcomers texts from Revelation 2–3, the paper rarely cited, quoted, or alluded to 'whoever has an ear, let them hear what the Spirit says to the churches'. One significant exception appears in a refutation of the Oneness doctrine:[124]

At the same time, let not a false sentimental charity close our eyes and deafen our ears to the solemn fact that God has pronounced a fearful penalty against those who add or take from His Holy Word. Rev. 22.17, 18. The Anti-trinitarians are guilty of both these

---

[121] *TBM* 2.23 (October 1, 1908), p. 1.

[122] *TBM* 4.82 (March 1, 1911), p. 4.

[123] *TBM* 4.82 (March 1, 1911), p. 4.

[124] See chapter 1 of this work for a short explanation of the Oneness dispute.

sins. He that hath ear [*sic*] let him hear what the spirit saith unto the churches. Rev. 2:6; Isa. 6:8-10.[125]

Perhaps, the rarity of the appearance of 'whoever has an ear, let them hear what the Spirit says to the churches' indicates a particular weight this text carried in *The Bridegroom's Messenger*, which might uncover their firmness concerning the trinitarian debate. In other words, *The Bridegroom's Messenger* was so confident in their pneumatic discernment of the Oneness issue that they pronounced their critique to be the words of the Spirit.

*Rev. 13.9-10*

*The Bridegroom's Messenger* referenced the hearing formula from Rev. 13.9-10 and offered a couple of interpretations.[126] On the one hand, some read Rev. 13.9-10 through a futuristic lens – represented by E.T. Slaybaugh – who concluded that it was a warning against anyone who will attempt to fight the beast or Antichrist in the 'tribulation'.[127] If the saints fight the beast, they will be killed, and therefore will need patience in the face of persecution. On the other hand, F. Bartleman– in the midst of World War I – was critical of anyone who used a sword:

> 'Deliver me from blood-guiltiness, O God' Ps. 51:14. Truly a stern warning for these present days, for 'whosoever hateth his brother is a murderer' (I Jno 3:15), and we cannot wish death of any man without hating him. Here is a supreme test on the church today, and multitudes are failing. 'If any man shall kill with the sword, with the sword must he be killed. He is the patience and the faith of the saints.' – Rev. 13:10. 'They loved not their lives even unto death.' – Rev. 12:11.[128]

Thus, although there were different interpretative presuppositions, both Slaybaugh and Bartleman discerned that having an ear to hear implied that the saints were to act nonviolently and have patience in the face of persecution and violence.

---

[125] *TBM* 9.181 (April 1, 1916), p. 1.

[126] *TBM* 5.99 (December 1, 1911), p. 3; *TBM* 8.168 (March 1, 1915), p. 1; *TBM* 8.175 (October 1, 1915), p. 4; *TBM* 9.176 (November 1, 1915), p. 4.

[127] *TBM* 7.161 (September 1, 1914), p. 4.

[128] *TBM* 8.168 (March 1, 1915), p. 1.

Discerning the Mark of the Beast

*The Bridegroom's Messenger* connected Christian identity to being sealed by God: 'I have the seal of God in my forehead, which is the baptism of the Holy Ghost, with Bible evidence of speaking in other tongues as the Spirit gives utterance'.[129] Being sealed of God suggested becoming baptized with the Holy Spirit, being (full/perfect) overcomers, and identifying with the Bride of Christ: 'Praise God, I am sealed unto the day of our redemption, for this is the seal with which we are sealed, even the Spirit of Truth'.[130]

Conversely, *The Bridegroom's Messenger* considered the mark of the beast as an identifier. First, from a futuristic presupposition, Slaybaugh proposed that the mark of the beast would appear during the time of the tribulation when the Anti-Christ would rule over the earth.[131] The followers of the beast would have to wear a 'badge' and would be identified as subjects of the beast.[132]

Second, F. Bartleman who during World War I wrote:

Under the control of the warring nations, also the souls of men are the mere property of their respective rulers. England is struggling for conscription also, and even the United States is beginning to threaten the same thing, a compulsory military service. That does not look much like the time 'when wars shall be no more.' There is to be no liberty of conscience for the individual. In fact, such will be the 'anti-Christ's' order. The way is being paved. Men must obey. They must take the 'mark of the beast.' They are to be simply the separate parts of a great state machine, to be used up as ordered for the wild beast's glory. The nations of the world are but wild beasts today.'[133]

Bartleman believed that the church had an obligation not to be involved in war. Believers were to either identify with heaven and were sealed by God or identified with country or state, participated in war, and were marked by the beast:

---

[129] *TBM* 3.49 (November 1, 1909), p. 3.

[130] *TBM* 2.27 (December 1, 1908), p. 3.

[131] See *TBM* 6.127 (February 15, 1913), p. 4; *TBM* 7.154 (May 1, 1914), p. 4; *TBM* 9.176 (November 1, 1915), p. 4.

[132] *TBM* 7.154 (May 1, 1914), p. 4.

[133] *TBM* 9.179 (February 1, 1916), p. 4.

German militarism and English imperialism together spell 'devilism.' 'England's menace' is not nearly so serious as the 'Christian menace,' the menace to the Christian spirit through hatred of the enemy in war, especially in England. London is plastered with the placard, 'Our war on German trade.' Thank God, the true Christian is neither 'made in Germany,' nor in England. We are 'made in heaven.' There is no 'mark of the beast' there.[134]

He added,

Nationalism forces men to take a spirit of patriotism and militarism. It is the 'mark of the beast.' The command is to murder, to destroy our fellowmen, to people hell [*sic*]. What will the church do about it? Will she side with the world, or with heaven? Will she vote to destroy men, or to save them?[135]

There was no middle ground when it came to discerning between those of God or those of the beast:

The church must ultimately take the 'mark of the beast,' the anti-Christ, or that of Christ fully. There must be complete separation to one or the other. She cannot 'serve two masters.' … The early church occupied a position of separation from nationalism completely, separated unto God. And so must the church of the end.[136]

A Christian in war or politics is pretty much in the position of old Lot in Sodom in the final analysis. They will throw him out. He must ultimately take the 'mark of the Beast' (Anti-Christ), or that of Christ'.[137]

Bartleman was not the only Pentecostal to discern the mark of the beast to be an identifying marker in *The Bridegroom's Messenger*. One missionary testified concerning those who were performing idol worship:

---

[134] *TBM* 8.168 (March 1, 1915), p. 1.

[135] *TBM* 9.180 (March 1, 1916), p. 4.

[136] *TBM* 9.179 (February 1, 1916), p. 4.

[137] *TBM* 9.180 (March 1, 1916), p. 4.

We were on the road this morning. Thousands of people were passing to and fro, marked with the mark of the beast; not satisfied with having it on their foreheads, they had marked chins, cheeks and other parts of the body, the whole thing a dreadful sight, and the air thick with influence of powers not of God.[138]

The mark of the beast was interpreted to be an identifying mark given to those who were doing evil whether participation in war or idol worship.

Third, a Pentecostal offered a narrative where she was at a store, and the sales clerk asked 'have you the mark?' The Pentecostal unsure of the meaning replied, no. The clerk then explained that those who had the mark could purchase anything in that store. The testimony concludes with the question, 'Is not the above, which is authentic, a fulfillment of Scripture? (See Rev. 13.16, 20.4)'.[139] This testimony uncovers an eschatological expectation, which many Pentecostals held that the end of time was near, but this testimony did not reveal an escapist attitude. This Pentecostal was not surprised that the time of the mark of the beast had already arrived.

Finally, these testimonies reveal a variety of interpretations of the mark of the beast. They discerned that the mark of the beast identified anyone who participated in evil activities. Any attempt to calculate the number of the beast, 666, was absent from *The Bridegroom's Messenger*. Their discernment was focused on the identities and activities of those who did or did not have the mark.

Babylon

*The Bridegroom's Messenger* included expositions on Revelation 17–18, including Babylon, the great whore, and the beast upon which she rides. Babylon was a diversely interpreted image in the paper where at times it was hard to discern whether the writer was reflecting on a physical, spiritual, futuristic, or present reality. First, E.T. Slaybaugh noted that whenever Revelation described a mystery, one would find an interpretation that followed. He appealed to the great whore of Revelation 17 because even though the woman was a mystery in Rev. 17.5, the angel in 17.7 provided an interpretation.[140] Second, working

---

138 *TBM* 4.94 (September 15, 1911), p. 3.
139 *TBM* 7.153 (April 15, 1914), p. 2.
140 *TBM* 6.125 (January 15, 1913), p. 4.

from another interpretative stream, Elizabeth Sexton anticipated the literal rebuilding of the city of Babylon, which she believed to be a sign of the coming of Jesus.[141] One interpreter remarked, 'Will Babylon be rebuilt? Personally I have not the slightest hesitation about the matter, especially as recent developments all seem to indicate that the city of Revelation 18 is about to come into existence'.[142] Third, others described the beginnings of World War I as: (1) the red horse coming forth and taking peace from the earth, (2) Babylon falling in a single hour, and (3) the work of demons where smoke came forth from the pit and locusts emerged upon the earth.[143] Fourth, some such as F. Bartleman used the imagery of Babylon to criticize the war and to discourage believers from participating in it. He wrote, '"Babylon is falling" both political and spiritual, and what the Christian needs to find is a way out'.[144] When critiquing nationalism and patriotism, Bartleman asked 'Is not this a daughter of "Mother Harlot"'.[145] Fifth, another stream of interpretation in *The Bridegroom's Messenger* found Babylon to be the church of Rome:

> No one would dispute the fact that Rome is, or rather will be, the hub of the 'Christian world' (but not of the true church of the Lord Jesus Christ.) The book of Revelation shows us once more in the end of this age Rome in the lead and having for a little time her power restored. The woman in Rev. 17 sitting upon a scarlet-colored beast, full of names of blasphemy, arrayed in purple and scarlet (the predominant colors in the Romish worship,) the woman drunken with the blood of the saints, and with the blood of the martyrs of Jesus, the woman having her seat upon the seven mountains and her name, Babylon the Great, the Mother of Harlots and abominations of the earth – that woman is Rome. And Rome will be the hub of apostatized Christendom.[146]

Sixth, others considered idealist interpretations of Babylon who was identified (1) as any 'wicked body of people ruling over the kings of

---

[141] *TBM* 4.74 (November 15, 1910), p. 1; *TBM* 9.187 (October 1, 1916), pp. 1, 4.

[142] *TBM* 5.113 (July 1, 1912), p. 4.

[143] *TBM* 8.167 (February 1, 1915), p. 2.

[144] *TBM* 8.168 (March 1, 1915), p. 1.

[145] *TBM* 9.180 (March 1, 1916), p. 4.

[146] *TBM* 4.87 (June 1, 1911), p. 4.

the earth (Rev. 17.5 and 18)',[147] or (2) as those who had a spirit of fanaticism in the church.[148] One common theme in all these interpretations was that Babylon represented a body of wicked people, and the readers were exhorted to come out of her.

Finally, when examining the beast that the great whore rides (Rev. 17.9-11), Slaybaugh integrated a futuristic expectation with a historical understanding: he deciphered the identity of the beasts through the lens of the past Roman emperors.[149] He uncovered that the 'sixth' was Domitian who ruled when John wrote Revelation, and Nerva – who succeeded Domitian – was the 'seventh'. Slaybaugh suggested that the 'eighth' would be one the seven Roman emperors who will be resurrected and will return to earth to become 'the Antichrist'. Based on the evidence of the sword wound, Slaybaugh proposed that the 'eighth' would be Nero.[150]

Thus, Babylon became a diversely interpreted theme in *The Bridegroom's Messenger*. It offered interpretations that were futuristic, contextual, historical, literal, and spiritual. The mystery was open to discernment from the entire community. The community needed wisdom and the mind of the Spirit, which could only be given by the seven Spirits to discern the identity of Babylon and to come out of her.

## Discerning the Mysteries

### *Revelation 1*
E.T. Slaybaugh noted that Revelation was a 'mystery revealed', which for him meant that any 'mystery' in Revelation would be revealed in the text. Interpreters in *The Bridegroom's Messenger* usually discerned the mystery of the seven stars to be the messengers or ministers of the seven churches.[151] Slaybaugh, affirming this interpretation, also connected the seven stars of Rev. 1.20 with the twelve stars in the crown of the women clothed with the sun (Rev. 12.1):

---

[147] *TBM* 7.159 (August 1, 1914), p. 4.

[148] *TBM* 5.117 (September 1, 1912), p. 4.

[149] *TBM* 9.176 (November 1, 1915), p. 4.

[150] *TBM* 9.176 (November 1, 1915), p. 4.

[151] *TBM* 1.4 (December 15, 1907), p. 1; *TBM* 6.125 (January 15, 1913), p. 4; *TBM* 7.159 (August 1, 1914), p. 4.

By carefully considering Rev. 1:20, we learn that the seven ministers (see Geek [*sic*]) of the seven churches are represented by the
seven stars in the right hand of Jesus: and, therefore, if prime
ministers of the body of Christ are represented by stars, it is strikingly significant that these twelve stars upon the head of the
women are a sign of the 'twelve apostles of the Lamb'.[152]

Thus, the mystery of the seven stars was revealed by Jesus and eluci-
dated in the image of the women clothed with the sun.[153]

### Revelation 10

L.V. Kenny commented on the mystery of Rev. 10.7 that was pronounced by the mighty angel and found the mystery to be revealed
with the seventh trumpet in Revelation 11. She believed that the
mighty angel of Revelation 10 was the same angel who sounded the
seventh trumpet. Thus, the seventh trumpet – the mystery of Rev.
10.7 – represents the resurrection of the dead, the ending the great
tribulation, and the inauguration of the millennial reign of Jesus.[154]

### Pneumatically

*The Bridegroom's Messenger* offered one exposition on Rev. 11.8 by E.T.
Slaybaugh. Reading primarily through a futuristic lens, he interpreted
the two witnesses as two incarnate HB prophets who will appear during the tribulation period and will witness to the people of Israel,
while bringing judgment upon the forces of the antichrist. When discerning the meaning of Rev. 11.8, Slaybaugh wrote:

> They are as wicked as the Sodomites and Egyptians (and for this
> reason Jerusalem is 'spiritually called Sodom and Egypt' – V. 8.;
> and in a few days sudden destruction shall overtake them as it
> overtook the Sodomites and Egyptians; for 'after three days an
> [*sic*] a half the spirit of life from God' enters into them, and they
> ascend up to heaven in a cloud (Rev. 11:11-12).[155]

In this excerpt πνευματικῶς was translated 'spiritually', representing the spiritual position of Israel. He interpreted it through an HB

---

[152] *TBM* 7.159 (August 1, 1914), p. 4.

[153] *TBM* 6.125 (January 15, 1913), p. 4.

[154] *TBM* 5.99 (December 1, 1911), p. 4.

[155] *TBM* 7.155 (May 15, 1914), p. 4.

*[handwritten margin note, left side: but they still ascend to heaven?]*

*[handwritten mark in left margin next to "10.7" paragraph: ✗]*

lens where the evil condition of Israel and their judgments will be like Sodom and Egypt.

Spirit and the Bride

The Spirit and the Bride appeared in *The Bridegroom's Messenger* in contexts that imply participation of the community with the Spirit:

> If the Spirit of God says 'Come,' it cannot be a meaningless empty word, but a real, genuine spiritual call. And does it mean any the less than this for the Birde [*sic*] to say 'Come?' Verily no. It shall be as genuine on the part of the Bride as on the part of the Spirit, with the supernatural power of God back of it. How many of us are willing to heed the injunction 'And let him that heareth say Come,' and thus have the privilege with the Spirit and the Bride of sharing His highest honour and glory when he comes.[156]

Thus, once again the church had the opportunity to participate with the Spirit to fulfill their role as the Bride by calling out with the Spirit, 'come'.

## Summary

*The Bridegroom's Messenger* offered a robust interpretation of pneumatic discernment. They believed that the Spirit was an integral part of their lives. Understanding, discernment, wisdom, the mind of the Spirit, and knowledge were all given by the Spirit. One needed to be 'in the Spirit' to hear what the Spirit was saying to the church. The discernment process was open to the entire community, and they were urged to search the scriptures, listen to the voice of the Spirit, and to utilize a sanctified mind.

The richest contributions of the paper concerning Revelation's pneumatology occurred in contexts of pneumatic discernment. Perhaps the best example was Hubbell who exhorted the church to pray for the eyes of the Lamb – the seven Spirits. Only if they received the seven Spirits would they receive perfect knowledge and wisdom. Otherwise, the church would only be utilizing a lesser measure of wisdom. Exposition on the four living creatures, who represented the perfect overcomers, built upon this theme because they had received

*four living creatures = four perfect overcomers*

---

[156] *TBM* 6.123 (December 15, 1912), p. 4. See *TBM* 8.165 (December 1, 1914), p. 4.

*[handwritten: Perfect wisdom]*

perfect wisdom and knowledge; they had access to the seven Spirits
– the seven eyes of the Lamb.

Other significant contributions include discernment of nonviolence in the face of persecution (Rev. 13.9-10). The dualism found
between those who were marked by the beast because they participated in the war or idol worship and those who were sealed by God.
The most diversely interpreted image in *The Bridegroom's Messenger* was
Babylon. Babylon represented evil in their world, and the church
needed wisdom to discern the evil surrounding them.

Therefore, *The Bridegroom's Messenger* described the Spirit as being
involved in their discernment, knowledge, wisdom, and interpretation. The process of discernment was open to the entire community.
The inclusivity of the paper allowed for a diversity of interpretations
that at times disagreed with each other. For example, the editors of
*The Bridegroom's Messenger* wrote a note that they did not agree with
every comment made by E.T. Slaybaugh,[157] but they continued to
provide him space. The paper itself seems to provide a model of the
process of discernment of some early Pentecostals. *The Bridegroom's
Messenger* desired to provide a space for anyone to testify because the
editors of the paper trusted that the Spirit would be their eyes, offering wisdom and discernment to them and allowing them to see the
truth.

## The Whole Truth

*The Whole Truth* was established in 1907 and published by the Church
of God in Christ.[158] Unfortunately, only a single issue of this periodical has survived from October 1911. This extant issue offers a
glimpse into these Pentecostals' belief of the Spirit's role in their lives
and a brief look into their interpretations of Revelation. In this one
issue, language from Revelation appeared, including: 'in the Spirit',
'let anyone who has an ear ...', overcomers, the Lamb, and the lake
of fire.[159]

---

[157] See the editor's note in *TBM* 6.137 (August 1, 1911), p. 4.

[158] Alexander, *Pentecostal Healing*, pp. 111-12.

[159] For quotes and references of Revelation, see *TWT* 4.4 (October 1911), pp.
2-3.

## Pneumatic Discernment

The issue is full of references to the Spirit as their teacher and guide. *The Whole Truth* seemed to hold a worldview that integrated the actions of the Spirit with the life of the community. The Spirit led their worship services,[160] and the Spirit would speak and teach through individuals, 'The Holy Ghost, through Elder C.H. Mason began to teach great things'.[161] Offering summaries of the revival services, one testified, 'The Spirit begins to teach us to wait on the Lord. Singing through the pastor, Elder C.H. Mason.'[162] There was a dynamic relationship between the Spirit and ministers, 'Repentance is the message of the Spirit to the people tonight, for the time is at hand. Sermon by the pastor.'[163]

The Spirit provided wisdom, knowledge, and discernment to the community. The Spirit 'convinced all, and made us know that he had ordained perfect praise out of the mouths of babes'.[164] When offering guidance, the Spirit would use those in the community, 'As the Spirit spoke through Elder E.R. Driver many were made to see the light'.[165] J. Bowe testified, 'Many sightseers and game-makers came to the meeting, but the great power and wisdom, through the Holy Spirit of God, disappointed them all and bound and rebuked the wicked spirits of unbelief and sent them away and brought life of liberty, joy and gladness to many precious souls'.[166] Another testimony added, 'The Lord used little Brother John McTee in every service either in preaching or teaching the word. It was rich, without mixture, simple, child-like wisdom'.[167] Thus, these testimonies suggest a dualism between the wisdom of the world and the wisdom of the Spirit. Those who did not have the wisdom of the Spirit had worldly wisdom. The wisdom of the Spirit was comprised of characteristics such as life, liberty, joy, gladness, light, belief, and it was described as being child-like.

---

[160] *TWT* 4.4 (October 1911), p. 1.

[161] *TWT* 4.4 (October 1911), p. 3.

[162] *TWT* 4.4 (October 1911), p. 1.

[163] *TWT* 4.4 (October 1911), p. 3.

[164] *TWT* 4.4 (October 1911), p. 4.

[165] *TWT* 4.4 (October 1911), p. 1.

[166] *TWT* 4.4 (October 1911), p. 4.

[167] *TWT* 4.4 (October 1911), p. 4.

## The Spirit and Discernment in Revelation

'In the Spirit' and If Anyone Has an Ear

Many references to 'in the Spirit' are found in this one issue of *The Whole Truth*, which encompassed: prayer and supplication, becoming 'deep in the Spirit', being 'taught in the Spirit', and 'singing in the Spirit'.[168] Hymns received in the Spirit included calls to hear and to repent, which resembles the language in Revelation 1–3. C.H. Mason offered numerous occurrences where he asked the readers to hear the Spirit:

> Hear him while he calls
> Hear him while he calls;
> Oh ye sinners, while you wait,
> Hear him while he calls.[169]

Or such as this 'new song' while 'in the Spirit':

> O repent, O sinner,
> Repent just now;
> The Voice of the Lord is calling you;
> Repent of all thou hast done.[170]

This hymn not only offers an example of being 'in the Spirit', but also that the Spirit offered the wisdom of Jesus. This hymn was perhaps influenced by Revelation evidenced by its emphasis upon Jesus, the Lamb, and the attribution of wisdom, glory, and honor to the Lamb. Other hymns received 'in the Spirit' included:

> Hear ye the word of the Lord
> O hear ye the word of the Lord,
> He speaks to you now in his word;
> O hear you the word of the Lord.[171]

Jesus was attributed wisdom from a hymn while 'in the Spirit':

> Jesus, my Savior, there's wisdom in him;
> Glory and honor to the Lamb!

---

[168] *TWT* 4.4 (October 1911), pp. 1, 4.
[169] *TWT* 4.4 (October 1911), p. 1.
[170] *TWT* 4.4 (October 1911), p. 3.
[171] *TWT* 4.4 (October 1911), p. 1.

Power of Jesus, coming the more
Into the souls of men.[172]

There were also a few appearances of 'whoever has an ear …':

> The Lord used Pastor D.W. Jones on Sunday of meeting in preach-
> ing from the text, 'Train up a child in the way it should go, and
> when it is old it will not depart therefrom.' It was pointed and
> edifying to all who had ears to hear what the Spirit said to the
> Church.[173]

This testimony expresses that the Spirit was dynamically involved in
the minister's sermon, while opening up discernment to the hearers.
It was possible to hear a sermon without hearing what the Spirit was
saying.

### Summary

This one issue of *The Whole Truth* offers a small picture of the spirituality of these early Pentecostals. The paper was filled with 'in the
Spirit' language. Singing, preaching, prayer, teaching, wisdom, and
knowledge were all performed 'in the Spirit' and given to the community by the Spirit. Revelation appeared to be a central influence of
this paper. The numerous quotations of 'in the Spirit' alongside mention of 'whoever has an ear …', and the attribution of wisdom to the
Lamb all confirm the influence of Revelation on these believers.

## The Church of God Evangel

*The Evening Light and Church of God Evangel* – later named *The Church
of God Evangel* – was first published on March 1, 1910, edited by A.J.
Tomlinson, and was the primary denominational publication of the
Church of God (Cleveland, TN). Being a denominational publication, *The Church of God Evangel* publicized institutional doctrine and
teaching. Revelation was referred to and engaged at numerous points
throughout the literature.[174]

---

[172] *TWT* 4.4 (October 1911), p. 1.

[173] *TWT* 4.4 (October 1911), p. 4.

[174] For explicit references and quotations of Revelation, see *COGE* 1.1 (March
1, 1910), p. 1; *COGE* 1.2 (March 15, 1910), pp. 2-3; *COGE* 1.4 (April 15, 1910), p.
3; *COGE* 1.7 (June 1, 1910), pp. 1-3, 6; *COGE* 1.8 (June 15, 1910), p. 2; *COGE*
1.12 (August 15, 1910), pp. 3, 6; *COGE* 1.15 (October 1, 1910), pp. 1, 5; *COGE*

## Pneumatic Discernment

*The Church of God Evangel* demonstrated a wide belief that God gave knowledge, wisdom, and guidance to the church.[175] When the church faced issues of discernment, they believed that the Word and the

---

1.16 (October 15, 1910), p. 8; *COGE* 1.17 (November 1, 1910), p. 5; *COGE* 1.18 (November 15, 1910), p. 2; *COGE* 1.20 (December 15, 1910), pp. 1, 4-5; *COGE* 3.14 (September 15, 1912), p. 3; *COGE* 5.5 (January 31, 1914), p. 6; *COGE* 5.9 (February 28, 1914), p. 7; *COGE* 5.11 (March 14, 1914), p. 5; *COGE* 5.12 (March 21, 1914), p. 6; *COGE* 5.15 (April 11, 1914), p. 2; *COGE* 5.23 (June 6, 1914), pp. 4-5; *COGE* 5.24 (June 13, 1914), pp. 7-8; *COGE* 5.25 (June 20, 1914), pp. 5, 7; *COGE* 5.26 (June 27, 1914), p. 7; *COGE* 5.28 (July 11, 1914), p. 7; *COGE* 5.29 (July 18, 1914), p. 7; *COGE* 5.34 (August 22, 1914), pp. 2-3; *COGE* 5.35 (August 29, 1914), p. 1; *COGE* 5.39 (September 26, 1914), p. 6; *COGE* 5.41 (October 10, 1914), pp. 4-5; *COGE* 6.3 (January 16, 1915), p. 3; *COGE* 6.4 (January 23, 1915), p. 1; *COGE* 6.6 (February 6, 1915), p. 4; *COGE* 6.19 (May 8, 1915), p. 2; *COGE* 6.20 (May 15, 1915), p. 4; *COGE* 6.21 (May 22, 1915), p. 2; *COGE* 6.25 (June 19, 1915), p. 3; *COGE* 6.26 (June 26, 1915), pp. 3-4; *COGE* 6.28 (July 10, 1915), p. 1; *COGE* 6.29 (July 17, 1915), p. 1; *COGE* 6.30 (July 24, 1915), p. 1; *COGE* 6.32 (August 7, 1915), p. 3; *COGE* 6.37 (September 11, 1915), p. 1; *COGE* 6.38 (September 18, 1915), p. 3; *COGE* 6.39 (September 25, 1915), p. 1; *COGE* 6.40 (October 2, 1915), p. 3; *COGE* 6.46 (November 13, 1915), p. 4; *COGE* 6.49 (December 4, 1915), pp. 1-3; *COGE* 6.50 (December 11, 1915), pp. 1, 4; *COGE* 7.8 (February 19, 1916), p. 1; *COGE* 7.11 (March 11, 1916), p. 1; *COGE* 7.13 (March 25, 1916), p. 4; *COGE* 7.20 (May 13, 1916), p. 4; *COGE* 7.23 (June 3, 1916), p. 2; *COGE* 7.28 (July 8, 1916), pp. 3-4; *COGE* 7.29 (July 15, 1916), p. 4; *COGE* 7.30 (July 22, 1916), pp. 2, 4; *COGE* 7.32 (August 5, 1916), pp. 3-4; *COGE* 7.36 (September 2, 1916), p. 1; *COGE* 7.39 (September 23, 1916), p. 2; *COGE* 7.41 (October 4, 1916), p. 1; *COGE* 7.47 (November 18, 1916), p. 4; *COGE* 7.50 (December 9, 1916), p. 4; *COGE* 8.2 (January 3, 1917), p. 1; *COGE* 8.10 (March 10, 1917), p. 2; *COGE* 8.11 (March 17, 1917), p. 4; *COGE* 8.13 (March 31, 1917), p. 3; *COGE* 8.14 (April 14, 1917), pp. 3-4; *COGE* 8.15 (April 21, 1917), p. 2; *COGE* 8.16 (April 28, 1917), pp. 1-2; *COGE* 8.18 (May 12, 1917), pp. 1, 4; *COGE* 8.21 (June 2, 1917), p. 4; *COGE* 8.23 (June 16, 1917), p. 1; *COGE* 8.26 (July 7, 1917), p. 1; *COGE* 8.28 (July 21, 1917), p. 2; *COGE* 8.30 (August 4, 1917), p. 1; *COGE* 8.31 (August 11, 1917), p. 1; *COGE* 8.33 (August 25, 1917), p. 4; *COGE* 8.35 (September 8, 1917), pp. 1-2; *COGE* 8.36 (September 15, 1917), p. 3; *COGE* 8.40 (October 13, 1917), p. 1; *COGE* 8.44 (November 10, 1917), p. 1; *COGE* 9.2 (January 12, 1918), p. 3; *COGE* 9.6 (February 9, 1918), p. 1; *COGE* 9.11 (March 16, 1918), pp. 1, 4; *COGE* 9.12 (March 23, 1918), p. 3; *COGE* 9.19 (May 11, 1918), p. 1; *COGE* 9.22 (June 1, 1918), pp. 1-3; *COGE* 9.23 (June 8, 1918), p. 1; *COGE* 9.26 (June 29, 1918), pp. 1-2, 4; *COGE* 9.30 (July 27, 1918), p. 1; *COGE* 9.32 (August 10, 1918), p. 2; *COGE* 9.35 (August 31, 1918), pp. 1, 3-4; *COGE* 9.36 (September 7, 1918), p. 2; *COGE* 9.40 (October 5, 1918), p. 2; *COGE* 9.41 (October 12, 1918), pp. 1-2; *COGE* 9.42 (October 19, 1918), p. 2; *COGE* 9.44 (November 2, 1918), pp. 3-4; *COGE* 9.45 (November 9, 1918), p. 1; *COGE* 9.46 (November 16, 1918), pp. 1, 3; *COGE* 9.47 (November 23, 1918), p. 3; *COGE* 9.48 (November 30, 1918), p. 2; *COGE* 9.50 (December 14, 1918), p. 4; *COGE* 9.51 (December 21, 1918), p. 4.

[175] *COGE* 1.1 (March 1, 1910), p. 4; *COGE* 1.11 (August 1, 1910), p. 6; *COGE* 8.13 (March 31, 1917), p. 2.

Holy Spirit must settle the issue.[176] Sam C. Perry considered that the Holy Spirit was the 'only one safeguard' and under the Spirit's guidance there is 'a fuller understanding of God's plan for us, as revealed in His Word'.[177] The Word and Spirit were cooperative in guiding the church, 'The Word of God is given as a guide through this world of darkness and error. The Holy Ghost is given to empower us and bring us through as conquerers [*sic*].'[178] There was 'no friction nor crosses' between the Word and Spirit because the Spirit 'always guides, instructs or teaches in perfect harmony with Christ the Head'.[179] The church participated with the Spirit and Word, 'the human and the Divine are co-workers … there is a blending of the two'.[180] *The Church of God Evangel* cautioned readers to be intentional in discerning works that were falsely attributed to the Spirit:

> It is a very difficult matter however, to distinguish always the work of the Holy Spirit through the human, from the efforts of the human without the Spirit. Often the human runs ahead of the Holy Spirit, and speaks, acts and manifests what is contrary to the Holy Spirit. Just at this point and in this error many simple hearted, honest followers of Jesus have been led astray.[181]

The paper exhorted that the church needed 'deep crucifixion of the natural and discernment given of the Holy Ghost'.[182] The Spirit did not always guide the church to 'pleasant places'.[183] Error never originated from the Spirit of Truth but from influences that sway the human mind,[184] 'if we refuse His plan for guidance He is under no obligation to do it'.[185] Tomlinson remarked that error and false teaching result when the church refuses to 'be quiet while He instructs'.[186]

---

[176] *COGE* 5.48 (December 5, 1914), p. 3.

[177] *COGE* 5.1 (January 3, 1914), p. 6.

[178] *COGE* 7.3 (January 15, 1916), p. 3. See also *COGE* 1.14 (September 15, 1910), p. 4.

[179] *COGE* 5.21 (May 23, 1914), p. 2.

[180] *COGE* 1.2 (March 15, 1910), p. 5.

[181] *COGE* 6.41 (October 9, 1915), p. 2.

[182] *COGE* 1.2 (March 15, 1910), p. 5.

[183] *COGE* 8.49 (December 15, 1917), p. 1.

[184] *COGE* 5.18 (May 2, 1914), p. 3. See *COGE* 8.1 (January 18, 1917), p. 3; *COGE* 8.13 (March 31, 1917), p. 2.

[185] *COGE* 5.20 (May 16, 1914), p. 2.

[186] *COGE* 6.51 (December 18, 1915), p. 1.

The Spirit of Wisdom[187] offers wisdom to the church.[188] Tomlinson believed that 'Wisdom is one of the main drive wheels of success for the Church of God',[189] and was necessary for God's ministers and members.[190] The paper often created a dualism between the wisdom of God[191] and worldly wisdom, 'Jesus has given the church wisdom, but many seek worldly wisdom instead of Jesus'.[192] Anyone who lacked wisdom would make mistakes,[193] and 'many suffer and bring on unnecessary persecution for the lack of wisdom'.[194] In one issue of the paper, Tomlinson asked the church to pray so that God would stop the Great War, and called for 'a humble confession of guilt and lack of wisdom'.[195] Receiving wisdom was contingent upon the actions of individuals who were urged to seek wisdom through prayer, 'Pray for wisdom – 'Pray! Pray! Pray! Earnestly for the gift of wisdom.'[196]

[187] *COGE* 5.20 (May 16, 1914), p. 6.
[188] *COGE* 7.27 (July 1, 1916), p. 1.
[189] *COGE* 6.34 (August 21, 1915), p. 1.
[190] *COGE* 7.39 (September 23, 1916), p. 3; *COGE* 8.29 (July 28, 1917), p. 3.
[191] God had infinite wisdom, see *COGE* 5.11 (March 14, 1914), p. 1; *COGE* 5.29 (July 18, 1914), p. 1; *COGE* 5.34 (August 22, 1914), p. 1; *COGE* 5.40 (October 4, 1914), p. 1; *COGE* 5.49 (December 12, 1914), p. 4; *COGE* 5.51 (October 10, 1914), p. 2; *COGE* 6.16 (April 17, 1915), p. 1; *COGE* 6.51 (December 18, 1915), p. 1; *COGE* 6.52 (December 25, 1915), p. 1; *COGE* 7.14 (April 1, 1916), p. 1; *COGE* 7.22 (May 27, 1916), p. 3; *COGE* 8.11 (March 17, 1917), p. 1; *COGE* 8.25 (June 30, 1917), p. 1; *COGE* 8.32 (August 18, 1917), p. 1; *COGE* 9.42 (October 19, 1918), p. 2; *COGE* 9.45 (November 9, 1918), p. 2; *COGE* 9.51 (December 21, 1918), p. 1.
[192] *COGE* 1.1 (March 1, 1910), p. 8.
[193] *COGE* 6.15 (April 10, 1915), p. 3.
[194] *COGE* 6.48 (November 27, 1915), p. 4.
[195] *COGE* 5.39 (September 26, 1914), p. 3.
[196] *COGE* 5.5 (January 31, 1914), p. 3. See also *COGE* 5.49 (December 12, 1914), p. 1; *COGE* 6.23 (June 5, 1915), p. 1; *COGE* 6.34 (August 21, 1915), p. 1; *COGE* 7.29 (July 15, 1916), p. 2; *COGE* 7.33 (August 12, 1916), p. 2.

## The Spirit and Discernment in Revelation

'In the Spirit'

'In the Spirit' appeared in *The Church of God Evangel* to describe experiences such as being carried away,[197] walking,[198] singing,[199] speaking,[200] fellowship,[201] union with God,[202] resurrected,[203] or buried[204] 'in the Spirit'.[205] Two testimonies explained visionary experiences much akin to John's experience 'in the Spirit' from Revelation. First, Nellie Pettitt explained that she was carried away 'in the Spirit' and heard, 'Look up'; she described that 'a mountain appeared in view, on top of which was a beautiful white city with a wall around it. There was a beautiful white road, which was very straight, leading to the city. Jesus was standing in the road, just outside the city, beckoning with His hand to come.'[206] Another testified that a member of the church was carried away 'in the Spirit' and explained that the Spirit began to speak through this individual warning and calling for repentance: 'Some one is rejecting the Spirit the last time'.[207] M.S. Lemons considered Rev. 1.9-10, 'If you will read Revelation you will find out what John saw and heard when he was in the Lord's day. This simply means he (John) was carried over into this day, or rather had a vision of "The Lord's Day," and the things that were to transpire during that day.'[208] F.J. Lee commented that 'the Lord's Day' was a reference to

---

[197] *COGE* 1.1 (March 1, 1910), p. 7; *COGE* 5.38 (September 19, 1914), p. 8.

[198] *COGE* 7.7 (February 12, 1916), p. 3; *COGE* 9.5 (February 2, 1918), p. 3; *COGE* 9.6 (February 9, 1918), p. 2.

[199] *COGE* 5.39 (September 26, 1914), p. 5; *COGE* 9.40 (October 5, 1918), p. 3.

[200] *COGE* 8.37 (September 22, 1917), p. 2.

[201] *COGE* 9.8 (January 19, 1918), p. 3.

[202] *COGE* 8.17 (May 5, 1917), p. 3.

[203] *COGE* 1.9 (July 1, 1910), p. 4.

[204] *COGE* 1.9 (July 1, 1910), p. 4.

[205] For quotes of 'in the Spirit' from Revelation, see *COGE* 1.5 (May 1, 1910), p. 6; *COGE* 1.7 (June 1, 1910), p. 3; *COGE* 1.11 (August 1, 1910), p. 6; *COGE* 5.28 (July 11, 1914), p. 7; *COGE* 5.43 (October 24, 1914), p. 6; *COGE* 8.13 (April 7, 1917), p. 3; *COGE* 9.9 (March 2, 1918), p. 1; *COGE* 9.50 (December 14, 1918), p. 3.

[206] *COGE* 1.1 (March 1, 1910), p. 7.

[207] *COGE* 5.38 (September 19, 1914), p. 8.

[208] *COGE* 1.2 (March 15, 1910), p. 2.

Sunday and concluded, 'All writers refer to it as Sunday in the century following the Apostolic times. Brit. 22:653'.[209]

## The Seven Prophetic Messages and If Anyone Has an Ear

A.J. Tomlinson examined the false teaching of Balaam as part of a multiple issue editorial, where Balaam's teaching includes eating food sacrificed to idols and committing fornication.[210] Tomlinson warned that some honest people believed that they were following the Spirit's guidance, but were, in fact, confusing the Spirit with the spirit of Balaam. Tomlinson directed the church to seek the gifts of the Spirit – wisdom and discernment.[211] On another occasion and looking at the false teaching of Jezebel in Thyatira, Tomlinson observed that Jezebel's false teaching was condemned not the prophetess Jezebel, a woman, for teaching.[212] J.J. Culpepper testified that he attended a meeting within another denomination without praying and seeking the Lord. At the meeting, the speaker cursed at the crowd, and Culpepper commented 'I had done got the poison and was under condemnation because I had disobeyed the Word of the Lord, "Come out from among them, and be ye separate"'.[213] Culpepper then quoted Rev. 2.2 and said that he 'repented and fasted and prayed and God forgave me'.[214] In a final testimony, Mrs. W.B. Bell invited the readers to examine themselves, check their ears, and hear Rev. 2.29.[215]

## Discerning the Mark of the Beast

Although this publication rarely used the terminology of being sealed by God as an identity marker of the saints,[216] *The Church of God Evangel* did offer some discussion on the mark of the beast. A.J. Tomlinson read the bestial texts against his contemporary context, especially when commenting on World War I. Tomlinson offered a few general

---

[209] *COGE* 5.28 (July 11, 1914), p. 7.
[210] *COGE* 5.34 (August 22, 1914), p. 2.
[211] *COGE* 5.35 (August 29, 1914), p. 3.
[212] *COGE* 6.37 (September 11, 1915), p. 1.
[213] *COGE* 7.28 (July 8, 1916), p. 4.
[214] *COGE* 7.28 (July 8, 1916), p. 4.
[215] *COGE* 6.49 (December 4, 1915), p. 2.
[216] *COGE* 1.6 (May 15, 1910), p. 1; *COGE* 5.22 (May 30, 1914), p. 5.

(used carefully)

conflict here between U.S. as beast and chosen by God

observations concerning the book of Revelation: (1) it was a 'wonderful book', (2) it used 'figurative language',[217] (3) it was a 'difficult book' to understand, (4) it contained 'hidden mysteries', and (5) belonged to the 'last days' but was being fulfilled in their contemporary setting. Tomlinson read Revelation through the lens of Rev. 1.8, observing that 'there is something good for us' in each text of Revelation even 'the subject before us – The Mark of the Beast'.[218] Tomlinson responded to the fear that some had already received the mark unknowingly by supporting the government's war efforts, 'Some are afraid to accept too much and sign too many papers for the government for fear they will accept the mark of the beast'.[219] Tomlinson wrote, 'the millions of soldiers on the battlefields are not there from choice, but because of exercise of the authority',[220] which he believed imitated the authority of the beast from Revelation. Tomlinson proposed that a nation's authority exposed in World War I was a crucial indicator of the beast:

> The revelator tells us that to this beast is given power to make war with the saints and overcome them. This war is already on. The saints are now being overcome and forced into army camps against their will. They are overcome now in this sense. The exercise of authority is overcoming them. Mothers and wives are being overcome as their sons and husbands are dragged off to war contrary to their wishes. This prophecy is already being fulfilled in a measure.[221]

Tomlinson concluded that the mark of the beast would appear when the saints are overcome (the 'time of preparation').[222] Tomlinson con-

---

[217] *COGE* 9.6 (February 9, 1918), p. 1. Tomlinson adds, 'There are three classes of interpreters of this book. One class wants to make it all figurative and apply it according to their knowledge of things. Another class wants to make it literal and apply it to a time they will never see. A third class claims it is both figurative and literal and that it is its own interpreter as to what is figurative and what is literal.'

[218] *COGE* 9.6 (February 9, 1918), p. 1.

[219] *COGE* 9.4 (January 26, 1918), p. 1. Tomlinson concluded, 'Render to Caesar the things that are Caesar's, and to God the things that are God's' because 'we are not responsible for what the tax is used'.

[220] *COGE* 9.6 (February 9, 1918), p. 1.

[221] *COGE* 9.6 (February 9, 1918), p. 1.

[222] *COGE* 8.40 (October 13, 1917), p. 1.

templated a practical issue of food cards during World War I, 'LON-
DON IS BEWILDERED BY COMPULSORY RATION PLAN …
Food Cards For Every One, Young and Old, Rich and Poor, Will be
Required'.[223] Apparently, some members of the church had specu-
lated whether these food cards were the mark of the beast, and Tom-
linson responded:

> I will say that it is well enough for us to be on our guard. I do not
> say this is the mark, but I do say that the spirit of the anti-christ is
> already working and it is becoming emboldened so as to march
> into our own towns and cities and commanding prices and placing
> a limit to the amount you purchase … [it] has too much the ap-
> pearance of it for me to want to wear a tag in order to purchase
> food.[224]

On another occasion, Tomlinson was hesitant to pinpoint the identity
of the mark of the beast:

> The time is ripening for the literal revelation of the anti-christ or
> the beast and people who do not love the truth as given in God's
> Word expose themselves to delusion and deception. I would not
> say just what the 'Mark of the Beast' is, but evidently it is some-
> thing that has the appearance of offering a benefit to those who
> receive it … The offer of the mark of the beast will have such
> attractions and give such imparting knowledge and wisdom that
> many many will be ensnared in its coils.[225]

He asked the church to pray for God's wisdom when considering the
possibility that the church was giving indirect support to the war effort by purchasing necessities such as food or clothing that contained
increased taxes used to fund participation in World War I.[226]

Despite Tomlinson's overall caution toward precisely identifying
the mark of the beast, at one point he did consider the resemblance
between the mark of the beast and labor unions, fraternal societies,
associations, and lodges.[227] He noted that each offered better standing

---

[223] *COGE* 9.6 (February 9, 1918), p. 1.

[224] *COGE* 9.6 (February 9, 1918), p. 1.

[225] *COGE* 5.15 (April 11, 1914), p. 2.

[226] *COGE* 9.4 (January 26, 1918), p. 1.

[227] *COGE* 5.15 (April 11, 1914), p. 3; *COGE* 8.26 (July 7, 1917), p. 1; *COGE*
8.40 (October 13, 1917), p. 1.

*handshake - organizations = antichrist* [handwritten]

in the world, and the inside workings of these groups presented an opportunity to make one wiser or a better citizen among businesses or friends from a social and financial point of view. He saw a similarity between the handshake or 'grip' and the mark in that 'the unwritten work is placed in their minds and thus they are joining in with the antichrist company whether these are the real marks of the beast or not for all such organizations are antichristian in their origins'.[228]

*? number and # God's way of controlling this? 101* [handwritten, right margin]

Finally, Tomlinson advised his readers that one could only escape this mark if they were in close touch with the Lord. He warned that one's safety was in 'the hollow of God's hand, and the only way you can get in there is to hear His voice and obey and follow Him',[229] and that 'to be in close touch with the Lord and obtain from Him knowledge and understanding, and revelations if need be for protection'.[230] He believed 'to the Church of God belongs knowledge and wisdom. We must know God will let us know.'[231] He warned his readers that they should keep from the very appearance of the mark of the beast. Tomlinson was restrained when commenting on the mark of the beast and allowed Revelation to speak to his own context. While he wanted to avoid offering firm identifications of the mark of the beast, Tomlinson was willing to provide some possible associations in his context that represented characteristics of the mark and the beast. He suggested that Revelation criticized the authority that governments and militaries had over their people and was convinced that the activities of countries involved in War World I resembled those of the beast.

*In this time - not ours* [handwritten, left margin]

*Doesn't this contradict our command to honor govt.?* [handwritten]

Furthermore, E.W. Simpson discussed the satanic trinity – Satan, the beast, and false prophet – where he interpreted the beast from Revelation and Daniel to symbolize a government 'composed of evil spirits that came from heaven with Satan and have power to thansform [*sic*] themselves into angels of light and become traps to catch the souls of people'.[232] The beast was the

> body of evil into different things as gods of gold and silver, houses and land, fine church edifices, dress, jewelry, theater, circus,

---

[228] *COGE* 5.15 (April 11, 1914), p. 3.

[229] *COGE* 5.15 (April 11, 1914), p. 3.

[230] *COGE* 9.6 (February 9, 1918), p. 1.

[231] *COGE* 9.6 (February 9, 1918), p. 1.

[232] *COGE* 5.41 (October 10, 1914), p. 4.

picture shows, bad literature, dime novels, tobacco and snuff, whiskey, and soft drinks, pride, pleasure seeking, etc. making the people believe it is all right to serve or use them.[233]

In another testimony, R.E. Winsett testified to a vision:

> I saw a vision of a trimmed olive tree. I saw a peculiar looking beast with long bluish silken hair, shaped somewhat like a bear, which went up to the olive tree and ate the green branches; but it didn't bother the branches whose leaves had withered and some decayed, it only ate the green ones. Neither did it eat the tree. My interpretation is this: There is going to be a sifting time and many movements which seem to have the power of God now and are apparently green, will be trimmed off because they do not measure up to the full bible standard. Only one tree will remain. I beheld this tree until it became a beautiful well formed tree; all of its branches were green and beautiful. The beast, of course, is the beast of whom the Bible tells us; who caused all, both small and great, whose names were not found written in the Lamb's Book, to receive his mark. He is devouring all who do not adhere to the truth of God's Word, but have ways, doctrines and systems of their own instead of the Bible ways, doctrines, and systems.[234]

Winsett's visionary experience alludes to imagery in Revelation, particularly the imagery of the two olive trees and the beast (Revelation 11, 13). Winsett viewed the beast as a reality in the contemporary world that threatened the church. Winsett creatively recontextualized the beast, describing the beast with bluish, silken hair that had the appearance of a bear. Only those who had the 'Bible standard' were able to stand against it.

Conversely, Z.D. Simmons read Revelation dispensationally. He suggested that the church would be caught away before the rise of the beast who 'will make a covenant with Israel for one week (seven years of complete time) as their Messiah king seated in the temple at Jerusalem (Dan. 9:27; 2 Thess. 2:3-12) and is the chief ruler in the federated kingdoms over all the earth'.[235] Sam C. Perry assured the

---

[233] *COGE* 5.41 (October 10, 1914), p. 4.
[234] *COGE* 8.48 (December 8, 1917), p. 3.
[235] *COGE* 7.20 (May 13, 1916), p. 4.

readers that the mark of the beast should not be feared until the antichrist 'comes on the scene of action and gets control over the kingdoms of earth', after which the 'faithful bride' will be 'taken' from the earth.[236] Contra Tomlinson, Perry held that the food cards were not connected to the mark of the beast because the mark would be plainly seen on either the hand or the forehead and would not be stamped upon anyone before they could recognize it. He wrote, 'That mark means allegiance to the beast, the anti-christ, his government, his religion and all. It means the strictest worship of the beast, or anti-christ himself and of his image also.'[237] Hence, Perry located the threat of the beast in the future that was removed from his church. Howard Juillerat put forth a similar futuristic reading when explaining the beast in Revelation 17. He first portrayed it in historical categories:

> We know that Rome was the kingdom or nation ruling the world at that time; the five before her that most completely ruled the earth were, Egypt, Assyria, Babylon, Persia, and Greece; these were fallen. From the cruelties of Pharaoh down to the iron of Caesar we see the characteristics of the Beast. Haven't they gained their enemies by conquest with the accompanying war, bloodshed and devastation?[238] *So... where does the U.S. fall in here?*

When looking at the beast from Revelation and Daniel, Juillerat asserted that Daniel's beasts embodied all that John saw. Concerning the beast from Rev. 17.8, he determined that (1) 'The seventh kingdom or empire, the last to have world dominion continues a short time', which will be three and a half years or 42 months,[239] and (2) 'this eighth is of the seven, then he must come from some of the rulers of the past'. Juillerat suggested that the eighth could be Nero, Nimrod, or Antiochus Epiphanes who all had the 'spirit of Antichrist and may be used as types of the last great tyrant'.[240] This one terrible tyrant would be the Antichrist who is yet to come. In the face of the Antichrist, Juillerat comforted his readers writing, 'Now if this is true, then those who are ready for the rapture will go with their Lord and

---

[236] *COGE* 9.12 (March 23, 1918), p. 3.

[237] *COGE* 9.12 (March 23, 1918), p. 3.

[238] *COGE* 9.26 (June 29, 1918), p. 1.

[239] *COGE* 9.26 (June 29, 1918), p. 2.

[240] *COGE* 9.26 (June 29, 1918), p. 2.

escape the terrible reign of this Beast'.[241] Therefore, it is notable that, for Juillerat, the beast represented 'conquest with the accompanying war, blood-shed and devastation', but he did not associate the beast with the contemporary warring kingdoms; rather, he offered hope of escape.

Thus, *The Church of God Evangel* had ample reflection regarding the beast and his mark where the majority of the interpreters were cautious about giving precise identifications. Often the beast was associated with powerful entities and governments (such as warring nations) who had the authority to demand the acceptance of their mark. *The Church of God Evangel* offered two interpretative approaches. One viewed the beast-like qualities in the world, while the other followed a much more dispensational reading. It is striking that Tomlinson – as the editor of the paper and while strongly disagreeing with the dispensational script – allowed dissonant voices to appear in the publication. *testing/ Spirit to provide discernment?*

### Discerning the Mystery

*The Church of God Evangel* identified the seven stars as pastors or ministers who 'warn you of the things that will wreck your lives and drag you down to hell'.[242] A.J. Tomlinson believed World War I to be a 'mystery' being revealed by God. Tomlinson found that the seals were being opened:

> The Pale horse and his rider are dashing rapidly and wildly over the world to-day and trampling the millions of earth's inhabitants mercilessly under their feet. God has a few saints scattered here and there who are treading the paths of peace and stealthily making their way into sublimity of His holy presence gathering from the clefts and hidden recesses the hidden mysteries and bringing them to light for God's glory and the advancement of His noble cause.[243]

---

[241] *COGE* 9.26 (June 29, 1918), p. 2.

[242] *COGE* 7.29 (July 15, 1916), p. 4. See also *COGE* 5.29 (July 18, 1914), p. 7; *COGE* 5.34 (August 22, 1914), p. 2; *COGE* 8.31 (August 11, 1917), p. 1.

[243] *COGE* 5.38 (September 19, 1914), p. 1. See also *COGE* 9.11 (March 16, 1918), p. 1:

> The leaders and war lords of every land are pushing on the war. This is the opening of the second seal and it is wide open, too. No one can question this if they know their Bibles and the condition of the world today. We can hardly

## Babylon

*The Church of God Evangel* contained two streams of interpretations of Babylon. First, Babylon was referred to as 'mystic Babylon'[244] or 'the spirit of Babylon',[245] which was defined as the 'church married to the world' and who 'prevails to-day in the end of this age'.[246] In one testimony, a sister under the influence of the Holy Spirit read Revelation 18 in tongues, and the congregation followed along in their English bibles. This experience was a sign that 'demonstrated plainly how when the called out ones left mystic Babylon, they would come to the Lord's church and be closely joined in love and caught up to meet the Lord in the air.'[247] Another testified concerning the contemporary landscape writing, 'It grieves our hearts to see the spiritual whoredom of Babylonian sects on the one hand, and the spiritual fornication on the other'.[248] Those who were in Babylon needed 'to be warned to flee the wrath to come!'[249] An eschatological aspect was present where 'Babylon, the glory of the kingdoms must soon fall' so that the kingdom of Christ would come.[250] Second, *The Church of God Evangel* looked at Babylon through a futuristic lens where 'great Babylon' would be destroyed at the end of the 'great tribulation' and represented 'all false forms of religion'.[251]

---

say that the third seal is wide open yet, but it is certainly broken sufficient so that the black horse is loosed from his stall and his rider has already got the balances in his hands. It looks to me like the cry of 'A measure of wheat for a penny, and three measures of barley for a penny' is already raised, when we cannot buy any flour without buying about three times as much corn meal. All indications are that it will be but a short time till the fourth seal will be opened which will disclose the pale horse and his rider whose name is Death. Already I fancy I see him as he is loosed in his stall, pawing and champing his bits, because he wants to go.

[244] *COGE* 1.7 (June 1, 1910), p. 6; *COGE* 1.18 (November 15, 1910), p. 2. See also *COGE* 8.40 (October 13, 1917), p. 1.
[245] *COGE* 8.13 (March 31, 1917), p. 3.
[246] *COGE* 1.7 (June 1, 1910), p. 6.
[247] *COGE* 1.18 (November 15, 1910), p. 2.
[248] *COGE* 1.2 (March 15, 1910), p. 4.
[249] *COGE* 9.44 (November 2, 1918), p. 3.
[250] *COGE* 9.26 (June 29, 1918), p. 4.
[251] *COGE* 7.20 (May 13, 1916), p. 4; *COGE* 9.44 (November 2, 1918), p. 4.

The Throne Room Vision *Seven horns, seven eyes = Holy Spirit*

John A. Giddens referred to Rev. 5.1-10, 'having seven horns and seven eyes, (power and wisdom), which are the seven Spirits of God sent into all the earth'.[252] The capitalization of the seven Spirits suggests that the seven eyes and seven horns signified the Holy Spirit, and the parenthesis indicates that the Spirit had (or was) full wisdom and power.

**Summary**

*The Church of God Evangel* revealed a desire to seek the Spirit in their discernment. They believed that God through the Spirit had given wisdom to them for discernment and that the Word and Spirit could resolve concerns. The paper cautioned that not every person who claimed to be speaking for the Spirit was speaking for the Spirit. Revelation was used to warn against the false teaching of Balaam. The church should be in the Spirit to discern these deceptions. The bestial texts were widely featured. The paper warned against the beast-like authority of the nations that drafted individuals to participate in violence. Tomlinson revealed restraint when wrestling with the identification of the mark of the beast and the beast, while observing various bestial realities in the world. Others read the bestial texts through a dispensational lens, which put the threat of the mark and the beast in the future. *The Church of God Evangel* permitted dissenting interpreter voices in the publication allowing the readers of the paper to discern difficult texts together.

## The Pentecostal Holiness Advocate and The Apostolic Evangel

The Fire-Baptized Holiness Church, following the Pentecostal outpouring, transformed its *Live Coals* publication into *The Apostolic Evangel*. J.H. King edited *The Apostolic Evangel* (there are six extant issues from 1907–1912). When the Fire-Baptized Holiness church became part of the Pentecostal Holiness Church in 1917, *The Pentecostal Holiness Advocate* was created and edited by G.F. Taylor.[253] These periodicals will be surveyed together because they share denominational

---

[252] *COGE* 1.2 (March 15, 1910), p. 3.

[253] Alexander, *Pentecostal Healing*, pp. 123-31; McQueen, *Toward a Pentecostal Eschatology*, pp. 124-27.

roots, and some of the articles that appeared in *The Apostolic Evangel* were later reprinted in *The Pentecostal Holiness Advocate*. These publications displayed influences of Revelation that included: the Bride, the Lamb, the millennium, the great tribulation, the beast, and the marriage supper.[254]

## Pneumatic Discernment

Discernment in *The Pentecostal Holiness Advocate* was considered to be a dynamic process that embraced the Word and the Spirit, 'Oh, hallelujah, the Spirit and the Word agree, so let us stand fast, and hold to what we know to be the truth'.[255] God, in infinite wisdom, would

---

[254] For explicit references and quotations to Revelation, see *AE* 1.1 (February 15, 1909), p. 6; *AE* 1.8 (June 1, 1909), pp. 2-3, 8; *AE* 1.9 (June 15, 1909), pp. 7-8; *AE* 1.18 (November 1, 1909), pp. 1, 7; *AE* 3.22 (January 1, 1912), pp. 1-2, 8; *PHA* 1.1 (May 3, 1917), p. 7; *PHA* 1.3 (May 17, 1917), pp. 2, 6; *PHA* 1.4 (May 24, 1917), pp. 2, 8-9, 15; *PHA* 1.5 (May 31, 1917), pp. 3, 15; *PHA* 1.6 (June 7, 1917), p. 16; *PHA* 1.7 (June 15, 1917), pp. 4, 12; *PHA* 1.8 (June 21, 1917), pp. 2, 5; *PHA* 1.9 (June 28, 1917), pp. 9, 14; *PHA* 1.10 (July 5, 1917), pp. 4, 16; *PHA* 1.11 (July 12, 1917), pp. 2-3, 6; *PHA* 1.12 (July 19, 1917), p. 16; *PHA* 1.13 (July 26, 1917), pp. 3, 15; *PHA* 1.14 (August 2, 1917), p. 15; *PHA* 1.15 (August 9, 1917), p. 8; *PHA* 1.16 (August 16, 1917), pp. 3, 16; *PHA* 1.18 (August 30, 1917), p. 8; *PHA* 1.19 (September 6, 1917), pp. 12, 16; *PHA* 1.21 (September 20, 1917), p. 7; *PHA* 1.22 (September 27, 1917), pp. 12-13; *PHA* 1.23 (October 4, 1917), p. 15; *PHA* 1.25 (October 18, 1917), p. 7; *PHA* 1.28 (November 8, 1917), pp. 7, 9; *PHA* 1.29 (November 15, 1917), pp. 3, 8; *PHA* 1.30 (November 22, 1917), pp. 3, 8; *PHA* 1.33 (December 13, 1917), pp. 7, 16; *PHA* 1.34 (December 20, 1917), pp. 2, 5-7; *PHA* 1.35 (December 27, 1917), pp. 12, 16; *PHA* 1.37 (January 10, 1918), p. 8; *PHA* 1.39 (January 24, 1918), p. 2; *PHA* 1.40 (January 31, 1918), p. 7; *PHA* 1.41 (February 7, 1918), pp. 2, 5; *PHA* 1.42 (February 14, 1918), p. 8; *PHA* 1.43 (February 21, 1918), pp. 1, 6; *PHA* 1.44 (February 28, 1918), pp. 4, 7; *PHA* 1.45 (March 7, 1918), p. 4; *PHA* 1.46 (March 14, 1918), pp. 2, 4, 7; *PHA* 1.47 (March 21, 1918), pp. 5-6; *PHA* 1.50 (April 11, 1918), pp. 3, 9; *PHA* 1.52 (April 25, 1918), p. 11; *PHA* 2.1 (May 2, 1918), p. 6; *PHA* 2.4 (May 23, 1918), pp. 3, 7; *PHA* 2.5 (May 30, 1918), p. 7; *PHA* 2.6 (June 6, 1918), pp. 9-10; *PHA* 2.7 (June 13, 1918), p. 13; *PHA* 2.8 (June 20, 1918), p. 4; *PHA* 2.9 (June 27, 1918), pp. 5, 9; *PHA* 2.10 (July 4, 1918), pp. 4-5; *PHA* 2.12 (July 18, 1918), pp. 4, 7-9; *PHA* 2.14 (August 1, 1918), p. 2; *PHA* 2.15 (August 8, 1918), pp. 9-10, 12; *PHA* 2.16 (August 15, 1918), p. 6; *PHA* 2.17 (August 22, 1918), p. 4; *PHA* 2.19 (September 5, 1918), p. 10; *PHA* 2.20 (September 12, 1918), p. 6; *PHA* 2.21 (September 19, 1918), p. 12; *PHA* 2.23 (October 3, 1918), p. 7; *PHA* 2.24 (October 10, 1918), p. 5; *PHA* 2.26 (October 24, 1918), pp. 4, 7; *PHA* 2.27 (October 21, 1918), pp. 2-3, 8-9; *PHA* 2.20-31 (November 21-28, 1918), p. 7; *PHA* 2.32 (December 5, 1918), p. 6; *PHA* 2.32 (December 12, 1918), pp. 8-10, 16; *PHA* 2.33-34 (December 19-25, 1918), p. 6.

[255] *PHA* 1.6 (June 7, 1917), p. 6. See also *PHA* 1.15 (August 9, 1917), p. 3; *PHA* 1.43 (February 21, 1918), p. 4.

give wisdom to the 'true' church by the Spirit.[256] Prayer was necessary for guidance, and understanding came not 'from the head, but from the heart'.[257] The Spirit provided interpretation of the scripture[258] and taught the church all things, guiding them into all truth.[259] J.H. King offered a testimony where he reflected upon discerning the will of God. He said it was difficult to know God's will and wrongly discerning might lead to injury to the cause of Christ.[260] If one wrongly discerned, God would 'let us suffer greatly to show us the foolishness of our thoughts and ways, and the folly of charging Him as the author of all our silly mistakes'.[261] King warned against attributing one's actions and deeds to God when God had nothing to do with those actions. King believed that discernment necessitated 'the largest portion of our life to get rid of the foolishness and nonsense, which Satan heaped up in us during our sinful days. "With the aged is wisdom." Sin is nonsense, righteousness is wisdom. "It is the wisdom of the wise to depart from evil."'[262]

## The Spirit and Discernment in Revelation

'In the Spirit'

The 'in the Spirit' phrases appeared in *The Pentecostal Holiness Advocate*, but there was rarely any reflection on Revelation. The uses of the 'in

---

[256] *AE* 1.4 (April 3, 1907), p. 3; *PHA* 1.1 (May 3, 1917), pp. 4-5; *PHA* 1.5 (May 31, 1917), p. 7; *PHA* 1.6 (June 7, 1917), p. 11; *PHA* 1.12 (July 19, 1917), p. 3; *PHA* 1.25 (October 18, 1917), p. 7; *PHA* 1.37 (January 10, 1918), p. 7; *PHA* 1.41 (February 7, 1918), p. 3; *PHA* 1.42 (February 14, 1918), p. 3; *PHA* 1.42 (February 14, 1918), p. 3; *PHA* 1.44 (February 28, 1918), p. 3; *PHA* 1.48 (March 28, 1918), p. 7; *PHA* 1.50 (April 11, 1918), p. 9; *PHA* 2.2 (May 9, 1918), p. 10; *PHA* 2.19 (September 5, 1918), p. 1; *PHA* 2.21 (September 19, 1918), p. 13; *PHA* 2.22 (September 26, 1918), p. 10; *PHA* 2.33-34 (December 19-25, 1918), pp. 2-3, 9. For other references to wisdom, see *PHA* 1.12 (July 19, 1917), p. 8; *PHA* 1.28 (November 8, 1917), p. 1; *PHA* 1.33 (December 13, 1917), p. 3; *PHA* 1.37 (January 10, 1918), p. 7.

[257] *AE* 1.1 (February 15, 1909), p. 2.

[258] *AE* 1.4 (April 3, 1907), p. 4.

[259] *AE* 1.4 (April 3, 1907), pp. 1, 4. See *PHA* 1.3 (May 17, 1917), p. 2; *PHA* 1.10 (July 5, 1917), p. 11; *PHA* 1.13 (July 26, 1917), p. 2; *AE* 1.18 (November 1, 1909), p. 2; *PHA* 1.43 (February 21, 1918), p. 3.

[260] *AE* 3.22 (January 1, 1912), p. 5.

[261] *AE* 3.22 (January 1, 1912), p. 5.

[262] *AE* 3.22 (January 1, 1912), p. 5.

the Spirit' phrases included: to judge,[263] prayer and supplication,[264] great demonstrations,[265] being cold,[266] to walk,[267] to think,[268] to preach,[269] free,[270] and fellowship 'in the Spirit'.[271] The pages of the periodical were sent 'in the Spirit'.[272] Following the death of Brother Gaines, *The Pentecostal Holiness Advocate* recorded: 'We feel like while Bro. Gaines is no more with us in the flesh, he is with us in the Spirit walking, talking, shouting, and dancing for God'.[273]

Discerning the Mysteries

Revelation 1

*The Pentecostal Holiness Advocate* considered the seven prophetic messages as referring to seven church ages where each church age had its failures.[274] The paper suggested that it was the last age, the Laodicean age.[275] Elizabeth A. Sexton, editor of *The Bridegroom's Messenger*, in a guest editorial wrote that the seven prophetic messages addressed the whole church.[276] Another testimony added, 'we are living in the church age' where 'the Holy Spirit deals with the church in special ways, in fact, He is the Leader of the church; we read in Revelation an exhortation for those who have ears to hear what the Spirit says unto the churches; it should be our daily prayer to hear what the Spirit says to us'.[277]

*The Pentecostal Holiness Advocate* observed that the seven lampstands represented the seven churches, and the seven stars signified the pastors of the seven churches:

---

[263] *PHA* 1.23 (October 4, 1917), p. 11.

[264] *PHA* 1.2 (May 10, 1917), p. 4.

[265] *PHA* 1.5 (May 31, 1917), p. 9.

[266] *PHA* 1.15 (August 9, 1917), p. 8.

[267] *PHA* 2.14 (August 1, 1918), pp. 2-3.

[268] *PHA* 2.14 (August 1, 1918), p. 3.

[269] *PHA* 2.14 (August 1, 1918), p. 3.

[270] *PHA* 2.16 (August 15, 1918), p. 10.

[271] *PHA* 2.22 (September 26, 1918), p. 16.

[272] *PHA* 1.2 (May 10, 1917), p. 7.

[273] *PHA* 2.21 (September 19, 1918), p. 14.

[274] *PHA* 1.8 (June 21, 1917), p. 8; *PHA* 1.33 (December 13, 1917), p. 8.

[275] *PHA* 1.4 (May 24, 1917), p. 2; *PHA* 1.18 (August 30, 1917), p. 8; *PHA* 1.33 (December 13, 1917), p. 13; *PHA* 1.46 (March 14, 1918), p. 2.

[276] *PHA* 1.34 (December 20, 1917), p. 6.

[277] *PHA* 2.19 (September 5, 1918), p. 1.

When Jesus appeared to John on Patmos, the churches were represented by candlesticks, each bearing seven lights, the perfect number. These were properly arranged around Him, thus speaking of organization. The pastors of the churches were represented by stars; and the stars are thoroughly organized.[278]

## Revelation 10

G.F. Taylor wrote on Rev. 10.1:

In Rev. 10.1 we read of a being in the person of an angel. He is no other than the Jehovah Angel. He is clothed with a cloud, which is never attire of other than the Deity. The rainbow is over His head, which indicates the glory of the Eternal. He holds a parchment in His hand, which is no other than a deed to the whole world. He places one foot upon the sea. This act signifies to take possession of (Joshua 1:3). He delivers the deed to the saints, who are to appropriate the world as their own.[279]

While Taylor viewed the mighty angel as a divine figure, it is hard to identify whether Taylor believed that the 'Jehovah Angel' was the Holy Spirit or Christ.

### The Mark of the Beast

The mark of the beast in *The Pentecostal Holiness Advocate* contained an element of finality: 'those who receive the mark of the Antichrist will put themselves beyond the reach of the atonement'.[280] L.R. Graham in a lengthy sermon on 'Division' offered a section dedicated to 'markings' where he considered the mark of the beast:

In order to buy or sell they must have one of three marks or signs, had the mark, or the name of the beast, or the number of his name. To some these may be the same. The definition of the word, is impressed mark, engraving. It is a character mark. The person that does the marking is concealed. The marking whether visible or invisible, is not clear. Its location being in the forehead or in the hand spells two factors: Capital and Labor.[281]

---

[278] *PHA* 1.10 (July 5, 1917), p. 16.
[279] *AE* 1.1 (February 15, 1909), p. 6; *PHA* 2.12 (July 18, 1918), p. 8.
[280] *PHA* 1.46 (March 14, 1918), p. 1.
[281] *PHA* 2.5 (May 30, 1918), p. 7.

It is not clear whether this interpretation is wholly futuristic; however, the article did not reveal any indication that the threat was imminent. Another engagement with the mark occurred in the 'Editorial Thoughts' section of the paper that cited *The Raleigh Christian Advocate*. The section explored the possibility that the Kaiser was the Antichrist based on his title, gematria, and the number of the beast – 666:

> We are not disposed to deny that he is 'a beast,' whether he is the particular one or not; but all such interpretations of Scripture are more curious than valuable. The latest interpretation that has come under our observation may be stated as follows: Take the name: 'William von Hohenzollern, King of Prussia, Emperor of all Germany,' and substitute the numeral equivalent for the letters, this a-1, b-2, c-3, etc., and we have the following:
>
> 23-9-12-12-9-1-13, 22-15-14, 8-15-8-5-14-26-15-12-5-18-14, 11-9-14-7, 15-6, 16-18-21-19-19-9-1, 5-13-16-5-18-15-18, 15-6, 1-12-12, 7-5-18-13-1-14-25.
>
> Add all these numerals together, and you have 666, which is the number of the beast. This is an interesting and peculiar coincident; but we present it purely as a curiosity, and not as an interpretation of Scripture. – *The Raleigh Christian Advocate*.'[282]

This excerpt demonstrates a few aspects of discerning and calculating the number of the beast. First, their discernment process led to gematria. The article pointed the readers through the process of calculating 666 using gematria and based on a particular chosen title of the Kaiser. Second, despite equating von Hohenzollern's title to the number of the beast, this article discerned that this was not an interpretation of the text, rather concluding it was a 'curiosity'. Von Hohenzollern was likely 'a beast', and his particular title offered a 'peculiar coincident' for the readers when explored with gematria. Third, the placement of this article in *The Pentecostal Holiness Advocate* is noteworthy because this article seemed to be less interested in discovering

---

[282] *PHA* 2.16 (August 15, 1918), p. 1. See also *PHA* 1.43 (February 21, 1918), p. 1, on the Kaiser as the antichrist.

the beast-like qualities of the current powers in the world and more concerned with the future implications of the bestial texts.[283]

An article by A.P. Sexton represents the dispensational interpretations of *The Pentecostal Holiness Advocate*. Sexton suggested that it did not matter which side won the Great War. The war was merely 'paving the way for Antichrist. The "one man" rule is becoming more and more imminent.'[284] Following the war, 'one universal government' and 'one creed religion' will rule the world both 'politically and religiously', which will be established under ten 'principle heads'.[285] The end of the war will create a 'supposed peace' where the beast will rise as 'head ruler' who will combine all 'fleets, navies, and armies'.[286] A sign of this development for Sexton was that 'the pope of Rome, and the Kaiser of Germany (the would be world despots), are closely allied. Who can resist, or make war with him!'[287] The antichrist 'will control all commerce, and without receiving the mark of the beast either in the hand or forehead, you can not buy nor sell!'[288] Thus, this interpreter suggested that the beast and his mark would use World War I as an opportunity to rise to power and rule the entire world through economic, political, military, and religious power. However, this threat, for Sexton, was confined to the future without consequence to the present. Sexton offered the hope of escape to the church: 'We can only hope in God, Christ is soon coming, and may we hear Him say, "Arise, my love, my dove, my fair one, and come away." "The winter is past, and the time of the singing of birds is at hand."'[289]

[283] See *PHA* 1.43 (February 21, 1918), p. 1, where Taylor wrote, 'The final Antichrist will not come until the Bride of Christ is in the air'.

[284] *PHA* 1.10 (July 5, 1917), p. 4. See also *PHA* 1.4 (May 24, 1917), p. 8; *PHA* 1.31 (November 29, 1917), p. 3. *The Pentecostal Holiness Advocate* often used 'antichrist' instead of 'beast', see *PHA* 1.50 (April 11, 1918), p. 11.

[285] *PHA* 1.4 (May 24, 1917), p. 8.

[286] *PHA* 1.10 (July 5, 1917), p. 4.

[287] *PHA* 1.10 (July 5, 1917), p. 4.

[288] *PHA* 1.10 (July 5, 1917), p. 4.

[289] *PHA* 1.10 (July 5, 1917), p. 4. See also *PHA* 1.4 (May 24, 1917), p. 15, which comments that the bride would escape the great tribulation.

Babylon

Babylon was thought to be a symbol of evil throughout scripture: 'We find Babylon spoken of in Genesis, another in Daniel, and another in Revelation. Each of these was established for the purpose of opposing the church. They all exalted themselves against God. The first two have fallen, the other will fall (Rev. 18:2.).'[290] One testimony anticipated the rebuilding of Babylon that would be completed 'probably within the next decade. Everything is working towards the re-establishment of both Jerusalem and Babylon – and both are again needed that "Scripture may be fulfilled".'[291] Some in the paper, limited Babylon to a future time when it would be the 'capitol city of the Antichrist, and the system of his religion, and never stop until they burn that city with fire'.[292]

V.P. Simmons wrote an article on 'Comeoutism'.[293] 'Comeoutism' was a dilemma in *The Pentecostal Holiness Advocate* that offer two responses: (1) following a Pentecostal experience, should Pentecostals leave their established churches and 'lay the foundation for another sect' and that would divide 'Christ's flock'; or (2) should Pentecostals remain in their churches 'under the devil's leadership' and 'be found clinging to a "body of death"' that would 'paralyze … efforts of spiritual reform'.[294] The term seems to allude to Revelation that exhorts the churches to 'come out of her, my people'. Simmons commented on the history of interpretation looking at sixteenth-century reformers who determined that the Church of Rome was the great whore from Revelation 17. The Reformers separated themselves from her to become the 'true people of God'. Simmons believed the process of discernment included:

> Prayerful humility with divine guidance … long patience, with
> prayerful solitude, with faithful warnings to those in the church
> that stand in the way of spiritual work, with the fullest reliance
> upon God for his guidance … then watch for the Holy Spirit's
> leadings; avoiding all haste of organization, or giving a human
> name to the work. Then as far as possible co-operating with other

---

[290] *PHA* 2.32 (December 12, 1918), p. 9.

[291] *AE* 1.9 (June 15, 1909), p. 1.

[292] *PHA* 1.4 (May 24, 1917), p. 9.

[293] *AE* 1.8 (June 1, 1909), p. 3; *PHA* 2.15 (August 8, 1918), p. 10.

[294] *AE* 1.8 (June 1, 1909), p. 3.

Remember-The Church is the body of Christ — not the body of people?

154    *Testimonies of Wesleyan-Holiness Pentecostalism*

Christian people, but positively never going into bondage to any. Whatever light you have received from the Word and from the Spirit, let your light shine even if they 'cast you out of the church'. It is sometimes better to be pushed out than to come out.[295]

Simmons demonstrated a discerning process, which utilized Revelation as a guide, and called on readers to pray, have patience, hear the warning, co-operate with other believers, and rely on guidance from God through the Word and the Spirit.

The Two Witnesses

G.F. Taylor offered an article on the two witnesses who, he believed, would appear during the great tribulation. They will prophesy for 1260 days to 'turn the Jews from their unbelief'.[296] He connected the two witnesses – two olives trees and two lampstands – with Zech 4.1-14:

> In Zechariah's vision, there was second restoration, the candlestick, the church, is gone, but one candlestick, which was a picture of the Jewish church at that time. The olive trees represented the Spirit of God helping in the work ... In Revelation, at the second restoration, the candlestick, the church, i sgone [*sic*] having been caught up to meet Jesus; and these two witnesses are both the candlesticks and the trees. They are sole light-bearers. They are witnesses of a peculiar sort. They have a peculiar work to do. In this work they stand alone. Of course, God is with them.[297]

Taylor considered that the two witnesses would be two saints 'capable of death, for they are soon put to death. Angels can not die, neither can the saints who have died once. "It is appointed unto man once to die." So we are driven to search heaven for two saints who have never died ... The one is Enoch, the other is Elijah.'[298] Despite determining that the two witnesses represented a fusion of the church and the Spirit, Taylor did not flesh out this connection rather finding his solution by means of a dispensational lens; thereby, Taylor did not allow the text to speak to the contemporary church.

---

[295] *AE* 1.8 (June 1, 1909), p. 3.

[296] *PHA* 1.14 (August 2, 1917), p. 15. Cf. *AE* 3.22 (January 1, 1912), pp. 1-2; *PHA* 1.44 (February 28, 1918), p. 7.

[297] *PHA* 1.14 (August 2, 1917), p. 15.

[298] *PHA* 1.14 (August 2, 1917), p. 15.

## Summary

*The Pentecostal Holiness Advocate* and *The Apostolic Evangel* are similar to Pentecostal literature previously surveyed inasmuch that it demonstrated a belief that God provided wisdom, knowledge, understanding, and discernment to the church by the Spirit, but only at select times did these publications consider the themes of discernment or pneumatology from Revelation. Generally, these two publications were controlled by a dispensational, futuristic interpretation and believed that 'the things mentioned in the Book of Revelation were to be in the future'.[299] G.F. Taylor who was committed to J.A. Seiss's dispensational interpretation was likely the reason for futuristic persuasion throughout the publication.[300] Taylor's outlook is perhaps best seen in a Question and Answer section of *The Pentecostal Holiness Advocate* during the Influenza epidemic when asked, 'Do you think that this disease is one of the seals of Revelation?' Taylor simply responded, 'I do not think any of the seals have opened yet'.[301]

*Interesting...*

## Summary of the Wesleyan-Holiness Stream

First, each periodical regarded the Spirit as being actively involved in their process of interpretation, discernment, and decision-making. They trusted that God by the Spirit and the Word offered guidance, wisdom, and discernment to the church. Rightly discerning and true knowledge originated from God while wrongly discerning resulted from worldly influences. The article by E.S. Hubbell offers perhaps the clearest exploration of pneumatic discernment in Revelation in the literature. Hubbell wrote that the church should ask for the seven Spirits – the seven eyes of the Lamb – for full wisdom and Lamb-like discernment.

Second, although a dispensational, futuristic interpretative lens influenced some in these periodicals, dispensationalism did not restrict

---

[299] *PHA* 1.44 (February 28, 1918), p. 4.

[300] See *PHA* 1.3 (May 17, 1917), p. 7, where Taylor – in an advisement (that reappeared in numerous other issues) for *Lectures on the Apocalypse* by J.A. Seiss – commented, 'All who wish to study Revelation should read these lectures. They are the best books that have ever been written on the subject, so far as is known.' At one point Taylor went as far to say 'In fact, I never knew anything about the subject until I read those lectures'. (PHA 1.14 [August 2, 1917], p. 15).

[301] *PHA* 2.33-34 (December 19-25, 1918), p. 16.

these Wesleyan-Holiness Pentecostals' interpretations of Revelation. Their interpretations were by no means monolithic; rather, this survey has revealed a diversity of readings. Many of these early Pentecostals made use of the different publications as an avenue for discerning their interpretations of Revelation. They used language and images from Revelation to describe their circumstances. Many contributors revealed a desire to hear the Spirit for their contemporary community. They believed that the lampstands represented the churches, and the seven stars were pastors or ministers. They regarded Christ as walking among churches as he walked among seven lampstands in Revelation. They reflected upon their pneumatic experiences in light of John's 'in the Spirit' experience. They longed for the seven Spirits – the seven eyes of the Lamb – to become their eyes so that they could discern. They believed that Babylon, Balaam, and Jezebel represented evil, false teaching, and sexual immorality in their contemporary world. Even in the most dispensational publication of the Wesleyan-Holiness stream – *The Holiness Pentecostal Advocate* – one finds non-dispensational readings of Revelation.

Third, the historical context of the Great War inspired an abundance of apocalyptic interest among these early Pentecostals. *The Bridegroom's Messenger* and *The Church of God Evangel* referred to Revelation as a way to reflect upon and criticize the violence of the World War I and the power of the nations. They considered the war as an unleashing of the four horsemen across Europe, and they utilized the bestial texts to critique the war efforts among the European powers that they believed were instigating a horrible war. While there were no examples of *The Pentecostal Holiness Advocate* using the bestial texts to critique the war, this publication mutually viewed the beast as an embodiment of complete power and authority, albeit confined to a future time.

Fourth, the mark of the beast became a dualistic identifying mark between those who followed God – having the seal of God – and those who followed the beast – having the mark of the beast. Those who had the mark of the beast were following it in economic, political, or military power. While some appealed to texts from Revelation to criticize the Great War, others suggested that the mark of the beast manifested as food cards, labor unions, and secret societies. It is striking that only once in all literature surveyed in the Wesleyan-Holiness

Stream was the number 666 mentioned. On that occasion, it was interpreted by using gematria, considering the beast-like qualities of the Kaiser.

Fifth, these early Pentecostals engaged the pneumatology of Revelation. Although the seven Spirits did not commonly appear in this literature, it was always acknowledged as a reference to the Holy Spirit. The seven Spirits were dynamically related to the Lamb as the Lamb's seven eyes and seven horns. The seven eyes represented the full wisdom and knowledge of the Spirit, and the seven horns symbolized the full power of the Spirit. The 'in the Spirit' phrases implied participation with the Holy Spirit. The Wesleyan-Holiness community realized that their pneumatic experiences closely correlated to experiences described in Revelation. Other pneumatological examples included G.F. Taylor's interpretation of the mighty angel in Rev. 10.1 as the 'Jehovah Angel', suggesting that the angel is a symbol of the Holy Spirit or Christ. Taylor also found the imagery of the two lampstands and the two olive trees as a fusion between the church and the Spirit, but he allowed his dispensational presupposition to control his interpretation and offered no comment concerning the contemporary church.

# 4

## DISCERNING THE TESTIMONIES OF FINISHED-WORK PENTECOSTALISM

In this chapter, I continue to examine the early Pentecostal (con)texts, turning to those who are part of the Finished-Work stream of Pentecostalism. Again, I have split this study into two chapters, following K. Alexander who discovered theological distinctives among the Wesleyan-Holiness Pentecostals and the Finished-Work Pentecostals.

### The Pentecost

*The Pentecost* was first published in 1908 and edited by J.R. Flower. In 1910, the editorial duties were given to associate editor, A.S. Copley.[1] This publication mostly contained teachings, sermonic materials, and missionary reports. There was a limited amount of reflection on Revelation, but *The Pentecost* included discussions by A.S. Copley on the seven Spirits and discernment in light of the false teaching of Jezebel and the great whore.[2]

---

[1] Archer, '*I Was in the Spirit on the Lord's Day*', p. 98.

[2] For explicit references and quotations to Revelation, see *TP* 1.1 (August 1908), p. 5; *TP* 1.2 (September 1908), p. 6; *TP* 1.4 (December 1908), p. 4; *TP* 1.5 (January-February 1909), p. 7; *TP* 1.6 (April-May 1909), p. 7; *TP* 1.7 (June 1909), pp. 7, 9; *TP* 1.9 (August 1909), pp. 6-8; *TP* 1.10 (September 1909), p. 3; *TP* 2.2 (January 1910), pp. 2, 5-7; *TP* 2.3 (February 1910), pp. 1, 3; *TP* 2.4 (March 1910), pp. 2, 4-6; *TP* 2.5 (April 1910), pp. 1-4, 7; *TP* 2.9-10 (September-October 1910), pp. 8, 13; *TP* 2.11-12 (November-December 1910), pp. 10-11.

## Pneumatic Discernment

*The Pentecost* observed that God engaged humanity so that they might understand.[3] It was through the Spirit that the church was able to hear God.[4] The Spirit was the church's guide and teacher.[5] The Spirit and Word were dynamically involved in the discerning process, 'It is not all spirits that agree with the word, but The Spirit and The Word agrees'.[6] When considering anyone who attempted to discern the Word without the Spirit, *The Pentecost* concluded that the 'letter killeth, but the Spirit giveth life'.[7]

## The Spirit and Discernment in Revelation

### 'In the Spirit'

There was not much reflection on the 'in the Spirit' phrases in *The Pentecost*, but contributors described that they lived,[8] walked,[9] sung,[10] and were free[11] 'in the Spirit'.

### The Seven Spirits

In a multi-issue series, A.S. Copley studied the seven 'types' of the Holy Spirit, two of which – fire and eyes – were reliant on Revelation 4–5. First, the seven Spirits were the seven lamps of fire burning before the throne (Rev. 4.5). He offered three categories of the Spirit: 'separation', 'dedication', and 'fire'.[12] (1) Separation was from the world of darkness, (2) dedication was sanctification where a believer offered 'deliberate, well-weighted, prayer-steeped dedication' to the Lord and the Word, and (3) fire was a living flame that was the love of God, and the Word of God was a lamp burning brightly.[13]

Second, Copley studied the Spirit as the seven eyes citing Rev. 4.5; 5.6; Isa. 11.2-3; Zech 4.10. He wrote that the number seven signifies,

---

[3] *TP* 1.3 (November 1908), p. 1.

[4] *TP* 1.12 (November 1909), p. 5.

[5] *TP* 2.4 (March 1910), p. 6.

[6] *TP* 1.11 (October 1909), pp. 2, 8.

[7] *TP* 1.11 (October 1909), p. 8.

[8] *TP* 1.5 (January-February 1909), p. 5.

[9] *TP* 1.5 (January-February 1909), p. 5; *TP* 1.12 (November 1909), p. 5; *TP* 2.6 (May 1910), p. 5.

[10] *TP* 1.7 (June 1909), p. 9.

[11] *TP* 1.11 (October 1909), p. 6.

[12] *TP* 1.9 (August 1909), p. 7.

[13] *TP* 1.9 (August 1909), p. 7.

'completeness, fullness, symmetry dispensationally. It includes the divine number three and the human number four. It therefore represents God's perfect dealings with men in the earth ... The number seven cannot be divided'.[14] Seven indicated the Spirit's 'perfection and fullness of wisdom, knowledge, power, love and tender watch-care over His cause and people and His just judgment against the wicked and all sin'.[15] As the seven eyes, no one was able to hide, 'Every little secret wicked device will be hunted out and judged, for the seven eyes of the Lord are diligent and untiring in their search'.[16] The seven eyes had the ability to discern 'good' against a false goodness that was a 'sham' or 'born of selfishness' because '[d]ivine wisdom discerns the genuine'.[17] The readers were exhorted to '[t]ake His very affections for your heart and His wisdom for your mind ... Remember that the seven Eyes of the Lord, the fullness of God, are at the disposal of your faith'.[18] Copley concluded, 'The leading lesson here is the untiring, never failing, universal wisdom of God in guarding and directing His own. Oh, it is so safe to trust the Dear Holy Spirit and His Word'.[19]

### Babylon and Jezebel

A.S. Copley studied Jezebel from Rev. 2.10 and connected her to the great whore who received judgment in Revelation 17, 'The woman of the parable, without question, is the combined body of false teachers, false prophets, false christs and false systems of the "present evil age"' who had 'stealthily scattered her poison along with truth everywhere'.[20] He believed that the 'parable' of Jezebel 'teaches that alongside of and intermixed with truth, error finds its place and plays its part'.[21] Copley inquired, 'Who of us has not imbibed it unconsciously? Who of us is entirely free from error today?'[22] He lamented, 'Sad! Sad! Sad! Jezebel is still at work, and will continue until

---

[14] *TP* 2.2 (January 1910), p. 5.
[15] *TP* 2.2 (January 1910), p. 5.
[16] *TP* 2.2 (January 1910), p. 5.
[17] *TP* 2.2 (January 1910), p. 5.
[18] *TP* 2.2 (January 1910), p. 5.
[19] *TP* 2.3 (February 1910), p. 5.
[20] *TP* 1.6 (April-May 1909), p. 7.
[21] *TP* 1.6 (April-May 1909), p. 7.
[22] *TP* 1.6 (April-May 1909), p. 7.

she is consigned to the lake of fire. (Rev. 19:20).[23] Copley believed that Jezebel and the great whore characterized false teachings throughout history, which the church continued to face. He was concerned with the subtle nature of false teaching and the way that truth and falsehood could not be easily discerned. Copley offered instructions to the readers to discern and urged the church to be filled with the love of God, to be prayerful, humble, dependent on God, and to seek truth earnestly against error.[24]

## Summary

While *The Pentecost* rarely commented on Revelation, it does offer an engaging and lengthy exploration of the seven Spirits. Copley explores the relationship between the seven Spirits and the Lamb as well as the seven Spirits and the one on the throne. Copley observes an allusion to Zechariah 4 and the seven eyes of the Lord. The seven Spirits represent the full wisdom and knowledge of God that was available to the church.

## The Latter Rain Evangel

*The Latter Rain Evangel* was first published in 1908 by William H. Piper at the Stone Church in Chicago.[25] This monthly publication primarily contained lengthy 'lecture' series, sermonic materials, and missionary reports. *The Latter Rain Evangel* had many references to Revelation including 'in the Spirit', the Bride, the millennium, the marriage supper of the Lamb, the mark of the beast, and the great tribulation.[26]

---

[23] *TP* 1.6 (April-May 1909), p. 7.

[24] For other examples of Babylon as evil, apostasy, and corruption, see *TP* 1.3 (November 1908), p. 5; *TP* 1.11 (October 1909), p. 5.

[25] W.E. Warner, 'Publications', *DPCM*, p. 744.

[26] For explicit references and quotations to Revelation, see *LRE* 1.4 (January 1909), pp. 18, 22; *LRE* 1.7 (April 1909), pp. 18-19; *LRE* 1.8 (May 1909), p. 19; *LRE* 1.9 (June 1909), pp. 15, 18; *LRE* 1.10 (July 1909), p. 5; *LRE* 2.1 (October 1909), p. 20; *LRE* 2.2 (November 1909), p. 24; *LRE* 2.3 (December 1909), pp. 6, 20-22, 24; *LRE* 2.6 (March 1910), pp. 4, 6-7; *LRE* 2.8 (May 1910), p. 13; *LRE* 2.10 (July 1910), pp. 8, 12-13, 16, 18; *LRE* 2.11 (August 1910), p. 13; *LRE* 2.12 (September 1909), pp. 4-9; *LRE* 3.1 (October 1910), pp. 17, 20-21; *LRE* 3.2 (November 1910), pp. 2, 14, 16-17; *LRE* 3.3 (December 1910), pp. 2-7; *LRE* 3.4 (January 1911), pp. 5-12; *LRE* 3.5 (February 1911), pp. 2-7, 9, 11; *LRE* 3.6 (March 1911), pp. 2-6, 17, 21; *LRE* 3.7 (April 1911), pp. 2-8, 16; *LRE* 3.8 (May 1911), pp. 13-18; *LRE* 3.9 (June 1911), pp. 4-10, 17, 24; *LRE* 3.10 (July 1911), pp. 6-10, 12; *LRE* 3.11 (August 1911), pp. 5-13; *LRE* 3.12 (September 1911), pp. 14-19, 22; *LRE* 4.2 (November

## Pneumatic Discernment

*The Latter Rain Evangel* writes that the Spirit was directly involved in their discerning and interpretation process. The Holy Spirit was their teacher who led the church, provided the scriptures, illuminated their understanding, revealed the way, and guided their judgment and conscience.[27] The Spirit was 'the Spirit of wisdom', and the Spirit provided divine wisdom to the church.[28] Discernment required participation in both the Word and the Spirit.[29] Interpretation of the Word, which was inspired by the Holy Spirit, necessitated the illumination of the Spirit.[30] Prayer was an essential component of the process of discernment along with the Word,[31] 'Seek direction from the Lord with your mind open toward God's book, and your heart open toward God's Spirit'.[32] The Spirit's voice was gentle, and hearers must

---

1911), p. 19; *LRE* 4.3 (December 1911), pp. 2, 19-22; *LRE* 4.5 (February 1912), pp. 6-12; *LRE* 4.6 (March 1912), p. 13; *LRE* 4.8 (May 1912), pp. 8, 24; *LRE* 4.12 (September 1912), p. 6; *LRE* 5.1 (October 1912), pp. 7, 17; *LRE* 5.2 (November 1912), pp. 22-24; *LRE* 5.3 (December 1912), pp. 14, 18; *LRE* 5.4 (January 1913), pp. 17-20; *LRE* 5.5 (February 1913), p. 5; *LRE* 5.9 (June 1913), pp. 15-19; *LRE* 5.11 (August 1913), p. 23; *LRE* 6.3 (December 1913), p. 23; *LRE* 6.6 (March 1914), p. 11; *LRE* 6.7 (April 1914), pp. 5-6; *LRE* 6.9 (June 1914), p. 17; *LRE* 6.11 (August 1914), p. 6; *LRE* 7.5 (February 1915), p. 10; *LRE* 7.7 (April 1915), pp. 5-6, 20; *LRE* 7.8 (May 1915), pp. 12-13; *LRE* 7.9 (June 1915), pp. 10-11, 18; *LRE* 7.10 (July 1915), pp. 3, 8, 17, 19; *LRE* 8.1 (October 1915), pp. 2, 11-12; *LRE* 8.2 (November 1915), pp. 14, 23; *LRE* 8.3 (December 1915), p. 8; *LRE* 8.4 (January 1916), pp. 6, 18; *LRE* 8.6 (March 1916), pp. 4, 10-11; *LRE* 8.7 (April 1916), p. 21; *LRE* 8.8 (May 1916), pp. 4, 7, 22; *LRE* 8.10 (July 1916), pp. 16-17; *LRE* 8.11 (August 1916), p. 22; *LRE* 9.1 (October 1916), p. 7; *LRE* 9.2 (November 1916), p. 22; *LRE* 9.3 (December 1916), pp. 7-8, 11; *LRE* 9.4 (January 1917), pp. 6-7; *LRE* 9.5 (February 1917), p. 23; *LRE* 9.6 (March 1917), pp. 11, 24; *LRE* 9.8 (May 1917), pp. 14-16; *LRE* 9.9 (June 1917), pp. 3-4; *LRE* 10.1 (October 1917), pp. 6-8; *LRE* 10.2 (November 1917), pp. 4-6; *LRE* 10.4 (January 1918), pp. 8, 20; *LRE* 10.5 (February 1918), pp. 2-5, 22; *LRE* 10.6 (March 1918), pp. 2, 11; *LRE* 10.7 (April 1918), p. 6; *LRE* 11.1 (October 1918), pp. 21-22; *LRE* 11.2 (November 1918), pp. 12-13, 15; *LRE* 11.3 (December 1918), p. 8.

[27] *LRE* 2.5 (February 1910), p. 21. See also *LRE* 2.3 (December 1909), p. 13.

[28] *LRE* 2.11 (August 1910), p. 11. See also *LRE* 2.11 (August 1910), p. 23; *LRE* 3.3 (December 1910), pp. 12, 14; *LRE* 3.9 (June 1911), p. 24; *LRE* 5.3 (December 1912), p. 18; *LRE* 5.11 (August 1913), p. 13; *LRE* 6.5 (February 1914), p. 20; *LRE* 7.9 (June 1915), p. 22; *LRE* 9.3 (December 1916), p. 19.

[29] *LRE* 3.3 (December 1910), p. 7; *LRE* 3.12 (September 1911), p. 10; *LRE* 4.1 (October 1911), p. 11.

[30] *LRE* 4.1 (October 1911), p. 6.

[31] *LRE* 4.7 (April 1912), p. 4; *LRE* 5.4 (January 1913), p. 18; *LRE* 5.6 (March 1913), p. 9; *LRE* 8.6 (March 1916), p. 22.

[32] *LRE* 1.6 (March 1909), p. 5.

listen intently to hear.[33] *The Latter Rain Evangel* suggested that the
Spirit assists the community in discerning between the activities of
God, the human spirit, or an evil spirit.[34] There was a dualism between worldly or 'intellectual' discernment and 'spiritual' discernment, 'So few people understand the workings of Pentecost because
they are trying to work it out intellectually, but spiritual things are to
be discerned by the *spirit*'.[35]

## The Spirit and Pneumatic Discernment in Revelation

### 'In the Spirit'

*The Latter Rain Evangel* referred to John's experience 'in the Spirit' and
used the language: live,[36] walk,[37] sing,[38] call,[39] liberty,[40] carried away,[41]
see,[42] laugh,[43] cry,[44] and unity[45] 'in the Spirit'.[46] Life should be lived 'in
the Spirit', 'Beloved, let us walk in the Spirit, talk in the Spirit, think
in the Spirit, sing in the Spirit, preach in the Spirit, testify in the Spirit,
doing all things in the Spirit and in the understanding, and you will
see Jesus; He is in the midst of the seven Spirits. Rev. 1:12-16'.[47] The
entire book of Revelation was given to John while he was in a state
of ecstasy, and the church could participate in these experiences in a
'preparatory' manner, 'We have preparatory experiences. These
things are mysteries. They are all lying in between the initial experience, the baptism of the Holy Spirit and the ultimate translation of

---

[33] *LRE* 11.2 (November 1918), p. 21.

[34] *LRE* 10.10 (July 1918), p. 17. See also *LRE* 2.10 (July 1910), p. 22.

[35] *LRE* 1.9 (June 1909), p. 18.

[36] *LRE* 3.2 (November 1910), p. 18.

[37] *LRE* 5.6 (March 1913), p. 12.

[38] *LRE* 4.4 (January 1912), p. 5.

[39] *LRE* 5.12 (September 1913), p. 14.

[40] *LRE* 3.4 (January 1911), p. 13; *LRE* 8.6 (March 1916), p. 22.

[41] *LRE* 1.9 (June 1909), p. 15; *LRE* 1.6 (March 1909), p. 4; *LRE* 8.3 (December 1915), p. 14.

[42] *LRE* 6.5 (February 1914), p. 4.

[43] *LRE* 5.11 (August 1913), p. 22.

[44] *LRE* 3.4 (January 1911), p. 10; *LRE* 5.11 (August 1913), p. 22.

[45] *LRE* 4.5 (February 1912), p. 17; *LRE* 10.3 (December 1917), p. 12.

[46] *LRE* 3.8 (May 1911), pp. 13-14 referred to John being 'in the Spirit'.

[47] *LRE* 3.9 (June 1911), p. 10.

the saints. Some day we will go into a state of ecstasy forever.'[48] Revelation 'is the book of all books that requires to be unfolded to us by the operation in us of that same Spirit who on Patmos Isle gave it to John'.[49] Mrs. Wesley Stowell had a visionary experience; like John, she saw the Lord come into her room and was carried away to heaven 'in the Spirit' and was healed.[50]

### The Seven Spirits

D.W. Myland observed that Revelation was a book of sevens, indicating 'the perfection of completeness and the completeness of perfection'.[51] *The Latter Rain Evangel* observed an influence of the sevenfold Spirit from Isaiah 11.[52] The seven Spirits were the 'Spirit of *truth*, Spirit of *light*, Spirit of *life*, Spirit of *holiness*, Spirit of *love*, Spirit of *power*, Spirit of *wisdom*, but His first operation is always as the Spirit of *truth* to make us know, and to illuminate our minds'.[53]

### Discernment in the Seven Prophetic Messages

Though some in *The Latter Rain Evangel* imagined living in the Laodicean age,[54] others such as D.W. Myland proposed that the seven churches were 'typical' and 'representative' of the 'church phases'. These phases could be traced amongst individuals in congregations, 'if you have the eyes of the Spirit you don't have to be in an assembly long before you can select the people that represent the seven phases of these churches'.[55] Myland considered the issue of discernment in Ephesus.[56] Ephesus was commended for their ability to discern and test apostles and those who professed to be apostles. They were zealous in discernment; nevertheless, the church of Ephesus was condemned for their lack of a 'deep spirituality', 'it is possible to have

---

[48] *LRE* 6.9 (June 1914), p. 17.

[49] *LRE* 3.5 (February 1911), p. 3. See also *LRE* 3.10 (July 1911), p. 9; *LRE* 9.6 (March 1917), p. 24; *LRE* 11.1 (October 1918), p. 21.

[50] *LRE* 9.11 (August 1917), p. 15.

[51] *LRE* 3.3 (December 1910), p. 6; *LRE* 11.1 (October 1918), p. 22.

[52] *LRE* 3.5 (February 1911), p. 3; *LRE* 11.1 (October 1918), p. 22.

[53] *LRE* 3.3 (December 1910), p. 7.

[54] *LRE* 1.7 (April 1909), p. 16; *LRE* 8.10 (July 1916), p. 16.

[55] *LRE* 3.5 (February 1911), p. 2.

[56] *LRE* 7.11 (August 1915), pp. 19-22.

discernment, an insight to things, and be able to understand prophecies and much that is in this Book, and yet not be spiritually minded. There is such a thing as intellectual enlightenment.'[57]

Opening one's ears to the Spirit was crucial for discernment:

> You ought to thank God all your lives for ears (physical) to hear the words of the Spirit, and the spiritual ears to hear the voice of the Spirit. As Jesus told John on the Isle of Patmos, 'If any man hath an ear to hear, let him hear what the Spirit is saying to the churches'. The trouble is not with God these days, but with the churches ... she has no longer an ear to hear what God is saying to her ... God reaches the soul through the ear-gate, the physical nature, by the voice of the Spirit and the Word.[58]

The church was exhorted to pray so that they might have their 'spiritual ear' to hear. Some were unable to hear the Spirit because their 'spiritual ear ... has become dead through trespasses and sin'.[59]

## Discerning the Mark of the Beast

When examining the number 666, W.H. Cossum wrote, 'He would be six; seven is a number of a divine perfection; six is less than that, and it is repeated thrice, meaning he is aiming at the very highest merely human perfection. He is not divine as Christ but seeks to imitate him as far as possible.'[60] Some considered the mark as a dualistic identifier in Revelation, 'Be careful whose mark you have, whether the mark of God's protection and love or the mark of the beast'.[61] Cossum discovered a 'distinct line of demarkation [*sic*] between the Christ and the Antichrist until each has a mark on his people'.[62] Elizabeth Sisson suggested that those who would participate in the first resurrection:

> kept the garments white, singularly unworldly, for they 'had not worshipped the beast' – the great Antichristal power – which, while it heads up in a person at the end of this age, yet as 'principalities ... powers ... world-rulers of this darkness' (Eph. 6:12,

---

[57] *LRE* 7.11 (August 1915), p. 21.

[58] *LRE* 1.9 (June 1909), p. 18.

[59] *LRE* 3.5 (February 1911), p. 2.

[60] *LRE* 2.12 (September 1909), p. 9.

[61] *LRE* 3.12 (September 1911), p. 16.

[62] *LRE* 2.12 (September 1909), p. 4.

R.V.) 'that spirit of Antichrist' John said even in his day was now
'now already in the world'. I. Jno. 4:3. But these souls in training
for first resurrection 'had not worshipped' this world-power; 'in
their fore-heads' was not the sign of its worry, care, greed or ava-
rice; 'in their hands' no unclean trickery of deed or pen had put
its mark.[63]

*The Latter Rain Evangel* considered the economic aspects of the mark
of the beast. Some believed that no one would be able to make 'mer-
cantile pursuits' without taking the mark.[64] During World War I, H.H.
Cox predicted the economic hardship for believers who would not
take the mark of the beast, 'It will be pretty hard on God's children,
will it not, to have their money piled up in the bank and not be able
to use it unless they take the mark of the beast ... They will either
have to let it go and take martyrdom, or take the mark of the beast.
We are facing that time now. Look at Europe with its clashing arms.'[65]
Another unnamed contributor also interpreted the Great War, economic hardship, and the Influenza virus as the unleashing of the four
horsemen from Revelation 6:[66]

> Already we can see the shadowing of the tribulation days; already
> we can hear the distant roar of the oncoming storm. We can feel
> the stealthy encroachment of the antichristian systems which will
> permit none to buy or sell excepting those who come under its
> allegiance. Hundreds and thousands of Christians will be deceived
> ... The warning voice will have to be lifted in secret, but the wise
> shall understand and be able to discern the false from the true.[67]

---

[63] *LRE* 2.3 (December 1909), p. 20.

[64] *LRE* 1.7 (April 1909), p. 19.

[65] *LRE* 8.8 (May 1916), p. 3.

[66] *LRE* 11.2 (November 1918), p. 13, writes:

The world has seen a literal fulfillment of these verses within the last few years.
War, famine, pestilence, have followed each other in rapid succession ... Every
home has been visited by the bearer of a pair of balances, rich and poor alike
have had their portions measured out to them ... Now the rider on the pale
horse follows in the wake of stalking pestilence, and his trail is marked by thousands who have been slain by his ruthless hand. The plague of Influenza is
sweeping the world, leaping from city to city, and from camp to camp, leaving
its blight and destruction on every hand.

See also *LRE* 7.9 (June 1915), p. 18; *LRE* 8.10 (July 1916), p. 16.

[67] *LRE* 11.2 (November 1918), p. 13.

*The Latter Rain Evangel* examined the two beasts. The two beasts along with the dragon formed the 'trinity of evil'.[68] The dragon was Satan. The first beast was the antichrist who represented both a man who will rise in the future as well as imperial and commercial power.[69] The second beast was the false prophet who will head all religious systems and unite all the 'isms'; the second beast was associated with the great whore in Revelation 17.[70] The two beasts embodied 'a world-wide devil-inspired imperialism linked with a devil-inspired false religious system each undoubtedly represented by a personal leader of great power'.[71] D.W. Myland attempted to discern the two beasts as contemporary figures and proposed that 'the Papacy and Mohammedanism' anticipated the rise of the two beasts that would 'culminate in, and combine together, to produce the fullness of the power of the Antichrist'.[72] Cossum pondered whether there would be anything able to encompass all that is described of these great powers and responded:

> 'Yes!' The spirit of federation, commercially, religiously and na-
> tionally! The spirit of combine represented by Rockefeller, Mor-
> gan, and the great trust idea is finding an enlarged sphere in the
> call for international federation with a world president ... the
> world-wide man is in the field feted of all nations, and the type is

---

[68] *LRE* 2.12 (September 1909), p. 8.

[69] *LRE* 2.12 (September 1909), p. 8.

[70] *LRE* 2.12 (September 1909), p. 8; *LRE* 8.1 (October 1915), p. 5; *LRE* 10.2 (November 1917), p. 4.

[71] *LRE* 2.12 (September 1909), p. 8.

[72] *LRE* 3.3 (December 1910), p. 3. Myland, in *LRE* 3.3 (December 1910), pp. 2-5, offered a lengthy exposition on four views of Revelation, which included: (1) the 'Praeterist' school, which proposed that all the prophecies were fulfilled around the time of the destruction of Jerusalem. (2) The 'Presentist or the Historical school' suggested that the prophecies from Revelation covered the whole church period and were being fulfillment throughout the ages and was advocated by Dr. H. Gattan Guinness. (3) The 'Futurist school' was the opposite of the 'Praeterist' school and resolved that everything will be fulfilled in the future, which was pro-moted by G.H. Pember. (4) The 'Comprehensive or Harmonic School', the school that Myland followed, put forth that 'the Praeterist, the Historic and the Futurist schools are in the main correct, except as they deny each other', which was advocated by Rev. Mr. Baxter of England. Although Myland followed the Harmonic school in his readings of Revelation, he tended to gravitate toward the futuristic approach, e.g. he wrote, 'Look at Revelation 13! Most of that is yet future; nearly every phase of it' (p. 5).

developing. He will soon appear he will evolve in a few successive stages into the Antichrist.[73]

## Babylon

*The Latter Rain Evangel* suggested that Babylon symbolized evil, commercialism, false religion, and a capital city in the great tribulation.[74] Babylon was 'a great system, false Christian system of confusion, building up to heaven and blaspheming heaven, and taking the name of God upon it, as the pope now does'.[75] Cossum observed a correlation between the imperial and commercial power of beasts from Revelation 13 and the description of the Babylon in Revelation 17–18:

> We find then that there are two prominent powers of the antichristian empire, first the imperial and commercial power shown in the first beast of Rev. 13 the beast of Rev. 17 and the great city of Rev. 18, and second, the religious power shown in the second beast of Rev. 13 who is called also the false prophet in Rev. 16 and 19 and who is evidently the mother of harlots of Rev. 17.[76]

Some interpretations considered the seven heads as referring to Rome, 'Now Papal Rome and all other false systems, religious, social, industrial and political ... all these go to make up Babylon'.[77] Cossum wrote:

> Yes and No. It is Rome in partial fulfillment, but in Rev. 17 John is very evidently seeing a time beyond Rome, for the final Babylon is an age-end picture ... the spirit of Babel was recognized as being in these great empire capitol cities ... So if John calls Rome Babylon, I presume he understood why he called it Babylon, and I think we can discover that these four empires [Babylon, Rome, Medo-Persia, and Greece] were simply used one after the other to

---

[73] *LRE* 2.12 (September 1909), p. 9.

[74] *LRE* 2.8 (May 1910), p. 7; *LRE* 2.12 (September 1909), p. 9; *LRE* 3.1 (October 1910), pp. 17-21; *LRE* 4.5 (February 1912), p. 7.

[75] *LRE* 4.3 (December 1911), p. 20.

[76] *LRE* 2.12 (September 1909), p. 8.

[77] *LRE* 4.3 (December 1911), pp. 20-21.

represent the world-wide infidel power against God. And so John, living in the time of Rome, here sees it as Babylon.[78]

Mysteries

*Revelation 1*
*The Latter Rain Evangel* interpreted the seven stars as pastors of the churches[79] and exhorted, 'Let us be stars ever shinning with the light of the knowledge of the truth'.[80] When considering the vision of Christ in Revelation 1, the paper observed, 'His eyes are a flame of fire, which means perfect discernment, revelation and understanding'.[81]

*Revelation 10*
Only once in this periodical did anyone comment on Revelation 10 where the mighty angel who reveals the mystery was identified as the 'covenant angel' from the HB and was identified as Jesus.[82]

**Summary**
*The Latter Rain Evangel* believed that the Spirit was central to the discerning process. The church needed to be 'in the Spirit' to interpret Revelation because John was 'in the Spirit' when he received the Revelation. Similarly, the church was exhorted to open their ears to hear the seven Spirits, and likewise to discern, not intellectually, but spiritually. The bestial texts were often considered in *The Latter Rain Evangel* having varying interpretations. Some interpretations were dispensational[83] and located the danger of the two beasts in the future.[84] Some of the dispensational interpretations still attempted to hear Revelation for their church. For example, Minnie F. Abrams wrote, 'if we do not learn how to overcome before the time of the tribula-

---

[78] *LRE* 3.1 (October 1910), p. 21.

[79] *LRE* 3.3 (December 1910), p. 6; *LRE* 3.5 (February 1911), p. 3.

[80] *LRE* 3.5 (February 1911), p. 3.

[81] *LRE* 4.5 (February 1912), p. 9.

[82] *LRE* 3.11 (August 1911), p. 5.

[83] *LRE* 3.5 (February 1911), p. 3, reveals Seiss's influence on *The Latter Rain Evangel*, although he was not often referenced in the literature.

[84] E.g. *LRE* 8.8 (May 1916), p. 9, '"Are we in The Great Tribulation?" ... No, but we are amid the beginning of events and elements which will yet combine to launch it'.

tion, we shall undoubtedly be left in the tribulation to learn that lesson'.[85] Sisson concurred writing that all believers were in 'training' for the first resurrection and must avoid worshipping the beast or taking his mark because the spirit of the antichrist was already present in the world. Others looked at Revelation as unfolding before their eyes in economic hardship, World War I, and the epidemic of the Influenza virus.

## Word and Witness

*Word and Witness* was a monthly publication edited by E.N. Bell. It began publication in 1912 and was combined with *The Weekly Evangel* in 1915.[86] This publication contained testimonials, teachings, hymns, and sermonic materials and numerous references to Revelation.[87]

### Pneumatic Discernment

The Spirit was identified as a teacher and guide who reveals the 'deep things of God' and Christ to the church.[88] Leadership was crucial for discernment because God 'ruled' the church through elders or pastors who were filled with the Spirit and ordained by God.[89] Since there was an excess of false teaching in the world, no one was able to preach the gospel unless they had received discernment to distinguish between the 'antichrist spirit' and genuine teaching.[90] *Word and Witness* condemned anyone who sought to follow the Spirit only while belittling the Word because the Spirit and the Word agree,[91] 'It

---

[85] *LRE* 2.6 (March 1910), p. 17.

[86] *The Christian Evangel* started on July 19, 1913. During the time of overlap between *Word and Witness* and *The Christian Evangel*, many articles were printed in both publications, see McQueen, *Toward a Pentecostal Eschatology*, p. 156.

[87] For explicit references and quotations to Revelation, see *WW* 9.1 (January 1913), p. 4; *WW* 9.2 (February 1913), p. 4; *WW* 9.3 (March 1913), pp. 2-3; *WW* 9.6 (June 1913), pp. 3, 8; *WW* 9.7 (July 1913), p. 2; *WW* 9.10 (October 1913), pp. 1-2; *WW* 9.11 (November 1913), pp. 1-2; *WW* 10.1 (January 1914), pp. 2-3; *WW* 10.3 (March 1914), p. 2; *WW* 10.4 (April 1914), p. 1; *WW* 10.5 (May 1914), p. 1; *WW* 10.7 (July 1914), p. 1; *WW* 10.8 (August 1914), p. 1; *WW* 12.5 (May 1915), pp. 4-5; *WW* 12.6 (June 1915), p. 5; *WW* 12.9 (September 1915), pp. 5-6; *WW* 12.10 (October 1915), p. 3.

[88] *WW* 9.2 (February 1913), p. 4; *WW* 9.5 (May 1913), p. 1; *WW* 9.6 (June 1913), p. 6; *WW* 10.7 (July 1914), p. 2.

[89] *WW* 9.6 (June 1913), p. 2.

[90] *WW* 10.3 (March 1914), p. 1. See also *WW* 9.2 (February 1913), p. 4.

[91] *WW* 9.12 (December 1913), p. 3. See also *WW* 9.3 (March 1913), p. 2.

is unwise and shows lack of balance to set the Spirit in contrast to the word or the word in contrast to the Spirit'.[92]

## The Spirit and Pneumatic Discernment in Revelation

'In the Spirit'

Pentecostals of the *Word and Witness* saw their experiences as correlating with John's 'in the Spirit' experience. They would walk,[93] be carried,[94] fellowship,[95] dance,[96] pray,[97] and grieve[98] 'in the Spirit'.[99] There were visionary experiences that echoed John's experiences in Revelation. An unnamed person from Dallas, Texas testified:

> Last Sunday morning he was carried away in the Spirit, like the Apostle John, and beheld the Holy City, the New Jerusalem, coming down from God out of heaven, prepared as a bride adorned for her husband, all exactly as described in the book of Revelation. He said: 'I saw the innumerable company of angels, singing around the throne, and was permitted to join in the song.' (We heard him singing in tongues at the time he was in the Spirit).[100]

Fred Lohman testified to a visionary experience where many images from Revelation were described:

> Around the altar souls saw visions of Him who is walking today among the Candlesticks, holding the stars in His right hand.' Numbers seemed to hear that voice as the sounding of 'great waters' and like John fell at his feet as dead ... Many saw visions of Jesus coming in the clouds of heaven with power and great glory. Some times the Spirit would move like the gentle breeze, fanning every soul with the breath of Heaven ... At the same time several in the Spirit were hearing the 'tramp, tramp' of a mighty army, and

---

[92] *WW* 9.12 (December 1913), p. 3. See also *WW* 12.5 (May 1915), p. 4.

[93] *WW* 8.8 (October 1912), p. 2.

[94] *WW* 10.5 (May 1914), p. 2; *WW* 12.5 (May 1915), p. 7.

[95] *WW* 12.9 (September 1915), p. 7.

[96] *WW* 9.1 (January 1913), p. 3; *WW* 9.2 (February 1913), p. 3; *WW* 10.7 (July 1914), p. 1; *WW* 12.11 (November 1915), p. 1.

[97] *WW* 9.6 (June 1913), p. 2.

[98] *WW* 10.4 (April 1914), p. 2.

[99] *WW* 8.8 (October 1912), p. 3; *WW* 8.10 (December 1912), p. 3; *WW* 9.11 (November 1913), p. 2; *WW* 12.5 (May 1915), p. 3; *WW* 12.6 (June 1915), p. 4.

[100] *WW* 8.8 (October 20, 1912), p. 3.

two saw the mighty armies of Heaven riding forth on White Horses ... The Spirit has been revealing in many ways that God is sifting out a people from among all the factions, tribes, and kindreds of earth whom He will send forth in love, clothed with power and might to do exploits and wonders in the name of Jesus.[101]

### Discernment in the Seven Prophetic Messages

*Word and Witness* proposed that the last age had arrived – the Laodicean age.[102] During this last age, the church was being called to hear the Spirit and to be 'full overcomers' who turned from 'lukewarmness, hypocrisy, blindness, shallowness of life, and strange and unsound teachings'.[103] There was an urgency to become 'full overcomers' since the final church age had arrived. One contributor considered the church in Ephesus and wrote, 'See that even professing apostles were tried by the church at Ephesus, and God commends them for such zeal and faithfulness'.[104] Occurring in a discussion of church discipline, this reference to Ephesus seemed to be encouraging the Pentecostal churches to test and try those who were in leadership.

### Summary

*Word and Witness* offers multiple examples of Pentecostals turning to Revelation to describe their pneumatic experiences. The language and images – such as being carried away, New Jerusalem, visions of the resurrection Christ, large armies, and the rider on a white horse – recall Revelation. *Word and Witness* had an eschatological outlook. There was urgency to become full overcomers and discern false teaching like those in Ephesus.

---

[101] *WW* 9.2 (February 20, 1913), p. 1. For other visionary experiences that might be influenced by Revelation, see *WW* 9.2 (February 1913), p. 3; *WW* 10.1 (January 1914), p. 3.

[102] *WW* 12.5 (May 1915), p. 4.

[103] *WW* 12.5 (May 1915), p. 4.

[104] *WW* 9.6 (June 1913), p. 2.

## The Weekly/Christian Evangel

In 1913 the Assemblies of God created *The Christian Evangel* under the leadership of E.N. Bell (editor) and J.R. Flower (associate editor).[105] The name of the periodical was changed to *The Weekly Evangel* in 1915.[106] The influence of Revelation can be seen throughout the publication, largely whenever considering futuristic aspects of Revelation.[107]

---

[105] McQueen, *Toward a Pentecostal Eschatology*, pp. 162-63. Although E.N. Bell halted his editorial duties from October 1915 to December 1917, he remained a major contributor throughout the publication.

[106] The publication changed its name again in 1919 to *The Pentecostal Evangel.* Footnote citations will reflect the appropriate publication cited.

[107] For explicit references and quotations to Revelation, see *CE* (January 4, 1914), p. 2; *CE* (April 19, 1914), p. 1; *CE* 49 (July 11, 1914), p. 1; *CE* 51 (July 25, 1914), p. 2; *CE* 53 (August 8, 1914), p. 2; *CE* 54 (August 15, 1914), p. 2; *CE* 56 (August 29, 1914), pp. 1-2; *CE* 57 (September 5, 1914), pp. 1-2; *CE* 58 (September 12, 1914), p. 3; *CE* 59 (September 19, 1914), p. 2; *CE* 60 (September 26, 1914), p. 2; *CE* 62 (October 10, 1914), pp. 2-3; *CE* 63 (October 17, 1914), pp. 1-3; *CE* 65 (October 31, 1914), pp. 2, 4; *CE* 66 (November 7, 1914), pp. 1-3; *CE* 67 (November 14, 1914), pp. 2-3; *CE* 68 (November 21, 1914), p. 3; *CE* 70 (December 12, 1914), p. 1; *CE* 71 (December 19, 1914), pp. 1-3; *CE* 72 (December 26, 1914), p. 1; *CE* 74 (January 16, 1915), pp. 1, 3; *CE* 75 (January 23, 1915), pp. 2-3; *CE* 76 (January 30, 1915), p. 3; *CE* 78 (February 20, 1915), p. 3; *WE* 81 (March 13, 1915), p. 2; *WE* 83 (March 27, 1915), pp. 1, 3; *WE* 85 (April 10, 1915), p. 1; *WE* 86 (April 17, 1915), pp. 1-2; *WE* 87 (April 24, 1915), p. 4; *WE* 88 (May 1, 1915), p. 2; *WE* 90 (May 15, 1915), p. 3; *WE* 92 (May 29, 1915), p. 2; *WE* 93 (June 5, 1915), p. 3; *WE* 94 (June 12, 1915), p. 2; *WE* 95 (June 19, 1915), p. 3; *WE* 96 (June 26, 1915), p. 4; *WE* 97 (July 3, 1915), pp. 2-3; *WE* 99 (July 17, 1915), p. 2; *WE* 101 (July 31, 1915), p. 3; *WE* 102 (August 7, 1915), p. 1; *WE* 103 (August 14, 1915), pp. 1, 3; *WE* 107 (September 11, 1915), p. 3; *WE* 109 (September 25, 1915), pp. 2-3; *WE* 111 (October 16, 1915), pp. 1-2; *WE* 112 (October 23, 1915), p. 4; *WE* 116 (November 20, 1915), pp. 1-2; *WE* 117 (November 27, 1915), pp. 2-3; *WE* 118 (December 4, 1915), p. 3; *WE* 121 (January 1, 1916), p. 1; *WE* 122 (January 8, 1918), p. 11; *WE* 124 (January 22, 1916), pp. 6, 8; *WE* 125 (January 29-February 5, 1916), p. 8; *WE* 126 (February 12, 1916), p. 9; *WE* 127 (February 19, 1916), p. 10; *WE* 128 (February 26, 1916), pp. 6-8, 10, 12; *WE* 129 (March 4, 1916), p. 7; *WE* 130 (March 11, 1916), pp. 7, 9; *WE* 131 (March 18, 1916), pp. 7, 10; *WE* 132 (March 25, 1916), pp. 7-8; *WE* 133 (April 1, 1916), pp. 6, 8; *WE* 134 (April 8, 1916), pp. 7-9; *WE* 136 (April 22, 1916), p. 14; *WE* 137 (April 29, 1916), p. 6; *WE* 138 (May 6, 1916), pp. 6, 8; *WE* 139 (May 13, 1916), pp. 6-8; *WE* 140 (May 20, 1916), pp. 8-9, 13; *WE* 141 (May 27, 1916), pp. 6, 8; *WE* 142 (June 3, 1916), p. 9; *WE* 143 (June 10, 1916), p. 5; *WE* 147 (July 8, 1916), p. 6; *WE* 148 (July 17, 1916), pp. 7, 9; *WE* 149 (July 22, 1916), p. 3; *WE* 150 (July 29, 1916), pp. 5, 8; *WE* 151 (August 5, 1916), pp. 6, 8-9, 11; *WE* 153 (August 19, 1916), pp. 6, 11, 14; *WE* 156 (September 9, 1916), pp. 8-9, 13; *WE* 157 (September 16, 1916), p. 9; *WE* 159 (September 30, 1916), p. 8; *WE* 162 (October 28, 1916), pp. 4, 6-7, 9; *WE* 164 (November 11, 1916), p. 3; *WE* 165 (November 18, 1916), pp. 6, 10; *WE* 166 (November 25, 1916), p. 10; *WE* 167 (December 2,

## Pentecostals and Pneumatic Discernment

*The Christian/Weekly Evangel* put forth a process to discern God's will: (1) submit to God, (2) study the Word, (3) corroborate with the providences of God, and (4) heed the voice of the Spirit.[108] The Spirit taught, guided, illuminated, and gave wisdom to the church:[109] 'It is

---

1916), pp. 7, 9-10; *WE* 168 (December 9, 1916), pp. 7-10; *WE* 169 (December 16, 1916), pp. 5, 11, 13; *WE* 170 (December 23, 1916), p. 10; *WE* 171 (January 6, 1917), p. 3; *WE* 172 (January 13, 1917), pp. 3-4, 6, 8, 10, 12-13; *WE* 173 (January 20, 1917), pp. 1, 4, 10, 13; *WE* 174 (January 27, 1917), pp. 4, 7, 13; *WE* 176 (February 10, 1917), p. 2; *WE* 178 (February 24, 1917), p. 11; *WE* 179 (March 3, 1917), p. 14; *WE* 180 (March 10, 1917), pp. 1, 5-6, 9; *WE* 181 (March 17, 1917), p. 8; *WE* 183 (March 31, 1917), pp. 5, 9; *WE* 184 (April 7, 1917), p. 6; *WE* 184a (April 10, 1917), pp. 3, 6; *WE* 186 (April 21, 1917), pp. 9-10; *WE* 187 (April 28, 1917), pp. 2, 5, 8; *WE* 188 (May 5, 1917), pp. 2, 12-13, 16; *WE* 189 (May 12, 1917), pp. 4-5; *WE* 190 (May 19, 1917), p. 5; *WE* 191 (May 26, 1917), pp. 6, 9; *WE* 192 (June 2, 1917), pp. 3, 8; *WE* 193 (June 9, 1917), pp. 6-7; *WE* 194 (June 16, 1917), pp. 1-2; *WE* 195 (June 23, 1917), pp. 4-5, 9; *WE* 196 (June 30, 1917), pp. 3-5, 9; *WE* 197 (July 7, 1917), pp. 3, 6-7; *WE* 198 (July 14, 1917), pp. 1, 13; *WE* 199 (July 21, 1917), pp. 3-4, 6, 8, 10; *WE* 200 (July 28, 1917), pp. 9, 12; *WE* 201 (August 4, 1917), p. 2; *WE* 202 (August 11, 1917), pp. 8-9; *WE* 203 (August 18, 1917), pp. 7, 9-12; *WE* 204 (August 25, 1917), pp. 6, 10; *WE* 205 (September 1, 1917), pp. 2-3; *WE* 206 (September 8, 1917), pp. 6, 8-9; *WE* 207 (September 15, 1917), pp. 6, 8-9; *WE* 208 (September 29, 1917), pp. 3, 8; *WE* 210 (October 13, 1917), p. 4; *WE* 211 (October 20, 1917), p. 9; *WE* 213 (November 3, 1917), pp. 2-3, 5, 7, 9; *WE* 214 (November 11, 1917), pp. 2, 9; *WE* 215 (November 17, 1917), pp. 4, 7, 12; *WE* 216 (November 24, 1917), pp. 3-4, 7-8; *WE* 217 (December 1, 1917), pp. 3, 8; *WE* 219 (December 15, 1917), pp. 7-8; *WE* 220 (December 12, 1917), pp. 7, 9, 13; *WE* 221 (January 5, 1918), p. 8; *WE* 222 (January 12, 1918), pp. 2-3, 7, 12; *WE* 223 (January 19, 1918), pp. 5, 7; *WE* 224 (January 26, 1918), pp. 2-3; *WE* 225 (February 2, 1918), pp. 1, 4, 6, 8; *WE* 226 (February 9, 1918), pp. 2-3; *WE* 227 (February 16, 1918), pp. 2, 12; *WE* 228 (February 23, 1918), p. 9; *WE* 231 (March 16, 1918), p. 2; *WE* 232 (March 23, 1918), pp. 12, 14-15; *WE* 233 (March 30, 1918), pp. 3, 8-9, 11-12; *WE* 234-235 (April 6, 1918), pp. 7, 9; *WE* 236-237 (April 20, 1918), pp. 1-5, 8, 12; *WE* 238-239 (May 4, 1918), pp. 1, 3, 12; *WE* 240-241 (May 18, 1918), pp. 3, 9; *CE* 242-243 (June 1, 1918), pp. 5, 9, 12; *CE* 244-245 (June 15, 1918), pp. 3, 5, 14; *CE* 246-247 (June 29, 1918), p. 9; *CE* 248-249 (June 27, 1918), p. 9; *CE* 250-251 (August 10, 1918), pp. 5, 7; *CE* 252-253 (August 24, 1918), pp. 2, 7, 9; *CE* 254 (September 7, 1918), p. 1; *CE* 255 (September 21, 1918), p. 6; *CE* 256-257 (October 5, 1918), p. 9; *CE* 258-259 (October 19, 1918), pp. 5-7; *CE* 260-261 (November 2, 1918), pp. 6, 8-9, 12; *CE* 262-263 (November 16, 1918), pp. 1, 4-5; *CE* 264-265 (November 10, 1918), pp. 2, 5; *CE* 266-267 (December 14, 1918), p. 7; *CE* 268-269 (December 28, 1918), pp. 2, 5.

[108] *WE* 190 (May 19, 1917), p. 9.

[109] *CE* 58 (September 12, 1914), p. 3; *CE* 63 (October 17, 1914), p. 1; *CE* 67 (November 14, 1914), p. 1; *CE* 71 (December 19, 1914), p. 2. *CE* 72 (December 26, 1914), p. 2; *CE* 76 (January 30, 1915), p. 1; *WE* 91 (May 22, 1915), p. 4; *WE* 99 (July 17, 1915), p. 4; *WE* 123 (January 15, 1916), p. 14; *WE* 196 (June 30, 1917), p. 3; *WE* 207 (September 15, 1917), p. 5.

the Spirit's gracious safeguard, like the eyes of the body, enabling it to see where are the dangers and pitfalls, and to avoid them'.[110] Spirit baptism provided illumination to believers.[111] Discernment required the Spirit and the Word because the Spirit and the Word agree, negating either the Spirit or Word led to worry and disappointment.[112] The Spirit spoke in a 'still, small voice':[113]

> Every voice that brings unrest and causes a sense of hurry and worry is a false, deluding voice, and is *not* the voice of the Holy Spirit. *God's voice speaks in stillness and brings peace within.* The voice of the Spirit already speaks in harmony with the written Word of God. Any impression or 'leading' that goes beyond or contradicts Scripture is not from the Holy Spirit, but some other spirit ... The power to hear and distinguish the voice of the Holy Spirit will come most easily to the one who cultivates the habit of silent waiting upon God.

> 'Be still and thy Beloved will speak.
> When He hath found a silent heart.'[114]

Wisdom is needed:

> Wisdom is understanding, is discernment. Wisdom is comprehensive, discrimination, perception. Wisdom sees relatively. Wisdom discerns not only good, but sees every value in true relation to all others. Wisdom comprehends both sides of a question and sees between or into matters. Wisdom not only looks at a matter, but looks into it. Wisdom deals with both spiritual and non-spiritual matters. Wisdom sees into both.[115]

---

[110] *WE* 197 (July 7, 1917), p. 5.

[111] *CE* 71 (December 19, 1914), p. 3.

[112] *CE* 72 (December 26, 1914), p. 3; *CE* 73 (January 9, 1915), p. 2; *WE* 144 (June 17, 1916), p. 3; *WE* 158 (September 23, 1916), p. 6.

[113] *WE* 207 (September 15, 1917), p. 7.

[114] *WE* 195 (June 23, 1917), p. 3.

[115] *WE* 157 (September 16, 1916), p. 3.

## The Spirit and Discernment in Revelation

'In the Spirit'

Beyond being carried away 'in the Spirit',[116] *The Weekly/Christian Evangel* referred to: walking,[117] dancing,[118] praying,[119] loving,[120] living,[121] singing,[122] talking,[123] being free,[124] being kept,[125] being deepened,[126] and having unity[127] and liberty[128] 'in the Spirit'. Reflecting on John as a model, believers needed to be 'in the Spirit' to receive revelation:

> The Spirit in these days is showing in a general manner things to come, but to those who seek Him, He will show in a particular manner. But those who seek must be in the Spirit … And there has been in every subsequent outpouring of the Spirit illumination and revelation … And as the time draws near, those who live in the Spirit may expect fuller revelation to be given in secret to be held as a secret.[129]

Alice Flower studied the process of writing Revelation 'in the Spirit':

> In a peculiar sense; he [God] is the author for John was simply the amanuensis to record what was dictated by the angel … It is a sign

---

[116] *CE* 79 (February 27, 1915), p. 1; *WE* 89 (May 8, 1915), p. 1; *WE* 91 (May 22, 1915), p. 1; *WE* 206 (September 8, 1917), p. 8; *WE* 223 (January 19, 1918), p. 7.

[117] *WE* 191 (May 26, 1917), p. 8; *WE* 217 (December 1, 1917), p. 2.

[118] *CE* (December 14, 1913), p. 2; *WE* 85 (April 10, 1915), p. 4; *WE* 100 (July 24, 1915), p. 2; *WE* 114 (November 6, 1915), p. 1.

[119] *CE* 59 (September 19, 1914), p. 4; *WE* 151 (August 5, 1916), p. 6; *WE* 171 (January 6, 1917), p. 1.

[120] *CE* 71 (December 19, 1914), p. 2.

[121] *CE* 80 (March 3, 1915), p. 3; *WE* 191 (May 26, 1917), p. 8; *WE* 206 (September 8, 1917), p. 8.

[122] *CE* 60 (September 26, 1914), p. 4; *WE* 90 (May 15, 1915), p. 1; *WE* 96 (June 26, 1915), p. 1; *WE* 135 (April 15, 1916), p. 14; *WE* 166 (November 25, 1916), p. 14; *WE* 172 (January 13, 1917), p. 15; *WE* 202 (August 11, 1917), p. 16.

[123] *WE* 111 (October 16, 1915), p. 3.

[124] *WE* 99 (July 17, 1915), p. 2; *WE* 202 (August 11, 1917), p. 12.

[125] *WE* 168 (December 9, 1916), p. 5.

[126] *CE* 57 (September 5, 1914), p. 3.

[127] *CE* 2.13 (March 28, 1914), p. 5; *CE* 51 (July 25, 1914), p. 4; *CE* 70 (December 12, 1914), p. 3.

[128] *WE* 169 (December 16, 1916), p. 9.

[129] *WE* 206 (September 8, 1917), p. 8.

book. And perhaps this is the reason it has been a book of mystery to many. And those who do interpret very widely in their understanding thereof. It is being delved into now as never before and the Holy Ghost is making manifest to our hearts many of the hitherto misunderstood things.[130]

The Spirit was instrumental in the process of discerning the great mysteries and signs of the book of Revelation, and the congregation needed to be 'in the Spirit' to receive revelation.

The Seven Spirits

The seven Spirits represent the complete Spirit and might allude to the description of the seven-fold Spirit in Isa. 11.2-3.[131] On two occasions, E.N. Bell contemplated the seven Spirits while responding in the Question and Answer section of the paper:

They are the 'seven eyes … sent forth into all the earth.' 5:6. The Lamb has these seven eyes according to this verse and 3:1. There are hints that this number seven is purely figurative, standing for the complete omniscience and omnipresence of the Holy Spirit operating from and in behalf of Christ the Lamb. In Rev. 1:4-5 we have grace and peace (1) 'From Him who is, (2) and from the seven Spirits, (3) and from Jesus Christ.' There seems to be a clear reference here to the Trinity, and if there is, then the seven Spirits would of necessity refer to the manifold workings of the Holy Spirit.[132]

They are the seven lamps burning before the throne (Rev. 4:5); they are the seven eyes of God sent forth into all the earth (Rev. 5:6), and Jesus, the Lamb, has all these eyes, praise God![133]

Bell affirmed the divine nature of the seven Spirits and observed the close relationship between God, the Lamb, and the Spirit in Revelation. Seven was used to signify the complete and perfect knowledge of the Spirit. A final mention of the seven Spirits is found in a hymn:

---

[130] *WE* 166 (November 25, 1916), p. 10.
[131] *WE* 172 (January 13, 1917), p. 13.
[132] *WE* 167 (December 2, 1916), p. 9.
[133] *WE* 203 (August 18, 1917), p. 9.

Yes, the bloodwashed shall behold
All the radiance of the Throne,
Radiance of the Seven-fold Light (Rev. 4:5)
Of the Father and the Son

O the Radiance of the Throne
Radiance of consuming flame,
Radiance of the lowly Lamb
Through eternal years the same.[134]

If Anyone has an Ear

*The Seven Prophetic Messages*
*The Weekly/Christian Evangel* considered the theme of discernment in
the seven prophetic messages:

> This is the picture given by the Holy Ghost, and let him who reads
> or hears, take heed. 'If any man hath an ear, let him hear.' Not
> only is the warning in the Word, but it is the duty of God's serv-
> ants to warn. Every preacher of the Gospel has the Word of God
> in his possession, and in the Word there is set forth in clear lan-
> guage the impending reign of the beast and the fearful results fol-
> lowing.[135]

Having complete knowledge, the seven Spirits aided the church in
their discernment, 'The Spirit marks the church at Sardis for rebuke
and exhortation. No community, no church, no individual can hide
from him whose eyes are as a flame of fire. We are living in a searching time. God is searching. Christ is searching out the condition of
the churches.'[136]

Many advocated that they were living in the Laodicean age, 'the
visible church as a whole is obsessed with the spirit of lukewarmness
and indifference. Cold creeds and lifeless forms have largely taken
the place of Living Bread and Loving Service.'[137] Stanley Frodsham
pressed that if the church was in the last age, they should hear the
Spirit for themselves, 'We condemn the Laodicean Church, yet in our
hearts we too are saying, "We are rich and have need of nothing,"

---

[134] *WE* 221 (January 5, 1918), p. 8.
[135] *WE* 208 (September 29, 1917), p. 8.
[136] *WE* 197 (July 7, 1917), p. 6.
[137] *CE* 70 (December 12, 1914), p. 1.

and yet how poor we are'.[138] Similarly, Andrew Urshan urged the church to hear the Spirit's message, 'Cold represents never having had the fire, like a person who was never converted. Warmness represents the fire of God in it.' The lukewarm person

> has a little bit of lukewarm love for the Bible, but he has a great love for the newspapers … He takes the Bible, yawns and yawns, and pretty soon goes to sleep. That is the kind of love he has for the Bible; but he will read the newspaper, and get into the spirit of war … he is killing the other fellow in his mind and heart. He has in him the spirit of politics more than the Spirit of Jesus Christ.[139]

Urshan held that the fire came through Pentecost:

> The man who is a HOT Christian is a holy man; he has the right-eousness of Jesus in him. Not only on the inside is the holy fire burning, but outside also is the shinning life of Jesus … He is not 'blind,' either he has eyes to see Jesus when He comes. Hallelujah! … He needs no 'eyesalve.' He has seven eyes – he can see from behind too. Hallelujah!'[140]

Discerning false teaching in the seven prophetic messages was also studied. Nelsie Hodges warned against desiring to seek out false doctrines above passion and love for Christ:

> We may have intense zeal for souls to be saved. We may be red-hot in our denunciations of fake doctrines and teachers; we may be able to pour forth strong prophecies, and much speaking in tongues; we may be able to exercise keen spiritual discernment, but if there is the lack of a pure passionate devotion to the person of Jesus Christ and a deep love toward Him, then all the rest, ex-cellent though it may be, counts for very little in the sight of God. Rev. 2:1-4.[141]

A.P. Collins wrote an article titled, 'The Overcomer – The New Name' where he proposed that the false teachings of Balaam, the Nicolaitans, and the prophetess Jezebel were contrary to the Word of

---

[138] *CE* 266-267 (December 14, 1918), p. 7.

[139] *WE* 192 (June 2, 1917), p. 3.

[140] *WE* 195 (June 23, 1917), p. 5.

[141] *WE* 180 (March 10, 1917), p. 6.

God and a 'curse' to the church in Thyatira.[142] Collins exhorted that Jesus will fight against these false teachings with the sword of his mouth (his word) and called each believer to discern, 'only the individual can know whether he has fully obeyed the Word of God ... No life can fulfill this word but the Christ life'. Whoever discerned rightly would become overcomers who 'are made partakers of the divine nature'.[143] D.W. Kerr examined the 'Nicolaitan tendency' from a historical perspective. Looking at church history, he concluded that ecclesial governmental systems became a hindrance to the moving of the Spirit:

> Church history, however, shows that unless the ministry of the church has an ear to hear what the spirit says to the churches, and sets itself against the tendency to 'lord over God's heritage,' this form of government however mild it may be in its beginning, soon becomes rigid, despotic and intolerant. The Nicolaitan spirit (which thing the Lord hates) has manifested itself during the church age in different forms and degrees of centralized administrations which cast their dark shadows across the path of spiritual progress, saying 'thus far and no further'.[144]

Thus, there were numerous expositions on discernment in the seven prophetic messages. Discernment required the church to hear the seven Spirits as the seven flames. As the seven eyes of the Lamb, the church was urged to see with the perfect knowledge of the Spirit. The church was warned against lukewarmness and false teachings, issues that appear in the seven prophetic messages.

*Rev. 13.9-10*

In *The Christian Evangel*, some contributors contemplated participation in the war effort in light of Rev. 13.9-10. An unnamed author wrote:

> Our Lord Jesus Christ taught the blessedness of the peace-maker, that violence should not be resisted with violence that those who take the sword should perish with the sword. This is Christianity,

---

[142] *WE* 140 (May 20, 1916), p. 9.
[143] *WE* 140 (May 20, 1916), p. 9.
[144] *CE* 70 (December 12, 1914), p. 3.

and only a civilization built upon the basis of the teaching of Jesus Christ can bear the name 'Christian'.[145]

Similarly, a brother McCafferty judged that the Christians were not of the world, but that their citizenship was in heaven:

> Hear the Spirit say, 'If any man have ears to hear, let him hear. He that leadth into captivity shall go into captivity. He that [ki]lleth with the sword must be killed with the sword.' Here is the patience and faith of the saints. Rev. 13.[9-10]. Shall we [f]ight with the sword? Shall we as Christians go to war?[146]

McCafferty called on the church to hear the Spirit as they discerned whether to participate in the war. He incorporated the phrase, 'hear the Spirit say', with Rev. 13.9-10, deeming it necessary to hear the Spirit in this process of discernment. This is not surprising considering the repeated invitations to hear the Spirit in the seven prophetic messages. Both of these contributors discerned that involvement in the war would lead to death and captivity, and thereby must be avoided.

### Discerning the Mark of the Beast

The bestial texts received much attention in *The Weekly/Christian Evangel*. These texts were regularly read through a futuristic lens where the beast would rise in the great tribulation and would mark his follows with the mark of the beast – 666. Conversely, those who were allegiant to Christ – the head of the true church – would be distinct by having the seal of Christ.[147] Articles by J.R. Flower and responses in the Question and Answer section by E.N. Bell encompassed the majority of the examinations and will be surveyed first.

First, E.N. Bell offered numerous responses dealing with the beast and the mark. (1) When asked, what was the mark of the beast, Bell responded that the Spirit would guide the church:

> It may be the name of the Beast or the number of his name marked in the hand or in the forehead. Rev 13:16-17. We do not yet know what his name is. The number is 666. Some ancient manuscripts read 616. But this need not bother us. The true child of

---

[145] *CE* 79 (February 27, 1915), p. 3.

[146] *CE* 74 (January 16, 1915), p. 1. See also *CE* 75 (January 23, 1915), p. 2.

[147] *WE* 173 (January 20, 1917), p. 4; *WE* 226 (February 9, 1918), p. 5.

God led by God's Spirit will know the beast because he will step
in between us and God, demand that we obey him instead of God,
that we put [his] authority above the authority of Christ. Any man
who does this is an anti-christ, and the great anti-Christ will
out[strip] all before him in exalting himself above Christ and
God.[148]

(2) Bell considered 666:

Some ancient manuscripts give the number as 616. Some say the
number 666, in Roman figures, is on the crown of the pope. Some
say the word Napoleon stands for 666. There are many specula-
tions over this number: but this editor confesses that he has never
seen any that satisfied him it was right. I do not know how this
number will be revealed or which number, 616 or 666, is correct?[149]

(3) When asked, 'Is taking the mark of the Beast when a man has to
sign up for it?', Bell replied, 'Sign up for what? I don't know of anything a customer has to sign up for, nor do I know of anything we
have to sign at the present which is the mark of the Beast. We cannot
take the mark of the Beast until the Anti-Christ Beast appears and
gets supreme power. No one has such power yet.'[150] (4) Bell observed
economic features associated with the beast, 'most of them will take
the mark of the beast in order to get bread, to do business and save
themselves from persecution, and the result is shown in Rev. 14:9-
12'.[151] (5) When contemplating the second beast, he wrote, 'He is the
religious high-priest and false prophet who aids the first beast, the
political anti-Christ'.[152] (6) Similarly, the beast in Rev. 16.13 'is "the
beast" of Rev. 13.11, who is associated with the Anti-christ beast of
Revelation 13:1. The Anti-christ is a great political ruler, while this
second beast is a sort of high priest in religion who makes religion
aid the Anti-christ. See Rev. 19:20.'[153] (7) The beast described in Rev.
17.8 'is the Antichrist the last head of the ten-horned, ten-toed world

---

[148] *CE* 264-265 (November 10, 1918), p. 5.
[149] *WE* 134 (April 8, 1916), p. 8.
[150] *WE* 230 (March 9, 1918), p. 9.
[151] *CE* 258-259 (October 19, 1918), p. 5.
[152] *WE* 151 (August 5, 1916), p. 8.
[153] *CE* 248-249 (June 27, 1918), p. 9.

kingdom which will fight Jesus Christ when He comes. It will have 10 kings and he will be head or chief, an emperor over the kings'.[154] (8) After being asked if the Kaiser was the beast, Bell answered, 'this writer does not believe the Kaiser with all these anti-Christian principles is the Anti-Christ'.[155] (9) One individual enquired concerning the possibility that the mark was present in the world asking, 'Is it taking the Mark of the Beast to give to the Red Cross Work? Is it not a Catholic affair?' Bell responded, 'Not at all so … It is not a church society, but all churches contribute to it'.[156]

In sum, Bell offered a variety of short responses that mostly appeared in the Question and Answer section of the publication. Overall, Bell approached the bestial texts from a futuristic position. While the political power and economic aspect of the beasts were noted, Bell denied the possibility that the beasts existed in his present world. However, if any anticipatory beast-like features were present, the Spirit would assist the church in discerning them.

Second, J.R. Flower offered a few articles commenting on the beast and his mark. (1) In an article titled 'The Mark of the Beast', Flower wrote:[157]

> The form of those 'perilous times' in the beast rising up out of the sea, who had given unto him great power and authority over all the earth so that no man might buy or sell except he had a mark upon him, placed there by the authority of the beast. In fact the power of this beast is to be so great that all men on earth must worship his image, and whosoever will not worship this image shall be killed.[158]

He suggested that the beast was similar to the 'Romish church':

> At the present time she is manifesting undoubtedly, the spirit of the Beast and the false prophet of Revelation 13, and it is apparent to all who are closely watching her moves and listening to her alarming utterances that she has never changed in spirit and, had

---

[154] *WE* 234-235 (April 6, 1918), p. 9.

[155] *CE* 244-245 (June 15, 1918), p. 3.

[156] *WE* 224 (January 26, 1918), p. 9.

[157] *CE* 49 (July 11, 1914), p. 2. This article was also printed in *WW* 10.7 (July 1914), p. 1.

[158] *CE* 49 (July 11, 1914), p. 2; *WW* 10.7 (July 1914), p. 1.

she the authority and influence which she seeks, would again rule with an iron hand in suppressing all opposition to her heathenish practices, and all aggressive Christianity which she could not control.[159]

Flower noted that during the 'dark centuries', the Roman church persecuted anyone 'who dared to worship God in a manner contrary to the dictates of the Roman Hierarchy'.[160] The remaining portion of this article mentioned reports of persecution by the Roman Catholic Church in Chicago, Illinois and Cumberland, Maryland, which confirmed that the Roman Church envisaged the 'spirit of the beast'.

(2) In 'Rumors of War', Flower put forth that the ten kingdoms represented the countries participating in the Balkan and European wars. He advocated that the beast that received the head wound was the Roman Empire and was slain for centuries but was rising in power. The Roman Empire 'will be an important part of the new confederation of nations composing the kingdom of the beast'.[161] Flower speculated that the other kingdoms might include 'The Triple Entente (England, France and Russia) and the Triple Alliance (Italy, Austria-Hungary and Germany) and the four Balkan states made just ten kingdoms'.[162] Flower called on the readers to discern the 'spirit of the beast' that was already present in the world, mainly the Roman Catholic Church. He concluded the article by writing, 'We are watching every development of the crisis in Europe with the greatest of interest, with our newspapers in one hand and the Bible in the other, checking off each prophecy as it is being fulfilled, knowing of a surety that the coming of the Lord cannot be long delayed'.[163]

(3) Responding to those that believed the Great War was the battle of Armageddon, Flower wrote, 'these people are a little ahead of the times and are not thoroughly acquainted with prophecy' because Armageddon will be fought at the close of the great tribulation.[164]

---

[159] *CE* 49 (July 11, 1914), p. 2; *WW* 10.7 (July 1914), p. 1.

[160] *CE* 49 (July 11, 1914), p. 2; *WW* 10.7 (July 1914), p. 1.

[161] *CE* 53 (August 8, 1914), p. 2. This article was also printed in *WW* 10.8 (August 1914), p. 1.

[162] *CE* 53 (August 8, 1914), p. 2; *WW* 10.8 (August 1914), p. 1.

[163] *CE* 53 (August 8, 1914), p. 2; *WW* 10.8 (August 1914), p. 1.

[164] *CE* 56 (August 29, 1914), p. 1.

Flower commented that the war had 'a close relationship to Armageddon in that it is the beginning of the great wars which will wind up in the battle of Armageddon. It is altogether probable that the Antichrist will appear at any moment.'[165] When considering the four horsemen, Flower believed that the first seal – the rider on the white horse – was the antichrist and therefore the opening of the following seals – war, famine, and pestilence – could only be more devastating in the great tribulation than the hardship experienced in the Great War. Flower offered an overtly futuristic reading of the bestial texts. He warned that the 'spirit of the beast' was already present in the world manifesting as the Roman church and in the formation of the ten kingdoms, which anticipated the coming of the beast.

Third, other significant contributions in *The Weekly/Christian Evangel* include (1) F. Bartleman who wrote an article studying the events of World War I as the opening of the seven seals in Revelation.[166] Bartleman proposed that Rome and other religious factions represented the beasts from Revelation, 'Rome is raising up her head again. If ever the Moslem, the "False Prophet," declares a "holy war" it will be now. It is his last stand. Even England, titled "Defender of the Faith," has at last sold out to Rome.'[167] Because of the nations' moral degeneration, oppression, and tyranny 'the hour of her judgment has come'.[168] 'The United States has a score of kings where European countries have but one. That is about the only difference. We are ruled by the money gods.'[169]

(2) A.G. Miniely wrote an article titled, 'The Mark of the Beast':

One of the great signs of the soon coming of Jesus and the mark of the beast is swiftly coming to a head in this land (Canada), which used to be called freeborn. Wives and mothers and all women are called upon to hiss at every man who is eligible to recruit. I hereby relate a few paragraphs from a local paper. 'The influence of women is so great that the country calls them to use this power to urge the young men to do their duty and make them

---

[165] *CE* 56 (August 29, 1914), p. 1.

[166] See also *WE* 102 (August 7, 1915), p. 1.

[167] *CE* 93 (June 5, 1914), p. 2. This article was also printed in *WW* 12.6 (June 1915), p. 5.

[168] *CE* 93 (June 5, 1914), p. 2; *WW* 12.6 (June 1915), p. 5.

[169] *CE* 93 (June 5, 1914), p. 2; *WW* 12.6 (June 1915), p. 5.

ashamed to stay at home while others fight for them. It is the bounden duty of every woman to ostracise such men.' ... Further, they are making a house to house canvass to learn who means to fight. Churches are used for recruiting services for the king. The antichrist is getting possession of the House of God and is setting up his image in the hearts of the people ... Pray for the brethren in patriotic, devil-crazed Canada. Pray for a brother who backslid and is now at the front, who now desires to get back, and desires prayer.[170]

For Miniely, it seems that dispensational eschatology influenced her readings of the text where the events in Canada were only anticipatory of the true, final antichrist. However, Miniely presented an interpretation that endeavored to contextualize Revelation as a way to criticize those who were persuading believers to become involved in the war. Although not explicitly stated, it is possible that Miniely supposed those going to fight in the war, who backslid, might have received the mark of the beast albeit in an anticipatory manner.

(3) Emily S. Hubbell wrestled with the interpretation that the Great War was the battle of Armageddon and that the Kaiser was identified as the beast. She quoted some contemporary proponents of this interpretation:

The Minneapolis man, having a talent for numerical puzzles, took the word 'Kaiser' and gave each letter of the word a number according to its place in the alphabet thus – 11, 1, 9, 19, 5, 18. After each of these numbers he placed the figure 6. Then he added the numbers together. The sum he found is 666. That happens to be the precise number of months there were in Kaiser Wilhelm's age when the war started. And wonderful to relate, it is the same as the number of the beast given in the twelfth chapter of Revelation. And thus we have a key to the duration of the war. Any reader may pick up his Bible and read the passage for himself.[171]

Following this report, Emily Hubbell retorted, 'A little study will show that this war cannot be the Bible Armageddon'. While Hubbell did not respond to the calculations performed by the Minneapolis man to identify the beast with the 'Kaiser', it is unlikely that she would

---

[170] *WE* 140 (May 20, 1916), p. 13.
[171] *WE* 216 (November 24, 1917), p. 3.

have agreed because such a conclusion suggests that the beast would have been active in her contemporary world.

In sum, *The Christian/Weekly Evangel* offered various reflections on the bestial texts that were broadly limited to futuristic interpretations. The descriptions of the beast throughout the publication expressed themes of political, religious, and economic power. While there were some attempts to relate these texts to their contemporary context (whether it was the Roman church or the Great War), these readings were qualified with phrases such as the 'spirit of the beast'.

Babylon

The whore of Babylon was identified as the false church and contrasted against the women clothed with the sun. The woman clothed with the sun represented the overcomers, while the whore represented the false church that was untrue to Christ, 'She goes after other lovers, rides in worldly glory on the back of political power through rulers, the beast kings of the earth. She is ecclesiastical Babylon which many hold to be Rome.'[172] E.N. Bell, in the Question and Answer section and citing the Scofield Bible wrote, that there are two Babylons: an ecclesiastical Babylon and a political Babylon.[173] The ecclesiastical Babylon was 'Apostate Christendom, headed up under the papacy; and political Babylon, which is the Beast's confederate empire'.[174] Bell proposed that ecclesiastical Babylon – the great whore – will be destroyed by political Babylon – the beast – so 'that the Beast may be the only object of worship'.[175] Elizabeth Sisson reflected on Babylon's prophetic role following War World 1:

> If we make a study of the 18th [chapter] of Revelation and the ruin of the great city there portrayed, we see there must come a time of unexampled world-prosperity to make such a city. To develop that marvelous wealth and luxury there must be peace universal, or something akin to it. In this description of the downfall of Babylon, we notice it has been a city of unequalled wealth: the merchantmen of the whole earth are made 'rich' (Rev. 19:3)

---

[172] *WE* 133 (April 1, 1916), p. 8. Cf. *WE* 95 (June 19, 1915), p. 3; *WE* 173 (January 20, 1917), p. 4.

[173] *WE* 197 (July 7, 1917), p. 9.

[174] *WE* 197 (July 7, 1917), p. 9.

[175] *WE* 197 (July 7, 1917), p. 9.

through her abundance and her commercial 'power' ... Her commerce in gold and silver, jewelry, linen, silk and co[s]tly manufacture[s] (verse 12) has commanded the [waste] of the world ... The city whose wreck is here described is not on the earth today in such power and wealth, and it will take a very booming time of peace and prosperity to build her and make her. It may be brief, for we have come upon an age of tremendous rapid[ity] in reconstruction and changes ... This answers the question, 'After the wars, what?' An [hour] of great prosperity.'[176]

Sisson discerned, following the turmoil of the war, that a time of peace and great prosperity would envelop the earth. Although prosperity was on the horizon, Sisson was not placated; rather, she warned the hearers to beware of the coming abundance manifested in manufacturing and commercial power because it would be closely associated with the image of Babylon from Revelation.

Revelation 11

There was a limited amount of engagement concerning the two witnesses in *The Weekly/Christian Evangel*. E.N. Bell denied that the two witnesses symbolically represented the church or the first resurrection saints, but suggested that they were two real men perhaps Elijah and Enoch.[177] When asked 'Why is the place where our Lord was crucified called spiritually Sodom and Egypt?', Bell responded, 'This is Jerusalem and it is because she has darkness like Egypt and sin like Sodom'.[178]

**Summary**

*The Christian/Weekly Evangel* widely approached Revelation from a dispensational perspective. The paper's editorial policies probably generated this uniformity while influences from Scofield and Seiss were present.[179] In articles that might have strayed from the dispen-

---

[176] *CE* 264-265 (November 10, 1918), p. 2.

[177] *WE* 121 (January 1, 1916), p. 1.

[178] *CE* 252-253 (August 24, 1918), p. 9.

[179] There were many advertisements for the Scofield Bible found in the literature. For influences of Scofield and Seiss on Revelation, see *WE* 197 (July 7, 1917), p. 9; *CE* 246-247 (June 29, 1918), p. 12. See also *WE* 198 (July 14, 1917), pp. 2-6, where W.W. Simpson critiqued Scofield's dismissal of tongue speech.

sational script, editorial notes appeared that 'corrected' these inter-pretations.[180] Outside a dispensational framework stood the seven prophetic messages, where numerous contributors discovered mean-ingful reflections for their community. These texts called upon the church to discern false teachings by the seven Spirits – perfect knowledge – and exhorted them to receive the Pentecostal fire of the seven Spirits – the seven flames before the throne.

Some dispensational scripts propose that the rapture would occur in Revelation 4, suggesting that the 'events' of Revelation 4–22 would transpire in the future. While overall *The Christian/Weekly Evangel* fol-lowed the dispensation script, variant interpretations to the script ap-peared in the publication that located the rapture later in Revelation. These discrepancies in the script are seen in the readings of J.R. Flower and E.N. Bell. On the one hand, Flower was convinced that the first seal describes the coming of the antichrist. Thereby, anything following Revelation 3 must take place in the future. On the other hand, Bell allowed for some openness in the paper when he sug-gested that the rapture could occur as late as Rev. 12.5.[181] Bell's open-ness permitted other interpreters to read Revelation in light of the Great War, especially in relation to the opening of the seven seals in Revelation 6.[182] Conversely, Flower responded to the horrors of War World I by asserting it could only be much worst in the great tribula-tion.

On account that the bestial texts appear in Revelation 13, these scriptures were always limited to the future. *The Christian/Weekly Evangel* observed military, religious, political, and economic aspects of the beast. The paper noted that the clearest example of the beast in their world was the Roman church that had both religious and po-litical power. However, these interpretations were anticipatory. The 'spirit of the beast' – not the beast – was present in the world.

---

[180] E.g. *CE* 68 (November 21, 1914), p. 4; *WE* 109 (September 25, 1915), p. 3.

[181] See *WE* 196 (June 30, 1917), pp. 4-5; *WE* 213 (November 3, 1917), p. 9; *WE* 217 (December 1, 1917), p. 8; *WE* 233 (March 30, 1918), p. 9.

[182] See *WE* 102 (August 7, 1915), p. 1; *WE* 204 (August 25, 1917), p. 6; *WE* 234-235 (April 6, 1918), p. 7.

## Summary of the Finished-Work Stream

First, the Spirit guided, illuminated, and assisted in the process of discernment on behalf of the church. The Spirit was needed to interpret the Word and spoke in a still, small voice. The Spirit provided wisdom, knowledge, and illumination to the church. The Assemblies of God publications offered a method for discernment that included looking to the Word, discerning God's will, working within God's providence, following the Spirit, and prayer.

Second, throughout much of the Finished-Work stream, there was a strong presence of dispensational eschatology. Despite this strong presence, parts of Revelation were read in a non-dispensational manner. Each publication in the Finished-Work stream reflected on either the pneumatology or the seven prophetic messages, exploring how these texts spoke to their communities. This survey has shown that there was some disagreement concerning the location of the rapture in Revelation, which allowed for some interpretative space in Revelation. This space allowed for interpretations that compared Revelation to economic hardship, World War I, and the Influenza epidemic.

Third, with the start of the Great War, there was an escalation of eschatological speculation. Primarily, those in the Finished-Work stream considered the imminence of the great tribulation, the rise of the beast, and the catching away of the saints. Revelation 13.9-10 was used to critique involvement in the war. When considering the beast, many observed military, political, economic, and religious elements. *The Latter Rain Evangel* offered the most divergent reading where readers were warned not to take the mark of the beast, which seemed to be a real possibility. Beyond this, the Finished-Work stream was continually reluctant to contextualize any bestial texts without including some sort of clarification that any similarities to the beast discovered in their present reality were only proleptic of a future reality. Thereby, when contributors referred to any person, institution, federation, or country that contained beast-like qualities, they qualified it with 'the spirit of the beast' or 'the spirit of the antichrist' that was already present in the world.

Fourth, the Finished-Work stream offered some reflections on the seven Spirits. The seven Spirits were always considered to be a reference to the Holy Spirit. A.S. Copley in *The Pentecost* offered one of the most comprehensive examinations of the seven Spirits in the early Pentecostal literature. Copley, in a multi-issue series on the seven 'types' of the Holy Spirit, explored the seven Spirits as the seven torches and the seven eyes. The seven Spirits signified perfection and were dynamically involved in the community. The seven Spirits perfectly guided the church as the seven eyes of the Lamb to discern the false teaching of Balaam, the Nicolaitans, Jezebel, or Babylon. As the seven torches, the Spirit provided fire to the church so that they might become hot. The church needed to hear the Spirit's messages. Other pneumatological contributions among the publications comprised of being 'in the Spirit'. Those in the community needed to be 'in the Spirit' to interpret the message, as John was 'in the Spirit' to receive it. Some testified of visionary experiences that contained similar language and imagery with that found in Revelation.

## Conclusions from the Early Pentecostal (Con)text(s)

This examination of the early Pentecostal intertexts offers an opportunity to dialogue with the theological heart of the Pentecostal (con)text, while also forming me as a Pentecostal interpreter concerning pneumatic discernment that attunes my ears to hear notes of the Apocalypse in a distinct fashion. As a Pentecostal interpreter, the diverse interpretative spectrum of the early Pentecostal periodical literature provides space to interpret the (inter)text of the Apocalypse in a new context, creating space for the Pentecostal community to hear anew.

Both streams of the early Pentecostal movement reveal a scaling interpretative continuum of reading Revelation dispensationally. Some of the periodicals such as *The Apostolic Faith* scaled far away from dispensational readings. *The Bridegroom's Messenger*, *The Latter Rain Evangel*, and *The Church of God Evangel* stood near the center of the scale where each publication permitted dispensational and non-dispensational interpretations to stand together. *The Pentecostal Holiness Advocate* and *The Christian/Weekly Evangel* scaled far toward the dispensational side that often isolated the text (especially Revelation

4–22) from the life of the community.[183] This survey confirms a tendency in the Wesleyan-Holiness stream to include non-dispensational and dispensational interpretations alike, while the Finished-Work stream tended to permit testimonies and articles that were dispensational. However, this survey also reveals that neither stream of the early Pentecostal movement was monolithic and did not allow dispensational eschatology to control their interpretations of Revelation entirely.

The pneumatology of Revelation was explored in the early Pentecostal literature to varying degrees, though at no point did any Pentecostal deny that the seven Spirits referred to the Holy Spirit. The church was called to have an ear to hear the Spirit in the seven prophetic messages, which took form in addressing false teachings, exhorting the church to be hot rather than cold or lukewarm, and calling the church to turn back to their first love. The perfect knowledge and wisdom of the seven Spirits, as the seven eyes of the Lamb, would guide the church in discernment and give them eyes to see. Outside explicit references to pneumatic discernment in Revelation, the early Pentecostals on numerous occasions commented on the Spirit as being actively involved in discernment, interpretation, and decision-making.

Both streams of the early Pentecostal movement shared in critiquing violent participation in World War I. While both streams appealed to Revelation to address violent action, they differed in their approaches, which seems to be determined by the extent of the influence of dispensational eschatology upon them. This can be seen in interpretations of Revelation 13. On the one hand, those who scaled away from dispensational thought suggested that the nations which drafted soldiers were stamping them with the mark of the beast. On the other hand, those who revealed a strong presence of dispensational thought did on occasion appeal to Rev. 13.9-10 but overall avoided any comment on the possibility that the beast was present in their contemporary context. This distinction becomes more noticeable when considering that contributors in both streams acknowledged the supreme military and political power of the beast, but only

---

[183] Some of the other less voluminous literature examined does not offer enough interpretive evidence on Revelation to determine where exactly they fit in the scale.

those who were not captive to dispensational thought read the bestial texts against World War I.

# 5

2/18/2021

# DISCERNING THE BIBLICAL INTERTEXT: PNEUMATIC DISCERNMENT IN THE APOCALYPSE

## Introduction

This chapter will examine the narrative thread of pneumatic discernment in the Apocalypse. I seek to employ a narrative critical method reading strategy that intertextually emerges from the Pentecostal (con)text and that is reassessed in light of the literary theory of intertextuality. My intertext, formed in the Pentecostal (con)text, will navigate this exploration of the universe of the text, selecting (sub)texts that intersect with pneumatic discernment and the Apocalypse. Such an approach to the interpretation of scripture is for and in the Pentecostal community. This chapter will explore the prologue, the four major divisions of Revelation, and the epilogue. Attention will be given to the character of the Spirit as presented in the Apocalypse, especially the intersections of the Spirit and discernment.

## Structure

While there are a variety of possibilities when considering the structure of the Apocalypse, the four reoccurring ἐν πνεύματι ('in the Spirit') phrases appear to be significant literary markers that reveal a narrative structure. The structure forming around these four ἐν πνεύματι ('in the Spirit') phrases is as follows:

I.   Prologue (1.1-8)
II.  ἐν πνεύματι – On Patmos on the Lord's Day (1.9–3.22)

III. ἐν πνεύματι – In Heaven (4.1–16.21)
IV. ἐν πνεύματι – In the Wilderness (17.1–21.8)
V. ἐν πνεύματι – On a Great Mountain (21.9–22.5)
VI. Epilogue (22.6-21)

*new geographical setting*

The appearance of each literary marker is associated with a new geographical setting. The repetitions of ἐν πνεύματι ('in the Spirit') unite the narrative structurally, creating a sense of unity of the whole narrative around the Spirit. The very structure of Revelation provides support that the Spirit is crucial to the creation and discernment of ✱ this narrative.[1]

## Literary Genre

The introductory words of the Apocalypse seem to be associated with the narrative's genre. The occurrence of ἀποκάλυψις ('revelation') in 1.1 seems to orient the hearers concerning the type of literary work that they are encountering; however, ἀποκάλυψις as a technical indicator of a genre is debated.[2] Whereas Revelation does share

---

[1] For Pentecostal interpreters who conclude that ἐν πνεύματι ('in the Spirit') shapes the structure, see Waddell, *Spirit of the Book of Revelation*, pp. 138-50; Herms, 'Invoking the Spirit', pp. 106-109; Thomas, *The Apocalypse*, pp. 2-6; Archer, 'I Was in the Spirit on the Lord's Day', p. 119. Other interpreters who structure the Apocalypse around these literary markers include: M.C. Tenney, *Interpreting Revelation* (Grand Rapids, MI: Eerdmans, 1957), pp. 32-33; W.R. Kempson, 'Theology in the Revelation of John' (PhD Dissertation: Southern Baptist Theological Seminary, Louisville, KY, 1982), pp. 83-86, 103-12; Mazzaferri, *The Genre of the Book of Revelation*, pp. 302-303; Bauckham, *Climax of Prophecy*, pp. 3-5; C.R. Smith, 'The Structure of the Book of Revelation in Light of Apocalyptic Literary Conventions', *NovT* 36.4 (1994), pp. 373-93; J.R. Michaels, *Revelation* (Downers Grove, IL: InterVarsity Press, 1997), p. 26; J.A. Filho, 'The Apocalypse of John as an Account of a Visionary Experience: Notes on the Book's Structure', *JSNT* 25.2 (2002), pp. 213-34. G.E. Ladd, *A Commentary on the Revelation of John* (Grand Rapids, MI: Eerdmans, 1972), pp. 14-17, proposes the above structure, but bases it on the recursions of 'come and see'. J.L. Trafton, *Reading Revelation: A Literary and Theological Commentary* (Macon, GA: Smyth & Helwys Publishing, 2005), p. 10, concludes that ἐν πνεύματι is the central marker in the structure of Revelation; however, Trafton breaks the second major division (4.1–16.21) at 11.19 and inserts one additional division from 12.1–16.21. Trafton's proposal fails to convince because ἐν πνεύματι does not appear in 12.1, calling into question the addition of another structural divide in a literary structure that revolves around the occurrences of ἐν πνεύματι.

[2] See J.J. Collins, 'Towards the Morphology of a Genre: Introduction', *Semeia* 14 (1979), p. 9, who offers a widely accepted definition of apocalyptic.

similarities with some apocalyptic literature,[3] it also breaks from those conventions.[4] The discussion of the genre is further complicated by the fact that Revelation is called a prophecy numerous times[5] and the epistolary features in the text imply that it is a letter.[6] Revelation seems to be artistically shaped by a variety of literary (but not clearly defined) conventions, suggesting that the genre of Revelation cannot be narrowly defined. Though conventions of genre commonly orient hearers to a piece of literature, perhaps the unique nature of Revelation's genre is disorienting to hearers,[7] preparing them for the unconventional universe that they are entering. How the text breaks from boundaries placed upon it should caution anyone from creating rigorous constraints concerning genre, and recognize the tension and uncertainty that lies within the literary conventions of the Apocalypse. Perhaps, Revelation could be loosely described as an apocalyptic prophecy, sent in the form of a letter to the seven churches of

---

[3] E. Schüssler Fiorenza, *Revelation: Vision of a Just World* (Minneapolis, MN: Fortress Press, 1991), p. 23, comments, 'Revelation employs stock images, conventional topoi or places, scriptural figures, and proofs, as well as literary techniques developed in apocalyptic literature'.

[4] G. Linton, 'Reading the Apocalypse as an Apocalypse', *SBL Seminar Papers* 30 (1991), p. 11, shows that there is no evidence that ἀποκάλυψις ('revelation') was used as a generic indicator of genre prior to the assumed date of Revelation, and thereby it is highly improbable that it is being used in this manner. Notable differences between the Apocalypse and apocalyptic literature include: (1) John is not a pseudonym, (2) the appearance of other genres (prophetic and letter), (3) there is a prominence of visual imagery in Revelation unlike some other apocalyptic literature, and (4) the heavenly journey motif is not central in Revelation. See also Newton, *The Revelation Worldview*, pp. 101-18.

[5] Revelation 1.3; 22.7, 10, 18, 19.

[6] Mazzaferri, *The Genre of the Book of Revelation*, concludes that the HB (especially the prophetic literature) is the primary source influencing Revelation while significantly diminishing the influence of apocalyptic. Unlike apocalyptic, prophecy will become a repeated self-descriptor throughout Revelation. So also D. Hill, 'Prophecy and Prophets in the Revelation of St. John', *NTS* 18 (1971–1972), pp. 401-18. Beale, *The Book of Revelation*, p. 39, challenges those who bifurcate Revelation 1–3 and 4–22 assuming that 1–3 is a letter while 4–22 should be considered a different category of genre. Beale notes that themes introduced in 1–3 continue and are developed throughout the remainder of the work, suggesting that the entire work should be considered a letter.

[7] I. Paul, 'The Revelation to John', in I.H. Marshall, S. Travis, and I. Paul (eds.), *Exploring the New Testament: A Guide to the Letters & Revelation* (Downers Grove, IL: InterVarsity Press, 2nd edn, 2002, 2011), II, p. 325, also points out the disorienting nature of the Apocalypse's genre.

Asia that narrates John's visionary experience to the churches ἐν πνεύματι ('revelation').[8]

## Prologue – Revelation 1.1-8

The opening line of the narrative – Ἀποκάλυψις Ἰησοῦ Χριστοῦ ('Apocalypse of Jesus Christ') – suggests that Jesus Christ is both being revealed and that he is the revealer. Although Jesus is the first character identified as a revealer, the hearers quickly learn in 1.1 that others – God, his angel, and John – will assist in the process of revelation.[9] The chain of revelation will be complete when it reaches his servants.[10] Revelation 1.3 introduces the first of seven beatitudes in Revelation, which expresses the significance of reading, hearing, and keeping the words of this prophecy. It seems unlikely that reading, hearing, or keeping are passive exercises but call for active hearing that involves obedience on behalf of the hearers.[11] ὁ γὰρ καιρὸς ἐγγύς ('for the time is near') sets the narrative in a context of eschatological urgency.[12]

---

[8] Smalley, *Revelation*, p. 8, describes the genre 'as apocalyptic deepened by prophetic insight, and also as prophecy intensified by apocalyptic vision'. J.R. Michaels, *Interpreting the Book of Revelation* (Grand Rapids, MI: Baker Book House, 1992), pp. 31-32, makes the point that Revelation's genre is creatively distinctive from other literary works in the ancient world, 'If a letter, it is like no other early Christian letter we possess. If an apocalypse, it is like no other apocalypse. If a prophecy, it is unique among prophecies.' See Archer, *'I Was in the Spirit on the Lord's Day'*, p. 123, who explores the liturgical elements in Revelation. She writes, 'It is within the context of the worshipping church that an ἀποκάλυψις ('apocalypse') and προφητείας ('prophecy') can be given and received, heard and discerned'.

[9] The chain of revelation is God to Jesus to his angel to John.

[10] Beale, *The Book of Revelation*, p. 183, finds that the phrase, τοῖς δούλοις αὐτοῦ ('to his servants'), refers to the entire community of faith who all have a prophetic vocation rather than referring to a select group of prophets.

[11] See again Martin, *The Unheard Voice of God*, pp. 52-79. Resseguie, *The Revelation of John*, pp. 64-65, comments that the exhortation to hear anticipates the seven-fold hearing formula in the seven prophetic messages, and that later in the narrative, hearing will include discernment. See Ruiz, *Ezekiel in the Apocalypse*, p. 190, who also finds an association between the 'hermeneutical imperatives' in Revelation. Hearing tends to imply obedience in much of the Johannine literature, G. Schneider, 'ἀκούω', *EDNT*, I, pp. 52-54; Smalley, *Revelation*, p. 31.

[12] Ruiz, *Ezekiel in the Apocalypse*, p. 190; Smalley, *Revelation*, p. 31.

In the epistolary address in 1.4, the hearers are introduced to the ones who are hearing this prophecy, the seven churches in Asia. While the seven churches might be limited to the churches in Asia, seven seems to function in a representative manner for the whole church.[13] The prophecy is from God, the seven Spirits, and Jesus Christ. The seven Spirits appear between God, ὁ ὢν καὶ ὁ ἦν καὶ ὁ ἐρχόμενος ('the one who is, who was, and who is coming'), and Jesus Christ, revealing a close relationship with the seven Spirits, God, and Jesus. Considering that God is the giver of the revelation (of Jesus Christ) and that Jesus is the revealer (1.1), it seems that the seven Spirits will be significant in the process of this revelation.[14] The appearance of the seven Spirits between God and Jesus Christ suggests that this is not a reference to seven angelic beings[15] but to the divine Holy Spirit where seven represents fullness and completeness.[16] Further evidence of the role of the Spirit in discernment is found in the

---

[13] K.H. Rengstorf, 'ἑπτά', *TDNT*, II, pp. 632-33.

[14] J.L. Mangina, *Revelation* (BTC; Grand Rapids, MI: Brazos Press, 2010), p. 46, writes, 'Naming the Spirit first underscores Jesus' character as Spirit-conceived and Spirit-anointed messiah (Luke 1:35, 3:22). If in a certain sense the Spirit exists for the sake of Christ, in another sense Christ exists for the sake of the Spirit, who makes the community of his followers participants in his *apokalypsis*.'

[15] For this position, see Charles, *The Revelation of St. John*, I, p. 11; Schweizer, 'πνεῦμα', pp. 449-51; R.H. Mounce, *The Book of Revelation* (NICNT; Grand Rapids, MI: Eerdmans, 2nd edn, 1977, 1997), pp. 46-48; A. Yarbro Collins, *The Apocalypse* (Wilmington, DE: Michael Glazier, 1979), p. 7; Aune, *Revelation 1–5*, pp. 34-35; L.L. Thompson, *Revelation* (ANTC; Nashville, TN: Abingdon Press, 1998), p. 49; M.E. Boring, *Revelation* (Interpretation; Louisville, KY: Westminster John Knox Press, 2011), p. 75; Koester, *Revelation*, p. 226. See also Oecumenius, 'Revelation', ACC, XII, p. 4.

[16] Schreiner, *Magnifying God in Christ*, p. 155, observes it is striking that grace and peace are attributed to the seven Spirits on account that grace and peace are divine prerogatives of the Father and the Son (not angelic beings) in the NT. The previous survey of early Pentecostal reception history (in)formed this interpretative decision. For scholars who find the seven Spirits as referring to the Holy Spirit, see Swete, *The Apocalypse of St. John*, p. clxv; Beckwith, *The Apocalypse of John*, pp. 426-27; G.B. Caird, *The Revelation of Saint John* (BNTC; Peabody, MA: Hendrickson, 1966), p. 15; L. Morris, *Revelation* (TNTC; Grand Rapids, MI: Eerdmans, 2nd edn, 1969, 1987), p. 49; Ladd, *Revelation of John*, p. 25; Bruce, 'The Spirit in the Apocalypse', pp. 333-34; G.R. Beasley-Murray, *The Book of Revelation* (NCBC; London: Marshall, Morgan, & Scott, 1974), pp. 55-56; J.P.M. Sweet, *Revelation* (TPINTC; Philadelphia, PA: Trinity Press Internation, 1979, 1990), p. 64; Gause, *Revelation*, p. 31; R.W. Wall, *Revelation* (Peabody, MA: Hendrickson, 1991), p. 57; Bauckham, *Climax of Prophecy*, p. 164; de Smidt, 'Hermeneutical Perspectives', p. 28; Beale, *The Book of Revelation*, p. 189; Keener, *Revelation*, pp. 69-70; P. Prigent, *Commentary on the Apocalypse of St. John* (trans. Wendy Pradels; Tübingen: Mohr

intertext of Isa. 11.2.[17] In Isa. 11.2, the Spirit and the messiah have a close relationship, and three of the seven attributes of the Spirit are wisdom, understanding, and knowledge (σοφίας, βουλῆς, γνώσεως). Hence, the seven Spirits are closely associated with the messiah and with wisdom, knowledge, and understanding.

Following the 'trinitarian' introduction and the description of the person of Jesus Christ (who is the faithful witness, the one who was raised from the dead, and the one who is ruling over the kings of the earth), the narrative breaks into a doxology (1.5-6). The first description of the seven churches is:

ἀγαπῶντι ἡμᾶς καὶ λύσαντι ἡμᾶς ἐκ τῶν ἀμαρτιῶν ἡμῶν ἐν τῷ αἵματι αὐτοῦ καὶ ἐποίησεν ἡμᾶς βασιλείαν, ἱερεῖς τῷ θεῷ καὶ πατρὶ αὐτοῦ.

To the one who loves us and who has freed us from our sins by his blood, and who made us a kingdom and priests to God and his Father.

The church discovers that their identity is connected to the actions of Jesus Christ.

Another aspect of discernment includes the doxology and recognizing to whom worship belongs. The opening doxology (1.6-7), exhibits the proper response to the divine throne, the seven Spirits, and Jesus: worship. The doxology offers discernment to the churches through a doxology. In the doxology, Ἰδοὺ ('behold') draws the

---

Siebeck, 2001), p. 117; G.R. Osborne, *Revelation* (BECNT; Grand Rapids, MI: Baker Academic, 2002), p. 61; M. Jauhiainen, *The Use of Zechariah in Revelation* (Tübingen: Mohr Siebeck, 2005), pp. 86-89; R. Stefanović, *Revelation of Jesus Christ* (Berrien Springs, MI: Andrews University Press, 2nd edn, 2002, 2009), pp. 63-64; Smalley, *Revelation*, p. 31; Waddell, *Spirit of the Book of Revelation*, pp. 176-77; Resseguie, *The Revelation of John*, p. 66; B.K. Blount, *Revelation* (NTL; Louisville, KY: Westminster John Knox Press, 2009), pp. 34-35; Skaggs and Benham, *Revelation*, pp. 21-22; Mangina, *Revelation*, pp. 43-44; Fee, *Revelation*, pp. 5-6; Thomas, *The Apocalypse*, p. 92; P.A. Rainbow, *Johannine Theology: The Gospel, The Epistles, and the Apocalypse* (Downers Grove, IL: InterVarsity Press, 2014), pp. 238-39; P.S. Williamson, *Revelation* (CCSS; Baker Academic: Grand Rapids MI, 2015), pp. 44-46; and Thomas and Macchia, *Revelation*, pp. 475-76.

[17] Victorinus, *Commentary on the Apocalypse* (Lexington, KY: CreateSpace Independent Publishing Platform, unknown), p. 5, seems to be the earliest commentator (in the latter half of the third century) who identifies the seven Spirits with Isa. 11.2. See also Apringius of Beja, 'Tractate on the Apocalypse', *ACC*, XII, pp. 3-4; Bruce, 'The Spirit in the Apocalypse', p. 334; Waddell, *Spirit of the Book of Revelation*, pp. 14-16.

churches' ear to discern these prophetic words.[18] The appearance of ἔρχεται μετὰ τῶν νεφελῶν ('coming with the clouds') might bring to mind Dan. 7.13 and Zech 12.10.[19] In Daniel, ὅμοιον υἱὸν ἀνθρώπου ('one like the son of humanity') comes and establishes his kingdom revealing an eschatological expectation;[20] however, this eschatological expectation creates a tension. Although the church anticipates the coming of ὅμοιον υἱὸν ἀνθρώπου ('one like the son of humanity'), they discern that Jesus is already present in their communities and that they are already participating in his kingdom.[21] The present tense verb ἔρχεται ('coming') adds another layer to this tension implying that the coming of Jesus is already in process. The appearance of ἔρχεται recalls Rev. 1.4 where 'the coming one' (ἐρχόμενος) is in the present tense and joins the coming of the one on the throne with the coming of ὅμοιον υἱὸν ἀνθρώπου ('one like the son of humanity').[22] The stage is set with eschatological urgency.

## ἐν πνεύματι – Revelation 1.9–3.22

### Revelation 1.9-20

Following the prologue, the narrative transitions to its first ἐν πνεύματι ('in the Spirit') section. The narration shifts to a first-person ('Εγὼ 'Ιωάννης, 'I, John') where John identifies himself as the narrator as well as a character in the narrative. John writes that he is on Patmos διὰ τὸν λόγον τοῦ θεοῦ καὶ τὴν μαρτυρίαν 'Ιησοῦ ('on account of the word of God and the witness of Jesus').[23] While John is on Patmos, he is also ἐν πνεύματι ἐν τῇ κυριακῇ ἡμέρᾳ ('in the Spirit on the Lord's Day').[24] First, ἐν πνεύματι ('in the Spirit') is likely

*[margin note: The coming one is already here]*

---

[18] Prigent, *The Apocalypse*, p. 121; Resseguie, *The Revelation of John*, p. 68.

[19] The hearers might notice a slight alteration in Revelation from Zechariah and Daniel. While these texts anticipated judgment alone, it is possible that the 'mourning' in Rev. 1.7 denotes an element of repentance and forgiveness. The opportunity of repentance is available for everyone, even for those who pierced him, see Koester, *Revelation*, pp. 219-20.

[20] See Bauckham, *The Theology of the Book of Revelation*, pp. 318-22, for a discussion of Dan. 7.13; Zech. 12.10; and Rev. 1.7.

[21] Koester, *Revelation*, p. 229.

[22] Trafton, *Reading Revelation*, p. 22.

[23] Resseguie, *The Revelation of John*, p. 71.

[24] Thomas, *The Apocalypse*, p. 100.

connected to the activity of the seven Spirits given the close proximity in which they are mentioned (1.4, 10). Second, the seven Spirits are an integral part of the revelation of Jesus Christ owing to the fact that the revelation takes place ἐν πνεύματι.[25] Third, ἐν πνεύματι denotes that John's prophecy is divinely inspired because it is mediated by a divine source: the Spirit.[26] Fourth, the appearance of ἐν πνεύματι τῇ κυριακῇ ἡμέρᾳ ('in the Spirit on the Lord's day') without explanation possibly indicates some familiarity on behalf of the churches, perhaps even referring to a worship context.[27] Fifth, it is possible that τῇ κυριακῇ ἡμέρᾳ ('on the Lord's day') alludes to the HB, 'Day of the Lord', יהוה יום;[28] though, τῇ κυριακῇ ἡμέρᾳ ('on the Lord's day') as a possible echo of 'the day of the Lord' (יום יהוה) has been discounted primarily based on semantic evidence. While ἡμέρα τοῦ κυρίου ('the day of the Lord', 'Lord's day') commonly appears in both the LXX and NT when alluding to 'the day of the Lord' (יהוה יום), the phrase τῇ ἡμέρᾳ κυριακῇ ('the day of the Lord', 'Lord's day')

---

[25] Thomas, *The Apocalypse*, p. 100; Thomas and Macchia, *Revelation*, p. 476, write, 'The discernment in the Spirit is the means by which the revelation given through Christ is received by John. This discernment then extends to a wider circle to involve the churches so that they would have the wherewithal to understand the words of Christ and the revelations that follow.'

[26] Bauckham, *The Theology of the Book of Revelation*, p. 117. See also E. Schüssler Fiorenza, 'The Words of Prophecy: Reading the Apocalypse Theologically', in S. Moyise (ed.), *Studies in the Book of Revelation* (New York, NY: T&T Clark, 2001), pp. 6-9.

[27] So Archer, *'I Was in the Spirit on the Lord's Day'*, p. 131, who cites Jn 4.23 and writes:

> Perhaps in identifying himself as being ἐν πνεύματι, John is making a statement about the significance of worship as the point of contact between heaven and earth. John is *in* a state of worship *when* he receives the apocalypse. He did not worship ἐν πνεύματι in hope of receiving an apocalypse; he worshipped ἐν πνεύματι because that is how worship takes place ... Both John and the hearers receive the apocalypse in the context and setting of worship.

Keener, *Revelation*, p. 84, comments, 'perhaps "in the Spirit" begins here not with a visionary state, as in 4:2 and 21:10, but initially in worship that led to a visionary state'. It has been suggested that τῇ κυριακῇ ἡμέρᾳ refers to Sunday and/or Easter, for a full examination of the interpretative options, see R. Bauckham, 'The Lord's Day', in D.A. Carson (ed.), *From Sabbath to Lord's Day: A Biblical, Historical and Theological Investigation* (Grand Rapids, MI: Zondervan, 1982), pp. 221-50.

[28] S. Bacchiocchi, *From Sabbath to Sunday: A Historical Investigation of the Rise of Sunday Observance in Early Christianity* (Rome, Italy: Pontifical Gregorian University Press, 1977), pp. 111-31; Stefanović, *Revelation*, pp. 94-98; Thomas, *The Apocalypse*, pp. 100-101.

*on every day the Lord's day?*

appears only in Revelation leaving an element of uncertainty to its meaning. Based on this evidence, if Rev. 1.10 alluded to 'the day of the Lord' (יוֹם יהוה), then ἡμέρα τοῦ κυρίου (not τῇ ἡμέρᾳ κυριακῇ) would be expected.[29] However, this argument fails to convince because it does not take into account that ἡμέρα τοῦ κυρίου never appears in the Johannine literature. The lacuna of this language in the Johannine literature allows the possibility that ἡμέρα τοῦ κυρίου echoes יוֹם יהוה in a new and creative way where the very language is being reshaped. The echoes of יוֹם יהוה transform reality into eschatological time where the יוֹם יהוה is proleptically experienced already on account of the activity of the Spirit.[30] This eschatological setting communicates a sense of urgency for discernment, and the pneumatological elements suggest that discernment occurs ἐν πνεύματι.[31]

*how is this not seen as acting as the word of God the very thing the icons argued? Why does he keep reinventing his wheel?*

In the inaugural vision (Rev. 1.12-18), ὅμοιον υἱὸν ἀνθρώπου ('one like the son of humanity') is introduced who reveals a μυστήριον ('mystery') to John. As John turns to see ὅμοιον υἱὸν ἀνθρώπου, among a variety of associations, the churches might perceive this figure's adeptness in discernment, his wisdom, and 'discriminating insight' represented by his white hair and fiery eyes.[32] One response seems appropriate for John when encountering this majestic figure: falling down as though dead.[33] Throughout this entire sequence (1.9–3.22), John remains in this reverential position possibly indicating that discernment should at least begin in prostration, if it is not the required posture. Falling down also implies worship. Discerning to

*Prostration for worship & discernment*

---

[29] So Bauckham, 'The Lord's Day', pp. 221-50. See also Aune, *Revelation 1–5*, pp. 83-84 for the development of τῇ κυριακῇ ἡμέρᾳ.

[30] Thomas, *The Apocalypse*, p. 101.

[31] See D.A. deSilva, *Seeing Things John's Way: The Rhetoric of the Book of Revelation* (Louisville, KY: Westminster John Knox Press, 2009), pp. 180-85, on the emotive aspects of the eschatological setting. See also Keener, *Revelation*, p. 84, who writes, '"The Lord's Day" here may also involve a play on words: In worship, John was experiencing a foretaste of the future day of the Lord, when believers' suffering would give way to the kingdom (1:9)'.

[32] Smalley, *Revelation*, p. 54; See also Ladd, *Revelation of John*, p. 33; D.L. Barr, *Tales of the End: A Narrative Commentary on the Book of Revelation* (Santa Rosa, CA: Polebridge Press, 1998), p. 40; Osborne, *Revelation*, p. 90; Stefanović, *Revelation*, p. 104; Resseguie, *The Revelation of John*, pp. 76-77; Skaggs and Benham, *Revelation*, p. 29.

[33] For prostration as a liturgical action, see Archer, *'I Was in the Spirit on the Lord's Day'*, pp. 132-33.

whom one's worship should be directed will become a theme as the narrative progresses, and from this point, the churches are clearly shown who should be worshipped: the resurrected Jesus. In this thick intertext, the churches would likely recognize the closeness of the description of the one like a son of man with the Ancient of Days in Daniel.[34] μυστήριον ('mystery') appears only in Daniel of all the HB books (LXX).[35] Identifying Jesus as the revealer of a mystery in Revelation would not be surprising, considering that God is the revealer of mysteries in Daniel (2.47).[36] These echoes might attune the ears of the churches to the need of wisdom from God for interpretation.[37]

The interpretative conundrum of the mystery of the seven stars and the seven ἄγγελοι lies in the interpretation (and translation) of ἄγγελοι as either seven 'angels' or seven human 'messengers'.[38] One interpretative possibility considers that since ἄγγελοι (and its derivatives) throughout Revelation mostly refer to angelic beings, ἄγγελοι in Rev. 1.9–3.22 would also refer to literal angelic beings.[39] When considering the relationship of these angelic beings to the church, the interpretative options vary, including: guardian angels, angels who represent the church as heavenly counterparts, or angels who are representatives of the church's spiritual condition.[40] However, this interpretative option fails to convince because: (1) the seven prophetic

---

[34] For a fuller examination of the HB allusions in the inaugural vision, see Moyise, *The Old Testament in the Book of Revelation*, pp. 37-44.

[35] See Beale, *The Book of Revelation*, pp. 216-17.

[36] καὶ ἀποκριθεὶς ὁ βασιλεὺς εἶπεν τῷ Δανιηλ ἐπ' ἀληθείας ὁ θεὸς ὑμῶν αὐτός ἐστιν θεὸς θεῶν καὶ κύριος τῶν βασιλέων καὶ ἀποκαλύπτων μυστήρια ὅτι ἠδυνήθης ἀποκαλύψαι τὸ μυστήριον τοῦτο (Dan. 2.47, Th).

[37] See Dan. 2.20-23, 27-30, 47; 4.8-9, 18; 5.11-16; 8.5, 15, 17, 23, 27; 9.2, 13, 23-25, 10.1, 10.11-12, 14; 11.24-25, 30, 33-35; 12.3-4, 10.

[38] For a thorough discussion of the interpretative options of ἄγγελοι, see E. Ferguson, 'Angels of the Churches in Revelation 1–3: Status Quaestionis and Another Proposal', *BBR* 21.3 (2011), pp. 371-86. See also Aune, *Revelation 1–5*, pp. 108-12.

[39] See Beasley-Murray, *The Book of Revelation*, p. 68; Schüssler Fiorenza, *Vision of a Just World*, pp. 52-53; Michaels, *Revelation*, pp. 63-64.

[40] See Beckwith, *The Apocalypse of John*, p. 446; Caird, *Revelation of St. John*, pp. 24-25; Ladd, *Revelation of John*, p. 32; Sweet, *Revelation*, p. 73; Mounce, *The Book of Revelation*, p. 63; Smalley, *Revelation*, pp. 57-58; F. Tavo, *Woman, Mother, and Bride: An Exegetical Investigation into the 'Ecclesial' Notions of the Apocalypse* (Belgium: Peeters, 2007), pp. 94-97. It is important to note that many of these angelic interpretative options merge and it is difficult to create sustaining categorical lines. See also E.

messages are addressed to the embodied churches in Asia, not angelic beings.[41] Similarly, how is it possible that the prophetic messages are addressed to angelic beings if the addressees receive both praise and criticism? (2) This interpretation generalizes the usage of ἄγγελοι in Revelation. In this narrative section (1.9–3.22), the only ἄγγελοι that appear are the ἄγγελοι τῶν ἑπτὰ ἐκκλησιῶν ('angels, messengers of the seven churches'). It seems possible then that the ἄγγελοι τῶν ἑπτὰ ἐκκλησιῶν designate a particular category of ἄγγελοι that is distinctive from the other categories of ἄγγελοι that appear elsewhere in Revelation.[42] Likewise, it does not seem that ἄγγελοι function as 'heavenly' or 'spiritual' representatives of the church in any other place in Revelation, thereby challenging the evidence that the ἄγγελοι in Rev. 1.9–3.22 are the same as the ἄγγελοι in other parts of Revelation. In other words, however one interprets the ἄγγελοι τῶν ἑπτὰ ἐκκλησιῶν (whether angelic beings, guardian angels, heavenly/spiritual representatives of the church, or human messengers), the ἄγγελοι do not function in this manner outside the seven prophetic messages.

A second interpretative option explores the ἄγγελοι τῶν ἑπτὰ ἐκκλησιῶν as human messengers.[43] Evidence for this interpretation includes: (1) viewing the seven ἄγγελοι as human messengers avoids the difficulties of the addressees being angelic beings. (2) This option acknowledges that the ἄγγελοι τῶν ἑπτὰ ἐκκλησιῶν function in a particular manner separate from other ἄγγελοι in the narrative. (3) Further evidence might be found in the intertext of Daniel (an intertext continuing to ring in the hearers' ears, as the one like a son of

---

Ferguson, 'Some Patristic Interpretations of the Angels of the Churches (Apocalypse 1–3)', *Studia Patristica* 63 (2013), pp. 95-100, who surveys interpretations of the ἄγγελοι τῶν ἑπτὰ ἐκκλησιῶν in the Patristics.

[41] Smalley, *Revelation*, p. 58, reveals an exegetical tension, asking how the prophetic messages can be addressed to the living Johannine community, and the wider church, if it is addressed to angelic beings? Smalley writes, 'He is not writing in the first place to angels'.

[42] Aune, *Revelation 1–5*, pp. 108-12.

[43] See W.H. Brownlee, 'The Priestly Character of the Church in the Apocalypse', *NTS* 5 (1958–59), pp. 224-25; Mangina, *Revelation*, pp. 56-57. For one of the earliest modern, critical interpretations of the ἄγγελοι as human messengers, see H.L. Strack and P. Billerbeck, *Kommentar zum Neuen Testament aus Talmud und Midrasch* (Munich: Beck, 1926), III, p. 791.

man offers this revelation). In multiple accounts in Daniel, there is a contrast between the wise ones of Babylon and Daniel's wisdom. The Babylonians continually fail to discern the dreams and visions that are presented to them, while Daniel is able to discern dreams and visions by the wisdom of God.[44] This theme culminates in Dan. 12.3 where 'the discerning [ones]'[45] are promised that they will shine brightly as the stars (ὡς οἱ ἀστέρες).[46] As this text intersects with the seven ἀστέρες ('stars') that are the seven ἄγγελοι τῶν ἑπτὰ ἐκκλησιῶν in Rev. 1.20, the ἄγγελοι τῶν ἑπτὰ ἐκκλησιῶν resonate with the wise or discerning stars (ἀστέρες) in Dan. 12.3. These ἀστέρες/ἄγγελοι would then represent the wise or discerning messengers (ἄγγελοι) in the seven churches. That these addressees are both human and full of wisdom/discernment would then offer a possible solution as to why the seven ἄγγελοι are the recipients of the seven prophetic messages. Wisdom and discernment are required to receive the words of this prophecy. Furthermore, the specificity of the *seven* ἀστέρες/ἄγγελοι should not assume exclusivity among members of the seven churches. To the contrary, the *seven* stars that are *seven* messengers would be inclusive in the same manner that the *seven* churches represent the whole church. It is possible as well then that the *seven* Spirits have a relationship with the *seven* ἀστέρες/ἄγγελοι implying that the Spirit has sanctified the discerning ones in wisdom, understanding, and knowledge (Isa. 11.2).[47]

---

[44] The text describes Daniel as having the

ἕως οὗ ἦλθεν Δανιηλ οὗ τὸ ὄνομα Βαλτασαρ κατὰ τὸ ὄνομα τοῦ θεοῦ μου ὃς πνεῦμα θεοῦ ἅγιον ἐν ἑαυτῷ ἔχει καὶ τὸ ἐνύπνιον ἐνώπιον αὐτοῦ εἶπα. Βαλτασαρ ὁ ἄρχων τῶν ἐπαοιδῶν ὃν ἐγὼ ἔγνων ὅτι πνεῦμα θεοῦ ἅγιον ἐν σοὶ καὶ πᾶν μυστήριον οὐκ ἀδυνατεῖ σε ἄκουσον τὴν ὅρασιν τοῦ ἐνυπνίου οὗ εἶδον καὶ τὴν σύγκρισιν αὐτοῦ εἰπόν μοι (Dan. 4.8-9, Th).

The context would be significant because, following the interpretation of Daniel, King Nebuchadnezzar loses his mind/intellect (φρένες) and acts like an animal because he admired his own glory rather than giving glory to God, see U. Wilckens, 'σοφία', *TDNT*, VII (1971), p. 489.

[45] J. Goldingay, *Daniel* (WBC; Nashville, TN: Thomas Nelson, 1996), p. 308, translates the participle הַמַּשְׂכִּלִים as 'the discerning'.

[46] On Dan. 12.3 in Rev. 1.20, see Brownlee, 'Priestly Character', pp. 224-25; Beale, *The Book of Revelation*, pp. 216-19; Prigent, *The Apocalypse*, p. 146.

[47] Mangina, *Revelation*, p. 57. See Victorinus, *Commentary on the Apocalypse*, p. 8.

Jesus reveals the final element of this mystery: the seven lampstands are the seven churches. This imagery recalls Zechariah 4, albeit slightly altered. In Zechariah, there is a single lampstand with seven branches while, in Revelation, there are seven lampstands. At the junction of Zechariah 4 and Revelation, the churches discover a close relationship between the seven Spirits and the seven (Spirit-filled) churches.[48] In this textual collision and among the many activities of the seven Spirits in the seven churches, the Spirit empowers (Zech. 4.6) the churches' discernment offering to them wisdom, understanding, and knowledge (Isa. 11.2). Similarly, as Jesus has revealed this mystery to John, Jesus (who is walking among them) will assist the churches in discerning. Thus, the inaugural scene introduces a μυστήριον ('mystery') setting the stage, in a sense, for the process of pneumatic discernment for the rest of the narrative.[49]

## Revelation 2–3

Without a break in the narrative, the resurrected Jesus openly speaks to the seven churches.[50] The repetition of τάδε λέγει ('thus says'), which introduces the words of Jesus that are actively spoken by the Spirit in each prophetic message, suggests that the churches are receiving more than simple 'letters', but that they are receiving prophetic messages.[51] Recognizing the prophetic nature of these messages informs the churches that discernment and wisdom will be

---

[48] Cf. esp. Zech. 4.6. See Bauckham, *Climax of Prophecy*, pp. 163-66; Blount, *Revelation*, p. 43. The pneumatic implications become more explicit in Rev. 5.6 where the seven eyes are the seven Spirits, see the discussion below.

[49] G.K. Beale, *The Use of Daniel in Jewish Apocalyptic Literature and in the Revelation of St. John* (Lanham, MD: University Press of America, 1984), p. 169, writes, 'μυστήριον is used in close association with the *idea* of "interpretation," since it introduces the interpretation of the vision in v. 20' (emphasis original).

[50] Thomas, *The Apocalypse*, p. 109.

[51] In the HB prophetic literature, many prophetic oracles began with τάδε λέγει, see Beale, *The Book of Revelation*, p. 229. Michaels, *Revelation*, pp. 64-65, writes that the seven messages 'are not letters, however, in any sense of the word. The whole book of Revelation presents itself as one long letter ... Rather they are the oracles of a prophet, given in the name of the divine Being who speaks through them ... chapters 2–3 of Revelation should be called "the seven messages".' D.A. deSilva, 'Out of Our Minds? Appeals to Reason (Logos) in the Seven Oracles of Revelation 2–3', *JSNT* 31.2 (2008), p. 130, observes that the repetitious descriptions of the glorified Christ and τάδε λέγει serve to add authority to the speaker and draw the hearers' attention to his prophetic words. Williamson, *Revelation*, p. 56, adds, 'Strictly speaking, rather than letters, they are prophetic messages from

needed in their hearing.[52] Perhaps, this is why narratively, prior to the seven prophetic messages in Rev. 1.20, the churches are drawn to Dan. 12.3 and the discerning ones (the seven ἀστέρες/ἄγγελοι). It will become apparent at the conclusion of each prophetic message that, although John writes to each church, every church is called to discern each prophetic message pneumatically.[53]

## Ephesus

The hearers in Ephesus immediately discover that this is not a typical letter; they are receiving the words of the one who holds the seven stars and who walks in the midst of the seven lampstands.[54] The subtle shift in language from ἔχων ('having', 1.16) to κρατῶν ('holding', 2.1) indicates the firmness with which Christ holds the seven stars.[55] Encountering Jesus who holds the seven stars recalls the inaugural vision where John falls down as dead. Would such language suggest that those in the churches would prostrate themselves as they encounter the resurrected Jesus and hear his prophetic words?

---

the risen Lord, addressed to seven churches'. See also Beasley-Murray, *The Book of Revelation*, p. 72; Boring, *Revelation*, p. 85. Concerning prophecy, Schüssler Fiorenza, 'The Words of Prophecy', p. 8, writes, 'Strictly speaking the "words of prophecy" do not represent John's discourse but rather claim to be divine discourse. The *real* author of the Apocalypse is not John, but G\*d, the risen Jesus, and the Spirit.'

[52] Sweet, *Revelation*, p. 78, comments, 'The theme of the letters is discernment and fidelity'. Bauckham, *The Theology of the Book of Revelation*, p. 122, notes, 'the function of prophecy addressed to the churches is to expose the uncomfortable truth, just as the two witnesses torment the inhabitants of the earth by bringing home to them their sin (11:10)'. Contra Schüssler Fiorenza, 'The Words of Prophecy', p. 8, who finds that John writes with authority and warns those who add or subtract from his prophecy because 'he seems to want to forestall the testing of his work, since it was a commonplace assumption that prophecy required the discernment of the spirits and testing of the prophets'.

[53] Gause, *Revelation*, p. 45. See also Tavo, *Woman, Mother, and Bride*, pp. 54-62.

[54] For a discussion on (the at times over-stated influence of) the historical setting upon the interpretations of the seven prophetic messages, see Moyise, *The Old Testament in the Book of Revelation*, pp. 24-36; C.R. Koester, 'The Message to Laodicea and the Problem of Its Local Context: A Study of the Imagery in Rev. 3.14-22', *NTS* 49.3 (2003), pp. 407-24. See also Michaels, *Interpreting Revelation*, pp. 35-40. For a survey of the historical setting of the seven churches, see W.M. Ramsay, *The Letters to the Seven Churches of Asia and Their Place in the Plan of the Apocalypse* (Grand Rapids, MI: Baker Book House, 1904, 1963); C.J. Hemer, *The Letters to the Seven Churches* (JSNTSup 11; Sheffield: Sheffield Academic Press, 1986).

[55] P. von der Osten-Sacken, 'κρατέω', *EDNT*, II, p. 314.

The position of οἶδα ('I know') as the first words of Jesus in the Greek text communicates the significance of his knowledge.[56] Jesus, with his fiery eyes and having absolute, divine discernment, knows the situation in Ephesus fully.[57] Jesus sees their works. The church has vigorously tested (ἐπείρασας) those falsely calling themselves apostles (λέγοντας ἑαυτοὺς ἀποστόλους).[58] The appearance of ἀποστόλους ('apostles') suggests that these deceivers are claiming to be sent from God. However, while the church rightly discerned these lies, the work of discernment alone does not fully reveal the condition of the church in Ephesus because they have abandoned their first love.[59] In the Johannine literature, love is wholistic.[60] Whereas distinguishing between love for God and love for others might be possible, the Johannine literature is familiar with a more integrated understanding of love. Love for God is interconnected to loving others.[61] This integrated perspective reveals that love is a vital component of the church's discernment. Discernment is not only the ability

---

[56] Bauckham, *The Theology of the Book of Revelation*, p. 123, writes,

Like the description of Christ at the head of the first message, to Ephesus (2:1), they relate to Christ's knowledge of all the churches. They characterized him as the one who gives truthful evidence. Those who accept his evidence against them repent. It proves salvific. To those who reject it, the evidence itself becomes their condemnation. The witness becomes the judge.

Aune, *Revelation 1–5*, p. 143, adds, 'Yet in spite of the conventional formulaic use of οἶδα, something much deeper is being referred to, namely, the knowledge that the exalted Jesus has for all human affairs upon the earth'.

[57] Aune, *Revelation 1–5*, p. 122, comments, 'The οἶδα clause makes it clear that the exalted Christ is fully aware of the conduct of all members and factions of each of the seven congregations'. See also Boring, *Revelation*, pp. 88-89; Bauckham, *The Theology of the Book of Revelation*, p. 122; Stefanović, *Revelation*, p. 117.

[58] The community might be following a custom in the Johannine community of testing (δοκιμάζετε) the spirits (1 Jn 4.1-6). Thomas, *The Apocalypse*, pp. 114-15, puts forth three aspects of discernment in the Johannine community: (1) discernment is the responsibility of the whole community, (2) pneumatic confession should be in conformity with the confession, 'Jesus Christ coming in the flesh', and (3) pneumatic activity is expected to demonstrate continuity with the community's experience in the belief and experience of Jesus. See also Ladd, *Revelation of John*, p. 38; Smalley, *Revelation*, p. 61.

[59] Mangina, *Revelation*, p. 59.

[60] E.g. Jn 8.32; 10.4-5, 14; 14.7, 9, 17; 17.3; 1 Jn 3.3-7, 11-24. See Wall, *Revelation*, p. 71; Smalley, *Revelation*, p. 61.

[61] Gause, *Revelation*, p. 79 n. 10; Osborne, *Revelation*, pp. 116-17; Fee, *Revelation*, p. 27.

to recognize deceptions but must be carried out in love. The Truth of God is tightly connected to the love of God. Thus, the judgment of the community in Ephesus is not inconsequential. If they have indeed lost their love, despite their tremendous abilities to discern, they might already be losing their identity as a lampstand. Where even the remarkable discernment of the Ephesian church has failed in recognizing their lack of love, Jesus has discerned perfectly.[62] Jesus' prophetic words create a 'crisis of discernment' in the church. How will they know if/when their lampstand is removed?[63] How will they know if/when they returned to their first love? Jesus' prophetic words create space for continuous discernment; the churches must now continually ask themselves, if they have heeded Jesus' prophetic message.

Revelation 2.6 creates a tension in the churches because Jesus' exhortation to love is contrasted with Jesus' 'hate'; Jesus commends the church for *hating* the works of the Nicolaitans, which Jesus also *hates*.[64] The location of this commendation, first, reminds the churches that returning to their first love implies in no way abandoning their vigilance in discerning false teachings.[65] Second, this commendation might remind the discerning ones that Jesus' hatred of the Nicolaitans' works would not exclude them from his love. Whereas the testimony of Jesus Christ would include a variety of aspects, central to his testimony is the love of God and Jesus for the world; again a love that is apparently missing in the Ephesian discerners.[66] Hence,

---

[62] Keener, *Revelation*, pp. 111-12, observes, 'Yet part of discernment involves knowing what we must discern, and the tragedy of the Ephesian church's failure on this count is a tragedy of human nature that recurs through history and in our own time. The same church that rightly "hated" the works of the Nicolaitans (2:6) wrongly abandoned their earlier commitment to "love" (2:4).'

[63] Koester, *Revelation*, p. 270, writes:

The metaphor of moving the lampstand creates a crisis of discernment … How would readers experience the effect of such threats? As long as the congregation at Ephesus continues to gather, the readers will find it difficult to conclude that their lampstand has been moved. Yet, this lack of closure also means that the imagery continues to serve as a warning about the way a loss of love threatens to bring a loss of identity.

See also Beale, *The Book of Revelation*, pp. 231-32; Thompson, *Revelation*, p. 65.

[64] F.J. Murphy, *Fallen is Babylon: The Revelation to John* (Trinity Press: Harrisburg, PA, 1998), p. 117.

[65] Ladd, *Revelation of John*, p. 40.

[66] E.g. Jn 3.16.

even though the Ephesian church has discerned the lies in the teachings of the Nicolaitans, they are in danger of becoming equated with the Nicolaitans because they are falsely representing the testimony of Jesus.   *because they do not love.*

Revelation 2.7 – ὁ ἔχων οὖς ἀκουσάτω τί τὸ πνεῦμα λέγει ταῖς ἐκκλησίαις ('Let the one having an ear, hear what the Spirit is saying to the churches') – puts all the churches on alert. Not only are the hearers in Ephesus called to hear Jesus' prophetic words, but every church is also called to discern what the Spirit is saying.[67] The inclusion of all the churches indicates the communal aspect of discernment: discernment occurs in community, and every church is exhorted to participate in the process. Although there is the communal element of this address, the communal aspect does not remove individual responsibility. Each one (ὁ ἔχων) is exhorted to hear the Spirit.[68]

Jesus and the Spirit have a dynamic, synergistic relationship where their words are coterminously spoken in the prophetic messages.[69] Anyone who hears the prophetic words of Jesus is hearing the Spirit speak. The Spirit is the source of divine truth who makes it available to those who have an ear to hear. The active sense of the Spirit's words (λέγει) suggests the need for unceasing discernment, hearing, and obedience, and indicates that the voice of the Spirit is not statically constrained by the words written down on a page.[70] Whereas

---

[67] A.-M. Enroth, 'The Hearing Formula', *NTS* 36 (1990), p. 603; Skaggs and Benham, *Revelation*, pp. 31-32; Sorke, *Identity and Function of the Seven Spirits*, p. 67. G.L. Stevens, *Revelation: The Past and Future of John's Apocalypse* (Eugene, OR: Pickwick Publishers, 2014), p. 282. Morris, *Revelation*, p. 62, adds, 'The plural *churches* shows that the message is not only for those Asian Christians so long ago but for every one who "has an ear"'. Contra Wilson, *The Victor Sayings in the Book of Revelation*, p. 71.

[68] Smalley, *Revelation*, p. 64.

[69] Thomas, *The Apocalypse*, p. 121, observes, 'the interpretive, discerning process to which [the hearers] are called is not only a Christological endeavor but is also a Pneumatological one as well'. Enroth, 'The Hearing Formula', p. 601. Ruiz, *Ezekiel in the Apocalypse*, p. 198. Mazzaferri, *The Genre of the Book of Revelation*, p. 310, '… especially apparent in the letters, [is] that Christ's τάδε λέγει is τί τὸ πνεῦμα λέγει'.

[70] Ruiz, *Ezekiel in the Apocalypse*, p. 199, writes, 'Thus, the attitude of attentive reflection is a constant duty of believers'. Bauckham, *The Theology of the Book of Revelation*, p. 125, adds, 'The churches must be exposed to the power of the divine truth in the Spirit's words of prophecy, if they are to be the lampstands from which

John has a visionary experience ἐν πνεύματι ('in the Spirit') and en-counters the resurrected Jesus, the Spirit dynamically speaks the seven prophetic messages to all the churches. John's description that he was ἐν πνεύματι becomes all the more significant because while the Spirit is the catalyst enabling John to receive this visionary proph-ecy, the continual call to hear the Spirit suggests that the churches become ἐν πνεύματι to receive, discern, and hear.[71] Furthermore, the similarity in language between the opening formula (τάδε λέγει) and the concluding hearing formulas (τὸ πνεῦμα λέγει) emphasizes the prophetic nature of the seven messages. Such a connection denotes that the Spirit is speaking (actively) the entire prophecy, the whole Apocalypse. These are the words of God.

As the Spirit calls the churches to discern, they learn that the over-comers will be able to eat from the tree of life in the paradise of God, which recalls Genesis 3.[72] Even though the serpent promised Eve that she would become like God if she ate the fruit of the tree, it was Eve's desire to become wise (שׂכיל, Gen. 3.6) that persuaded her to

---

the seven Spirits can shine the light of truth in to the world'. Prigent, *The Apocalypse*, pp. 160-61, comments that the repetitions to hear in each prophetic message (re)calls the community to discernment, 'It implies ... the assertion that the text is not immediately intelligible. To understand it requires the effort of reflection, or rather the illumination of inspiration. The prophetic discourse elicited by the Spirit is only intelligible to those who have been visited by that same Spirit.' Thomas and Macchia, *Revelation*, p. 476, comment, 'The Spirit speaks the words of Jesus and provides the wisdom for discerning these words in life. Not only does the Spirit speak the words of Jesus, but these words are also discerned (understood, contex-tualized) in the Spirit (2:7, 11, 17, 29; 3:6, 13, 22). The discernment not only is conceptual but involves wisdom for life. It involves repentance, patient endurance, and faithful living.' See also Sweet, *Revelation*, p. 82.

[71] See Ruiz, *Ezekiel in the Apocalypse*, p. 196; Prigent, *The Apocalypse*, pp. 160-61; Koester, *Revelation*, p. 270, who writes:

The Spirit mediates the word of the risen Christ in two ways. First, the Spirit enables *John* to receive the words of the risen Christ through his vision. John said that he received his message while 'in the Spirit' (1:9). This expression lik-ens him to the biblical prophets, who were moved by the Spirit to convey a word from God. Second, the Spirit enables *the readers* to receive the risen Christ's words through John's text. Communication is complete when the word given to John in visionary form is received by the readers in written form. In this process the Spirit shares Christ's authority: both speak (*legei*) as one (2:1, 7).

[72] Thompson, *Revelation*, p. 66. It is possible that there are eucharistic under-tones in this text especially in light of Jn 6.52-59 where eating Jesus' flesh and drinking his blood leads to eternal life and being raised on the last day.

eat the fruit of the tree and disobey God.[73] Perhaps, the churches would discern that the wisdom of God requires obedience to God.[74] Upon hearing the call to overcome for the first time, the churches would likely conclude that overcoming involves returning to love, while continuing to discern. Thus, the first prophetic message focuses on and introduces pneumatic discernment as a central issue.

### Smyrna

In the second prophetic message, the churches again encounter the resurrected Jesus and are reminded that Jesus knows (οἶδα). First, Jesus knows all things from the first to the last and knows the church's tribulation, suffering, and slander (βλασφημίαν); even in the midst of the church's suffering, they are not abandoned.[75] From Jesus Christ's perceptive, the lampstand in Smyrna is not poor but in fact rich. Material status does not accurately define the church's condition because, from Jesus' point of view, they are rich. Second, Jesus knows the identity of those who claim to be Jews, but are not.[76] Despite perceptions and appearances, the resurrected Jesus reveals that those who persecute the church cannot in any way be identified as Jews. Third, whoever appears to be persecuting the church and casting its members into prison, from Jesus' perspective, is Satan, the Devil, who is behind their tribulation.[77] The church is offered an opportunity to see through Christ's fiery eyes and discern a reality that is contrary to appearances.[78] Jesus perceives a reality different from what is expected. He sees beyond appearances, and the church is invited to share in Jesus' perspective, to see through his eyes.

---

[73] Skaggs and Benham, *Revelation*, p. 35.

[74] Smalley, *Revelation*, p. 64.

[75] βλασφημίαν ('slander') will be used in association with the beast, the prostitute, and the inhabitants of the earth in Revelation, see P.L. Mayo, *Those Who Call Themselves Jews': The Church and Judaism in the Apocalypse* (PTMS 60; Pickwick: Eugene, OR, 2006), p. 65.

[76] The text does not address the entire historical Jewish community in Smyrna; rather it addresses those in Smyrna who claim to be Jews, but clearly are not because they slander the church. These identify with the synagogue of Satan.

[77] Mayo, *Those Who Call Themselves Jews'*, p. 66.

[78] The community's persecution should not be minimized by viewing it from a cosmic perspective. The text directs the churches to recognize the deeper structures behind the evil actions of people against the churches. That the earthly powers work in conjunction with these sinister forces suggests that the churches' faithful witness to those who persecute them confronts those deeper structures.

The prophetic words in Rev. 2.10 tell of a coming test, a tribulation for ten days that reveals Jesus Christ's ability to foresee what will come upon the church. It seems possible that this text brings to mind Daniel and his friends' testing for ten days (Dan. 1.12-15).[79] The church in Smyrna finds itself in a comparable situation as Daniel who avoided the luxurious accommodations of their adversaries for ten days. Following Daniel and his friend's testing by avoiding the finer foods, they were in fact stronger than the others.[80] The church in Smyrna is stronger and richer despite appearances.[81] While those in Smyrna do not partake in aspects of a luxurious life, they are nevertheless rich as with Daniel and his friends. As the churches are encouraged by Jesus to be faithful even until death, they identify that when gazing through the fiery eyes of Jesus Christ, one discovers a much different perspective. If the church is faithful, they will receive a crown of life and will not be harmed by the second death, a promise no doubt holding much hope for those who are facing tribulation.

The churches again learn that the prophetic words of the resurrected Jesus are in fact the very words of the Spirit actively spoken to the community. While the churches remember that hearing the Spirit includes discerning rightly in love, they now learn that hearing  the Spirit involves seeing the world from a divine perspective. As the second call to hear the Spirit occurs, those in Smyrna are called to discern pneumatically. Discerning from Christ's perspective uncovers the source of the church's persecution – Satan – and the true reality of their wealth: they are rich despite appearing to be poor. As Jesus foresees an escalation in their persecution (being thrown into prison for ten days), the church is called to remain faithful, even to the point of death. Hence, for the second time, the churches learn how critical pneumatic discernment is among the churches.

Pergamum

The prophetic words to Pergamum come from the resurrected Jesus. For a third time, the churches learn that the resurrected Jesus knows

---

[79] Murphy, *Fallen is Babylon*, p. 125; Beale, *The Book of Revelation*, pp. 242-43; Keener, *Revelation*, p. 116. As the narrative progresses, the hearers will learn that 'ten' has negative associations.

[80] See Prigent, *The Apocalypse*, pp. 168-69.

[81] Trafton, *Reading Revelation*, p. 36.

(οἶδα). He has discerned the situation in Pergamum. As Jesus is holding (ὁ κρατῶν) the seven stars in his hand, the church holds (κρατεῖς)
to his name.[82] Jesus continues to have his hand on John who continues to be prostrated before him. The appearance of the seven stars
suggests that Jesus firmly holds the discerning ones in his hand. The
hearers are encountering the prophetic words of the resurrected Jesus, the sharp sword (from his mouth).[83] Jesus Christ's words are full
of discernment and are actively spoken by the Spirit.

Reference to Antipas as ὁ μάρτυς μου, ὁ πιστός μου ('my faithful
witness') reveals persecution occurring in Pergamum, and the reappearance of 'faithful witness' recalls the prologue where Jesus Christ
is the faithful witness (1.5). Much in the same manner as Smyrna, the
church in Pergamum is given an opportunity to share in Christ's sight
and discern that their persecution originates from Satan. Literally,
the name of Satan surrounds the name of Antipas forming an inclusio that emphasizes Satan's activity in the death of Antipas.[84] Specifically, it is Satan's throne that is located in Pergamum signifying that
(1) Satan's throne stands in conflict with the divine throne. (2) The
position of Satan's throne in Pergamum indicates a location of Satan's power.[85] (3) Pergamum is the only location in the prophetic messages where a member of the community has been killed, revealing
the severity of the situation.[86] (4) The appearance of Satan's throne,
rather than the synagogue of Satan, suggests that the opposition to
the church derives from a group other than those calling themselves
Jews. The presence of a throne in Smyrna suggests that some power

---

[82] Osborne, *Revelation*, p. 141.

[83] Although ἐκ τοῦ στόματος αὐτοῦ ('from his mouth') is missing, another
reference to Jesus' sword recalls the inaugural vision and the sword that comes
from Jesus' mouth, see Aune, *Revelation 1–5*, p. 181. Archer, *'I Was in the Spirit on the
Lord's Day'*, pp. 146-47, adds, 'That the sword comes from Jesus' mouth speaks to
the power and accuracy of his discerning words ... Jesus' discernment, like the
sword coming from his mouth, is pointed and sharp.' See also M. Wilcock, *The
Message of Revelation* (Downers Grove, IL: InterVarsity Press, 1975), p. 48;
Bauckham, *The Theology of the Book of Revelation*, p. 123.

[84] Sweet, *Revelation*, p. 88.

[85] Smalley, *Revelation*, p. 68.

[86] Koester, *Revelation*, p. 292.

– perhaps political/government – opposes the church; however, the precise source of their persecution is not identified in the text.[87]

While Jesus holds (ὁ κρατῶν) the seven stars and some in the church hold (κρατεῖς) to Jesus' name, others in Pergamum hold (κρατοῦντας) to the teachings of Balaam.[88] The relationship between 'holding' and discernment becomes clearer in that those holding (κρατοῦντας) to the teachings of Balaam certainly have not discerned.[89] Revelation identifies Balaam as a teacher (τὴν διδαχὴν Βαλαάμ, ἐδίδασκεν τῷ Βαλὰκ). 'Teaching' only appears in the seven prophetic messages in Revelation, and each occurrence is associated with false teaching.[90] In the Johannine literature, any teaching that is not of Jesus, the Father, or the Paraclete is viewed negatively.[91] In Numbers, Balaam (a non-Israelite) was not a teacher but a prophet, who 'heard the words' and 'knew the knowledge' of God, having the Spirit of God upon him.[92] Balaam entertained Balak's offer to sacrifice on his behalf and curse the people of Israel, but Balaam refused. While Balaam's character is ambiguous in Numbers 22–24, the conclusion of Numbers describes that Balaam's 'word' led the people of Israel to sexual immorality (Num. 31.16). Other appearances of Balaam in the HB described him as cursing the people of Israel and one who practiced divination.[93] He was both a Spirit-empowered prophet as well as one who cast a stumbling block for Israel. Is it possible then that Balaam is an example of a Spirit-empowered prophet who

---

[87] Barr, *Tales of the End*, p. 57, writes when addressing the historical interpretative options of the throne, 'It is perhaps best to say we can no longer discern the precise significance of the symbol, but we ought not to miss the political implications of the *throne*'. Koester, *Revelation and the End of All Things*, p. 58, comments 'it can best be understood in more general terms as the power that threatens the church'.

[88] Archer, *'I Was in the Spirit on the Lord's Day'*, p. 148.

[89] Archer, *'I Was in the Spirit on the Lord's Day'*, p. 149, writes, 'As Jesus has discerned, the church in Pergamum must also engage in proper discernment both of those who instruct as well as the content of their instruction'.

[90] Revelation 2.14-15, 20, 24.

[91] So Thomas, *The Apocalypse*, p. 147. Thomas points out that the one exception is John ('the Baptist') who is called 'Rabbi' (Jn 3.26).

[92] Numbers 24.2, 16.

[93] See Num. 31.16; cf. Num. 25.1; Deut. 23.4-5; Josh. 13.22; Neh. 13.2; Mic. 6.5. In the two other references to Balaam in the NT (2 Pet. 2.15; Jude 11), Balaam is accused of wrong doings for wages (μισθός).

knew the knowledge of God but ultimately led the people of God to a path of destruction?[94] The prophetic activity of Balaam's vocation in the HB is juxtaposed with his role as a teacher in Revelation. The dialogical juxtaposition of teaching and prophecy might reveal a prophetic characteristic to the teaching and a pedagogic function to prophecy. The relationship between teaching and prophecy challenges the churches to discern all prophetic and pedagogic activity, testing prophecy and teaching in light of the teaching of Jesus, the Spirit, and the Father. Furthermore, the churches are challenged to hold together the tension found in Balaam; a prophet used by God who led Israel astray. It is possible that some prophets and teachers in the churches, who have prophesied the very words of Jesus, who have the knowledge of God, who even have the Spirit upon them, could lead the community into false teaching.[95] This seems to be the case with the Balaamites in Pergamum. In the Johannine literature, the test of true teaching is Jesus, the Spirit, and the divine throne.

A second enigmatic occurrence of the Nicolaitans appears in the messages. Although the churches are not given the details of the Nicolaitan false teachings, they learn that the church in Pergamum (unlike the church in Ephesus) is unable to discern the Nicolaitan false teaching. The churches are reminded again of the necessity of constant and continual discernment. The call for repentance and discernment carries with it a sense of urgency. Jesus reveals that he is coming quickly and when he arrives he will make war against the Nicolaitans with the sword of his mouth, his discerning words. When Jesus comes, his truth will cut through deceptive teachings.

The call to discern Jesus' prophetic words becomes explicit once again, as all the churches are called to hear the Spirit. The reappearance of the Nicolaitans recalls the message to Ephesus, exhorting the churches to discern in love. The call to discern in Pergamum, as in Smyrna, includes perceiving the true reality of those who oppose the church, and that it is Satan who is persecuting them. The church must

---

[94] John 11.51.

[95] Thomas, *The Apocalypse*, p. 139, writes, 'Perhaps the intertext that results in v. 14, where despite Balaam's faithful prophesying he is only remembered for his leading the children of Israel astray, would convey to the hearers a warning that despite any prophetic activity that comes from their own Balaam, in the end all that will be remembered is his own involvement in leading "Israel" astray'.

also pneumatically discern false teachings in the community including the teachings of the Nicolaitans and Balaam. The church is called to discern pneumatically, to hear the prophetic words of Jesus, and to repent. Thus, if the church discerns, they will become overcomers and eat the hidden manna that brings life. Eating the hidden manna contrasts those in Pergamum, who eat food sacrificed to idols.[96] Another promise to the overcomers is that they will be given a white stone with a new name written on it that no one knows (οἶδεν) unless it is received. Thus far, forms of οἶδα have been exclusively associated with Jesus Christ's divine knowledge. Perhaps the promise 'to know' (οἶδα) implies that the overcomers will have a share in the (divine) knowledge of the resurrected Jesus.

## Thyatira

As in the previous three messages, this prophetic message is addressed to 'the discerning' in Thyatira. The hearers for the first time learn that the resurrected Jesus is the 'Son of God' alongside some more familiar descriptions: he has eyes of fire and thereby is able to see the lampstand's situation.[97] The church receives overwhelming praise for their ἔργα, καὶ τὴν ἀγάπην καὶ τὴν πίστιν καὶ τὴν

---

[96] See Mounce, *The Book of Revelation*, p. 82; Koester, *Revelation*, p. 291. Also, Prigent, *The Apocalypse*, p. 177; Boring, *Revelation*, p. 90; Archer, *'I Was in the Spirit on the Lord's Day'*, p. 151; Williamson, *Revelation*, p. 74, observe eucharistic elements in this passage. Wilson, *The Victor Sayings in the Book of Revelation*, p. 123, proposes an association between the manna and Jesus as the bread of life.

[97] Many scholars observe a connection between Christ's fiery eyes and his ability to discern the deception in Thyatira, see Mounce, *The Book of Revelation*, p. 85, who writes, 'The blazing eyes suggest the penetrating power of Christ's ability to see through the seductive arguments of Jezebel and those who were being led astray by her pernicious teaching'. Gause, *Revelation*, p. 58, adds, 'He is able to see the secrets and seductions of the false prophetess ... These sins which were supposedly done in secret are exposed to the eyes of the Son of God, whose eyes are as a flame of fire'. Rowland, *Revelation*, p. 64, notes a correlation between Christ's fiery eyes and the seven Spirits as fiery torches, 'The eyes of Christ are the ever searching Spirit of God sent out into the world (5.6), which will equip him to exercise judgment (19.11f.), to be "a searcher of hearts and minds" and to know "the deep secrets of Satan"'. See also Stefanović, *Revelation*, p. 134; Fee, *Revelation*, pp. 38-39; Smalley, *Revelation*, p. 72; Skaggs and Benham, *Revelation*, pp. 41-42; Archer, *'I Was in the Spirit on the Lord's Day'*, p. 152.

διακονίαν καὶ τὴν ὑπομονήν ('works, love, faith, service, and forti-tude'). Unlike the church in Ephesus, those in Thyatira are full of love, and their last works are greater than their first.[98]

Despite the good works of those in Thyatira, the church has not discerned the deceptive teaching and prophecy of 'Jezebel'.[99] Upon hearing the name Jezebel, the churches would recall the book of Kings where Jezebel notoriously murdered the prophets and accom-modated the false prophets of Baal at her table. When taking a piece of land from Naboth for Ahab, Jezebel was cunning and manipulated the elders and leaders to have Naboth murdered. She was accused of being a sorcerer and fornicator who incited Ahab to evil. She even seemed to have played a part alongside Ahab when he brought Baal worship to Israel.[100] Whereas the churches might recall these (in-ter)texts, Jesus' accusation contains continuity and discontinuity with this HB figure. Although sexual immorality and idol worship are pre-sent in the HB narrative, Jezebel is described as a prophet in Revela-tion.[101] Her prophetic activity might bring to mind Balaam where even those who have spoken on behalf of God can speak falsely in the churches and lead them astray. Similarly, it further reveals a rela-tionship between teaching and prophecy: the teaching of Jezebel flows from her role as a prophet. However, her teaching and proph-ecy are deceptive.[102] Deception has been rampant throughout the messages. Some have falsely called themselves apostles and others call themselves Jews. Already, Revelation has been called a prophecy (1.3), and John, the one delivering the prophecy, is a prophet. While the church is hearing what the prophetess – Jezebel – is saying (ἡ

---

[98] Osborne, *Revelation*, p. 154, points out that only in Rev. 2.4, 19 does ἀγάπην ('love') appear in Revelation, emphasizing the contrast between the two prophetic messages.

[99] E. Schüssler Fiorenza, *The Book of Revelation: Justice and Judgment* (Philadelphia, PA: Fortress Press, 1985), p. 223, observes that Jezebel is critiqued based on her false prophecies and not on the basis of being a woman prophet.

[100] See 1 Kgs 16.31; 18.4, 13, 19; 21.5-15, 25; 2 Kgs 9.7, 22; cf. 19.2.

[101] Beale, *The Book of Revelation*, p. 261. This is especially noteworthy consider-ing Jezebel in the HB was not a prophet, so Keener, *Revelation*, pp. 133-34. Tavo, *Woman, Mother, and Bride*, p. 115, notes that the deceptive activity of Jezebel aligns her character with the dragon who deceives the whole world. Thomas, *The Apocalypse*, p. 147, comments, 'For Jesus to name this woman "Jezebel" is enough to alert the hearers to her true identity and perhaps to suggest that their discern-ment with regard to this figure was lacking'.

[102] Bauckham, *The Theology of the Book of Revelation*, p. 122.

λέγουσα), it seems that they are unable to hear what the Spirit and Jesus are saying (τάδε λέγει, τί τὸ πνεῦμα λέγει).[103] Therefore, the church is exhorted to discern vigilantly, to hear the prophetic words of Jesus, to look through the fiery eyes of Jesus, and to discern the active voice of the Spirit. The Thyatiran works do not protect them from the deceptive prophecy of Jezebel or false teachings.[104] Hence, the seven prophetic messages reveal a dynamic context where discernment must accompany works and works must be accompanied by discernment. Love without vigilant discernment is under the threat of judgment in the same manner that a church full of discernment that fails to love will be judged.

Jesus reveals to the community that Jezebel's works will lead directly to her judgment. While the text does not reveal the opportunities given to Jezebel to repent, it displays her unwillingness. Her lack of repentance leads to the judgment of Jezebel, her children, and her followers.[105] In Thyatira, the purpose of judgment is: γνώσονται πᾶσαι αἱ ἐκκλησίαι ὅτι ἐγώ εἰμι ὁ ἐραυνῶν νεφροὺς καὶ καρδίας, καὶ δώσω ὑμῖν ἑκάστῳ κατὰ τὰ ἔργα ὑμῶν ('all the churches will know, themselves, that I am the one searching minds and hearts, and I will give to each of you according to your works'). A significant aspect of discernment is that the churches themselves will know (γνώσονται)[106] that Jesus Christ's discerning fiery eyes are able to see the inner most being and the heart, nothing can be hidden from him against the inability of the churches to know.[107] The Son of God, the

---

[103] Murphy, *Fallen is Babylon*, p. 135, observes a connection between Jezebel 'saying' (λέγουσα) and 'the deep things of Satan as they say' (ὡς λέγουσιν). Smalley, *Revelation*, p. 74, observes that πλανᾷ appears elsewhere in Revelation of Satan, the beast, and Babylon. See also Bauckham, *The Theology of the Book of Revelation*, p. 124; Resseguie, *The Revelation of John*, p. 93; deSilva, 'Out of our Minds?', p. 140.

[104] C.G. González and J.L. González, *Revelation* (Louisville, KY: Westminster John Knox Press, 1997), p. 31.

[105] While this could be a reference to her literal children, it seems more appropriate in this context to interpret 'children' as those who follow her deceptive teaching, see Smalley, *Revelation*, p. 75. Koester, *Revelation*, p. 307, adds, 'readers are left to discern when and how Christ will enact justice. The question of discernment is significant because the language in Revelation is surprisingly vague.'

[106] The middle voice verb, γνώσονται, emphasizes the knowledge of the churches.

[107] νεφροὺς καὶ καρδίας is literally kidneys and hearts meaning the inner being, thoughts, and emotions. Aune, *Revelation 1–5*, p. 206, notes that this alludes to

ἐγώ εἰμι ('I am'), is able to discern the evil in the churches and it will not be tolerated. Among a variety of associations with ἐγώ εἰμι in the Johannine literature, one includes that Jesus is the Truth (Jn 14.6) who is able to judge the deceptions of Jezebel truly. Truth is christologically conditioned in the Johannine literature. The churches are called upon to see the truth of Jesus (the truth of the Truth) and repent from Jezebel's works.[108]

Jesus' fiery eyes are also able to discern those in Thyatira who do not 'have' (ἔχουσιν) these false teachings and who do not know the deep things of Satan (ἔγνωσαν τὰ βαθέα τοῦ Σατανᾶ). This creates a differentiation between those who do not know (γνώσονται) that Jesus is searching minds and hearts, and those who do not know (ἔγνωσαν) the deep things of Satan. Perhaps, what is *not known* is as significant as what *is known*. What should be *not known* is the deep things of Satan. Similarly, 'as they say' (ὡς λέγουσιν) contrasts what the Spirit says (λέγει) who actively speaks the words of Jesus.[109] While the text does not reveal the precise identity of the deep things of Satan, once again the churches learn that false teaching ultimately derives from Satan.[110] In Thyatira, Satan and Jezebel's activity is subtle ('hidden') and deceitful, which urges diligent discernment in the churches.

For those in Thyatira who continue in love and who discern, Jesus Christ will not add any more to them. Rather, they are to hold

---

Jer. 17.10. Aune helpfully points out that the exalted Jesus possesses Yahweh's omniscience from the Jeremiah passage. Sweet, *Revelation*, p. 95, writes concerning the situation in Thyatira, '[Jezebel's] refusal to repent, and their refusal to disown her, raised the issue of discernment in its sharpest form'. Skaggs and Benham, *Revelation*, p. 43, add, 'Christ describes himself as he who searches hearts and minds, which suggests that his judgment is based on the knowledge of a person's inner condition as well as their outward deeds. Such discernment exposes the deception of false teachers who would appear holy, even exercising spiritual gifts.' See also Beale, *The Book of Revelation*, p. 264; Stefanović, *Revelation*, p. 135; Blount, *Revelation*, p. 64.

[108] Smalley, *Revelation*, p. 75, proposes that the 'right-thinking and correctly behaving members' in Thyatira are called upon 'to repent *on behalf of* Jezebel's activity, which has nothing to do with their own practices'.

[109] Keener, *Revelation*, p. 135, comments, 'But as the true searcher of hearts, Jesus notes the course of their revelations: Satan (2:24)'. Mangina, *Revelation*, p. 65, adds, 'It is a matter of knowledge, of the Spirit (Jezebel is a prophet like John), of having deep insight into the things not only of God but of Satan'.

[110] Koester, *Revelation*, p. 308.

(κρατήσατε) to what they know. They are to continue to discern false teachings vigilantly and continue in love, faithfulness, endurance, and service. The fourth promise to the overcomers assures that the churches will receive authority over the nations and the morning star. Overcoming for the church in Thyatira is tied to overcoming the deceit of Jezebel and Satan. For the fourth time, the words of Jesus are spoken dynamically by the Spirit. On this occasion, the prophetic message has emphasized the need to hear the Spirit and Jesus in place of the words of Jezebel.[111] Whereas Ephesus was condemned for lack of love in discernment, the church in Thyatira loved but lacked discernment. Both contexts ultimately result in Jesus' judgment.

## Sardis

The churches encounter the fifth prophetic message that is addressed to the discerning one in Sardis. The churches learn that Jesus has the seven Spirits and the seven stars.[112] The seven stars are associated with the seven messengers of the seven churches who are identified as the discerning ones. The appearance of the seven Spirits recalls the seven Spirits before the throne, ἐν πνεύματι ('in the Spirit'), and the calls to hear the Spirit. Hence, Jesus holds the seven Spirits and seven stars, suggesting a close relationship among the seven stars, Jesus, the divine throne, and the seven Spirits.[113]

---

[111] Archer, *'I Was in the Spirit on the Lord's Day'*, pp. 156-57, writes, 'The Spirit's call for discernment requires the church to discern the words of Jesus from the words of those like "Jezebel" who claim to speak prophetically. The giving, receiving, and discerning of the word – all elements of the church's worship – must take place under the guidance of the Holy Spirit.'

[112] Aune, *Revelation 1–5*, p. 219, proposes that the καὶ in Rev. 3.1 is epexegetical concluding that the seven Spirits do not refer to the Spirit; however, his argument fails to convince because the seven stars and the seven Spirits appear as distinct images in the narrative. While they do have a close relationship, they are not equated. See Tenney, *Interpreting Revelation*, p. 63, who comments, 'His possession of the seven spirits of God and the sevens stars, His complete wisdom and His complete control of the leadership of the church'. See also Gause, *Revelation*, p. 63; Fee, *Revelation*, p. 46.

[113] Skaggs and Benham, *Revelation*, p. 45, comment, 'The seven spirits represent the Holy Spirit, who plays an important role in discernment and prophecy'. Archer, *'I Was in the Spirit on the Lord's Day'*, p. 157, adds:

Further, the prophetic messages are clearly identified as the words of the Spirit. Therefore, in this opening address to Sardis, the intimate connection between Jesus, the Spirit, and the community is prominent … perhaps this connection

For the fifth time, the churches are reminded that the resurrected Jesus knows (οἶδα). He has discerned the works of those in Sardis, and it is not a positive assessment. From the perspective of Jesus Christ's fiery eyes, the lampstand in Sardis is dead despite their name of being alive. Their works are directly associated with their dead identity.[114] Again, the appearance of the lampstand is at odds with the perception of Jesus.[115] Distinct from the previous prophetic messages, the resurrected Jesus does not reveal the precise issue plaguing the church in Sardis. The fact that Jesus' address is cryptic seems designed to inspire self-critical discernment on behalf of the churches because they are charged to discern for themselves the reason for their necromantic state.[116] In order to repent, come alive, keep, and obey, the churches must discern their state from Jesus' perspective.

If they do not discern, Jesus threatens that he will come as a thief, swift and in anonymity, urging attentive discernment on the part of the churches. As with Thyatira, the whole community is in danger of Jesus' judgment because, as Jesus knows everyone's works, he also knows those who have not soiled their clothes, who walk with Jesus

---

between Jesus, the Spirit, and the community is also intended to add reinforcement to the important role that the Spirit plays in the Apocalypse. The ascription affirms the presence of Jesus within their midst, who is intimately connected with the Spirit and holds the churches close to himself.

[114] Ladd, *Revelation of John*, p. 56, notes that their works lack 'the life-giving Holy Spirit'. J.W. Fuller, '"I Will Not Erase his Name from the Book of Life" (Revelation 3:5)', *JETS* 26.3 (1983), p. 303, differentiates between their 'heavenly' and 'earthly' reputation' (ὄνομα). See also Beasley-Murray, *The Book of Revelation*, pp. 94-95; Sweet, *Revelation*, p. 98.

[115] I. Boxall, *The Revelation of St. John* (BNTC; Peabody, MA: Hendrickson, 2006), p. 68, comments, 'Appearances can be fiendishly deceptive! ... [W]hat appears to be a thriving community from one perspective may look very different from the divine perspective'. See also Resseguie, *The Revelation of John*, p. 95; Trafton, *Reading Revelation*, p. 45.

[116] Koester, *Revelation*, p. 318, writes, 'The problem of discernment is like that in earlier warnings ... Yet the disturbing vagueness helps to rob the readers at Sardis of the complacency that they mistake for true security'. So also Mangina, *Revelation*, p. 65, who comments, 'What exactly was going on in Sardis remains obscure, of course, and yet this obscurity is to our benefit. Rather than seeking to discern what was happening behind the text, this letter (like all the letters) invites present-day churches to ask themselves whether their impressive human appearance masks a radical deficiency "in the sight of my God" (3:2).'

Christ (who is walking among the lampstands), and who are worthy.[117] It seems that among the possible implications for being dressed in white, one aspect is that those who have not soiled their clothes have rightly discerned. While Jesus knows (οἶδα), the churches do not know (γνῷς) when Jesus will come, establishing a distinction between Jesus Christ's knowledge and that of the church.[118] As some in Sardis have a name that is not true to their reality, if they overcome, are worthy, and have white garments, then Jesus will confess their names before his Father and the angels. Continuing in the roundabout of Daniel, upon hearing of the seven stars, those who do not overcome will be removed/blotted out of the scroll, like those who were removed from the scroll in Dan. 12.1-2, who will not shine like the stars.[119] Those who will be blotted out do not have discernment or wisdom, are not overcomers, and will not shine like the (seven) stars.

For the fifth time, the churches are exhorted to discern the active words of the Spirit, the prophetic words of Jesus. After hearing this hearing formula again, the churches are reminded that they must love in their discernment and discern in love, while being attentive to the perspective of Jesus offered prophetically to the churches. Remembering these previous exhortations by the resurrected Jesus is all the more important considering that no particular issue is raised in Sardis. The church is tasked to discern their condition pneumatically: what does it mean to be dead or alive?

## Philadelphia

The sixth message is addressed to the discerning one in Philadelphia, and the churches again encounter the resurrected Jesus who is holy and true. The prophetic witness of Jesus is true because Jesus is the

---

[117] Aune, *Revelation 1–5*, p. 222, finds 'walking' to be synonymous with discipleship in the Johannine literature (cf. Jn 12.35; 1 Jn 1.6-7; 2.6, 11); 'walking' might allude to Enoch and Noah who 'walked' with God implying an 'unmediated relationship to God'.

[118] Smalley, *Revelation*, p. 83, notes that the second-person singular of γνῷς implies urgent action. Each individual member is implicated by Christ's words. Wall, *Revelation*, pp. 80-81, adds, 'Spiritual renewal is "mind renewal" ... to repent (*metanoeō*) literally refers to a person's intellectual reorientation, a "change of one's mind". The experience of conversion enables the congregation to know ...'

[119] Beale, *The Book of Revelation*, p. 281, observes that this text alludes to Dan. 12.1-2. See also B.M. Metzger, *Breaking the Code: Understanding the Book of Revelation* (Nashville, TN: Abingdon Press, 1993), p. 40.

Truth.[120] Jesus has the key of David and is able to open and close doors.[121] The churches are reminded that Jesus knows (οἶδα). As before, Jesus knows the true identity of those who say that they are Jews but are not; rather, they are liars and from the synagogue of Satan. Those calling themselves Jews, who are persecuting those with a little power, will bow before those in Philadelphia. Again, appearances are not as they seem because those with little power rarely have anyone bow before them.[122] Furthermore, the purpose of bowing and their judgment results in knowing (γνῶσιν) that Christ loves the church.[123] Judgment leads to knowledge. Jesus again warns that judgment will come upon those who are undiscerning of their false reality. As with Thyatira, all the churches will know that Jesus searches hearts and minds. Whereas the overcomers in Smyrna are promised a crown, those in Philadelphia are wearing a crown already.[124] The ones who have a little power will become a pillar in the temple of God, denoting eschatological strength and will receive a 'new name'.[125]

---

[120] On truth as a heavenly reality in Revelation, see W. Howard-Brook and A. Gwyther, *Unveiling Empire: Reading Revelation Then and Now* (The Bible & Liberation Series; Maryknoll, NY: Orbis Books, 1999), pp. 134-35.

[121] Boxall, *The Revelation of St. John*, p. 72, observes a connection between the open door in Rev. 3.8 with the door to heaven in 4.1: 'the "open door" will provide John with privileged access to the heavenly throne-room, and with it to heavenly mysteries otherwise hidden from him. The same privileged access is offered to the faithful Philadelphians, and indeed all who heed the words of this message, enabling them to see their own difficult situation from God's perspective, and thus make sense of it.'

[122] H.O. Maier, *Apocalypse Recalled: The Book of Revelation After Christendom* (Minneapolis, MN: Fortress Press, 2002), p. 173, notes the irony present in this text. Boxall, *The Revelation of St. John*, p. 72, comments, 'From the world's perspective, therefore, the Church is weak. But true power is revealed as something very different throughout the Apocalypse: it is wielded by a Lamb which is slaughtered, and by followers who are equally prepared to lay down their lives.'

[123] The churches might also detect Isa. 45.14 where there is a presence of both bowing and knowing, see Fekkes, *Isaiah in the Book of Revelation*, pp. 134-35.

[124] Archer, *'I Was in the Spirit on the Lord's Day'*, p. 163. Andrew of Caesarea, 'Commentary on the Apocalypse', in T.C. Oden (ed.), *Greek Commentaries on Revelation* (trans. W.C. Weinrich; Madison, WI: InterVarsity Press), p. 125, adds, 'And, moreover, the Holy Spirit is the key of the book of the Psalms and of every prophecy, for through him the treasures of knowledge are opened'.

[125] Resseguie, *The Revelation of John*, p. 100, comments, 'This name is a puzzle to be solved, and the reader must wait to learn more (cf. 19:12)'.

For a sixth time, the churches are called to hear, obey, and reflect upon the words of the Spirit. They are reminded that the prophetic words of the resurrected Jesus are actively spoken by the Spirit and are delivered to the discerning ones from John who is ἐν πνεύματι ('in the Spirit').[126] The hearers in Philadelphia are exhorted to discern the lies of those who claim to be Jews and to remain vigilant in their faithfulness and discernment. Although the church in Philadelphia does not receive any criticism, they are exhorted to continue in pneumatic discernment, to continue to hear the Spirit, or else they could lose their crown.[127]

## Laodicea

The seventh and final prophetic message is addressed to the church in Laodicea. The lampstand is hearing the words of the resurrected Jesus spoken by the Spirit and written by John, the prophet. The churches encounter ὁ Ἀμήν, ὁ μάρτυς ὁ πιστὸς καὶ ἀληθινός, ἡ ἀρχὴ τῆς κτίσεως τοῦ θεοῦ ('the Amen, the faithful and true witness, the origin of God's creation'). Christ is 'the Amen', the final word of truth, which is appropriate for the final prophetic message. The combination of 'true' and 'faithful' with witness suggests that a faithful witness requires divine truthfulness. Jesus, as the true and faithful witness, offers a witness that is true to the churches. The truth of Jesus, who is identified as the Truth, confronts the deceit among the churches.[128] Hence, the truthfulness of a faithful witness springs

---

[126] Fee, *Revelation*, p. 61, adds:

This reflects John's Trinitarian understanding of God as Father, Son ... and Holy Spirit. Whereas it is Christ who is speaking in each case to the seven churches, each letter also includes the admonition, by which it can begin to fall on deaf ears, is John's emphatic way of telling all the churches – then and now – that what God the Father has to say to the church through Christ the Son is ultimately communicated through the Spirit.

[127] Osborne, *Revelation*, p. 199, observes, 'They could still lose their "crown" and in that light had to "hold fast" to all they "had" (3:11). The way to "hold fast" is to continue to "heed" this message from the Spirit.'

[128] See Bauckham, *The Theology of the Book of Revelation*, p. 122, who observes, 'Christ in his exposure of the truth to the churches appears in the role of "the faithful witness", and "the Amen" (3:14), that is, the divine truthfulness'. Macchia also comments on a connection between pneumatic discernment and faithful witness, 'The discernment of the words of Christ in the Spirit among the faithful is part of their consecration unto God as the lampstands of the temple. The Spirit functions most intimately with the risen Christ to consecrate the people of God

forth from hearing the Spirit who, in the Johannine literature, is the Spirit of Truth and who speaks the words of Jesus, the Truth.[129]

Jesus Christ has discerned that the works of those in Laodicea are lukewarm. While the text does not offer a precise identification of hot, cold, or lukewarm, the churches become aware that hot and cold are viewed positively and lukewarm negatively. Being that the church is lukewarm, Jesus reacts in a startling matter and vomits them from his mouth.[130] Once again the churches are reminded that viewing the world through Christ's fiery eyes exposes a much different reality.[131] Contrary to the seven Spirits who speak (λέγει) with wisdom, understanding, Truth, and knowledge, the Laodicean church speaks (λέγεις) with misperceptions. While the church says, I am (εἰμι) rich, prosperous, and in need of nothing, the resurrected Jesus says that they do not know (οὐκ οἶδας).[132] Considering the repetitions of οἶδα ('I know', with Jesus as the subject) and λέγει ('saying', with the Spirit

---

for life and witness' (Thomas and Macchia, *Revelation*, p. 476). See also Archer, *'I Was in the Spirit on the Lord's Day'*, p. 165.

[129] John 16.13.

[130] Koester, 'The Message to Laodicea', pp. 407-24, has convincingly critiqued the historical interpretation that hot and cold derived from the water supplies of Hierapolis and Colossae, see Hemer, *The Letters to the Seven Churches*, pp. 186-91. Koester has put forth dining imagery as a preferable option and comments:

> Drawing on the imagery of a meal, the author expected readers to know that cold and hot beverages stand in contrast to their environment and that diners find them refreshing. In contrast, the temperature of a cup of lukewarm water or wine is more like that of its surrounding it does not distinguish itself to the touch. When applied to the Christians at Laodicea the imagery suggests that their works in no way distinguish them from others in their society. In the previous messages the risen Christ commends works of perseverance, faith, and love (Rev 2.2, 19; 3.8) – the kind of works that would be positively regarded as hot or cold. Subsequent verses will identify the lukewarm quality of the Laodicean Christians with a complacency born of prosperity (p. 415).

[131] Gause, *Revelation*, p. 75, observes, 'These people were ignorant; they did not even know their spiritual condition (Revelation 3:17). Everything they boasted of, they actually needed.' Murphy, *Fallen is Babylon*, p. 158, compares the criticisms in Laodicea and Sardis where '[b]oth messages admit that things are *apparently* going well in each of the two churches but assert that appearances are deceptive'.

[132] Metzger, *Breaking the Code*, p. 45, notes the deception in their claims and their 'proud, smug self-complacency'. Prigent, *The Apocalypse*, p. 216, adds, 'To a community which prides itself on acceding to riches reserved for the beneficiaries of a higher knowledge, our author retorts that this superior spiritualism is in reality nothing but misery in the eyes of Christ'. Skaggs and Benham, *Revelation*, p. 53, 'Christ rebuked the Laodiceans for their self-sufficiency, complacency and lack of spiritual self-discernment'.

as the subject), the appearance of these terms here with the Laodiceans as the subject of the verb suggests an element of arrogance in their words. Arrogance confirmed by the repetition of the first person singular εἰμι ('I am'). In other words, those in Laodicea imagine that they have the true perception of the resurrected Jesus and the Spirit, but in truth, they are unable to recognize their pitiful state.[133]

As with the church in Smyrna, material wealth does not offer a legitimate assessment of one's reality.[134] Although the states of wealth and poverty in Laodicea and Smyrna are antithetical,[135] both churches are offered an opportunity to see with the eyes of Jesus Christ. From the perception of Jesus, Smyrna is rich despite their poverty, and those in Laodicea are poor despite their wealth. Where the discernment in Laodicea has failed, Jesus' knowledge has not.[136] Material affluence (or lack thereof) is deceptive.[137] If the church continues to discern wrongly, then they will continue to believe that they are able to see, clothed, and rich.[138] Conversely, if the churches perceive through Jesus Christ's eyes, then they will recognize that they are in fact poor, blind, and naked. A correlation is created between the Laodicea's blindness and their inability to discern their reality from Jesus' perspective.[139] For the church in Laodicea, they must anoint their

---

[133] Aune, *Revelation 1–5*, p. 259, writes, 'The ignorance of the Laodicean church is in explicit contrast with the knowledge of the risen Christ emphasized in v 15a'. See also Smalley, *Revelation*, p. 99; Archer, *'I Was in the Spirit on the Lord's Day'*, p. 167. For a comparison of γινώσκω and οἶδεν in Revelation, see appendix 1 of this monograph. Osborne, *Revelation*, p. 207 n. 16, concludes that whenever οἶδα appears and Christ is the subject, it refers to divine knowledge; whenever οἶδα occurs with other characters as the subject, 'it has the classical meaning of theoretical knowledge'.

[134] See P. Richard, *Apocalypse: A People's Commentary on the Book of Revelation* (trans. P. Berryman; Maryknoll, NY: Orbis Books, 1994, 1998), p. 63.

[135] So Beale, *The Book of Revelation*, p. 305. See also M.G. Reddish, *Revelation* (Macon, GA: Smyth & Helwys, 2001), p. 82.

[136] Koester, *Revelation*, p. 346.

[137] Resseguie, *The Revelation of John*, p. 101.

[138] See A. Yarbro Collins, *Crisis & Catharsis* (Philadelphia, PA: Westminister Press, 1984), pp. 132-34; P.B. Duff, *Who Rides the Beast?: Prophetic Rivalry and the Rhetoric of Crisis in the Churches of the Apocalypse* (Oxford: Oxford University Press, 2001), pp. 61-70, for a discussion of wealth in Revelation.

[139] Beale, *The Book of Revelation*, p. 306, observes, 'The picture of the "eye salve" for regaining sight emphasizes the Laodiceans' lack of spiritual discernment (cf. John 9:39-41)'. Stefanović, *Revelation*, p. 154 observes,

blinded eyes to see. Revelation 3.19 denotes that the resurrected Jesus judges the churches because he loves them.[140]

Finally, there is a correlation created between pneumatic discernment and repentance: if the church discerns the prophetic words of Jesus, then they will repent.[141] Discernment requires vigilance, zeal, and love; it is perhaps because of their lackluster discernment that the church in Laodicea has arrived at such a pitiful state. The exhortation to repent accompanies the call to hear Jesus' voice. The churches have already been exhorted on six occasions that the Spirit is dynamically speaking the prophetic words of Jesus Christ.[142] 'Hearing', having been defined as keeping and obeying, is now expanded to include an opportunity for fellowship with the resurrected Jesus who is at the door knocking and waiting to be invited in.[143]

---

What the Laodiceans need above all is eyesalve to clearly discern their real spiritual condition'. Skaggs and Benham, *Revelation*, p. 54, 'Spiritual blindness seems to have been the cause of the church's problem in that they did not discern their condition ... Although they sell eye salve to help physical eye problems, the Laodiceans, themselves, needed God's eye salve to heal their spiritual blindness. The resulting sight would make repentance possible, for change cannot occur unless the problem is recognized ... He advises the Laodiceans to change their perspective of what is valuable, useful and effective, which ... will result in holiness and spiritual insight.

Mangina, *Revelation*, p. 67, comments, 'the lukewarm church, the church that imagines that it has everything, neither needs nor expects anything of him. The pathos of this situation lies in the absolute dichotomy between reality and perception, so that the community that is the most "wretched, pitiable, poor, blind, and naked" is at the same time the one most impervious to help.' Archer, *'I Was in the Spirit on the Lord's Day'*, pp. 167-68, adds, 'The hearers know that Jesus' eyes are like flames of fire (1.14), which are capable of searching the minds and hearts of the churches (2.18, 23). Jesus' eyes do not miss a thing; conversely, the Laodiceans' eyes have missed everything.' See also Boxall, *The Revelation of St. John*, p. 77; Williamson, *Revelation*, p. 94.

[140] Smalley, *Revelation*, p. 101.

[141] Sweet, *Revelation*, p. 108.

[142] Archer, *'I Was in the Spirit on the Lord's Day'*, p. 169, notes, 'Their inability to discern their own condition has not only blinded their eyes but also plugged their ears to Jesus' knocking'. See also Boxall, *The Revelation of St. John*, p. 78.

[143] Thomas, *The Apocalypse*, p. 197, writes, 'This image of hearing his voice pushes the hearers toward discerning their own status before and relationship with the resurrected Jesus'. The hearers might even recall Jn 10.2; 18.37. Sweet, *Revelation*, p. 109 and González and González, *Revelation*, p. 37, who observe the eucharistic elements in this text. If so, the eucharist might be a space for self-critical discernment, to hear the Spirit, and to perceive through the eyes of Jesus in the churches.

The seventh and final promise is to sit on Jesus' throne. The resurrected Jesus states that he overcame (ἐνίκησα, aorist active), and thereby becomes the standard for overcoming. Overcoming would include aspects of Jesus' life, death, and resurrection, as well as his wisdom and discernment. For the seventh time, the churches are exhorted to hear the Spirit who is speaking the prophetic words of Jesus, the Truth.[144] Hearing would likely be connected to the ability to hear Jesus knocking at the door. Pneumatic discernment in Laodicea would include, first, discerning the true and faithful witness of Jesus in order that they might recognize the deceptive reality in which they are living. Second, to repent and buy eye slave from Jesus in order that they might be able to perceive through his eyes. Third, hear Jesus who is knocking at the door and hear the Spirit who is speaking the prophetic words of Jesus to the churches.

Summary of Revelation 2–3

The seven prophetic messages are directed to every church, and discernment is the central theme throughout.[145] Discernment is communal on account that the entire church is exhorted to discern every message. The sevenfold repetition of the hearing formula (ὁ ἔχων οὖς ἀκουσάτω τί τὸ πνεῦμα λέγει ταῖς ἐκκλησίαις, 'Let the one having an ear, hear what the Spirit is saying to the churches') along with the sevenfold repetition of οἶδα ('I know') emphasizes the call for pneumatic, prophetic discernment.[146] Each prophetic message ex-

---

[144] Beale, *The Book of Revelation*, p. 306, comments, 'The exhortation to spiritual discernment at the end of the other letters and here in 3:22 has … particular relevance for this church since its members, perhaps above all others, have become anesthetized and insensitive to their spiritual plight. Consequently, they are complacent in their ignorance.'

[145] Bauckham, *The Theology of the Book of Revelation*, p. 122. Newton, *The Revelation Worldview*, pp. 136-37, writes:

One of the major themes in the messages to the seven churches is the need to discern between the two: seeing through the claims of 'those who *claim* to be apostles but are not' (2:2), 'those who *say* they are Jews and are not, but are a synagogue of Satan' (2:9; 3:9), 'Jezebel, who *calls* herself a prophet' (2:20), churches that 'have a *name* of being alive' but are dead (3:1; italics added), and those which *think* they are rich and prosperous but are actually 'wretched, pitiable, poor, blind, and naked' (3:17).

[146] Enroth, 'The Hearing Formula', p. 602. Thomas and Macchia, *Revelation*, p. 487.

horts the churches to self-reflection, to hear the Spirit, and to perceive the world with the fiery eyes of Jesus. Jesus (who knows all), who is the true and faithful witness, who is the Truth, confronts the churches with his true witness. The Spirit (of Truth) dynamically and actively conveys Jesus' true and faithful witness to the churches. The Spirit and Jesus speak in tandem in the seven prophetic messages. The Spirit's role in discernment is further emphasized by the appearance of ἐν πνεύματι ('in the Spirit') in the opening of this literary section, associating the whole R/revelation with the activity of the Spirit. Particular issues of discernment in the seven prophetic messages include: (1) testing false teaching/prophecy, (2) recognizing the true reality of their opponents by identifying them with the synagogue of Satan, Balaam, the Nicolaitans, or Jezebel, (3) examining the manners in which the churches engage in discernment, foremost in love, and (4) perceiving the church's true reality, which included recognizing poverty as wealth, wealth as poverty, or being alive as being dead.

## ἐν πνεύματι – Revelation 4.1–16.21

There is a subtle shift in narration from the resurrected Jesus, who spoke conterminously with the Spirit throughout the seven prophetic messages, back to John. This shift is indicated by the appearance of εἶδον ('I saw') that functions as a literary marker in Revelation and draws the hearers' attention to the scenes that follow. In the following scene, Jesus opens a door offering access to heaven to John (4.1).[147] John's narration recapitulates the opening scene on Patmos as he hears: ἡ φωνὴ ἡ πρώτη ἣν ἤκουσα ὡς σάλπιγγος λαλούσης μετ᾽ ἐμοῦ, λέγων, Ἀνάβα ὧδε, καὶ δείξω σοι ἃ δεῖ γενέσθαι μετὰ ταῦτα ('the first voice, which I heard as a trumpet, speaking to me, saying, "Come up here, and I will show you what is necessary to happen after this"'). The churches would remember John's encounter with the resurrected Jesus on Patmos as well as John's discerning prostration. As

---

[147] So Yarbro Collins, *The Apocalypse*, p. 34, who also notes that the door represents access to God. Thomas, *The Apocalypse*, p. 202, observes that Jesus is the door of the sheep (Jn 10.9). See also Resseguie, *The Revelation of John*, p. 106.

the resurrected Jesus assisted John and the church in their discernment, the churches anticipate assistance from the resurrected Jesus here. Because Jesus knows (οἶδα), he will reveal to John ἃ δεῖ γενέσθαι μετὰ ταῦτα ('what is necessary to happen after this').[148]

While similar, there is an alteration in the scenes described in Revelation 4 and Revelation 1. John was described as being ἐν πνεύματι ('in the Spirit') on Patmos, and then he heard a voice and saw 'one like the son of man'. In Revelation 4, John hears a voice like a trumpet and then is ἐν πνεύματι immediately. The reappearance of ἐν πνεύματι (4.2) indicates that the narrative progresses to its next literary section while also reminding the churches that the very structure of Revelation is pneumatically conditioned. With the appearance of ἐν πνεύματι, the narrative setting changes from Patmos to heaven.[149] Similarly, the appearance of ἐν πνεύματι reorients the hearers to the eschatological and pneumatological setting of Revelation. The literary repetition offers continuity between the description of John's pneumatic experience in Rev. 1.9 and 4.1.[150] The appearance of ἐν πνεύματι recalls the sevenfold repetition of the hearing formula – ὁ ἔχων οὖς ἀκουσάτω τί τὸ πνεῦμα λέγει ταῖς ἐκκλησίαις ('Let the one having an ear, hear what the Spirit is saying to the churches'), denoting that the seven Spirits are central to the process of discernment.

## Revelation 4–5

In heaven, the churches encounter a majestic sight that is recounted as a throne in heaven. The throne in heaven is the same throne introduced in 1.4 along with the seven Spirits. The throne evokes the promise to the overcomers who will have a place with Jesus and his Father on their throne (3.21), while also standing in stark opposition to the throne of Satan in 2.13.[151] Beyond the descriptions of the

---

[148] Murphy, *Fallen is Babylon*, p. 188, observes, 'John's visit to heaven changes his perspective on the world. He now sees things very differently, from heaven's viewpoint.'

[149] Similar setting changes occur in the two remaining occurrences of ἐν πνεύματι in 17.3; 21.10.

[150] Sweet, *Revelation*, p. 115; Thomas, *The Apocalypse*, p. 203.

[151] Sweet, *Revelation*, p. 117. Boring, *Revelation*, p. 103, observes the political nature of the throne. The heavenly vision reveals who really rules. There are other thrones in the narrative that function to parody the sovereignty of God. See R.

throne itself, the identity of the one sitting on the throne is clouded in mystery. John describes the one on the throne with metaphorical language, including precious jewels and a rainbow. Anthropomorphic language is avoided in Revelation to preserve the mystery while also conveying glory, mercy, sovereignty, and regal splendor.[152] The identity of the one on the throne is further revealed in the appearance of theophanic elements: καὶ ἐκ τοῦ θρόνου ἐκπορεύονται ἀστραπαὶ καὶ φωναὶ καὶ βρονταί ('and coming from the throne are lightning, sounds, and thunder'). The theophanic elements express awe, authority, and the divinity of the one on the throne, while also distinguishing the heavenly throne from all other thrones.[153]

John sees before the throne seven fiery torches that are the seven Spirits. (1) The churches would recall the prologue where the seven Spirits appear before the throne. The seven Spirits likely intersect with Isa. 11.2, which attributes wisdom, understanding, and knowledge to the Spirit.[154] (2) The location of the seven Spirits before the throne (re)emphasizes the close relationship between the seven Spirits and the one on the throne, revealing further the character of the seven Spirits. It would also be true that the activities of the seven Spirits further depict the identity of the one on the throne.[155] (3) It

---

Farmer, 'Divine Power in the Apocalypse to John: Revelation 4–5 in Process Hermeneutic', *SBL Seminar Papers* 32 (1993), pp. 91-97, who explores the nature of the divine throne's power.

[152] For a thorough examination of the circumlocution for God's name in Revelation, see L. Gallusz, *The Throne Motif in the Book of Revelation* (LNTS 487; London: T&T Clark, 2014), pp. 113-27. Caird, *Revelation of St. John*, p. 63, observes that the presence of the rainbow alludes to the Noahic covenant and that an element of mercy frames all the actions from the throne. Aune, *Revelation 1–5*, p. 285, comments that the stones describing the divine throne likely serve to evoke colors. Koester, *Revelation*, p. 367, adds that the language used to describe the one on the throne appeals to the HB. See also Sweet, *Revelation*, p. 117; Gause, *Revelation*, p. 89; Bauckham, *The Theology of the Book of Revelation*, p. 32; Boxall, *The Revelation of St. John*, p. 84.

[153] See Bauckham, *The Theology of the Book of Revelation*, pp. 41-42, who points out that there is a literary function of the theophanic elements (cf. 8.5; 11.19; 16.18, 21). Resseguie, *The Revelation of John*, p. 110, notes that as the theophanic elements reappear in increased form, the readers are oriented to the linear progression of the plot.

[154] Sweet, *Revelation*, p. 118.

[155] Yarbro Collins, *The Apocalypse*, p. 36, comments, 'The presence of these torches enhances the majesty of the enthroned one and evokes a worshipful mood in the readers'. Thomas, *The Apocalypse*, p. 210, writes, 'the Spirit's identity cannot be understood apart from his intimate relationship with God. This is to say, "the

might not be pushing the imagery too far to suggest that the seven fiery torches are connected to the fiery eyes of the resurrected Jesus.[156] (4) Similarly, the seven fiery torches (seven Spirits) denote a relationship between the seven churches (the seven lampstands) and the seven Spirits.[157]

The text describes 24 elders who are sitting on 24 thrones and orbiting the throne. (1) Narratively, the numeral 24 seems to be connected to the identity of 24 elders,[158] and there are similarities between the 24 elders and the overcomers. The 24 elders have obtained many of the promises to the overcomers: atop their heads are crowns, they are clothed in white robes, and they sit upon thrones (2.10; 3.5, 21).[159] (2) The numeral 12 has functioned symbolically in scripture for the people of God. Thereby, the number 24 might be seen as a combination of 12 and 12, possibly a combination of the 12 tribes of Israel and the 12 disciples. Such a juxtaposition of the 12 tribes of Israel with 12 disciples suggests that the 24 elders represent the full people of God and that one group has not displaced the other.[160] (3) The fact that the 24 elders have obtained the promises to the overcomers implies that they have heard and obeyed the prophetic words of Jesus spoken by the Spirit. They have pneumatically

---

Seven Spirits of God" which Jesus "has" are indeed "the seven Spirits *of God*". Morris, *Revelation*, p. 87, observes that the present participle, καιόμεναι, denotes the continuous activity of the Spirit. See also Gause, *Revelation*, pp. 90-91; Blount, *Revelation*, p. 91.

[156] So Wilson, *The Victor Sayings in the Book of Revelation*, p. 73. This possibility will seem clearer when the hearers learn that the seven Spirits are the seven eyes of the Lamb (5.6). See also Wall, *Revelation*, p. 93, who notes, 'The pentecostal use of "fire" as a metaphor for the empowerment of the Spirit may help explain John's image of "blazing lamps," here in apposition to the "sevenfold Spirit," as an element of God's reign (cf. Acts 1:6-8; 2:1-4; 1 Cor. 4:20-21)'.

[157] Beasley-Murray, *The Book of Revelation*, p. 115; Bauckham, *Climax of Prophecy*, p. 165; Waddell, *Spirit of the Book of Revelation*, p. 177; Gallusz, *The Throne Motif*, p. 106.

[158] For an overview of the interpretative options of the 24 elders, see L.W. Hurtado, 'Revelation 4–5 in the Light of Jewish Apocalyptic Analogies', *JSNT* 25 (1985), pp. 105-24; Koester, *Revelation*, pp. 360-61.

[159] Gallusz, *The Throne Motif*, pp. 190-91, comments that the descriptions of the 24 elders reveal a close relationship between them and the overcomers, and in particular, the appearance of 24 thrones are 'inseparable' from, and only hold significance in relation to, the divine throne.

[160] Gause, *Revelation*, pp. 89-90; Boring, *Revelation*, p. 106; Blount, *Revelation*, p. 90; L.T. Stuckenbruck, 'Revelation 4–5: Divided Worship or One Vision?', *SCJ* 14 (Fall 2011), pp. 239, 242-43.

discerned and thereby are exemplars in discernment. As exemplars in discernment, the elders offer interpretative assistance to John in the narrative.[161] The elders' discernment is illustrated further in their worshipful acknowledgment that all power and authority ultimately belongs to the one on the throne.[162]

John encounters four living creatures who are in the midst of and around the throne, who also function as exemplars in discernment. These four creatures might recall the four creatures with four faces in Ezekiel and the seraphim in Isaiah. The description of the faces of the creatures and the numeral four denote that these creatures represent creation.[163] The appearance of the four living creatures and the 24 elders around the throne discloses that the activity of the one on the throne is not far removed from creation. The abundance of eyes upon the four creatures signifies that they have knowledge and discernment because they are able to see everything, even the divine throne.[164] The hymn of the four living creatures reveals that one of

---

[161] Thompson, *Revelation*, p. 91, comments that the elders function in two primary ways: (1) to 'render homage' to the one on the throne and the Lamb, and (2) to explain things to John (5.5; 7.13). See also Osborne, *Revelation*, p. 229.

[162] Their worship is embodied as they bow before the throne, cast their crowns before the one on the throne, and hold censors and harps in their hands. Blount, *Revelation*, p. 90, comments, 'Here in this heavenly worship scene, believers find the complete and sure picture of how humanity is to orient itself in faithful response before God'. See also Hurtado, 'Revelation 4–5 in the Light of Jewish Apocalyptic Analogies', p. 115; Resseguie, *The Revelation of John*, p. 110; Boring, *Revelation*, pp. 106-107; Koester, *Revelation*, p. 362; S. Grabiner, *Revelation's Hymns: Commentary on the Cosmic Conflict* (LNTS 511; New York, NY: T&T Clark, 2015), pp. 90-91.

[163] On the function of the numeral four, see Bauckham, *Climax of Prophecy*, pp. 30-32; Boxall, *The Revelation of St. John*, p. 90. Mangina, *Revelation*, p. 78, notes that there is no estrangement between humanity and the rest of creation; all worship the creator together. Thomas, *The Apocalypse*, p. 212, writes, 'it is significant that things do not revolve around humankind, but rather in this context it is clear that humankind is simply a part of this heavenly vision. God is central.'

[164] Sweet, *Revelation*, p. 120, observes a connection between the living creatures covered with eyes and the Spirit – the seven eyes of the Lamb – in 5.6. Beale, *The Book of Revelation*, p. 330, identifies the four creatures as having 'divine omniscience'. Thomas, *The Apocalypse*, p. 214, writes, 'The combination of the close proximity of the four living creatures to the throne and their being full of eyes ensures that their knowledge of God is accurate. And since true knowledge of who God is inevitably leads to true worship of God, their worship is indeed true worship (Jn 4.23).' Cf. Beckwith, *The Apocalypse of John*, p. 502; Sweet, *Revelation*, p. 120; Metzger, *Breaking the Code*, p. 50; Prigent, *The Apocalypse*, p. 232; Keener, *Revelation*, p. 175; Osborne, *Revelation*, p. 233; Smalley, *Revelation*, p. 122.

their essential functions is to offer worship to their creator.[165] The triad of holiness – holy, holy, holy – continues to emphasize the otherness of the one on the throne.[166] The hymn of the four living creatures offers a fuller characterization of the one on the throne: holy, eternal, all-mighty, Lord, and God. Hence, thus far, the hymns in Revelation function to offer understanding and a discerning activity.[167] This point is furthered owing to the fact that the four living creatures, the source of the hymn, are identified as exemplars of discernment and thereby convey divine truthfulness in their hymns. The manner in which the divine truthfulness is mediated – via a hymn – reveals that worship is one of the ways in which creation comes to know the creator.[168] Taking into consideration that hymns function as discernment, Revelation establishes that 'true knowledge of who God is is inseparable from worship of God'.[169]

Furthermore, Revelation 5 transitions to another scene of John's heavenly vision introduced by the appearance of εἶδον ('I saw') in

---

[165] Bauckham, *The Theology of the Book of Revelation*, p. 33, comments, 'Their ceaseless worship at the heart of all reality, around the divine throne, represents the theocentric nature of all reality, which exists to glorify God'.

[166] Metzger, *Breaking the Code*, p. 51; Koester, *Revelation*, p. 370. The hymn alludes to Isaiah 6 with a slight adjustment because rather than saying that the whole earth is filled with God's glory, the churches encounter a familiar description of God: ὁ ὢν καὶ ὁ ἦν καὶ ὁ ἐρχόμενος. Fekkes, *Isaiah in the Book of Revelation*, p. 148, considers that the change in the wording is associated with an eschatological promise.

[167] Aune, *Revelation 1–5*, p. 316, comments that the hymns function 'to interpret the significance of eschatological events'. Archer, *'I Was in the Spirit on the Lord's Day'*, p. 181, writes, 'The hymn has a pedagogic function as it emphasizes the person and character of God'. Sweet, *Revelation*, p. 116, identifies the 24 elders' hymn as an 'interpretative comment'. See also Farmer, 'Divine Power in the Apocalypse', p. 95; Keener, *Revelation*, p. 171; Smalley, *Revelation*, p. 124; Skaggs and Benham, *Revelation*, p. 64; Gallusz, *The Throne Motif*, pp. 103-104.

[168] Aune, *Revelation 1–5*, p. 308, observes that this is the first occurrence in Revelation where the terms πεσοῦνται and προσκυνήσουσιν are paired together, implying that the terms 'are used to describe two stages of a single act of adoration and thus are very nearly synonymous'. See also Mounce, *The Book of Revelation*, p. 126.

[169] Bauckham, *The Theology of the Book of Revelation*, pp. 32-33, adds, 'These most elemental forms of perception of God not only require expression in worship: they cannot be truly experienced except as worship'.

Rev. 5.1.[170] John sees the one on the throne who has 'on' his hand an opisthograph that is sealed with seven seals.[171] The plot thickens and a conflict arises as a mighty angel preaches (κηρύσσοντα) that there is no one in heaven, earth, or under the earth who is worthy to open the scroll. The extent of the angel's search heightens the drama all the more.[172] Devastated by this development, John weeps because he is unable to receive the scroll and 'discern the message until the seals [of the scroll] are broken'.[173] In the midst of John's sorrow, one of the elders comes to John and inspires hope because there is one who overcame.[174] Where John's knowledge has failed, the elder knows of one who is worthy to open the scroll: the Lion of the tribe of Judah and the Root of David, who overcame (ἐνίκησεν).[175]

The appearance of the Lion and the Root evokes HB intertexts that will assist the churches in their discernment. The Lion of the tribe of Judah recalls Gen. 49.8-12 where Judah is described as a lion's whelp who is a violent conqueror, whose clothes are stained with blood, and who will rule over his brothers and the people.[176] Upon

---

[170] P.J. Achtemeier, 'Revelation 5:1-14', *Int* 40.3 (1986), p. 283, believes that Revelation 5 is the climax of the narrative even though it appears early in the narrative. He proposes a second climax in Rev. 21.1. See also Smalley, *Revelation*, pp. 126-27.

[171] For a thorough discussion of the interpretative possibilities of the scroll, see Beale, *The Book of Revelation*, pp. 339-48. L. Baynes, 'Revelation 5:1 and 10:2a, 8-10 in the Earliest Greek Tradition: A Response to Richard Bauckham', *JBL* 129.4 (2010), pp. 801-16, helpfully notes an allusion to Zech. 5.1-4 and the scroll in Revelation 5; however, her conclusion that Zech. 5.1-4, rather than Ezekiel 2.8–3.3, is the 'source' text does not take into account the polyvalent nature of the allusions in Revelation. See also R. Stefanović, *The Backgrounds and Meanings of the Sealed Book of Revelation 5* (Berrien Springs, MI: Andrews University Press, 1996).

[172] Thomas, *The Apocalypse*, p. 221. Aune, *Revelation 1–5*, p. 347, notes a hint of irony in this text where a 'mighty' angel should be able to open a scroll.

[173] Koester, *Revelation*, p. 383.

[174] Aune, *Revelation 1–5*, p. 349, comments that the appearance of ἐνίκησεν without an object suggests that 'his victory is unlimited and absolute'.

[175] Koester, *Revelation*, p. 362, notes that one of the functions of the elders is to interpret visions, 'An elder explains the identity of the Lion of Judah and multitude in white (5:5; 7:13-14). Elsewhere, they disclose the meaning of visions through hymns about the Creator and his coming conflict with the destroyers of the earth (4:10-11; 11:16-18).'

[176] See Bauckham, *Climax of Prophecy*, pp. 179-85, for a discussion of the messianic implications of the Lion; he proposes that the Lion represents conquest through destructive power. Koester, *Revelation*, p. 375, observes two meanings in the Lion: kingship and power. See also L.L. Johns, *The Lamb Christology of the Apocalypse of John: An Investigation into Its Origins and Rhetorical Force* (WUZNT 167;

hearing of the Root of David, echoes of Isa. 11.1-10 would remind the churches of the messianic expectations in Isaiah.[177] Isaiah 11.2 has already intersected with the seven Spirits which connects the power of the messiah to the seven Spirits. The messiah will judge the earth with the rod of his mouth and the wicked with the רוּחַ ('spirit, breathe') of his lips (Isa. 11.4).[178] The messiah will permeate the entire earth with the knowledge of Yahweh (Isa. 11.10). The relationship of the two intertexts – Gen. 49.8-12 and Isaiah 11 – creates a tension.[179] It is significant that Isa. 11.7 portrays a lion eating straw in the eschatological kingdom, while also describing a lamb who lives unharassed by the wolf. The image of a gentle lion in Isa. 11.7 is dialectically fused with the fierce, violent conquering lion evoked in Gen. 49.8-12. The Lion of Judah and the Root of David is both a powerful, vicious conqueror who will establish a peaceful and just kingdom and a tamed predator who uses his razor-edged teeth to devour straw. The dialectic functions in a manner where neither element overtakes the other; rather, as the churches consider and reconsider the Lion and the Root, the identity of the messiah is formed and reformed in their imagination. As the intersections of Isaiah 11 and Revelation continue to be explored, this roundabout indicates that the power of the messiah is closely interrelated with the seven Spirits. The Spirit is the instrument of the messiah's judgment, his savage bite, while also providing attributes such as wisdom, under-

---

Tübingen: Mohr Siebeck, 2003), pp. 164-67, who concludes that the lion represents a 'powerful aggressive force'.

[177] Beale, *The Book of Revelation*, pp. 351-52. See also Fekkes, *Isaiah in the Book of Revelation*, pp. 150-55. An allusion to David has already appeared in Rev. 3.7.

[178] The proposal of Bauckham that the Root of David is 'the messianic conqueror of the nations' seems to place too much emphasis on Isa. 11.4 without hearing the other aspects of the echo of Isaiah 11, see Bauckham, *Climax of Prophecy*, p. 181. In fact, some of the 'violent' imagery in Isa. 11.4 (righteous judgment, striking with the rod of his mouth, striking the wicked) appear, albeit modified, in Revelation (the sword of his mouth, destroying the destroyers of the earth; Rev. 1.16; 2.12; 19.15, 21). For other HB texts that might intersect with the Root imagery, see N. Gulley, 'Revelation 4 and 5: Judgment or Inauguration?', *JATS* 8.1-2 (1997), pp. 75-77.

[179] Gause, *Revelation*, p. 96, writes on the combination of the Lion/Root, 'The total impact of this symbolism is to show military power and royalty. At the same time He is the banner of peace. The two Old Testament passages cited emphasize [the] Messiah's mission to the Jews and to the Gentiles.'

standing, and knowledge. The knowledge, wisdom, and understanding of the seven Spirits are connected to the way that the messiah operates in the world.

John hears the Lion and the Root, and the appearance of 'hearing' recalls the sevenfold call to hear the Spirit in the seven prophetic messages. This connection suggests (1) that the churches must continue their discernment and (2) that 'hearing' requires participation in the Spirit. As these images of the Lion and the Root (re)form in the churches' imagination, John turns and sees (εἶδον) in the midst of the throne: ἀρνίον ἑστηκὸς ὡς ἐσφαγμένον, ἔχων κέρατα ἑπτὰ καὶ ὀφθαλμοὺς ἑπτά, οἳ εἰσιν τὰ ἑπτὰ πνεύματα τοῦ θεοῦ, ἀπεσταλμένοι εἰς πᾶσαν τὴν γῆν ('a Lamb standing as slaughtered, having seven horns and seven eyes, which are the seven Spirits of God sent into the whole earth').[180] Is it possible that John's hearing (his pneumatic discernment) is directly connected to the transformation of his perception of the Lamb? Hearing (the Spirit) transforms perceptions, and pneumatic discernment includes the ability to recognize the Root and Lion as the slaughtered Lamb. The textual intersections in the intertextual web that is Revelation continue to form and reform messianic expectations. The task of struggling with these tensions reveals, in part, the process of discernment.[181] What John hears and

---

[180] The Lamb is ἐν μέσῳ τοῦ θρόνου ('in the midst of the throne'); however, the Lamb is not described as κύκλῳ ('around') like the four living creatures in 4.6. Therefore, it seems that the Lamb sits on the throne in Rev. 5.5, see Michaels, *Revelation*, p. 95; Gallusz, *The Throne Motif*, pp. 153-55. Some ancient manuscripts omit ἑπτά ('seven') in Rev. 5.6, and the external textual evidence is split. The harder reading seems to be the omission of ἑπτά considering that τὰ πνεύματα τοῦ θεοῦ ('the Spirits of God') never appear in Revelation, while τὰ ἑπτὰ πνεύματα τοῦ θεοῦ have appeared in 1.4; 3.1; 4.5. This would seem to indicate that the copyists added ἑπτά to align with the previous appearances. However, B.M. Metzger, *A Textual Commentary on the Greek New Testament* (Germany: United Bible Society, 1975), p. 736, contends another possible reason for the omission is that the repetition of ἑπτά in 5.6 might have confused the copyists leading to the omission. Other internal considerations point to τὰ ἑπτὰ πνεύματα τοῦ θεοῦ as being original on account that even if ἑπτὰ was omitted, τὰ πνεύματα τοῦ θεοῦ would likely be a reference to τὰ ἑπτὰ πνεύματα τοῦ θεοῦ. See also Beale, *The Book of Revelation*, p. 356.

[181] Resseguie, *The Revelation of John*, p. 118, identifies 'hearing and seeing' as a 'hermeneutical key' in the narrative.

sees creates a 'trialectical'[182] tension, as the narrative fuses together three intertexts – the Lion, the Root, and the slaughtered Lamb.[183] The process of discernment leads the churches to reflect upon the Spirit-empowered Root and ferocious Lion who has transformed into a slaughtered Lamb.[184] The Lion's savage strength must be reconsidered in relation to the (supposed) vulnerability of the Lamb while the vulnerability of the Lamb is reformed in light of the Lion's strength.[185] The wounded Lamb's power is expressed in the Lamb's ability to stand upon the throne, to take the scroll, and to open its seals. The detail that the Lamb was slaughtered implies that the Lamb had died; however, standing upon the throne signifies that the Lamb has overcome death and is resurrected.[186] The death and resurrection

---

[182] I am playing on the commonly used description of 'dialectic' to emphasize that this image is much more a triad or 'trialectic'.

[183] M. Barker, 'Enthronement and Apotheosis: The Vision in Revelation 4-5', in P.J. Harland and R. Hayward (eds.), *New Heaven and New Earth: Prophecy and the Millennium: Essays in Honor of Anthony Gelston* (The Netherlands: Brill, 1999), p. 222, concludes that the Lamb alludes to the servant of Isaiah. Aspects of the servant include being exalted and having wisdom and understanding (Isa. 52.13-14, LXX).

[184] Reddish, *Revelation*, p. 109, points out that a variety of allusions form the image of the Lamb in Revelation 5 and concludes, 'Rather than seeing the lamb imagery in Revelation as being drawn from only one source or having only one meaning, a better approach is to acknowledge the multivalent character of this powerful symbol'. Farmer, 'Divine Power in the Apocalypse', p. 94 n. 104, observes that the power of the Lamb (seven horns) recalls the power of the Lion (Gen. 49.9-10) and the wisdom of the Lamb (seven eyes) recalls the Root (Isa. 11.1-2).

[185] Moyise, 'Does the Lion Lie Down with the Lamb?', pp. 181-94, is critical of interpretations that ignore the violence of Revelation on account of the sacrificial Lamb, observing that the Lamb acts violently in the narrative at times. Moyise proposes an 'ethical' and 'ideological' approach to the violence. Ford, *Revelation*, p. 89 (So also Murphy, *Fallen is Babylon*, p. 193. J.D. Charles, 'An Apocalyptic Tribute to the Lamb (Rev 5:1-14)', *JETS* 34.4 (1991), p. 467), notes that the animalistic imagery of the Lamb (i.e. weakness or vulnerability) should not solely characterize the Lamb in Revelation; rather, the Lamb is powerful, which is revealed by the Lamb's horns. Some interpretations appeal to other apocalyptic works, particularly the image of the 'apocalyptic ram' to illustrate the power of the Lamb. See Johns, *Lamb Christology*, pp. 108-49, for a thorough examination of the 'lamb' in the HB. Along with a variety of HB echoes, the churches might recall the FG where Jesus is the Lamb of God who takes away the sin of the world and was crucified at the time when the Passover lambs were slaughtered (cf. Jn 1.29; 19.14), see N. Hillyer, '"The Lamb" in the Apocalypse', *EQ* 39.4 (1967), p. 230; Yarbro Collins, *The Apocalypse*, p. 40; Mounce, *The Book of Revelation*, p. 132; Fee, *Revelation*, pp. 80-81.

[186] Gause, *Revelation*, p. 97, comments, 'Here is another of the great paradoxes of Revelation. He has been slain and He is standing. His standing is witness of His being alive even though he has been slain.'

of the Lamb denote the manner in which the Lion/Root/Lamb overcame and why the Lamb is worthy to take and to open the sealed
scroll.[187] The tension created by this intertext further describes what
overcoming entails to the seven churches.[188] The Lamb overcame in
his death and resurrection by the power and wisdom of the Spirit.
The assumed weakness of the sacrificial Lamb becomes the powerful
jaws of the Lion exerted to overcome. On the one hand, the strength
of the Lamb forces the churches to reconsider the power of the Lion
and the Root; however, neither the strength of the Lion nor the wisdom of the Root is supplanted; it is transformed.[189] On the other
hand, as the churches reconsider the strength of the Lion and the
wisdom of the Root, the vulnerability and the wisdom of the Lamb
is redefined. Sacrificial death is power. The images continue to be
dialogically formed and reformed.

As the churches wrestle with the trialectical imagery, the text, as
with the Lion and the Root, joins the power and the wisdom of the
Lamb to the seven Spirits again. The Lamb has seven eyes and seven
horns that are the seven Spirits of God sent into the world.

First, the appearance of the seven eyes evokes another intertext.
In Zechariah 4, the seven eyes are the seven eyes of Yahweh.[190] In
Revelation, the seven eyes of Yahweh are attributed to the slaughtered Lamb representing divine omniscience.[191] Attributing the seven
eyes of Yahweh to the Lamb denotes the Lamb's divine status as well
as the dynamic relationship of the Lamb, the seven Spirits, and the
one on the throne.[192] The seven Spirits of God that are the seven
torches before the divine throne in Revelation 4 kaleidoscopically
transform into the seven eyes and seven horns of the Lamb.[193] The

---

[187] J.-P. Ruiz, 'Revelation 4:8-11; 5:9-14: Heavenly Hymns of Creation and
Redemption', *SBL Seminar Papers* (1995), p. 218.

[188] Resseguie, *The Revelation of John*, p. 119, adds, 'The sacrificial Lamb represents the way God displays power and wisdom in this world'.

[189] Against Caird, *Revelation of St. John*, p. 74; Johns, *Lamb Christology*, pp. 171-
204.

[190] Bauckham considers Zechariah 4 to be the most important allusion for Revelation's pneumatology.

[191] See Jauhiainen, *The Use of Zechariah in Revelation*, pp. 84-85.

[192] Bruce, 'The Spirit in the Apocalypse', p. 335; Gause, *Revelation*, p. 97; Keener,
*Revelation*, p. 187; Blount, *Revelation*, p. 112; Fee, *Revelation*, p. 81.

[193] See Bruce, 'The Spirit in the Apocalypse', p. 334, who concludes that it is
not incongruent for two different symbols in one vision to denote the same reality.

fusion of the seven eyes of Yahweh, the Lamb, and the seven Spirits reveals a 'trinitarian' quality to divine omniscience and wisdom, where the seven Spirits might be the very embodiment of divine knowledge. Zechariah 4 reveals further the pneumatic nature of the power of the Lamb, 'it is not by might nor by power, but by the Spirit' (Zech 4.6). The Lamb overcomes and establishes his kingdom by the power of the Spirit.[194]

Second, the relationship between the seven fiery torches and the fiery eyes of the resurrected Jesus is further evident on account that the seven Spirits are the seven eyes of the Lamb.[195] The seven (fiery) eyes represent the Lamb's complete and perfect knowledge. Such a connection between the wisdom of Jesus and the Spirit suggests that the divine knowledge (οἶδα) of the resurrected Jesus is directly connected to the activity of the seven Spirits. Hence, if the seven churches desire discernment or to know like Jesus Christ knows (οἶδα), then they must hear the seven Spirits and see with the seven eyes of the Lamb.[196]

Third, the seven Spirits, the רוח ('spirit, breathe') of the Root's lips, will judge the wicked and fill the earth with the knowledge of Yahweh (Isaiah 11).[197] The seven Spirits in Isaiah are juxtaposed with

---

Bauckham, *Climax of Prophecy*, p. 164, points out that 'the ambiguous phraseology' of Rev. 5.6 allows for the identification of the seven horns and seven eyes to be identified as the seven Spirits, which conveys that the Lamb and the Spirit have perfect knowledge of what is going on in the world and are able to act powerfully. So also Bruce, 'The Spirit in the Apocalypse', p. 334 n. 6; Waddell, *Spirit of the Book of Revelation*, p. 177.

[194] Wall, *Revelation*, pp. 93, 103, observes the similarities between the seven Spirits and the Paraclete in the FG.

[195] While I disagree with Koester that the seven Spirits are angelic beings, he observes that the seven Spirits before the throne, the seven fiery torches, and the fiery eyes of the resurrected Jesus are fused together, becoming the seven eyes of the Lamb, Koester, *Revelation*, pp. 386-87. See also Charles, 'An Apocalyptic Tribute to the Lamb (Rev 5:1-14)', p. 468; Metzger, *Breaking the Code*, p. 53.

[196] Bauckham, *Climax of Prophecy*, p. 165, writes, 'The horns and the eyes of the Lamb are the power and discernment of their prophetic witness, which is their faithfulness to the witness Jesus bore'. See also Wilckens, 'σοφία', p. 524; Metzger, *Breaking the Code*, p. 53; Stuckenbruck, 'Revelation 4–5', p. 241 n. 17. Thomas, *The Apocalypse*, p. 226. Cf. *TBM* 6.133 (May 15, 1913), p. 4; Trafton, *Reading Revelation*, p. 65.

[197] Prigent, *The Apocalypse*, p. 252, concludes a combination of Zech. 4.10 and Isa. 11.2 in this imagery. Beale, *The Book of Revelation*, p. 355, finds Isaiah 11 as a key echo here where seven attributes of the Spirit are present. See also Sweet,

the seven Spirits in Revelation who are identified as the seven torches before the divine throne as well as the seven eyes and seven horns of the Lamb who are sent out into the world.[198] Such an association suggests that the seven Spirits are the *modus operandi* of the divine throne and the Lamb, accomplishing the divine will on and in the world.[199] The seven Spirits accomplish this task because they are identified as the complete power and perfect wisdom of the Lamb and the one on the throne.[200] The seven Spirits, who go out into all the earth, complete the eschatological reality anticipated in Isa. 11.1-10 by filling the earth with the knowledge of Yahweh. The knowledge of Yahweh that is the knowledge of the Lamb includes the Lamb's sacrificial death and resurrection.[201] As the seven Spirits are sent into the earth, this perfect knowledge is made available to the whole earth and to the seven churches. Thus, pneumatic discernment would entail seeing with the eyes of the Lamb, seeing with the eyes of Yahweh, seeing through the fiery eyes of the resurrected Jesus (the seven fiery torches), and discerning by the seven Spirits of God. As these intertexts continue to circle around and around, the role the seven Spirits in discernment appears to be all the more crucial. The seven Spirits

*Revelation*, p. 128; Gause, *Revelation*, p. 97; S. Laws, *In the Light of the Lamb* (Wilmington, DE: Michael Glazier, 1988), pp. 28-29.

[198] Sweet, *Revelation*, p. 129, finds that 'sent out' alludes to the FG, '*sent out into: sent (apestalmenos)* is a keyword in John's Gospel, cf. 20.21f., "As the Father sent me out, so I send you … Receive the Holy Spirit." The hearers would understand the symbolism in terms of their own mission and witness … Already the seven spirits have been linked with the torches or lamps (4.5), which symbolize the churches (1.20; 2.1; 3.1).'

[199] Osborne, *Revelation*, p. 257, finds a similar theme in Jn 14.26; 15.26; 16.7 where the Father and Jesus send out the Spirit to carry out their mission in the world. Stuckenbruck, 'Revelation 4–5', p. 241, adds, 'Through Jesus as the Lamb, God's spirits become present and see conditions that affect the entire world'. B. Quash, 'Holy Seeds: The Trisagion and the Liturgical Untilling of Time', in R. Rashkover and C. Pecknold (eds.), *Liturgy, Time and the Politics of Redemption* (United Kingdom, Europe: SCM Press, 2006), p. 151, observes that the actions of the Lamb – death and resurrection – are interconnected with the knowledge of the Lamb. Quash defines the Lamb's life and knowledge as the Lamb's true and faithful witness, which the followers are called to follow. See also Beasley-Murray, *The Book of Revelation*, p. 124; Bauckham, *Climax of Prophecy*, p. 164; Beale, *The Book of Revelation*, p. 355; Skaggs and Benham, *Revelation*, p. 63.

[200] Ladd, *Revelation of John*, p. 88; Thomas, *The Apocalypse*, p. 227.

[201] Bauckham, *The Theology of the Book of Revelation*, p. 64, observes, 'When the slaughtered Lamb is seen "in the midst of" the divine throne in heaven (5:6 cf. 7:17), the meaning is that Christ's sacrificial death *belongs to the way God rules the world*'.

are sent throughout the earth by the divine throne, and the seven Spirits are the source of the Lamb's power, wisdom, and omnisci-ence.[202]

Next, John sees the Lamb take the scroll from the one on the throne because he is worthy and has the eyes to see – the seven Spir-its.[203] Following this, the four living creatures and the 24 elders, hav-ing harps and golden bowls full of incense, fall and worship the Lamb. While the churches continue to ponder the implications of seeing the Lamb, another hymn appears that assists in their interpre-tation.[204] The Lamb is worshipped because he is worthy. The Lamb's worthiness is connected to his death and resurrection.[205] The world-wide implications of his actions are confirmed because redemption is available to every tribe, tongue, people, and nation.[206]

In reaction to the activities of the Lamb, those full of discernment offer an appropriate response – worship. Majestically, John sees all of creation – those above the earth, on the earth, under the earth, and countless angels – offer worship to the Lamb and the one on the throne.[207] Worshipping the Lamb is not an alternative to worshipping

---

[202] Beasley-Murray, *The Book of Revelation*, p. 124; Johns, *Lamb Christology*, pp. 160-61.

[203] E. Schüssler Fiorenza, 'Redemption as Liberation: Apoc 1:5f and 5:9f', *CBQ* 36.2 (1974), pp. 220-32.

[204] Beale, *The Book of Revelation*, p. 352, asserts that the hymns in Revelation 4–5 function as 'interpretative summaries of the meaning of the preceding visionary portrayals'. See also Caird, *Revelation of St. John*, p. 74; Sweet, *Revelation*, p. 131.

[205] Schüssler Fiorenza, 'Redemption as Liberation', pp. 220-32, proposes that redemption in Revelation is liberation. On this see also A.J. Bandstra, '"A Kingship and Priests": Inaugurated Eschatology in the Apocalypse', *CTJ* 27.1 (1992), pp. 10-25. While Bandstra mostly follows Schüssler Fiorenza's thesis that redemption is liberation, Bandstra asserts that the liberation is not confined to the eschaton but has inaugural aspects in Revelation. See also L.A. Powery, 'Painful Praise: Exploring the Public Proclamation of the Hymns of Revelation', *Theology Today* 70.1 (2013), p. 72.

[206] Mangina, *Revelation*, p. 92, writes, 'Here the churches of Asia Minor should be able to see themselves, or if they do not, then they need to let themselves be corrected by the voice of the Spirit'. See also G. Schimanowski, '"Connecting Heaven and Earth": The Function of Hymns in Revelation 4–5', in R.S. Boustan and A.Y. Reed (eds.), *Heavenly Realms and Earthly Realities in Late Antique Religions* (Cambridge: Cambridge University Press, 2009), p. 82.

[207] Resseguie, *The Revelation of John*, p. 123, notes a tension in the plot. In the seven prophetic messages, it is clear that not every creature offers worship to God and the Lamb; however, in Revelation 5, it seems as if everyone is worshipping God and the Lamb.

the one on the throne; rather, the worship of the one on the throne is incorporated with the worship of the Lamb.[208] It is possible that worshipping the Lamb includes worship of the seven Spirits, who are intimately connected to the Lamb.[209] The next hymn offers an explanation of the Lamb's power and the implications of the Lamb's actions for the church and the earth.[210] The hymn describes seven attributes of the Lamb, one of which – wisdom – finds its first appearance in the narrative.[211] Attributing wisdom explicitly to the Lamb shapes wisdom in a particular manner. As has already been suggested, the Lamb's wisdom is dynamically characterized as the seven Spirits. The wisdom of the Lamb is accessible to the churches in the present, especially considering that the seven Spirits are providing the power and wisdom of the Lamb to the world and to the churches.[212] The divine seven Spirits, the source of divine wisdom, make available divine wisdom to the churches.[213] The interpretative nature of this hymn and the sevenfold attributes of the Lamb reveal further the identity of the Lamb.[214] With a final affirmation, 'Amen', this majestic

---

[208] Bauckham, *The Theology of the Book of Revelation*, p. 60, demonstrates that Revelation is carefully monotheistic even though the Lamb is worshipped, 'John does not wish to represent Jesus as an alternative object of worship alongside God, but as one who shares in the glory due to God. He is worthy of divine worship because his worship can be included in the worship of the one God.'

[209] Frank Macchia has argued that since the Lamb is worshipped and the seven Spirits are identified as the eyes of the Lamb, then the seven Spirits are an object of worship and thereby should be considered as divine, see Thomas and Macchia, *Revelation*, p. 492.

[210] Grabiner, *Revelation's Hymns*, pp. 223-24, has shown the function of hymns in the larger narrative threads in Revelation. While Grabiner's work focuses on 'cosmic conflict', it seems that other narrative threads (i.e. discernment, wisdom, interpretation) are also advanced in these hymns.

[211] Schimanowski, '"Connecting Heaven and Earth"', pp. 77-78.

[212] Against Beale, *The Book of Revelation*, p. 364, who identifies Daniel's understanding of wisdom to be unique in relation to other HB books and alludes to Daniel 2 where 'power' and 'wisdom' appear together. He suggests it is an 'apocalyptic' usage in Daniel 2 and Revelation 5 and thereby has an 'eschatological association with the divine kingdom'.

[213] Koester, *Revelation*, p. 391, writes, 'Wisdom (*sophia*) is ascribed to the slaughtered Lamb, as it is to God elsewhere (5:12; 7:12), and it fits a context in which readers face competing truth claims (2:2, 9, 20, 24; 3:9). John assumes that evil works through deception, so wisdom is needed to unmask it (12:9; 13:14; 18:23) … Revelation … identifies true wisdom with the slaughtered Lamb, who brings God's purposes to fulfillment.'

[214] Osborne, *Revelation*, p. 263, comments, 'In this book, "wisdom" points to the God-given ability to interpret the symbols (Rev. 13.18; 17.9)'.

scene comes to an end, and the churches are given a moment to re-flect. Has their wisdom and perception been formed by the wisdom of the Lamb, the seven Spirits, and the one on the throne?

## Summary of Revelation 4–5

Revelation 4–5 offers a variety of implications for the study of pneu-matic discernment. First, Revelation 4 begins another major section of the narrative signified by the appearance of ἐν πνεύματι. This reminds the churches of the previous appearance of ἐν πνεύματι, drawing their attention to the role of the Spirit in discernment.

Second, the depictions of the Spirit reveal a plurality of activities of the Spirit. (1) The seven Spirits are the seven torches before the throne. (2) Intertextually, Isa. 11.1-10 and Zechariah 4 seem to be caught in the web that is the seven Spirits, highlighting features of omniscience, wisdom, knowledge, power, and might. The images of the Root and the Lamb reveal the central role of the Spirit for the messiah's wisdom, knowledge, and power. (3) The seven Spirits are the eyes of the Lamb offering an imaginative picture of the wisdom of the Lamb and the activity of the seven Spirits in the world (5.6). The Spirit who is sent into the world provides discernment and wis-dom for the churches. (4) The seven Spirits create a 'trinitarian' con-nection between the Lamb and the one on the throne where the di-vine Holy Spirit dynamically enacts the activities of the Lamb and the throne. (5) Narratively, the hearers might consider the connection between the fiery eyes of the resurrected Jesus and the seven fiery torches, where the seven fiery torches are the discriminating insight of Jesus (1.14; 4.5).

Third, hymns function in Revelation 4–5 to interpret and to char-acterize images in the text that need to be interpreted. The hymns in Revelation communicate a dimension of knowledge that is not solely cognitive. The knowledge of God is closely associated with the wor-ship of God, revealing the pneumatic, relational, and participatory nature of knowledge. Characters who are exemplars in discernment – including the 24 elders and the four living creatures – offer hymns that assist the churches in discernment. As these characters appear later in the narrative, it will alert the churches to have an ear to hear.

Fourth, the trialectic formed in the Lion/Root/Lamb offers an opportunity for the churches to 'hear' the Spirit that transforms their perceptions. The portrait of the Lion/Root/Lamb includes elements of self-sacrifice, messianic expectations, kingship, power, might, wisdom, peace, justice, non-violence and a close relationship with the seven Spirits. The tension and juxtaposition of these images form the churches in a manner that (re)defines the power and wisdom of the Lamb. If the churches desire the wisdom of the Lamb, they must discern the trialectical portrait created by the Lion/Root/Lamb that struggles with these intertexts.

## Revelation 6–9

Revelation 6–9 describes the opening of the seven seals by the Lamb. A narrative interlude occurs in Revelation 7 that momentarily pauses the opening sequence where the 144,000 and the great crowd are sealed. Following the opening of the seventh seal, the narrative progresses to describe the sounding of seven trumpets (Revelation 8–9).

First, in the series of the seven seals, the opening of the fifth seal describes: ὑποκάτω τοῦ θυσιαστηρίου ψυχὰς τῶν ἐσφαγμένων ('under the altar the lives of the ones who had been slaughtered').[215] The ψυχὰς ('lives') cry out for justice: Ἕως πότε, ὁ δεσπότης ὁ ἅγιος καὶ ἀληθινός, οὐ κρίνεις καὶ ἐκδικεῖς τὸ αἷμα ἡμῶν ἐκ τῶν κατοικούντων ἐπὶ τῆς γῆς; ('How long, holy and true Lord, until you judge and avenge our blood on those who dwell on the earth?'). The appearance of ἐσφαγμένων ('slaughtered') creates a relationship between the Lamb (ἐσφαγμένον in 5.6) and the ψυχὰς.[216] (2) Witness

---

[215] For a discussion of ψυχή where the term is defined as a 'person' and a 'whole being' rather than representing a disembodied soul in Revelation, see L.L. Lichtenwalter, '"Souls Under the Altar": The "Soul" and Related Anthropological Imagery in John's Apocalypse', *JATS* 26.1 (2015), pp. 57-93. Thomas, *The Apocalypse*, p. 248, notes that in the Johannine literature ψυχή conveys more than a disembodied spirit (cf. Jn 10.11, 15, 17; 13.37, 38; 15.13; 1 Jn 3.16). D.E. Aune, *Revelation 6–16* (WBC; Nashville, TN: Thomas Nelson, 1998), p. 404, comments that the position of the souls under the altar represents that they are near to God. Koester, *Revelation*, pp. 398-99, writes that the martyrs' location under the altar reveals their deaths are sacrificial, 'Such sacrificial imagery reverses common perceptions of the martyrs' death. They might appear to have died pointlessly at the hands of their adversaries, but their location under the altar shows that God receives those who are slaughtered on account of their witness.'

[216] So Barr, *Tales of the End*, p. 86; Murphy, *Fallen is Babylon*, p. 209; Thomas, *The Apocalypse*, p. 248. S.J. Pattemore, *The People of God in the Apocalypse: Discourse, Structure, and Exegesis* (SNTSup 128; Cambridge: Cambridge University Press, 2004), p. 78, writes, 'These are people whose story is, at least with regard to their death, like the story of the Lamb'.

has appeared to describe John and Antipas (1.2, 5, 9; 2.13),[217] while Jesus is the true and faithful witness (3.14).[218] The close associations of the ψυχὰς ('lives') with Jesus suggests that the ψυχὰς are also true and faithful witnesses. Such a connection might indicate that the seven Spirits, who are the seven eyes of the Lamb, are the source of the true witness of the ψυχὰς.[219] The true witness of the ψυχὰς would even include their words spoken under the altar, which is a lament confronting the injustice in the world.[220] Although the ψυχὰς must wait for justice, their lamenting witness reveals that God will not allow injustice to continue indefinitely.[221] However, the time for the fullness of divine justice has not yet arrived, and the ψυχὰς must wait until their fellow servants, who are about to die, are finished.[222] In their wait, the ψυχὰς are given white garments, connecting them

---

[217] Caird, *Revelation of St. John*, p. 84, considers the possibility that the language of witness might recall specific individuals in the community (e.g. Antipas) and perhaps some individuals from the HB who had died on account of their testimony. See also Pattemore, *The People of God*, pp. 78-79.

[218] Barr, *Tales of the End*, p. 86.

[219] The relationship of their witness and their death also extends to the Lamb, see Pattemore, *The People of God*, p. 77, for a discussion of the souls sacrificial identity.

[220] A.A. Boesak, *Comfort and Protest* (Philadelphia, PA: Westminster Press, 1987), p. 68, writes, 'The martyrs are dead, but their witness is still alive. Their voices can still be heard; they still inspire the church.' Blount, *Revelation*, p. 134, adds, 'Even in lament, they witnessed'.

[221] For a discussion of persecution and the response to wait, see Schüssler Fiorenza, *Justice and Judgment*, pp. 46-51. See also Koester, *Revelation*, p. 399.

[222] Pattemore, *The People of God*, p. 89, writes, 'the faithfulness of their witness is in some way connected with the period until the full establishment of God's kingdom and the vindication for which the martyrs pray'. Koester, *Revelation*, pp. 400-401, helpfully notes that the word 'number' is absent in the Greek text; preferring to translate ἕως πληρωθῶσιν καὶ οἱ σύνδουλοι αὐτῶν καὶ οἱ ἀδελφοὶ αὐτῶν οἱ μέλλοντες ἀποκτέννεσθαι ὡς καὶ αὐτοί, 'their fellow servants and brethren – who were to be killed as they were – were finished'. This interpretation indicates for Koester that 'God's justice will take place when the faithful on earth have finished bearing witness'. Koester finds a similar theme later in the Apocalypse, 'John tells of God's readiness to bring justice when the witnessing of the faithful is finished. He makes this point again by saying that the time (*chronos*) of waiting will continue until God's purposes are finished (*telein*, Rev. 10:6-7), and this will occur when the faithful have been able to finish (*telein*) giving their testimony (11:7).'

to the overcomers (3.4-5).[223] Thus, the ψυχὰς ('lives') have heard the Spirit; they are true and faithful witnesses; they have been slaughtered; they have pneumatically discerned; and they are exemplars of discernment for the churches, shaping true witness into the protest of injustice.

Second, Revelation 7 interrupts the recounting of the breaking of the seven seals, creating tension and anticipation.[224] The interruption of the seven seals occurs in order that the servants of God might be sealed, which signifies their protection (7.3).[225] The seal placed on the foreheads of the servants serves as an identifying mark.[226] John hears that the servants are numbered as 144,000 from every tribe of Israel. While it is possible the 144,000 refer to ethnic Israel,[227] the numerology of 144,000 contains multiples of 12 (12 x 12 x 1,000) that recalls the 24 elders and seems to represent the whole people of God.[228]

[223] Beale, *The Book of Revelation*, p. 394, comments that those under the altar are told to wait, but the giving of the white robes functions as a symbol of their promised vindication. Thomas, *The Apocalypse*, p. 252, notes, 'the gift of the white robe conveys the idea that the promises made to those who overcome are being fulfilled before their very eyes'. See also Smalley, *Revelation*, pp. 164-65; Pattemore, *The People of God*, p. 87; Lichtenwalter, '"Souls Under the Altar"', p. 79.

[224] Bauckham, *The Theology of the Book of Revelation*, pp. 80-81, proposes that the opening of the seals 'is a literary device enabling John to narrate a series of visions which *prepare for* the revelation of the contents of the scroll'. So also Resseguie, *The Revelation of John*, p. 136. Barr, *Tales of the End*, pp. 83-84, does not find this to be an 'interlude' rather finding continuity between the narrative sections because it answers the question, who is able to stand?

[225] Resseguie, *The Revelation of John*, p. 125, writes, 'As the seals are unsealed, the saints are sealed'. Murphy, *Fallen is Babylon*, pp. 218-19, proposes that there is continuity between the seven seals and the servants of God being sealed: both the sealed scroll and the servants belong to God.

[226] Sweet, *Revelation*, p. 146. Aune, *Revelation 6–16*, p. 479, notes that the sealing represents their protection and ownership.

[227] R. Skaggs and T. Doyle, 'Revelation 7: Three Critical Questions', in M. Labahn and O. Lehtipuu (eds.), *Imagery in the Book of Revelation* (Leuven: Peeters, 2011), pp. 166-68.

[228] For a thorough discussion of the 144,000, see Beale, *The Book of Revelation*, pp. 416-23. See C.R. Smith, 'The Portrayal of the Church as the New Israel in the Names and Order of the Tribes in Revelation 7.5-8', *JSNT* 39 (1990), pp. 11-18; C.R. Smith, 'The Tribes of Revelation 7 and the Literary Competence of John the Seer', *JETS* 38.2 (June 1995), pp. 213-18, for a discussion of the order of the tribes based on maternal descent. See R. Bauckham, 'The List of the Tribes in Revelation 7 Again', *NTS* 42 (1991), pp. 99-115, for a response to Smith. See also Boxall, *The Revelation of St. John*, p. 124, who compares Revelation's tribal listings with other HB listings. Mounce, *The Book of Revelation*, p. 158, proposes that the numerical formula represents completeness.

Reminiscent of the hearing/seeing formula in Rev. 5.4-5, John hears the sealing of the 144,000 and then turns to see a great crowd.[229] The juxtaposition of what John hears (the 144,000) and what John sees (a great crowd) offers another opportunity to hear the Spirit and perceive with the eyes of the Lamb.[230] The particularity of the 144,000 from the 12 tribes of the sons of Israel morph dialogically into the great crowd from every nation, tribe, people, and language and reveals the particularity yet also inclusivity of the people of God.[231]

Furthermore, the churches are assisted in their discernment by the depiction, actions, and hymns of the great crowd ἑστῶτες ἐνώπιον τοῦ θρόνου καὶ ἐνώπιον τοῦ ἀρνίου, περιβεβλημένους στολὰς λευκάς, καὶ φοίνικες ἐν ταῖς χερσὶν αὐτῶν ('standing before the throne and before the Lamb, having been clothed with white robes and having palm branches in their hands'). (1) The hymn that is sung to the one on the throne and to the Lamb characterizes the crowd as a model of discernment and recalls other exemplars of discernment such as the elders, the four living creatures, and the angels. The hymn of the great crowd attributes wisdom to the one on the throne and the Lamb, revealing that true wisdom ultimately belongs to and derives from the one on the throne and the Lamb (who has seven eyes that are the seven Spirits).[232] (2) The great crowd is standing before the throne and the Lamb. The seven Spirits are also before the throne, suggesting that the great crowd has a close relationship with the seven Spirits, the Lamb, and the one on the throne.[233] (3) The

---

[229] Bauckham, *Climax of Prophecy*, pp. 215-16, proposes that the hearing/ seeing in Revelation 7 corresponds to the Lion/Lamb in Revelation 5.

[230] Murphy, *Fallen is Babylon*, p. 221, writes, 'Although 144,000 is a very large number, it is limited, in contrast to the multitude seen in the next vision (7:8)'. Boring, *Revelation*, p. 130, observes that 144,000 is not a small number in its own right and conveys 'the impression of a vast throng beyond all reckoning'.

[231] Smalley, *Revelation*, pp. 185-86, is critical of Bauckham who proposes that the 144,000 represent a militant group of martyrs, see Bauckham, *Climax of Prophecy*, pp. 215-20. Rather, Smalley concludes that the 144,000 'are worshippers more than soldiers' and that martyrdom never appears in the contexts of the 144,000. Smalley concludes, 'The numbering in this passage affirms that the eschatological hopes of Israel are realized in the church ... They are representatives equally of the Christian community in its completeness'. See also Pattemore, *The People of God*, pp. 125-40.

[232] Wilckens, 'σοφία', p. 524.

[233] Gallusz, *The Throne Motif*, pp. 163-66.

great crowd is dressed in white, which connects them to the over-comers, the 24 elders, and the ψυχὰς ('lives') under the altar.[234] (4) Prior to the interlude, those afflicted by the seals asks – τίς δύναται σταθῆναι? ('who is able to stand?', Rev. 6.17). The irony that the great crowd is standing while others are unable to stand in 6.17 would not be lost on the hearers.[235]

The process of discernment continues, and an elder is introduced to assist John in interpreting the great crowd. In Revelation 5, an elder assisted John in interpreting the Lion, the Root, and the Lamb.[236] Here, the elder aids in the discernment of the 144,000/great crowd by first asking:[237] Οὗτοι οἱ περιβεβλημένοι τὰς στολὰς τὰς λευκὰς τίνες εἰσὶν καὶ πόθεν ἦλθον? ('Who are these who are clothed in white robes and from where did they come?'). John, recognizing that the elder is a discerning interpreter, responds, Κύριέ μου, σὺ οἶδας ('your honor, you know').[238] John's response reveals the limits of the prophet's knowledge; even he needs assistance in discernment.[239] The reappearance of οἶδα ('I know') recalls the sevenfold repetition in the seven prophetic messages where Jesus knows (οἶδα) and has perfect discernment. Jesus' perfect discernment is represented in the imagery of the Lamb who has the seven eyes, the seven Spirits of God. It might not be going too far to propose that the elder knows (οἶδα) by the seven Spirits, revealing continuity between the way the resur-rected Jesus knows and the way the elder knows. Following this ex-change, the elder assists John in discerning the crowd: Οὗτοί εἰσιν οἱ ἐρχόμενοι ἐκ τῆς θλίψεως τῆς μεγάλης, καὶ ἔπλυναν τὰς στολὰς αὐτῶν καὶ ἐλεύκαναν αὐτὰς ἐν τῷ αἵματι τοῦ ἀρνίου ('These are the ones who are coming out of the great tribulation, and they have washed their robes and have made them white in the blood of the

---

[234] Pattemore, *The People of God*, p. 143. Blount, *Revelation*, p. 155, proposes that washing, making white, and overcoming/conquering function as 'euphemisms' for witness in Revelation.

[235] Trafton, *Reading Revelation*, pp. 69-70, 78.

[236] J. Lambrecht, 'The Opening of the Seals (Rev 6,1–8,6)', *Biblica* 79.2 (1998), p. 212.

[237] Bauckham, *Climax of Prophecy*, p. 229.

[238] Wall, *Revelation*, pp. 119-20. Aune, *Revelation 6–16*, p. 472, proposes a similar scene in Ezek. 37.3.

[239] Thomas, *The Apocalypse*, p. 272.

Lamb').[240] (1) In the seven prophetic messages, those who do not repent from their adultery with Jezebel will experience great tribulation, and Jesus knows (οἶδα) the tribulation of those in Smyrna (2.22).[241] (2) In Dan. 12.1-3, it is the discerning ones who were described as coming through tribulation.[242] The intersection of Dan. 12.1-3 and the 144,000/great crowd connects the great crowd to the discerning ones in Daniel. (3) In Isa. 1.18, Israel was stained by the crimson and scarlet that was their injustice and sin, which Yahweh promised to make white as wool and snow.[243] In Revelation, the blood-stained, unjust slaughter of the Lamb poetically enacts a participatory cleansing for the great crowd.[244] (4) The elder offers a hymn that assists in discernment. The hymn in Rev. 7.15-16 reveals further the identity of the one on the throne, the Lamb, and the great crowd.[245] The hymn confirms a close relationship with the one on the throne, the Lamb, and the great crowd. The great crowd offers worship to the one on the throne and the Lamb, and they provide protection, sustenance, and living water to the great crowd.[246]

---

[240] Murphy, *Fallen is Babylon*, p. 226, writes, 'Such a lengthy explanation, when explanations in general are rare in Revelation, indicates the significance of the vision'.

[241] Pattemore, *The People of God*, p. 147, writes, 'there are those who will succumb to great tribulation (like Jezebel), in contrast to the crowd, which has "come through" it'.

[242] Aune, *Revelation 6–16*, p. 474. Smalley, *Revelation*, p. 197, notes a relationship between the ones coming out of the tribulation in Revelation and those in Dan. 11.35; 12.1. In Daniel, the wise ones are made white. See also Bauckham, *Climax of Prophecy*, p. 227; Beale, *The Book of Revelation*, p. 433.

[243] Fekkes, *Isaiah in the Book of Revelation*, pp. 166-69, concludes that Isa. 1.18 is a 'secondary' influence preferring an allusion to Exodus 19.

[244] Bauckham, *Climax of Prophecy*, p. 227; Pattemore, *The People of God*, pp. 152-53.

[245] Archer, *'I Was in the Spirit on the Lord's Day'*, pp. 198-99, writes, 'The hymn, like those in the first worship scene, affirms the character of God; yet, in light of the martyrs' experience, the hymn's theological focus is all the more important. What happens to the faithful on earth does not take away from the character of God; that is, God is always to be worshipped.'

[246] In the FG, the 'living waters' recall Jesus and the Samaritan woman who was also offered 'living water' (Jn 4.14; cf. 7.39). See Boxall, *The Revelation of St. John*, p. 128; Thomas, *The Apocalypse*, pp. 276-77. Strikingly, this passage contains the only other appearances of ἐν πνεύματι ('in the Spirit') in the Johannine literature (Jn 4.23). Sweet, *Revelation*, p. 154, notes allusions to Jn 4.10; 6.35; 7.37-39. See Fekkes, *Isaiah in the Book of Revelation*, pp. 170-74 for a discussion of Isa. 25.8; 49.10 and Rev. 7.16-17.

Third, after the Lamb opens the seventh seal, there is silence for half an hour that is followed by the appearance of seven angels who have seven trumpets.[247] The first four trumpets cause devastation and destruction over one-third of the earth, and the final three trumpets are designated as the final three 'woes'. An eagle provides a warning of the final three trumpets as woes.[248] The woes are aptly named because of the demonic hordes that accompany them. The extended depictions of the demonic hordes slow the plot development causing anguish even in the hearers. In the face of the excruciating judgments, this narrative section concludes by noting that the inhabitants of the earth do not repent.[249] This conclusion reveals, at least in part, that the purpose of these judgments is repentance, though repentance has not occurred to this point in the judgment series.[250] The churches would recall that Jesus rebukes (ἐλέγχω) and disciplines (παιδεύω) the ones whom he loves and will judge Jezebel and her followers so that they would know that Jesus searches the minds and hearts (2.22-23; 3.19).[251] Is it possible that the central purpose of the Lamb's wrath in these judgments includes the hope that the inhabitants of the earth would recognize that the Lamb loves them? Whatever the possible outcomes, the inhabitants of the earth do not repent from their evil works. The text creates a relationship between worshipping demons, idols made of gold, silver, bronze, stone, or wood, and evil works such as murder, sorcery, immorality, and theft.[252] The inhabitants of the earth are unable to discern that the

---

[247] M. Kiddle, *The Revelation of St. John* (MNTC; New York, NY: Harper and Brothers, 1940), p. 144, describes the silence as a 'brilliant device for deepening the suspense'.

[248] Thomas, *The Apocalypse*, p. 291, points out the continuity between ἑνὸς ἀετοῦ ('one eagle'), ἑνὸς ἐκ τῶν τεσσάρων ζῴων, ('one of the four living creatures') and εἷς ἐκ τῶν πρεσβυτέρων ('one of the elders'). This observation might serve to place ἑνὸς ἀετοῦ as another character who interprets events in the narrative.

[249] Bauckham, *The Theology of the Book of Revelation*, p. 82, proposes that judgments alone do not bring about repentance. Koester, *Revelation*, p. 462, writes, 'The martyrs may have asked God to bring justice against those who shed their blood, but these visions show that if justice is reduced to wrath, then nothing changes'.

[250] Koester, *Revelation*, p. 468.

[251] Beale, *The Book of Revelation*, p. 520.

[252] Smalley, *Revelation*, pp. 442-43, comments, 'that which is not of God, if worshipped, becomes a demonic power'. For an examination of the demonic in the Johannine literature, see J.C. Thomas, 'The Role and Function of the Demonic in the Johannine Tradition', in C.S. Keener, J.S. Crenshaw, and J.D. May (eds.), *But*

idols that they worship are demonic. This inability to discern is even more damning considering that paradoxically the demons who torment the inhabitants of the earth are, from the divine perspective, the idols that they worship.[253] The astounding rhetorical effect upon the hearers would be difficult to miss. Furthermore, considering the presence of false teachings, idol worship, and sexual immorality in the seven churches, this text confronts the churches to discern from the perspective of the Lamb and to hear the Spirit. The evil works of idolatry and immorality are more dangerous than the churches have been able to recognize. They must pneumatically discern.

## Summary of Revelation 6–9

First, the ψυχὰς ('lives') under the altar serve to reveal that their witness is closely related to their death. They witness in a similar manner to Jesus, and their witness is faithful and true. The true witness of the ψυχὰς incorporates their lament even as they are located under the altar.

Second, the elder assists the churches in their pneumatic discernment. The 144,000/great crowd resemble the discerning ones in Daniel and have come out of the great tribulation. They wear white garments, wash them in the blood of the Lamb, and participated in the sacrifice of the slaughtered Lamb. The 144,000/great crowd are exemplars of discernment. They worship the Lamb and the one on the throne in hymns, which offers discernment to the churches.

Third, the conclusion of the seven seals and the seven trumpets reveals that the purpose of these judgments is related to repentance and knowledge that the Lamb loves them. Idolatry and evil works are equated with demon worship. As the churches were exhorted to discern in the seven prophetic messages, the relationship between evil works and demons unveils severe consequences if the churches are not vigilant in their discernment. The inhabitants of the earth are worshipping demons, and demons are the ones who enact torture and judgment.

---

*These Are Written ... Essays on Johannine Literature in Honor of Professor Benny C. Aker* (Eugene, OR: Wipf & Stock, 2014), pp. 27-47.
[253] Caird, *Revelation of St. John*, p. 124.

## Revelation 10–11

As the churches continue to discern the implications of idol worship, demonic activity, and judgment, another narrative interlude occurs between the sixth and seventh trumpets.[254] The setting changes from heaven (where it has been located since 4.1) to earth.[255] In this narrative interlude, the churches encounter a majestic figure, a mighty angel who is coming down from heaven. The mighty angel is enormous and able to stand with one foot on the earth and the other foot on the sea. The angel comes on a cloud, has a rainbow upon his head, his face shines like the sun, and his legs are like pillars of fire. Each of these characteristics recalls the divine attributes that have appeared earlier in Revelation. The attribution of these divine characteristics to an angel causes some ambiguity as to the mighty angel's identity. One stream of interpretation identifies the mighty angel as a divine figure, including (1) Christ,[256] (2) a 'christophany' like the angel of Yahweh,[257] or (3) the Holy Spirit.[258] The primary criticism of this interpretative stream is that ἄγγελος ('angel') does not occur in any other place in Revelation to describe a divine figure. Hence, there is a sharp distinction between angels and the divine characters in Revelation.[259] However, it should be noted that no other angel in Revelation receives a description as close to a divine character as the mighty angel in Revelation 10. For this mighty angel shares divine characteristics with Christ (coming on a cloud and having a shining face), with the one on the throne (rainbow), and perhaps, with the seven Spirits (who are the seven torches) in accord with the appearance of fire

---

[254] Koester, *Revelation*, pp. 463, 488, writes, 'the interruption of judgment after the sixth plague will clarify the nature of the conflict: God's design is not to destroy the earth, but to destroy *the destroyers* of the earth (11.18)'; 'The interlude in Rev 10–11 redefines the question raised by the martyrs – how *long* will God delay in bringing justice – by showing *why* God's judgment seems to be delayed'.

[255] Resseguie, *The Revelation of John*, p. 152.

[256] The interpretation that the mighty angel is Christ has been common in church history, see Kovacs and Rowland, *Revelation*, pp. 118-19.

[257] Beale, *The Book of Revelation*, pp. 522-26.

[258] Waddell, *Spirit of the Book of Revelation*, pp. 154-61.

[259] Bauckham, *Climax of Prophecy*, pp. 118-49. So also Morris, *Revelation*, pp. 133-34, who observes that the mighty angel is not worshipped and thereby unlikely to be divine.

(feet as fire).[260] Thus, while there is evidence that the mighty angel is a divine character, it is difficult to settle on any particular divine figure considering the presence of several divine characteristics from different characters used to describe the mighty angel.[261] One way forward with this interpretative option is to consider the way in which the mighty angel reflects divine characteristics from each divine being in Revelation, suggesting that the mighty angel reflects the activities of the seven Spirits, the one on the throne, and the resurrected Jesus.

Beyond the ambiguity associated with the mighty angel's appearance, he delivers a scroll; a scroll that is unsealed. The appearance of a scroll recalls the sealed scroll that the Lamb was able to take from the one on the throne. The inability of anyone, except for the Lamb, to take and open the scroll returns the narrative to a central plot point. Narratively, it seems best to interpret the angel's scroll as the sealed scroll from Revelation 5.[262] The Lamb has completed the process of opening and unsealing the scroll, which is narrated in Revelation 6–9. John is now able to take the scroll and prophesy.[263] It is not surprising that the mighty angel is the messenger of this prophecy considering the mighty angel's close relationship with the divine Spirit, Jesus, and the one on the throne.[264]

The mighty angel, raising his right hand towards heaven, swears to the creator, the eternal one that

χρόνος οὐκέτι ἔσται ἀλλ᾽ ἐν ταῖς ἡμέραις τῆς φωνῆς τοῦ ἑβδόμου ἀγγέλου, ὅταν μέλλῃ σαλπίζειν, καὶ ἐτελέσθη τὸ μυστήριον τοῦ θεοῦ, ὡς εὐηγγέλισεν τοὺς ἑαυτοῦ δούλους τοὺς προφήτας.

---

[260] It is possible that the fire would recall the fiery eyes of the resurrected Jesus; however, as has been considered in this monograph, there appears to be an association between the fiery eyes of Jesus and the seven Spirits as the seven torches.

[261] Waddell, *Spirit of the Book of Revelation*, pp. 158-59.

[262] For a discussion of the (two) scroll(s), see Mazzaferri, *The Genre of the Book of Revelation*, pp. 268-73; Bauckham, *Climax of Prophecy*, pp. 243-50; Waddell, *Spirit of the Book of Revelation*, pp. 150-61. See Beale, *The Book of Revelation*, p. 527, for literary parallels between Revelation 5 and Revelation 10.

[263] The scene recalls the prophetic call narratives in the HB, on this see Mazzaferri, *The Genre of the Book of Revelation*, pp. 264-96.

[264] Archer, *'I Was in the Spirit on the Lord's Day'*, p. 207. See Waddell, *Spirit of the Book of Revelation*, p. 162.

time will no longer be but in the days of the voice of the seventh angel, when the angel is about to trumpet, the mystery of God will be completed as pronounced to the servants and prophets themselves.[265]

The appearance of χρόνος ('time') might recall (1) the eschatological and pneumatological time in which Revelation was set; it is the Lord's day (ἐγενόμην ἐν πνεύματι ἐν τῇ κυριακῇ ἡμέρᾳ', 1.10).[266] (2) Jezebel was given χρόνον ('time') to repent. (3) The ψυχὰς ('lives') under the altar who asked 'How long?', and were told to wait a little longer (literally, χρόνον μικρόν) until their fellow-servants complete (ἀναπαύσονται) their witness.[267] With these themes of time converging in the narrative, the mighty angel's proclamation reveals that the time for repentance, the time for witness, and the delay in judgment is coming to an end.

The previous appearance of μυστήριον ('mystery') in Revelation occurred in the context of the resurrected Jesus assisting the churches in discerning the mystery of the seven stars and seven lampstands.[268] As mystery appears again, the churches (i) would be prepared to interpret the mystery and (ii) would expect assistance in the process. The appearance of mystery recalls Daniel's mystery, which was to be sealed up until it is *revealed* to the discerning ones in the last days.[269] However, the mystery in Revelation 10 is not *revealed* but is ἐτελέσθη ('completed'). If these HB intertexts are evoked, then the text subverts the expectations of the churches. The appearance of ἐτελέσθη might intersect with Jn 19.30 where Jesus' final words on the cross is narrated: τετέλεσται, καὶ κλίνας τὴν κεφαλὴν παρέδωκεν τὸ πνεῦμα ('it is completed and having bowed his head, he handed over the Spirit'). Such an intertextual observation would

---

[265] Smalley, *Revelation*, p. 263.

[266] Bauckham, *Climax of Prophecy*, p. 265, proposes, 'The answer is that there is now to be no more delay before the final period which will bring in the kingdom, the Danielic "time, times and half a time"'.

[267] Ladd, *Revelation of John*, p. 144.

[268] Thomas, *The Apocalypse*, p. 317, comments, 'In Rev. 1.20 it is the mystery of the seven stars and the seven lampstands that is explained by the resurrected Christ, an example of the pneumatic interpretation needed for understanding this Revelation. The occurrence of "the mystery of God" in 10.7 would alert the hearers to the fact that something else is in need of (divine) explanation.'

[269] Beale, *The Book of Revelation*, p. 540.

unite the mystery of God in Revelation with the death of Jesus upon the cross and the giving of the Spirit.[270] The mystery of God no longer awaits revelation, because the mystery of God has been revealed in the person of Jesus and the giving of the Spirit. Additionally, if the churches anticipate an ἀποκάλυψις ('Apocalypse') upon hearing of a mystery, then they might recall the prologue, which claims that the entire narrative is the Ἀποκάλυψις Ἰησοῦ Χριστοῦ ('Apocalypse of Jesus Christ'). Jesus Christ is the mystery of God who has been revealed, is being revealed, and is the revealer. The connections to the prologue could be considered further because the Ἀποκάλυψις Ἰησοῦ Χριστοῦ ('Apocalypse of Jesus Christ') originates from God (ἣν ἔδωκεν αὐτῷ ὁ θεὸς) just as the mystery in Revelation 10 is of/from God. As the mystery of God was proclaimed to the servants and prophets, the Ἀποκάλυψις Ἰησοῦ Χριστοῦ ('Apocalypse of Jesus Christ') is shown to his servants (δεῖξαι τοῖς δούλοις αὐτοῦ, 'to show his servants' ... ἐσήμανεν ἀποστείλας διὰ τοῦ ἀγγέλου αὐτοῦ, 'signified on account of sending his angel'), including his servant, John (καὶ τῷ δούλῳ αὐτοῦ Ἰωάννῃ).[271] Therefore, the mystery of God is the resurrected Jesus who is encountered ἐν πνεύματι ('in the Spirit') on Patmos. The mystery of God is the Lion, the Root, and the Lamb who is standing on the divine throne and who has the seven eyes and seven horns who are the seven Spirits of God. At the sounding of the seventh trumpet, the completion of this mystery will occur, suggesting that there continues to be mysterious elements associated with Jesus.[272]

---

[270] Thomas, *The Apocalypse*, p. 317, writes, 'The implications with regard to the relationship between Jesus' death and the completion of the mystery of God in the Apocalypse are not difficult to see, for the one is coterminous with and makes the other possible'.

[271] Boxall, *The Revelation of St. John*, pp. 156-57, adds, 'The mysterious scroll of Ezekiel, the sealed scroll of Daniel, and other prophetic revelations, are now becoming clear in the light of "the revelation of Jesus Christ"'.

[272] Koester, *Revelation and the End of All Things*, p. 103, writes, 'The element of "mystery" pertains not so much to the goal of God's saving purposes as it does to the means by which God will attain the goal. Therefore, the visions in Revelation 11 will disclose to readers how the suffering of God's servants mysteriously helps to bring about the conversion of the ungodly.'

The mystery of God was proclaimed (εὐηγγέλισεν) to the servants and prophets.[273] Prophets here suggests HB prophets as well as other Christian prophets.[274] Revelation 10.7 offers the first appearance of any form of εὐηγγέλισεν ('proclaim') in the Johannine literature. While it is possible that εὐηγγέλισεν would refer to God's triumph over evil[275] or the establishment of God's kingdom on earth,[276] there are christological (and pneumatological) elements on account of the relationship of Jesus with this mystery.[277] The scene concludes with John being commanded to take the scroll from the mighty angel, eat the scroll, and consequently prophesy.[278] The bitter and sweet nature of this prophecy is conveyed, at least in part, in Revelation 11.

The scene in Revelation 11 opens with καί ('and'), which links the prophecy in Revelation 11 to the prophetic call in Revelation 10.[279]

---

[273] Thomas, *The Apocalypse*, p. 318. For other cognates of τελέω ('completed') in Revelation, see Rev. 10.7; 11.7; 15.1; 15.8; 17.17; 20.3; 20.5; 20.7. Cf. Jn 4.34; 5.36; 17.4.

[274] Hill, 'Prophecy and Prophets', p. 409; Mounce, *The Book of Revelation*, p. 208; J. Roloff, *The Revelation of John* (trans. John Alsup; Minneapolis, MN: Fortress Press, 1984, 1993), p. 481; Koester, *Revelation*, p. 481.

[275] Mazzaferri, *The Genre of the Book of Revelation*, p. 284, writes, 'Therefore εὐαγγέλιον αἰώνιον εὐαγγελίσαι connotes no proclamation of the gospel in the normal NT sense [Why, indeed should angels preach the NT gospel?], but a patent warning of divine triumph over evil in classical OT style. This confirms that in 10:7 εὐαγγέλιζειν shares the latter sense as well.'

[276] So Bauckham, *Climax of Prophecy*, pp. 261-62, who proposes that in Revelation the change from ἀποκαλύπτω

> makes it clear that to the prophets themselves it remained a secret, while also suggesting its character as the good news of the coming of God's kingdom. This is the significance of בשׂר (translated by εὐαγγελίζομαι in Jewish Greek) in its theological significant Old Testament occurrences (Isa 40:9; 41:27; 52:7; 61:1) … It is the significance which εὐαγγελίζομαι has in Revelation's only other use of the verb (14:6).

[277] Wall, *Revelation*, p. 138, writes that mystery in the NT 'usually refers to the content of the gospel message, the core of which is the atoning death and exaltation of Christ'. Smalley, *Revelation*, p. 266 proposes that εὐηγγέλισεν simply means the 'divine purposes for salvation'. See also Ladd, *Revelation of John*, p. 145; Mounce, *The Book of Revelation*, p. 207.

[278] Bauckham, *Climax of Prophecy*, p. 265, notes that the fourfold formula appears in regard to the church thus far in the narrative (Rev. 5.9; 7.9). The slight change in the formula in subsequent appearances refers to the nations themselves (11.9; 13.6; 14.6; 17.15).

[279] Murphy, *Fallen is Babylon*, pp. 257-58; Smalley, *Revelation*, p. 271.

The prophecy John receives from the mighty angel is presented in the form of a narrative that portrays the story of the two witnesses. The first scene in Rev. 11.1-2 tells of the measuring of the temple (ναός), the altar, and the worshippers. Measuring seems to be related to protection,[280] and the temple, altar, and worshipers function to represent the people of God.[281] Protection recalls those who have received the seal of God on their forehead.[282] Although it is possible to interpret the temple literally and the holy city as Jerusalem, 'the setting of the story is cosmic rather than local'.[283] The protection of the temple, altar, and worshippers is not extended to the outer courts.

---

[280] M. Jauhiainen, 'The Measuring of the Santuary Reconsidered (Rev 11,1-2)', *Biblica* 83.4 (2002), pp. 507-26, by way of creative lexical exploration, concludes that the temple of God represents the faithful people of God, but that the altar, worshippers, outer courts, and the holy city are not measured and thereby represent the 'corrupt cult and idolatrous/syncretistic Christians'. Jauhiainen critiques the spiritual/physical protection interpretation, which is helpful. However, his conclusion gives too much weight (based on HB readings) to those who are not measured as being the unfaithful church. By doing so, he also overlooks a potential literary connection between the souls under the altar and this altar. Similarly, Jauhiainen ignores the positive connotations of worship that are directed toward God (worship that is seemingly directed toward God here since it occurs in God's temple) in the Apocalypse.

[281] Koester, *Revelation*, p. 495, notes that the overcomers are promised to be pillars in the temple of God (3.12), 'The congregations of Jesus' followers are the earthly counterpart. Their community is God's temple on earth, where true worship takes place, and the redeemed serve as priests (1:6; 5:10).' Tavo, *Woman, Mother, and Bride*, pp. 191-92, observes that the imagery should be interpreted specifically as 'the church at worship'. Thomas, *The Apocalypse*, p. 324, notes that ναός appears in the FG in reference to Jesus' body (2.19-21). See also Smalley, *Revelation*, p. 272. R. Dalrymple, 'The Use of καί in Revelation 11,1 and the Implications for the Identification of the Temple, the Altar, and the Worshippers', *Biblica* 87.3 (2006), pp. 387-94, proposes that the altar and the worshippers, although both images are part of the temple, should be distinguished from one another. He considers that the 'altar' is 'composed of those who will suffer martyrdom' (cf. Rev. 6.9-10), and the 'worshippers' are 'those who remain faithful to the end' (p. 393). Dalrymple helpfully observes the relationship between the altar in Revelation 11 and the altar in Revelation 6; however, his proposal does not address the 'outer court' and the 'holy city'.

[282] Sweet, *Revelation*, p. 175, writes, 'the parallel delay between the sixth and seventh unsealings, when the servants of God were sealed (7.3), suggests that bearing witness is what they were sealed *for*; chs. 8 and 9 have told us what they were sealed against'. So also Aune, *Revelation 6–16*, p. 604.

[283] Koester, *Revelation*, p. 506. See also C.H. Giblin, 'Revelation 11.1-13: Its Form, Function and Contextual Integration', *NTS* 30 (1984), p. 439; Schüssler Fiorenza, *Vision of a Just World*, p. 77.

The outer courts and the holy city will not be measured and will be trampled for 42 months. Since the outer courts remain part of the temple, the outer courts, along with the holy city, also seem to signify the people of God.[284] The imagery suggests a tension between protection and persecution. While it is possible that the demarcation between the measured temple and the trampled outer courts denotes *spiritual* protection for the churches even during *physical* harm,[285] Revelation does not reveal a bifurcation between the spiritual and physical person. Another interpretative possibility would be to allow the tension to remain. The people of God are protected and are also trampled; a tension of protection and persecution appeared in the depiction of the great crowd who are sealed by God but come through the great tribulation.[286] The people of God are protected yet they experience war and persecution.[287] The characterization of the city as holy would align the city with those who have washed their garments in the blood of the Lamb. The holiness of the city also implies for the Johannine literature that they have been sanctified in T/truth (Jn 17.17-19); they have the χρῖσμα ('anointing') from the Holy One (1 Jn 2.20) and thereby know all things. In the Johannine literature, the holiness of the people of God is closely associated with T/truth, knowledge, and the χρῖσμα.

After measuring the temple, the people of God morph into yet another image, the two witnesses:

καὶ δώσω τοῖς δυσὶν μάρτυσίν μου, καὶ προφητεύσουσιν ἡμέρας χιλίας διακοσίας ἑξήκοντα, περιβεβλημένοι σάκκους. Οὗτοί εἰσιν αἱ δύο ἐλαῖαι καὶ αἱ δύο λυχνίαι αἱ ἐνώπιον τοῦ κυρίου τῆς γῆς ἑστῶτες.

And I will give to my two witnesses and they will prophesy for 1260 days while wearing sackcloth. These are the two olive trees

---

[284] See Tavo, *Woman, Mother, and Bride*, pp. 193-96, for a helpful discussion concerning the outer court as being part of the temple.

[285] So Aune, *Revelation 6–16*, p. 604; Osborne, *Revelation*, p. 411.

[286] So Thomas, *The Apocalypse*, p. 327. This tension will be further supported by the narrative of the two witnesses who are unharmed until their witness is complete.

[287] Smalley, *Revelation*, p. 273; Blount, *Revelation*, p. 205.

and the two lampstands, which stand before the Lord of the earth (11.3-4).

First, the resurrected Jesus interpreted the mystery of the seven lampstands as the seven churches in Rev. 1.20, and the reappearance of the lampstand suggests that the two witnesses represent the churches.[288] Already, Zechariah 4 has intersected with the seven Spirits (as the seven eyes and the seven torches), and the intertext circles back around in the description of the two witnesses as the two lampstands and two olive trees. In Zech 4.14, it is not by might nor by power, but it is by the Spirit (Zech 4.6) that the two branches (the two anointed ones) are able to complete their task.[289] In Revelation, the seven Spirits (as the seven torches, the seven eyes, and the seven horns who go out into the world) intersect with the two lampstands and the two olive trees – the two anointed ones. The seven Spirits, as the seven torches, light up the lampstand, the church, empowering their witness.[290] The seven Spirits are characterized in Revelation in such a manner that, as the seven eyes and the seven horns of the Lamb, the seven Spirits supply the Lamb's power and wisdom to the churches. The pneumatic power of the two witnesses is closely associated with their capacity to see with the seven eyes of the Lamb.

Second, the two witnesses act in conjunction with and are identical to one another. The witnesses deliver their prophetic message in the tradition of HB prophets. The actions of the two witnesses recall Moses and Elijah, but any attempt to distinguish one witness from the other is unconvincing.[291] It is not insignificant that the opponents

---

[288] Koester, *Revelation*, p. 509, writes, 'The imagery also encourages readers to see their own vocation in this vision … the witnesses in Rev 11 neither retreat from nor assimilate to a context that challenges them. Instead, they challenge others with the claims of God'. Thomas, *The Apocalypse*, p. 330, identifies the divine voice as the one who assists in Rev. 11.4. See also Beale, *The Book of Revelation*, p. 574.

[289] See K.A. Strand, 'The Two Olive Trees of Zechariah 4 and Revelation 11', *AUSS* 20.3 (1982), pp. 257-61.

[290] Waddell, *Spirit of the Book of Revelation*, p. 177, writes, 'the seven flames which burn before the throne also inhabit the church(es), lighting up the lampstand(s)'. Tanner, 'Climbing the Lampstand-Witness-Trees', p. 81, notes that the appearance of lampstands should invoke an association with the Spirit. See also Jauhiainen, *The Use of Zechariah in Revelation*, p. 90; Thomas, *The Apocalypse*, p. 330.

[291] Minear, 'Ontology and Ecclesiology', pp. 96-97; Giblin, 'Revelation 11.1-13', p. 442. Koester, *Revelation*, p. 507, adds, 'Rather than asking whether readers can identify the figures, we might ask how the text encourages readers to identify

of Moses and Elijah included Jezebel and Balaam. The distinction between true and faithful witnesses against the false prophets and false teachers is reiterated.[292] 'Two' witnesses likely alludes to Deut. 19.15 and indicates that their witness is trustworthy.[293] The two witnesses are clothed in sackcloth representing lament and repentance.[294] The judgments that the two witnesses enact upon the inhabitants of the earth recall the plagues inflicted by the seven seals and the seven trumpets.[295] It is possible that the fire that comes from the mouth of the two witnesses recalls the seven Spirits – the seven torches – who empower their witness.[296]

Third, the witness of the two witnesses is prophecy.[297] The connection between prophecy and witness becomes nearly indistinguishable here. Whereas the two witnesses embody the whole church, prophecy becomes the vocation of the church.[298] As the Spirit em-

---

with them, since they embody the public testimony and perseverance to which the Christian community is called'.

[292] On this see Pattemore, *The People of God*, pp. 162-63. See also Bauckham, *Climax of Prophecy*, p. 277.

[293] Cf. Jn 8.17. On the 'two-witness' theme in the FG, see K.A. Strand, 'The Witnesses of Rev 11:3-12', *AUSS* 19.2 (1981), pp. 127-35. See also Mounce, *The Book of Revelation*, p. 217; Blount, *Revelation*, p. 208.

[294] Prigent, *The Apocalypse*, p. 351; Skaggs and Benham, *Revelation*, p. 115.

[295] Michaels, *Revelation*, pp. 139-40, goes as far as to propose that 'the echoes of the first four trumpets suggest that John's prophecy of the witnesses be read as a conscious transformation of the entire trumpet series ... the people of God themselves become the executors of divine judgments'. See also Koester, *Revelation*, p. 506.

[296] Trafton, *Reading Revelation*, p. 108, observes that the hearers would recall both the resurrected Jesus who has a sword coming from his mouth and the fire, smoke, and sulfur coming from the mouths of the demonic hordes (1.16; 9.17-18; 19.15, 21).

[297] Mazzaferri, *The Genre of the Book of Revelation*, p. 306, proposes that 'μάρτυς equals προφήτης'. So also Aune, *Revelation 6–16*, p. 610; Smalley, *Revelation*, pp. 275-76.

[298] Boring, *Revelation*, p. 142, writes, 'all members of the Christian community participate in the body of Christ and thus in the breathe/Spirit that animates the body; and thus they receive the gifts of the Spirit, including prophecy ... In the vision of 11:1-13, John pictures the whole church in their role as the eschatological prophetic People of God; he affirms the "prophethood of all believers".' See also Waddell, *Spirit of the Book of Revelation*, pp. 177-78.

powers the church's witness, the Spirit empowers the church's prophesy.[299] The appearance of prophecy recalls the seven prophetic messages where the resurrected Jesus and the Spirit speak conterminously.[300] The two witnesses, when prophesying, speak the words of the Spirit that are at the same time the words of Jesus. In the two witnesses, there is a dynamic union between the church, Jesus, and the Spirit. The way the two witnesses prophetically speak the words of Jesus suggests that their witness is faithful and true (3.14). The truthfulness of the church's witness would be related to the seven Spirits as the seven eyes of the Lamb – the wisdom of the Lamb – who empower the witness of the church.

Fourth, in the seven prophetic messages, the churches were urged to discern false prophecies (from Jezebel) and false teachings (Balaam and Nicolaitans) that were prevalent in their communities. The integration of true witness and true prophecy in the two witnesses expands the theme of discernment in the churches. A test of discernment becomes, does the church speak in tandem with Jesus and the Spirit? Thus, discernment is, at least in part, the ability of the seven churches to recognize the words of the Spirit and Jesus and thereby speak conterminously with them.[301] The church must distinguish between true and false witness/prophecy by comparing their Spirit-empowered witness/prophecy with false witness/prophecy.[302] In the

---

[299] See Blount, *Revelation*, p. 206; Koester, *Revelation*, pp. 509-10.

[300] Thomas, *The Apocalypse*, p. 331.

[301] Waddell, *Spirit of the Book of Revelation*, p. 171.

[302] Koester, *Revelation*, p. 508:

In Revelation, witnessing and prophesying serve the same end, which is to direct people to God. Discerning which prophetic messages were valid was a matter of dispute in the congregations addressed by Revelation. A woman at Thyatira claimed special knowledge and called herself a prophet while adopting a latitudinarian approach to polytheism (2:20), and later visions show a prophet doing signs and wonders in the service of the beast (13:11-18; 16:13; 19:20; 20:10). Revelation draws on biblical and early Christian traditions that insisted that true prophecy moves people to worship God, while false prophecy draws people away from God (cf. Deut. 13:1-11; Zech. 13:2-3; Philo, *Spec. Laws* 1.315; 2 Pet. 2:1), works against faith in Jesus (1 John 4:1-3; 1 Cor 12:1-3; Matt 24:11; Acts 13:6-8), and is characterized by conduct that is incongruent with the faith (*Did.* 11:7-12; Matt 7:15-20; 24:11, 24; Aune, *Prophecy*, 217-29). Revelation also identifies the 'spirit of prophecy' with 'the witness' that the community has received from Jesus and makes to Jesus. The point of such witness is that people 'worship God' (Rev 19:10). As members of the Christian community bear witness, they share a prophetic vocation.

same manner that the resurrected Jesus and the Spirit confront sin, false teachings, false prophecy, false perspectives, and evil works in the seven prophetic messages, so too do the two witnesses, as they prophesy, expose the truth to the inhabitants of the earth concerning their sin, evil works, false perceptions, and false teachings. Such a provoking witness seems to be a primary reason why the inhabitants of the earth describe the prophecy of the two witnesses as torturous. The churches' witness, analogous with the witness of the resurrected Jesus and the Spirit, confronts the world with Spirit-empowered T/truth.[303]

Fifth, the two witnesses will prophesy for 1260 days. Whereas the mighty angel declared that there would be no more time, the churches encounter another, limited time-period. The designation of 1260 days and 42 months recalls Daniel's time, times, and a half a time, which is a three and a half year period.[304] In Revelation, the 1260 days in which the two witnesses will prophesy aligns with the 42 months that the nations will trample the outer courts and the holy city. It is striking that these two different time increments occur to describe the same three and a half year period, suggesting that the same realities can appear differently depending on one's perspective.[305] The perspective of the two witnesses is contrasted with the perspective of the inhabitants of the earth.[306] The inhabitants of the earth perceive time as 42 months, which will be associated with evil characters in the narrative, while the two witnesses perceive time as 1260 days, which will be associated with the church and the Spirit. A similar distinction occurred in the seven prophetic messages where Jesus' discerning perception was compared to the perception of the churches. 1260 days is the time for pneumatic witness; 1260 days is the time of

---

[303] Bauckham, *The Theology of the Book of Revelation*, p. 122.

[304] See R.C. Waddell, 'What Time is it? Half-past Three: How to Calculate Eschatological Time', *JEPTA* 31.2 (2011), pp. 141-52, concerning three and a half years from Daniel as 'eschatological time' in Revelation. See also Beale, *The Book of Revelation*, pp. 565-68, concerning 42 months and Daniel.

[305] Thomas, *The Apocalypse*, p. 329. Waddell, *Spirit of the Book of Revelation*, p. 169, adds, 'the span of three and a half years serves as a symbolic amount of time in which the church will face the threat of the beast (forty-two months), yet throughout this same span of time, the church can trust that she will be protected by God (1260 days)'. See also Bauckham, *Climax of Prophecy*, p. 284; Murphy, *Fallen is Babylon*, p. 262.

[306] Resseguie, *The Revelation of John*, p. 161, notes that the point of view varies in this section.

the Spirit.[307] Conversely, the church's pneumatic witness also occurs for 42 months; 42 months is a treacherous time when the temple – the church – is trampled. The two witnesses follow the example of their Lord, experiencing persecution, opposition, and death during the 42 months. Therefore, the eschatological and pneumatological time of the Apocalypse is the time when the two witnesses prophesy, when the churches witness, when the churches are empowered by the Spirit, when the churches are trampled, and when the beast overcomes the churches.[308] During the churches' maligned trampling, they have not been abandoned because the Spirit is present among them.[309] The scroll, the prophecy of John, is bitter because the churches are situated in a time of trampling, war, persecution, and the beast, but the scroll is sweet because, at the very same time, the Spirit is with the churches.

Furthermore, the eschatological and pneumatological time in which the two witnesses prophesy is limited. When the two witnesses have finished their Spirit-empowered, true and faithful witness, the beast from the abyss will make war on them and overcome them.[310] The beast, appearing for the first time, is characterized as one who makes war and kills. The introduction of the beast presents a new conflict in the plot: the beast is the one who opposes the church. However, the fuller characterization of this adversary will wait until Revelation 13. The two witnesses, following in the way of other faithful witnesses, die. Although this narrative does not seem to imply that every faithful witness will die on account of their witness, it does

---

[307] See Waddell, 'What Time is it?', p. 150, who concludes, 'It is the time between the advents of Christ – the time that is already and not yet. It is a time for faithful endurance of saints, a time for the church to prophesy by the power of the Spirit and a time to bear witness to the world about the Lamb of God. Evil is rampant in the world, but it will not last forever.'

[308] Minear, 'Ontology and Ecclesiology', p. 97, observes a connection between the conflict described in Revelation 11 and 'tribulation'.

[309] This aligns with the Paraclete passages in the Farewell materials in the FG (Jn 16.4-15).

[310] It is possible that the articular construction of τὸ θηρίον ('the beast') indicates that the churches were already familiar with the beast without receiving any other introduction in the Apocalypse. Trafton, *Reading Revelation*, p. 109, notes that narratively the abyss has been a place from where demonic and evil forces originate. For a discussion of the beast and Daniel, see Beale, *The Book of Revelation*, pp. 587-89.

reveal that the churches' witness will at times lead to death.[311] Once the beast kills the two witnesses, they lay in the street located in the great city without receiving a proper burial.[312] The narrative has been set in the holy city since 11.2 and now changes to the great city.[313] Similar to the holy city, the great city seems to allude to more than a geographical location. Whereas the holy city represented the people of God, the great city appears to represent the beast, the inhabitants of the earth, and anyone who opposes the churches.[314] While the churches consider the implications of this sudden change in setting, the text offers an opportunity to discern the identity of the great city pneumatically: τῆς πόλεως τῆς μεγάλης, ἥτις καλεῖται πνευματι-κῶς Σόδομα καὶ Αἴγυπτος, ὅπου καὶ ὁ κύριος αὐτῶν ἐσταυρώθη ('the great city, which is Spiritually called Sodom and Egypt, where even their Lord was crucified', 11.8).

πνευματικῶς has numerous translations including 'allegori-cally',[315] 'figuratively',[316] 'prophetically',[317] 'spiritually',[318] 'Spiritu-ally',[319] or 'pneumatically'.[320] Considering that πνευματικῶς is a cog-nate of πνεῦμα and that every previous occurrence of πνεῦμα refers to the Holy Spirit to this point in Revelation, the appearance of

---

[311] Koester, *Revelation*, p. 507, writes, 'by holding firmly to the testimony that comes *from* Jesus, people become witnesses *to* Jesus and the God who sent him, whether or not they die violently for the faith (1:2, 9; 6:9; 12:11, 17; 20:4)'.

[312] Thomas, *The Apocalypse*, p. 335, notes the singular term, τὸ πτῶμα ('mouth'), emphasizes the singularity of their witness. See Aune, *Revelation 6–16*, p. 622, on the significance of being refused burial in the ancient world.

[313] Giblin, 'Revelation 11.1-13', pp. 439-40.

[314] So Tavo, *Woman, Mother, and Bride*, p. 210, who finds further evidence in the imagery of Babylon, see Rev. 14.8; 16.19; 17.5; 18.2.

[315] Ladd, *Revelation of John*, p. 157; Beasley-Murray, *The Book of Revelation*, p. 186; Mounce, *The Book of Revelation*, p. 226; Sweet, *Revelation*, p. 187.

[316] Caird, *Revelation of St. John*, p. 138.

[317] Bauckham, *Climax of Prophecy*, p. 169; Aune, *Revelation 6–16*, p. 581; Smalley, *Revelation*, p. 246; Waddell, *Spirit of the Book of Revelation*, p. 181.

[318] Mounce, *The Book of Revelation*, p. 226; Beale, *The Book of Revelation*, p. 592.

[319] Waddell, *Spirit of the Book of Revelation*, p. 181, translates πνευματικῶς 'Spiritually'. He considers that those who translate πνευματικῶς 'prophetically' 'capture the correct connotation but obscure the agent of the prophetic perspec-tive, the Spirit of prophecy'. See also Bauckham, *Climax of Prophecy*, p. 169; Osborne, *Revelation*, p. 427; Koester, *Revelation*, p. 500; Herms, 'πνευματικῶς', pp. 136-37.

[320] Thomas, *The Apocalypse*, p. 336.

πνευματικῶς describes that the churches are to discern the great city via the Spirit.[321] At the climax of this narrative, the churches are exhorted to change their perspective in the most explicit manner: to view the world literally through the Spirit – through the eyes of the Lamb and through the fiery eyes of Christ. The fact that this narrative thread reappears at this crucial moment reveals that pneumatic discernment is one of the most significant themes of the Apocalypse, if not the most.[322] Robby Waddell adds:

> In the center of the Apocalypse, John places the story of the two witnesses, and in the center of this brief narrative, John describes the spiritual insight of the church discerning the reality of the great city. The Apocalypse is intended to reveal to the church the true identity of Jesus as king of kings and lord of lords. Despite apparent perceptions, the beast is not the ultimate authority. If a person fears God and gives him glory then there is no longer any need to fear the beast. Like John, who was in the Spirit when he saw visions, the church must also see Spiritually.[323]

The great city is πνευματικῶς Sodom, Egypt, and the place where their Lord was crucified. Pneumatic perception is then the ability to recognize that the great city is more than a geographical location.[324] The great city is a trans-geographical, trans-cosmological reality where one location transforms into four.[325] The great city is a kaleidoscopic web that the churches are directed to perceive with the eyes

---

[321] Minear, 'Ontology and Ecclesiology', p. 96, comments that this text 'is a way of perceiving reality'. Bauckham, *Climax of Prophecy*, p. 169, describes πνευματικῶς as 'Spirit-given perception'. Waddell, *Spirit of the Book of Revelation*, p. 182, writes, 'the church is being called to discern true reality via the assistance of the Spirit'. See also U. Vanni, 'The Ecclesial Assembly "Interpreting Subject" of the Apocalypse', *RSB* 4.2 (1984), p. 83; Keener, *Revelation*, pp. 294-95; Thomas, *The Apocalypse*, p. 335.

[322] Waddell, *Spirit of the Book of Revelation*, p. 182 writes, 'this prophetic perspective is a major (and perhaps the primary) purpose of the book'. See also Roloff, *The Revelation of John*, p. 133.

[323] Waddell, *Spirit of the Book of Revelation*, pp. 182-83.

[324] In the HB, the great city appeared in reference to Nineveh (Jon. 1.2, 3.2, 3.3, 4.11), Judah (Jer. 22.8), and Resen (Gen. 10.12). See also Josh. 10.2.

[325] Waddell, *Spirit of the Book of Revelation*, p. 183. See Minear, 'Ontology and Ecclesiology', p. 96.

of the seven Spirits. The process of wrestling with the great city reveals, in part, the ability of the churches to see with the eyes of the Lamb; it is a process of pneumatic discernment.

The kaleidoscopic web would recall a variety of (inter)texts. (1) Sodom, in Genesis, has sinned against the Lord and is described as being wicked. Their sin includes harming strangers rather than offering hospitality to them.[326] Once Sodom was destroyed, the prophets in the HB continued to refer to Sodom as an example of evil works.[327] The prophets warned that those who followed in the ways of Sodom would share in their destruction and judgment.[328] Sodom is associated with sin, violence, injustice, wickedness, arrogance, bitterness, and oppression.[329] (2) Egypt is an embodiment of slavery and bondage. While initially a location of refuge for the people of Israel, Egypt notoriously enslaved the Israelites. Following the deliverance of Israel from Egypt, the law commanded that the Israelites should not oppress or enslave anyone because of their own enslavement in Egypt.[330] The prophets describe Egypt as an image of oppression and slavery, violence, the shedding of innocent blood, judgment, idolatry, and assimilation.[331] (3) The place where their Lord was crucified seems to direct the churches to the Gospel(s). While it is possible to view this reference as an allusion to Jerusalem (either literally or symbolically), this interpretation does not take into account that the location of Jesus' death was the place of the skull – Golgotha.[332]

---

[326] Cf. Gen. 10.19; 13.13; 18.20. Revelation names Sodom without mention of Gomorrah. Most prophetic literature paired Sodom with Gomorrah with the exception of Ezekiel (16.46, 48, 49, 53, 55, 56).

[327] In the Torah, the only other mention of Sodom is in Deut. 29.23; 32.32 where it seems to have already become a metaphorical reality.

[328] Deuteronomy 29.23; Isa. 1.9-10; 13.19; 49.18; 50.40; Lam. 4.6; Amos 4.11; Zeph. 2.9.

[329] Isaiah 3.9; Jer. 23.14; Lam. 4.6; Ezek. 16.46-56; cf. Deut. 32.32.

[330] Exodus 22.21, 23.9; Deut. 6.12, 7.8, 8.14, 13.5, 10.

[331] Deuteronomy 17.16; 28.68; Isa. 19.1, 20; 31.1-9; 45.14; 52.4; Ezekiel 20; 27.7; 29; 30.13; Jeremiah 2; 7; 34.13; 42–44; Joel 3.19.

[332] John 19.17. Cf. Mt. 27.33; Mk 15.22; Lk. 23.33. This is not to deny the influence and predominance of Jerusalem because the place of the skull is associated with Jerusalem. However, this detail suggests that the great city includes more than Jerusalem. See Smalley, *Revelation*, p. 282 who notes that ὅπου ('where') appears in every other place in Revelation at the beginning of a clause that introduces a reality that is either symbolic, spiritual, divine (12.6, 14; 14.4) or satanic (2.13; 20.10; cf. 17.3, 9). See also Beale, *The Book of Revelation*, p. 592.

The place of the skull recalls the crucifixion of Jesus as well as the authorities guilty of Jesus' unjust death. Therefore, when seen in the Spirit, the medley that is Egypt, Sodom, the place of the skull, and the great city functions as a trans-geographical and trans-temporal representation of oppression, slavery, violence, evil, and death. The great city conveys much more than a location on a map; rather, the great city and the beast who operates there represent anyone who promotes violence, oppression, evil, and death. Conversely, the holy city is a trans-geographical location that personifies the anointed church and the presence of the Spirit. As with the holy city, the two witnesses prophesy to the nations and experience opposition that ultimately leads to their death in the great city at the hands of the beast. Jesus (who is referred to as the ναός, 'temple', in the FG) is crucified in the same murderous city in which the two witnesses die.[333] Thus, even in their death, the church discovers solidarity in their Lord.[334] While the churches wrestle with the tension of the holy city and great city, they learn that the two witnesses will be raised to life. The time that the two witnesses lay in the street loosely resembles the time that their Lord was in the grave.[335] The witnesses followed their Lord in death, and now they will follow their Lord in resurrection and ascension.[336] The Spirit of life comes upon the two witnesses and raises them to life.[337] In their resurrection and by means of the Spirit, the two witnesses are publicly vindicated.[338]

Following the resurrection and ascension of the two witnesses, there is an earthquake. The great city crumbles in the face of God's judgment. This judgment is the completion of the second woe. There remains one final trumpet and one last woe. The anticipation of the

---

[333] Bauckham, *The Theology of the Book of Revelation*, p. 86, adds, the great city 'is any and every city in which the church bears it prophetic witness to the nations'.

[334] Bauckham, *Climax of Prophecy*, p. 171. It has been demonstrated elsewhere that the two witnesses follow the life, death, resurrection, and ascension of Jesus. This is not the only occurrence in Revelation wherein an aspect of Jesus' story is transformed; Rev. 11.9 changes the three days associated with the death of Jesus to three and a half days that the two witnesses are dead.

[335] Aune, *Revelation 6–16*, p. 609.

[336] Wall, *Revelation*, p. 146.

[337] Caird, *Revelation of St. John*, p. 138. Koester, *Revelation*, p. 510.

[338] Giblin, 'Revelation 11.1-13', p. 444; Fee, *Revelation*, p. 154. See also Osborne, *Revelation*, p. 430; Koester, *Revelation*, p. 511.

final trumpet recalls the mighty angel in Revelation 10 who proclaimed that the mystery of God would be completed when the last
trumpet sounded. Narratively, the completion (τελέσωσιν) of the
prophecy of the two witnesses is connected to the completion
(ἐτελέσθη) of the mystery of God. This is evident because it is not
until the two witnesses complete their witness, die, and are resurrected that the pneumatological and eschatological time (42 months
and 1260 days in which the church is situated) is completed, and the
(seventh) trumpet sounds.[339] As the mystery of God was closely associated with the person, death, and resurrection of Jesus, this mystery now incorporates the ministry of the two witnesses who, in
prophesying to the nations, participate in revealing the mystery of
God – Jesus Christ. Following the earthquake and in conjunction
with the ascension of the two witnesses, the nations are fearful and
give glory to God. Although it is possible to interpret the nations'
fear as cowardice,[340] it seems more likely that their fear is related to
repentance.[341] The completion of the church's witness, the completion of the mystery of God, leads to a repentant fear in the inhabitants of the earth, repentance that the series of judgments could not
accomplish. Hence, the mystery of God is closely associated with the
person of Jesus Christ who sends the seven Spirits to empower the
church's true, faithful, prophetic witness on earth. Despite opposition in the great city and by the beast, their witness ultimately leads
to the repentance of the nations, ushering in the final trumpet and
the establishment of God's kingdom on earth (11.15-19).[342] It is not

---

[339] L.L. Thompson, *The Book of Revelation: Apocalypse and Empire* (Oxford:
Oxford University Press, 1990), p. 67, concludes that the seventh trumpet describes
a worship scene.

[340] Beale, *The Book of Revelation*, pp. 597-98; Smalley, *Revelation*, p. 284.

[341] Giblin, 'Revelation 11.1-13', p. 446; Bauckham, *Climax of Prophecy*, pp. 278-
79; Aune, *Revelation 6–16*, pp. 628-29; Stefanović, *Revelation*, p. 361. Thomas, *The
Apocalypse*, p. 339, adds that in the FG, fear is interrelated to further understanding
and the deepening of one's faith. Resseguie, *The Revelation of John*, p. 166, notes that
the angel holding the everlasting gospel calls for a 'two-step' response: fear God
and give God glory (14.7).

[342] Wall, *Revelation*, p. 139. Beasley-Murray, *The Book of Revelation*, p. 188, adds,
'When the seventh seal is opened, there was silence in heaven (8:1). When the seventh trumpet is blown, there were loud voices in heaven.' Yarbro Collins, *The
Apocalypse*, p. 74, notes that the third woe, although not named, continues the theme
of judgment, which is described as the destruction on the destroyers of the earth.

as if the two witnesses are responsible for the completion of the mystery in and of themselves. Rather, the churches dynamically participate with the Spirit and Jesus to complete the mystery of God.

## Summary of Revelation 10–11

First, the central role of the Spirit in the process of discernment is explicitly revealed in the appearance of πνευματικῶς. The seven churches were continually exhorted to hear the Spirit, to view their context from the divine perspective, and to know as the resurrected Jesus knows. At the climax of the narrative, the churches are directed to discern via the Spirit. The occasion for pneumatic discernment exhorts the seven churches to view the world through the eyes of the Lamb, with the seven Spirits. The repetitive calls in the seven prophetic messages for discernment and the placement of πνευματικῶς in the center of this narrative reveal that pneumatic discernment is perhaps the most significant theme in the Apocalypse.

Second, the intersection of the two lampstands, the two olive trees, and the seven Spirits functions to characterize the Spirit-anointed and Spirit-empowered church. The seven Spirits who are the torches, the seven eyes, and the sevens horns of the Lamb provide wisdom, anointing, and power to the churches. The Spirit assists in the churches' true and faithful witness and provides wisdom in their discernment.

Third, the mighty angel is the triune divine messenger who delivers the unsealed scroll to John. The mighty angel announced that the mystery of God will be completed. The appearance of ἐτελέσθη ('completed') seems to unite the mystery of God with the death of Jesus on the cross and the giving of the Spirit in the FG. The mystery has been revealed in Jesus and continues to be revealed in the Ἀποκάλυψις Ἰησοῦ Χριστοῦ ('Apocaylpse of Jesus Chrsit'). The completion of the mystery of God is connected to the completion of the prophecy of the two witnesses and the sounding of the seventh trumpet. The completion of their witness recalls the response to the ψυχὰς ('lives') under the altar who must wait for justice until their fellow-servants are finished. The mystery of God continues to be revealed in the dynamic activity of the Spirit in the churches, as the churches follow their Lord in death and resurrection, the nations fear and give glory to God.

Fourth, the setting of the Apocalypse describes that John ἐγενόμην ἐν πνεύματι ἐν τῇ κυριακῇ ἡμέρᾳ ('was in the Spirit on the Lord's Day'), which sets the Apocalypse in eschatological and pneumatological time. As the churches encounter time in Revelation 11, the eschatological time that is the day of the Lord and the pneumatological time that is ἐν πνεύματι ('in the Spirit') is transformed into the 42 months and the 1260 days. The time increments represent the same reality from two perspectives. The church is trampled for 42 months, but the Spirit of life provides strength (seven horns), wisdom (seven horns), and fire (seven torches) to the lampstands for 1260 days. The churches are simultaneously living in the time of the Spirit (1260 days) and the time of the beast (42 months).

## Revelation 12–14

Revelation 12–14 continues in the second major ἐν πνεύματι ('in the Spirit') structural section of Revelation. If the climactic scene described in Revelation 11 is viewed as the contents of the scroll *in nuce*,[343] then Revelation 12–14 continues to (re)tell John's prophecy, albeit from a cosmic perspective. Since the seven prophetic messages, the narrative has challenged the perceptions of the churches. Revelation 12–14 functions as a way for the churches to view the contents of the scroll from another perspective, from a cosmic perspective that is, perhaps, analogous with seeing πνευματικῶς. If this is the case, then Revelation 12–14 shapes the pneumatic discernment of the churches. The churches are lead through a process of viewing (again) with pneumatic perception the conflict between the beast and the people of God.[344]

Revelation 12

The woman clothed with the sun who has the moon under her feet and a crown of twelve stars on her head is identified as a sign.[345] While a variety of narratives could be recalled concerning the identity

---

[343] Bauckham, *Climax of Prophecy*, p. 266.

[344] See Koester, *Revelation*, p. 565, who observes a theme of perception in this section.

[345] See Thomas, *The Apocalypse*, p. 352, for a discussion of 'signs' and their occurrences in the FG.

of the woman,[346] this intertextual medley echoes Eve who encoun-tered a serpent,[347] the mother of Jesus who birthed the messiah,[348] Hagar who found nourishment and protection in the wilderness,[349] while also seeming to represent the people of God.[350] While it is pos-sible to choose one of the above interpretative options, the text cre-ates a collage with these distinctive heroines that converges in this one transmutative image[351] – a woman clothed with the sun who finds protection in the wilderness for 1260 days.[352] In much the same man-ner as the temple, the outer court, and the two witnesses (Revelation 11), the woman in the wilderness and her children are protected by God, while being pursued by the dragon for 1260 days. The antago-nist of the woman is a great red dragon who has seven heads, ten

[346] The Greco-Roman background material concerning the woman and the dragon is extensive, see for example, A.Y. Collins, *The Combat Myth in the Book of Revelation* (Missoula, MT: Harvard Theological Review, 1976); S.J. Friesen, 'Myth and Symbolic Resistance in Revelation 13', *JBL* 123.2 (2004), pp. 281-313. How-ever, D. Treacy-Cole, 'Women in the Wilderness: Rereading Revelation 12', in R.S. Sugirtharajah (ed.), *Wilderness: Essays in Honour of Frances Young* (New York: T&T Clark, 2005), p. 45, prefers to consider intersections from the HB: 'Revelation owes much to a mythopoetic restyling of the Hebrew Bible motifs … It is curious that the model for the Woman Clothed with the Sun is drawn from non-Jewish tradi-tions'. .

[347] For an examination of Genesis 3–4 and Revelation 12, see P.S. Minear, 'Far as the Curse is Found: The Point of Revelation 12:15-16', *NovT* 33.1 (1991), pp. 71-77.

[348] See R.E. Murphy, 'An Allusion to Mary in the Apocalypse', *TS* 10.4 (1949), pp. 565-73.

[349] Treacy-Cole, 'Women in the Wilderness', pp. 45-58, convincingly argues that the woman clothed with the sun would evoke Hagar based on Hagar's wilderness experiences.

[350] See Koester, *Revelation*, pp. 560-63. See also I. Paul, 'The Value of Paul Ricoeur's Hermeneutic of Metaphor in Interpreting the Symbolism of Revelation Chapters 12 and 13' (PhD Thesis: St. John's College, Bramcote, Nottingham), pp. 165-79, for a thorough examination of HB echoes of Revelation 12–13.

[351] I agree with Thomas, *The Apocalypse*, p. 360, who notes the polyvalent nature of this image, 'It is as though in the emerging image of the woman clothed with the sun that the promises regarding the messianic seed given to Eve, Israel, and Mary converge in this one image'. Koester, *Revelation*, p. 560, helpfully adds, 'Instead of asking how readers are to identify the woman, we will ask how the text invites them to identify *with* her so that they see the action from her perspective'. See also Tavo, *Woman, Mother, and Bride*, p. 229.

[352] Treacy-Cole, 'Women in the Wilderness', pp. 45-58, notes that the wilder-ness is a location of protection and nourishment. So also Thomas, *The Apocalypse*, p. 362, who observes that the wilderness is a positive location in the Johannine literature where witness, salvific healing, provision, and protection occur.

horns, and seven diadems. The great dragon, the ancient serpent is called (ὁ καλούμενος) the Devil, Satan, and the deceiver of the whole earth (12.9).[353] It would not be missed by the hearers that in Rev. 11.8 the great city was called (καλεῖται) πνευματικῶς Sodom, Egypt, and the place where their Lord was crucified. It is possible that the dragon's deception is connected to the flood that comes from its mouth, suggesting that the attacks of the dragon include its deceitfulness.[354] The dragon also recalls the serpent in the garden. In Genesis 3, the serpent deceived Eve into believing that the wisdom obtained from the tree was warranted, despite having to disobey God's command. Evoking Genesis 3 characterizes any supposed 'wisdom' from the dragon to stand in opposition to God's commandments.[355] It seems that some of the churches have already accepted the dragon's 'wisdom', having obtained the 'deep things of Satan' (2.24) from Jezebel who, like the dragon, is characterized as a deceiver.[356] The association of Satan with the opponents of the seven churches extends to those who persecuted the churches, who were liars, and who were part of the synagogue and the throne of Satan. The seven churches are therefore warned of the dragon's wiles. The dragon is the ever-morphing, trans-temporal adversary of the woman. Whereas the Lamb and the Spirit offer divine wisdom, the dragon propagates falsehood, deceit, and fraudulent wisdom.[357]

---

[353] For a full characterization of the dragon, see Bauckham, *Climax of Prophecy*, pp. 185-98; P.G.R. de Villiers, 'Prime Evil and its Many Faces in the Book of Revelation', *NeoT* 34.1 (2000), pp. 57-85.

[354] Sweet, *Revelation*, p. 204, writes, 'the phrase, repeated in v. 16, suggests that the *flood* is Satan's "river of lies" (Caird); cf. 16.13, and contrast the word issuing from the *mouth* of the Son of man (1.16 etc.), and the fire from the *mouth* of the two witnesses (11.6), which represents the word and Spirit of Truth.' So also Smalley, *Revelation*, p. 332, who writes, 'The floods of deceit and destruction are then replaced by the river of the water of life, flowing from the heavenly throne'. See also Caird, *Revelation of St. John*, p. 159; Beale, *The Book of Revelation*, p. 673; Keener, *Revelation*, p. 323; Blount, *Revelation*, p. 241.

[355] Beale, *The Book of Revelation*, p. 673; Koester, *Revelation*, p. 564.

[356] P.B. Duff, 'Wolves in Sheep's Clothing: Literary Opposition and Social Tension in the Revelation of John', in D.L. Barr (ed.), *Reading the Book of Revelation* (Atlanta, GA: SBL, 2003), p. 73.

[357] H. Koester, 'Revelation 12:1-12: A Meditation', in W.H. Brackney and C.A. Evans (eds.), *From Biblical Criticism to Biblical Faith: Essays in Honor of Lee Martin McDonald* (Macon, GA: Mercer University Press, 2007), p. 143, writes, '… discernment: they are able to recognize those governmental agencies that are committed

The woman clothed with the sun has twelve stars in her crown. The appearance of stars recalls the seven stars in Revelation 1, and as discussed above, the seven stars (intersecting with Daniel 12) seem to represent the discerning ones in the seven churches.[358] The churches might also recall the stars in Gen. 37.9 that are closely connected to the 12 tribes of Israel. The star imagery reappears when the dragon knocks one-third of the stars from heaven to earth (12.4). The appearances of stars in Revelation 12 might indicate that the stars on the crown of the woman, the stars that the dragon knocks from heaven, and the stars among the seven churches are closely related, if not representing the same entity.[359] Perhaps, knocking the stars from heaven represents the dragon's deceptive activities among the seven churches, where even the discerning ones are susceptible to the dragon's deception. The magnitude of those effected by the dragon – one-third – confirms the widespread issues of deceit, false teachings, and false prophecies among the seven churches, while also urging the churches to discern the workings of the dragon.[360] Despite the scope of the deceit of the dragon, the narrative immediately establishes that the dragon is a defeated adversary. Neither the Lamb nor the one on the throne combats the dragon; rather, it is Michael alone, a servant, who defeats the dragon.[361]

---

to justice, equity, and fairness. Thus Christians can sing hymns and are at the same time able to locate in their own world the powers of evil and chaos … it is a challenge to the Christian community to use our powers of insight to discern the powers of evil that are ruling the world in which we live.' See also Caird, *Revelation of St. John*, p. 159.

[358] Smalley, *Revelation*, p. 315, observes a connection between the twelve stars in Revelation 12 and the seven stars in Revelation 1. See also Beale, *The Book of Revelation*, pp. 635-37, who observes that stars in Daniel seem to function to represent the people of Israel and angels; he also notes that in Daniel angels can represent people. See Daniel 7; 8.10-11; 10.20-21; 12.1, 3.

[359] Beale, *The Book of Revelation*, p. 637.

[360] Three of the seven churches were dealing explicitly with false teaching/prophecy even though Ephesus resisted the deception of false teachings. Others in the churches were exhorted to wake up and to discern the divine reality that included the identity of their opponents, their state of poverty or wealth, or if they are alive or dead.

[361] Blount, *Revelation*, p. 226, writes, 'John's point is a simple one: for all the dragon's great strength, it is never, even narratively, on a par with God. God need not engage the battle directly because God's representatives are sufficient for the task.' See also Osborne, *Revelation*, p. 469.

Another hymn appears that assists the churches in discernment in Revelation 12. The hymn announces the coming of God's kingdom and subsequently the defeat of the dragon. The victory of the kingdom of God over the dragon is closely connected to overcoming. Overcoming recalls the sevenfold repetition in the seven prophetic messages. The appearance further describes overcoming as well as identifies the one whom the overcomers overcome – the dragon. Overcoming the dragon would include overcoming the deception of the dragon along with the dragon's persecution. The process to overcome is threefold (12.10-12). (1) They overcome by the blood of the Lamb, which connects overcoming with the sacrificial death of the slaughtered Lamb.[362] (2) They overcome by the word of their witness, which implies that the overcomers are true and faithful witnesses. The overcomers' witness is true because they had an ear to hear the Spirit and, like the two witnesses, their witness is empowered by the Spirit. The true, pneumatic witness of the overcomers overcomes the deceit of the dragon. (3) As the Lamb, Antipas, and the two witnesses, the witness of the overcomers can lead to death and persecution. As the victory of the Lamb was achieved through sacrifice, so too is victory possible for the overcomers, if they follow the Lamb in self-sacrifice and true and faithful witness.[363]

## Revelation 13

The narrative of the dragon continues when John sees a beast rise from the sea as the dragon stands on the seashore. Narratively, it is possible that the origin of the beast (the sea) has been created by the flood from the dragon's mouth.[364] Thereby, the beast would be closely associated with, if not the personification of, the deceitful attacks of the dragon. This sea beast has seven heads, ten horns, and ten crowns and looks like a leopard, bear, and lion, recalling the beasts in Daniel 7; however, Daniel's beasts form one beast in Revelation.[365] The beast

---

[362] Pattemore, *The People of God*, p. 95, writes, 'Once again the historical death of Christ forms the centre point of the story ... Victory is through death. Not a cosmic super-hero but a slain Lamb is the key player.'

[363] Pattemore, *The People of God*, pp. 95-96, observes a close connection between the ψυχὰς under the altar and the overcomers, concluding that they are essentially the same characters.

[364] Michaels, *Revelation*, p. 159.

[365] Koester, *Revelation*, p. 580, comments, 'Yet Revelation does not simply repeat Daniel 7; the writer recasts it ... in Revelation those four beasts become a single

recalls the enemy of the two witnesses in Rev. 11.7 and the location of the beast's murderous activities – the great city, Egypt, Sodom, and the place where their Lord was crucified. Reference to the great city alerts the churches that the sea beast must be discerned πνευματικῶς.[366]

First, the churches must discern πνευματικῶς the power and authority of the beast. The beast receives authority and power from the dragon. The beast's throne represents its political authority that is closely associated with the beast's military might.[367] The throne that the beast occupies (given by the dragon) recalls other thrones in Revelation such as the divine throne in heaven and Satan's throne (2.13). Satan's throne is located in Pergamum where the church is experiencing persecution, even the death of Antipas.[368] Viewing the beast πνευματικῶς and recognizing the close relationship of the beast and Satan suggests that the beast might have participated in the death of Antipas, and thereby that the beast is actively operating among the seven churches. This close relationship would also imply that the beast is active in Pergamum, the location of Satan's throne. Pergamum would be πνευματικῶς part of the kaleidoscopic web that is the great city where the beast is actively warring against the church (11.7).[369] Violence, death, and persecution are the works of Satan and the works of the beast, which occur trans-geographically in the great city. However, in the face of this opposition, those with pneumatic discernment would recognize that the beast's military power is a guise, considering that the source of the beast's fragile power is the dragon who is defeated by Michael. After hearing the question, Τίς ὅμοιος τῷ θηρίῳ, καὶ τίς δύναται πολεμῆσαι μετ' αὐτοῦ; ('Who is like the beast, and who is able to war against him?', 13.4), the discerning ones might respond, 'Michael' who was able to defeat the

---

beast, so that readers see the tyrannical qualities of many empires as part of the same reality'. See also Moyise, *The Old Testament in the Book of Revelation*, pp. 52-54.

[366] Michaels, *Revelation*, p. 158.

[367] Schüssler Fiorenza, *Vision of a Just World*, p. 83, writes, 'If Revelation takes its meaning from Daniel 7, then the beast embodies all political powers of the time'. See also J. Ellul, *Apocalypse: The Book of Revelation* (trans. George W. Schreiner; New York, NY: The Seabury Press, 1977), pp. 93-97; Rowland, *Revelation*, p. 113; Murphy, *Fallen is Babylon*, p. 297.

[368] Schüssler Fiorenza, *Vision of a Just World*, p. 83.

[369] Koester, *Revelation*, p. 586, writes, 'Where persecution occurs, the beast is present; where Christians are put to death, Satan reigns (2:13)'.

dragon.[370] As the churches anticipate a conflict with the beast following the narratives of the two witnesses and the woman in the wilderness, they would recognize that the beast's power has already been (at
least partly) subjugated. Ultimate power and authority belong to the
Lamb who has seven horns (the seven Spirits) and to the one who
sits on the throne.[371]

Second, the churches must discern πνευματικῶς the deceptions
of the beast. The beast deceives through his own death (13.3, ὡς
ἐσφαγμένην) and resurrection (13.3, 12 ἐθεραπεύθη cf. 13.14,
ἔζησεν), which parodies the Lamb who was slaughtered (5.6,
ἐσφαγμένον) and who was raised to life (2.8 ὃς ἐγένετο νεκρὸς καὶ
ἔζησεν).[372] In a manner like the Lamb, the beast reveals its power
through its death and resurrection. The hymnic worship of the people reveals the impact of the beast's resurrection. The worship of the
beast is closely tied to the deception of the beast, denoting a correlation between false worship and deceit. The connection would not
be lost on the seven churches where some in the churches were deceived by the Nicolaitans, Jezebel, and Balaam to cause them to participate in false worship.[373] Worship therefore becomes an essential
feature in the process of discernment:

> Prophetic discernment is necessary to distinguish between true
> and false worship; that is, 'only those committed to worship of
> the true Power see past the façade to the satanic reality'. While the
> whole world celebrates in their song the power of the beast and
> their perceived notion that no one can war against him, the
> churches have learned through the true songs of worship pre-
> sented in the narrative that worship is only to be given to God and
> the Lamb, who exercise all power and authority.[374]

Are some in the churches worshipping the beast? Are the churches
deceived by the miraculous power and authority of the beast? To
whom are those in the churches directing their worship? Do they

---

[370] Osborne, *Revelation*, p. 498.

[371] Trafton, *Reading Revelation*, p. 126.

[372] W. Foerster, 'θηρίον', *TDNT*, (1965), VIII, pp. 134-35. Cf. Bauckham,
*Climax of Prophecy*, p. 452; Murphy, *Fallen is Babylon*, p. 303.

[373] Osborne, *Revelation*, p. 497.

[374] Archer, *'I Was in the Spirit on the Lord's Day'*, p. 229, who quotes Howard-
Brook and Gwyther, *Unveiling Empire*, p. 215. See also Koester, *Revelation*, p. 577.

worship the murderous, violent, haughty, and slanderous beast? Or
do they worship the Lamb who overcomes through sacrificial death
and resurrection, who sits upon the divine throne, and who has seven
eyes and seven horns that are the seven Spirits, who knows all and
who is all-powerful?[375]

Third, the churches must discern πνευματικῶς the duration of
the beast's rule. The beast will reign for 42 months, recalling previous
three and a half-year designations; 42 months is the time that the holy
city will be trampled, connecting the time of trampling with the reign
of the beast. The 42 months of the beast suggests that its power is
limited; the beast will not reign forever and is not invincible.[376] These
limitations of time also indicate that the beast cannot compare to the
eternal one. Conversely, 1260 days represents the time of the Spirit
where the two witnesses offer pneumatic witness, and the woman is
protected in the wilderness. For 1260 days, the seven Spirits who are
the seven eyes of the Lamb will be active among the seven churches
to assist the churches in discerning the deceptions of the beast.

Additionally, the description of the sea beast concludes with a call
for pneumatic discernment:[377]

Εἴ τις ἔχει οὖς ἀκουσάτω.
εἴ τις εἰς αἰχμαλωσίαν, εἰς αἰχμαλωσίαν ὑπάγει·
εἴ τις ἐν μαχαίρῃ ἀποκτανθῆναι αὐτὸν ἐν μαχαίρῃ
ἀποκτανθῆναι.
ὧδέ ἐστιν ἡ ὑπομονὴ καὶ ἡ πίστις τῶν ἁγίων.

Let anyone who has an ear, hear
If anyone goes into captivity,
  into captivity they go.
If anyone is killed with the sword,

---

[375] See Schüssler Fiorenza, *Vision of a Just World*, p. 84; Michaels, *Revelation*, p.
159; Reddish, *Revelation*, pp. 265-68; Maier, *Apocalypse Recalled*, p. 179; deSilva, *Seeing
Things John's Way*, pp. 198-99.

[376] Koester, *Revelation*, p. 585.

[377] V. Westhelle, 'Revelation 13: Between the Colonial and Postcolonial, a
Reading from Brazil', in D. Rhoads (ed.), *From Every People and Nation: The Book of
Revelation in Intercultural Perspective* (Minneapolis: Fortress Press, 2005), p. 196, writes,
'Listen to what the Spirit says, and you will discern the beast behind the adorn-
ments. Do you know what you see? Do you see what you know?'

with the sword, they are killed.
Here is the fortitude and the faith of the saints (13.9-10).

(1) The significance of the reoccurrence of the familiar hearing formula – Εἴ τις ἔχει οὖς ἀκουσάτω ('Let anyone who has an ear, hear') – would not be lost on the hearers.[378] The sevenfold hearing formula at the conclusion of each of the prophetic messages calls upon the churches to discern pneumatically. The Spirit actively conveyed the words of Jesus in seven prophetic messages. Thus, the churches are reminded that they are hearing the very words of Jesus spoken dynamically by the Spirit. Pneumatic discernment is needed for all that has proceeded, which is not surprising considering the deceitful deeds of the beast.[379] (2) This is the first of three occurrences of ὧδέ ἐστιν ('here is') in this narrative section. The appearance of ὧδέ ἐστιν alongside Εἴ τις ἔχει οὖς ἀκουσάτω connects these important literary markers. The close appearance of these exhortations suggests that whenever ὧδέ ἐστιν occurs, it should be regarded as an invitation for pneumatic discernment, to hear the Spirit. (3) The call for pneumatic discernment contains a poetic couplet: εἴ τις εἰς αἰχμαλωσίαν, εἰς αἰχμαλωσίαν ὑπάγει· εἴ τις ἐν μαχαίρῃ ἀποκτανθῆναι αὐτὸν ἐν μαχαίρῃ ἀποκτανθῆναι. There is a sense of irony present in the text because the beast who is slaughtered by a sword, does not die but lives.[380] The context of this couplet suggests

---

[378] Gause, *Revelation*, p. 183, comments, 'verse 9 is an exhortation of the Lord by the Holy Spirit'. Boxall, *The Revelation of St. John*, p. 192, comments, 'The command serves as a literary device alerting the readers, and therefore the audience, to a saying which requires particular attention'. Pattemore, *The People of God*, p. 172, adds, 'Here within the mytho-symbolic vision of the beasts is the Spirit-inspired voice of prophecy, not only in the direct address that follows, but in the story itself to which it points'. See also Bauckham, *The Theology of the Book of Revelation*, p. 117; G. Campbell, 'Findings, Seals, Trumpets, and Bowls: Variations upon the Theme of Covenant Rupture and Restoration in the Book of Revelation', *WTJ* 66.1 (2004), p. 91.

[379] Ruiz, *Ezekiel in the Apocalypse*, pp. 200-204; Thomas, 'Pneumatic Discernment', p. 106.

[380] Koester, *Revelation*, p. 588, observes a double meaning in this text. On the one hand, the faithful in confrontations with the beast might experience death or captivity. On the other hand, the beast who kills with the sword will experience the judgment of Christ with the sword of his mouth. So also Sweet, *Revelation*, pp. 212-13. Some comparisons have been made between the beast who is killed with a sword and Nero who was killed with a dragger. However, despite the possibilities of some legends that Nero would return, Nero remained dead. The beast, however,

that these prophetic words, like the prophetic messages, are addressed to the churches.[381] Unlike the beast, the churches are urged to take a non-violent stance toward the attacks of the beast. The churches must not kill with a sword, as the beast kills. This non-violent stance follows in the tradition of Jesus, Antipas, and the two witnesses who did not physically resist the beast.[382] Thus, non-violence is fused together with the call for pneumatic discernment, endurance, and faithfulness in the face of persecution.[383] Death and captivity are possible outcomes of the churches' faithful witness. Faithfulness and endurance are needed in the face of such opposition.

The theme of deception continues with another beast who is from the earth. The explicit association of the beast from the earth who looks like a lamb but speaks as a dragon characterizes the earth beast as one who is deceitful and a liar.[384] The beast from the earth creates a false religious system accompanied by signs and wonders;

---

is resurrected and the beast's resurrection is witnessed by the whole earth. A similar point is made by P.S. Minear, 'The Wounded Beast', *JBL* 72.2 (1953), p. 97, who challenges some assumptions of interpreting the beast as Nero. So also Thomas, 'Pneumatic Discernment', p. 120, who writes, 'There is also the fact that by the time of the Apocalypse, Nero is surely dead, and despite arguments to the contrary, there is no evidence that the tradition of Nero's return included the idea of his death and resurrection, an idea that is clearly present in the description of the beast in Revelation 13'. For a discussion of *Nero Redivivus*, see H.-J. Klauck, 'Do They Never Come Back?: Nero Redivivus and the Apocalypse of John', *CBQ* 63.4 (2001), pp. 683-98.

[381] Caird, *Revelation of St. John*, p. 169.

[382] Aune, *Revelation 6–16*, p. 750, observes, 'in Revelation the fates of captivity and the sword (i.e., death) are the fated consequence of those who practice the qualities of faith and endurance'. Beale, *The Book of Revelation*, p. 705, writes, 'They are to stand more strongly in their faith because of their discernment (v 9) that such persecution is intended by the devil to cause them to compromise'. See also Thomas, *The Apocalypse*, p. 396, who comments, 'Such pneumatic discernment reveals that they are not to resist the fates marked out for them, but rather accept them as somehow integral to their prophetic witness and as part of God's will and plan for the believing community'.

[383] Resseguie, *The Revelation of John*, p. 186.

[384] Smalley, *Revelation*, p. 345, writes, 'John is speaking of deceit and falsehood at any time and in any place. The second beast appears to be harmless as a ram; but his truly evil nature is evinced when he speaks with the authority of the dragon and with the alluring, deceptive voice of a serpent.' Wall, *Revelation*, p. 172, adds, 'when the believer listens intently to the "word of God and the testimony of Jesus Christ," now conveyed through the Paraclete in Christ's absence, the false claims of Rome or of Jezebel are distinctly heard as belonging to the Evil One'. See also Koester, *Revelation*, p. 590.

practices that might have been occurring in the seven churches.[385] Hence, as with the sea beast and the dragon, the churches must discern πνευματικῶς the deceitful earth beast.

First, the churches must discern πνευματικῶς the activities of the earth beast which parody the activities of the seven Spirits.[386] (1) The earth beast performs signs and wonders, tangible manifestations that deceive the whole earth. The signs and wonders of the earth beast parody the signs and wonders of the two witnesses who are empowered by the Spirit.[387] These false signs cause the whole world to worship the beast and deceive the world to believe that these experiences originate from the true God and the true Spirit.[388] The ability of the earth beast to manipulate fire recalls the seven torches who are the seven Spirits. The earth beast produces phenomena that mimic the power of the seven Spirits – the seven torches.[389] The attribution of signs and wonders to the beast reveals to the seven churches that miraculous manifestations are not the sole identifying markers of one's legitimacy toward God.[390] The false prophetic activity of the earth beast encourages vigilant discernment on behalf of the churches to recognize the activity of the Spirit against the activity of

---

[385] Smalley, *Revelation*, p. 346.

[386] See Thomas, 'Pneumatic Discernment', pp. 107-11.

[387] Aune, *Revelation 6–16*, p. 679, observes that the occurrences of σημεῖα (in the plural) in Revelation are always associated with false miracles (13.13-14; 16.14; 19.20).

[388] Newton, *The Revelation Worldview*, p. 137, writes, 'The land beast uses signs to deceive "the inhabitants of the earth" (13:13-14). These signs appeal to the senses and cause people to *think* they are perceiving or experiencing spiritual reality when they are actually worshiping a false god.'

[389] While it is possible that these descriptions evoke a parody between the earth beast and the two witnesses, this does not take into account the dynamic relationship between the Spirit and the two witnesses. The seven Spirits empower the two witnesses, and the seven torches ignite the fire that comes from the mouth of the witnesses. It is the Spirit who raises the two witnesses from death. See also Foerster, 'θηρίον', p. 134; Sweet, *Revelation*, pp. 214, 216; Gause, *Revelation*, p. 183; O. O'Donovan, 'The Political Thought of the Book of Revelation', *TynB* 37 (1986), p. 81; Wall, *Revelation*, p. 167; Richard, *Apocalypse*, p. 111; Smalley, *Revelation*, p. 348.

[390] Boring, *Revelation*, p. 161, writes, 'John never denies the reality of the impressive miracles worked by this beast, knowing in accord with biblical theology in general that the truth of faith is not proven or disproven by displays of miraculous power or the lack of it'. See also Boxall, *The Revelation of St. John*, p. 195.

the earth beast.[391] It is possible that the seven churches are encountering the false signs and wonders of the earth beast, manifesting as Jezebel, the Nicolaitans, and Balaam. (2) The mimicry of the earth beast even extends to the Spirit's life giving power. Whereas πνεῦμα ζωῆς ἐκ τοῦ θεοῦ ('the Spirit of life from God') raised the two witnesses from death to life (11.11), the earth beast gives πνεῦμα ('spirit') to the image of the beast (13.15).[392] However, the life-giving power of the earth beast is ultimately an imitation, considering that the earth beast would rather take life from whoever does not worship the image of the beast than offer life to the inhabitants of the earth.

Second, the churches must discern πνευματικῶς the religious systems of the earth beast. While the sea beast was worshipped based on its resurrection, the earth beast creates an image of the beast that everyone is required to worship or face death.[393] The churches would recall the relationship between demonic worship and idolatry in Revelation 8.[394] The earth beast's cultic work extends to a marking that is placed on the head or the right hand of those who worship the image of the beast. The placement of the mark of the beast upon the forehead parodies the seal of God that is placed upon the foreheads of the 144,000/great crowd.[395] The churches would recall that worship belongs to God alone.[396] These two opposing marks function to create a dualism of identity: one identifies either with the beast or with God. One worships either God or the beast.[397] These conflicting markings reveal that pneumatic discernment is required to recognize

---

[391] Beale, *The Book of Revelation*, p. 708.

[392] Sweet, *Revelation*, p. 216.

[393] Moyise, *The Old Testament in the Book of Revelation*, p. 55. Mangina, *Revelation*, p. 166, notes, 'As the prophetic Spirit exposes the truth in all things, so the false prophet spins a web of lies, inviting us to debase ourselves by worshipping the beast rather than the Creator'.

[394] E. Schüssler Fiorenza, 'The Followers of the Lamb: Visionary Rhetoric and Social-Political Situation', *Semeia* 36 (1986), p. 139. See also Koester, *Revelation*, p. 603.

[395] So Aune, *Revelation 6–16*, pp. 766-68, who offers an examination of markings in the ancient world. C. Rowland, 'Revelation', *The New Interpreter's Bible* (Nashville, TN: Abingdon Press, 1998), XII, p. 658, notes the public aspects concerning both the markings and the worship implied. See also Beasley-Murray, *The Book of Revelation*, p. 218; Schüssler Fiorenza, *Vision of a Just World*, p. 86; Boring, *Revelation*, p. 161.

[396] Blount, *Revelation*, p. 257.

[397] Moyise, *The Old Testament in the Book of Revelation*, p. 55.

the identity of those who follow the beast and those who follow the Lamb.[398]

Third, the churches must discern πνευματικῶς the economic implications of the earth beast. The mark of the beast is inclusive of everyone – rich or poor, small or big – in determining if anyone can buy or sell. The religious character of the mark of the beast, which requires worship of the image of the beast, is brought together with economic implications.[399] A primary feature of Jesus' exhortation in the seven prophetic messages is that earthly statuses such as wealth or poverty, when viewed through the eyes of the resurrected Jesus, appear differently. Those in the seven prophetic messages who are rich, from the divine perspective, are poor; those who are poor, from the divine perspective, are rich.[400] Economics are addressed again; those who do not worship the beast will receive limitations on commerce, which suggests that one's identity is revealed by buying and selling. Having an ear to hear the Spirit in this text calls upon the churches to examine the ways in which they partake in commerce. Everyone is urged to examine their own situation as they consider if their wealth has been accumulated at the cost of receiving the mark of the beast and worshipping the image of the beast. Those marked by the beast have no limitations placed upon their purchases, while those who have been sealed by God do not have equal purchasing liberties.[401]

---

[398] Rowland, *Revelation*, p. 119, comments, 'Idolatry represents a life that is completely submerged in the economic and cultural life of the present so that it cannot see that it is forfeiting its own soul'. Archer, *'I Was in the Spirit on the Lord's Day'*, p. 232, writes, 'In marking his followers, the actions of the beast parody God's actions, and the community must engage in pneumatic discernment'.

[399] Schüssler Fiorenza, *Vision of a Just World*, p. 87.

[400] Cf. Rev. 2.9; 3.17-18.

[401] Koester, *Revelation*, p. 605, comments, 'The vision presses for clarity about the readers' commitments, asking whether their identities are determined by the power to purchase goods in the market or by the power of the Lamb, whose blood has purchased them for God's kingdom (5:9)'. D.A. deSilva, 'The "Image of the Beast" and the Christians in Asia Minor: Escalation of Sectarian Tension in Revelation 13', *Trinity Journal* 12.2 (1991), p. 205, writes, 'The mark of the beast, which is the key to this world's economy, is set antithetically against the seal of God, the key to association with the Lamb in 14.1'. See also Rowland, *Revelation*, p. 113; Pattemore, *The People of God*, p. 174.

Fourth, the description of the earth beast concludes with another explicit call for pneumatic discernment in 13.18 that is expressed by the reappearance of ὧδε ... ἐστίν ('here is'):[402]

ὧδε ἡ σοφία ἐστίν·
ὁ ἔχων νοῦν ψηφισάτω τὸν ἀριθμὸν τοῦ θηρίου,
ἀριθμὸς γὰρ ἀνθρώπου ἐστίν· καὶ ὁ ἀριθμὸς αὐτοῦ ἑξακόσιοι
ἑξήκοντα ἕξ.

Here is wisdom
Let the one who has discernment, calculate the number of the beast,
For it is a number of a human, and the number is six hundred and sixty-six (13.18).

In Revelation, wisdom appeared in 5.12 and 7.12 and was attributed to God and to the Lamb[403] and is one of the attributes of the seven Spirits in Isa. 11.2. Hence, the seven Spirits who provide wisdom, understanding, and endurance to the churches is needed to calculate this enigmatic number.[404] This is confirmed in the next words of this text where the exhortation for understanding (ὁ ἔχων νοῦν) recalls the sevenfold repetition that exhorts the seven churches to have an ear to hear the Spirit (ὁ ἔχων οὖς) and recalls a similar formula found in 13.9-10, which dynamically unites the call for wisdom and understanding with faithfulness, endurance, and having an ear to hear the Spirit.[405] The number 666 is ἀριθμὸς ἀνθρώπου suggesting that the

---

[402] Thomas, 'Pneumatic Discernment', p. 115; Ellul, *Apocalypse*, p. 98, translates this final exhortation, '"It is the moment to have discernment"'.

[403] Ruiz, *Ezekiel in the Apocalypse*, p. 207, adds, 'Thus two distinct but related meanings are assigned to wisdom: it is an attribute of God whereby he orders history, executing his plan of salvation; and it is the human activity of deciphering, interpreting and understanding the way that plan is revealed, in the imagery of Revelation. The two senses are related: the task of human wisdom is to be attentive to the unfolding of the divine wisdom.'

[404] Contra Aune, *Revelation 6–16*, p. 769, who concludes that this text does not call for divine assistance. So Beale, *The Book of Revelation*, p. 726, who comments, 'Believers must be spiritually on the alert to discern such deceptive manifestations, which are not expected by those not cultivating divine wisdom'. See also Prigent, *The Apocalypse*, p. 423; Osborne, *Revelation*, p. 519; Smalley, *Revelation*, p. 350.

[405] Ruiz, *Ezekiel in the Apocalypse*, p. 207, writes, 'From its use in a doxological, liturgical setting, it is clear that wisdom is a divine quality, which belongs to God and to Christ. In 13,18 and 17,9, σοφία occurs in a different context: what was described as a divine attribute in 5,12; 7,2 is associated with νοῦς and together they

number is either a human(ly) number (i.e. able to be understood by humans) or the number of a human (i.e. the number of a person).[406] What interpretative options might be considered when calculating 666?[407]

(1) The appearance of 666 recalls 1 Kgs 10.14, which depicts the pinnacle of Solomon's success when the queen of Sheba visited him to test and affirm Solomon's wealth and wisdom. Solomon's accumulation of wealth surpassed the wealth of all other kings, and Solomon was declared to be the wisest of all kings. Solomon's wisdom originated from Yahweh (1 Kgs 10.23-24). 1 Kings 10.14 reports that Solomon received gold in the sum of 666 talents, in addition to the wealth he received from traders, merchants, kings, and governors (1 Kgs 10.14-15). However, in 1 Kings 11, Solomon's political and economic success, which was celebrated in 1 Kings 10, is staunchly criticized because of Solomon's marriages to those from other nations, which lead him to idolatry and an unfaithful heart toward Yahweh. Echoes of the 666 gold reverberate when 666 appears in Rev. 13.18.[408] This intertextual intersection suggests a correlation between economics, idolatry, and political success, which coincides with the beast who, by military and political power, causes the whole earth to worship the image of the beast, while preventing anyone from buying or selling who would not worship its image. It might not be pushing the intertext too far to suggest that perhaps Solomon, who was guilty of false worship and who had unlimited purchasing power, had 'received' such a mark, himself.

---

form part of an admonition to the faithful to apply themselves to a process of reflection.' C. Rotz, *Revelation: A Commentary in the Wesleyan Tradition* (NBBC; Kansas City: Beacon Hill Press, 2012), p. 209, observes an echo of Dan. 12.10 where the wise will understand. See also Wall, *Revelation*, p. 170; J. Lambrecht, 'Rev 13,9-10 and Exhortation in the Apocalypse', in A. Denaux and J. Delobel (eds.), *New Testament Textual Criticism and Exegesis: FS J. Delobel* (Leuven: Peeters, 2002), pp. 331-47.

[406] Cf. Rev. 21.17. See also Beale, *The Book of Revelation*, p. 724; Thomas, 'Pneumatic Discernment', p. 116.

[407] For an examination of the interpretative possibilities of the calculation of the number of the beast, see Aune, *Revelation 6–16*, pp. 771-73.

[408] Bede the Venerable, 'The Exposition of the Apocalypse', in W.C. Weinrich (ed.), *Latin Commentaries on Revelation* (trans. W.C. Weinrich; Downers Grove, IL: InterVarsity Press), p. 157, observes the appearance of 666 in 1 Kings 10 and comments that the beast would enact a tax.

Solomon's failure is especially significant considering that Solomon had received divine wisdom; however, his divinely inspired wisdom was not adequate to prevent him from participating in false worship. Since calculating 666 requires wisdom (13.18), these echoes of Solomon caution the churches that divine wisdom in and of itself is not sufficient to avoid false worship.[409] Discernment lacking the love of God resonates with an exhortation from Jesus to the church in Ephesus. The church in Ephesus abandoned their first love, despite being able to recognize false apostles and being able to discern the false teachings of the Nicolaitans. Perhaps, in a similar manner to Solomon, some in the churches have keen discerning abilities; nevertheless, because of their desire for economic advantage, they have compromised with the beast by offering false worship to the image of the beast. They love success more than they love God, and without love for God, divinely inspired wisdom and pneumatic discernment are found lacking.

(2) Another interpretative possibility for 666 arises with the appearance of the term ψηφισάτω ('calculate'), which implies counting.[410] 666 is a triangular number that recalls another triangular number in the Johannine literature, 153 (Jn 21.11), which is the sum of the fish that Peter and John caught following the resurrection of Jesus. Triangular numbers are categorized as numbers that are the sum of consecutive digits, and, when visualized as a geometrical shape, form an equilateral triangle. For example, 153 is the sum of the numbers from 1 to 17, while 666 is the sum of the numbers from 1 to 36:

---

[409] W. Brueggemann, *1 & 2 Kings* (S&HBC; Macon, GA: Smyth & Helwys Publishing, 2000), pp. 142-43, writes:

Thus the key issue is that the heart of the king was diverted from Yahweh so that he no longer had the 'discerning heart' requested in 3:9. That is, the splendid establishment of Solomon that we have seen described and celebrated in detail was no longer reflective of Yahwistic loyalty, neither in terms of its actual cultic practices nor in terms of its social policies that had little contact with the neighborly covenantalism of Moses.

[410] G. Braumann, 'ψῆφος', *TDNT*, IX, p. 607.

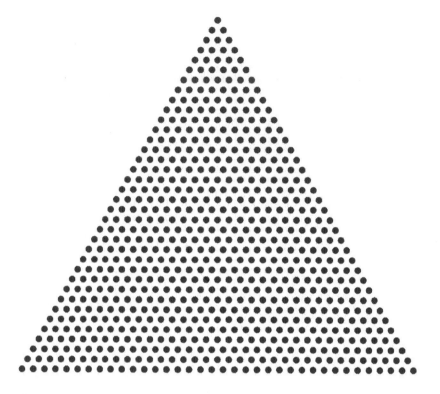

The striking feature of 666 is that 36, the final number in the sequence, is also a triangular number (the sum of the numbers from 1 to 8), which categorizes 666 as a 'doubly triangular number'. Doubly triangular numbers are exceptionally rare, and 666 is the eighth such doubly triangular number: 1, 6, 21, 55, 120, 231, 406, and 666. Perhaps, the triangular number in 13.18 appears in association with the triadic nature of the two beasts and the dragon. It also seems that the churches must wait in tension to discover additional implications of 666 in relation to the 'eighth' such doubly triangular number owing to the fact that the 'eighth' describes the beast later in the narrative.[411]

---

[411] Cf. Rev. 17.11. F.H. Colson, 'Triangluar Numbers in the New Testament', *JTS* 16.61 (1914), p. 71, observes that the doubly triangular number is the 'king amongst numbers'. See also Thomas, 'Pneumatic Discernment', pp. 120-23, who concludes, 'owing to the significance of 36, which was especially honored among the ancients, and the fact that 666 is the triangular number of that triangular number, it might not be going too far to see in the number of the beast, a number that would be understood as of cosmic proportions; perhaps a king amongst numbers!' On the meaning of triangular numbers, see R.A. Culpepper, 'Designs for the Church in the Imagery of John 21:1-14', in J. Frey *et al.* (eds.), *Imagery in the Gospel*

(3) Another interpretative possibility for 666 associated with counting is gematria. Gematria is a system where each letter of the alphabet is assigned a corresponding numerical value.[412] Totals are determined by adding together each of the assigned numerical values of each letter found in a term. An example of calculating 666 via gematria is the calculation of θηρίον. θηρίον, when transliterated into Hebrew letters – תריון – equals 666 (ת = 400 + ר = 200 + י = 10 + ו = 6 + ן = 50).[413] Gematria invites the churches to a process of discernment where a variety of names or terms could be (and have been) calculated as 666.[414] It is an invitation to a process where the

---

*of John: Terms, Forms, Themes, and Theology of Johannine Figurative Language* (Tübingen: Mohr Siebeck, 2006), pp. 383-94, who concludes that the symbolic meaning of 153 has been lost.

[412] See B.M. Metzger, *The Text of the New Testament: Its Transmission, Corruption, and Restoration* (Oxford: Oxford University Press, 3rd edn, 1992), p. 190 n. 1. For examples of gematria used in the ancient world, see A. Deissmann, *Light from the Ancient East* (Ann Arbor, MI: Baker Book House, 1978), pp. 276-78.

[413] See U. Wilckens, 'χάραγμα', *TDNT* (1974), IX, pp. 416-17. It is important to note that θηρίου ('beast'), transliterated into Hebrew (תריו), equals 616 in the genitive (the case that the term appears in Rev. 13.18). This could explain the textual variant, 616, that appeared in some early manuscripts, see E.F. Lupieri, *A Commentary on the Apocalypse of John* (trans. M.P. Johnson and A. Kamesar; Grand Rapids, MI: Eerdmans, 1999, 2006), p. 216; Koester, *Revelation*, p. 598. For a discussion of the textual variant, see Metzger, *Textual Commentary*, pp. 749-50.

[414] While nearly every Caesar who ruled in the first or second century has been named as the beast (see M. Oberweis, 'Die Bedeutung der neutesta-mentlichen "Rätselzahlen" 666 (Apk 13:18) und 153 (Joh 21:11)', *ZNW* 77.3-4 (1986), p. 228), Nero is one solution that has received much attention, see especially Bauckham, *Climax of Prophecy*, pp. 384-452. The Greek title, Νέρων Καίσαρ, when transliterated into Hebrew, נרון קסר, adds up to 666. Further evidence for Nero is the textual variant, 616, which if the title 'Caesar Nero' is transliterated from Latin (rather than Greek) into Hebrew the sum is 616. While Nero fits within the polyvalent nature of this text; the solution 'Caesar Nero' does have some difficulties. First, there is no evidence that Nero was calculated to be 666 in early church interpreters, outside the possibilities that 616 refers to Nero. This point is significant considering that many early church interpreters used gematria to discern this text, see Weinrich (ed.) *Revelation*, pp. 210-13, contra F.X. Gumerlock, 'Nero Antichrist: Patristic Evidence for the Use of Nero's Naming in Calculating the Number of the Beast (Rev 13:18)', *WTJ* 68.2 (2006), pp. 347-60. Second, there is no explicit reference to Nero in the Apocalypse. Third, the convenience of Nero can ignore the difficult process of discernment that would have been required to arrive at נרון קסר. Fourth, as Smalley, *Revelation*, p. 352 astutely remarks Nero 'by no means exhausts the interpretation and significance of 666, which in any case is broader and deeper'. Concerning the 'unusual spelling' of נרון קסר for Nero, see Mounce, *The*

churches encounter an equation with a 'solution' that lacks any other explicit variables ($x = 666$). There is no other explicit evidence disclosed in Revelation of a name or a term that should be calculated as 666.[415] The invitation directs the churches to consider a variety of individuals, nations, or systems that might be manifestations of the beast, suggesting that the identity of the beast is polyvalent and fluid. This polyvalent characteristic of the beast is not surprising regarding the expansive actions of the beast. The beast receives worship from the whole earth, has complete military and political authority, and achieves board control over the economy, preventing anyone who does not take the mark from buying or selling. These actions seem to expand beyond any one individual.

(4) A final interpretative possibility to be explored when calculating 666 is the 'symbolic' significance of 666.[416] In Revelation, other numbers have 'symbolic' values, e.g. seven represents completeness. When considering 666, it is possible that 666 accentuates the triple sixes (six, six, six), rather than the value of six hundred and sixty-six. If 666 denotes triple sixes, then it is possible that six represents incompleteness: six falls one short of the complete seven; six is the penultimate number. The threefold repetition (six, six, six) adds emphasis to such incompleteness. However, while numbers have symbolic meaning in Revelation, there does not seem to be evidence that six represents incompleteness in any other location in the narrative. In fact, the first appearance of the numeral six describes the six wings of the four living creatures (4.8). Though the sixth seal and sixth trumpet are penultimate in their respective septet series, neither the sixth seal nor trumpet are comprised of any inherently incomplete

---

*Book of Revelation*, p. 262 and D.R. Hillers, 'Revelation 13:18 and a Scroll from Murabba'at', *BASOR* 170 (1963), p. 65.

[415] Andrew of Caesarea, 'Commentary on the Apocalypse', p. 163, writes, 'For, were it necessary, as some of the teachers say, that such a name be clearly known, the seer would have revealed it'. Caird, *Revelation of St. John*, p. 174, notes, 'A sum has only one correct answer, but an answer may be the answer to many sums'. See also Oberweis, '"Rätselzahlen"', p. 228, who adds, 'Gerade die Vielfalt der vorgeschlagenen Interpretationen unterstreicht, dass mit dem angewandten gematrischen Verfahren keine letztgültige Klarheit zu erlangen ist'.

[416] For this interpretation, see P.S. Minear, *I Saw a New Earth: An Introduction to the Visions of the Apocalypse* (Washington, DC: Corpus Books, 1968), pp. 258-60; Beale, *The Book of Revelation*, pp. 718-28; Smalley, *Revelation*, pp. 350-53.

elements and do not seem to convey a distinct meaning that is separate from the other enumerated seals/trumpets.[417] In other words, the sixth seal/trumpet awaits the completion represented in the seventh seal/trumpet along with seals/trumpets 1–5.

The four interpretative options described above suggest that the calculation of 666 can be and has been approached from numerous vantages points, where each interpretative option conveys an element of the beast. While it is possible to settle on one interpretative option, it seems that the text invites the churches to discern the polyvalent character of the beast.[418] The polyvalent solutions seem to subvert any certainty of discovering *the* beast and *the* number. Despite the polyvalent nature of the beast, or perhaps because of it, the text directs the churches to a careful and diligent process of calculation and discernment. What does this process of pneumatic discernment entail? (1) Calculating the number of the beast involves ears that are attuned to other texts, which seems to include 1 Kings 10-11. (2) Calculating 666 is a laborious process of calculation.[419] Pneumatic discernment is not a simple or easy process; rather, it requires toil and

---

[417] Further evidence against this option includes the *seven* churches on account that the sixth church does not represent incompleteness. Another avenue explored in this option is the number, 888, which is the sum of the letters in the name, Jesus. While there might be some comparison or contrast between 666 and 888, in Revelation the numeral 8 will have a negative conation specifically in relation to the eighth in Revelation 18. It is also difficult to determine that if the churches utilized gematria to calculate the number of Jesus (888), they would then have utilized gematria to calculate 666.

[418] Rowland, *Revelation*, p. 114, adds, 'We are probably right to refuse to be tied down to one possible interpretation of this enigmatic passage'. Such an interpretative possibility is noticeable in Paul, 'The Value of Paul Ricoeur's Hermeneutic', p. 202, who writes:

> This process of universalising creates images that are trans-historical, even whilst they spring from specific historical referents. This apocalyptic imagery has at its heart a certain ambiguity towards its historical context, being rooted in it and yet struggling to transcend it at the same time. And it is ambiguity which at once makes the imagery in Rev 12 and 13 appear to be universally applicable to every oppressive regime that there has ever been, and so makes the commentator reluctant to tie it to the one situation of its origin ... So any ambiguity concerning the historical context of Revelation is an ambiguity that flows from the nature of the text itself.

See also Boesak, *Comfort and Protest*, pp. 93-94; Thompson, 'Spirit Possession', pp. 147-48.

[419] Smalley, *Revelation*, p. 352, goes as far to identify the process of calculating by gematria as 'torturous'.

struggle. (3) Since Revelation does not offer explicit indicators to whom the number refers, the numerous interpretative options can generate uncertainty, obscurity, and disorientation.[420] While aspects of the identity of the beast are exposed in the calculation of its number, the vision of the churches remains hazy. (4) This uneasiness and uncertainty arouse vigilant discernment on behalf of the churches. Though the calculation of the beast might disorient the churches, the uncertainty that accompanies this disorientation is not so the churches will embark on an impossible task. This process is not frivolous, even though the churches might not arrive at a definite and certain answer. Rather, frivolousness results from any solution that terminates the process of discernment or ceases calculation.[421] This process of discernment, which is detailed, attentive, and laborious sharpens the discerning skills of the churches, shaping them into careful and attentive discerners who are dependent on the wisdom of the Spirit. The text is disorienting, and in this moment of disorientation, the Spirit re(dis)orients the churches by providing wisdom, truth, understanding, endurance, and discernment of the Lamb from God.[422]

---

[420] This point is especially significant in comparison to the overt identification of the dragon as Satan, the Devil, and the deceiver of the whole earth. E.B. Allo, *L'Apocalypse* (Paris: Lecoffre, 1921), p. 193, proposes that this text is intentionally obscured to protect the author and the churches should Revelation fall into the wrong hands. He writes 'Ce n'est donc pas la simple habitude apocalyptique, c'est un calcul de prudence qui l'a fait parler dans cette façon obscure'. While I agree with Allo concerning the obscurity found in the mark of the beast, it is beyond the scope of this study to comment on the intentions of the author. Koester, *Revelation and the End of All Things*, pp. 159-61, notes that Revelation is not concealing its message from Roman captors because a 'city set on seven hills' was a common description for Rome 'that not even the most obtuse Roman censor would have missed the point'. Contra Beasley-Murray, *The Book of Revelation*, p. 219, who suggests that number is not a riddle and would have been known to the readers.

[421] Sweet, *Revelation*, p. 217, goes as far to say, 'So the call for *wisdom* is not to decipher the number, but to recognize its significance, and act'. Ellul, *Apocalypse*, p. 98, similarly comments, 'wisdom or discernment does not have to do with deciphering the number 666 itself: it is a matter of discerning what is happening around us'. See also Wilcock, *The Message of Revelation*, pp. 128-31; A.F. Johnson, *Revelation* (EBC; Grand Rapids, MI: Zondervan, 1996), p. 138.

[422] Some early church interpreters followed a similar approach: Irenaeus, 'Against Heresies', in P. Schaff (ed.), *The Complete Ante-Nicene & Nicene and Post-Nicene Church Fathers Collection* (Catholic Way Publishing, Kindle edn), 5.30.3, writes, 'It is therefore more certain, and less hazardous, to await the fulfilment of the prophecy, than to be making surmises, and casting about for any names that may present themselves, inasmuch as many names can be found possessing the number

While the polyvalent nature of the beast is revealed in the interpretative possibilities described above, the calculation of 666, the
number of the beast, must not be calculated apart from the previous
descriptions of the beast in the text. The text has already offered
clues to the beast's identities. As the churches reflect on these characteristics of the beast, they might recognize manifestations of the
beast among them. The beast makes war on and murders the two
witnesses. In Philadelphia and Pergamum, the beast manifests in association with the throne of Satan and one who strikes with the
sword (cf. 13.7). In Smyrna, those who slander the church correspond to the blasphemous activities of the beast (cf. 13.5). In Ephesus, Pergamum, and Thyatira, Jezebel, Balaam, and the Nicolaitans
spread deceit, lies, and false teaching that is similar to the beast who
deceitfully propagates false worship through signs and wonders that
mimic the divine Spirit (cf. 13.12-15). In Laodicea, the enticement of
economic success is closely associated with the beast who persuades
the world to worship the image of the beast through buying and selling (cf. 13.17). Those who have pneumatic discernment recognize
that the beast is identified as: whoever is falsely worshipped, whoever
persecutes and murders, whoever creates false images, whoever has
absolute military power, whoever controls commerce, whoever deceives the world with false teachings, false prophecy, false religion,
and signs and wonders, whoever blasphemies God, whoever slanders
the people of God, and whoever deceitfully mimics the one on the
throne, the Lamb, and the seven Spirits.

Revelation 14

The mark of the beast – 666 – on the forehead or right hand contrasts the seal of God that is the name of God and located on the
forehead of the 144,000.[423] The appearance of the 144,000 recalls the
scene in Revelation 7 where the 144,000 morph dialectically into the

---

mentioned; and the same question will, after all, remain unsolved'. See also *COGE*
9.6 (February 9, 1918), p. 1.

[423] A. Corell, 'The 144,000 Sealed', in M. Parvio, E. Segelberg, and J.L. Womer
(eds.), *Ecclesia, Leiturgia, Ministerium: Studia in Honorem Toivo Harjunpää* (Helsinki:
Loimaan Kirjapaino, 1977), p. 34. Bauckham, *Climax of Prophecy*, pp. 398-400, concludes that the contrast between 666 and 144,000 extends to the type of numbers;
triangular numbers such as 666 represent the beast, and square numbers such as
144 represent the people of God. However, 144,000 is not a square number; rather,
the number 144 is a square number. See also Schüssler Fiorenza, *Justice and Judgment*,
p. 181; Beale, *The Book of Revelation*, p. 733; Smalley, *Revelation*, p. 349.

great crowd who represent the whole people of God.[424] Having the name of God on the heads of the 144,000 reveals that they belong to God. There is a dualism between those who identify with God, the Lamb, and the seven Spirits, on the one hand, and those who identify with the evil trinity, on the other hand.[425]

First, 'following the Lamb' identifies the 144,000 with the Lamb's witness and sacrificial death, while denoting that they are the Lamb's disciples.[426] The 144,000 follow the Lamb in witness conveying that they too are true and faithful witnesses. Perhaps, the 144,000, like the two witnesses, were slaughtered by the beast but have been resurrected and ascended.[427] This connection is striking considering that the two witnesses were ascending in their last appearance in the narrative (11.12), and now the 144,000 are found at an elevated location atop Mount Zion. Such a connection might imply that, narratively, the two witnesses have morphed into the 144,000. There is no lie (ψεῦδος) in the mouth of the 144,000, contrasting the 144,000 against the antagonists in Revelation who are characterized as liars and deceivers.[428] The opponents include those in the seven prophetic messages as well as the dragon, the sea beast, and the earth beast.[429] Thus, there is a sharp divide between the people of God and the

---

[424] See Trafton, *Reading Revelation*, p. 133.

[425] Corell, 'The 144,000 Sealed', pp. 32, 34, observes a relationship between the name given to the overcomers and the name of God on the 144,000 foreheads.

[426] M.G. Reddish, 'Followers of the Lamb: Role Models in the Book of Revelation', *PRS* 40.1 (2013), pp. 66-67. ἀκολουθέω is often associated with discipleship in the FG, so Thomas, *The Apocalypse*, p. 426. See also Boxall, *The Revelation of St. John*, p. 202.

[427] Revelation 3.14. Bauckham, *The Theology of the Book of Revelation*, p. 79, writes, 'Thus, the victory of the Lamb's army is the victory of truthful witness maintained as far as sacrificial death'. See also Murphy, *Fallen is Babylon*, p. 320. Smalley, *Revelation*, p. 360 comments:

> The point at issue in this context is the faithful and true *witness* which the faithful bear in their ongoing testimony to God's love shown in Jesus, even to the point of sacrifice (cf. 1.5-6; 2.13). Against the pressures to compromise with idolatrous falsehood (13.18; 14.9-11), the saints are called to maintain with enduring integrity the sharp distinction which exists between truth and error, and between the service of God and the worship of idols.

[428] Pattemore, *The People of God*, p. 190.

[429] Schüssler Fiorenza, *Justice and Judgment*, p. 191; Rowland, *Revelation*, p. 120; P.G.R. de Villiers, 'The Composition of Revelation 14:1–15:8: Pastiche or Perfect Pattern?', *NeoT* 38.2 (2004), p. 217.

people of the beast, which is revealed in one's truthfulness or one's falsehood.[430] Perhaps, like the Lamb, whose seven eyes are the seven Spirits, the truthfulness of the witness of 144,000 derives from a close relationship with the seven Spirits. As the seven Spirits empower the two witnesses, the seven Spirits empower the true and faithful witness of the 144,000 that 'prevails over' the lies and the deceit of the dragon.[431] Whereas the 144,000 are characterized as exemplars in discernment, their discernment extends to their ability to learn or to understand (μαθεῖν, 14.3) the song of the Lamb.[432] The medium of their understanding, a song, further reveals that songs and hymns are instruments of discernment for the churches.

Second, the 144,000 are pure because they resist improper sexual relationships. The purity of the 144,000 recalls those who were washed in the blood of the Lamb. While it is possible that this text refers to actual improper sexual activity, other examples of sexual activity in Revelation suggest that the purity of the 144,000 conveys more than purity in physical relations.[433] The 144,000 have not fornicated with Jezebel;[434] they have not followed the teaching of Balaam;[435] they have not defiled their garments as those in Sardis;[436] they have not been enticed by false teachings or false prophecies. The 144,000 are pure because they have been sanctified in truth (Jn 17.17-19); they are virgins because they have not been seduced by deception.

---

[430] Thomas, *The Apocalypse*, p. 428.

[431] Bauckham, *Climax of Prophecy*, p. 237, observes, 'Their witness to the truth prevails over the lies and deceit of the devil and the beast. For those who reject this witness, it becomes legal testimony *against* them, securing their condemnation. This negative function of witness is present in Revelation. But entails also a positive possibility: that people may be won from illusion to truth.' Howard-Brook and Gwyther, *Unveiling Empire*, p. 219, add, 'Just as they sing with one voice of thunder, so too do they speak with a united voice that is free from imperial propaganda, that voice of sweet deception which tempted all to worship the icon of the Beast (13:5, 12-15)'.

[432] Koester, *Revelation*, p. 609, translates μανθάνω as 'understand'. See also K.H. Rengstorf, 'μανθάνω', *TDNT*, IV, pp. 407-408.

[433] See Schüssler Fiorenza, *Justice and Judgment*, pp. 190-91; Koester, *Revelation*, pp. 610-11.

[434] Schüssler Fiorenza, *Justice and Judgment*, pp. 190-91.

[435] Howard-Brook and Gwyther, *Unveiling Empire*, p. 218; Pattemore, *The People of God*, pp. 186-87.

[436] Revelation 3.4. Prigent, *The Apocalypse*, p. 434.

The following characterization further suggests that the 144,000 are inclusive of the whole people of God that is not exclusive to one's sex or sexual activity:

οὗτοι οἱ ἀκολουθοῦντες τῷ ἀρνίῳ ὅπου ἂν ὑπάγῃ· οὗτοι ἠγοράσ-θησαν ἀπὸ τῶν ἀνθρώπων ἀπαρχὴ τῷ θεῷ καὶ τῷ ἀρνίῳ.

These ones are following the Lamb whenever the Lamb goes. These ones were bought from the first-fruits of humanity to God and to the Lamb (14.4).

The appearance of ἠγοράσθησαν ('bought') implies that the economic activity of the 144,000 is contrary to those who have the mark of the beast and who are provided unlimited purchasing power. However, those who are sealed by God are purchased (ἠγοράσθησαν) by the Lamb, worship God, belong to God, and are protected by God.[437] On the one hand, those who are marked by the beast appear to receive economic success and opportunity; on the other hand, the 144,000 are purchased by God and are protected by God, while those who are marked by the beast will be judged by God (14.9-11).[438]

Third, the appearance of another angel who proclaims the everlasting gospel (εὐαγγέλιον αἰώνιον εὐαγγελίσαι) recalls the mighty angel in Revelation 10 who proclaimed the mystery of God.[439] The mystery of God was completed in the seventh trumpet and was proclaimed to the prophets. The mystery of God was closely associated with Jesus Christ, who is revealed and is being revealed, and the giving of the Spirit. These two appearances of εὐαγγέλιον ('proclaim') in Revelation form an inclusio that encompasses the narrative of the

---

[437] Howard-Brook and Gwyther, *Unveiling Empire*, pp. 218-19; Boring, *Revelation*, p. 168; Osborne, *Revelation*, p. 530.

[438] Pattemore, *The People of God*, p. 182, writes:

Ch. 13 poses the problem: if the sealing marked God's people for pro-tection, how is it that those with the mark of the beast are the ones who enjoy security and prosperity? Rev. 14:1 returns to an emphatic statement of the thesis ... Despite appearances, in reality it is those who resist the beast and its mark who are owned by God, who share companionship with the Lamb, and who are marked as conquerors. Once again the apocalyptic images of the vision are tied to the reality of the lives of the audience.

[439] Boxall, *The Revelation of St. John*, p. 206, who observes a connection between the gospel in Revelation 10 and 14.

two witnesses, the woman in the wilderness, the dragon, the two beasts, and the 144,000, suggesting that these narratives encompass the εὐαγγέλιον, at least in part. Revelation 14 offers two proper responses to the εὐαγγέλιον: fear God and worship God. God is the one to whom all worship should be directed and the one who is to be feared because God created all things.

Fourth, the gospel proclamation also contains pronouncements of judgment. The judgment includes: the whoring of Babylon and those who worship the beast and its image, who have received its mark. The sexual theme appears again and although the condemnation of actual sexual relationships is possible, the presentation of Babylon alongside the two beasts – who enticed the inhabitants of the earth through the deception, signs and wonders, false worship, and political and military power – suggests that Babylon's πορνείας ('whoring') encompasses more than physical, sexual activity. The πορνείας ('whoring') of Babylon contrasts with the purity of the 144,000.[440] Outside of a variety of possible HB intertexts that could be considered in association with Babylon,[441] the first appearance of Babylon characterizes the city as (1) a city of idolatry and whoring which will be judged for these evil works.[442] (2) The whoring of Babylon reminds the churches of the false teachings and prophecies of Jezebel, the Balaamites, and the Nicolaitans,[443] which attests further that Babylon's sin is related to false prophecy or teachings. (3) In Rev. 9.20-21, sexual immorality appeared as an evil work that was closely connected to false worship and demonic activity, denoting that Babylon's whoring is demonic. (4) The appearance Βαβυλὼν ἡ μεγάλη recalls the great city in Rev. 11.8, which πνευματικῶς is dynamically characterized as Egypt, Sodom, the place where their Lord was cru-

---

[440] Schüssler Fiorenza, *Vision of a Just World*, p. 88.

[441] See P.F. Gregory, 'Its End is Destruction: Babylon the Great in the Book of Revelation', *CTQ* 73.2 (2009), pp. 143-52.

[442] Pattemore, *The People of God*, p. 187, also observes the sexual purity metaphor will become clearer when the hearers encounter the pure bride, the church who is adorned for her husband, the Lamb, for a full discussion of the sexual purity and fornication dialectic in the Apocalypse, see Pattemore, *The People of God*, p. 188.

[443] See D.A. deSilva, 'A Sociorhetorical Interpretation of Revelation 14:6-13: A Call to Act Justly Toward the Just and Judging God', *BBR* 9 (1999), pp. 109-10. Trafton, *Reading Revelation*, p. 134.

cified, and the location of the beasts and the dragon. This close association exposes the great city as another kaleidoscopic location that includes Babylon the great. This literary connection indicates that the beast who killed the two witnesses in the great city is associated with Babylon. On the one hand, in Babylon, there is opposition, oppression, murder, false teachings and prophecy, and demon worship. On the other hand, Babylon is judged and the people of God offer faithful, true, and Spirit-empowered witness in this trans-geographical location.

For a third time, ὧδε ('here [is]') appears in this short narrative section bringing together the need for discernment with the previous two appearances of ὧδε.[444] This third appearance indicates that the call for discernment is structured around the descriptions of the two beasts, the 144,000, and Babylon. Discernment requires having an ear to hear the Spirit, wisdom, knowledge, understanding, calculation, and faithful endurance, which now includes keeping the commandments of God. In what will be the final occurrence of endurance in the narrative,[445] endurance denotes keeping the commandments of God in the face of false worship, prophecy, and teachings from the beast, in addition to withstanding the beast's murderous attacks. As the whole earth worships the image of the beast, enduring discernment is required to identify the false signs and wonders of these beasts who operate in the great city, Babylon.[446]

Following this call for pneumatic discernment, the Spirit interjects with an affirmation: ναί, λέγει τὸ πνεῦμα ('Yes, says the Spirit').[447] Whereas much emphasis has been placed on discernment and hearing the Spirit throughout Revelation, the rhetorical effect of the Spirit's interjection would not be missed by the hearers.[448] Hearing

---

[444] Beale, *The Book of Revelation*, p. 766.

[445] Osborne, *Revelation*, p. 543.

[446] This is the seventh and final appearance of endurance in the Apocalypse (1.9; 2.2, 3, 19; 3.10, 13.10).

[447] Murphy, *Fallen is Babylon*, p. 325, writes, 'The choice Christians face is so crucial that the Spirit intervenes to confirm the truth of the beatitude (14:13)'.

[448] deSilva, 'A Sociorhetorical Interpretation of Revelation 14:6-13', p. 111, writes, 'the Spirit testifies to the truth of what the voice has said, acting thus as the faithful witness to the truth which is a primary role of the Spirit in Johannine discourse'. Thomas, *The Apocalypse*, p. 440, comments, 'Owing to the numerous ways in which the Spirit has spoken to and communicated with the hearers throughout the Apocalypse, the numerous times that they have received divine assistance in

the Spirit in this text recalls the sevenfold exhortations to hear what the Spirit is saying to the churches. This interjection reminds the churches that, as they hear the words of this prophecy, they are simultaneously hearing the Spirit, and, ναί ('Yes'), the Spirit's words are true. This interjection reveals that the Spirit has an independent voice and is not confined to speak the words of Jesus solely, even though the Spirit spoke only the words of Jesus in the seven prophetic messages.[449] The Spirit's affirmation connects the churches' vigilant pneumatic discernment and their true and faithful witness to the possibility of death, comforting those who die for their witness.[450]

Following the Spirit's interjection, the churches again encounter ὅμοιον υἱὸν ἀνθρώπου ('one like the son of humanity') which recalls the opening scene of Revelation where ὅμοιον υἱὸν ἀνθρώπου had fiery discerning eyes and revealed the mystery of the seven stars and seven lampstands. ὅμοιον υἱὸν ἀνθρώπου has a sharp sickle and reaps a ripe grain harvest from the earth. While it is possible that the grain harvest represents a negative judgment,[451] this grain harvest recalls the 144,000 who are described as the first fruits, suggesting that the grain harvest has positive connotations.[452] A second corresponding harvest follows the description of the grain harvest – a grape harvest – that is reaped by two angels. The angel who has a sickle reaps the grapes and places the grapes into τὴν ληνὸν τοῦ θυμοῦ τοῦ θεοῦ τὸν μέγαν ('the great winepress of the wrath of God', 14.19),which reminds the churches of Babylon's judgment, specifically τοῦ οἴνου τοῦ θυμοῦ τῆς πορνείας αὐτῆς ('of the wine of wrath of her whoring', 14.8).[453] Evoking the winepress of God's great wrath implies that these judgments are directed to those who would not repent from

---

such discernment, it would certainly not surprise the hearers to hear directly from the Spirit at this point'. See Sorke, *Identity and Function of the Seven Spirits*, pp. 74-75.

[449] Bauckham, *The Theology of the Book of Revelation*, p. 117.

[450] Archer, *'I Was in the Spirit on the Lord's Day'*, p. 237, adds, 'It is not insignificant that the crucial task of discernment to ensure that the churches' works are pleasing to Jesus is here connected to the death of the faithful'.

[451] See Beale, *The Book of Revelation*, pp. 772-76.

[452] Ladd, *Revelation of John*, p. 200; Schüssler Fiorenza, *Vision of a Just World*, p. 90; Bauckham, *Climax of Prophecy*, p. 291; Smalley, *Revelation*, p. 374; Thomas, *The Apocalypse*, p. 443; Koester, *Revelation*, pp. 624, 628-29.

[453] Bauckham, *Climax of Prophecy*, p. 291; Thomas, *The Apocalypse*, p. 445; Koester, *Revelation*, pp. 625, 630.

their πορνείας ('whoring') with Babylon (14.8, 10). The judgment is vast, violent, and bloody.[454] The winepress is located outside the city indicating that those in the city are protected from the judgment of the grape harvest. This protected city recalls the holy city which is measured and protected by God (11.2).[455]

## Summary of Revelation 12–14

First, discernment is a primary theme in Revelation 12–14, accentuated by a threefold appearance of ὧδε ('here [is]'). Each of the recurrences of ὧδε dynamically joins together: if anyone has an ear, hear what the Spirit is saying to the churches, wisdom, understanding, faith, endurance, calculation, and keeping the commandments of God; this is in addition to the call to discern πνευματικῶς. The climax of the churches' discernment in this section concludes with an interjection from the Spirit who affirms their discernment and promises rest for those who die confronting the beast. Having an ear to hear the Spirit requires that those in the churches have both patient endurance in the face of physical violence as well as pneumatic discernment in the face of the deception of the dragon and the beasts. Whilst discerning the deceitful activities of the beast, the Spirit offers wisdom, discernment, and understanding to the churches in order that they might identify the beast and calculate the number of the beast.

Second, this narrative section introduces and expands on the primary antagonists in the Apocalypse, which are identified as the dragon, the sea beast, and the earth beast. A common characterization of the evil trinity is deceit. They use miracles, signs and wonders, and economic enticements to coerce the inhabitants of the earth to worship the image of the beast. This evil trinity persecutes and makes war on the churches, murders the inhabitants of the earth, has absolute military power, extensive control over commerce, and blasphemies and slanders the people of God, while deceitfully mimicking the

---

[454] Koester, *Revelation*, pp. 630-31, proposes that the amount of blood partly derives from the violence and brutality in the world.

[455] Mounce, *The Book of Revelation*, p. 281, observes, 'The judgment of God, portrayed ideally as taking place outside the holy city, extends to all people everywhere who find themselves beyond the pale of divine protection'. Boxall, *The Revelation of St. John*, p. 215, adds that the trampling of the grapes is a direct response to the trampling of the holy city. So also González and González, *Revelation*, p. 97; Trafton, *Reading Revelation*, p. 140.

divine trinity. However, the source of its power and authority, the dragon, is a defeated foe.

Third, the characterization of the evil triumvirate offers a tension. On the one hand, the beasts and the dragon are monstrous entities that would be easily recognizable, especially considering their murderous, oppressive, slanderous, blasphemous, and ruling activities. The beast clearly marks its followers. On the other hand, the satanic trinity deceitfully mimics the divine trinity. The beast has the ability to perform signs and wonders, even giving πνεῦμα ('spirit') to the image of the beast. The beast dies and is resurrected like the slaughtered Lamb. This mimicry alerts the churches that the differentiation between the actions of the evil trinity and the holy trinity can be difficult to distinguish. The text suggests that the manifestations of the beast are not always obvious and thereby require vigilant pneumatic discernment.[456] The process required to calculate 666 suggests that pneumatic discernment is a laborious and challenging process, which might not lead to a clear solution.

## Revelation 15–16

The next scene depicts another sign in heaven: seven angels with the seven bowls of plagues of God's wrath,[457] which narratively picks up on the last septet that ended in Revelation 11. The people of God have morphed once again in this narrative stretch from the two witnesses to the 144,000 atop Mount Zion, and now they have ascended to heaven and have kaleidoscopically transformed into the overcomers who surround a glassy sea. Following the description of the grain and grape harvests, it seems that the description of the overcomers recapitulates the grain harvest, while the seven plagues of God's wrath correspond to the grape harvest. The seven bowls will complete the wrath of God expressing finality. As the seventh trumpet

---

[456] Koester, *Revelation and the End of All Things*, p. 136, Koester helpfully pens, 'John did not make such a sharp distinction because the alternatives were obvious to his readers, but because the alternatives were not obvious'. Rowland, *Revelation*, p. 114, adds, 'It is easy to confuse the way of the beast and the way of the Messiah … So watchfulness is essential to avoid being taken in by false messiahs and end up supporting injustice and oppression'. See also Grabiner, *Revelation's Hymns*, p. 197; Archer, *'I Was in the Spirit on the Lord's Day'*, pp. 234-35.

[457] Koester, *Revelation*, p. 631, writes, 'Heavenly signs like those of the woman and dragon disclose God's purposes (12:1, 3), whereas the signs performed by the beast's agents are deceptive (13:13-14; 16:14; 19:20)'.

completed (ἐτελέσθη) the mystery of God, the seven bowls will complete (ἐτελέσθη) the wrath of God.[458] The occurrence of ὁ θυμὸς τοῦ θεοῦ ('the wrath of God', 15.1) recalls τὴν ληνὸν τοῦ θυμοῦ τοῦ θεοῦ τὸν μέγαν ('the great winepress of the wrath of God') used to press the grape harvest (14.19-20), suggesting that these judgments are closely connected, if not describing the same events.

The scene in Rev. 15.2 describes the overcomers who are in heaven and surround a glassy sea mixed with fire. The glassy sea and fire recall the glassy sea and the seven torches before the divine throne in Revelation 4.[459] A variety of texts converge with the appearance of the overcomers. (1) The hymn in Rev. 12.11 describes the overcomers who overcome the universal deceit of the dragon. Overcoming included the word of their witness, the blood of the Lamb, and that they did not love their lives until death. (2) The overcomers have harps in their hands implying continuity between the overcomers and the 24 elders. Additionally, the overcomers stand by the glassy sea, suggesting that there is a connection between the 144,000/great crowd who stand before the divine throne (where the glassy sea is located) and the overcomers.[460] (3) As the slaughtered Lamb overcame and stands on the divine throne, it is possible that the overcomers died – in a conflict against the beast – and now stand, as they have been resurrected.[461] (4) It is noteworthy that the sevenfold call to overcome and the sevenfold call to hear the Spirit were joined together in the seven prophetic messages. The overcomers overcame, in part, because they discerned the voice of the Spirit (which is coterminous with the voice of Jesus) against the deceitful words of the beast.[462] Hence, the close association of overcoming and hearing the

---

[458] Sweet, *Revelation*, p. 239; Osborne, *Revelation*, p. 561.

[459] Mangina, *Revelation*, p. 181, suggests that the fire represents 'the pentecostal fire'.

[460] Michaels, *Revelation*, p. 182, observes a possible connection between the song of the 144,000 in Rev. 14.2-3 to the song of Moses and the song of the Lamb. See also Boxall, *The Revelation of St. John*, p. 218.

[461] Smalley, *Revelation*, p. 385; Thomas, *The Apocalypse*, p. 452.

[462] Koester, *Revelation*, p. 634, astutely comments:

Satan and his allies seek to dominate the world by deception and coercion (12:9; 13:14; 18:23), and the beast conquers the faithful by slaying them (11:7; 13:7). This creates a crisis of perception, since it would appear that the beast has

Spirit in the seven prophetic messages indicates that overcoming requires pneumatic discernment. The ones whom the people of God overcome include the beasts and the dragon who embody deception, coercion, political and military authority, false worship, and unlimited economic power.[463]

The overcomers sing the song of Moses and the song of the Lamb (15.3-4).[464] Moses alludes to Israel's deliverance out of Egypt. However, while the churches might have anticipated a song resembling the text of Exodus 15[465] or perhaps Deuteronomy 32,[466] they hear a new song intersecting with a variety of HB texts.[467] Those who hear the song πνευματικῶς recognize that Egypt is πνευματικῶς part of the collage that is the great city, which kaleidoscopically morphs into Babylon, Sodom, and the place where their Lord was crucified.[468] As the overcomers stand by the glassy sea, they have been delivered out of the great city, which is the location of the beast; the one whom the overcomers overcome. The song of Moses and the Lamb assists the churches in their discernment as with other hymns in Revelation. The assistance entails a characterization of God who is great, marvelous, just and true, the king of the nations, holy, who

---

triumphed and that resistance is futile. Yet the visions from heaven alter the readers' perspectives by showing that those who witness to God, even at the cost of their lives, are true conquerors. Capitulating to a lie is defeat, while refusing to do so is a victory, since it means that deception and coercion have not suppressed the truth.

[463] Archer, 'I Was in the Spirit on the Lord's Day', p. 239.

[464] Thomas, *The Apocalypse*, p. 452.

[465] See Bauckham, *Climax of Prophecy*, pp. 296-307, who offers an extended examination of Rev. 15.2-4 and considers Rev. 15.2-4 to be a 'beneath the surface' use of a 'Jewish exegetical method' in interpreting Exodus 15.

[466] See Ford, *Revelation*, p. 257.

[467] See S. Moyise, 'Singing the Song of Moses and the Lamb: John's Dialogical Use of Scripture', *AUSS* 42.2 (2004), pp. 347-60, who proposes that the song of the Lamb intersects with a variety of HB intertexts and evokes Israel's deliverance from Egypt, while creating a dialogical tension in the churches who should resolve neither the song of Moses into the song of the Lamb nor the song of the Lamb into the song of Moses.

[468] See Caird, *Revelation of St. John*, p. 197.

is to be feared, glorified, and worshipped by all nations.[469] The appearance of the truthfulness of God serves to contrast the deception and lies propagated by the trinity of evil.[470]

Following the hymn, the seven angels pour out the contents of the seven bowls.[471] The first bowl is poured on those who are marked by the beast and who worship the image of the beast. The mark of the beast recalls the number of the beast, 666. The churches were directed to discern the polyvalent manifestations of the beast and the bestial works in Revelation 13. If anyone does not discern the bestial activities and thereby takes the mark of the beast, then they will be inflicted with sores. Those who have received a mark on their body from the beast now receive a mark of judgment.[472] The next two bowls impact the sea and the waters, which are followed by a hymn that briefly interrupts the sequence to assist the churches in discerning. The hymn indicates that the wrath of God is just, even as these horrific judgments occur because whoever receives this judgment, killed the saints and the prophets (16.6).[473] The affirmation – ναί – from the altar recalls the response of the Spirit in 14.13,[474] suggesting an intimate relationship between the ψυχὰς ('lives') under the altar and the Spirit. The affirming response from the ψυχὰς implies that their previous cry for justice (6.10) is being answered.[475] God's justice is antithetical to the oppression, false worship, deceitfulness, slander,

---

[469] Blount, *Revelation*, p. 289, observes that the appearance of fear, glorify, and worship recalls the everlasting gospel proclaimed in Revelation 14.

[470] Smalley, *Revelation*, p. 387, comments, 'God is all-powerful; and, as Sovereign over the universe, he enables his servants to conquer the evil deception of the beast'. See also Schüssler Fiorenza, *Vision of a Just World*, p. 92; Koester, *Revelation*, p. 636.

[471] Aune, *Revelation 6–16*, p. 881, observes that the occurrence of ἐτελέσθη forms an inclusio around vv. 1-8.

[472] Smalley, *Revelation*, pp. 400-401.

[473] Murphy, *Fallen is Babylon*, p. 331, writes, 'Truth is not merely abstract, a matter of doctrine with tenuous connection to real life. Truth manifests itself in the establishment of justice on earth.'

[474] Michaels, *Revelation*, p. 185; Archer, *'I Was in the Spirit on the Lord's Day'*, p. 246.

[475] D.A. deSilva, 'Final Topics: The Rhetorical Functions of Intertexture in Revelation 14:14–16:21', in F.W. Duane (ed.), *Intertexture of Apocalyptic Discourse in the New Testament* (Atlanta: SBL, 2002), p. 230, writes, 'the victims of human injustice themselves speak as witnesses ... to God's unfailing commitment to bring justice'. See also Aune, *Revelation 6–16*, p. 888.

and murder of the beast and of Babylon. God will not allow their injustices to continue forever.[476]

The next three bowls are poured on humanity, the throne of the beast and its kingdom, and the river Euphrates (16.8-16). The attack on the throne of the beast denotes that its throne cannot withstand the might of God. The throne of the beast was erected on lies and deception. As the throne of the beast is destroyed, the discerning hearers would recall that the beast received its throne and its authority from the dragon – a defeated foe. The penultimate bowl accentuates the deceptive work of the evil trinity. Out of the mouths of the dragon, the beast, and the false prophet come three unclean spirits like frogs. The earth beast is identified as the false prophet, which confirms the earth beast's associations with false religion and worship,[477] while connecting the false prophet to other deceitful antagonists such as Jezebel, the Nicolaitans, and Balaam. The origins of the unclean spirits – from their mouths – recall (1) the dragon who attacked the woman in the wilderness with a flood from its mouth, (2) the beast who blasphemed God from its mouth, while standing in contrast to (3) the true witness of Christ that comes out of his mouth like a sword, and (4) the 144,000 who do not have a lie in their mouths.[478] The occurrence of πνεύματα ('spirits') suggests that the unclean, demonic spirits subtly and deviously impersonate τὰ ἑπτὰ πνεύματα ('the seven Spirits').[479] As the seven Spirits go out into all the earth, these demonic spirits go out to the kings of the whole earth to deceive them. Likewise, these unclean spirits deceive through signs

---

[476] Thomas, *The Apocalypse*, p. 470, comments, 'If the hearers are tempted to misunderstand these wrathful activities of God as too severe, they are immediately reassured that they come from the hand of a righteous God whose ways are "true and righteous" (15.3)'. See also deSilva, 'Final Topics', p. 225.

[477] Stefanović, *Revelation*, p. 495.

[478] Thomas, 'The Role of the Demonic in the Johannine Tradition', p. 41. See also Caird, *Revelation of St. John*, p. 206; Sweet, *Revelation*, p. 249; Resseguie, *The Revelation of John*, p. 213.

[479] Boxall, *The Revelation of St. John*, pp. 231-32, comments:

The capacity of this satanic trinity to deceive and lead astray runs like a shocking thread throughout the second half of this book. It is Revelation's bold claim that, far from being crystal clear to the undiscerning eye, the dividing line between good and evil, truth and falsehood, is very subtle indeed. True discernment requires divine revelation, an apocalyptic unveiling of the true state of affairs such as this book claims to mediate.

and wonders like the beast who parodied the seven Spirits.[480] Strikingly, this is the first appearance of an 'unclean spirit' in the Johannine literature and clearly ties 'unclean' to falsehood, deception, and war.[481]

In Rev. 16.16, Harmageddon in Hebrew seems to translate as 'Mount Megiddo'.[482] Strikingly, the term καλούμενον ('called') recalls the great city that is καλεῖται πνευματικῶς ('called Spiritually') Sodom, Egypt, and the place where their Lord was crucified, suggesting that Harmageddon is another piece of the geographical collage that constructs the great city. Hence, as the churches continue to discern with the eyes of the Spirit, they would recognize that the great city has expanded its territory to include the location where these deceitful spirits gather the whole earth to war against God kaleidoscopically. Upon πνευματικῶς discerning Mount Megiddo, the churches might detect a contrast between the 144,000 who stand on Mount Zion and those who are deceived by these unclean spirits.[483] Furthermore, there is likely an element of satire present in this text because Megiddo is not a mountain at all but a *plain* where numerous

---

[480] Minear, *I Saw a New Earth*, p. 148, writes, 'It was primarily a test of discernment, for Christians were more vulnerable to unconscious than to conscious treasons. They were susceptible especially to demonic spirits (parody of the Holy Spirit) which performed miracles (parody of genuine charismata) through the work of false prophets (16:13-16).' See also Beale, *The Book of Revelation*, p. 834; Sorke, *Identity and Function of the Seven Spirits*, p. 269.

[481] This association between cleanness, holiness, and discernment aligns closely with Jesus' prayer in the Farewell materials: ἁγίασον αὐτοὺς ἐν τῇ ἀληθείᾳ· ὁ λόγος ὁ σὸς ἀλήθειά ἐστιν ('sanctify them in the T/truth. Your W/word is Truth', Jn 17.17). See also Beale, *The Book of Revelation*, p. 831; Thomas, 'The Role of the Demonic in the Johannine Tradition', p. 41.

[482] J. Day, 'The Origin of Armageddon: Revelation 16:16 as an Interpretation of Zechariah 12:11', in S.E. Porter, P. Joyce, and D. Orton (eds.), *Crossing the Boundaries: Essays in Biblical Interpretation in Honour of Michael D. Goulder* (Leiden: Brill, 1994), p. 320, observes in the context of Zech. 12.11, where the eschatological battle occurs on the plain of Megiddo, the false prophets and unclean spirits (רוח הטמאה) will be cleansed from the land (Zech. 13.2). M. Jauhiainen, 'The OT Background to Armageddon (Rev 16:16) Revisited', *NovT* 47.4 (2005), pp. 380-93, engages Day and proposes that the reference to 'in Hebrew' suggests that Harmageddon should be translated 'the mountain of slaughter' and alludes to the destruction of Babylon.

[483] Keener, *Revelation*, p. 396; Thomas, 'The Role of the Demonic in the Johannine Tradition', pp. 41-42.

battles have occurred.[484] As the churches examine Mount Megiddo πνευματικῶς, they might recognize that there is no comparison between Mount Megiddo and Mount Zion. The mountain of the trinity of evil is merely a plain of war and death. The appearance of Mount Megiddo also recalls the eschatological battle described in Zechariah 12 where the unclean spirits and false prophets would be cleansed from the land. In other words, the activity of these demonic spirits to coerce the kings of the earth to war through deceit becomes their own annihilation.

The sixth bowl contains an interjection in the form of a beatitude, which seems to originate from the resurrected Jesus, Ἰδοὺ ἔρχομαι ὡς κλέπτης ('Behold, I am coming as a thief'), which urges the churches to diligent pneumatic discernment (16.15).[485] A similar exhortation occurred in the prophetic message to Sardis (3.3).[486] This exhortation implies that watchfulness (3.3) and not soiling one's garments (3.4) involves overcoming the deceitfulness of the satanic trinity that is manifested as these unclean/demonic spirits.[487] Those who have pneumatically discerned the fraudulent activities of the evil trinity are fully clothed and pure. Conversely, those who have been deceived by the enticements of the evil trinity and their spawn have soiled garments or have become naked.[488]

The bowl series concludes with another appearance of theophanic elements, which completes the wrath of God (16.17-21). An earthquake splits the ἡ πόλις ἡ μεγάλη ('the great city') into three parts. ἡ πόλις ἡ μεγάλη ('the great city') recalls the great city that experienced an earthquake in 11.13; the intertextual collage that includes Egypt, Sodom, the place where their Lord was crucified, the beast, Babylon, and Harmageddon.[489] The trans-geographical and trans-temporal location of murder, death, and opposition has fallen.

---

[484] See Judg. 5.19; 2 Kgs 9.27; 23.29.

[485] Sweet, *Revelation*, p. 247, writes, 'The danger of deception and the threat of Christ's coming is primarily for *them* – lest he come and find them asleep in spite of warning'. Mounce, *The Book of Revelation*, pp. 300-301, adds, 'The kind of spiritual preparedness that Christ requires is the discernment that cuts through the deceptive propaganda of Satan and his henchmen'.

[486] Smalley, *Revelation*, p. 411. Trafton, *Reading Revelation*, p. 149.

[487] Beale, *The Book of Revelation*, p. 837.

[488] Smalley, *Revelation*, pp. 411-12.

[489] See Bauckham, *Climax of Prophecy*, pp. 205-207.

As these cities intersect with Babylon who is fallen (14.8), the churches would discern that any city of tyranny is ultimately and already doomed.[490] The seventh bowl describes colossal hail pouring down on the people. The response of the people is to blaspheme God rather than repent.[491] Strikingly, at least some, despite these dreadful judgments, keep their lives to voice their blasphemous response to God. Again, revealing a stark contrast between the beast who murders anyone who does not exalt the image of the beast and God whose judgments allow the people to voice their blasphemy against God. Previously, blasphemy was an action of the beast; thus, as these characters respond with blasphemy thrice (16.9, 11, 21), it exposes that anyone who worships the beast also takes on the characteristics of the beast.[492]

## Summary of Revelation 15–16

First, the overcomers are characterized as overcoming the beast, which aligns with the description of the overcomers in Revelation 12. Among the possible implications of overcoming, a central aspect includes pneumatically discerning the deception of the triumvirate of evil. This element of discernment is closely associated with the sevenfold call to hear the Spirit in the seven prophetic messages. The overcomers have recognized the voice of the Spirit.

Second, the characterization as deceptive and deceitful of the enemy of the people of God, of the whole world is further revealed in the relationship between the unclean, deceitful, demonic spirits who come from the mouths of the trinity of evil to deceive the whole world. The demonic spirits are active in Harmageddon which seems to be part of the great city as a location of war, deception, and judgment.

---

[490] Smalley, *Revelation*, p. 415.

[491] Gause, *Revelation*, p. 217, comments, 'They treat justice as if it were injustice'. Boxall, *The Revelation of St. John*, p. 220 writes, 'these plagues ... reveal yet again the madness of worshipping the monster'.

[492] Thomas, *The Apocalypse*, p. 477. So also Caird, *Revelation of St. John*, p. 202; Resseguie, *The Revelation of John*, pp. 211-12. Mangina, *Revelation*, p. 183, observes, 'The wrath of God brings to light things long hidden. It exposes truths that the earth-dwellers would prefer to suppress.'

## ἐν πνεύματι – Revelation 17.1–21.8

In Revelation 17, another literary marker, ἐν πνεύματι ('in the Spirit'), occurs that advances the narrative to the next major structural section. As with the previous occurrences of ἐν πνεύματι, the geographical location shifts and in this scene John is in the wilderness.[493] As the churches encounter ἐν πνεύματι, they are reminded that the whole of the Apocalypse is to be discerned via the Spirit; the churches must see πνευματικῶς.[494] Other literary markers that direct the churches to careful pneumatic discernment that appear in this literary section include: mystery, ὧδε ('here [is]'), νοῦς ('discernment'), ὁ ἔχων ('the one having'), and σοφίαν ('wisdom').[495]

### Revelation 17

One of the angels who had one of the seven bowls offers a detailed characterization of the great πόρνη ('whore') who rides a scarlet beast. First, the πόρνη ('whore') is in the wilderness. The geographical location serves to provide a contrast between the woman in the wilderness, who is protected by God (Revelation 12), and the πόρνη ('whore').

Second, the woman is a πόρνη ('whore') suggesting that she commodifies sex and that her success is dependent upon her clients;[496] relations with her are transactions that are economically conditioned.[497] The description of the attire of the πόρνη ('whore'), which

---

[493] Boring, *Revelation*, p. 179, writes, 'the "wilderness" is the place of refuge for the People of God, from which perspective they can see the city for what it is'. Boxall, *The Revelation of St. John*, p. 241, adds that the wilderness 'is the place to which he must go in order to learn true discernment, albeit with angelic assistance'.

[494] Smalley, *Revelation*, p. 428, writes, 'Spiritual perception is an important part of John's apocalyptic drama'.

[495] Sweet, *Revelation*, p. 253, comments, 'his concern is with the church, and with discernment'.

[496] Bauckham, *Climax of Prophecy*, pp. 346-47, observes, 'The basic notion, of course, is that those who associate with a harlot pay her for the privilege ... she is a rich courtesan, whose expensive clothes and jewelry (17.4) indicate the luxurious lifestyle she maintains at her lovers' expense'. For an examination of the 'whore' in the first century, see J.A. Glancy and S.D. Moore, 'How Typical a Roman Prostitute is Revelation's "Great Whore"?', *JBL* 130.3 (2011), pp. 551-69.

[497] Ellul, *Apocalypse*, p. 191, comments, 'Prostitution is the diabolic parody of love'.

includes fine and luxurious jewelry, adornments, and regal clothing,[498] implies that she has been successful in her profession. The purple and scarlet color of her garments contrast with the white garments of the people of God and the cosmic attire – the sun – of the woman in the wilderness.[499] The πόρνη ('whore') commits πορνείας ('whoredom') with the kings of the earth. While πορνείας ('whoredom') might refer to sexual relationships, thus far in Revelation πορνείας ('whoredom') has also been associated with false worship and idolatry (2.21; 9.21).[500] The πορνείας ('whoredom') of the πόρνη ('whore') with the kings and inhabitants of the earth is tied to the judgment of Babylon who is already fallen (14.8). The description of the πορνείας ('whoredom') of the πόρνη ('whore') in Revelation 17 suggests that the πορνείας ('whoredom') of the πόρνη ('whore') includes economic elements.[501] While it is possible that the economic aspect of the great whore's πορνείας ('whoredom') recalls only imperial cultic practices,[502] it seems Revelation offers a more robust view of idolatry where economic prosperity, military power, or political success, themselves, are forms of πορνείας ('whoredom').[503]

*I do not see where it says this about military power?*

---

[498] See Mounce, *The Book of Revelation*, p. 310; Aune, *Revelation 17–22*, p. 935; Stevens, *Revelation*, pp. 466-67.

[499] Cf. 1.14; 2.17; 3.4-5; 3.18; 4.4; 6.11; 7.9, 13-14; 19.14. Minear, *I Saw a New Earth*, p. 151; Roloff, *The Revelation of John*, p. 197.

[500] Newton, *The Revelation Worldview*, p. 129.

[501] E. Schüssler Fiorenza, 'Babylon the Great: A Rhetorical-Political Reading of Revelation 17–18', in D.L. Barr (ed.), *The Reality of Apocalypse: Rhetoric and Politics in the Book of Revelation* (Atlanta, GA: SBL, 2006), p. 262. See also Beale, *The Book of Revelation*, p. 856.

[502] So Beale, *The Book of Revelation*, pp. 853-57.

[503] See Ruiz, *Ezekiel in the Apocalypse*, p. 331, who comments, 'The remainder of Rev 17 and 18 makes it unmistakably clear that such idolatry is not restricted to the cultic sphere, that it is a reality with profound roots in the economic and political arena as well'. See also I.W. Provan, 'Foul Spirits, Fornication and Finance: Revelation 18 from an Old Testament Perspective', *JSNT* 64 (1996), pp. 81-100; K. Siitonen, 'Merchants and Commerce in the Book of Revelation', in M. Labahn and O. Lehtipuu (eds.), *Imagery in the Book of Revelation* (Leuven: Peeters, 2011), pp. 151-57. See also O'Donovan, 'The Political Thought of the Book of Revelation', pp. 84-86 who observes that trade with Babylon is fornication with her.

Third, the success of the πόρνη ('whore') is more extensive than economic or commercial because her scarlet and purple clothing suggests that she has obtained some political power.[504] The political influence of the πόρνη ('whore') is further confirmed by her enthronement upon the beast and upon many waters. That the women is sitting (καθημένης) contrasts other characters who have been described as sitting on thrones, especially the one sitting on the throne who has universal sovereignty.[505] However, the throne of the πόρνη ('whore') – a scarlet beast and many waters – represents that her rule is a different type of rule.[506] The throne of the πόρνη ('whore') is a seven-headed and ten-horned scarlet beast, which recalls the seven-headed and ten-horned beast described in Revelation 13 and the seven-headed, ten-horned red dragon who appeared in Revelation 12.[507] The association of the πόρνη ('whore') with these characters suggests that the πόρνη ('whore') participates in the activities of the beast and dragon, such as murder, slander, blasphemy, false worship, mimicry of the divine, deception, and coercion. However, the characterization that the woman is enthroned on the beast denotes that the beast is subordinate in some manner to the πόρνη ('whore'), which is remarkable considering that the beast represents complete military and political authority. The other throne of the πόρνη ('whore') – the many waters – recalls the water from the mouth of the dragon used to attack the woman in the wilderness along with the origins of the beast.[508] The imagery suggests that the ruling power of the πόρνη ('whore') is associated with the deceit of the dragon and the beast.

[504] See Ellul, *Apocalypse*, p. 194; Gause, *Revelation*, p. 221; Ruiz, *Ezekiel in the Apocalypse*, pp. 324-27; González and González, *Revelation*, p. 112.

[505] Smalley, *Revelation*, p. 428, comments, 'Babylon is a representation of the misuse of power, and of the wrongful desire to usurp the throne of God'. See Thomas, *The Apocalypse*, pp. 492-93, who observes a possible echo of Ps. 29.10 where Yahweh is enthroned upon the flood. For an examination of καθημένης ('sitting'), see Ruiz, *Ezekiel in the Apocalypse*, pp. 306-309.

[506] B.R. Rossing, *The Choice Between Two Cities: Whore, Bride, and Empire in the Apocalypse* (HTS; Harrisburg, Pa: TPI, 1999), pp. 67-68. See also Ford, *Revelation*, p. 277; Aune, *Revelation 17–22*, p. 934; Resseguie, *The Revelation of John*, p. 220; Koester, *Revelation*, p. 684.

[507] Beale, *The Book of Revelation*, p. 853. Smalley, *Revelation*, p. 429.

[508] See Ruiz, *Ezekiel in the Apocalypse*, pp. 308-309.

Fourth, the appearance of γέμον βδελυγμάτων καὶ τὰ ἀκάθαρτα τῆς πορνείας αὐτῆς ('being full of detestable things and the uncleanness of her whoring') suggests these evil deeds have some commonality with each other. The term βδελυγμάτων ('detestable things') appeared in contexts of idolatry in the HB (LXX), while the appearance of ἀκάθαρτα ('uncleanness') recalls the ἀκάθαρτα spirits who originated from the mouths of the evil trinity and who deceived the kings of the whole earth to go to war.[509] The association of βδελυγμάτων ('detestable things') and ἀκάθαρτα ('uncleanness') brings together idolatry and deception. The πόρνη ('whore') operates through deceit and idolatry to coerce the kings and the inhabitants of the earth to do her bidding, which includes war, false worship, political power, and economic achievement.[510]

Fifth, the πόρνη ('whore') is described as having a golden cup, which recalls the wine of her πορνείας ('whoring') and suggests this wine is the contents of her golden cup. The color of the cup, gold, conditions her wine economically.[511] The πόρνη ('whore') used the wine of her πορνείας to intoxicate the inhabitants of the earth (17.2), suggesting that the πόρνη ('whore') uses economic enticements to intoxicate them; and thereby, while inebriated, the πόρνη ('whore') beguiles the tipsy nations.[512] However, as the churches expect her cup to be full of wine, the cup of πόρνη ('whore') is filled with the blood of the saints and the witnesses of Jesus. The wine of her πορνείας ('whoring') transforms into the blood of the saints, suggesting that her πορνείας, her intoxication, her wealth, and her enticements are achieved through oppression and violence.[513] ἔχουσα ποτήριον χρυσοῦν ἐν τῇ χειρὶ αὐτῆς ('having a golden cup in her hand') recalls the cup of the wine of God's wrath, implying that her vile drink is

---

[509] Beale, *The Book of Revelation*, p. 856; Thomas, *The Apocalypse*, p. 497.

[510] Smalley, *Revelation*, p. 430. See M.C. Baines, 'The Identity and Fate of the Kings of the Earth in the Book of Revelation', *RTR* 75.2 (2016), pp. 73-88.

[511] Rowland, 'Revelation', p. 686, comments, 'To commit "fornication" or be "intoxicated" risks compromising both our ability to discern truth and justice and our sense of integrity. The book of Revelation is a challenge to see ourselves as we are seen by God and to see others without the corrupting lens of self-interested exploitation.'

[512] Bauckham, *Climax of Prophecy*, p. 347; Koester, *Revelation*, p. 673.

[513] Aune, *Revelation 17–22*, p. 938.

related to her judgment. In her cup, there is a convergence of seduction, intoxication, false worship, violence, and economic enticements, while also indicating that God will judge anyone who partakes from her golden cup.[514]

Following the detailed introduction of the πόρνη ('whore'), the narrative offers her name,[515] which is a mystery, that is inscribed upon her forehead. The appearance of 'mystery' recalls the two previous appearances of mystery in Revelation (1.20; 10.7) where the resurrected Jesus and the mighty angel assisted the churches in discernment, denoting that the churches will receive assistance in their discernment here.[516] The mystery is described as Βαβυλὼν ἡ μεγάλη, ἡ μήτηρ τῶν πορνῶν καὶ τῶν βδελυγμάτων τῆς γῆς ('Babylon the great, the mother of whores and of the detestable things of the earth'). First, the appearance of Babylon the great further connects Babylon to the great city, which, when viewed πνευματικῶς (11.8), morphs into Sodom, Egypt, the place where their Lord was crucified, and Harmageddon.[517] Discerning the mystery of Babylon the great will require seeing with the seven Spirits, the seven eyes of the Lamb.

---

[514] See Beale, *The Book of Revelation*, p. 849. See also F. King, 'Travesty or Taboo?: "Drinking Blood" and Revelation 17:2-6', *NeoT* 38.2 (2004), pp. 303-25, who detects 'travesty' eucharistic elements in the cup and wine where the drinking of blood might recall John 6.

[515] de Villiers, 'Prime Evil', p. 66, notes, concerning the names of the beast and the πόρνη, 'Readers of the text are reminded in both these cases that they must avail themselves of the knowledge of these names. It is decisive that they know them. This is why, for example, it is said that the name of the beast requires wisdom.'

[516] Ruiz, *Ezekiel in the Apocalypse*, p. 334, writes:

John marks the identification of the Prostitute as a μυστήριον, taking full advantage of the theological and the hermeneutical weight of that term. The identification of the πόρνη is a μυστήριον because of the process in which the reader is invited to undertake: a μυστήριον calls for *hermeneia*. That does not mean we are dealing with a code, a cipher, or a message which was encrypted in order to protect either author or audience from the prying eyes of Roman officials, or that the enigma is merely an intellectual exercise or riddle.

Stefanović, *Revelation*, p. 513, adds, 'Only those endowed with divine discernment are able to grasp the full meaning of the name'. See also P.W. Cheung, 'The Mystery of Revelation 17:5 & 7: A Typological Entrance', *Jian Dao* 18 (2002), pp. 8-9; Boxall, *The Revelation of St. John*, p. 243; Smalley, *Revelation*, p. 431.

[517] Beasley-Murray, *The Book of Revelation*, p. 251; Roloff, *The Revelation of John*, p. 198; Thomas, *The Apocalypse*, p. 498.

Second, the mystery is upon her forehead, suggesting that her name is closely associated with her identity. The 144,000 belong to God and have God's name on their foreheads, while the inhabitants of the earth belong to the beast and have 666 on their foreheads.[518] Third, the connections between Babylon and the πόρνη ('whore') expose that the πόρνη ('whore') is already fallen and already judged (14.8; 16.19). Fourth, the πόρνη ('whore') is the mother of πορνῶν ('whores') and βδελυγμάτων ('detestable things'). As mother, the πόρνη stands in contrast to the woman in the wilderness who gave birth to the male-child.[519] Whereas the woman in the wilderness gave birth to the people of God, the πόρνη ('whore') births πορνῶν ('whores') who commit πορνείας ('whoredom') just as their mother. Her children are deceitful, murderous, unclean, and vile.[520] The πόρνη ('whore') also recalls Jezebel who is a mother (3.23), who is a false prophet, who deceives, and who entices the churches to commit πορνείας ('whoredom'); other false teachings in the churches associated with πορνείας ('whoredom') of the πόρνη ('whore') include the Nicolaitans and the Balaamites (3.14-15).[521] The association of these opponents with the πόρνη ('whore') implies that their false prophecy and teachings might have provided economic or political success to anyone who would follow the 'deep things of Satan', to anyone who would commit πορνείας ('whoredom') with the πόρνη ('whore'). The seductive activities of the πόρνη ('whore') extend beyond the churches to the whole earth; the whole earth is drunk on her deceitful activities. Fifth, the political and economic elements of the πόρνη ('whore') recall Jezebel's characterization in the HB who, as queen, cunningly coerced the elders and leaders to have Naboth killed to acquire a field.[522]

---

[518] Mounce, *The Book of Revelation*, p. 311; Resseguie, *The Revelation of John*, p. 222; Duff, *Who Rides the Beast?*, pp. 85-87.

[519] Gause, *Revelation*, p. 222.

[520] Smalley, *Revelation*, p. 432.

[521] A point made by Schüssler Fiorenza, 'Babylon the Great', p. 263. See also Blount, *Revelation*, p. 312; Resseguie, *The Revelation of John*, p. 222; Duff, *Who Rides the Beast?*, pp. 89-92.

[522] 1 Kings 21.5-15. See Beale, *The Book of Revelation*, p. 884, for an examination of the parallels between Jezebel in the HB and the great whore.

Sandwiched in-between the two appearances of mystery (17.5, 7), John, upon seeing the great πόρνη ('whore') riding on a scarlet beast, marvels a great marvel. Is it possible that John, the prophet and one who is ἐν πνεύματι ('in the Spirit'), is being seduced by the πόρνη ('whore') and tempted to worship her?[523] Strikingly, the same language – marveling – occurred in the description of the people who worshipped the beast (13.3; 17.8), whose names are not found in the book of life.[524] References to those who are written in the book of life appear in Rev. 13.8; 17.8. The contexts of these previous appearances explicitly contain calls for pneumatic discernment, suggesting that those whose names are written in the book of life have pneumatically discerned the deceitful façade of the beast and the whore.[525] Such an association suggests that John acts in a similar manner to the inhabitants of the earth.[526] He is lacking discernment and is in danger of wrongfully worshipping the whore and the beast.[527] John's misguided attempt to worship the whore reveals the depth of her deception. Thus, it is not by coincidence that the angel's next action is to expose the mystery of the great whore (πόρνη).[528] The angel's response is to direct John to discernment, which implies that false worship correlates directly to a lack of discernment.[529] In other words,

---

[523] Thomas, *The Apocalypse*, p. 502, writes, 'If John who is "in the Spirit" at the time, could be so tempted, could anyone be immune from such seduction?' See also Michaels, *Revelation*, pp. 193-94; Archer, *'I Was in the Spirit on the Lord's Day'*, pp. 255-56; Koester, *Revelation*, p. 676.

[524] Caird, *Revelation of St. John*, p. 213; Murphy, *Fallen is Babylon*, p. 357; Barr, *Tales of the End*, p. 133; Resseguie, *The Revelation of John*, p. 222.

[525] So Beale, *The Book of Revelation*, p. 867, who writes that those written in the book 'are not deceived by the beast and do not worship him. Their protection is shown by their possession of "an understanding having wisdom"; such wisdom discerns the falsehood of the beast and prevents them from being deceived into following him.' Also, Prigent, *The Apocalypse*, p. 491, adds, 'Only those whose names are in the book of life will find the discernment and the courage necessary to refuse this cult'.

[526] Gause, *Revelation*, p. 223; Ruiz, *Ezekiel in the Apocalypse*, p. 340; Resseguie, *The Revelation of John*, p. 223.

[527] Beale, *The Book of Revelation*, pp. 866-67.

[528] Murphy, *Fallen is Babylon*, p. 357.

[529] Ruiz, *Ezekiel in the Apocalypse*, p. 351, writes, 'The placement of the angel's offer to explain the μυστήριον between John's admission ἐθαύμασα … θαῦμα μέγα and καὶ θαυμασθήσονται οἱ κατοικοῦντες ἐπὶ τῆς γῆς implies that reflection on the vision as a μυστήριον is the only way out of θαῦμα. The

because John was unable to recognize the true identity of the πόρνη ('whore'), he was susceptible to her deceptions, which ultimately leads to false worship. The text via the angel unveils the character of the great whore, offering a pneumatic perception. If John the prophet who is ἐν πνεύματι ('in the Spirit') is unable to discern the deceptive appearance of the whore by the Spirit, then the churches who are also ἐν πνεύματι ('in the Spirit') will require assistance to recognize this evil.

First, the angel directs the churches to discern πνευματικῶς the scarlet beast. The scarlet color of the beast suggests a relationship between the whore, the beast, and the great red dragon.[530] The description that the beast was, is not, and is about to ascend from the bottomless pit and go to destruction expresses further that the beast parodies God who was, is, and is to come as well as the Lamb who died and is resurrected.[531] That the beast ascends from the bottomless pit unites the scarlet beast in Revelation 17 with the beast who arose from the abyss in 11.6 and overcame the two witnesses.[532] The connection to Revelation 11 further conveys that the ever-morphing beast must be discerned πνευματικῶς. This connection reveals another aspect of the kaleidoscopic nature of the great city where Babylon, the beast, the dragon, and the whore fuse into a unique transmutative reality along with Egypt, Sodom, the place where their Lord was crucified, and Harmageddon. The ever-shifting nature of evil urges pneumatic discernment.

Before the unveiling of the mystery of the seven heads and ten horns of the beast, the literary markers – ὧδε ('here [is]'), ὁ νοῦς ('discernment'), ὁ ἔχων ('the one having'), σοφίαν ('wisdom') – appear again directing the churches to pneumatic discernment.[533] The appearance of these discernment markers dynamically joins together having an ear to hear the Spirit, wisdom, knowledge, understanding,

---

μυστήριον requires explanation, hence the offer in 17.7. It also requires attentive reflection, hence the admonition in 17.9.'

[530] Bauckham, *Climax of Prophecy*, p. 404.

[531] Mounce, *The Book of Revelation*, p. 314. See also Trafton, *Reading Revelation*, p. 157.

[532] Yarbro Collins, *The Apocalypse*, pp. 120-21.

[533] Boxall, *The Revelation of St. John*, p. 239, observes that the call for wisdom occurs at the center of the vision in Revelation 17. See also Koester, *Revelation*, p. 677.

calculation, faithful endurance, and keeping the commandments of God. Specifically, the appearances of ὧδε ('here [is]'), νοῦς ('discernment'), σοφίαν ('wisdom') recall the calculation of the number of the beast – 666. The combination of these literary markers suggests that the pneumatic discernment of the beast will continue and is to be discerned in conjunction with the πόρνη ('whore'), while also indicating that the process will be challenging and might conclude with an identification that is fluid and polyvalent.[534]

Second, the seven heads of the beast must be examined πνευματικῶς, with νοῦς ('discernment') and with σοφίαν ('wisdom'). The seven heads of the beast are the seven mountains and the seven kings that the whore sits upon. While specific identifications of these seven kings with historical figures are possible, this enigmatic description seems to shroud any precise identifications of the kings.[535] (1) The appearance of seven mountains denotes that these seven heads represent political powers.[536] The seven mountains stand in contrast

---

[534] See Ruiz, *Ezekiel in the Apocalypse*, pp. 354-55; Wall, *Revelation*, p. 207; Murphy, *Fallen is Babylon*, p. 359; Keener, *Revelation*, p. 409; Cheung, 'The Mystery of Revelation 17:5 & 7', p. 7; Lupieri, *Apocalypse of John*, p. 270; Osborne, *Revelation*, p. 617; Thomas, *The Apocalypse*, pp. 506-507. Stefanović, *Revelation*, p. 524, comments, 'The understanding of the beast calls for spiritual discernment rather than brilliant mental and intellectual activity. It can only be imparted to the believers by the Spirit … Only through this divinely imparted wisdom, the faithful will be able to discern and comprehend …' J. Schmidt, 'Νους und σοφια in Offb 17', *NovT* 46.2 (2004), pp. 164-89, goes so far as to utilize gematria and explore Roman numerals to calculate the heads of the beast.

[535] So Caird, *Revelation of St. John*, pp. 218-19; Koester, *Revelation*, pp. 677-78. While it is possible to conclude that Domitian is the eighth representing *Nero redivivus* (another incarnation of Nero's atrocities having a 'despotic attitude to the church', e.g. Smalley, *Thunder and Love*, pp. 45-48), this interpretation fails to convince based on the evidence that in Revelation all seven heads of the beast oppress and oppose the church, not just two of the heads. For a thorough discussion of the interpretative options, see Aune, *Revelation 17–22*, pp. 946-49.

[536] Concerning the seven mountains, Aune, *Revelation 17–22*, p. 944, describes that the seven hills would 'be instantly recognizable as a metaphor for Rome'. However, Thompson, 'Spirit Possession', p. 148, observes, 'An angel explained the vision, but even that explanation was not univocal … John may have intended the vision to point unambiguously to the Roman Empire and its emperors, but the vision remains multivocal.' Beale, *The Book of Revelation*, p. 868, adds that ὄρος in Revelation 'always means "mountain"' and represents strength preferring to conclude that a reference to Rome might be 'secondary'. Koester, *Revelation*, pp. 683-84, comments, 'The whore is Rome, yet more than Rome … the vision depicts

to Mount Zion while also recalling Harmageddon. (2) That the seven mountains are at the same time seven kings conveys further that the seven heads represent kingly or political power. The dual imagery implies that while the seven heads manifest as human realities – kings – they are not limited to the identification of any seven particular kings. (3) The number seven, similar to other appearances in the narrative, conveys that the seven heads, seven mountains, and seven kings represent the full rule of the beast.[537] The beast has complete political power, while also denoting that the power of the whore is the scarlet beast upon which she is enthroned. (4) The description of the seven heads of the beast – five have come, one is, and one will be – implies that the manifestations of the beast are polyvalent. The churches have already encountered the beast as five heads, are presently encountering the beast as the head that is, and will continue to encounter the beast in the future as the seventh head.[538] (5) Since five heads have already fallen, and two remain, the time of the beast is nearing completion.[539] (6) The description that the final beast goes to destruction signifies that the beast, while a formidable adversary for a short time, is fated for destruction and death. As already characterized in the narrative, the beast's power is frail.[540]

Third, while the churches discern the seven heads of the beast, the narrative offers an additional enigmatic detail: there are more than seven heads because there is an eighth. The eighth recalls 666, which is the eighth doubly triangular number, and guides the churches to pneumatic discernment, a process that is laborious and challenging.[541]

---

forces that extend beyond Rome. The description of the whore combines prophetic critiques of a number of cities with elements from the imperial context, in which John wrote, creating a multifaceted image.' Smalley, *Revelation*, p. 430, adds again, '"Rome" does not entirely exhaust the meaning of "Babylon"'. See also Boxall, *The Revelation of St. John*, p. 244; Resseguie, *The Revelation of John*, p. 220.

[537] Smalley, *Revelation*, pp. 436-37.

[538] Thomas, 'The Mystery of the Great Whore', p. 128. See also Koester, *Revelation*, p. 691.

[539] Beasley-Murray, *The Book of Revelation*, p. 257; Bauckham, *Climax of Prophecy*, pp. 406-407; Mangina, *Revelation*, p. 197; Koester, *Revelation*, p. 691; Baines, 'The Identity of the Kings', p. 79.

[540] Beale, *The Book of Revelation*, p. 865, comments, 'It takes divine wisdom to discern the difference in the destinies of the Lamb and the beast'.

[541] Thomas, 'The Mystery of the Great Whore', p. 129.

The connection with the beast as the eighth doubly triangular number suggests that the eighth is the beast that is described in Revelation 13 whose number is 666.[542] The eighth is also ἐκ τῶν ἑπτά ('from the seven') suggesting that the identity of the eighth is intertwined with the seven heads, the seven mountains, and the seven kings but is not to be identified as any one of the seven heads.[543] The eighth – the beast whose number is 666 – presents a tension in the churches where there is both continuity and discontinuity between the eighth and its seven heads.[544] The identification of the eighth from the seven reveals that the beast manifests as kings, but is not any one king or mountain. The eighth encompasses the rule of all seven kings. The complete political rule of the seven kings is connected to the eighth, while the eighth, who encompasses the complete rule, is from these kings. The works of the eighth are not equated with any one king; rather, the works of the eighth manifest in the activities of the seven heads, the seven mountains, and the seven kings; they identify with the all-encompassing eighth.[545] The fluid and polyvalent connection between the eighth and the seven is not surprising considering that the calculation of the number of the beast suggests that the identity of the beast is polyvalent and fluid. The addition of an eighth disturbs the closeness of the end of the beast that was assumed with the description that the sixth is current and that the end of the reign of the beast will arrive with the seventh head. This additional detail extends the time of the beast ever so slightly; there will be one beyond completion.

Fourth, the churches need pneumatic wisdom and understanding to discern the identity of the ten horns of the beast which are ten kings. The appearance of ten horns recalls the ten-horned dragon and the ten-horned beast. The horns represent the complete power of the beast that is contrary to the power of the Lamb whose seven

---

[542] Bauckham, *Climax of Prophecy*, pp. 394-96.

[543] Mounce, *The Book of Revelation*, p. 316.

[544] Mangina, *Revelation*, p. 197, responds to the quests of uncovering the historical figure who is the eighth by commenting, 'The problem, perhaps, is not that we lack the key to deciphering the image, but that we insist on treating it as a cipher'.

[545] See Michaels, *Revelation*, pp. 198-99.

horns are the seven Spirits.[546] The identification of the ten horns challenges the churches with another enigma. The ten additional kings suggest that (i) the rule of the beast is even more expansive than the complete rule suggested by the seven heads of the beast, and (ii) as horns, the reign of these ten kings is powerful. The appearance of the ten kings might forge a connection to the kings from the east and the kings of the whole earth who are deceived by the unclean spirits of the trinity of evil (16.12, 14). This connection suggests that the beast manifests as these kings who participate in war which is a primary action of the beast (11.7; 13.7), while also revealing some discontinuity: it is the beast who deceives these kings to go to war. The discontinuity between the ten horns of the beast, and the beast itself is evident because, whereas the reign of the beast will last for 42 months (a relatively short time), the reign of these ten horns is even shorter lasting for only one hour.[547] In other words, the ten horns are not indistinguishable from the beast but seem to be manifestations of it. Not only is the character of the ten horns revealed by their violent actions but also in the ones whom they war against: the Lamb and the saints.[548] The kings' participation in war suggests that they have taken on the character of the beast and are deceived by the beast. However, neither the beast nor the ten kings have any power in comparison to the Lamb because the Lamb is the κύριος κυρίων καὶ βασιλεὺς βασιλέων ('lord of lords and king of kings'). The Lamb overcomes the ten horns, these ten kings, and the beast because the Lamb is all-powerful and is seated upon the divine throne. The Lamb has seven horns, his full strength, that are the seven Spirits.

Finally, the churches are guided through another laborious task of discernment as they return to discern πνευματικῶς the whore (πόρνη). (1) God's judgment is dynamically achieved in conjunction with the beast's evil intentions because God puts into the mind of the ten kings, who have one mind, to destroy the whore (πόρνη).[549]

---

[546] Mounce, *The Book of Revelation*, p. 319; R.C.H. Lenski, *The Interpretation of St. John's Revelation* (Augsburg Publishing House: Minneapolis, MN, 1943), pp. 502, 507-508.

[547] Thomas, 'The Mystery of the Great Whore', p. 130.

[548] Trafton, *Reading Revelation*, p. 159.

[549] Koester, *Revelation*, p. 694.

The beast that the whore rides upon hates the whore and will unite with the kings to destroy her horrifically. Those who perpetrate violence become victims of their own destructive practices.[550] (2) Whereas the whore is seated upon many waters, these waters transform into λαοὶ καὶ ὄχλοι καὶ ἔθνη καὶ γλῶσσαι ('people, crowds, nations, and tongues'). The fourfold appearance of the peoples conveys that the rule of the whore is universal.[551] The λαοὶ καὶ ὄχλοι καὶ ἔθνη καὶ γλῶσσαι have ambiguously appeared in the narrative as those who worship God (5.9; 7.9); those to whom prophetic witness is directed (10.11); and those who opposed God and the people of God (11.9). Their appearance in 11.9 connects the people to the great city which includes Babylon as its inhabitants.[552] Enigmatically, the whore is the great city who rules over the people who inhabit the great city. The judgment of the whore would impact each kaleidoscopic city associated with the great city as well as those who inhabit her.[553] The judgment of this transmorphic reality recalls the eschatological earthquake in Revelation 16 that broke the great city into three parts. Perhaps it would not be going too far to suggest that the three descriptions – (i) ἠρημωμένην ποιήσουσιν αὐτὴν καὶ γυμνήν ('will make her desolate and naked'), (ii) τὰς σάρκας αὐτῆς φάγονται ('they will eat her flesh'), (iii) αὐτὴν κατακαύσουσιν ἐν πυρί ('they will burn her with fire') – might correspond to the three parts of the great city. (3) A final detail in Revelation 17 reveals that the whore (πόρνη) gives power to the kings of the earth. Whereas the ten kings and the beast have authority and power, the whore is enthroned upon the kings of the earth and the beast, ruling over them. The whore rules over the rulers of the world. (4) The gruesome death of the whore is reminiscent of the death of Jezebel in 2 Kgs 9.36.[554] Anyone who refuses to repent from their πορνείας ('whoring') with the πόρνη ('whore') will share in her judgments.[555]

---

[550] Koester, *Revelation*, p. 693; Baines, 'The Identity of the Kings', p. 79.

[551] Smalley, *Revelation*, p. 440.

[552] Thomas, 'The Mystery of the Great Whore', pp. 133-34.

[553] Thomas, *The Apocalypse*, p. 516.

[554] Aune, *Revelation 17–22*, p. 957.

[555] Ruiz, *Ezekiel in the Apocalypse*, p. 367.

## Revelation 18

The appearance of μετὰ ταῦτα εἶδον ('after these things, I saw') suggests a progression in the narrative; yet, the revelation of the mystery of Babylon continues, specifically the description of her destruction. In Revelation 18 four hymns appear, three mourn Babylon's destruction and another hymn rejoices because of her judgment. The opening scene pronounces again that Babylon is fallen, fallen (cf. 14.8), suggesting that, while Babylon's destruction will be described in Revelation 18, Babylon has always been fallen.[556] As Revelation 18 depicts the fallen state of Babylon, it seems the narrative is offering another vantage point by which the churches should view the great whore described in Revelation 17. The first perspective imagines Babylon as a lavish, prosperous, and vile whore (πόρνη) who entices the whole world with her luxury, power, and πορνείας ('whoring'). The first perspective on Babylon is so alluring that her appearance entices even John. The second perspective reveals that Babylon is already judged and that those who have relationships with her will are already participating in her evil works and thereby judgments.[557] The marvel that is Babylon is only a façade. Babylon has always hosted demons and unclean spirits, birds, and beasts; Babylon is the lair of the beast.[558] Perhaps, this second perspective is viewing Babylon πνευματικῶς.[559]

---

[556] Mangina, *Revelation*, p. 211.

[557] Stevens, *Revelation*, p. 474, describes 18.1–19.10 as 'heaven's perspective'.

[558] Smalley, *Revelation*, p. 444, comments, 'so that the demons and evil spirits of this verse become a symbol for Babylon's devilish nature, masked until now behind a deceitful disposition towards idolatry'. Thomas, *The Apocalypse*, p. 521, adds, 'Babylon the Great in her fallen-ness is what she was before, a place of demonic deception that leads to idolatrous worship'.

[559] Ruiz, *Ezekiel in the Apocalypse*, p. 379, observes, 'The expression in 18,1 [μετὰ ταῦτα εἶδον] tells us that Rev 18 offers a different perspective than does Rev 17, but also that both present facets of the same vision. The features in Rev 18 which reflect the Prostitute metaphor reinforce that continuity.' Howard-Brook and Gwyther, *Unveiling Empire*, p. 177, add, 'What John sees in 17:1–19:10 is not something new. It is something that has already been announced as accomplished.' Rowland, *Revelation*, p. 143, writes, 'Babylon ... involves distorted perceptions and unjust acts, and which in its splendor seems invincible (18.10 and 19). It is in reality less than human in its savagery and the defacement of its own dignity and worth in pursuit of its glory (18.23).' Koester, *Revelation and the End of All Things*, p. 155, also writes, 'The portrayal of the harlot is designed to unmask the seductive powers that dull the readers' perceptions, startling them into a keener awareness of what faith means'. A similar point is made by P.B. Decock, 'Hostility Against the Wealth

Unveiling Babylon's true state is accompanied by an exhortation to come out of her.[560] While it is possible that this text beckons the churches to leave a physical location, it is more likely that the text is working, again, on a trans-temporal and trans-geographical level.[561] From the pneumatic perspective, wealth, success, and power that is achieved through deception and violence and in conjunction with the whore will be judged. The exhortation to come out of her suggests that the churches must abandon her fornication, drunkenness, and luxury. The churches must retreat to the holy city, which is (the location of) the people of God and is an alternative reality to the great city.[562]

First, the power and arrogance of Babylon are closely associated with her luxurious wealth, which must be discerned πνευματικῶς.[563] The kings of the earth, the merchants, and the seafarers mourn the loss of Babylon's wealth.[564] The kings of the earth who become drunk on Babylon's wine, who fornicated with her, and who shared

---

of Babylon: Revelation 17:1–19:10', in J.T. Fitzgerald, F.J. van Rensburg, and H.F. van Rooy (eds.), *Animosity, The Bible, and Us: Some European, North American, and South African Perspectives* (Atlanta, GA: SBL, 2009), pp. 284-85, who writes, 'What John is attempting to do is to shape his churches' perception of their situation … What John is offering is the gift of heavenly wisdom and insight into their situation (13:18; 17:9) … The Apocalypse must be situated in this tradition of revelatory experiences by which persons see their situation and the whole of reality in a new way, a heavenly way.'

[560] Koester, *Revelation*, p. 716, writes, 'The exhortation engages readers in a process of discernment in which they must continue to ask which commercial practices are incompatible with their commitments to God and the Lamb'. See S.M. Elliott, 'Who Is Addressed in Revelation 18:6-7', *Biblical Research* 40 (1995), pp. 98-113, who examines the addressees in Revelation 18.6-7 concluding these imperatives are directed toward the people of God.

[561] See Boxall, *The Revelation of St. John*, p. 257.

[562] M.J. Gorman, *Reading Revelation Responsibly: Uncivil Worship and Witness: Following the Lamb into New Creation* (Eugene, OR: Cascade, 2011), p. 181, writes, 'it calls us to rely on the discerning Spirit to distinguish the good (and the neutral) from the bad in order to remain *in* Babylon, but not *of* it'.

[563] Decock, 'Hostility Against the Wealth of Babylon', p. 268; E.P.C. Luan, 'The Acquisition and Use of Wealth: Some Reflections from Revelation 18', *Jian Dao* 41 (2014), pp. 272-73. Contra Provan, 'Foul Spirits, Fornication and Finance', pp. 81-100, who does not observe economic implications in Revelation 18.

[564] Decock, 'Hostility Against the Wealth of Babylon', p. 267, writes, 'The Apocalypse aims at destroying the perception in the churches that Babylon's wealth and power will last forever'. See also deSilva, *Seeing Things John's Way*, pp. 72-75; Koester, *Revelation*, p. 716. Luan, 'The Acquisition and Use of Wealth', pp. 270-71.

in her luxury mourn her destruction.[565] Ironically, these kings, who mourn, might be the same kings who executed Babylon's judgment (17.16).[566] The kings mourn because, in her destruction, they have abolished the source of their political and economic power. Her judgment becomes their judgment.[567] Babylon's lavish luxury (στρήνους, 18.3) is also shared with the merchants and seafarers.[568] No one will purchase their cargo anymore (18.11).[569] The lament of the merchants and the sea traders, who mourn the loss of their trade, conveys their self-absorbed disposition.[570] The extent of the wealth lost from the destruction of Babylon is exposed in the cargo list (18.12-13).[571] Many of the 28 cargo items listed are expensive imports representing luxury, while the number 28 (4 x 7) seems to represent every item (represented by seven) taken from the whole earth (represented by

---

[565] Yarbro Collins, *The Apocalypse*, p. 126.

[566] Ruiz, *Ezekiel in the Apocalypse*, p. 424, writes, 'God's transcendence might manifest itself in the judgment by which Babylon loses her might. Those who mourn that loss are the kings of the earth who shared in her activity, and who therefore share her loss.'

[567] See Baines, 'The Identity of the Kings', p. 79.

[568] Ladd, *Revelation of John*, pp. 236-37.

[569] The sea would recall the origins of the sea beast and the water that flows from the mouth of the dragon. By exploiting the origins of evil and deceit, the seafarers gained prosperity and wealth, see Provan, 'Foul Spirits, Fornication and Finance', p. 91.

[570] Wall, *Revelation*, p. 203, comments, 'The grief of those who lament the fall of Babylon (18.9-19) is centered not upon the loss of human life but upon the loss of the city and its great wealth. According to Revelation, at the foundation of evil's self-destruction is its love and concern for Mammon and self rather than for God and neighbor.' See also Beasley-Murray, *The Book of Revelation*, p. 268; Trafton, *Reading Revelation*, p. 167; Baines, 'The Identity of the Kings', p. 80.

[571] For a full examination of the 28 items, see Bauckham, *Climax of Prophecy*, pp. 350-71. Howard-Brook and Gwyther, *Unveiling Empire*, p. 173, observe that since the list includes some mundane items, 'the list depicts Babylon as appropriating *everything* from the entire earth'. Items listed in Revelation 18 also appear in Ezekiel 27, see Ruiz, *Ezekiel in the Apocalypse*, pp. 426-40, for a full examination of the lists in Ezekiel and Revelation. Many of the items that appear in the cargo list are some of the most costly items in the Roman world, leading Bauckham, *Climax of Prophecy*, p. 366, to conclude that Revelation 18 is a critique of Roman economics. Provan, 'Foul Spirits, Fornication and Finance', pp. 81-100, is critical of this proposal observing that Revelation offers a broader critique than Rome. While Provan's conclusion is helpful, it seems that he pushes the point too far as he ignores any economic implications in Revelation 18, limiting the critique to political and religious elements.

four).[572] It is also possible that the customers who buy as well as those who sell have received the mark of the beast.[573] If these characters bear the mark of the beast, then it seems that they offer false worship to the beast to join fully in these commercial activities.[574] The final of the 28 cargo items listed is σωμάτων καὶ ψυχὰς ἀνθρώπων ('bodies, even the lives of humans'), indicating that human lives have become commodities in Babylon.[575] This indifference toward human life and the economic associations align with the character of the beast and the whore who both murder and kill for their own gain. Those who trade with Babylon who have taken the mark of the beast participate in the murderous character of their masters – the dragon, the beast, and the whore.[576] Babylon has shed the blood of prophets, of saints, and of all who have been slaughtered on the earth (18.24). Whereas some in the churches might have fallen for her seductions, Babylon's indifference toward human life evokes a sense of solitary among those who are oppressed by Babylon.[577] Babylon is a trans-geographical location, which kaleidoscopically morphs into the place where their Lord was crucified – into Golgotha – suggesting that any indifference toward human life that is slaughtered in Babylon, in the great city, is equal to having indifference toward the death of their Lord. Thus, the church must discern by the Spirit and recognize the true state of Babylon. Does anyone in the churches sympathize with Babylon, the great city, and lament like the kings, merchants, and sea traders because of economic enticements? Does anyone lament the loss

---

[572] Some of the items listed also appeared to describe the attire of the great whore (Rev. 17.4; 18.16), see Caird, *Revelation of St. John*, p. 226; Ruiz, *Ezekiel in the Apocalypse*, p. 440.

[573] Trafton, *Reading Revelation*, p. 168. See Stevens, *Revelation*, p. 481.

[574] Another soft intertextual note might resound with Solomon in 1 Kings who obtained chariots representing his wealth and success, who is also associated with slavery and trade with Tyre; for this proposal, see Provan, 'Foul Spirits, Fornication and Finance', pp. 87-88.

[575] Bauckham, *Climax of Prophecy*, pp. 370-71, observes that the final 'item' offers comment on the entire list, 'It suggests the inhuman brutality, the contempt for human life, on which the whole of Rome's prosperity and luxury rests'. See also C.R. Koester, 'Roman Slave Trade and the Critique of Babylon in Revelation 18', *CBQ* 70.4 (2008), pp. 766-86; Luan, 'The Acquisition and Use of Wealth', pp. 255-98.

[576] Cf. Rev. 12.9-10, 17; 13.3, 6-7, 12-15, see Michaels, *Revelation*, p. 210.

[577] Bauckham, *Climax of Prophecy*, p. 349.

of certain items in the cargo list?[578] Upon discerning the state of Babylon, the churches must offer true and faithful witness to those who live in the great city and exhort everyone to come out of her even at the cost of their lives.

Second, the churches must discern πνευματικῶς the deception of Babylon. The appearance of unclean things to describe Babylon as the lair and prison of demons, unclean spirits, birds, and beasts, recalls the golden cup of the whore who deceived all the nations.[579] The deception of Babylon is associated with her wine that is used to enthrall the inhabitants of the earth as well as her sorcery (18.23).[580] Deception is the work of the trinity of evil and the unclean spirits who deceived all the kings of the earth (16.13-14; 17.4), suggesting Babylon is a lair of deception and war.[581] Her deception also recalls characters such as Jezebel, the Balaamitess, the Nicolaitans, the dragon, and the beasts.[582] The sorcery of Babylon suggests that she utilizes magic, perhaps not unlike the signs and wonders of the beast, to deceive the nations. Thus, in order to resist the allure of Babylon, the churches must recognize her true state by the Spirit.

Finally, following the three laments from the kings, the merchants, and the seafarers, the text jars the hearers' expectations as they hear a hymn rejoicing in Babylon's destruction. The three laments offered by the kings, merchants, and seafarers might have invoked sympathy amongst some in the churches, as they might have imagined losing their own wealth on account of Babylon's destruction. The two responses to the judgment of Babylon – lament or rejoice – reveal a stark dualism between those who follow the Lamb and those who follow the beast and Babylon. The final hymn voiced from the perspective of the saints, apostles, and prophets offers a pneumatic per-

---

[578] Koester, *Revelation*, p. 713.

[579] Yarbro Collins, *Crisis & Catharsis*, p. 121.

[580] Resseguie, *The Revelation of John*, p. 232, comments, 'Babylon's magic art of deception casts a spell that persuades people that she is sovereign and a god worthy of worship'. See also Bauckham, *Climax of Prophecy*, pp. 347-48; Osborne, *Revelation*, p. 658.

[581] Ruiz, *Ezekiel in the Apocalypse*, p. 387; Trafton, *Reading Revelation*, p. 170.

[582] Resseguie, *The Revelation of John*, p. 232; Koester, *Revelation and the End of All Things*, p. 164. In 2 Kgs 9.22, Jezebel was also accused of sorcery, see Keener, *Revelation*, p. 433.

spective on Babylon's destruction, suggesting those who are not entangled with Babylon's evil works are able to rejoice at her destruction.[583] Either the churches have been seduced by the deceptive activities of the whore and thereby mourn her judgment like the kings, merchants, and seafarers;[584] or the churches rejoice in her destruction because they have experienced her oppression and death, which is the price of her lavish lifestyle. Those who rejoice have an ear to hear the Spirit, recognize the great city πνευματικῶς, and overcome her deception, having come out of her, dissociating themselves from her commerce, fornication, sorcery, and drunkenness; otherwise, they will participate in her judgments.[585]

## Revelation 19.1-10

First, the scene in Revelation 19.1-10 continues to describe the heavenly response to the destruction of Babylon. The heavenly response stands in contrast to the laments of the kings, merchants, and seafarers who sympathize with Babylon.[586] The heavenly response originates from a great crowd, the 24 elders, the four living creatures, and the throne. Earlier in the narrative, the elders, four living creatures, and the great crowd (recalling the great crowd in Revelation 7 who morphed from the 144,000) were characterized as exemplars in discernment.[587] This discerning hymn reiterates that rejoicing is the true response to the destruction of Babylon. The hymn attributes ἀληθιναὶ to God denoting again that truth belongs to God, which contrasts the lies and deceit of the dragon, the beasts, and the whore.

---

[583] Bauckham, *Climax of Prophecy*, pp. 376-78, describes this as a 'hermeneutical trap'. See also Archer, *'I Was in the Spirit on the Lord's Day'*, p. 257.

[584] Luan, 'The Acquisition and Use of Wealth', pp. 271-72, observes that the three laments are told from the perspective of the kings, merchants, and seafarers.

[585] Boxall, *The Revelation of St. John*, p. 259, writes, 'viewed from a heavenly perspective, the appropriate response is not lament but a cry of "Hallelujah!" (19:1-3)'. See also D. Ramírez Fernández, 'The Judgment of God on the Multinationals: Revelation 18', in L.E. Vaage (ed.), *Subversive Scriptures: Revolutionary Readings of the Christian Bible in Latin America* (Valley Forge, PA: Trinity Press International, 1997), pp. 88-89.

[586] Archer, *'I Was in the Spirit on the Lord's Day'*, p. 259, writes, 'The heavenly liturgy beckons them to experience the destruction of Babylon proleptically and to discern it pneumatically ... Such celebration reminds them of their true identity as followers of the Lamb, as partakers in the heavenly liturgy even *now*, and as those who have ears to hear what the Spirit is saying to the churches.'

[587] Smalley, *Revelation*, p. 476; Koester, *Revelation*, p. 726.

Second, the pure, bright clothing worn by the saints are their τὰ δικαιώματα. The white color recalls the garments of the great crowd who washed their garments in the blood of the Lamb making them white. In the Johannine literature, sanctification and purity are accomplished in truth (Jn 17.17-19). The pure clothing of the saints combines just deeds with their truthfulness, which stands in contrast to the garments wore by the whore and connects her injustice to her deceitfulness. Among the possible implications of works in Revelation, one aspect would include that the saints have undertaken the challenging work of pneumatic discernment to recognize the deception of the whore and the beast, refusing to participate in their evil works. The difficult process of discerning the T/truth is a feature of the sanctification of the saints. The deeds of the saints are just, suggesting that the saints have taken on the character of God who is just (19.1).[588] In the seven prophetic messages, works were identified as good, bad, or incomplete.[589] The churches are offered a choice: either identify with the just God, be sanctified in truth, and perform just works, or do evil works, be seduced by deceit, and participate in idolatry, fornication, murder, war, and false worship.

Third, the description that οὗτοι οἱ λόγοι ἀληθινοὶ τοῦ θεοῦ ('these are the true words of God') in 19.9 indicates, again, that truthfulness is divinely conditioned.[590] While it is possible that ἀληθινοὶ ('true') describes the beatitude in 19.9 solely,[591] the declaration that these words are true seems to describe the whole of the Apocalypse.[592] The Apocalypse originates from God (1.1), and God is true.

---

[588] Murphy, *Fallen is Babylon*, p. 383; Beale, *The Book of Revelation*, p. 939; Resseguie, *The Revelation of John*, p. 235; Koester, *Revelation*, p. 738.

[589] Cf. Rev. 2.2, 5, 6, 19, 26; 3.1, 2, 8, 15, see Swete, *The Apocalypse of St. John*, p. 247; D. McIlraith, "'For the Fine Linen Is the Righteous Deeds of the Saints'": Works and Wife in Revelation 19:8', *CBQ* 61.3 (1999), pp. 513-23; Thomas, *The Apocalypse*, p. 566.

[590] Revelation 3.7, 14; 6.10; 15.3 16.7; 19.2, 9, 11; 21.5; 22.6, see Ruiz, *Ezekiel in the Apocalypse*, p. 509; Mangina, *Revelation*, p. 219.

[591] So Koester, *Revelation*, p. 731; See also Roloff, *The Revelation of John*, p. 213.

[592] Murphy, *Fallen is Babylon*, p. 384; Schüssler Fiorenza, *Vision of a Just World*, p. 102.

In response to these true words from God, John, in a surprising manner, wrongfully bows down to worship a fellow-servant (19.10).[593] This is a surprising response by John who recently marveled at the appearance of the great whore improperly. John previously fell before the feet of the resurrected Jesus (1.17), while the elders and living creatures fell before the one on the throne where both scenes described true and proper worship.[594] Bearing in mind these previous scenes, John's action of bowing before this fellow-servant is startling. The fellow-servant's rebuke assists the churches to discern that worship should be directed to God alone and never toward God's servants or the whore.[595] Worship is portrayed as a primary criterion of discernment; true prophecy directs one toward the worship of God.[596]

Fourth, following the rebuke, the fellow-servant utters, ἡ γὰρ μαρτυρία Ἰησοῦ ἐστιν τὸ πνεῦμα τῆς προφητείας ('for the witness of Jesus is the Spirit of prophecy'). (1) Clearly, another appearance of πνεῦμα ('Spirit') in the narrative suggests that the πνεῦμα τῆς προφητείας ('Spirit of prophecy') denotes the Holy Spirit.[597] The characterization of the Spirit as the Spirit of prophecy is not surprising because of the prophetic activity of the Spirit in the Apocalypse: (i) the Spirit of prophecy speaks the words of Jesus introduced by

---

[593] While it is possible that this fellow-servant is to be identified as an angel and thereby the scene critiques angelic worship occurring in the churches (so Bauckham, *Climax of Prophecy*, pp. 135-36), the text does not explicitly identify this fellow-servant as an angel. See also Prigent, *The Apocalypse*, pp. 528-33, who offers evidence that angel worship was not a central issue in the seven churches. Based on the depiction of the fellow-servant, Thomas, *The Apocalypse*, p. 570, identifies the fellow-servant with one of the ψυχὰς ('lives') from under the altar. See also Lenski, *Revelation*, p. 546.

[594] Archer, *'I Was in the Spirit on the Lord's Day'*, p. 266.

[595] J.-P. Ruiz, 'The Politics of Praise: A Reading of Revelation 19:1-10', *SBL Seminar Papers* 36 (1997), p. 376, writes, 'They were called upon, first, to discern the appropriate object of their worship. Second, they were challenged to consider just what activities constituted authentic worship.' See also Archer, *'I Was in the Spirit on the Lord's Day'*, p. 266.

[596] Bauckham, *Climax of Prophecy*, p. 135, writes, 'In a sense the theme of his whole prophecy is the distinction between true worship and idolatry, a distinction for which Christians in the contemporary situation needed prophetic discernment'. See also Koester, *Revelation*, p. 740.

[597] Contra Wilson, 'Revelation 19:10', pp. 191-202, who concludes that the testimony of Jesus is the 'essence' of prophecy.

the prophetic formula τάδε λέγει ('thus says'). (ii) The Spirit of prophecy speaks the whole of this prophecy that is received and given ἐν πνεύματι ('in the Spirit'). (iii) The Spirit of prophecy empowers the prophecy of the two witnesses.[598]

(2) While it is possible to choose between the objective or subjective genitive concerning the μαρτυρία 'Ιησοῦ ('witness of Jesus') – a choice between the witness Jesus bore or the witness about Jesus – such a distinction seems to be unnecessary.[599] The witness of Jesus is both from and about Jesus. The Spirit of prophecy is actively and dynamically involved in both the empowerment of the witness of the church about Jesus and the witness that originated with Jesus, who is the true and faithful witness. Since prophecy and witness are equated, anyone who offers a pneumatic, true, and faithful witness about Jesus is a prophet who is inspired by the Spirit of prophecy who likewise inspired the witness Jesus bore.[600] The prophetic Spirit is the medium by which the prophetic, true, and faithful words of Jesus are conveyed, and the Spirit is the source of the church's prophetic witness, a prophetic witness that communicates the very words of Jesus.[601] Thus, the witness of Jesus is pneumatic, prophetic, true, and faithful.[602] The witness of Jesus *is* the Spirit of prophecy. However, the prophetic voice of the Spirit is not reducible to the words of Jesus or the witness of the church because the Spirit has an independent voice in Revelation (cf. Rev. 14.13).[603]

(3) The Spirit of prophecy recalls the Spirit of Truth in the Johannine literature.[604] The truthfulness of the witness of Jesus, who is the

---

[598] See Mazzaferri, *The Genre of the Book of Revelation*, p. 310; Bauckham, *The Theology of the Book of Revelation*, pp. 118-21; de Smidt, 'The Holy Spirit in the Book of Revelation', p. 242; Waddell, *Spirit of the Book of Revelation*, pp. 189-94; Koester, *Revelation*, p. 732.

[599] See Murphy, *Fallen is Babylon*, p. 385; Michaels, *Revelation*, p. 213.

[600] See Bauckham, *The Theology of the Book of Revelation*, p. 119; Barr, *Tales of the End*, p. 136; Waddell, *Spirit of the Book of Revelation*, pp. 175-78, 189-90, 193-94.

[601] Bauckham, *Climax of Prophecy*, p. 190, writes, 'The Spirit of prophecy speaks through the Christian prophets bringing the word of the exalted Christ to his people on earth'.

[602] Thomas, *The Apocalypse*, p. 573.

[603] Bauckham, *The Theology of the Book of Revelation*, p. 117. Contra Schweizer, 'πνεῦμα', p. 510.

[604] Rainbow, *Johannine Theology*, p. 239. See also Caird, *Revelation of St. John*, p. 238, who notes that this test of truth or falsehood aligns with 1 John 4 where Caird

Truth,[605] is associated with the Spirit of Truth.[606] The truthfulness of the prophetic witness of the church is empowered by the Spirit of Prophecy, much like the truthfulness of the Lamb who sees all by the seven Spirits. The Spirit of Truth sanctifies the witness of the churches in the Truth.[607] Contrary to the Spirit of prophecy/Truth, stands the false prophecy of Jezebel, Balaam, and the Nicolaitans.[608] As the churches encounter false prophecy, a criterion for discernment is a process to recognize if a prophecy is from the Spirit of prophecy/Truth.[609]

## Revelation 19.11–21.8

The final part of the third ἐν πνεύματι ('in the Spirit') section describes a rider on the white horse and the judgment of the beast, the false prophet, and those who served them, which is followed by a description of the millennium, the final defeat of the deceitful dragon, and the descent of the New Jerusalem.

First, the rider on the white horse is (1) πιστὸς καὶ ἀληθινός ('Faithful and True').[610] The same descriptors appeared to characterize Jesus as the true and faithful witness (3.14), suggesting that this rider is the resurrected Jesus.[611] The rider who is true and faithful overcomes the deceit of the dragon with truth.[612] (2) The connection

observes a twofold test: (1) belief in Jesus who is the love of God incarnate and (2) conducting one's life in conformity with this belief. See also Wall, *Revelation*, pp. 223-24.

[605] Cf. Jn 14.6; Rev. 3.14; 19.11.

[606] Bauckham, *The Theology of the Book of Revelation*, p. 125, writes, 'The Spirit's prophetic ministry is both to expose the truth in this world of deceit and ambiguity, and to point to the eschatological age when the truth of all things will come to light'.

[607] K.E. Miller, 'The Nuptial Eschatology of Revelation 19–22', *CBQ* 60.2 (1998), p. 308; Thomas, *The Apocalypse*, p. 573.

[608] See Keener, *Revelation*, pp. 452, 460-61.

[609] Bruce, 'The Spirit in the Apocalypse', pp. 338-39; Koester, *Revelation and the End of All Things*, p. 172.

[610] Ladd, *Revelation of John*, p. 253, considers that 'faithful' and 'true' function synonymously.

[611] Smalley, *Revelation*, p. 488. See also Schüssler Fiorenza, *Vision of a Just World*, p. 105; Blount, *Revelation*, p. 350.

[612] Bauckham, *The Theology of the Book of Revelation*, p. 105, writes, 'While the devil and the beast reign, the earth is the sphere of deceit and illusion. Truth is seen first in heaven and then when it comes from heaven to earth. At 19:11, heaven opens and truth himself, the Word of God (19:13), rides to earth. This is the point

between the rider and the resurrected Jesus is further evident from his fiery eyes. The resurrected Jesus sees with perfect insight penetrating through deception with his fiery eyes that are the seven torches, the seven Spirits.[613] (3) From the mouth of the rider, who is Faithful and True, comes a sword, which likely represents the truth coming from his mouth.[614] A connection between the sword from the mouth of the rider and the Spirit might be discovered by way of Isaiah 11, an intertextual echo that resounded earlier in the narrative. In Isaiah 11, the רוח ('Spirit') of the mouth of the Root judges the nations.[615] This might indicate that the sword from the mouth of the one named True and Faithful is closely associated with, if not identified as, the seven Spirits of Truth/Prophecy. Contrary to the sword that comes from the mouth of the rider, the trinity of evil expels deceitful and lying spirits from their mouths.[616] In Revelation, there is power in speech and words.[617] (4) The rider also has a name that no one knows (οἶδεν) except for him. The appearance of οἶδεν ('I know') recalls the sevenfold description that Jesus knows in the seven prophetic messages. That only the rider knows this name implies that

---

at which the perspective of heaven prevails on earth finally dispelling all the lies of the beast.' See also Koester, *Revelation*, p. 735; de Villiers, 'Prime Evil', p. 81.

[613] Kiddle, *The Revelation of St. John*, p. 384; Thomas, *The Apocalypse*, p. 576. See also Resseguie, *The Revelation of John*, p. 237, who writes:

> The primary trait of Christ's blazing eyes is the ability to penetrate beneath the falsehoods and lies of this world and reveal what is 'true' – the second half of his title in 19:11. The war Jesus wages is against the falsehoods, deceptions, and lies of the beast and company that distort the truth of God's good creation. These penetrating eyes augment the imagery of the Lamb's seven eyes (5:6). While the seven eyes accent the Lamb's ability to see all, the fiery eyes suggest Christ's ability to see beneath the pretenses and falsehoods of this world.

[614] Wall, *Revelation*, p. 232; Prigent, *The Apocalypse*, p. 546; Boxall, *The Revelation of St. John*, p. 275. See also Thomas, *The Apocalypse*, p. 579, for an examination of truth in the FG and appearances in the Apocalypse.

[615] See Osborne, *Revelation*, p. 685. S. Laws, 'The Blood-Stained Horseman: Revelation 19,11-13', in E.A. Livingstone (ed.), *Studia Biblica 1978: III: Papers on Paul and Other New Testament Authors* (Sheffield: JSOT Press, 1980), p. 247, also observes that the blood-dipped garments on the white horse might echo the Lion in Gen. 49.1-12.

[616] See Resseguie, *The Revelation of John*, p. 239.

[617] See Blount, *Revelation*, p. 354; Koester, *Revelation*, p. 766; Newton, *The Revelation Worldview*, pp. 208-209.

there are limits to human knowledge and that there are aspects of the divine which remain mysterious.[618]

Second, following the judgment of the false prophet, the beast, and their followers, the dragon is chained for 1000 years. While chained, the dragon cannot deceive the nations until the millennium is completed. During the millennium, those who were beheaded, who witnessed to the word of God, who refused to worship the beast, and who refused the mark of the beast will sit upon the thrones.[619] Those who rule for 1000 years are identified as ψυχὰς ('lives'), which recalls the ψυχὰς ('lives') under the altar who were violently slaughtered and who cried for justice (6.9-11).[620] The throne that these ψυχὰς ('lives') are seated upon recalls a promise to the overcomers who will share Christ's throne (3.21).[621] After the millennium and similar to the actions of the unclean spirits at Harmageddon, the dragon is released, deceives the nations, and provokes them to war against the beloved city at Gog and Magog.[622] The similarities in these scenes

---

[618] Caird, *Revelation of St. John*, p. 242, comments, 'When they have joined all the glorious names that adorning wonder can ascribe to him, he still confronts them with an ultimate mystery'. Thomas, *The Apocalypse*, p. 577, suggests that the name 'both reveals and conceals'. See also Miller, 'Nuptial Eschatology', p. 313; Mangina, *Revelation*, p. 221.

[619] Boxall, *The Revelation of St. John*, p. 284, suggests that the thrones represent a kingdom with a shared rule with Christ that is contrary to the totalitarian regime of the beast or Babylon.

[620] Mangina, *Revelation*, p. 225; M. Waymeyer, 'The First Resurrection in Revelation 20', *MSJ* 27.1 (2016), pp. 29-32. So Lichtenwalter, '"Souls Under the Altar"', pp. 61-62, who observes an inclusio between the appearance of ψυχὰς ('lives') in 6.9-11 and 20.4. See also Skaggs and Benham, *Revelation*, p. 207.

[621] Aune, *Revelation 17–22*, p. 1084; D. Mathewson, 'A Re-examination of the Millennium in Rev 20:1-6: Consummation and Recapitulation', *JETS* 44.2 (2001), pp. 243-44.

[622] For an examination of the battle scenes in Rev. 19.11-21 and Rev. 20.7-20, see Mathewson, 'A Re-examination of the Millennium', pp. 237-51. Cf. J.K. Newton, 'Time Language and the Purpose of the Millennium', *Colloquium* 43.2 (2011), pp. 147-68. The beloved city is closely associated with the holy city in Rev. 11.1-2 and the city that is protected from winepress in Rev. 14.20. These cities seem to represent the people of God suggesting that they are protected by God against the attacks of Satan and those deceived by Satan. See Murphy, *Fallen is Babylon*, p. 402; Osborne, *Revelation*, pp. 702, 715; Smalley, *Revelation*, pp. 511-12; Trafton, *Reading Revelation*, p. 183. For an examination of early Pentecostal readings of Gog and Magog, see Jackson, 'Wesleyan Holiness and Finished Work Pentecostal Interpretations of Gog and Magog Biblical Texts', pp. 168-83.

suggest that the location of Gog and Magog is connected to Harmageddon, which is kaleidoscopically the great city, Egypt, Sodom, Babylon, and the place where their Lord was crucified. However, the actions of the dragon are once again foiled by fire that comes from heaven to consume all those who oppose the people of God. It is possible that this fiery judgment is connected to the seven Spirits who are identified as the seven fiery torches as well as the seven eyes of the Lamb who has fiery eyes, suggesting that the fire of the Spirit of Truth judges the deceit of the dragon in fiery judgment. This association with the fire of the Spirit might extend to the lake of fire where the dragon, the beast, and the false prophet are tormented; their deceit will be forever judged by the Spirit of Truth, the רוח ('Spirit') from the Root's mouth. In the final appearance of the dragon and the triumvirate of evil in the narrative, deception is once again described to be the leading characteristic of the dragon.[623] Accordingly, the primary enemy of the church (and the world) is deception, deceit, falsehood, and lies;[624] thereby, pneumatic discernment that originates with the Spirit of Truth and discloses the T/truth is necessary for the churches and the world to overcome the dragon. The true and faithful witness of the churches, who have discerned by the Spirit of Truth, torments the inhabitants of the earth because they confront those who have been deceived by the dragon with the T/truth from God.

Third, John is exhorted once again to write because these words are faithful and true. Among the variety of occasions when John was commanded to write in the Apocalypse, the command first appeared when John was exhorted to record the Apocalypse (1.3).[625] If this

---

[623] de Villiers, 'Prime Evil', p. 65, writes:

> The author wants to stress the waging of war against the saints *as a result of the deception* of the dragon. The story of the unchaining of the dragon and the story in the story about the attack of the nations are linked by the motif of deception. Deception is a significant (if not the most significant) feature of the characters of evil, as Revelation 12 and 13 with the history of the two beasts prove adequately. John wishes to stress that there are deeper structures behind the evil actions of people against God and the people of God. Evil never functions on its own and isolated from other forms of evil. There is an intricate link in the deeds of all those who oppose God's people.

[624] Boring, *Revelation*, p. 199.

[625] Revelation 1.11. Smalley, *Revelation*, p. 484.

exhortation to write refers to the whole Apocalypse, then once again as in Rev. 19.9, the whole prophecy self-identities as true. The description of the Apocalypse as true and faithful would not come as a surprise considering that it is the Ἀποκάλυψις Ἰησοῦ Χριστοῦ ('Apocalypse of Jesus Christ'). Jesus Christ is called True and Faithful, is the true and faithful witness, and is the Truth.[626] Hence, the Truth is revealing these true words and the Truth is the one who is being revealed in the Apocalypse. The Apocalypse, as truth, is a prophecy (1.3) that originates from God (1.1), is conveyed by the Spirit of prophecy/Truth (19.10), which is given and received while 'in the Spirit' of prophecy/Truth (1.10). Hence, as the churches reflect on the stark division between truth and falsehood throughout the narrative, the narrative self-identifies as the truth that is conveyed to the churches by the Spirit. In other words, hearing the Apocalypse ἐν πνεύματι ('in the Spirit') is hearing the T/truth from God. The Truth is conveyed by the Spirit of Truth, the Spirit of prophecy, the Spirit of wisdom, the Spirit of understanding, and the Spirit of knowledge, the seven Spirits who are the seven eyes of the Lamb, who are the seven eyes of Yahweh, who see and know all things. The Apocalypse is pneumatic discernment because the T/truth that is revealed in this prophecy shapes and forms the churches to recognize and to know the T/truth by and in the Spirit.[627] Hearing this prophecy is pneumatic discernment because the T/truth, which overcomes the deceit of the dragon, is a person who is called True and Faithful and revealed in this narrative.

## Summary of Revelation 17.1–21.8

First, the detailed description of the great whore, and the appearance of the literary markers, ὧδε ('here [is]'), νοῦς ('discernment'), σοφίαν ('wisdom'), urge the hearers to careful pneumatic discernment. The discernment of the whore is associated with the continued discernment of the beast that she rides upon. The process suggests that the

---

[626] Andrew of Caesarea, 'Commentary on the Apocalypse', p. 203, writes, 'They are "trustworthy and true" because they come from the Truth'.

[627] Rowland, 'Revelation', p. 686, writes, 'Reading Revelation may enable some people to see the truth of what they are doing'. See also Vanni, 'The Ecclesial Assembly', p. 84.

beast and the whore represent expansive military and political authority that facilitates her vast economic success. Her power, success, and wealth are seductive and can be difficult to identify. The description of the whore in Revelation 17 is followed by another perspective of the whore in Revelation 18. This pneumatic perspective directs the churches to recognize that the wealth, success, and power of the whore is fleeting and already judged. Babylon is fallen. Discernment is required to perceive the truth of the whore; otherwise, the undiscerning are in danger of participating in her whoring, which is her exploitation and her disregard for human life, and thereby share in her destruction.

Second, worship is a central element in relation to the whore (πόρνη). In Revelation πορνείας ('whoring') is associated with false worship. Some in the churches such as Laodicea were condemned for their dependence on their success and were exhorted to examine themselves, to purchase gold from Jesus, to overcome, and to hear the Spirit. The πορνείας ('whoring') of the πόρνη ('whore') has economic, military, and political implications, suggesting that wealth and power are forms of false worship. Perhaps, with the description of the whore, some in the churches would recognize that they have fallen prey to her seductions, not unlike John.[628] Some in the churches might also marvel at the whore πόρνη, might be drunk on her wine, might be whoring (πορνείας) with her, and might be filling their coffers to the brim. Some in the churches might lament, like the merchants, seafarers, and kings at the loss of such great wealth.

Third, deception is the primary characteristic of the antagonists in the narrative, which compels the churches to pneumatic discernment. Satan is the father of lies and a murderer from the beginning.[629] John on two occasions is tempted to worship wrongly, first, the whore and, second, a fellow-servant. When John wrongly worships these characters, immediately the text directs John to discernment in order that he might recognize these mistaken attempts of worship. Thus, false worship directly correlates to a lack of discernment.

---

[628] Caird, *Revelation of St. John*, p. 223, writes, 'This, we are to understand, is the true nature of the seduction exercised by the great whore. The kings of the earth were guilty of an economic dalliance, which involved the idolatrous worship of Mammon.' See also Ladd, *Revelation of John*, p. 221; Thomas, *The Apocalypse*, p. 524.

[629] John 8.44, see Beasley-Murray, *The Book of Revelation*, p. 341.

Fourth, in the midst of such deceit and deception, the Apocalypse offers two occasions where it self-identifies as being true and faithful. This prophecy is the Apocalypse of Jesus Christ who is the Truth. As the churches encounter the words of this prophecy that are conveyed to the churches in the Spirit of Truth/prophecy, they are encountering the T/truth. The Spirit of prophecy dynamically delivers the prophetic words of the Truth from God to the churches. The Spirit of prophecy empowers the true and faithful witness of the churches in order that they might overcome the deceit of the dragon, the beast, and the whore.

## ἐν πνεύματι – Revelation 21.9–22.5

The final major section of the narrative is indicated by the fourth appearance of ἐν πνεύματι ('in the Spirit') that describes the bride, New Jerusalem, the holy city. The description of the bride/New Jerusalem stands in contrast to that of the whore/Babylon.[630] This narrative section describes the fulfillment of many of the promises to the overcomers that appeared in the seven prophetic messages, suggesting that those who are part of the city have an ear to hear the Spirit and have overcome (the deception of) the dragon and the beast.[631] Strikingly, while there is a significant contrast between the New Jerusalem and Babylon, the description of the New Jerusalem lacks any literary makers (e.g. ὧδε, νοῦς, σοφίαν) that have previously directed the churches to pneumatic discernment in the narrative.

First, the holy city, the New Jerusalem, recalls the holy city in Rev. 11.1-2, which represents the people of God who were protected by

---

[630] Boxall, *The Revelation of St. John*, p. 242, writes, 'But the similarities between the two women underscores the Apocalypse's claim that what is evil and unjust can easily be taken for what is good and beneficial. It requires an apocalyptic unveiling such as this to reveal the true state of affairs.' Resseguie, *The Revelation of John*, p. 217, adds, 'The contrast between the good and evil woman is made not because the reader's choices are obvious but because the choices are subtle. Evil appears good. Stark, offensive, sexual language helps awaken the reader to the choices of the Apocalypse.' See also R. Zimmermann, 'Nuptial Imagery in the Revelation of John', *Biblica* 84.2 (2003), pp. 178-82.

[631] E. Schüssler Fiorenza, 'Composition and Structure of the Book of Revelation', *CBQ* 39.3 (1977), p. 360; J.A. du Rand, 'The New Jerusalem as Pinnacle of Salvation: Text (Rev 21:1-22:5) and Intertext', *NeoT* 38.2 (2004), p. 277.

God.[632] Further evidence of the relationship between the holy city and the people of God appears with the 12 gates and 12 foundations of the city that measure 144 cubits (12 x 12). The appearance of 144 recalls the 144,000 and the great crowd who also represented the whole people of God.[633] Both Babylon and the New Jerusalem represent a distinctive people, and those who are part of these cities reflect the character of each respective location.[634] The bride is a beautiful, bright city sanctified in the truth and adorned with many precious gems for her husband, while the adornments of the whore are achieved through deceitful enticements, exploitative economic practices, and the commodification of human beings.[635] Whereas Babylon exploited the earth to adorn herself in gems, the people of God are precious gems. Whereas Babylon is a lair of demons, beasts, deception, whoring, and murder, the New Jerusalem is pure, full of truth, and is the dwelling of God.[636]

Second, God and the Lamb are described as the temple, implying that there is no longer the need for mediated access to the presence of God that the temple and the Holy of Holies had provided to the people of God.[637] Furthermore, the people of God are personified as the city, as the New Jerusalem in the vision. One implication of such a depiction includes unmediated access to the presence of God, which would appear to include unmediated access to the truth, wisdom, discernment, and knowledge of God.[638] The measurements of the city, of the people of God, are identified as μέτρον ἀνθρώπου, ὅ

---

[632] Sweet, *Revelation*, p. 302.

[633] See Thompson, *Apocalypse and Empire*, p. 89; Aune, *Revelation 17–22*, pp. 1155-58; Beale, *The Book of Revelation*, p. 1070; K.L. Tõniste, 'Measuring the Holy City: Architectural Rhetoric in Revelation 21:9-21', *CBW* 34 (2014), p. 289.

[634] R.H. Gundry, 'The New Jerusalem: People as Place, Not Place for People', *NovT* 29.3 (1987), pp. 254-64; Pattemore, *The People of God*, pp. 197-212.

[635] Murphy, *Fallen is Babylon*, p. 417.

[636] Koester, *Revelation*, p. 828, writes, 'Demons dwell in Babylon (18:2), but New Jerusalem will be the dwelling of God (21:3)'. See also Schüssler Fiorenza, *Justice and Judgment*, p. 226.

[637] The cubit dimensions of the city recall the dimensions of the Holy of Holies, see Tõniste, 'Measuring the Holy City', pp. 288-90.

[638] Bauckham, *The Theology of the Book of Revelation*, p. 125, writes, 'To live faithfully and courageously according to the truth of God now requires a vision of that eschatological future. This the Spirit gives, first in terms adapted to the situation of each church in each of the seven messages, then much more fully in the great climax of John's whole visionary revelation: the vision of the New Jerusalem.'

ἐστιν ἀγγέλου ('a measure of a human that is of an angel'). Previously in the narrative, the angels (and other heavenly characters) have assisted John (and the churches) in their pneumatic discernment. In the New Jerusalem, heavenly measurements (ἀγγέλου) are equated to what might be termed 'humanly' (ἀνθρώπου) measurements. Such an association suggests that human insights have become indistinguishable from angelic insights in the New Jerusalem. Thus, those in the city have pneumatic discernment; they are like the (seven) stars; they are the wise ones, the discerning ones; they are associated with the seven angels.[639]

Third, in the middle of the city, there is a crystal river flowing from the divine throne. In the New Jerusalem, there is no longer a sea before the throne. While the crystal sea has an enigmatic function in the narrative, the crystal sea has appeared before the throne along with the seven torches, the seven Spirits. In the FG, water is associated with the Spirit. Thus, while there is some discontinuity in the new heavens and new earth in relation to the sea, there is some continuity in the description of the crystal sea and the crystal river that involves the Spirit. It is even possible that the crystal (κρυστάλλῳ, 4.5) sea has transformed into a crystal (κρύσταλλον, 22.1) river of life. On each side of the river of life is a tree of life that offers fruit to anyone who inhabits the holy city. The location of the tree by the river of life suggests that the tree is sustained by the river of life and is thereby pneumatically conditioned. Unlike the prohibition concerning the fruit of the tree in Genesis 3, the New Jerusalem freely offers the fruit of the tree of life (2.7).[640] The river of life and the tree of life provide full access to the Spirit of life. The Spirit of Truth sanctifies the bride in the water of life,[641] while the fruit from the tree and water nourish the people of God with T/truth, understanding, knowledge, and wisdom.[642]

---

[639] See again Revelation 2–3; Dan. 12.3.

[640] See Ellul, *Apocalypse*, p. 229.

[641] See Rossing, *The Choice Between Two Cities*, p. 143.

[642] Cf. Jn 7.39, see K.H. Rengstorf, 'ποταμός', *TDNT*, XI, pp. 604-607. See also Swete, *The Apocalypse of St. John*, p. 298; Smalley, 'The Paraclete', p. 295; Osborne, *Revelation*, p. 769; S.L. Rico, 'Thirsting for God: The Levitical Inheritance Motif in the Apocalypse', *WTJ* 74.2 (2012), pp. 428-30; Mangina, *Revelation*, p. 246.

Fourth, Rev. 21.5-7 describes that the overcomers will be the υἱός ('son') of the one on the throne. Strikingly, in the Johannine literature, the term υἱός ('son') is exclusively reserved to describe Jesus and his unique relationship with the Father. Such a description reveals that the overcomers will have a close and intimate relationship with the one on the throne in the New Jerusalem.[643] However, in keeping with the fact that υἱός ('son') occurs to describe the overcomers, 'Father' does not occur in 21.7. In Revelation, 'Father' is reserved to portray the relationship between Jesus and the Father.[644] Such a point apparently distinguishes between the extraordinary relationship of the overcomers with the one on the throne and the divine relationship between Jesus and the Father. There is both continuity and discontinuity in the relationship between the overcomers and the one on the throne and the relationship between Jesus and the Father. Among the possible implications of such a relationship between the overcomers and the one on the throne is that the overcomers will know (οἶδα) in ways similar to the υἱός ('son') and other heavenly characters, who perfectly know (οἶδα). The overcomers will receive a more complete knowledge that fulfills the promise in 2.17; they will receive a new name that no one knows (οἶδεν) except for them.

Fifth, a central aspect of pneumatic discernment throughout Revelation is the ability to recognize deceit, lies, and deception. In the New Jerusalem, the κοινὸν ('common'), the βδέλυγμα ('detestable things'), and the liars (ψεῦδος) are located outside the city, suggesting that their deceiving influence cannot defile those who are in the city.[645] While κοινὸν ('common') has not appeared to describe anyone or anything in the Johannine literature, its appearance here alongside βδέλυγμα ('detestable things') and liars suggests that this uncleanness is conditioned by deceitfulness (cf. 16.13).[646] Whereas the liars are located outside the city, the 144,000, who are (part of) the city, have no lie in their mouth, are pure because they have been sanctified in truth,

---

[643] Thomas, *The Apocalypse*, p. 630.

[644] So Koester, *Revelation*, p. 800. Cf. Rev. 1.6; 2.28; 3.5, 21; 14.1.

[645] Newton, *The Revelation Worldview*, p. 184, comments, concerning the New Jerusalem and the absence of the deception of the dragon, 'This implies that as a result people will become significantly freer to see spiritual reality and understand the revelation of God for themselves'.

[646] Murphy, *Fallen is Babylon*, p. 426; Skaggs and Benham, *Revelation*, p. 219.

belong to God having the name of God on their forehead, and have rejected the defiling deception of the triumvirate of evil and the whore.[647] Anyone who is a liar is not sanctified by the Spirit of Truth in the T/truth and thereby is not part of the holy city. In the New Jerusalem, the Spirit fills the whole earth with the light of the Lamb. The city is the dwelling place of the Truth, of the Spirit of Truth, and of the true God. Those who chose to distort the truth are outside the city.[648]

Finally, the Spirit of Truth is freely available, the overcomers have a more perfect knowledge, the fruit from the tree and the water of life are openly accessible, and deception is nowhere to be found in the city.[649] While the holy city envisions a future where discernment is immediately available, pneumatic discernment is already available to the churches. The seven Spirits are already sent out into the earth providing eschatological wisdom, understanding, truth, and knowledge; the churches are already hearing the Spirit of Truth; they can already see with the seven eyes of the Lamb; they already have access to the T/truth who is walking among them.

The eschatological reality described as the New Jerusalem presents an existence where there is unmediated access to truth, knowledge, understanding, and wisdom. While the pneumatic discernment in the present that is given by the eschatological Spirit offers a foretaste of the New Jerusalem, the immediate and unmediated access to pneumatic discernment, truth, wisdom, and knowledge provides a glimpse into a new manner of existence for the people of God that is portrayed in the New Jerusalem. This portrayal of unmediated access to the Truth and the Spirit of Truth raises the question, will there be a need for pneumatic discernment in the New Jerusalem? On the one hand, the people of God will have immediate access to God – to the wisdom, knowledge, and truth of God. This unmediated access expresses a radical discontinuity in the new heaven and earth that usurps the current condition of the churches where knowledge, understanding, truth, and wisdom are mediated realities that require discernment and interpretation. A reality where God is experienced in an unmediated manner is unfathomable. On the other

---

[647] Newton, *The Revelation Worldview*, p. 184.

[648] Newton, *The Revelation Worldview*, p. 185.

[649] Mangina, *Revelation*, p. 242.

hand, there seems to be continuity because even in the New Jerusalem there continues to be opportunities for pneumatic discernment, which include (but are not limited to): (i) the detailed description of the city, which requires discernment, (ii) the tension presented in the description of the nations who have been destroyed, who are located outside the city, who can find healing from the leaves of the tree of life, and who might be able to enter the city because of its opened gates,[650] and (iii) aspects of the divine persons remain shrouded in mystery because the one on the throne does not receive a fuller characterization even in the description of the New Jerusalem, suggesting that there remains divine mystery even in the New Jerusalem. These mysterious elements open the possibility for further revelation of God. In other words, in Revelation, discernment is closely associated with knowing a person because Truth is a person, and the New Jerusalem envisions a world where the people of God continue to discern God, albeit in a different (immediate) manner. Thus, full access to the knowledge of God does not suggest an existence where the people of God have obtained divine omniscience: they continue to be God's creation, not the creator. The New Jerusalem depicts a space and time, where, without deception, there is immediate access to the knowledge of God and to the T/truth of God by the Spirit of Truth in order that the people of God might continue to discern, to learn, and to know the infinite mysteries of the unfathomable God into the everlasting.[651]

---

[650] On the possibility of universal salvation for the kings of the earth, see Bauckham, *Climax of Prophecy*, p. 310. On the possibility that the kings of the earth will be judged, see R. Herms, *An Apocalypse for the Church and for the World: The Narrative Function of Universal Language in the Book of Revelation* (Berlin: de Gruyter, 2006), p. 14. For attempts that try to hold these two interpretative possibilities in tension, see D. Mathewson, 'The Destiny of the Nations in Revelation 21:1–22:5: A Reconsideration', *TynB* 53.1 (2002), pp. 121-42; Baines, 'The Identity of the Kings', pp. 73-88; M. Gilbertson, *God and History in the Book of Revelation: New Testament Studies in Dialogue with Pannenberg and Moltmann* (SNTS Monograph Series 124; Cambridge: Cambridge University Press, 2003), p. 107 n. 81, who writes, 'It is surely wiser to acknowledge the ambiguities of the text and to remember that the seer's aim is not to provide a neatly packaged historical survey, but rather an expanded perspective within which to view the present'.

[651] It seems that theosis might be a helpful avenue by which to explore this interpretative possibility further.

## Summary of Revelation 21.9–22.5

The New Jerusalem depicts the new heaven and the new earth where access to the Truth, the one on the throne, and the Spirit of Truth is unmediated. This immediate access to the truth, knowledge, and wisdom of God is signified in the description of the river of life, the tree of life, the title of υἱός ('son'), the absence of a temple, and the lack of falsehood. This unmediated access opens the possibility that discernment is complete. However, the people of God are not static characters who have obtained divine omniscience. The people of God in the New Jerusalem have full access to the truth, knowledge, understanding, discernment, and wisdom of God, which requires everlasting life to scratch the surface of the vast and full life of the divine mysteries.

## Epilogue – Revelation 22.6-21

The occurrence of δεῖξαι τοῖς δούλοις αὐτοῦ ἃ δεῖ γενέσθαι ἐν τάχει ('to show his servants what is necessary to happen soon') in Rev. 22.6 denotes the beginning of the epilogue on account that the wording corresponds exactly to the words in the prologue in Rev. 1.1.[652]

First, as in Rev. 19.9; 21.5, Revelation self-identifies as being true and faithful.[653] The narrative that is being heard is the revelation of the T/truth that is from God, which is conveyed in the Spirit of Truth/prophecy. The truthfulness of Revelation is established because God is true and the source of truth. The true God is ὁ θεὸς τῶν πνευμάτων τῶν προφητῶν ('the God of the Spirits of the prophets', 22.6). While it is possible that the phrase τῶν πνευμάτων τῶν προφητῶν ('the Spirits of the prophets') describes individual human spirits,[654] it seems the appearance of πνευμάτων ('Spirits'),

---

[652] Bauckham, *Climax of Prophecy*, p. 23.

[653] Murphy, *Fallen is Babylon*, p. 435, writes, 'It is fitting that the faithful and true Christ declares the words of Revelation faithful and true'. See Prigent, *The Apocalypse*, p. 635. See also Yarbro Collins, *The Apocalypse*, p. 152; Boesak, *Comfort and Protest*, p. 136; Michaels, *Revelation*, p. 250; Rowland, *Revelation*, p. 160.

[654] So Aune, *Revelation 17–22*, p. 1182. Concerning the possibility that there was a community of prophets, see Hill, 'Prophecy and Prophets', pp. 401-18; D.E. Aune, 'The Prophetic Circle of John of Patmos and the Exegesis of Revelation

based on the previous occurrences of πνεύματα ('Spirits') in Revelation, refers to the seven Spirits.[655] Previously, the Spirit conveyed the prophetic words of Jesus, empowered the prophecy of the two witnesses, and was identified as the Spirit of prophecy, while the seven Spirits are located before the throne, sent out into the world, and identified as the seven eyes and seven horns of the Lamb.[656] The appearance of prophecy, in a context where Revelation self-identifies as true and faithful, characterizes these prophets as true prophets because their prophecy derives from the Spirit of God.[657] The churches are blessed because they are encountering the prophetic, pneumatic truth.[658] True prophecy, inspired by the seven Spirits of Truth, encourages the churches to worship God, to stop lying, to become pure in truth, and to cease pursuing power and wealth. False prophets, who convey the deceit of the dragon, will be judged along with murderers, dogs, sorcerers, fornicators, and idolaters, denoting the destructive qualities of deception, deceit, and lying.[659]

Second, for a third time, John wrongly attempts to worship a character who is not divine, and on this occasion, it is an angel. John is again rebuked and is commanded to worship God alone. The churches have been warned against worshipping the whore, fellow-servants, and now angels in addition to earlier cautions against beast worship. The three occasions of John's error in worship rhetorically jolts the churches to pneumatic discernment, urging them to identify their own false worship practices, while also directing the churches to worship God alone. Deception was an underlying cause of John's worship of the whore, suggesting that the false worship among the churches correlates directly to deception and a lack of discernment.

---

22:16', *JSNT* 37 (1989), pp. 103-16. See also Smalley, *Revelation*, p. 576 who proposes that the addressees (the identity of ὑμῖν) are the seven ἄγγελοι of the seven churches.

[655] So Mazzaferri, *The Genre of the Book of Revelation*, p. 301; Michaels, *Revelation*, pp. 250-51; Skaggs and Benham, *Revelation*, p. 230; Thomas, *The Apocalypse*, p. 667.

[656] See Thomas, *The Apocalypse*, p. 667, who also observes a connection to 1 Jn 4.1, 2, 6.

[657] Ladd, *Revelation of John*, p. 289.

[658] For an examination of the seven beatitudes in Revelation, see V.P. Cruz, 'The Beatitudes of the Apocalypse: Eschatology and Ethics', in R.A. Muller and M. Shuster (eds.), *Perspectives on Christology: Essays in Honor of Paul K. Jewett* (Grand Rapids, MI: Zondervan, 1991), pp. 269-83.

[659] See Murphy, *Fallen is Babylon*, p. 438; Koester, *Revelation*, p. 839.

The truth revealed in Revelation is that no object, person, or system should be worshipped, only God should be worshiped.[660]

Third, the epilogue contains another interjection by the Spirit, which resounds with the voice of the bride: τὸ πνεῦμα καὶ ἡ νύμφη λέγουσιν· Ἔρχου ('the Spirit and the bride say, come'). These concluding remarks offer the discerning response of the churches who are shaped by the truth of the Spirit. The bride joins her words to the Spirit, suggesting that this is the pinnacle of pneumatic discernment. The bride has heard the Spirit and now imitates the voice of the Spirit.[661] The striking feature of such an association is that in the seven prophetic messages, the Spirit and Jesus spoke coterminously, implying that the epilogue envisions perfect harmony among the bride, the Spirit, and the resurrected Jesus. The second interjection, ὁ ἀκούων εἰπάτω· Ἔρχου ('let the one who is hearing, say come'), recalls the sevenfold hearing formula in the seven prophetic messages.[662] The association with the seven prophetic messages fuses together the bride with the one who hears the Spirit and the one who overcomes. This association suggests that hearing is not a passive activity but requires active discernment. The one who hears (the Spirit) echoes the voice of the Spirit, saying Ἔρχου ('come'). Anyone who hears, discerns, and obeys what the Spirit is saying, responds in concert with the Spirit and the bride. Thus, these responses are a test of discernment, revealing that those who discern the Truth of this

---

[660] Archer, *'I Was in the Spirit on the Lord's Day'*, pp. 285-86, writes, 'perhaps, false worship is more of an enticement than they realize. The call to worship God is thereby a call to communal self-discernment.' Koester, *Revelation*, p. 851, adds, 'In Revelation, the criterion for true prophecy is not simple prediction. False prophets are not denounced for making incorrect predictions but for promoting false worship (2:20; 13:11-18; 16:13-14; 19:20), whereas true prophets are like the witnesses clothed in sackcloth, who summon people to repentance (11:3, 10). True prophecy directs people to God and Jesus (19:10).' See also Caird, *Revelation of St. John*, p. 283; Smalley, *Revelation*, p. 569; Rotz, *Revelation*, p. 311.

[661] G. Biguzzi, 'The Chaos of Rev 22,6-21 and Prophecy in Asia', *Biblica* 83.2 (2002), p. 200, writes, 'John puts the ardent longing for Christ's Coming on the lips of the ideal Church, that is the Church that heeds what the Spirit says to her ... and who is preparing and adorning herself for her bridegroom (21,2) with the works of the saints (19,7d-8)'. See also Beasley-Murray, *The Book of Revelation*, pp. 344-45; Vanni, 'The Ecclesial Assembly', p. 84.

[662] Beale, *The Book of Revelation*, pp. 1143-44; Zimmermann, 'Nuptial Imagery', p. 177.

prophecy will respond by crying out accordingly, Ἔρχου ('come').[663] The third exhortation, ὁ διψῶν ἐρχέσθω ('let the one who is thirsty, come'), ὁ θέλων λαβέτω ὕδωρ ζωῆς δωρεάν ('let the one who desires the water of life, take freely'), indicates that the water of life and the tree of life (22.14) are freely obtainable in the present. The water of life and the tree of life are associated with the Spirit, suggesting that the Spirit is openly accessible to anyone who desires to drink. Among a variety of possible associations, partaking of the nourishment of the Spirit include: empowerment for true and faithful witness, sanctification in Truth, discernment, knowledge, wisdom, understanding, truth, resurrection, and life.[664]

Fourth, Rev. 22.18-19 offers a warning that anybody who adds or takes away from this prophecy will be severely punished. This warning verifies the self-identification that Revelation reveals Jesus, the divine Truth, who reveals the Truth from God that is conveyed in the Spirit (of Truth).[665] Since Revelation is the Truth, it should not be changed or altered; tampering with the Truth hinders the church's discernment. Anyone who takes from, adds to, or changes this divine Truth is a deceiver, reflecting the character of the evil trinity and the whore; and thereby, the deceiver will share in their judgments. Those who are sanctified in Truth do not lie and therefore would not act in such a deceptive manner as to alter the pneumatic Truth of God.[666]

## Summary of the Epilogue

The epilogue self-identifies as being true and faithful because it is revealing the Truth of God by the Spirit. The identification of Revelation as T/truth comes with a harrowing warning. Anyone who adds to or removes from this Truth is a deceiver like the dragon and will be punished. The Spirits of the prophets appears to refer to the

---

[663] Archer, *'I Was in the Spirit on the Lord's Day'*, p. 292, writes, 'to cry out for their Lord's return is also to participate in self-examination and discernment'. See also Rowland, 'Revelation', p. 734.

[664] Mounce, *The Book of Revelation*, p. 407, observes that in Rev. 7.14 the verb to wash appears in the aorist, and in 22.14 it appears as a present participation, which recalls the two washings found in John 13. On footwashing as a continual sign of the cleansing of post conversion sin in the Johannine community, see J.C. Thomas, *Footwashing in John 13 and the Johannine Community* (Cleveland, TN: CPT Press, 2nd edn, 1991; 2014).

[665] Michaels, *Revelation*, p. 257.

[666] Koester, *Revelation*, p. 857, comments, 'If the words are trustworthy and true (22:6), then alteration is an act of deception, which is contrary to the ways of God'.

seven Spirits. In the narrative, John seeks to wrongly worships the whore, a fellow-servant, and an angel, which directs the churches to examine their own worship practices. Such a point emphasizes that false worship is closely associated with deception, and thereby requires careful pneumatic discernment and at times direct assistance from God and God's servants. The churches are given an active test of pneumatic discernment. Upon hearing the Truth of the Apocalypse, the ones hearing this prophecy, along with the bride and the Spirit, should respond: Come!

# 6

# PNEUMATIC DISCERNMENT, THE APOCALYPSE, AND PENTECOSTAL THEOLOGY

The final section of this work attempts to construct overtures toward a theology of pneumatic discernment. The piece has examined the early Pentecostal (con)text in chapters three and four that then explored the intertext of the Apocalypse that now returns to dialogue with the Pentecostal (con)text. This theological construction, formed by the Pentecostal (con)text and the intertext of scripture, is for and in the Pentecostal community.

Internal evidence and literary markers appeared in the Apocalypse that direct the churches to pneumatic discernment. The first major structural section of the Apocalypse offers a sevenfold repetition of ὁ ἔχων οὖς ἀκουσάτω τί τὸ πνεῦμα λέγει ('let the one who has an ear, hear what the Spirit is saying'), establishing an immediate emphasis on discernment and the involvement of the Spirit in the process. When other significant literary markers appear that direct the churches to discern, such as πνευματικῶς, ὧδε ('here [is]'), σοφία ('wisdom'), νοῦν ('discernment'), ὁ ἔχων ('the one having'), μυστήριον ('mystery'), and ψηφισάτω ('calculate'), it seems that all these activities are accomplished in, with, and by the Spirit.[1] Beyond these explicit markers, other indicators in the text suggest that the whole of the Apocalypse is pneumatic discernment. The whole narrative is the Apocalypse of Jesus Christ, who is the Truth (Rev. 1.1,

---

[1] The connection between these literary markers becomes most explicit in Revelation 13.

Jn 14.6). The act of reading the narrative is an attempt to reveal (ἀποκάλυψις) the mystery (μυστήριον) of God. On occasion, the Apocalypse self-validates its own truthfulness.[2] The self-validation of the truthfulness of the Apocalypse does not assume that the churches have obtained the fullness of divine T/truth in the Apocalypse and that once received there is nothing more for the churches to do. Rather, the Apocalypse regards Truth as a person, while communicating this Truth with challenging and complex symbols and images that direct the churches to stop and discern.[3] The churches wrestle with the Truth as they hear, see, obey, have a mind, have wisdom, and discern in and by the Spirit.[4] If the medium is the message, then the Apocalypse is a medium of pneumatic discernment.

One aspect of postmodernism considers that everything is text. If all is text, then it tends to follow that all is interpretation.[5] While this work is not able to offer an exhaustive discussion, this chapter seeks to add to the postmodern conversation in light of this study of the Apocalypse on discernment, considering that if everything is interpretation, then perhaps everything is discernment.

Discernment, while an aspect of interpretation, more broadly examines interpretation of a process of decision making that attempts to discover the truthfulness or the meaningfulness of interpretations. Discernment is the process of 'sorting, evaluating, and distinguishing among competing voices'.[6] In the same manner that everything is interpretation, every community and every individual partake in some sort of process of discernment whether intentional or not:

> The fact is, of course, that whether consciously or not, in every case some process of discernment or evaluation is being followed.

---

[2] See Rev. 19.9; 21.5; 22.6.

[3] Again, see Ruiz, *Ezekiel in the Apocalypse*, p. 220, who goes as far as to say that the idiosyncratic Greek of the Apocalypse is intentionally difficult.

[4] Newton, *The Revelation Worldview*, p. 181, writes, 'John sees it as taking some level of spiritual discernment to actually receive God's revelation through the prophetic witnesses'.

[5] On this see J.K.A. Smith, *Who's Afraid of Postmodernism?: Taking Derrida, Lyotard, and Foucault to Church* (Grand Rapids, MI: Baker Academic, 2006).

[6] L.T. Johnson, *Scripture & Discernment: Decision Making in the Church* (Nashville, TN: Abingdon Press, 1983, 1996), p. 25. See also M.J. Cartledge, 'Charismatic Prophecy: A Definition and Description', *JPT* 2.5 (1994), pp. 95-96.

It may be wholly naive and credulous, or it may be stiflingly pedantic; but each time a claim to inspiration is made, the community and/or individuals who hear it do make up their minds one way or other about it. If then evaluation is inevitable, it is all the more necessary that the gift of discernment be taken seriously.[7]

J. Dunn recognizes the centrality of discernment, but also the neglect among many Christian communities.[8] If there is any hint that everything is discernment, then the neglect of discernment becomes ostensibly problematic.

The significance of discernment, as well as its neglect, seems to be generally true for the Pentecostal community as well.[9] Some have taken up the task, such as S. Land, who has proposed that the theological task should be described as 'discerning reflection' for the Pentecostal community.[10] A theological construction of pneumatic discernment is especially significant for the Pentecostal community because the Pentecostal theological process is discerning reflection. This study of the Apocalypse seeks to contribute to the conversation concerning the theological task for the Pentecostal community and perhaps any other community who describes their theological process as discerning reflection.

The issue of discernment in the contemporary context is one that is vast, and there is no way that this work, nor this chapter will be able to address the issues at hand fully. This chapter seeks to bring into conversation some theological overtures in the Apocalypse largely with, but not limited to, Pentecostal scholars who have worked

---

[7] J.D.G. Dunn, 'Discernment of Spirits – A Neglected Gift', *The Christ & The Spirit: Pneumatology* (Grand Rapids, MI: Eerdmans, 1979, 1998), II, p. 323.

[8] Hence, the title of Dunn's article, 'Discernment of Spirits – A Neglected Gift'.

[9] See C.M. Robeck, 'Discerning the Spirit in the Life of the Church', in W.R. Barr and R.M. Yocom (eds.), *Church in the Movement of the Spirit* (Grand Rapids: Eerdmans, 1994), pp. 29-49.

[10] Land, *Pentecostal Spirituality*, p. 23. See also S.E. Parker, *Led by the Spirit: Toward a Practical Theology of Pentecostal Discernment and Decision Making* (Cleveland, TN: CPT Press, 2015), originally published as S.E. Parker, *Led by the Spirit: Toward a Practical Theology of Pentecostal Discernment and Decision Making* (JPTSup 7; Sheffield: Sheffield Academic Press, 1996), who has made a significant contribution concerning discernment for the Pentecostal community. Cf. M. Turner, *The Holy Spirit and Spiritual Gifts in the New Testament Church and Today* (Peabody, MA: Hendrickson Publishers, Revised edn, 1996, 1998), pp. 323-25.

toward a theology of discernment. The theological overtures will in-clude: (1) pneumatic discernment and knowing the one on the throne, the Lamb, and the seven Spirits; (2) pneumatic discernment and the means of knowing the Truth: (i) experience, (ii) community, (iii) story, and (iv) hymns and lament; and (3) pneumatic discernment and the churches.

## Pneumatic Discernment and the One on the Throne, the Seven Spirits, and Jesus

The Truth unveiled in this narrative is identified as Jesus; the Truth originates from the true God; and the Truth is conveyed in and by the Spirit of Truth. In the Johannine literature, truth and wisdom are divinely conditioned, and thereby must be conveyed by a divine source. In Revelation, truth and discernment are pneumatically, chris-tologically, and theologically conditioned.[11]

The prophetic Truth that is from the true God is conveyed in and by the divine Spirit.[12] Divine truth, discernment, understanding, knowledge, and wisdom are attributes of the seven Spirits[13] and con-veyed ἐν πνεύματι ('in the Spirit') to the churches and to the world. John receives this prophetic vision ἐν πνεύματι ('in the Spirit'), and the narrative is structured around the appearances of four ἐν πνεύματι ('in the Spirit') phrases.[14] Since Revelation calls for discernment, it is not surprising that the structure of the narrative

---

[11] See esp. Newton, *The Revelation Worldview*, pp. 186-92 (186), for a discussion of truth as divine revelation. He writes, 'the picture of truth and knowledge sug-gested by Revelation as fundamental or ultimate is revelatory: the One who knows all shares with us a portion of his infinite knowledge, primarily through his chosen witnesses and prophets'.

[12] The role of the Spirit in discernment has been emphasized in Luke/Acts as well. See Johnson, *Scripture & Discernment*, pp. 68-80, 98-108; Thomas, 'Women, Pentecostals, and the Bible', pp. 41-56 See also P.G.R. de Villiers, 'Communal Discernment in the Early Church', *Acta Theologica* 17 (2013), p. 149, who writes, 'Discernment thus has to do with following the lead of the Spirit of God … The divine-human relationship in discernment is symbiotic, picturing a flawless unity between the divine and human. The Spirit is not portrayed in an impersonal man-ner … or on his own, but this phrase describes the Spirit as being in an intimate relationship with the apostles and elders so that their decision is also a decision of the Holy Spirit.'

[13] Cf. Isa. 11.2.

[14] Revelation 1.10; 4.2; 17.3; 21.10.

accentuates the role of the Spirit in the reception of this prophetic vision. The Spirit of prophecy dynamically and actively inspires the prophetic words contained in the Apocalypse, and all who hear the true words of God in this prophecy encounter the Spirit of Truth. The churches are directed to view the great city πνευματικῶς (11.8), that is to view the city with pneumatic perception. The churches are exhorted seven times to hear the Spirit who communicates prophetic Truth to the churches. The divine Spirit actively and dynamically 'speaks for God and for Christ. This is one reason the deity of the Spirit is so important.'[15] In Revelation, while the Spirit speaks coterminously with Jesus, the Spirit also has a distinctive voice. The Spirit interjects, while affirming a beatitude (14.13), and responds along with the bride to beckon the coming of Jesus (22.17). Even the witness of Jesus seems to include a witness concerning the Spirit, particularly the invitation to drink the water of life (22.17).[16] Truth is discerned and received ἐν πνεύματι ('in the Spirit') because the Spirit is the means by which divine discernment and truth are conveyed.

While the Spirit is central to the role of discernment in the Apocalypse, a stark distinction between the activity of the seven Spirits, the Lamb, and the one on the throne is artificial. The true words of this prophecy originate from the true God (6.10; 15.3; 16.7; 19.2). The seven Spirits are introduced alongside the one on the throne and Jesus in the prologue (1.4-5). As the seven torches, the seven Spirits, are located before the divine throne and the seven Spirits are identified as the seven eyes and the seven horns of the Lamb (4.5; 5.6). The seven Spirits are sent into the world to convey divine truth. The seven Spirits are identified as the *modus operandi* of the divine throne and the Lamb, accomplishing the divine will in the world. The seven Spirits fill the earth with the knowledge of God and the Truth from God, making known the one on the throne and Jesus. Even though the one on the throne is revealed, the characterization of the one on the throne contains elements of mystery throughout the narrative. There is no one able to look upon the scroll except for the divine Lamb who perceives with the seven Spirits. The rider on the white horse has a name that no one knows except for him. In Rev. 1.20 when the resurrected Jesus reveals the mystery of the seven stars and

---

[15] Thomas and Macchia, *Revelation*, p. 490.

[16] So Thomas and Macchia, *Revelation*, pp. 498-99.

seven lampstands, the identity of the seven stars remain mysterious. There are limits to human knowledge. Even when divine T/truth is revealed, there remains mystery because truth, wisdom, and knowledge are divinely conditioned.[17]

Seeing the world via the seven Spirits (πνευματικῶς) is analogous to perceiving the world as the Lamb, 'We cannot view the Spirit as our eyes until we first see the Spirit as the eyes of the Lamb. The Spirit links our wisdom to the Lamb's.'[18] Jesus is identified as the Truth who is named True and Faithful and who is the true and faithful witness. Jesus, as the Truth, is being revealed and Jesus is identified as the one who is revealing the Truth in Revelation.[19] The Lamb who shares the divine throne embodies the knowledge of God and the witness of Jesus. Truth is a person in the Apocalypse.[20] The resurrected Jesus has perfect insight and knows each situation of the seven churches, seemingly by means of the seven Spirits who are personified as the fiery eyes of the Lamb (Revelation 2–3). The sacrificial Lamb exemplifies pneumatic discernment for the churches in the person, life, ministry, death, and resurrection of Jesus. The wisdom of the Lamb includes love and liberation (1.5). The Lamb's wisdom includes hearing the vicious Lion and the regal Root while seeing a slaughtered Lamb upon the divine throne (Revelation 5). The wisdom of the Lamb – seeing πνευματικῶς – involves their Lord's death in the great city (Revelation 11). Thus, in Revelation all truth originates from the true God, is associated with Jesus, and is conveyed by the seven Spirits.

The association of God and pneumatic discernment appeared in the early Pentecostal literature. Early Pentecostals believed that Jesus

---

[17] See Newton, *The Revelation Worldview*, p. 195, who adds, 'According to Revelation, in this age human beings cannot independently attain to complete objective or absolute knowledge (at least about spiritual reality), due to their limitations as creatures, their bias as sinners, and the deception of the devil'.

[18] Thomas and Macchia, *Revelation*, p. 488.

[19] Newton, *The Revelation Worldview*, p. 166.

[20] F. Macchia, 'Pneumatological Feminist/Womanist Theologies: The Importance of Discernment', *Pneuma* 35 (2013), p. 71, writes, 'Since this Word is fundamentally a person (the Word or Son made flesh) and not a concept, the Word thus cannot be mastered or manipulated by anyone and, therefore, continues to inspire an expanding diversity of witnesses'.

and the Spirit were actively and dynamically teaching the church, offering truth, wisdom, and knowledge to the churches.[21] Hymns exhorted the churches to hear the active voice of the Lord in the Spirit:

Hear ye the word of the Lord
O hear ye the word of the Lord,
He speaks to you now in his word;
O hear you the word of the Lord.[22]

Mary Hubbell offered one of the best examples in the early Pentecostal literature that explores the role of the seven Spirits in the process of discernment that is (in)formed by Revelation 5. She discerned that, while every person has some sort of perception, it is only by pneumatic perception, by the seven eyes of the Lamb, that anyone is able to obtain 'perfect knowledge'.[23]

Jesus and the Spirit are central to Pentecostal theology and worship.[24] S. Land has considered that the story of the triune God shapes and forms the Pentecostal community, 'the acts of Jesus must be taken together with the acts of the Spirit and the story of God the Father throughout Scripture, for all three of these are part of the one story which should evoke and shape the christian life for the kingdom of God'.[25] Similarly, C. Pinnock comments on the centrality of the story of Jesus for discernment:

The gospel story helps us discern the movements of the Spirit. From this narrative we learn the pattern of God's ways. So wherever we see traces of Jesus in the world and people opening up to his ideals, we know we are in the presence of the Spirit. Wherever, for example, we find self-sacrificing love, care about community, longings for justice, wherever people love one another, care for the sick, make peace not war, wherever there is

---

[21] See chapters 3 and 4 of this work for numerous examples. See also Green, *Sanctifying Interpretation*, pp. 115-18, who explores early Pentecostal Christological readings of the HB and NT.

[22] *TWT* 4.4 (October 1911), p. 1.

[23] See again *TBM* 6.133 (May 15, 1913), p. 4.

[24] For example, the five-fold gospel.

[25] Land, *Pentecostal Spirituality*, p. 163.

beauty and concord, generosity and forgiveness, the cup of cold water, we know the Spirit of Jesus is present.[26]

The centrality of the role of the Spirit in Pentecostal theology and worship has been explored by S. Parker who describes discernment as 'following the leadings of the Spirit'. The process of discernment evaluates these 'leadings', determining if they are from the Spirit, from one's own urges, or from demonic forces.[27] The ability to know, to understand, to discern is dependent on the activity of the Spirit.[28] The Spirit actively and dynamically communicates truth and discernment to the church:[29]

> The Spirit also convicts the church where it has gone wrong and helps us grasp old truths in new ways. The Spirit helps us recognize signs of the times and position the words of Jesus in changing situations. The criterion cannot be equated with what we have thought so far, because we may not have been true to the gospel in our thinking. We may be standing in need of correction … Therefore, let us listen to what the Spirit of Jesus is saying to the churches (Rev. 2:7).[30]

One consideration that the Pentecostal community needs to explore further is that while the Spirit and Jesus are dominant features of Pentecostal worship and theology, Revelation connects Truth and discernment to the Spirit, to Jesus, and to the one on the throne. The quest for truth and wisdom should not be embarked (perhaps, cannot be pursued) apart from a desire to know the triune God more fully. Whatever issues of discernment a community encounters should be viewed in light of the gospel of the triune God. Thereby, when issues of decision-making and discernment arise in the Pentecostal community, the process of discernment should begin with attempting to

---

[26] C.H. Pinnock, *Flame of Love: A Theology of the Holy Spirit* (Downers Grove, IL: InterVarsity Press, 1996), pp. 209-10.

[27] Parker, *Led by the Spirit*, p. 7.

[28] See J.R. Levison, *Filled with the Spirit* (Grand Rapids, MI: Eerdmans, 2009), who explores the relationship of the Spirit and wisdom in the HB, the Pauline literature, and the FG.

[29] C.M. Robeck, 'Discernment: Insight into the Mind of Christ', *Pneuma* 11.2 (1989), p. 75, writes, 'for the church to speak and act prophetically in appropriate ways, the church must discern the mind of Christ through the Spirit who guides us into all truth (John 16:13)'.

[30] Pinnock, *Flame of Love*, p. 211. See also Green, *Sanctifying Interpretation*, p. 117.

hear the active Spirit and to recognize the Truth of God in light of the story of God.

The Spirit makes possible the ability to discern divine truth because divine truth is directly connected to knowing God;[31] in order to know the triune God, God must reveal God's-self to the churches. Theology, in a basic sense, is to know, to learn, to worship, to reflect on, and to study God, while theology, for Pentecostals, is discerning reflection. Everyone in the community is tasked to reflect on God discerningly because the process to know God is a primary task of pneumatic discernment in Revelation. Theology as discerning reflection begins with the exploration of the triune God in order that the church will know God better, and so the church will be the church: 'But the thing, which I here particularly mean is this: The knowledge of the Three-One God is interwoven with all true Christian faith; with all vital religion'.[32] Intentional and dedicated theological work continues to be needed among Pentecostal communities in order that they might know God more fully and be better prepared for the process of pneumatic discernment.

However, since the Apocalypse is the revelation of Jesus, since Jesus is the one who is being revealed in this apocalyptic, prophetic narrative, then the Apocalypse implies that knowing God is challenging. Knowing God resists and subverts simplicity and easily identifiable answers. The difficulty with such a beginning position for discernment is that discerning the divine activities might be one of the most challenging aspects of the process. The mysterious and challenging aspects of discernment associated with knowing God is a staunch reminder to the Pentecostal community that the work of theology and the work of discernment is a continuous process that is to

---

[31] Green, *Sanctifying Interpretation*, p. 163, writes, 'those depths of possibility hidden in the Scriptures are nothing less than the depths of God's own self-understanding. To search those depths is to share in the Spirit's searching of the deep things of God (1 Cor. 2.10) where Christ, our sanctification, is found. Therefore, as we are searching, we are participating in the divine life, knowing God as God knows God.' Newton, *The Revelation Worldview*, p. 165, comments, 'There is a moral dimension to human failure to know God and his will in the Bible (Prov 1:7; Rom 1:18–32; Rev 21:27)'.

[32] J. Wesley, 'On the Trinity: Sermon 55', *Sermons of John Wesley* (May 8, 1775); accessed via http://wesley.nnu.edu/john-wesley/the-sermons-of-john-wesley-1872-edition/sermon-55-on-the-trinity.

be revisited and reconsidered. Even in the New Jerusalem, there continues to be room for the churches to wrestle with the wisdom and knowledge of the triune God. Thus, since discernment is closely associated with knowing God, then discernment will contain elements that are mysterious and unknown concerning both pneumatic discernment and knowing God.[33]

## Pneumatic Discernment and the Means of Discerning the Truth in the Apocalypse

### Pneumatic Experience

In Revelation, pneumatic discernment begins with John's pneumatic experience on Patmos. John is ἐν πνεύματι ('in the Spirit') on the island of Patmos and receives the prophetic vision that is the Apocalypse of Jesus Christ (1.10). The prologue suggests that the churches must be ἐν πνεύματι ('in the Spirit') to receive a revelation of Truth.[34] Other indicators, including having an ear to hear the Spirit, as well as the appearance of πνευματικῶς, connect further these associations of pneumatic involvement and experience.[35] The first appearance of ἐν πνεύματι ('in the Spirit') occurs alongside ἐν τῇ κυριακῇ ἡμέρᾳ ('on the Lord's day'). This connection fuses together the church's liturgical setting (the Lord's Day) with the eschatological day of the Lord.[36] In the eschatological sense, the unmediated access to discernment that is represented in the New Jerusalem is already available to the churches by the eschatological Spirit. In these divine encounters, the churches are called to discernment.[37]

---

[33] See A. Yong, *Discerning the Spirit(s): A Pentecostal-Charismatic Contribution to Christian Theology of Religions* (JPTSup 20; Sheffield: Sheffield Academic Press, 2000), pp. 67-69.

[34] See Newton, *The Revelation Worldview*, pp. 167-68.

[35] See Rev. 2.7, 11, 17, 29; 3.6, 13, 22. Cf. Rev. 13.9.

[36] Thomas and Macchia, *Revelation*, p. 486, comment that such an eschatological outlook does not assume an escapist outlook; rather, the vision directs the churches to discern by the Spirit the world in which they live and offers another perspective from which to view the world.

[37] Johnson, *Scripture & Discernment*, pp. 102-104, notes the importance of pneumatic experiences in the Acts.

Pneumatic experience changes the way that the churches look at the world.[38] Pneumatic experience transforms the churches to see like the Lamb who sees with the seven Spirits (πνευματικῶς, 11.8). Pneumatic experience entails seeing the great city transform pneumatically and kaleidoscopically into a collage of trans-temporal realities and trans-geographical locations where time and space seem to break apart while deconstructing perceptions and realities. Pneumatic experience forms the churches to view the Lion and the Root as the slaughtered Lamb; overcoming morphs into sacrifice and death; poverty transforms into wealth and wealth into poverty, power becomes prostration, and the persecuted ones become the authorities. These experiences in the Spirit reshape the ways that the churches view reality and subvert the wisdom of the world. In this sense, the Spirit's role in discernment is not merely 'illumination'; rather, the Spirit of Truth actively and dynamically forms, transforms, and sanctifies the churches in Truth in order that they might see like the slaughtered Lamb and know the Truth from God.

The transforming experience of the Spirit changes the way that the churches view scripture.[39] In the Apocalypse, the seven eyes of Yahweh, representing divine discernment in Zechariah 4, become the seven eyes of the Lamb that are identified as the seven Spirits. The attributes of the Spirit-empowered messiah in Isaiah 11 transform into the seven Spirits who are divine wisdom and divine power (Revelation 5). The seven lampstands and seven eyes of Yahweh in Zech. 4.10 transmute into the seven Spirits who are the seven torches, who are sent out into the world to accomplish the divine will on earth and to fill the whole earth with the knowledge of God. The seven lampstands are identified as the seven churches in the Apocalypse who are dynamically empowered by the seven torches who are the power and wisdom of the Lamb. ἐν πνεύματι, the lion, the bear, the leopard, and the horned beast of Daniel 7 mutate into one beast who is composed of a leopard, a bear, and a lion (13.2). Thus, while there might be a variety of possible reasons as to why the HB texts appear

---

[38] See G. Twelftree, *Christ Triumphant: Exorcism Then and Now* (Sevenoaks: Hodder and Stoughton, 1985), pp. 181-82, who observes in the Pauline literature that the Spirit renews and transforms the mind of the church in order that they might have spiritual discernment, cf. Romans 7; 8; 12.2; 1 Cor. 12.1-3, 10.

[39] See Herms, 'πνευματικῶς', pp. 135-46.

differently in the Apocalypse, the narrative suggests that pneumatic experiences reshape the perceptions of the scriptures.[40]

While pneumatic experience is a central aspect of pneumatic discernment in Revelation, experience, including the miraculous and signs and wonders, is not the sole or primary identifying marker of discernment.[41] On the one hand, fire comes from the mouth of the two witness and is closely associated with their pneumatic witness; the Spirit is the giver of life in the Apocalypse, raising the two witnesses from the dead (11.5, 11). On the other hand, the beast is raised from a mortal head wound (13.3). The beast from the earth performs signs and wonders, even manipulating fire and thereby mimicking the prophetic activities of the divine Spirit and the two witnesses (13.11-15). The beast is even able to give πνεῦμα ('Spirit') to the image of the beast (13.15). The unclean spirits, the spawn of the evil triumvirate, perform signs and wonders (16.14). Hence, the beasts and the unclean spirits are able to perform signs and wonders in the Apocalypse, even mimicking the activities of the divine Spirit.[42] The possibility that the dragon and its minions are able to mimic the activity of the triune God indicates that the churches must discern their experiences, even those experiences that occur in the churches, that

---

[40] Fowl, *Engaging Scripture*, p. 100, observes a similar occurrence in the FG. The disciples could not understand the meaning of Jesus' actions and words in Jn 2.22 and 12.6 until after the giving of the Spirit (who brings remembrance of all things, Jn 14.26) and the resurrection of Jesus. Remembrance allows scripture 'to be understood in new and unanticipated ways'. So also Levison, *Filled with the Spirit*, pp. 402-403.

[41] See Macchia, 'Pneumatological Feminist/Womanist Theologies', pp. 68-69. F. Martin, 'Discernment of Spirits, Gift of', *DPCM*, (1988), p. 246, writes,

> The age of enlightenment with its 'closed system' of thinking tended even in religious circles to reduce discernment to prudence or character evaluation. With the abundant reappearance of spiritual manifestations, the true role of discernment has become once again apparent. Because the Spirit of God moves in the human heart, bestowing his gifts, especially that of prophecy, and because these can be counterfeited by Satan and by human spirit, we see the need once again to pray for the gift of discernment of spirits so that we may know 'those things given to us by God'.

[42] Dunn, 'Discernment of Spirits', p. 314, notes a similar outlook in the Pauline literature, writing 'Wherever he is confronted with prophecy as a living force, he is quick to indicate that prophetic inspiration alone is no guarantee that the inspired word is of the Spirit'. See also Johnson, *Scripture & Discernment*, p. 64; Fowl, *Engaging Scripture*, p. 104. Cf. 1 Cor. 2.13; 12.8-10; 14.29. See also *Did* 11.7-8; 12.1; *Shepherd of Hermas* 11.12-13, 16.

appear to be religious, ecstatic, or miraculous. The beast is able to impersonate the activity of the triune God; thereby, it is possible that the source of the churches' experiences is diabolic.[43] While signs and wonders play a role in discernment, the manner by which evil mimics the Spirit suggests that the churches' discernment should not be based solely on miraculous manifestations; experience, miracles, and signs and wonders are not, themselves, signs of discernment; rather, they require discernment. The spirits, the experiences, the miracles, and the signs and wonders must be tested.[44]

Pentecostals believe, like Revelation, that they experience the divine Spirit in their communities: 'Though often criticized for their emphasis on experience (and sometimes rightly so), Pentecostals can find in the Apocalypse confirmation that true worship *is* experiential, involving the whole person – body, mind and spirit – in encounter with God *in the Spirit*.'[45] While experience is a central aspect of Pentecostal worship, it is possible that some communities have not been intentional in their discernment of these experiences:

A people for whom the leading of the Spirit is so important must have means for discerning what is of the Spirit's leading and what

---

[43] See Johnson, *Scripture & Discernment*, pp. 136-39.

[44] Thomas and Macchia, *Revelation*, p. 490, write:

Experience as fallible cannot be that which fundamentally guides the substance of revealed wisdom. Experience does not occur within a vacuum but is mediated by social, cultural, and personal realities. How we construe our experiences profoundly influences what they mean to us and how they shape us. There is no such thing as an immediate experience of God in the absolute sense of the term. Our experiences are thus in constant danger of falsification or of being construed in support of self-serving agendas. Prophetic discernment based in revelation will thus play a seminal role in human experience of God. This role means that revelation must be determined first by God's own self-disclosure in Christ and the biblical witness to Christ. The Spirit's discernment is faithful to the words and actions of God and of the Lamb.

[45] Archer, *'I Was in the Spirit on the Lord's Day'*, p. 301. Waddell, *Spirit of the Book of Revelation*, p. 130, notes, 'Pentecostals believe they will encounter God when they read the Bible, and I have proposed that a revelation of Jesus is necessary in order to interpret scripture properly. Therefore, a reading of the biblical text, not unlike the christophany experienced by John, should involve a certain amount of fear and worship.' So also Parker, *Led by the Spirit*, p. 1, who comments, 'At the heart of Pentecostal practice is an experience of the Spirit's immediate presence, an experience that often involves claims to direct guidance from the Spirit for decisions and actions by Pentecostal believers'. See also Robeck, 'Discerning the Spirit', pp. 36-37; Green, *Sanctifying Interpretation*, p. 48.

is not. Yet when one seeks Pentecostal literature on discernment and decision making one finds very little. There is thus a further need to explore how Pentecostal discernment and decision making actually takes place and to elaborate the meaning and significance of these practices both for Pentecostals and the wider Christian community.[46]

J. Newton considers Pentecostal experience in light of the Apocalypse, commenting that while Pentecostals have an openness to spiritual experiences, they have not been fully attentive to Revelation's exhortation concerning discernment. Pentecostals have either uncritically accepted 'all claims to spiritual experience' or 'demonize their rivals'.[47] With the emphasis that is placed on experience in the Pentecostal communities and if there is any lack of intentionality in the discernment process, then the community is in danger of bestial deceptions. Revelation warns against an over-emphasis placed on experiences because some experiences originate from the beast. The Apocalypse alerts the churches that the Spirit *and* the beast perform signs and wonders. The Spirit *and* the beast raise the dead. The Spirit *and* the beast prophesy. The beast manipulates the churches through these signs and wonders to coerce the churches to worship the image of the beast.

Thus, the churches must be diligent in their pneumatic discernment to determine if a prophecy is the voice of the Lamb or the voice of the dragon, if the source of the signs and wonders is the Spirit or the false prophet. Some Pentecostals have described these experiences as associated with intuition.[48] Herein lies the trouble of discernment. Some such as S. Land have proposed that discernment is possible for those who have corporately experienced the Spirit of

---

[46] Parker, *Led by the Spirit*, p. 4. See also Dunn, 'Discernment of Spirits', pp. 312, 319-22 for this critique.

[47] Newton, *The Revelation Worldview*, p. 150. Concerning prophecy, Cartledge, 'Charismatic Prophecy', p. 89, notes, 'Most charismatics would stress the need to test prophecy, since they believe that a message contains a mixture of the human and the divine'.

[48] See Parker, *Led by the Spirit*, p. 213, discovers that intuition in discernment is one aspect of the transrational discernment in the Pentecostal community. See also J.C. Thomas, *The Devil, Disease and Deliverance: Origins of Illness in New Testament Thought* (Cleveland, TN: CPT Press, 1998, 2010), p. 312, on the intuitive aspect of discernment.

God.[49] While Land aligns closely with Revelation that the church is able to discern rightly only by the activity of the Spirit, the issue arises how does a community discern if their experiences originate from the Spirit or from the beast, if the beast is able to appear like the Lamb or the Spirit? S. Parker attempts to explore this tension of discernment by integrating ecstatic experience with structures, conjoining ecstasy with reason. He describes this type of knowing as 'affective knowing' or 'ecstatic reason'.[50] It seems one way forward concerning the tension between 'experience' and 'structure' is not to allow these categories to become mutually exclusive mediums of ways that the churches experience God. In other words, ecstatic experiences are not the only way to experience God.[51] Even in the 'structure', the Spirit is experienced, forming and sanctifying the churches in the Truth.[52] Such a reflection leads to the question, what other ways does the Apocalypse consider that the community experiences God (in order to know God and thereby discern if the signs and wonders originate from God)?[53]

## Community

The Apocalypse of Truth, of Jesus Church, is sent to the seven churches by John. The seven prophetic messages describe that Jesus walks among the churches and knows the situation in every church, while the Spirit actively speaks the prophetic words of Jesus to the churches. The seven prophetic messages offer a glimpse into the manner in which Jesus views the world. In community, the churches

---

[49] See Land, *Pentecostal Spirituality*, pp. 93-94.

[50] Parker, *Led by the Spirit*, p. 194, adds, 'Ecstatic reason recognizes dimensions of knowing that are less technically rational and more holistic in that both affective and cognitive dimensions of knowing are involved'. It seems that R. Moore's proposal of a 'Spirit-less Word' or a 'Word-less Spirit' anticipates the kinds of observations from Parker, see Moore, 'Canon and Charisma', p. 91.

[51] Parker, *Led by the Spirit*, p. 176. See also Robeck, 'Discerning the Spirit', p. 47.

[52] See A. Yong, 'Discerning the Spirit', *CC* 123.5 (2006), pp. 31-32.

[53] Fowl, *Engaging Scripture*, p. 114, observes:

Understanding and interpreting the Spirit's movement is a matter of communal debate and discernment over time. This debate and discernment is itself often shaped both by prior interpretations of scripture and by traditions of practice and belief. This means that in practice it is probably difficult, if not impossible, to separate and determine clearly whether a community's scriptural interpretation is prior to or dependent upon a community's experience of the Spirit. Experience of the Spirit shapes the reading of scripture, but scripture most often provides the lenses through which the Spirit's work is perceived and acted upon.

hear the prophetic witness from the prophet John who offers the witness from the true and faithful witness, Jesus Christ. The Spirit actively and dynamically speaks the witness of Jesus to the churches. Every prophetic message concludes with an exhortation to hear the Spirit, directing every church to pneumatic discernment.[54] While the matter of discernment varies among the churches, every church is urged to hear the Truth, to hear the Spirit, and to obey. Not only is the task of discernment laid upon each individual church, but the whole church is tasked to participate in the process of discernment of each message.[55] The communal aspect of discernment is further evident in the description of other characters in the narrative who aid in discernment. The elders, the fellow-servants, and the angels (cf. 10.1-11; 17.7-18; 19.9-10; 22.8) assist John in discerning the Root, Lion, Lamb (5.5), the 144,000, the great crowd (7.13-17), and the great whore. John is part of a prophetic community who seem to assist in the process of discernment (22.6, 9). The Truth that is conveyed by the Spirit is received in a communal setting; it is received in the churches.[56]

---

[54] Archer, *'I Was in the Spirit on the Lord's Day'*, pp. 302-303, writes,

It is not the *words* of this prophecy that the churches are called on to discern (hence the curse formula of 22.18-19); rather, by means of the prophecy they are called to discern their *own condition* (Revelation 2–3) as well as the *culture* around them. By means of the words of this prophecy, the Spirit aids the churches in properly discerning the insidious workings of the Dragon and beasts (Revelation 12–13), so that in their worship the churches can sing the song of Rev. 12.10-12. By means of the words of this prophecy, the Spirit aids the churches in properly discerning their true identity as the Bride of the Lamb, so that in their worship they can sing the songs of Rev. 19.6-8. The words of the prophecy are to be received *in the Spirit* because John receives them *in the Spirit*. The climactic statement – 'the testimony of Jesus is the S/spirit of prophecy' (19.10; also 12.17) – fuses together prophetic proclamation and worship.

[55] ὁ ἔχων οὖς ἀκουσάτω τί τὸ πνεῦμα λέγει ταῖς ἐκκλησίαις ('let the one having an ear, hear what the Spirit is saying to the churches').

[56] Dunn, 'Discernment of Spirits', p. 321, observes a communal aspect for discernment when reading 1 Thess. 5.12-22, writing, 'It is quite clear that those who are addressed in 5:12 and again 5:14-22 are the "brethren" – that is, the community at large, as a whole. It is the community as a whole that Paul calls on not to quench the Spirit, not to despise prophecy, but to test everything (5:19-22).' Dunn notes additional communal elements in 1 Cor. 2.12-16; So also Johnson, *Scripture & Discernment*, p. 64. See also D.C. Augustine *et al.*, 'Experience in Christian Faith and Life: Worship, Discipleship, Discernment, Community, and Justice', *Report of the Reformed-Pentecostal Dialogue* 63.1, p. 26; Johnson, *Scripture & Discernment*, p. 26.

S. Land describes the 'Spirit-filled community' as being the 'best safeguard' against deception.[57] Those who are part of the Pentecostal community come to know God through discipleship, living in truth, and through prayer.[58] The local community is the location where the testimonies are heard.[59] The local church is the 'locus of theology' where the church discerningly reflects on God.[60] The congregation is the central location for discerning and distinguishing between competing voices. Everyone who is a member of a local community is called to partake in the discernment process.[61] Everyone is tasked with reflecting discerningly on the mysteries of the triune God.[62] Everyone is called to have an ear to hear the Spirit, to encounter the Truth, and to recognize deceptive signs and wonders.[63]

Knowing God, the Spirit, and Jesus are closely associated with being in a community and knowing fellow believers. John writes this prophecy and sends it to the seven churches, when the prophecy is read aloud, the churches dynamically hear the voice of the Spirit and the voice of Jesus in the narrative, suggesting that the seven churches know God through the prophetic activities of fellow-servants in the community. Knowing God and thereby knowing the truth includes hearing from others in community. The Spirit works in and through those who are inspired in the community.[64]

---

[57] Land, *Pentecostal Spirituality*, p. 163. See also Parker, *Led by the Spirit*, pp. 70-130, 213-15, who explores practices of discernment in local Pentecostal communities, while also observing that the Pentecostal community has not always intentionally discerned and discussed the testimonies offered in their communities.

[58] See Land, *Pentecostal Spirituality*, p. 170.

[59] See Parker, *Led by the Spirit*, pp. 213-15. Parker considers multi-generational small groups as helpful spaces for the community to discern.

[60] See Johnson, *Scripture & Discernment*, p. 26, who adds, 'Theology is, rather, a task to be taken up by the church as such. Because everyone in this community is also required to do theology.'

[61] Robeck, 'Discerning the Spirit', p. 47.

[62] Green, *Sanctifying Interpretation*, p. 132, observes that the difficulties of scripture form the churches to recognize deception, 'I do *not* mean that God tries to deceive us with Scripture. We have an enemy who does that. I mean God tests us precisely in order to save us *from* deception. God tests us to teach us discernment – and discernment cannot be learned any other way.'

[63] See Thomas, 'What the Spirit is Saying to the Church', pp. 116-19.

[64] Green, *Sanctifying Interpretation*, p. 37, makes a similar point, 'Loving God is inseparable from loving neighbor. In fact, loving our neighbor just *is* the way we love God.' See also T.J. Gorringe, *Discerning Spirit: A Theology of Revelation* (Philadelphia, PA: Trinity Press, 1990), pp. 76-79.

The discernment of the prophetic activity occurs in the seven churches and is addressed to the seven stars who are identified as the seven angels. The seven stars to whom each message is addressed represent the discerning ones in the community, suggesting that there is a 'structure' and a tradition for discernment in the seven churches. For the Johannine literature, the 'structures' for discernment also recall the appearance of 'what you have seen and have heard' in 1 John for the community's discernment.[65] Parker and Land have both explored the impact of tradition on the process of discernment.[66] All churches have some sort of tradition that defines their identity and structure, which guides each church in their discernment process. While the discussion has generally focused on the traditions that have formed the Pentecostal community, it seems that the Apocalypse offers an avenue to be attentive to those traditions that have been received by the wider church.[67] The whole church community is exhorted to hear the Spirit in each prophetic message. The churches come to know the activities of the triune God more fully in the stories of God's workings among all the churches. The Pentecostal community is exhorted to have an ear to hear the testimonies offered by believers in other churches, to hear those things that they have seen and heard, and to hear the activities of the Spirit among them in order that the church might discern faithfully.[68]

---

[65] Cf. 1 Jn 2.24; 3.11, see Dunn, 'Discernment of Spirits', p. 325. Levison, *Filled with the Spirit*, pp. 410-15, observes that the 'principle of discernment' in 1 John that most matters is the 'possession' of the Spirit in addition to keeping the commandments, loving, and confessing that Jesus came in the flesh.

[66] See also Land, *Pentecostal Spirituality*, p. 88. Parker, *Led by the Spirit*, pp. 203, 217-18, writes:

A practical theology of discernment and decision making must look at the role of traditions in determining and guiding Spirit leading experiences. The impact of tradition is already seen in, for instance, the role of leaders and membership stratification in keeping down charismatic excesses, the use of music to guide worship, and stories about the character of the Holy Spirit ... 'Testimonies' also participate in and expand traditions regarding what it means to be a Spirit led people, offering a kind of reflection on Pentecostal practice in the process.

[67] See Chapter 1 of this monograph for a discussion of Pentecostals and church tradition.

[68] Land, *Pentecostal Spirituality*, p. 222, writes, 'Contemporary Pentecostals should explore what it would mean to be in experiential continuity with the early movement in light of the claim to be in continuity with the apostolic church. Apostolic succession takes on new meaning in this light.' A. Yong, 'The Holy Spirit and the World Religions: On the Christian Discernment of Spirit(s) "After" Buddhism',

## Hymns and Story

In the narrative, hymns, songs, and laments appear as means of discernment. The mysterious figure who is on the throne becomes better known via a hymn (4.8-11). The elder who is an exemplar in discernment offers a hymn when discerning the identity of the great crowd (7.14-17). Overcoming is most fully described in hymnic materials (12.10-12; 15.3-4). In Revelation, 'The hymns are profoundly theological and thereby become melodic vehicles for catechesis. It is largely through the music of the Apocalypse that the hearers are formed in their understanding of God.'[69] Hymns thread the narrative, assisting the churches in discerning and revealing God.

Some of the hymnic material in the Apocalypse includes laments. The souls under the altar lament the injustice in the world, asking how long until the injustice will be judged and the blood that has been shed avenged (6.10)? The souls under the altar are associated with the overcomers (if not identified as the overcomers) and would thereby be identified as exemplars in discernment. Their lamenting discernment expresses, on the one hand, that the souls recognize injustice, evil, and exploitation in the world; the rampant injustice is not the way the world should be.[70] Oppression and death are contrary to the ways of the Lamb. On the other hand, their lament recognizes that it is God who will transform the injustices of this world into justice. The complaint is directed to the one on the divine throne because the Lamb is the only one who is able to overcome the injustice of the beast and establish a kingdom of justice.[71] The response

---

*Buddhist-Christian Studies* (2004), pp. 203-205, offers one of his five theses for discernment to include biblical and ecclesial traditions. Yong's other criterion include: (2) norm of Jesus Christ, (3) discernment should examine contexts of activity, (4) discernment should be dialogical, dialectical, and dynamic emerging freshly for new contexts, and (5) discernment should be judged ethically and morally on this side of the eschaton. See also Newton, *The Revelation Worldview*, p. 142.

[69] Archer, *'I Was in the Spirit on the Lord's Day'*, pp. 313-15.

[70] W. Brueggemann, 'The Costly Loss of Lament', *JSOT* 11.36 (1986), p. 62, writes, 'Lament occurs when the dysfunction reaches an unacceptable level, when the injustice is intolerable and change is insisted upon'. See also S.A. Ellington, 'The Costly Loss of Testimony', *JPT* 8.16 (2000), pp. 48-59.

[71] Brueggemann, 'The Costly Loss of Lament', p. 64:

A community of faith which negates laments soon concludes that the hard issues of justice are improper questions to pose at the throne, because the throne seems to be only a place of praise. I believe it thus follows that if justice questions are improper questions at the throne (which is a conclusion drawn through liturgic use), they soon appear to be improper questions in public

from the one on the throne to the lament from the souls under the altar is that they must wait.

However, Revelation does not suggest, in the time of waiting lament, that the churches should be silent or passive; rather, the churches are called to true and faithful witness where the Spirit of Truth dynamically confronts the deceit of the world. If the souls under the altar represent the overcomers, then overcoming the deceit of the beast and dragon would include confronting their injustice with lament. Lament is an aspect of the churches' discerning, pneumatic witness. The churches' lament reveals that they recognize the evil in the world, while confronting the injustice of the beast. If lament is absent within the community, then the churches are not offering a true and faithful witness;[72] the churches are not discerning nor are they properly responding to the evil and the injustice in the world. Without lament, the church is not discerning the ways of the Lamb.

John experiences the Spirit on Patmos and encounters the Truth from God. John receives a prophetic vision where he conveys his experience to the churches in the form of an apocalyptic, prophetic narrative that is sent to the seven churches (to all churches).[73] Truth, knowledge, and discernment in the Apocalypse are presented as an apocalyptic, prophetic narrative that contains hymns and lament, revealing that the means by which one knows and discerns, as well as the means by which Truth is communicated.[74] It is not that the narrative, hymns, and laments merely express truth, these genres are truth. Truth is narrative; knowledge is hymnic; lamentation is wise.[75]

---

places, in schools, in hospitals, with the government, and eventually even in the courts.

[72] Brueggemann, 'The Costly Loss of Lament', pp. 63-64, writes, 'When the lament form is censured, justice questions cannot be asked and eventually become invisible and illegitimate'.

[73] Thomas and Macchia, *Revelation*, p. 486. See the discussion of Revelation's genre as disorientation above in chapter 5.

[74] Johnson, *Scripture & Discernment*, pp. 102-108, observes the centrality of story and testimony in Acts for discernment and writes concerning Acts 15, 'What is remarkable, however, is that the text is confirmed by the narrative, not the narrative by the Scripture. As Peter had come to a new understanding of Jesus' words because of the gift of the Spirit, so here the Old Testament is illuminated and interpreted by the narrative of God's activity in the present.'

[75] Smith, *Thinking in Tongues*, p. 64.

368 Pneumatic Discernment, the Apocalypse, and Pentecostal Theology

These means of knowing – narrative, hymn, apocalyptic, prophetic, and lamentation – resist didactic, rationalistic, or objective
forms of knowledge, which do not offer a sense of certainty in the
churches' discernment. At times, these means of knowing even offer
a sense of disorientation and frustration. Despite the hymnic discernment of the elders to characterize the one on the throne more fully,
the mystery remains. The one on the throne is not fully revealed.
These epistemological mediums suggest that discernment is challenging and difficult, which might lead the churches to uncertainty, disorientation, and frustration.

One striking example of this disorientation and frustration is the
calculation of the number of the beast. This monograph has illustrated that there are a variety of conceivable interpretative possibilities to calculate the number of the beast, including associations with
Solomon, triangular numbers, first-century emperors, and symbolic
explanations. While there are a variety of interpretative options, the
text offers neither any explicit evidence to the calculation of the number nor *the* identity of the beast. The number 666 becomes an equation that reveals a solution without any other explicit variables for
calculation. The identity of the beast cannot be readily determined
because of the polyvalent and fluid character of the beast. At times,
the churches are left in uncertainty and disorientation. At times, there
are no answers. Certainty is not afforded to the churches and that is
precisely the reason for discernment.[76] The text does not offer any
definitive solution to *the* beast or *the* number. The numerous interpretative possibilities without an explicit solution can lead the churches
to uncertainty and disorientation.[77]

The process of wrestling with the text shapes the churches into
true and faithful discerners, while also directing the churches that
they are not always privileged to easy or definite answers in their
pneumatic discernment. The churches are directed to calculate, to

---

[76] See Green, *Sanctifying Interpretation*, p. 39.

[77] Johnson, *Scripture & Discernment*, p. 111, writes:

We cannot know if the decisions we make here and now are correct. We only
know that they are the best we are able to make, and that in the future we might
both regret them and need to change them. The reason has nothing to do with
our sinfulness and everything to do with the fact that faith has to do with the
Living God, who always moves ahead of us in surprising and sometimes shocking ways.

wrestle, to discern, to struggle, and to labor with this text even if there is not a definitive solution.[78] This process is frustrating and disorientating to anyone who desires to know the identity of *the* beast.[79] The disorientation in the apocalyptic text might be closely associated with seeing through the eyes of the Lamb – with the seven Spirits. The Spirit does not save the churches from the frustration and the uncertainty; rather, the Spirit works in it, offering divine wisdom and pneumatic perception even in their disorientation. The leading of the text to a state of uncertainty, disorientation, and frustration is not so the churches will discontinue their quest to discern the beast; rather, such uncertainty seems to have a formative result. The Spirit of Truth sanctifies the churches in Truth, forming the churches in the midst of their uncertainty, disorientation, and frustration. An aspect of the frustration is that the process can be time extensive.[80] Pneumatic discernment is a process because solutions are not always immediately knowable; '*Discernment may require further research or knowledge*',[81] and the process might be 'slow and messy'.[82] Whoever stops discerning on account of being unable to determine the answer hinders the formative function of the text.[83] Such a response to a difficult task reveals

---

[78] See Pinnock, *Flame of Love*, pp. 218-19, who writes:

> The truth once delivered to the saints is sufficient for every age, but we need time to reflect on it in order to gain better comprehension. Mature knowledge does not come quickly or easily, given the limitations of human nature and our fallenness. It takes time to penetrate profound matters and make them our own … But seeking truth is exciting and promising. God has so much more to tell us than we have grasped thus far.

[79] S. Felix-Jager, 'Inspiration and Discernment in Pentecostal Aesthetics', *JPT* 23.1 (2014), p. 102, makes a helpful point, 'Coming into discernment with an agenda conflates the end result and defeats the purpose of discernment in the first place. Because of our pneumatological imagination, our past experiences of the Spirit will speak into our comparative process and will give us the necessary promptings to know if God inspired the work or not.'

[80] Green, *Sanctifying Interpretation*, p. 148.

[81] Augustine, *et al.*, 'Experience in Christian Faith and Life', p. 23. See Johnson, *Scripture & Discernment*, pp. 88-89, 107, who observes the time required for discernment in the Acts narrative. See also R. Williams, 'Making Moral Decisions', *Cambridge Companion to Christian Ethics* (Cambridge: Cambridge University Press, 2001), p. 4; Fowl, *Engaging Scripture*, p. 118; Parker, *Led by the Spirit*, p. 226.

[82] Johnson, *Scripture & Discernment*, p. 111.

[83] Robeck, 'Discerning the Spirit', p. 39, comments, 'an unwillingness to cooperate in the discernment process is itself an indication that something is wrong. Those who claim inspiration must be open to assessment, review, and critique.'

the identity of a group.[84] Thus, the process of pneumatic discernment resists certainty and subverts the assumption that meaning is easily captured. The process of discernment does not seem to have a definite solution. The process of discernment is as important (perhaps even more important) as obtaining *the* answer.[85]

For early Pentecostals, discernment and knowledge were not solely cognitive processes but integrated the head and heart, 'Error does not start with the head, but with the heart';[86] similarly, 'So few people understand the workings of Pentecost because they are trying to work it out intellectually, but spiritual things are to be discerned by the *spirit*'.[87] J.H. King recognized inherent difficulties in attempting to know God's will and that one's discernment might bring uncertainty and frustration. Despite these difficulties, King wrote that discernment is 'the largest portion of our life'.[88] C. Green has uncovered some early Pentecostal voices that commented on the struggles in interpreting texts. For example, D.W. Myland commented, 'when you have these paradoxes in scripture, that we call them, seeming contradictions, this is where you get the greatest illumination of truth',[89] also observing that the Spirit did not always guide the church to 'pleasant places'.[90] A.J. Tomlinson explored different possible interpretations of the mark of the beast, while resisting a single identification of *the* beast or *the* mark.[91]

---

[84] Johnson, *Scripture & Discernment*, p. 17.

[85] Land, *Pentecostal Spirituality*, p. 163, writes, 'Out of the heart affected toward God the Father, through God the Son, and in God the Holy Spirit the mouth speaks'.

[86] *TBM* 6.121 (November 15, 1912), p. 4.

[87] *LRE* 1.9 (June 1909), p. 18. See also *TBM* 3.56 (February 15, 1910), p. 1, which records: 'We are so unwilling to admit our conclusions are wrong, and that there is a realm of the Spirit where we cannot live mentally except through constant supernatural illumination and revelation by the Spirit. But human wisdom is 'folly' with God. Stop this human effort of talking, reading, studying, and mental conceptions, till the power of the Spirit gets control of your mind.'

[88] *AE* 3.22 (January 1, 1912), p. 5.

[89] *LRE* 4.8 (May 1912), p. 14, cited in Green, *Sanctifying Interpretation*, p. 118. Cf. *LRE* 6.9 (June 1914), p. 17.

[90] *COGE* 8.49 (December 15, 1917), p. 1.

[91] See again *COGE* 9.6 (February 9, 1918), p. 1. It is important to note that not all early Pentecostals described the elements of uncertainty: 'Friends, if you profess to know the Spirit of God, and do not recognize Him when He comes, there is cause for you to be anxious about your own spiritual condition', *AF* 1.2 (October

L. McQueen has shown that early Pentecostals used lament in their communities but has also critiqued the contemporary Pentecostal community for abandoning lament as part of their liturgical practice. McQueen proposes that the 'recovery of lament is essential for the re-visioning of Pentecostal spirituality and theology'.[92] It seems that the Apocalypse aligns with McQueen's proposal concerning lament. If the Pentecostal community has lost its lament, then the question arises, has the Pentecostal community lost its ability to discern? Is the community able to distinguish between injustice and justice? Does the community recognize the difference between the ways of the Lamb and the ways of the beast? Has the church been deceived by the allure of the beast or the whore? If the churches are deceived, then the churches will likely not lament the injustices in the world. Thus, lament becomes one marker of discernment because it measures the churches' ability to recognize the ways of the beast and confront injustice.

Story, testimony, and lament have been and continue to be significant elements of the Pentecostal (con)text. For Pentecostals, narrative is a 'fundamental and irreducible mode of understanding'.[93] Story is a way of knowing for Pentecostals; it is a way of doing theology; and testimony is the means by which the community shares their story.[94] The Pentecostal ethos of narrative resounds closely with the

---

1906), p. 2. Another example might be the interpretative approach of E.T. Slaybaugh who noted that Revelation was a 'mystery revealed', meaning for him that any 'mystery' in the Apocalypse would be revealed in the text. However, the editors of *The Bridegroom's Messenger* wrote a note in the paper that the editors of the paper did not agree with every comment made by E.T. Slaybaugh, see *TBM* 1.4 (December 15, 1907), p. 1; *TBM* 6.125 (January 15, 1913), p. 4; *TBM* 6.137 (August 1, 1913), p. 4; *TBM* 7.159 (August 1, 1914), p. 4.

[92] McQueen, *Joel and the Spirit*, pp. 70-76, 93-95 (94). See also Ellington, 'The Costly Loss of Testimony', pp. 51-55.

[93] Smith, *Thinking in Tongues*, pp. 52-53, 67. See also S.C. Torr, 'Lamenting in Tongues: Glossolalia as a Pneumatic Aid to Lament', *JPT* 26.1 (2017), pp. 30-47, who considers glossolalia, particularly 'signs too deep for words', as an avenue of lament between the space of silence and speech.

[94] See K.J. Archer, 'Pentecostal Story: The Hermeneutical Filter for the Making of Meaning', *Pneuma* 26.1 (2004), pp. 36-59; Archer, 'A Pentecostal Way of Doing Theology', pp. 301-14. For the role of testimony in Pentecostalism, see Bridges Johns, *Pentecostal Formation*, pp. 126-27; Ellington, "Can I Get a Witness", pp. 1-14.

way pneumatic discernment is presented in Revelation. Truth is a person and Truth is a story. Revelation, as a story, follows the tradition of the greater gospel story that reveals the triune God in a story.[95]

This narrative way of knowing resists modernistic or rationalistic means of knowing, that desire certainty.[96] The difficulties inherent with narrative knowledge would resonate with the frustration felt when interpreting the Apocalypse. The certainty desired in a modernistic epistemology resists knowledge that is narrative, hymnic, apocalyptic, or prophetic. The frustration, uncertainty, and disorientation form the churches through the anxiety and resistance of the decision-making process.[97] These resistances in the texts, which lead the churches to frustration and uncertainty, are not a plight but a 'creational gift':

> ... to be *Pentecostal* is to be empowered by God for that human work of listening and speaking ... The truth is that we must *struggle*, both in our attempt to understand and in our attempts to make ourselves understood. If our words come too easily – as they did for Job's friends, for example, and for so many of Jesus' friends and enemies – it is a sure sign that we are keeping God at bay, suppressing the Spirit's effort to transform us through our speaking and listening.[98]

---

[95] Macchia, 'Pneumatological Feminist/Womanist Theologies', p. 69, writes, 'Wise discernment is possible only as we seek to harmonize ourselves in our practices with that which is before us in the gospel of Christ (fivefold or otherwise). Experience is vital to this discernment and this process, but an appeal is always made to that which transcends and confronts us in divine-human encounter.'

[96] See Robeck, 'Discernment', p. 76, notes, 'discernment is a gift to the *whole* church. And like all other gifts in an age known for partial knowledge (1 Cor. 13:9) and less than perfect understanding, it is a gift which itself must be discerned within the larger context of *koinōnia* ... the motivation behind this gift is to discover the mind of Christ, in a spirit of love.' See also Smith, *Thinking in Tongues*, p. 67.

[97] On this point, see Parker, *Led by the Spirit*, pp. 199-200, 225-26, who follows P. Tillich. So also Johnson, *Scripture & Discernment*, p. 17, who writes, 'Whichever way the decision goes, the process of reaching it will show us the true identity of the group. The decision, furthermore, will give more definite shape to the group's identity than it had in earlier unchallenged times.'

[98] Green, *Sanctifying Interpretation*, pp. 47-48. He later adds, 'Struggling to read Scripture faithfully, we find ourselves doing exactly what we are made to do' (p. 125). Parker, *Led by the Spirit*, pp. 194-95, adds:

> While some have suggested that certain Pentecostal practices may avoid these kinds of existential ambiguities and choices (Hunter 1984), attempts to rid oneself of all ambiguity and responsibility for choice through claiming the 'leading

Uncertainty, mystery, and disorientation seem to be part of the fabric of pneumatic discernment as it is presented in the Apocalypse. If any church considers that the Apocalypse is too difficult a text to interpret or if any community ceases to wrestle with difficult texts, or if any church views the Apocalypse, or any text as a code that is easily cracked with the correct cipher, then these communities terminate the affective dimension of the discernment process.[99] If any community is troubled by the disorientation that the Apocalypse communicates, then it reveals an element of resistance in the community toward the text, 'some of what seems to be wrong or strange in the Scriptures is in point of fact simply a reflection of what is wrong and strange in *us*'.[100] If the contemporary churches are guilty of neglecting discernment, one source might be the ignorance of wrestling with difficult texts such as the Apocalypse, the avoidance of uncertainty, the evasion of disorientation, the inability to let the mystery be.[101]

---

of the Spirit' is neither healthy nor true to the nature of the Spirit. Pentecostal attempts to avoid ambiguity through appeal to charismatic manifestations or fleeces are misguided; the divine Spirit cannot be forced or coerced by the human spirit (Tillich 1963: 112). Even a rigorous application of the criteria drawn from Tillich cannot determine unambiguously whether particular experiences are revelatory (though they provide helpful guidelines for such determinations). While this is due partly to the ambiguity in Tillich, it should be noted that it also is due to ambiguity in the experiences themselves. This means there will always be some claims to Spirit leading that will be difficult to judge regardless of the criteria to which one appeals.

[99] See also Johnson, *Scripture & Discernment*, p. 138, who adds, 'When bylaws and customs, or codes and unreflected Scripture citations replace the testing of the Spirit in the church, or, more tragically, when the church proceeds on the assumption that there is no work of the Spirit to *be* tested, then the church may reveal itself in the process of reaching a decision, but it won't be as a community of faith in the Spirit'.

[100] Green, *Sanctifying Interpretation*, p. 126.

[101] A similar point is made by Dunn, 'Discernment of Spirits', p. 323, 'it was not a simple matter of pronouncing Yes or No, Right or Wrong! It was inevitably a much more delicate process altogether. This is no doubt one of the main reasons why the gift has been neglected today; it is so difficult and time-consuming to exercise.' See also Robeck, 'Discerning the Spirit', pp. 38-40, who notes that the Spirit is likened to the wind in the gospel of John, suggesting that the Spirit is 'unpredictable, perhaps serendipitous in its movement … those who expect to discern the presence of the Spirit must be open to the unpredictable, to the new, and to the spontaneous'. Parker, *Led by the Spirit*, p. 226, adds, 'It is not the role of the Spirit to remove one's humanity and one cannot and should not try to escape all ambiguity through appeal to the Spirit's leading'. See also Green, *Sanctifying Interpretation*, p. 48, who writes: 'The problem is, some of us sometimes talk as if the Spirit saves us from the trouble of interpretation and mediation, taking over

## Conclusion

Therefore, pneumatic discernment is the process to know, to recognize, and to discern God. Truth, discernment, and wisdom are divinely conditioned in Revelation. Truth is a person, is from God, is conveyed by the Spirit of Truth, is encountered in an apocalyptic, prophetic narrative 'in the Spirit'. The Spirit is encountered both in the ecstatic encounter as well as the 'structures', including traditions, local congregations, and liturgies.[102] In keeping with the paradigm provided by the Apocalypse, the means of knowledge are not merely rationalistic or didactic; rather, they are hymnic, story, and experiential. One must discern the mysteries of the triune God to worship God, and worshipping God includes coming to know God more fully.[103] Coming to know God more fully and pneumatic discernment are, themselves, acts of worship. Hymns and songs are needed to reflect on the infinite mysteries of the one on the throne, while telling the redemptive story of the Lamb, 'in the Spirit', that form the churches in discernment and Truth.[104] In their formation, the churches are directed to create means of knowing that includes liturgies; creative mediums are crucial for the formation of the churches, which include hymns, songs, prayers, sermons, sacrament, poetry, and art.[105] It is not that these mediums of discernment merely tell about

---

our mouths or our ears so that we are freed from the difficulties of judgment, meaning-making, and communication – as if by the Spirit we are taken up beyond human, worldly limits'. On this point see also Smith, *Thinking in Tongues*, p. 48.

[102] So Robeck, 'Discerning the Spirit', p. 39, who does give priority to the canon of scripture. See Parker, *Led by the Spirit*, p. 222, who writes, 'An integrative model of discernment and decision making recognizes that reason and the Spirit are not inextricably opposed to each other'. See also Fowl, *Engaging Scripture*, p. 115, who writes, 'both the practice of testifying or bearing witness and the practice of listening wisely to such testimony are essential to a community's ability to "read the Spirit"'.

[103] Land, *Pentecostal Spirituality*, p. 25, writes:

Doctrinal language about God must be in response to something actually discerned in God. But this means to thank, to praise, to invoke, and to petition God. This is why Barth can say, 'Theological work must really and truly take place in the form of a liturgical act'. This is implicit in Barth's reflection on the fact that we are not only to speak the words Jesus gives us; but we must also receive him and the life of service he confers in and through the words ...

[104] On this point, see esp. Archer, '*I Was in the Spirit on the Lord's Day*', pp. 313-14.

[105] See also Felix-Jager, 'Inspiration and Discernment', pp. 85-104 (92), on art and discernment in the Pentecostal community.

Jesus, or about the Spirit, or about God. Rather, when the churches hear the story, when the churches hear the testimony, the churches dynamically hear God. The churches hear the Spirit of Truth in the voices of fellow-believers and the words of Jesus, the Truth, in their narratives, hymns, worship, and lament.[106] Knowing the triune God is closely associated with knowing each other, which is connected to the way that the churches discern the world.

The contemporary churches are directed to wrestle with these texts. The narrative is apocalyptic and prophetic because the process of discernment is challenging and frustrating which might guide the churches to uncertainty.[107] The Apocalypse presents a way of knowing that seems to be much different from any other way of knowing in the NT. In the world of the Apocalypse, the knowing is the discernment. The disorientation is the orientation and the orientation is disorienting. This apocalyptic uncertainty is formative and revelatory. The Spirit dynamically and actively speaks to the churches through different (pneumatic) means that form and shape the churches in order that they might recognize the activities of God and be able to

---

[106] McQueen, *Joel and the Spirit*, p. 95, writes, 'Lament testifies to the limit of words and subverts the merely rational modes of constituting the world. Lament acknowledges that the answers are beyond us and hopes for God who will one day make all things right.' Ellington, 'The Costly Loss of Testimony', pp. 57-58, adds, 'Testimony, I would argue, is both a primary resource that allows the psalmist to explore the experience of God's silence, hiddenness and absence and a necessary response to divinely answered laments. Without testimony it becomes difficult if not impossible to explore openly and candidly the circumstance of lament, because testimony to God's saving acts in the past provides the necessary hope that permits both an honest appraisal of the present and hope for the future.'

[107] Yong, *Discerning the Spirit(s)*, pp. 254-55, writes:

Pentecostal-charismatic discernment is guided and shaped but not dictated by aesthetic, ethical, or theological norms which are cognitionally articulated. Even if precisely applied, these norms cannot pierce through the deceptiveness of radical evil since 'Satan himself masquerades as an angel of light' (2 Cor. 11.14). Rather, the discernment of spiritual things is ultimately a spiritual act that transcends purely rational ways of knowing (1 Cor. 2.10-15). The actual processes of discerning the Spirit(s) draws from and integrates perceptual feelings, affective impulses and cognitive judgments into spiritual insights. Even when the combination of evaluations at all of these levels in the end results in nothing more than an intuitive judgment that is inevitably imprecise, Pentecostals and charismatics are constrained to 'hold on to the good [and] avoid every kind of evil' (1 Thess. 5.21) ... because they are cognizant that no human judgment is infallible, they are free to acknowledge that discerning the spirits in the religions is a profoundly complex and ambiguous affair.

distinguish bestial, deceptive signs and wonders from true signs and wonders. Ignorance of the apocalyptic words written in this prophecy would seem to be connected to a lack of discernment, knowledge, wisdom and understanding among the churches.

## Pneumatic Discernment and Church

In the narrative of the two witnesses, the two lampstands (the two olive trees) are ignited by the seven Spirits who are the seven torches, the seven eyes, and the seven horns of the Lamb. The eyes of the Lamb, representing pneumatic discernment, empower the churches' witness in order that their witness might be true. The seven Spirits are sent out into the world to fill the whole earth with the knowledge of Yahweh. This mission of the Spirit seems to extend to the churches where the seven Spirits enable the prophetic witness of the churches to fill the earth with the knowledge of God and the Lamb. In their Spirit-empowered, true and faithful witness, the churches make known God, the Spirit, and the Lamb to the inhabitants of the earth. The churches are able to participate in such a task because the seven Spirits provide the wisdom of the Lamb and the knowledge of God to the churches; the seven Spirits form the churches in truthfulness and faithfulness; the seven Spirits enable the churches to become mediators of divine truth, knowledge, wisdom, and discernment. All believers who witness about Jesus are inspired by the Spirit of prophecy and can be identified as prophets.[108] As part of their

---

[108] Newton, *The Revelation Worldview*, pp. 137-38, helpfully summarizes some of the issues of discernment in Revelation:

Symptoms of false spirituality may include opposition to the church, verbal ('slander') or physical (2:9, 10; 11:9, 10; 12:10; 16:6; 17:6; 18:24; 19:2), propagation of teaching that involves compromise with the non-Christian culture, especially in the area of idolatry (9:20; 18:4; 21:8; 22:15), moral impurity (2:14, 20; 3:4; 9:21; 17:4; 18:3, 9; 19:2; 21:8, 22; 22:11, 15), attachment to material luxury (3:17; 18:3, 7, 9, 14), and spiritual lassitude and/or self-satisfied complacency (3:1-2, 15-17). More explicitly, false spirituality is revealed in worship of the beast and receiving his mark (13:4-6, 8, 15-18; 14:9-11; 16:2; 19:4), blasphemy (13:5; 17:3), and cursing God during the plagues of his judgment (16:9, 11, 21). True spirituality, on the other hand, is shown by moral purity (3:4; 14:4; 18:4; 22:11), repentance (3:19; 11:13), good deeds (2:5, 26; 14:13; 19:8), keeping God's commands (12:17; 14:12; 22:14), worship and fear of the true God only (4:8, 11; 11:13, 18; 14:7; 15:3, 4; 19:5, 6, 10; 22:9), prayer (8:3, 4), and persevering faith in and fervent love for Jesus, expressed in open testimony, even under pressure (1:9; 2:3, 4, 10, 13, 25; 3:8, 10, 11, 20; 5:9-13; 6:9-11; 11:7, 15; 12:11,

witness, the two witnesses paradigmatically follow the Lamb, imitating his life, ministry, death, resurrection, and ascension. In following the Lamb, the two witnesses do not love their lives even unto death; such actions are part of their prophetic witness to the world.

In the dynamic witness of the churches, the nations encounter the Truth of God, which confronts the deception of the beast, causing the nation's perception of the world to become unstable. The challenging, mysterious, difficult, and strange wisdom of the Lamb subverts the wisdom of the world. In the dynamic witness of the churches, the nations are exposed to the deconstructing and transforming power of the wisdom and knowledge of God. The nations are confronted with the seven fiery flames of the Spirit that are the fiery eyes of the resurrected Jesus. The רוח of the one named True and Faithful uses the fire of judgment to confront anyone who is deceived by the beast.[109] The churches participate with the Spirit of Truth who strikes like a sword of Truth, causing anguish in those who are deceived. The agony of the nations is eased only when the churches' witness is complete, and the beast slaughters the two witnesses. The violence of the beast and the nations is contrary to the ways of the slaughtered Lamb. The narrative of the two witnesses concludes, not with the death of the church, but with their resurrection and vindication that is followed by an earthquake of judgment upon the nations who finally give glory to God. It is not the judgments of God alone that open the eyes of the deceived, but the earthquake in conjunction with the true witness of the churches. The fiery judgment of the seven Spirits, who confront the nations with Truth and through the witness of the churches, leads to the conversion of the nations.

The seven Spirits are filling the earth with the knowledge of God and the Truth of Jesus by means of the churches' prophetic witness. In this sense, the two witnesses are exemplars of pneumatic discernment. As exemplars of pneumatic discernment and as the two witnesses represent the churches, the seven prophetic messages urge the seven churches to fulfill their prophetic calling, to hear the Spirit, to

---

17; 13:10; 14:4, 12; 16:15; 17:14; 19:10; 20:4). Poverty is also commended as a mark of spirituality (2:9).

[109] See Isa. 11.4; Rev. 19.11.

anoint their eyes with a salve to see clearly, and to be sanctified in Truth in order that the churches might participate with the seven Spirits in filling the earth with wisdom and Truth.[110]

One issue related to discernment in the seven prophetic messages includes the ability to recognize the activities of deceivers, liars, false teachers, and false prophets among the churches. The identities of the false teachers and false prophets are undisclosed in the narrative, being referred to only as Jezebel and Balaam.[111] These pseudonyms fuse together false worship, sexual immorality, and economic exploitation.[112] The false worship, deception, exploitation, and oppression of the opponents described in the seven prophetic messages suggest that they are expressions, if not manifestations, of a larger deceptive and exploitative system; a system represented by the beast, the dragon, and the whore. The whole world worships the beast because of its military might and political authority, and John is tempted to worship the whore on account of her enticing wealth.[113] The enticements of the beasts, dragon, and whore include military activity, political power, and economic wealth. The connection between false worship and power, authority, and wealth suggests that these evil enticements are, themselves, temptations of false worship, and their allure is immensely seductive. Some in the churches have been deceived; some are lead astray by Balaam who – despite being inspired by the Spirit of Yahweh – caused the people of Israel to commit sexual immoralities; some are deceived by bestial signs and wonders; some have fallen for the seductions of the whore. Even John is susceptible to the allure of power and luxury. John is tempted to worship wrongfully on three occasions, marveling at the great whore (17.6-7), bowing before a fellow-servant (19.9-10), and later before an angel (22.8). In John's attempt to worship wrongfully, the angels and fellow-servants rebuke him, assist him in discernment, and immediately direct John to worship God alone, suggesting that even if the churches participate in false worship, even if they are deceived by the allure of

---

[110] Thomas and Macchia, *Revelation*, p. 486.

[111] As well as the Nicolaitans.

[112] Cf. Numbers 22–24; 31.16; 1 Kgs 16.31; 18.4, 13, 19; 21.5-15, 25; 2 Kgs 9.7, 22; 19.2. Cf. Newton, *The Revelation Worldview*, p. 142.

[113] The *Didache* 11 teaches that those who exploit for economic gain are false prophets.

the whore, or mistakenly worship an angel or fellow-servant, God actively assists in the discernment process.

The most detailed assistance in discerning that John receives is associated with the true identity of the whore who rides a beast. The deceitfulness and the enticement of the whore correlate directly to false worship. The enticements of the whore and beast include economic success, violent exploitation, and oppression. As John is tempted and lacks the ability to recognize the true identity of the whore, it seems that the churches are also encountering these deceitful enticements.[114] On account of the deceptive activities of the opponents, the churches are exhorted seven times to discern by the Spirit and to overcome the deceit of the dragon and the beast (Revelation 12). The façade of these enticements is deconstructed with pneumatic perception, exhibiting that any false teacher who persuades the churches toward false worship, directs them to worship power, violence, status, luxury, and money. While fornication has numerous possible associations in the seven prophetic messages, fornication with the great whore includes achieving luxury and power. While eating food sacrificed to idols might be interpreted in a variety of ways, it includes partaking of food that is purchased with the mark of the beast; a mark that is acquired through beast worship. Those who exploit for economic gain have taken the mark and eaten abundantly, while those who fornicate with the whore have need of nothing. Revelation unifies false teachings as the deception that directs the churches to worship power, military might, luxury, and violence rather than God. The churches must recognize their own participation in these systems of exploitation and turn toward the worship of God alone.[115]

Additionally, some in the churches are deceived by their own (mis)perceptions. While the prophetic words to the church in Smyrna are positive, lacking any critical remark, the church is challenged to recognize with pneumatic perception that they are rich despite their

---

[114] Newton, *The Revelation Worldview*, p. 181.

[115] See W.K. Kay, *Pentecostalism: A Very Short Introduction* (Oxford: Oxford University Press, 2011), pp. 71-73, who observes a Pentecostal worldview that includes a belief in invisible beings – angelic and demonic – who operate behind earthly institutions in the world.

poor material condition.[116] Conversely, the rich in Laodicea perceive themselves to be rich, but they are poor, naked, and pitiful when perceived with the seven eyes of the Lamb. With pneumatic perception, the riches of the Lamb subvert the wealth and luxury of the whore. In Philadelphia, those from the synagogue of Satan will bow before those who are weak, who have no position or authority. πνευματικῶς, the sacrificial power of the Lamb confronts the imperial power of the beast. The church in Sardis has a reputation of being alive, but with the eyes of the Lamb, they are dead. With the eyes of the Lamb, the life of the Lamb revisions how the life of the world appears. The church in Ephesus rightly discerned the false teachings of the Nicolaitans, even hating their deception and aligning with the perception of the Lamb. Yet, the church in Ephesus has lost its first love. With pneumatic perception, the love of the Lamb overcomes the hate of the beast. Other challenges to perception that occur in the narrative include the Root and Lion who with pneumatic perception (literally what John sees) appear as the slaughtered Lamb. The great city transforms with pneumatic perception, πνευματικῶς, into Sodom, Egypt, and the place where their Lord was crucified. With pneumatic perception, 42 months and 1260 days offer two perceptions of one reality. On the one hand, 42 months represent the time of the beast; for 42 months, the churches experience persecution during the reign of the beast; for 42 months, the churches are trampled. On the other hand, 1260 days represent the time of the Spirit; for 1260 months, the churches are ἐν πνεύματι ('in the Spirit'); for 1260 days, the churches witness; for 1260 days, the Spirit prophetically empowers the churches' witness and discernment. Thus, the narrative guides the churches to view the world from a pneumatic perception, with the seven eyes of the Lamb, πνευματικῶς.[117]

---

[116] Johnson, *Scripture & Discernment*, p. 139, writes, 'there is as much need for self-discernment and self-criticism as there is for discernment of the other's story'.

[117] This seems to resound with Acts 21 when Agabus dramatically prophesied that Paul would be bound. Some in the community interpreted the prophecy of Agabus as a warning against Paul's journey to Jerusalem, while Paul discerned that the prophecy was confirmation that he would not return from his journey to Jerusalem; on this point, see Augustine *et al.*, 'Experience in Christian Faith and Life', p. 24.

Another aspect of pneumatic discernment is associated with those who are experiencing persecution in the seven prophetic messages. Even though the resurrected Jesus does not criticize the churches in Philadelphia and Pergamum, they are exhorted to have an ear to hear the Spirit. Those who oppose the churches are identified as Satan, the dragon, who gives his authority to the beast (13.2). From the pneumatic perspective, the opponent of the churches is the dragon who is Satan. The dragon has murdered Antipas, who is a faithful witness. John, a faithful witness, is experiencing tribulation. Jesus, the true and faithful witness, is crucified in the great city. The two witnesses are slaughtered by the beast where their Lord is crucified. With pneumatic perception, the violent powers who oppose the churches slaughtered Jesus in the same trans-temporal and trans-geographical location that the two witnesses are slaughtered. Such a change in perspective, seems to address the question, how does the church offer witness to those who persecute them? In the face of persecution, the churches are called to discern that those who persecute them identify with Satan. The narrative describes the dragon and his minions as the ones who deceive the nations to coerce them to violence (16.14; 19.19; 20.7), suggesting that the violent character of the nations is connected to their deception. Thus, in the face of this persecution, the churches discover solidarity with Antipas, John, and with their Lord. It is on account of their true and faithful witness that the churches experience opposition. In the church's dynamic, pneumatic witness the nations encounter the Spirit and the Truth who overcome the deception of the dragon, that is connected to the conversion of the nations.

In sum, the challenge laid before the church is that the power of the beast is awesome, and the allure of the whore is seductive. Revelation urges the churches to discern, warning that any system that uses violence, political authority, or economics to control, to manipulate, and to deceive identifies with the beast, is empowered by the dragon, and is seduced by the whore. The authority of the beast mimics the power of God, suggesting that the churches must be cautious with whom they identify. While Revelation does not offer an explicit identification of *the* beast or *the* whore, the churches are directed to discern beast-like and whorish qualities operating in the world. These beast-like and whorish qualities include: the appearance of having all power and authority, a desire for worship, the ability to perform signs

and wonders, deception and manipulation, a haughty and blasphemous demeanor, and luxurious enticements. A church that worships
the beast and the whore is unable to recognize that these beast-like
qualities are demonic and satanic.

*The Bridegroom's Messenger* describes an individual who claimed to
be the angel John saw on Patmos and offered three aspects of the
process of discernment: (1) search the scriptures, (2) listen to the
voice of the Spirit, and (3) utilize a 'sanctified mind'.[118] Some early
Pentecostals described false doctrines as metaphorically a 'dragon'
that devours those who get out of the scriptures. A.J. Tomlinson
warned his readers that some honest people believed that they were
following the Spirit's guidance but were in fact confusing the divine
Spirit with the spirit of Balaam.[119] Moreover, Tomlinson, along with
some other Pentecostals, discerned that the nations who participated
in war were bestial.[120] Some early Pentecostals believed that the
church had an obligation not to be involved in war and were openly
critical of any country who participated in such violence. Believers
could either identify with God or identify with the beast; those who
identified with the beast were nationalistic and advocated participation in war.[121] F. Bartleman proclaimed, 'We are ruled by the money
gods.'[122] M. Galmond in *The Apostolic Faith* created a dualism between
the poor and rich. Galmond envisioned that the rich would oppress
the poor by taking the mark of the beast, allowing the rich to purchase all the available food. A violent conflict would ensue on account of the rich's oppression. Galmond associated the mark of the
beast with economic exploitation, greed, and violence.[123]

---

[118] See again *TBM* 2.45 (September 1, 1909), p. 2.

[119] *COGE* 5.34 (August 22, 1914), p. 2; *COGE* 5.35 (August 29, 1914), p. 3.

[120] See for example again *TBM* 8.168 (March 1, 1915), p. 1; *COGE* 9.6 (February 9, 1918), p. 1; *WE* 216 (November 24, 1917), p. 3. See Andrew Urshan in *WE*
192 (June 2, 1917), p. 3. Cf. *CE* 74 (January 16, 1915), p. 1; *CE* 75 (January 23,
1915), p. 2. See also Johnson, 'The Mark of the Beast', pp. 184-202.

[121] See again *TBM* 8.168 (March 1, 1915), p. 1; *TBM* 9.179 (February 1, 1916),
p. 4; *TBM* 9.180 (March 1, 1916), p. 4.

[122] *CE* 93 (June 5, 1914), p. 2; *WW* 12.6 (June 1915), p. 5.

[123] See again *AF* 1.2 (October 1906), p. 2. See M.W. Dempster, 'Reassessing the
Moral Rhetoric of Early American Pentecostal Pacifism', *Crux* 26.1 (1990), p. 28,
who observes, 'In order to reveal the structural evil that war represented and per-
petuated, two groups within the power structure were favorite targets of early pentecostal pacifists: the ruling politicians and the rich class'.

The apocalyptic, prophetic narrative warns the churches that the whore and beast are active among the churches, while directing the churches to wrestle discerningly with these beast-like and whorish characteristics infiltrating their communities.[124] If the Pentecostal communities have trouble discerning the manifestations of the beast in the world, it is perhaps associated with an interpretative lens that approaches the Apocalypse as a decipherable script, conveying a detailed report of future events,[125] an interpretative approach that usually does not investigate the beast-like qualities manifesting in the contemporary world.[126] When approaching the Apocalypse, many Pentecostals have lost the 'for us' approach, ignoring that 'there is something good for us' in each text of the Apocalypse.[127] If there is any possibility that the Apocalypse directs the churches to pneumatic discernment – a process that is formative, time-consuming, and difficult, then the churches might be resisting an affect of the text. Moreover, if the churches encounter the Spirit in the process, then avoiding the process of discernment resists a way in which the churches experience the Spirit. Churches that evade this formative process are not fully prepared by the Spirit of Truth to discern difficult issues that confront the churches.

Many of these early Pentecostal testimonies reveal a reading of the Apocalypse that discerned the activity of the beast among them in the manifestation of nationalism, political authorities, economics, and violent military conquest.[128] A reading that has been abandoned among several contemporary US Pentecostal congregations. The

---

[124] Another avenue concerning the ability to discern demonic activity against the activities of God concerns the origins of illness. On this, see Thomas, *The Devil, Disease and Deliverance*, pp. 301-302, 309-12, who observes concerning illness that the origins of illness are not always clear. The community is tasked in discerning if an illness originates from God, on account of sin, or from diabolic forces. Cf. Twelftree, *Christ Triumphant*, pp. 180-82. See also Levison, *Filled with the Spirit*, pp. 383-85, who explores the dualistic nature of deceit and truth in the FG.

[125] See Williams, 'Making Moral Decisions', p. 6, who writes, 'the self-discovery we have been thinking about in the process of making certain kinds of decisions is also a discovery of the world that shapes us'.

[126] See McQueen, *Toward a Pentecostal Eschatology*, pp. 287-91.

[127] As Tomlinson approaches the Apocalypse when interpreting the mark of the beast, see *COGE* 9.6 (February 9, 1918), p. 1.

[128] See Dempster, 'Reassessing the Moral Rhetoric of Early American Pentecostal Pacifism', pp. 28-30. See also Yong, *Discerning the Spirit(s)*, pp. 234-43, on the diabolic activities in the systems of government.

Apocalypse offers a critique to anyone in the church who is undiscerningly participating in 'the capitalist priority of economic self-interest' and who participates in a system that propagates war and exploitation.[129] The description of the whore, along with the kings and merchants of the earth, who gather wealth and cargo from the four corners of the earth is hauntingly similar to the western economy of consumption,[130] economic success that rides on the back of violence and influence. Such associations urge the churches to be wary of economic systems that vastly depend on consumption for prosperity and primarily serve individual self-interest. This criticism of exploitative luxury does not suggest that the Apocalypse views all wealth as inherently evil. The bride has many of the same adornments as the whore. However, uncritical participation in any economic system that exploits the world for self-serving consumption is whorish. Uncritical participation in any political system that uses its military power to kill those who oppose it violently is bestial. The church that participates in these bestial and whorish systems also participates in their worship cult, marveling at the vast wealth of the whore, worshipping the image of the beast, and chanting hymns of the mighty acts of their régime and the opulence of their economies. The churches that worship the beast and the whore lose the seal of God upon their foreheads, exchanging the seal of God for the number 666, while becoming a 'war church' and a 'harlot church'.[131]

As a Pentecostal, my community has shaped me to recognize the centrality of scripture in worship and life. The Pentecostal community has formed me to be attentive to the voice of the Spirit in my church and my life. The Pentecostal community has molded me to hear testimonies from those in the community and to discern by the Spirit what is being spoken. I have heard testimonies from scripture

---

[129] D.C. Augustine, 'Pentecostal Communal Economics and the Household of God', *JPT* 19.2 (2010), p. 223.

[130] See esp. Augustine, 'Pentecostal Communal Economics', pp. 219-42, who observes that economics are a spiritual matter, which are an external expression of the inner life of individuals and communities, commenting, 'In this spiritual discipline one is committed to sharing possessions with one's neighbor and redisturbing wealth according to human needs rather than political and economic benefits. The development of this type of civic consciousness requires our personal spiritual transformation' (p. 224).

[131] See J.J. Shuman, 'Pentecost and the End of Patriotism: A Call for the Restoration of Pacifism among Pentecostal Christians', *JPT* 4.9 (1996), pp. 70-96.

and testimonies from early Pentecostals who describe the bestial manifestations that are active in the world, manifestations that include violence, militaristic oppression, nationalism, and exploitative economic. It is vital that the Pentecostal community hear these testimonies and discern the beast-like and whorish activities in their world.

For whoever might be deceived by these bestial deceptions, the Apocalypse indicates that God does not abandon the churches. The Spirit is actively speaking the Truth to the churches, confronting their deception and sin.[132] The question arises, how is God by the Spirit speaking Truth to the churches? While these are not the only ways the churches experience God, the Apocalypse considers that the Spirit speaks to the churches through experience, prophetically through those in the community, through hymns and laments, and through the apocalyptic and narrative texts. The way of the Lamb is sacrifice; it is not individual gain achieved through exploitation. The power of the slaughtered Lamb is the seven Spirits, perceiving the haughtiness, blasphemy, violence, oppression, and exploitation of the trinity of evil and the whore.[133] The wealth of the Lamb, the jewels of the bride, is her sacrificial love, wisdom, discernment, holiness, and sanctification. The one on the throne creates life for every nation, people, tribe, and tongue. Through this apocalyptic narrative, the churches encounter the Truth from God by the seven Spirits of Truth, which is a sanctifying experience that washes away the corrupting influences of deceit, violence, oppression, and exploitation.

---

[132] Shuman, 'Pentecost and the End of Patriotism', p. 92, writes:

Participation in the stories of Israel and of Jesus rightly calls into question the supposition that Christians must calculate ways to protect themselves and to control their own existences; it names as a lie the notion that human existence in a world filled with violence necessarily relativizes the way of life presented in Jesus' life, death, and resurrection. Such deceptive illusions are at the root of Christian participation in human violence.

[133] P. Alexander, 'Speaking in the Tongues of Nonviolence: American Pentecostals, Pacifism, and Nationalism', *BLT* 57.1 (2012), p. 12, writes, 'Pentecostals should be truth tellers who speak as honestly as their perceptions allow about the good, the bad, the ugly, and the beautiful in any nation'.

The seven Spirits offer wisdom, truth, and discernment to the churches in order to empower their true, faithful, prophetic, pneumatic witness.[134] The churches overcome deceit with Truth and violence and oppression with lamenting witness (13.9-10).[135] The churches are not able to offer a true, faithful, and prophetic witness, following the paradigm of the two witnesses, unless they have discerned by the seven Spirits beast-like and whorish works in the world. A true, prophetic, and faithful witness confronts violence and oppression in the great city. If the contemporary church is deceived and worshipping the beast, their witness is invalid. If the whore has seduced the contemporary church, they have lost their prophetic voice. Churches that worship political power, military might, or economics are deceived by the beast, seduced by the whore, and are not able to offer a prophetic or true witness to the world.[136]

## Pneumatic Discernment of the Apocalypse and Acts 15 in Intertextual Dialogue

In the final section of this theological construction, I seek to bring into dialogue the hermeneutical paradigm of Acts 15 with the theological overtures of pneumatic discernment of the Apocalypse considered in this chapter. J.C. Thomas has offered a metaphor of the scriptures where he likens the canon to a 'black gospel choir'.[137] Thomas considers that each biblical book of the canon offers a distinct voice. Interpreters should hear single voices on their own terms

---

[134] On this point, Yong's pneumatological approach to the theology of religions would find some support in the Apocalypse because the seven Spirits go out into the whole earth to fill the earth with the knowledge of God, see Yong, *Discerning the Spirit(s)*. See also Felix-Jager, 'Inspiration and Discernment', pp. 95-96, who explores a similar line of thought as Yong in Acts 17.22-31. He describes Paul's sermon as a transformative moment where the elements of truth that were apparent with the Athenians are seen anew after encountering the truth of the resurrected Christ.

[135] See M.W. Mittelstadt, 'Spirit and Peace in Luke-Acts: Possibilities for Pentecostal/Anabaptist Dialogue Christian Ethics Interest Group', *Didaskalia* 20 (2009), pp. 17-40, who explores peace and non-violence in Luke-Acts.

[136] Newton, *The Revelation Worldview*, pp. 164-65, writes, 'People become deceived, or deceive themselves, because of their own limited, self-interested, power-driven perspective on issues of truth. However, John attributes this also to spiritual factors and sees that it can be overcome, at least in part, by revelation.'

[137] See Thomas, 'What the Spirit is Saying to the Church', pp. 120-28.

before hearing all the voices of the canon together in the full gospel choir. In the full choir, hearers might hear sounds of harmony or dissonance.[138] For Thomas, the dissonance found in the canon must be allowed to stand to avoid artificially harmonizing voices with one another. Following Thomas' metaphor, I seek to hear two voices of the biblical canon, the voices of Revelation and Acts 15, as a sort of duet. I will bring the hermeneutical paradigm of Acts 15 into dialogue with the findings of this study on account of the impact of Acts 15 in Pentecostal hermeneutics and decision-making.[139]

First, one point of harmony between the process of discernment in Acts 15 and the Apocalypse is associated with the activity of the Spirit who speaks and guides the community. In Revelation and in Acts 15, the Spirit substantially impacts the decisions of the churches and is explicitly involved in the discernment process. The Spirit actively and dynamically speaks the words of Jesus in the Apocalypse to the seven churches, assisting the churches in their discernment; whereas in Acts 15, the Spirit directs the churches in discernment, affirming the decision made by the Jerusalem council.

On points of diversity, the Apocalypse offers an emerging trinitarian view of God's activities in the process of discernment. The Apocalypse of Jesus Christ, who is the Truth, originates from the true God and is conveyed by the Spirit of Truth who goes out into all the earth. The wisdom and knowledge of Yahweh is attributed to the Lamb and the seven Spirits. While Jesus and God appear in the narration of Acts 15, the Pentecostal hermeneutical paradigms based on Acts 15 have not yet fully explored the role of Jesus or God in the process of discernment, focusing on the affirmation of the Spirit in the process of discernment.

Thereby, it would appear that the Pentecostal hermeneutical paradigms would be well served to reflect further on the role of the divine in the process of discernment from a trinitarian perspective. Revelation explicitly associates the one on the throne, the Spirit, and

---

[138] See Thomas, *The Devil, Disease and Deliverance*, for a proto-attempt of this hermeneutical model. See also R.L. Coleman, 'The Lukan Beatitudes (Luke 6.20-26) in the Canonical Choir: A 'Test Case' for John Christopher Thomas' Hermeneutical Proposal', *JPT* 26.1 (2017), pp. 48-67, for an engagement with and attempt at this hermeneutical model.

[139] See again Thomas, 'Women, Pentecostals, and the Bible', pp. 41-56; Archer, *A Pentecostal Hermeneutic*. See also Archer, *'I Was in the Spirit on the Lord's Day'*, for an application of the triadic model to the study of the Apocalypse.

Jesus with the Truth. The voice of the Spirit is not isolated from the voice of Jesus or the voice of the one on the throne, even though the Spirit speaks independently. Divine Truth is a person, suggesting that particular issues of discernment are integrally bound to the process of knowing the triune God more fully.

Second, the role of the community in the process of discernment offers another point of harmony between Acts 15 and the Apocalypse. In the Apocalypse, the prophetic words of Jesus – spoken in tandem by the Spirit – are heard in the seven churches. In Acts 15, the community offers testimonies of pneumatic experiences to the community that have occurred among them. John testifies to the things that he hears and sees, while Paul, Barnabas, Peter, and the others testify to the things that they experience. Much like the Apocalypse, the experiences among the communities require discernment and at the same time become evidence for the community's discernment when these experiences originate from the Spirit.

Some points of diversity between the communities reflected by these texts include the ecclesiastical systems of leadership. Acts 15 offers a more established hierarchy of leadership in the church in Jerusalem. James clearly holds a significant place of leadership, and there are elders and apostles, implying systems of governance. The Apocalypse, along with the rest of the Johannine literature, does not offer evidence of an established ecclesial governance. In the Apocalypse, John is a prophet, but does not claim an explicit position of leadership over the communities. The Apocalypse suggests that every member is (at least potentially) a prophet. The Apocalypse is addressed to the seven ἄγγελοι ('angels') of the seven churches – the wise and discerning ones; however, it is not altogether clear that these seven ἄγγελοι ('angels') function in any leadership role in the community. Even though the seven ἄγγελοι ('angels') are characterized as the discerning ones, the seven prophetic messages exhort every church and each individual hearer ('anyone who has …') to be active in hearing and discerning.

Thus, while the communities clearly have different systems of governance, both texts indicate the importance of community in the process of discernment. The rich dissonance heard in these texts gives evidence that in the construction of a Pentecostal approach to discernment, the discerning community might appear differently in different contexts, and both texts offer room for a variety of individuals to testify in the community. Hence, the Pentecostal hermeneutical task is boarder than any individual interpretative community, suggesting a need for the hearing of diverse and global voices in the process of discernment.

Third, the role of scripture appears in both biblical voices. There is unity in both Acts 15 and Revelation in relation to the way in which pneumatic experiences transform the ways that the scriptures are interpreted and discerned. On the one hand, among a variety of texts that could be included as evidence concerning the Gentiles in the HB, the Jerusalem council cites the LXX version of Amos 9.11-12, which confirms the community's experience, but does not explicitly mention the Gentiles. On the other hand, as discussed above, the Apocalypse does not overtly quote the HB at any point, but transforms the language, imagery, and language of the HB, reforming it in a pneumatological and eschatological context. Both voices suggest that their pneumatic experiences directly impact, even transform, the way that the churches view scripture.

Furthermore, the Apocalypse seems to understand itself uniquely as prophetically inspired, even self-validating its own prophetic truthfulness. If Pentecostals regard the Apocalypse as scripture, then the Apocalypse offers some overtures toward considering the role of scripture in the process of discernment. (1) The Apocalypse reveals Jesus Christ and the Truth that is from God and is conveyed in and by the Spirit. When hearing the Apocalypse, the churches hear the active voice of the Spirit who is coterminously speaking the words of Jesus. The churches are encountering divine communication when they hear the Apocalypse. (2) As the churches are hearing the Spirit and Jesus actively speak in tandem to the churches, they are exhorted to discern. The churches are exhorted to discern via the apocalyptic narrative that they encountering.

Thus, in a theological construction of pneumatic discernment for the Pentecostal community, scripture becomes an encounter with the divine Spirit who actively conveys the truth of Jesus from the true God. Scripture does not offer a merely objective view of Truth. Truth is a story, Truth is a person, and Truth is divinely conditioned. Story subverts simplistic, modernistic, or objective understandings of discernment, T/truth, understanding, and knowledge. Scripture assists in the process of discernment, while also being in need of discernment.[140] The discernment of scripture, like the Apocalypse, can be a process that is frustrating, laborious, and challenging. However, any frustration experienced in the process of interpreting particularly difficult texts prepares and forms the Pentecostal community to discern a variety of challenging issues they encounter currently.

## Summary

First, pneumatic discernment in the Apocalypse begins with the triune God. Discernment is the process of coming to know the seven Spirits, Jesus Christ, and the one on the throne more fully. The process of knowing God is crucial to distinguish between the activities of God and the beast. Discernment begins with the triune God because discernment, truth, knowledge, and wisdom originate from the true God, is a person – Jesus who is the Truth, and is conveyed by the seven Spirits of Truth to the seven churches. In other words, Truth and discernment are theologically, christologically, and pneumatically conditioned.

Second, the Truth of God is discerned by the Spirit in pneumatic experience, in the community, through hymns and laments, and through narrative. The means by which discernment is conveyed resists rationalistic and simplistic approaches. Rather, the process of discernment might be challenging, difficult, and lengthy where the churches are led to uncertainty. In this process, the seven Spirits of Truth sanctify the churches in the Truth from the true God.

Third, pneumatic discernment must become a vital part of the life of the church; otherwise, the church is in danger of no longer being the church. The church encounters deceptions, misperceptions, and bestial and whorish manifestations among their communities. The characteristics of the beast and whore include violence, exploitation, and oppression. The beast parodies the activities of the triune God, performing signs and wonders, masquerading as a lamb, and even raising the dead. The whore seduces the whole world with her appearance of luxury. The deceptive nature of the beast and whore

---

[140] Gorringe, *Discerning Spirit: A Theology of Revelation*, p. 24, writes, 'To discern the Spirit, the Christian theologian claims, we turn to scripture, and yet scripture itself needs to be read with a discerning eye'.

warns the churches that they must diligently discern. While the explicit identity of the beast is masked, the churches are tasked to recognize the beast-like qualities in their churches. When the churches recognize the bestial manifestation in the world, the church is able to offer a true, faithful, prophetic, and lamenting witness that confronts oppression, violence, and economic exploitation.

Fourth, in the canonical choir, the Apocalypse and Acts 15 offer melodies that contain both harmony and dissonance concerning pneumatic discernment. A construction of a Pentecostal hermeneutical model should continue to explore the role of (1) the Spirit, the one on the throne, and Jesus in the process of discernment, (2) pneumatic experiences in discerning, (3) the community, particularly the possibility of various ecclesial models of governance, as well as the incorporation of diverse and global testimonies in the community, and (4) scripture that is narrative, prophetic, apocalyptic, pneumatic, christological, and theological, both assisting in the process of discernment, while also necessitating careful and diligent discernment.

# CONCLUSIONS AND SUGGESTIONS FOR FURTHER RESEARCH

## Conclusions

First, the methodology of this work has attempted to move the conversation forward concerning Pentecostal hermeneutics engaging the most up to date studies in Pentecostal hermeneutics. The methodology employed has attempted to move the conversation forward concerning Pentecostal hermeneutics by (1) integrating intertextuality with the Pentecostal community as a way to dialogue with the Pentecostal (con)text that has a formative impact on the Pentecostal interpreter; and (2) by bringing intertextuality into dialogue with the method of narrative criticism that emerges from the Pentecostal (con)text.

Second, this monograph has proposed that the Pentecostal 'community' of the hermeneutical triad includes (i) a local community, (ii) early Pentecostal community, (iii) *Ecclesia Catholic*, and (iv) the scholarly (Pentecostal) community.

Third, this monograph offers the most comprehensive summary of the scholarly con(text) on the pneumatology of the Apocalypse in chronological order. The review of literature has revealed an overall lacuna concerning the study of the theme of pneumatic discernment in the Apocalypse.

Fourth, the chronological survey has traced the impact of Pentecostal scholars on the study of the pneumatology of the Apocalypse, particularly from 2006–2015, which begins with the publication of *The Spirit of the Book of Revelation* by R. Waddell that is followed by works from P. Benham and R. Skaggs, C. Tanner, J.C. Thomas, R. Herms, and F. Macchia.

Fifth, by means of *Wirkungsgeschichte*, this work has offered the first investigation of the impact of the Apocalypse on the early Pentecostal (con)text concerning pneumatic discernment and pneumatology of the Apocalypse from 1906–1918. Literatures from both the Wesleyan-Holiness and Finished-Work streams of the Pentecostal tradition were read with the discovery that there were slight differences among the two streams that were dependent on (i) the effect of dispensationalism on the stream, and (ii) if the dispensational script explained a particular passage of the Apocalypse.

Sixth, this work has offered a comprehensive intertextual, theological, and narrative analysis of the theme of pneumatic discernment in the Apocalypse from the Pentecostal (con)text. This monograph has shown that pneumatic discernment is a significant feature of the Apocalypse and that the process of interpreting this apocalyptic, prophetic narrative is, itself, a process of pneumatic discernment.

Seventh, this monograph has offered the first theological construction of pneumatic discernment of the Apocalypse that brought the findings of the intertextual, narrative reading into a conversation with the Pentecostal context.

## Suggestions for Further Research

In light of this study, several avenues of further research could be considered.

First, further theological considerations are required in the development of the literary theory of intertextuality, the Pentecostal (con)text, and narrative criticism in conjunction with Pentecostal hermeneutics.

Second, this work explores the early Pentecostal literature via *Wirkungsgeschichte* from 1906–1918 in the US leading to the question, what other (con)texts might be discovered in other Pentecostal texts beyond the first years of the Pentecostal movement?

Third, what other biblical books in addition to the Apocalypse would be advantageous for a study via *Wirkungsgeschichte*?

Fourth, this monograph has offered a limited examination via *Wirkungsgeschichte* of early church interpretations of the pneumatology and the theme of discernment. A more intentional examination via *Wirkungsgeschichte* might offer helpful insights into the interpretation of the Apocalypse, particularly the pneumatology and the theme of discernment.

Fifth, considering the significance of pneumatic discernment in the Apocalypse, it would be profitable to explore pneumatic discernment in other biblical books.

Sixth, this study has brought into conversation the paradigm of Acts 15 and some overtures of the Apocalypse concerning discernment and interpretation, what other biblical voices might assist in the discussion of Pentecostal hermeneutics? What other fruit might be produced if the Acts 15 paradigm is viewed in light of the entire Luke/Acts narrative?

# APPENDIX 1

## The Function of οἶδα and γινώσκω in the Apocalypse

In the seven prophetic messages, the seven-fold appearance of οἶδα ('I know') is primarily associated with Jesus' discerning knowledge (2.2; 2.9; 2.13; 3.1; 3.8; 3.15). Jesus is omniscient and is able to see everything, even the inner most thoughts and emotions of those in the church. In the seven prophetic messages, there are two other occurrences of οἶδα ('I know') where Jesus is not the subject. (1) In 2.17 with the promise to the church in Pergamum, the overcomers will receive a new name on the white stone, which 'no one knows' (οὐδεὶς οἶδεν) except for those who receive knowledge of this new name. This reveals an eschatological association where if the church overcomes as Christ overcame, then they too will have access to heavenly knowledge – οἶδα. The connection becomes more substantial in 19.12 where the hearers learn that the rider on the white horse has a name that no one knows (οὐδεὶς οἶδεν); this brings together the promise to the overcomers and the heavenly (Christological) knowledge repeated seven times in the seven prophetic messages. (2) In the message to Laodicea, the church is harshly critiqued for their undiscerning knowledge. At the very least the condemnation from Christ creates a contrast between what Christ knows and what the Laodiceans (do not) know; whereas the Laodiceans know themselves to be rich, they do not know (οὐκ οἶδας) that they are poor, blind, and naked: they do not know as Christ knows.

Outside the seven prophetic messages, οἶδα ('I know') occurs three times. (1) In 7.14 John responds to the elder's question with σὺ οἶδας ('you know'). The knowledge of the elder is true: he knows the identity of the great multitude. The location of the 24 elders in heaven (cf. Revelation 4–5) supports the evidence that οἶδα ('I know') is associated with heavenly knowledge. Furthermore, if the 24 elders are to be identified with the overcomers, it offers further evidence that the appearance of οἶδα ('I know') in 2.17 is a promise of heavenly knowledge. (2) In 12.12 a voice from heaven proclaims that the Dragon knows (εἰδώς) that his time is short. The knowledge of Satan, while not likely to be identified as divine, seems to come from a heavenly source indicated perhaps by the proclaimer of this hymn – the voice from heaven. Further evidence of the heavenly origins of the Dragon's knowledge might be in the usage of the perfect participle pointing to a particular moment. It is possible that this moment occurred while Satan was located in heaven (cf. 12.3). (3) In 19.12, no one knows (οὐδεὶς οἶδεν) the name of the rider on the white horse except for him, which again brings together both the discerning knowledge of Christ with the promise to the overcomers in 2.17.

γινώσκω ('I know') appears only in the seven prophetic messages and seems to be associated with the undiscerning knowledge of the churches or more general human knowledge. (1) In 2.23 following the judgment of Jezebel, her followers, and her children, the hearers learn that their judgment will serve so that all the churches will know themselves (γνώσονται) that Christ is omniscient, knowing the hearts and minds of all. Perhaps γινώσκω ('I know') appears here to distinguish between those who hear the Spirit, discern, and become overcomers and those who do not discern, do not hear the Spirit, and thereby face Christ's judgment, which brings them to knowledge. (2) In 2.24, γινώσκω ('I know') appears to describe those who do not know (ἔγνωσαν) 'the deep things of Satan' implying that those who know the deep things of Satan have not discerned by the Spirit. (3) In 3.3, the church again does not know (ἔγνωσαν) the hour when Jesus will come, revealing a lack of (heavenly?) knowledge. (4) Revelation 3.9 closely parallels 2.23 where the Jews will be judged in order that they will know (γνῶσιν) that Jesus loves the church meaning that they did not hear the Spirit, did not discern, and thereby Christ will judge them. If γινώσκω ('I know') carries with it a negative implication, then the judgment upon the church is all the more critical because all those in the churches, who cannot discern the false teachings of Jezebel, come to know something about Christ through judgment.

Therefore, it seems that Revelation connects οἶδα ('I know') with heavenly or cosmic knowledge based on the emphasis found in the repetitions of 'I know' (οἶδα) where Jesus is the subject, and the association with: overcomers, the elder's knowledge, the harsh critique of the Laodicean's lack of knowledge, and Satan's knowledge. It also seems that γινώσκω ('I know') is associated with knowledge of those who did not discern in the church, or more generally, humanity's incomplete knowledge. The church does not know the hour of his coming; some do not know the deep things of Satan; and finally, undiscerning knowledge will bring judgment.

# BIBLIOGRAPHY

## Early Pentecostal Periodicals

*The Apostolic Evangel* (J.H. King, Falcon, NC)
*The Apostolic Faith* (Azusa Street Mission, Los Angeles, CA)
*The Bridegroom's Messenger* (The Pentecostal Mission, Atlanta, GA)
*The Christian Evangel* (Assemblies of God, Plainfield, IN; Findley, OH)
*The Church of God Evangel* (Church of God, Cleveland, TN)
*The Latter Rain Evangel* (Stone Church, Chicago, IL)
*The Pentecost* (J. Roswell Flower, Indianapolis, IN)
*The Pentecostal Holiness Advocate* (Pentecost Holiness Church, Falcon, NC)
*The Whole Truth* (Church of God in Christ, Argenta, AR)
*Weekly Evangel* (Assemblies of God, St. Louis, MO; Springfield, MO)
*Word and Witness* (E.N. Bell, Malvern, AR; Findley, OH; St. Louis, MO)

## Other Works Cited

Achtemeier, P.J., 'Revelation 5:1-14', *Int* 40.3 (1986), pp. 283-88.
Alexander, K.E., *Pentecostal Healing: Models in Theology and Practice* (JPTSup 29; Dorset: Deo Publishing, 2006).
Alexander, P., 'Speaking in the Tongues of Nonviolence: American Pentecostals, Pacifism, and Nationalism', *BLT* 57.1 (2012), pp. 1-16.
Alkier, S., 'Intertextuality Based on Categorical Semiotics', in B.J. Oropeza and S. Moyise (eds.), *Exploring Intertextuality: Diverse Strategies for New Testament Interpretation of Texts* (Eugene, OR: Cascade Books, 2016), pp. 128-49.
Allen, G., *Intertextuality* (London: Routledge, 2nd edn, 2000, 2011).
Allo, E.B., *L'Apocalypse* (Paris: Lecoffre, 1921).

Anderson, A., *An Introduction to Pentecostalism: Global Charismatic Christianity* (Cambridge: Cambridge University Press, 2004).

Andrew of Caesarea, 'Commentary on the Apocalypse', in T.C. Oden (ed.), *Greek Commentaries on Revelation* (trans. W.C. Weinrich; Madison, WI: InterVarsity Press), pp. 113-208.

Apringius of Beja, 'Tractate on the Apocalypse', *ACC*, XII.

Archer, K.J., *A Pentecostal Hermeneutic for the Twenty-First Century: Spirit, Scripture, and Community* (JPTSup 28; New York, NY: T&T Clark, 2004).

—'Pentecostal Story: The Hermeneutical Filter for the Making of Meaning', *Pneuma* 26.1 (2004), pp. 36-59.

—'A Pentecostal Way of Doing Theology: Method and Manner', *IJST* 9.3 (2007), pp. 301-14.

—*A Pentecostal Hermeneutic: Spirit, Scripture and Community* (Cleveland, TN: CPT Press, 2009).

Archer, M., '*I Was in the Spirit on the Lord's Day': A Pentecostal Engagement with Worship in the Apocalypse* (Cleveland, TN: CPT Press, 2015).

Arrington, F.L., 'Hermeneutics', in *DPCM*, pp. 376-89.

Augustine, D.C., 'Pentecostal Communal Economics and the Household of God', *JPT* 19.2 (2010), pp. 219-42.

Augustine, D.C., *et al.*, 'Experience in Christian Faith and Life: Worship, Discipleship, Discernment, Community, and Justice', *Report of the Reformed-Pentecostal Dialogue* 63.1 (2013), pp. 2-44.

Aune, D.E., 'The Prophetic Circle of John of Patmos and the Exegesis of Revelation 22:16', *JSNT* 37 (1989), pp. 103-16.

—*Revelation 1–5* (WBC; Dallas, TX: Word Books, 1997).

—*Revelation 6–16* (WBC; Nashville, TN: Thomas Nelson, 1998).

—*Revelation 17–22* (WBC; Nashville, TN: Thomas Nelson, 1998).

Bacchiocchi, S., *From Sabbath to Sunday: A Historical Investigation of the Rise of Sunday Observance in Early Christianity* (Rome, Italy: Pontifical Gregorian University Press, 1977).

Baines, M.C., 'The Identity and Fate of the Kings of the Earth in the Book of Revelation', *RTR* 75.2 (2016), pp. 73-88.

Bandstra, A.J., '"A Kingship and Priests": Inaugurated Eschatology in the Apocalypse', *CTJ* 27.1 (1992), pp. 10-25.

Barker, M., 'Enthronement and Apotheosis: The Vision in Revelation 4-5', in P.J. Harland and R. Hayward (eds.), *New Heaven and New Earth: Prophecy and the Millennium: Essays in Honor of Anthony Gelston* (The Netherlands: Brill, 1999), pp. 217-27.

Barr, D.L., *Tales of the End: A Narrative Commentary on the Book of Revelation* (Santa Rosa, CA: Polebridge Press, 1998).

Bauckham, R., 'The Role of the Spirit in the Apocalypse', *EQ* 52.2 (1980), pp. 66-83.

—'The Lord's Day', in D.A. Carson (ed.), *From Sabbath to Lord's Day: A Biblical, Historical and Theological Investigation* (Grand Rapids, MI: Zondervan, 1982), pp. 222-50.

—'The List of the Tribes in Revelation 7 Again', *NTS* 42 (1991), pp. 99-115.

—*The Climax of Prophecy* (New York, NY: T&T Clark, 1993).

—*The Theology of the Book of Revelation* (Cambridge: Cambridge University Press, 1993).

—'Review of Robby Waddell, *The Spirit of the Book of Revelation*', *JPT* 17.1 (2008), pp. 3-8.

Baynes, L., 'Revelation 5:1 and 10:2a, 8-10 in the Earliest Greek Tradition: A Response to Richard Bauckham', *JBL* 129.4 (2010), pp. 801-16.

Beale, G.K., *The Use of Daniel in Jewish Apocalyptic Literature and in the Revelation of St. John* (Lanham, MD: University Press of America, 1984).

—*John's Use of the Old Testament in Revelation* (JSNTSup 166; Sheffield: Sheffield Academic Press, 1998).

Beale, G.K., *The Book of Revelation: A Commentary on the Greek Text* (NIGTC; Grand Rapids, MI: Eerdmans, 1999).

Beasley-Murray, G.R., *The Book of Revelation* (NCBC; London: Marshall, Morgan, & Scott, 1974).

Beckwith, I., *The Apocalypse of John* (New York, NY: Macmillan Company, 1919).

Bede the Venerable, 'The Exposition of the Apocalypse', in W.C. Weinrich (ed.), *Latin Commentaries on Revelation* (trans. W.C. Weinrich; Downers Grove, IL: InterVarsity Press), pp. 110-95.

Biguzzi, G., 'The Chaos of Rev 22,6-21 and Prophecy in Asia', *Biblica* 83.2 (2002), pp. 193-210.

Blount, B.K., *Revelation* (NTL; Louisville, KY: Westminster John Knox Press, 2009).

Boesak, A.A., *Comfort and Protest* (Philadelphia, PA: Westminster Press, 1987).

Boring, M.E., *Revelation* (Interpretation; Louisville, KY: Westminster John Knox Press, 2011).

Boxall, I., *The Revelation of St. John* (BNTC; Peabody, MA: Hendrickson, 2006).

Boxall, I., and R. Tresley (eds.), *The Book of Revelation and Its Interpreters: Short Studies and an Annotated Bibliography* (Lanham, MD: Rowman & Littlefield, 2016).

Braumann, G., 'ψῆφος', *TDNT*, IX, pp. 604-607.

Bridges Johns, C., *Pentecostal Formation: A Pedagogy Among the Oppressed* (JPTSup 2; Sheffield: Sheffield Academic Press, 1993).

—'Grieving, Brooding, and Transforming: The Spirit, the Bible, and Gender', *JPT* 23 (2014), pp. 141-53.

Brownlee, W.H., 'The Priestly Character of the Church in the Apocalypse', *NTS* 5 (1958–59), pp. 224-25.

Bruce, F.F., 'The Spirit in the Apocalypse', in B. Lindars and S. Smalley (eds.), *Christ and Spirit in the New Testament: Studies in Honour of Charles Francis Digby Moule* (Cambridge: Cambridge Press, 1973), pp. 333-44.

Brueggemann, W., 'The Costly Loss of Lament', *JSOT* 11.36 (1986), pp. 57-71.

—*1 & 2 Kings* (S&HBC; Macon, GA: Smyth & Helwys Publishing, 2000).

Bryant, H.O., *Spirit Christology in the Christian Tradition: From the Patristic Period to the Rise of Pentecostalism in the Twentieth Century* (Cleveland, TN: CPT Press, 2015).

Caird, G.B., *The Revelation of Saint John* (BNTC; Peabody, MA: Hendrickson, 1966).

Campbell, G., 'Findings, Seals, Trumpets, and Bowls: Variations upon the Theme of Covenant Rupture and Restoration in the Book of Revelation', *WTJ* 66.1 (2004), pp. 71-96.

Cartledge, M.J., 'Charismatic Prophecy: A Definition and Description', *JPT* 2.5 (1994), pp. 79-120.

—'Text-Community-Spirit: The Challenges Posed by Pentecostal Theological Method to Evangelical Theology', in K.L. Spawn and A.T. Wright (eds.), *Spirit and Scripture: Exploring a Pneumatic Hermeneutic* (London: T&T Clark, 2012), pp. 130-42.

Charles, J.D., 'An Apocalyptic Tribute to the Lamb (Rev 5:1-14)', *JETS* 34.4 (1991), pp. 461-73.

Charles, R.H., *A Critical and Exegetical Commentary on The Revelation of St. John* (ICC; Edinburgh: T&T Clark, 1920).

Cheung, P.W., 'The Mystery of Revelation 17:5 & 7: A Typological Entrance', *Jian Dao* 18 (2002), pp. 1-19.

Coleman, R.L., 'The Lukan Beatitudes (Luke 6.20-26) in the Canonical Choir: A 'Test Case' for John Christopher Thomas' Hermeneutical Proposal', *JPT* 26.1 (2017), pp. 48-67.

Collins, J.J., 'Towards the Morphology of a Genre: Introduction', *Semeia* 14 (1979), pp. 1-20.

Colson, F.H., 'Triangluar Numbers in the New Testament', *JTS* 16.61 (1914), pp. 67-76.

Corell, A., 'The 144,000 Sealed', in M. Parvio, E. Segelberg and J.L. Womer (eds.), *Ecclesia, Leiturgia, Ministerium: Studia in Honorem Toivo Harjunpää* (Helsinki: Loimaan Kirjapaino, 1977), pp. 28-43.

Cox, H., *Fire From Heaven: The Rise of Pentecostal Spirituality and the Reshaping of Religion in the Twenty-First Century* (Reading, MA: Addison-Wesley, 1995).

Cruz, V.P., 'The Beatitudes of the Apocalypse: Eschatology and Ethics', in R.A. Muller and M. Shuster (eds.), *Perspectives on Christology: Essays in Honor of Paul K. Jewett* (Grand Rapids, MI: Zondervan, 1991), pp. 269-83.

Culpepper, R.A., 'Designs for the Church in the Imagery of John 21:1-14', in J. Frey, *et al.* (eds.), *Imagery in the Gospel of John: Terms, Forms, Themes, and Theology of Johannine Figurative Language* (Tübingen: Mohr Siebeck, 2006), pp. 369-402.

Dalrymple, R., 'The Use of καί in Revelation 11,1 and the Implications for the Identification of the Temple, the Altar, and the Worshippers', *Biblica* 87.3 (2006), pp. 387-94.

Davies, A., 'What Does it Mean to Read the Bible as a Pentecostal', *JPT* 18 (2009), pp. 216-29.

Day, J., 'The Origin of Armageddon: Revelation 16:16 as an Interpretation of Zechariah 12:11', in S.E. Porter, P. Joyce and D. Orton (eds.), *Crossing the Boundaries: Essays in Biblical Interpretation in Honour of Michael D. Goulder* (Leiden: Brill, 1994), pp. 315-26.

de Smidt, K., 'The Holy Spirit in the Book of Revelation – Nomenclature', *NeoT* 28.1 (1994), pp. 229-44.

—'Hermeneutical Perspectives on the Spirit in the Book of Revelation', *JPT* 14 (1999), pp. 27-47.

de Villiers, P.G.R., 'Prime Evil and its Many Faces in the Book of Revelation', *NeoT* 34.1 (2000), pp. 57-85.

—'The Composition of Revelation 14:1–15:8: Pastiche or Perfect Pattern?', *NeoT* 38.2 (2004), pp. 209-49.

—'Communal Discernment in the Early Church', *Acta Theologica* 17 (2013), pp. 132-55.

Decock, P.B., 'Hostility Against the Wealth of Babylon: Revelation 17:1–19:10', in J.T. Fitzgerald, F.J. van Rensburg and H.F. van Rooy (eds.), *Animosity, The Bible, and Us: Some European, North American, and South African Perspectives* (Atlanta, GA: SBL, 2009), pp. 263-86.

Deissmann, A., *Light from the Ancient East* (Ann Arbor, MI: Baker Book House, 1978).

Dempster, M.W., 'Reassessing the Moral Rhetoric of Early American Pentecostal Pacifism', *Crux* 26.1 (1990), pp. 23-36.

deSilva, D.A., 'The "Image of the Beast" and the Christians in Asia Minor: Escalation of Sectarian Tension in Revelation 13', *Trinity Journal* 12.2 (1991), pp. 185-208.

—'A Sociorhetorical Interpretation of Revelation 14:6-13: A Call to Act Justly Toward the Just and Judging God', *BBR* 9 (1999), pp. 65-117.

—'Final Topics: The Rhetorical Functions of Intertexture in Revelation 14:14–16:21', in F.W. Duane (ed.), *Intertexture of Apocalyptic Discourse in the New Testament* (Atlanta: SBL, 2002), pp. 215-41.

—'Out of Our Minds? Appeals to Reason (Logos) in the Seven Oracles of Revelation 2–3', *JSNT* 31.2 (2008), pp. 123-55.

—*Seeing Things John's Way: The Rhetoric of the Book of Revelation* (Louisville, KY: Westminster John Knox Press, 2009).

Dix, G.H., 'The Seven Archangels and the Seven Spirits', *JTS* 28 (1926), pp. 233-50.

du Rand, J.A., 'The New Jerusalem as Pinnacle of Salvation: Text (Rev 21:1-22:5) and Intertext', *NeoT* 38.2 (2004), pp. 275-302.

Duff, P.B., *Who Rides the Beast?: Prophetic Rivalry and the Rhetoric of Crisis in the Churches of the Apocalypse* (Oxford: Oxford University Press, 2001).

—'Wolves in Sheep's Clothing: Literary Opposition and Social Tension in the Revelation of John', in D.L. Barr (ed.), *Reading the Book of Revelation* (Atlanta, GA: SBL, 2003), pp. 65-79.

Dunn, J.D.G., 'Discernment of Spirits – A Neglected Gift', in *The Christ & The Spirit: Pneumatology* (Grand Rapids, MI: Eerdmans, 1979, 1998), II, pp. 311-28.

Ellington, S.A., 'Pentecostalism and the Authority of Scripture', *JPT* 9 (1996), pp. 16-38.

—'The Costly Loss of Testimony', *JPT* 8.16 (2000), pp. 48-59.

—'"Can I Get a Witness": The Myth of Pentecostal Orality and the Process of Traditioning in the Psalms', *JPT* 20.1 (2011), pp. 1-14.

Elliott, S.M., 'Who Is Addressed in Revelation 18:6-7', *Biblical Research* 40 (1995), pp. 98-113.

Ellul, J., *Apocalypse: The Book of Revelation* (trans. G.W. Schreiner; New York, NY: The Seabury Press, 1977).

Emmerson, R.K., and B. McGinn (eds.), *The Apocalypse in the Middle Ages* (Ithaca, NY: Cornell University Press, 1992).

Enroth, A.-M., 'The Hearing Formula', *NTS* 36 (1990), pp. 598-608.

Ervin, H., 'Hermeneutics: A Pentecostal Option', *Pneuma* 3.2 (1981), pp. 11-25.

Farmer, R., 'Divine Power in the Apocalypse to John: Revelation 4–5 in Process Hermeneutic', *SBL Seminar Papers* 32 (1993), pp. 70-103.

Faupel, D.W., *The Everlasting Gospel: The Significance of Eschatology in the Development of Pentecostal Thought* (JPTSup 10; Sheffield: Sheffield Academic Press, 1996).

Fee, G.D., *Revelation* (NCCS; Eugene, OR: Cascade, 2011).

Fekkes, J., *Isaiah and Prophetic Tradition in the Book of Revelation: Visionary Antecedents and their Development* (JSNTSup 93; Sheffield: Sheffield Academic Press, 1994).

Felix-Jager, S., 'Inspiration and Discernment in Pentecostal Aesthetics', *JPT* 23.1 (2014), pp. 85-104.

Ferguson, E., 'Angels of the Churches in Revelation 1–3: Status Quaestionis and Another Proposal', *BBR* 21.3 (2011), pp. 371-86.

—'Some Patristic Interpretations of the Angels of the Churches (Apocalypse 1–3)', *Studia Patristica* 63 (2013), pp. 95-100.

Filho, J.A., 'The Apocalypse of John as an Account of a Visionary Experience: Notes on the Book's Structure', *JSNT* 25.2 (2002), pp. 213-34.

Fish, S., *Is There A Text in This Class? The Authority of Interpretative Communities* (Cambridge, MA: Harvard University Press, 1980).

Foerster, W., 'θηρίον', *TDNT* (1965), III, pp. 133-35.

Ford, J.M., 'For the Testimony of Jesus is the Spirit of Prophecy', *ITQ* 42.4 (1975), pp. 285-92.

—*Revelation* (ABC 38; Garden City, NY: Doubleday & Company, 1975).

Fowl, S.E., *Engaging Scripture: A Model for Theological Interpretation* (Eugene, OR: Wipf & Stock, 1998).

Friesen, S.J., 'Myth and Symbolic Resistance in Revelation 13', *JBL* 123.2 (2004), pp. 281-313.

Fuller, J.W., '"I Will Not Erase his Name from the Book of Life" (Revelation 3:5)', *JETS* 26.3 (1983), pp. 297-306.

Gallusz, L., *The Throne Motif in the Book of Revelation* (LNTS 487; London: T&T Clark, 2014).

Gause, R.H., *Revelation: God's Stamp of Sovereignty on History* (Cleveland, TN: Pathway Press, 1983).

Giblin, C.H., 'Revelation 11.1-13: Its Form, Function and Contextual Integration', *NTS* 30 (1984), pp. 433-59.

Gilbertson, M., *God and History in the Book of Revelation: New Testament Studies in Dialogue with Pannenberg and Moltmann* (SNTS Monograph Series 124; Cambridge: Cambridge University Press, 2003).

Glancy, J.A., and S.D. Moore, 'How Typical a Roman Prostitute is Revelation's "Great Whore"?', *JBL* 130.3 (2011), pp. 551-69.

Goldingay, J., *Models for Scripture* (Grand Rapids, MI: Eerdmans, 1994).

—*Daniel* (WBC; Nashville, TN: Thomas Nelson, 1996).

—'Authority of Scripture', *DBCI* (New York, NY: Routledge, 2007), pp. 30-32.

González, C.G., and J.L. González, *Revelation* (Louisville, KY: Westminster John Knox Press, 1997).

Gorman, M.J., *Reading Revelation Responsibly: Uncivil Worship and Witness: Following the Lamb into New Creation* (Eugene, OR: Cascade, 2011).

Gorringe, T.J., *Discerning Spirit: A Theology of Revelation* (Philadelphia, PA: Trinity Press, 1990).

Grabiner, S., *Revelation's Hymns: Commentary on the Cosmic Conflict* (LNTS 511; New York, NY: T&T Clark, 2015).

Green, C.E.W., *Toward a Pentecostal Theology of the Lord's Supper: Foretasting the Kingdom* (Cleveland, TN: CPT Press, 2012).

—*Sanctifying Interpretation: Vocation, Holiness, and Scripture* (Cleveland, TN: CPT Press, 2015).

Green, J.B., *Practicing Theological Interpretation: Engaging Biblical Texts for Faith and Formation* (Grand Rapids, MI: Baker Academic, 2011).

Gregory, P.F., 'Its End is Destruction: Babylon the Great in the Book of Revelation', *CTQ* 73.2 (2009), pp. 137-53.

Gulley, N., 'Revelation 4 and 5: Judgment or Inauguration?', *JATS* 8.1-2 (1997), pp. 59-81.

Gumerlock, F.X., 'Nero Antichrist: Patristic Evidence for the Use of Nero's Naming in Calculating the Number of the Beast (Rev 13:18)', *WTJ* 68.2 (2006), pp. 347-60.

Gundry, R.H., 'The New Jerusalem: People as Place, Not Place for People', *NovT* 29.3 (1987), pp. 254-64.

Hays, R.B., 'Reading the Bible with Eyes of Faith: The Practice of Theological Exegesis', *JTI* 1.1 (2007), pp. 5-21.

Hemer, C.J., *The Letters to the Seven Churches* (JSNTSup 11; Sheffield: Sheffield Academic Press, 1986).

Herms, R., *An Apocalypse for the Church and for the World: The Narrative Function of Universal Language in the Book of Revelation* (Berlin: de Gruyter, 2006).

—'Invoking the Spirit and Narrative Intent in John's Apocalypse', in K.L. Spawn and A.T. Wright (eds.), *Spirit and Scripture: Examining a Pneumatic Hermeneutic* (London: T&T Clark, 2012), pp. 99-114.

—πνευματικῶς and Antagonists in Revelation 11 Reconsidered', in G.V. Allen, I. Paul, and S.P. Woodman (eds.), *The Book of Revelation: Currents in British Research on the Apocalypse* (WUZNT; Tübingen: Mohr Siebeck, 2015), pp. 133-46.

Hill, D., 'Prophecy and Prophets in the Revelation of St. John', *NTS* 18 (1971–1972), pp. 401-18.

Hillers, D.R., 'Revelation 13:18 and a Scroll from Murabba'at', *BASOR* 170 (1963), p. 65.

Hillyer, N., '"The Lamb" in the Apocalypse', *EQ* 39.4 (1967), pp. 228-36.

Hollenweger, W.J., 'Pentecostals and the Charismatic Movement', in C. Jones, G. Wainwright and E. Yarnold (eds.), *The Study of Spirituality* (New York, NY: Oxford University Press, 1986), pp. 549-53.

—*The Pentecostals* (Peabody, MA: Hendrickson, 1988).

Horton, S.M., *What the Bible Says About the Holy Spirit* (Springfield, MO: Gospel Publishing House, 1976).

Howard-Brook, W., and A. Gwyther, *Unveiling Empire: Reading Revelation Then and Now* (The Bible & Liberation Series; Maryknoll, NY: Orbis Books, 1999).

Hurtado, L.W., 'Revelation 4–5 in the Light of Jewish Apocalyptic Analogies', *JSNT* 25 (1985), pp. 105-24.

Irenaeus, 'Against Heresies', in P. Schaff (ed.), *The Complete Ante-Nicene & Nicene and Post-Nicene Church Fathers Collection* (Catholic Way Publishing, Kindle edn).

Jackson, A.R., 'Wesleyan Holiness and Finished Work Pentecostal Interpretations of Gog and Magog Biblical Texts', *JPT* 25.2 (2016), pp. 168-83.

Jauhiainen, M., 'The Measuring of the Santurary Reconsidered (Rev 11,1-2)', *Biblica* 83.4 (2002), pp. 507-26.

—'The OT Background to Armageddon (Rev 16:16) Revisited', *NovT* 47.4 (2005), pp. 380-93.

—*The Use of Zechariah in Revelation* (Tübingen: Mohr Siebeck, 2005).

Jenson, R.W., 'Scripture's Authority in the Church', in E.F. Davis and R.B. Hays (eds.), *The Art of Reading Scripture* (Grand Rapids, MI: Eerdmans, 2003), pp. 27-37.

—*Canon and Creed* (Interpretation; Louisville, KY: Westminster, 2010).

Jeske, R.L., 'Spirit and Community in the Johannine Apocalypse', *NTS* 31 (1985), pp. 452-66.

Johns, J.D., 'Pentecostal and the Postmodern Worldview', *JPT* 7 (1995), pp. 73-96.

Johns, J.D., and C. Bridges Johns, 'Yielding to the Spirit: A Pentecostal Approach to Group Study', *JPT* 1 (1992), pp. 109-34.

Johns, L.L., *The Lamb Christology of the Apocalypse of John: An Investigation into Its Origins and Rhetorical Force* (WUZNT 167; Tübingen: Mohr Siebeck, 2003).

Johnson, A.F., *Revelation* (EBC; Grand Rapids, MI: Zondervan, 1996).

Johnson, D.R., 'The Mark of the Beast, Reception History, and Early Pentecostal Literature', *JPT* 25.2 (2016), pp. 184-202.

Johnson, L.T., *Scripture & Discernment: Decision Making in the Church* (Nashville, TN: Abingdon Press, 1983, 1996).

Kay, W.K., *Pentecostalism: A Very Short Introduction* (Oxford: Oxford University Press, 2011).

Keener, C.S., *Revelation* (NIVAC; Grand Rapids, MI: Zondervan, 2000).

—*Spirit Hermeneutics: Reading Scripture in Light of Pentecost* (Grand Rapids, MI: Eerdmans, 2016).

Kempson, W.R., 'Theology in the Revelation of John' (PhD Dissertation: Southern Baptist Theological Seminary, Louisville, KY, 1982).

Kiddle, M., *The Revelation of St. John* (MNTC; New York, NY: Harper and Brothers, 1940).

King, F., 'Travesty or Taboo?: "Drinking Blood" and Revelation 17:2-6', *NeoT* 38.2 (2004), pp. 303-25.

Kirk, J.R.D., 'Narrative Transformation', in B.J. Oropeza and S. Moyise (eds.), *Exploring Intertextuality: Diverse Strategies for New Testament Interpretation of Texts* (Eugene, OR: Cascade Books, 2016), pp. 165-75.

Klauck, H.-J., 'Do They Never Come Back?: Nero Redivivus and the Apocalypse of John', *CBQ* 63.4 (2001), pp. 683-98.

Koester, C.R., *Revelation and the End of All Things* (Grand Rapids, MI: Eerdmans, 2001).

—'The Message to Laodicea and the Problem of Its Local Context: A Study of the Imagery in Rev. 3.14-22', *NTS* 49.3 (2003), pp. 407-24.

—'Roman Slave Trade and the Critique of Babylon in Revelation 18', *CBQ* 70.4 (2008), pp. 766-86.

—*Revelation: Translation with Introduction and Commentary* (ABYC 38A; New Haven, CT: Yale University Press, 2014).

Koester, H., 'Revelation 12:1-12: A Meditation', in W.H. Brackney and C.A. Evans (eds.), *From Biblical Criticism to Biblical Faith: Essays in Honor of Lee Martin McDonald* (Macon, GA: Mercer University Press, 2007), pp. 138-44.

Kovacs, J., and C. Rowland, *Revelation* (BBC; Malden, MA: Blackwell Publishing, 2004).

Kretschmar, G., *Die Offenbarung des Johannes: Die Geschichte ihrer Auslegung im 1. Jahrtausend* (Stuttgart: Calwer Verlag, 1985).

Kristeva, J., 'Bakhtine, le mot, le dialogue et le roman', *Critique* 33 (1967), pp. 438-65.

—'Word, Dialogue, and Novel', in T. Moi (ed.), *The Kristeva Reader* (New York, NY: Columbia University Press, 1986), pp. 35-61.

Ladd, G.E., *A Commentary on the Revelation of John* (Grand Rapids, MI: Eerdmans, 1972).

Lambrecht, J., 'The Opening of the Seals (Rev 6,1–8,6)', *Biblica* 79.2 (1998), pp. 198-220.

—'Rev 13,9-10 and Exhortation in the Apocalypse', in A. Denaux and J. Delobel (eds.), *New Testament Textual Criticism and Exegesis: FS J. Delobel* (Leuven: Peeters, 2002), pp. 331-47.

Lamp, J.S., 'New Heavens and New Earth: Early Pentecostal Soteriology as a Foundation for Creation Care in the Present', *Pneuma* 36.1 (2014), pp. 64-80.

Land, S.J., *Pentecostal Spirituality: A Passion for the Kingdom* (JPTSup 1; Sheffield: Sheffield Academic Press, 1993).

—*Pentecostal Spirituality: A Passion for the Kingdom* (Cleveland, TN: CPT Press, 2010).

Landrus, H.L., 'Hearing 3 John 2 in the Voices of History', *JPT* 11.1 (2002), pp. 70-88.

Laws, S., 'The Blood-Stained Horseman: Revelation 19,11-13', in E.A. Livingstone (ed.) *Studia Biblica 1978: III: Papers on Paul and Other New Testament Authors* (Sheffield: JSOT Press, 1980), pp. 245-48.

—*In the Light of the Lamb* (Wilmington, DE: Michael Glazier, 1988).

Lenski, R.C.H., *The Interpretation of St. John's Revelation* (Augsburg Publishing House: Minneapolis, MN, 1943).

Levison, J.R., *Filled with the Spirit* (Grand Rapids, MI: Eerdmans, 2009).

Lichtenwalter, L.L., '"Souls Under the Altar": The "Soul" and Related Anthropological Imagery in John's Apocalypse', *JATS* 26.1 (2015), pp. 57-93.

Lieb, M., E. Mason, and J. Roberts (eds.), *The Oxford Handbook of the Reception History of the Bible* (Oxford: Oxford University Press, 2011).

Linton, G., 'Reading the Apocalypse as an Apocalypse', *SBL Seminar Papers* 30 (1991), pp. 161-86.

Longenecker, B.W., 'Revelation 19,10: One Verse in Search of an Author', *ZNW* 91.3-4 (2000), pp. 230-37.

Luan, E.P.C., 'The Acquisition and Use of Wealth: Some Reflections from Revelation 18', *Jian Dao* 41 (2014), pp. 255-98.

Lupieri, E.F., *A Commentary on the Apocalypse of John* (trans. M.P. Johnson and A. Kamesar; Grand Rapids, MI: Eerdmans, 1999, 2006).

Luz, U., *Matthew in History: Interpretation, Influence, and Effects* (Minneapolis, MN: Fortress, 1994).

—'A Response to Emerson B. Powery', *JPT* 14 (1999), pp. 19-26.

Macchia, F., 'Pneumatological Feminist/Womanist Theologies: The Importance of Discernment', *Pneuma* 35 (2013), pp. 61-73.

—'The Spirit of the Lamb: A Reflection on the Pneumatology of Revelation', in C.S. Keener, C.S. Jeremy and J.D. May (eds.), *But These are Written ... : Essays on Johannine Literature in Honor of Professor Benny C. Aker* (Eugene, OR: Wipf & Stock, 2014), pp. 214-20.

Maier, H.O., *Apocalypse Recalled: The Book of Revelation After Christendom* (Minneapolis, MN: Fortress Press, 2002).

Mangina, J.L., *Revelation* (BTC; Grand Rapids, MI: Brazos Press, 2010).

Martin, F., 'Discernment of Spirits, Gift of', *DPCM* (1988), pp. 244-47.

Martin, L.R., *The Unheard Voice of God: A Pentecostal Hearing of the Book of Judges* (JTPSup 32; Dorset: Deo Publishing, 2008).

—'The Function and Practice of Fasting in Early Pentecostalism', *PJT* 96 (2015), pp. 1-19.

Martin, R.F., 'Apocalypse, Book of the', *DPCM* (1988), pp. 11-13.

Mathewson, D., 'A Re-examination of the Millennium in Rev 20:1-6: Consummation and Recapitulation', *JETS* 44.2 (2001), pp. 237-51.

—'The Destiny of the Nations in Revelation 21:1–22:5: A Reconsideration', *TynB* 53.1 (2002), pp. 121-42.

Mayo, P.L., *'Those Who Call Themselves Jews': The Church and Judaism in the Apocalypse* (PTMS 60; Pickwick: Eugene, OR, 2006).

Mazzaferri, F.D., *The Genre of the Book of Revelation from a Source-Critical Perspective* (New York, NY: de Gruyter, 1989).

McIlraith, D., '"For the Fine Linen Is the Righteous Deeds of the Saints": Works and Wife in Revelation 19:8', *CBQ* 61.3 (1999), pp. 512-29.

McKay, J., 'When the Veil is Taken Away: The Impact of Prophetic Experience on Biblical Interpretation', *JPT* 5 (1994), pp. 17-40.

McLean, M.D., 'Toward a Pentecostal Hermeneutic', *Pneuma* 6.2 (1984), pp. 35-56.

McQueen, L.R., *Joel and the Spirit: The Cry of a Prophetic Hermeneutic* (JPTSup 8; Sheffield: Sheffield Academic Press, 1995).

—*Joel and the Spirit: The Cry of a Prophetic Hermeneutic* (Cleveland, TN: CPT Press, 2009).

—*Toward a Pentecostal Eschatology: Discerning the Way Forward* (JPTSup 39; Dorset: Deo Publishing, 2012).

Metzger, B.M., *A Textual Commentary on the Greek New Testament* (Germany: United Bible Society, 1975).

—*The Text of the New Testament: Its Transmission, Corruption, and Restoration* (Oxford: Oxford University Press, 3rd edn, 1992).

—*Breaking the Code: Understanding the Book of Revelation* (Nashville, TN: Abingdon Press, 1993).

Michaels, J.R., *Interpreting the Book of Revelation* (Grand Rapids, MI: Baker Book House, 1992).

—*Revelation* (Downers Grove, IL: InterVarsity Press, 1997).

Miller, K.E., 'The Nuptial Eschatology of Revelation 19–22', *CBQ* 60.2 (1998), pp. 301-18.

Minear, P.S., 'The Wounded Beast', *JBL* 72.2 (1953), pp. 93-101.

—'Ontology and Ecclesiology in the Apocalypse', *NTS* 12 (1966), pp. 89-105.

—*I Saw a New Earth: An Introduction to the Visions of the Apocalypse* (Washington, DC: Corpus Books, 1968).

—'Far as the Curse is Found: The Point of Revelation 12:15-16', *NovT* 33.1 (1991), pp. 71-77.

Mittelstadt, M.W., 'Spirit and Peace in Luke-Acts: Possibilities for Pentecostal/Anabaptist Dialogue Christian Ethics Interest Group', *Didaskalia* 20 (2009), pp. 17-40.

—*Reading Luke-Acts in the Pentecostal Tradition* (Cleveland, TN: CPT Press, 2010).

Moore, R.D., 'A Pentecostal Approach to Scripture', *Seminary Viewpoint* 8.1 (1987), pp. 4-5, 11.

—'Canon and Charisma in the Book of Deuteronomy', *JPT* 1 (1992), pp. 75-92.

—'Deuteronomy and the Fire of God: A Critical Charismatic Interpretation', *JPT* 7 (1995), pp. 11-33.

—*The Spirit of the Old Testament* (JPTSup 35; Dorset: Deo Publishing, 2011).

—'A Pentecostal Approach to Scripture', in L.R. Martin (ed.), *Pentecostal Hermeneutics: A Reader* (Leiden, The Netherlands: Brill, 2013), pp. 11-13.

Moore, R.D., J.C. Thomas, and S.J. Land, 'Editorial', *JPT* 1 (1992), pp. 3-5.

Moore, S.D., *Literary Criticism and the Gospels: The Theoretical Challenge* (New Haven, CN: Yale University Press, 1992).

Morris, L., *Revelation* (TNTC; Grand Rapids, MI: Eerdmans, 2nd edn, 1969, 1987).

Mounce, R.H., *The Book of Revelation* (NICNT; Grand Rapids, MI: Eerdmans, 2nd edn, 1977, 1997).

Moyise, S., *The Old Testament in the Book of Revelation* (JSNTSup 115; Sheffield: Sheffield Academic Press, 1995).

—'Intertextuality and the Study of the Old Testament in the New Testament', in S. Moyise (ed.), *The Old Testament in the New Testament: Essays in Honour of J.L. North* (JSNTSup 189; Sheffield: Sheffield Academic Press, 2000), pp. 14-41.

—'Does the Lion Lie Down with the Lamb?', in S. Moyise (ed.), *Studies in the Book of Revelation* (New York, NY: T&T Clark, 2001), pp. 181-94.

—'Does the Author of Revelation Misappropriate the Scriptures?', *AUSS* 40.1 (2002), pp. 3-21.

—'Singing the Song of Moses and the Lamb: John's Dialogical Use of Scripture', *AUSS* 42.2 (2004), pp. 347-60.

—*Evoking Scripture: Seeing the Old Testament in the New* (New York, NY: T&T Clark, 2008).

—'Models for Intertextual Interpretation of Revelation', in R.B. Hays and S. Alkier (eds.), *Revelation and the Politics of Apocalyptic Interpretation* (Waco, TX: Baylor University Press, 2012), pp. 31-45.

Murphy, F.J., *Fallen is Babylon: The Revelation to John* (Trinity Press: Harrisburg, PA, 1998).

Murphy, R.E., 'An Allusion to Mary in the Apocalypse', *TS* 10.4 (1949), pp. 565-73.

Newport, K.G.C., *Apocalypse & Millennium* (Cambridge: Cambridge University Press, 2000).

Newton, J.K., 'Time Language and the Purpose of the Millennium', *Colloquium* 43.2 (2011), pp. 147-68.

—*The Revelation Worldview: Apocalyptic Thinking in a Postmodern World* (Eugene, OR: Wipf & Stock, 2015).

O'Donovan, O., 'The Political Thought of the Book of Revelation', *TynB* 37 (1986), pp. 61-94.

Oberweis, M., 'Die Bedeutung der neutestamentlichen "Rätselzahlen" 666 (Apk 13:18) und 153 (Joh 21:11)', *ZNW* 77.3-4 (1986), pp. 226-41.

Oecumenius, 'Revelation', *ACC*, XII.

Oropeza, B.J., 'Intertextuality', *OEBI*, pp. 453-63.

Osborne, G.R., *Revelation* (BECNT; Grand Rapids, MI: Baker Academic, 2002).

Parker, S.E., *Led by the Spirit: Toward a Practical Theology of Pentecostal Discernment and Decision Making* (JPTSup 7; Sheffield: Sheffield Academic Press, 1996).

—*Led by the Spirit: Toward a Practical Theology of Pentecostal Discernment and Decision Making* (Cleveland, TN: CPT Press, 2015).

Pattemore, S.J., *The People of God in the Apocalypse: Discourse, Structure, and Exegesis* (SNTSup 128; Cambridge: Cambridge University Press, 2004).

Paul, I., 'The Value of Paul Ricoeur's Hermeneutic of Metaphor in Interpreting the Symbolism of Revelation Chapters 12 and 13' (PhD Thesis: St. John's College, Bramcote, Nottingham, 1998).

—'The Use of the Old Testament in Revelation 12', in S. Moyise (ed.), *The Old Testament in the New Testament: Essays in honour of J.L. North* (JSNTSup 189; Sheffield: Sheffield Academic Press, 2000), pp. 256-76.

—'The Revelation to John', in I.H. Marshall, S. Travis and I. Paul (eds.), *Exploring the New Testament: A Guide to the Letters & Revelation* (Downers Grove, IL: InterVarsity Press, 2nd edn, 2002, 2011), II, pp. 305-32.

Paulien, J., 'Dreading the Whirlwind: Intertextuality and the Use of the Old Testament in Revelation', *AUSS* 39.1 (2001), pp. 5-22.

Phillips, G.A., 'Poststructural Intertextuality', in B.J. Oropeza and S. Moyise (eds.), *Exploring Intertextuality: Diverse Strategies for New Testament Interpretation of Texts* (Eugene, OR: Cascade Books, 2016), pp. 106-27.

Pinnock, C.H., *Flame of Love: A Theology of the Holy Spirit* (Downers Grove, IL: InterVarsity Press, 1996).

—'The Work of the Holy Spirit in Hermeneutics', *JPT* 2 (1993), pp. 3-23.

—*The Scripture Principle* (Grand Rapids, MI: Baker Publishing, 2nd edn, 2006).

—'The Work of the Spirit in the Interpretation of the Holy Scriptures from the Perspective of a Charismatic Biblical Theologian', *JPT* 18 (2009), pp. 157-71.

Powell, M.A., *What is Narrative Criticism?* (Minneapolis, MN: Fortress, 1990).

—'Narrative Criticism', in J.B. Green (ed.), *Hearing the New Testament: Strategies for Interpretation* (Grand Rapids: Eerdmans, 1995), pp. 239-55.

Powery, E.B., 'Ulrich Luz's Matthew in History: A Contribution to Pentecostal Hermeneutics?', *JPT* 14 (1999), pp. 3-17.

Powery, L.A., 'Painful Praise: Exploring the Public Proclamation of the Hymns of Revelation', *Theology Today* 70.1 (2013), pp. 69-78.

Prigent, P., *Commentary on the Apocalypse of St. John* (trans. W. Pradels; Tübingen: Mohr Siebeck, 2001).

Provan, I.W., 'Foul Spirits, Fornication and Finance: Revelation 18 from an Old Testament Perspective', *JSNT* 64 (1996), pp. 81-100.

Quash, B., 'Holy Seeds: The Trisagion and the Liturgical Untilling of Time', in R. Rashkover and C. Pecknold (eds.), *Liturgy, Time and the Politics of Redemption* (United Kingdom, Europe: SCM Press, 2006), pp. 114-63.

Rainbow, P.A., *Johannine Theology: The Gospel, The Epistles, and the Apocalypse* (Downers Grove, IL: InterVarsity Press, 2014).

Ramírez Fernández, D., 'The Judgment of God on the Multinationals: Revelation 18', in L.E. Vaage (ed.), *Subversive Scriptures: Revolutionary Readings of the Christian Bible in Latin America* (Valley Forge, PA: Trinity Press International, 1997), pp. 75-100.

Ramsay, W.M., *The Letters to the Seven Churches of Asia and Their Place in the Plan of the Apocalypse* (Grand Rapids, MI: Baker Book House, 1904, 1963).

Reddish, M.G., *Revelation* (Macon, GA: Smyth & Helwys, 2001).

—'Followers of the Lamb: Role Models in the Book of Revelation', *PRS* 40.1 (2013), pp. 65-79.

Reed, D.A., *'In Jesus Name': The History and Beliefs of Oneness Pentecostals* (JPTSup 31; Dorset: Deo Publishing, 2008).

Rengstorf, K.H., 'ἑπτά', *TDNT*, II, pp. 627-35.

—'μανθάνω', *TDNT*, IV, pp. 390-466.

—'ποταμός', *TDNT*, XI, pp. 595-607.

Resseguie, J.L., *Narrative Criticism of the New Testament: An Introduction* (Grand Rapids, MI: Baker Academic, 2005).

—*The Revelation of John: A Narrative Commentary* (Grand Rapids, MI: Baker Academic, 2009).

Richard, P., *Apocalypse: A People's Commentary on the Book of Revelation* (trans. P. Berryman; Maryknoll, NY: Orbis Books, 1994, 1998).

Rico, S.L., 'Thirsting for God: The Levitical Inheritance Motif in the Apocalypse', *WTJ* 74.2 (2012), pp. 417-33.

Robeck, C.M., 'Discernment: Insight into the Mind of Christ', *Pneuma* 11.2 (1989), pp. 73-76.

—'Discerning the Spirit in the Life of the Church', in W.R. Barr and R.M. Yocom (eds.), *Church in the Movement of the Spirit* (Grand Rapids: Eerdmans, 1994), pp. 29-49.

—*The Azusa Street Mission and Revival: The Birth of the Global Pentecostal Movement* (Nashville, TN: Thomas Nelson, 2006).

Roloff, J., *The Revelation of John* (trans. J. Alsup; Minneapolis, MN: Fortress Press, 1984, 1993).

Rossing, B.R., *The Choice Between Two Cities: Whore, Bride, and Empire in the Apocalypse* (HTS; Harrisburg, Pa: TPI, 1999).

Rotz, C., *Revelation: A Commentary in the Wesleyan Tradition* (NBBC; Kansas City: Beacon Hill Press, 2012).

Rowland, C., *Revelation* (London: Epworth Press, 1993).

—'Revelation', in *The New Interpreter's Bible* (Nashville, TN: Abingdon Press, 1998), XII, pp. 501-736.

Ruiz, J.-P., *Ezekiel in the Apocalypse: The Transformation of Prophetic Language in Revelation 16, 17-19, 10* (Frankfurt am Main: Peter Lang, 1989).

—'Revelation 4:8-11; 5:9-14: Heavenly Hymns of Creation and Redemption', *SBL Seminar Papers* (1995), pp. 217-20.

—'The Politics of Praise: A Reading of Revelation 19:1-10', *SBL Seminar Papers* 36 (1997), pp. 374-93.

Schimanowski, G., *Die himmlische Liturgie in der Apokalypse des Johannes: Die frühjüdischen Traditionen in Offenbarung 4–5 unter Einschluss der Hekhalotliteratur* (Tübingen: Mohr Siebeck, 2002).

—'"Connecting Heaven and Earth": The Function of Hymns in Revelation 4–5', in R.S. Boustan and A.Y. Reed (eds.), *Heavenly Realms and Earthly Realities in Late Antique Religions* (Cambridge: Cambridge University Press, 2009), pp. 67-84.

Schmidt, J., 'Νους und σοφια in Offb 17', *NovT* 46.2 (2004), pp. 164-89.

Schneider, G., 'ἀκούω', *EDNT*, I, pp. 52-54.

Schreiner, T.R., *Magnifying God in Christ: A Summary of New Testament Theology* (Grand Rapids, MI: Baker Academic, 2010).

Schüssler Fiorenza, E., *The Book of Revelation: Justice and Judgment* (Philadelphia, PA: Fortress Press, 1985).

—*Revelation: Vision of a Just World* (Minneapolis, MN: Fortress Press, 1991).

—'The Words of Prophecy: Reading the Apocalypse Theologically', in S. Moyise (ed.), *Studies in the Book of Revelation* (New York, NY: T&T Clark, 2001), pp. 1-19.

—'Redemption as Liberation: Apoc 1:5f and 5:9f', *CBQ* 36.2 (1974), pp. 220-32.

—'Composition and Structure of the Book of Revelation', *CBQ* 39.3 (1977), pp. 344-66.

—'The Followers of the Lamb: Visionary Rhetoric and Social-Political Situation', *Semeia* 36 (1986), pp. 123-46.

—'Babylon the Great: A Rhetorical-Political Reading of Revelation 17–18', in D.L. Barr (ed.), *The Reality of Apocalypse: Rhetoric and Politics in the Book of Revelation* (Atlanta, GA: SBL, 2006), pp. 243-69.

Schweizer, E., 'πνεῦμα', *TDNT*, VI, pp. 332-455.

—'Die sieben Geister in der Apokalypse', *EvT* 6 (1951–1952), pp. 502-12.

Sheppard, G.T., 'Word and Spirit: Scripture in the Pentecostal Tradition – Part One', *Agora* 1.4 (1978), pp. 4-5, 17-22.

—'Word and Spirit: Scripture in the Pentecostal Tradition – Part Two', *Agora* 2.1 (1978), pp. 14-19.

Shuman, J.J., 'Pentecost and the End of Patriotism: A Call for the Restoration of Pacifism among Pentecostal Christians', *JPT* 4.9 (1996), pp. 70-96.

Siitonen, K., 'Merchants and Commerce in the Book of Revelation', in M. Labahn and O. Lehtipuu (eds.), *Imagery in the Book of Revelation* (Leuven: Peeters, 2011), pp. 145-60.

Skaggs, R., and P. Benham, *Revelation* (PCS; Dorset: Deo Publishing, 2009).

Skaggs, R., and T. Doyle, 'Revelation 7: Three Critical Questions', in M. Labahn and O. Lehtipuu (eds.), *Imagery in the Book of Revelation* (Leuven: Peeters, 2011), pp. 161-81.

Smalley, S.S., *Thunder and Love: John's Revelation and John's Community* (Waco, TX: Word, 1994).

—'The Paraclete: Pneumatology in the Johannine Gospel and Apocalypse', in R.A. Culpepper and C.C. Black (eds.), *Exploring the Gospel of John* (Louisville, KY: John Knox Press, 1996), pp. 150-73.

—*The Revelation to John: A Commentary on the Greek Text of the Apocalypse* (Downers Grove, IL: InterVarsity Press, 2005).

Smith, C.R., 'The Portrayal of the Church as the New Israel in the Names and Order of the Tribes in Revelation 7.5-8', *JSNT* 39 (1990), pp. 111-18.

—'The Structure of the Book of Revelation in Light of Apocalyptic Literary Conventions', *NovT* 36.4 (1994), pp. 373-93.

—'The Tribes of Revelation 7 and the Literary Competence of John the Seer', *JETS* 38.2 (June 1995), pp. 213-18.

Smith, J.K.A., 'The Closing of the Book: Pentecostals, Evangelicals, and the Sacred Writings', *JPT* 11 (1997), pp. 49-71.

—*Who's Afraid of Postmodernism?: Taking Derrida, Lyotard, and Foucault to Church* (Grand Rapids, MI: Baker Academic, 2006).

—*Thinking in Tongues: Pentecostal Contributions to Christian Philosophy* (Grand Rapids, MI: Eerdmans, 2010).

Sorke, I.W., *The Identity and Function of the Seven Spirits in the Book of Revelation* (Ann Arbor, MI: ProQuest LCC, 2009).

Spawn, K.L., and A.T. Wright, 'The Emergence of a Pneumatic Hermeneutic in the Renewal Tradition', in K.L. Spawn and A.T. Wright (eds.), *Spirit and Scripture: Exploring a Pneumatic Hermeneutic* (T&T Clark: London, 2012), pp. 3-22.

Spawn, K.L., and A.T. Wright (eds.), *Spirit and Scripture: Exploring a Pneumatic Hermeneutic* (London: T&T Clark, 2012).

Stefanović, R., *The Backgrounds and Meanings of the Sealed Book of Revelation 5* (Berrien Springs, MI: Andrews University Press, 1996).

—*Revelation of Jesus Christ* (Berrien Springs, MI: Andrews University Press, 2nd edn, 2002, 2009).

Stevens, G.L., *Revelation: The Past and Future of John's Apocalypse* (Eugene, OR: Pickwick Publishers, 2014).

Strack, H.L., and P. Billerbeck, *Kommentar zum Neuen Testament aus Talmud und Midrasch* (Munich: Beck, 1926).

Strand, K.A., 'The Witnesses of Rev 11:3-12', *AUSS* 19.2 (1981), pp. 127-35.

—'The Two Olive Trees of Zechariah 4 and Revelation 11', *AUSS* 20.3 (1982), pp. 257-61.

Stronstad, R., 'Pentecostal Experience and Hermeneutics', *Paraclete* 26.1 (1992), pp. 14-30.

Stuckenbruck, L.T., 'Revelation 4–5: Divided Worship or One Vision?', *SCJ* 14 (Fall 2011), pp. 235-48.

Sweet, J.P.M., *Revelation* (TPINTC; Philadelphia, PA: Trinity Press Internation, 1979, 1990).

Swete, H.B., *The Apocalypse of St. John* (New York, NY: The Macmillan Company, 1907).

Synan, V., *The Holiness-Pentecostal Movement in the United States* (Eerdmans: Grand Rapids, MI, 1971).

Tanner, C., 'Climbing the Lampstand-Witness-Trees: Revelation's Use of Zechariah 4 in Light of Speech Act Theory', *JPT* 20 (2011), pp. 81-92.

Tavo, F., *Woman, Mother, and Bride: An Exegetical Investigation into the 'Ecclesial' Notions of the Apocalypse* (Belgium: Peeters, 2007).

Tenney, M.C., *Interpreting Revelation* (Grand Rapids, MI: Eerdmans, 1957).

Thomas, J.C., 'Holy Spirit and Interpretation', *DBCI*, p. 165.

—'Pentecostal Interpretation', *OEBI*, II, pp. 89-97.

—*Footwashing in John 13 and the Johannine Community* (Cleveland, TN: CPT Press, 2nd edn, 1991; 2014).

—'Women, Pentecostals, and the Bible: An Experiment in Pentecostal Hermeneutics', *JPT* 5 (1994), pp. 41-56.

—'1998 SPS Presidental Address: Pentecostal Theology in the Twenty-First Century', *Pneuma* 20.1 (1998), pp. 3-19.

—*The Devil, Disease and Deliverance: Origins of Illness in New Testament Thought* (Cleveland, TN: CPT Press, 1998, 2010).

—'Reading the Bible From Within Our Tradition: A Pentecostal Hermeneutic as Test Case', in J. Green and M. Turner (eds.), *Between Two Horizons: Spanning New Testament Studies and Systematic Theology* (Grand Rapids, MI: Eerdmans, 2000), pp. 108-22.

—'Healing in the Atonement: A Johannine Perspective', *JPT* 14.1 (2005), pp. 23-39.

—'The Mystery of the Great Whore: Pneumatic Discernment in Revelation 17', in P. Althouse and R. Waddell (eds.), *Perspectives in*

*Pentecostal Eschatologies* (Eugene, OR: Pickwick Publications, 2010), pp. 111-36.

—'Pneumatic Discernment: The Image of the Beast and His Number: Revelation 13.11-18', in S.J. Land, R.D. Moore and J.C. Thomas (eds.), *Passover, Pentecost, and Parousia: Studies in Celebration of the Life and Ministry of R. Hollis Gause* (JPTSup 35; Dorset: Deo Publishing, 2010), pp. 106-24.

—*The Apocalypse: A Literary and Theological Commentary* (Cleveland, TN: CPT Press, 2012).

—'"What the Spirit is Saying to the Church" – The Testimony of a Pentecostal in New Testament Studies', in K.L. Spawn and A.T. Wright (eds.), *Spirit and Scripture: Exploring a Pneumatic Hermeneutic* (London: T&T Clark, 2012), pp. 115-29.

—'Revelation', in T.J. Burke and K. Warrington (eds.), *A Biblical Theology of the Holy Spirit* (Eugene, OR: Cascade Books, 2014), pp. 257-66.

—'The Role and Function of the Demonic in the Johannine Tradition', in C.S. Keener, J.S. Crenshaw and J.D. May (eds.), *But These Are Written ... Essays on Johannine Literature in Honor of Professor Benny C. Aker* (Eugene, OR: Wipf & Stock, 2014), pp. 27-47.

Thomas, J.C., and K.E. Alexander, '"And the Signs are Following": Mark 16.9-20 – A Journey into Pentecostal Hermeneutics', *JPT* 11.2 (2003), pp. 147-70.

Thomas, J.C., and F. Macchia, *Revelation* (THC; Grand Rapids, MI: Eerdmans, 2016).

Thompson, L.L., *The Book of Revelation: Apocalypse and Empire* (Oxford: Oxford University Press, 1990).

—*Revelation* (ANTC; Nashville, TN: Abingdon Press, 1998).

—'Spirit Possession: Revelation in Religious Studies', in D.L. Barr (ed.), *Reading the Book of Revelation: A Resource for Students* (Atlanta, GA: SBL, 2003), pp. 137-50.

Tõniste, K.L., 'Measuring the Holy City: Architectural Rhetoric in Revelation 21:9-21', *CBW* 34 (2014), pp. 269-93.

Torr, S.C., 'Lamenting in Tongues: Glossolalia as a Pneumatic Aid to Lament', *JPT* 26.1 (2017), pp. 30-47.

Trafton, J.L., *Reading Revelation: A Literary and Theological Commentary* (Macon, GA: Smyth & Helwys Publishing, 2005).

Treacy-Cole, D., 'Women in the Wilderness: Rereading Revelation 12', in R.S. Sugirtharajah (ed.), *Wilderness: Essays in Honour of Frances Young* (New York: T&T Clark, 2005), pp. 45-58.

Turner, M., *The Holy Spirit and Spiritual Gifts in the New Testament Church and Today* (Peabody, MA: Hendricks Publishers, Revised edn, 1996, 1998).

Twelftree, G., *Christ Triumphant: Exorcism Then and Now* (Sevenoaks: Hodder and Stoughton, 1985).

Vanni, U., 'The Ecclesial Assembly "Interpreting Subject" of the Apocalypse', *RSB* 4.2 (1984), pp. 79-85.

Victorinus, *Commentary on the Apocalypse* (Lexington, KY: CreateSpace Independent Publishing Platform, unknown).

von der Osten-Sacken, P., 'κρατέω', *EDNT*, II, pp. 314-15.

Waddell, R., and P. Althouse, 'The Pentecostals and Their Scriptures', *Pneuma* 38.1-2 (2016), pp. 115-21.

Waddell, R.C., *The Spirit of the Book of Revelation* (JPTSup 30; Dorset: Deo Publishing, 2006).

—'What Time is it? Half-past Three: How to Calculate Eschatological Time', *JEPTA* 31.2 (2011), pp. 141-52.

Wall, R.W., *Revelation* (Peabody, MA: Hendrickson, 1991).

Warner, W.E., 'Publications', *DPCM*, pp. 743-51.

Waymeyer, M., 'The First Resurrection in Revelation 20', *MSJ* 27.1 (2016), pp. 3-32.

Weinrich, W.C. (ed.), *Revelation* (ACC 12; Downers Grove, IL: InterVarsity Press, 2005).

—(ed.), *Greek Commentaries on Revelation* (ACT; Downers Grove, IL: InterVarsity Press, 2011).

—(ed.), *Latin Commentaries on Revelation* (ACT; Downers Grove, IL: InterVarsity Press, 2011).

Wesley, J., 'On the Trinity: Sermon 55', in *Sermons of John Wesley* (May 8, 1775).

Westhelle, V., 'Revelation 13: Between the Colonial and Postcolonial, a Reading from Brazil', in D. Rhoads (ed.), *From Every People and Nation: The Book of Revelation in Intercultural Perspective* (Minneapolis: Fortress Press, 2005), pp. 183-99.

Wilckens, U., 'σοφία', *TDNT* (1971), VII, pp. 465-528.

—'χάραγμα', *TDNT* (1974), IX, pp. 416-17.

Wilcock, M., *The Message of Revelation* (Downers Grove, IL: InterVarsity Press, 1975).

Williams, R., 'Making Moral Decisions', in *Cambridge Companion to Christian Ethics* (Cambridge: Cambridge University Press, 2001), pp. 3-15.

Williamson, P.S., *Revelation* (CCSS; Baker Academic: Grand Rapids MI, 2015).

Wilson, M.M., 'Revelation 19:10 and Contemporary Interpretation', in M.M. Wilson (ed.), *Spirit and Renewal: Essays in Honor of J. Rodman Williams* (JPTSup 5; Sheffield: Sheffield Academic Press, 1994), pp. 191-202.

—*The Victor Sayings in the Book of Revelation* (Eugene, OR: Wipf & Stock, 2007).

Yarbro Collins, A, *The Combat Myth in the Book of Revelation* (Missoula, MT: Harvard Theological Review, 1976).

—*The Apocalypse* (Wilmington, DE: Michael Glazier, 1979).

—*Crisis & Catharsis* (Philadelphia, PA: Westminister Press, 1984).

Yong, A., *Discerning the Spirit(s): A Pentecostal-Charismatic Contribution to Christian Theology of Religions* (JPTSup 20; Sheffield: Sheffield Academic Press, 2000).

—*Spirit-Word-Community: Theological Hermeneutics in Trinitarian Perspective* (Burlington, VT: Ashgate Publishing Limited, 2002).

—'The Holy Spirit and the World Religions: On the Christian Discernment of Spirit(s) "After" Buddhism', *Buddhist-Christian Studies* (2004), pp. 191-207.

—'Discerning the Spirit', *CC* 123.5 (2006), pp. 31-33.

Zimmermann, R., 'Nuptial Imagery in the Revelation of John', *Biblica* 84.2 (2003), pp. 153-83.

# INDEX OF BIBLICAL AND OTHER ANCIENT REFERENCES

## Old Testament

### Genesis

| | |
|---|---|
| 2.7 | 56, 83 |
| 3 | 210, 273 |
| 3.6 | 210 |
| 3–4 | 272 |
| 10.12 | 266 |
| 10.19 | 267 |
| 13.13 | 267 |
| 18.20 | 267 |
| 37.9 | 274 |
| 49.1-12 | 331 |
| 49.8-12 | 235, 236 |
| 49.9-10 | 238 |

### Exodus

| | |
|---|---|
| 15 | 302 |
| 19 | 250 |
| 22.21 | 267 |
| 23.9 | 267 |
| 25.31-40 | 61 |
| 40.4 | 61 |
| 40.24-25 | 61 |

### Numbers

| | |
|---|---|
| 22–24 | 376 |
| 31.16 | 376 |

### Deuteronomy

| | |
|---|---|
| 6.12 | 267 |
| 7.8 | 267 |
| 8.14 | 267 |
| 13.1-11 | 262 |
| 13.5 | 267 |
| 13.10 | 267 |
| 17.16 | 267 |
| 19.15 | 261 |
| 28.68 | 267 |
| 29.23 | 267 |
| 32 | 302 |
| 32.32 | 267 |

### Joshua

| | |
|---|---|
| 1.3 | 150 |
| 10.2 | 266 |

### Judges

| | |
|---|---|
| 5.19 | 306 |

### 1 Kings

| | |
|---|---|
| 3.9 | 286 |
| 10 | 285 |
| 10–11 | 290 |
| 16.31 | 217, 376 |
| 18.4 | 217, 376 |
| 18.13 | 217, 376 |
| 18.19 | 217, 376 |
| 21.5-15 | 217, 313, 376 |
| 21.25 | 217, 376 |

### 2 Kings

| | |
|---|---|
| 9.7 | 217, 376 |
| 9.22 | 217, 325 |
| 9.27 | 306 |
| 9.36 | 320 |
| 19.2 | 217, 376 |
| 23.29 | 306 |

### Psalms

| | |
|---|---|
| 29.10 | 310 |
| 51.14 | 122 |

### Isaiah

| | |
|---|---|
| 1.9-10 | 267 |
| 1.18 | 250 |
| 3.9 | 267 |
| 4.4 | 87 |
| 6 | 234 |
| 6.8-10 | 122 |
| 11 | 163, 236, 240, 331, 356 |
| 11.1-10 | 235, 241, 244 |
| 11.2 | 51-52, 53, 55, 77, 86, 100, 198, 205, 231, 236, 238, 240, 284, 349 |
| 11.2-3 | 158, 176 |
| 11.4 | 236, 375 |
| 11.7 | 236 |
| 11.10 | 236 |
| 13.19 | 267 |
| 19.1 | 267 |
| 19.20 | 267 |
| 25.8 | 250 |
| 31.1-9 | 267 |
| 40.9 | 257 |
| 41.27 | 257 |
| 45.14 | 223, 267 |
| 49.10 | 250 |
| 49.18 | 267 |
| 50.40 | 267 |
| 52.4 | 267 |
| 52.7 | 257 |
| 52.13-14 | 238 |
| 61.1 | 257 |

### Jeremiah

| | |
|---|---|
| 2 | 267 |
| 7 | 267 |
| 15.2 | 67 |
| 17.10 | 219 |
| 22.8 | 266 |
| 23.14 | 267 |
| 34.13 | 267 |
| 42–44 | 267 |

### Lamentations

| | |
|---|---|
| 4.6 | 267 |

### Ezekiel

| | |
|---|---|
| 2.8–3.3 | 235 |
| 2.10 | 79 |
| 3.2 | 79 |
| 16 | 68 |
| 16.46 | 267 |
| 16.46-56 | 267 |
| 16.48 | 267 |
| 16.49 | 267 |
| 16.53 | 267 |
| 16.55 | 267 |
| 16.56 | 267 |
| 20 | 267 |
| 23 | 68 |
| 27 | 323 |
| 27.7 | 267 |
| 29 | 267 |
| 30.13 | 267 |
| 37.1 | 56, 59 |
| 37.3 | 249 |
| 47.1 | 57 |

### Daniel

| | |
|---|---|
| 2 | 243 |
| 2.20-23 | 202 |
| 2.27-30 | 202 |
| 2.47 | 202 |
| 4.8-9 | 202, 204 |
| 4.18 | 202 |
| 5.11-16 | 202 |
| 7 | 68, 274, 275, 276, 356 |
| 7.13 | 199 |
| 8.5 | 202 |
| 8.10-11 | 274 |
| 8.15 | 202 |
| 8.17 | 202 |
| 8.23 | 202 |
| 8.27 | 202 |
| 9.2 | 202 |
| 9.13 | 202 |
| 9.23-25 | 202 |
| 9.27 | 142 |

10.1 202
10.11-12 202
10.14 202
10.20-21 274
11.24-25 202
11.30 202
11.33-35 202
11.35 250
12 274
12.1 250, 274
12.1-2 222
12.1-3 250
12.3 204, 206, 274, 337
12.3-4 202
12.10 202, 285

**Joel**
3.19 267

**Amos**
4.11 267
9.11-12 387

**Jonah**
1.2 266
3.2 266
3.3 266
4.11 266

**Zephaniah**
2.9 267

**Zechariah**
3.9 82
4 52, 53, 55, 57, 61, 62, 65, 76, 81, 83, 92, 93, 100, 160, 205, 240, 244, 260, 356
4.1-4 85
4.1-14 61, 72-73
4.2 65, 87, 91
4.6 61, 205, 240, 260

4.10 81, 86, 158, 24, 356
4.11-14 65, 153
4.14 260
5.1-4 235
12 306
12.10 199
12.11 305
13.2 305
13.2-3 262

**New Testament**

**Matthew**
3.11 73
7.15-20 262
24.11 262
24.24 262
27.33 267

**Mark**
15.22 267
16.9-20 24-25

**Luke**
1.35 197
3.22 198
23.33 267

**John**
1.29 238
2.19-21 258
2.22 357
3.16 208
4.10 250
4.14 250
4.23 200, 233, 250
4.34 257
5.36 256
6 312
6.35 250
6.52-59 210
7.37-39 250
7.39 250, 338
8.17 261

8.44 335
9.39-41 226
10.2 227
10.9 229
10.11 245
10.15 245
10.17 245
11.51 215
12.6 357
12.35 222
13 344
13.28 245
13.37 245
14.6 219, 329, 348
14.17 92
14.26 241, 357
15.13 245
15.26 56, 241
16.4-15 264
16.7 241
16.13 225
17.4 256
17.17 305
17.17-19 259, 294, 326
18.37 227
19.14 238
19.17 267
19.30 255
20.21f 241
21.11 89, 286

**Acts**
1.6-8 232
2 85-86
2.1-4 232
2.3 73
13.6-8 262
15 19, 20, 366, 385, 386, 387, 389, 392
17.22-31 384
21 379

**Romans**
7 356

8 356
12.2 356

**1 Corinthians**
2.10 354
2.10-15 374
2.12-16 361
2.13 357
12.1-3 356
12.3 56
12.8-10 357
14.29 357

**2 Corinthians**
3.17-18 119
4.20-21 232
11.14 374

**Ephesians**
6.12 164

**1 Thessalonians**
5.12 361
5.12-22 361
5.14-22 361
5.19-22 361
5.21 374

**2 Thessalonians**
2.3-12 142

**2 Peter**
2.1 262

**1 John**
1.6-7 222
2.6 222
2.10 88
2.11 222
2.20 259
2.24 363
2.27 88
3.11 363
3.15 122
3.16 245
4 329
4.1 342
4.1-3 262
4.2 56, 342
4.3 165
4.6 342

5.20        88

**3 John**
2           24

**Revelation**
1           109, 127,
            168, 230,
            274
1–3         58, 132,
            195
1.1         80, 194,
            196, 197,
            326, 333,
            342, 347
1.2         72, 264
1.1-8       78, 193,
            196
1.2         245, 265
1.3         195, 196,
            217, 333
1.4         52, 55,
            58, 71,
            86, 197,
            199, 200,
            230, 237
1.4-5       176, 351
1.5         245, 351
1.5-6       198, 293
1.6         258, 338
1.6-7       198
1.7         199
1.8         138
1.9         201, 230,
            245, 265,
            297, 374
1.9-10      137
1.9-20      199
1.9–3.22    78, 193,
            199, 201,
            202, 203
1.10        59, 63,
            200, 201,
            254, 333,
            349, 355
1.11        333, 349
1.12        70
1.12-13     81, 93

1.12-16     162
1.12-18     201
1.14        71, 215,
            227, 244,
            309
1.16        236, 261,
            273
1.17        327
1.19        69
1.20        65, 68,
            93, 127,
            204, 205,
            206, 241,
            255, 260,
            312, 351
2–3         84, 107,
            121, 205,
            228, 337,
            351, 361
2.1         241
2.1-4       178
2.2         138, 225,
            228, 243,
            297, 327,
            393
2.3         297, 375
2.4         217, 375
2.5         327, 375
2.6         122, 327
2.7         65, 336,
            354, 356
2.8         277
2.9         228, 243,
            283, 375,
            376, 394
2.10        159, 232,
            375
2.11        65, 356
2.12        236
2.13        230, 245,
            267, 276,
            293, 375,
            394
2.14        375

2.17        65, 309,
            339, 356,
            394, 395
2.18        73, 227
2.19        217, 225,
            297, 327
2.20        228, 243,
            262, 344,
            375
2.20-21     89
2.21        309
2.22        249
2.22-23     251
2.23        227, 395
2.24        219, 243,
            273, 395
2.25        375
2.26        327, 375
2.28        339
2.29        65, 138,
            356
3           188, 338
3.1         85, 176,
            220, 228,
            237, 241,
            327, 394
3.1-2       375
3.2         221, 327
3.3         306, 395
3.4         294, 306,
            375
3.4-5       247, 309
3.5         232, 339
3.6         65, 356
3.7         236, 327
3.8         223, 225,
            326, 375,
            394
3.9         228, 243
3.10        297, 375
3.11        224, 375
3.12        258
3.13        65, 356
3.14        224, 245,
            262, 293,
            326, 329

3.14-15     313
3.15        226, 327,
            394
3.15-17     375
3.17        225, 228,
            375
3.17-18     283
3.18        309
3.19        227, 251,
            375
3.20        121, 375
3.21        230, 232,
            332, 339
3.22        65, 228,
            356
3.23        313
4           75-76,
            87, 188,
            230, 239,
            244, 301
4–5         75, 158,
            230, 242,
            244, 394
4–11        58
4–22        188, 190-
            191, 195
4.1         223, 229,
            230, 253
4.1–16.2    78, 194,
            229
4.2         59, 76,
            230
4.4         309
4.5         52, 61,
            65, 70,
            76, 85,
            93, 158,
            176, 177,
            237, 241,
            244, 338,
            351
4.6         237
4.8         289, 375
4.8-11      365
4.10-11     235
4.11        375

| Ref | Pages |
|---|---|
| 5 | 79, 87, 92, 98, 234, 235, 238, 242, 243, 248, 249, 254, 352, 353, 357 |
| 5.1 | 79, 234 |
| 5.1-9 | 117 |
| 5.1-10 | 145 |
| 5.4-5 | 248 |
| 5.5 | 233, 235, 237, 362 |
| 5.6 | 65, 86, 93, 158, 176, 205, 216, 232, 233, 237, 239, 241, 244, 245, 277, 331, 351 |
| 5.7 | 69 |
| 5.8 | 55 |
| 5.9 | 257, 283, 320 |
| 5.9-13 | 375 |
| 5.10 | 258 |
| 5.12 | 67, 88, 243, 284 |
| 6 | 165, 188, 258 |
| 6–9 | 79, 245, 252, 254 |
| 6.9 | 265 |
| 6.9-10 | 258 |
| 6.9-11 | 332, 375 |
| 6.10 | 303, 327, 351, 365 |
| 6.11 | 84, 309 |
| 6.17 | 249 |
| 7 | 245, 248, 292, 326 |
| 7.2 | 284 |
| 7.3 | 89, 247, 258 |
| 7.3-4 | 107 |
| 7.8 | 248 |
| 7.9 | 257, 309, 320 |
| 7.12 | 67, 88, 243, 284 |
| 7.13 | 233 |
| 7.13-14 | 235, 309 |
| 7.13-17 | 362 |
| 7.14 | 345, 394 |
| 7.14-17 | 365 |
| 7.15-16 | 250 |
| 7.16-17 | 250 |
| 7.17 | 241 |
| 8 | 258, 282 |
| 8–9 | 245 |
| 8.1 | 61, 269 |
| 8.2-3 | 55 |
| 8.3 | 375 |
| 8.4 | 375 |
| 8.5 | 231 |
| 9 | 258 |
| 9.4 | 89 |
| 9.17-18 | 261 |
| 9.20 | 375 |
| 9.20-21 | 296 |
| 9.21 | 309, 375 |
| 10 | 79, 81, 83, 128, 149, 168, 253, 254, 255, 256, 257, 268, 295 |
| 10–11 | 253, 270 |
| 10.1 | 79, 80, 149, 156 |
| 10.1-11 | 80, 362 |
| 10.2 | 79 |
| 10.6-7 | 246 |
| 10.7 | 128, 255, 257, 312 |
| 10.11 | 320 |
| 11 | 56, 61, 62, 81, 84, 96, 128, 142, 187, 256, 257, 258, 260, 264, 270-71, 272, 300, 315, 352 |
| 11.1 | 70 |
| 11.1-2 | 81, 258, 332, 336 |
| 11.1-13 | 79, 81, 261 |
| 11.2 | 265, 293, 299 |
| 11.3 | 81, 344 |
| 11.3-4 | 259 |
| 11.3-13 | 62 |
| 11.4 | 93, 260 |
| 11.5 | 358 |
| 11.6 | 273, 315 |
| 11.7 | 246, 257, 276, 301, 319, 375 |
| 11.8 | 54, 82, 91, 92, 96, 97, 128, 265, 273, 296, 312, 351, 357 |
| 11.9 | 257, 268, 320, 375 |
| 11.10 | 344, 375 |
| 11.11 | 56, 78, 83, 92, 282, 358 |
| 11.11-12 | 128 |
| 11.13 | 306, 375 |
| 11.15 | 375 |
| 11.15-19 | 269 |
| 11.16-18 | 235 |
| 11.18 | 253, 375 |
| 11.19 | 194, 231 |
| 12 | 271, 272, 274, 275, 290, 307, 308, 310, 333, 378 |
| 12–13 | 272, 362 |
| 12–14 | 271, 299 |
| 12–22 | 58 |
| 12.1 | 127, 194, 300 |
| 12.1-6 | 89 |
| 12.1–16.21 | 194 |
| 12.3 | 300, 395 |
| 12.4 | 274 |
| 12.5 | 188 |
| 12.6 | 267 |
| 12.9 | 243, 301 |
| 12.9-10 | 324 |
| 12.10 | 375 |
| 12.10-12 | 275, 362, 365 |
| 12.11 | 56, 122, 265, 3001, 375 |
| 12.12 | 395 |
| 12.14 | 267 |
| 12.16 | 273 |
| 12.17 | 65, 265, 324, 362, 375, 376 |
| 13 | 67, 90, 93, 142, 166, 167, 182, 188, 191, 264, 275, 280, 290, 295, 302, 309, 318, 333, 347 |
| 13.1 | 181 |
| 13.1-8 | 67 |
| 13.2 | 357, 380 |
| 13.3 | 277, 314, 324, 358 |
| 13.3-4 | 89 |

| | | | | | | | |
|---|---|---|---|---|---|---|---|
| 13.4 | 276 | 14.3 | 57, 294 | 16.13-14 | 84, 325, | 17.11 | 287 |
| 13.4-6 | 375 | 14.4 | 267, 295, | | 344 | 17.14 | 376 |
| 13.5 | 292, 294, | | 375, 376 | 16.13-16 | 305 | 17.15 | 257 |
| | 375 | 14.6 | 257 | 16.14 | 281, 300, | 17.16 | 323 |
| 13.6 | 257 | 14.7 | 269, 375 | | 319, 358, | 17.17 | 257 |
| 13.6-7 | 324 | 14.8 | 89, 265, | | 380 | 18 | 126, 145, |
| 13.7 | 292, 301, | | 299, 307, | 16.15 | 57, 306, | | 167, 290, |
| | 319 | | 309, 313, | | 376 | | 309, 321, |
| 13.8 | 313, 375 | | 321 | 16.16 | 305 | | 322, 323, |
| 13.9 | 67, 279, | 14.9 | 89 | 16.17-21 | 306 | | 335 |
| | 280, 356 | 14.9-11 | 293, 295, | 16.18 | 231 | 18.1 | 321 |
| 13.9-10 | 68, 95, | | 375 | 16.19 | 265, 313 | 18.1–19.10 | 321 |
| | 122, 129, | 14.9-12 | 181 | 16.21 | 231, 307, | 18.2 | 84, 152, |
| | 179, 180, | 14.10 | 299 | | 375 | | 265, 337 |
| | 189, 191, | 14.12 | 375, 376 | 17 | 90, 125, | 18.3 | 323, 375 |
| | 279, 284, | 14.13 | 60, 65, | | 126, 142, | 18.4 | 375 |
| | 385 | | 71, 75, | | 153, 159, | 18.6-7 | 322 |
| 13.10 | 67, 88, | | 84, 297, | | 166, 167, | 18.7 | 375 |
| | 122, 297, | | 303, 329, | | 308, 309, | 18.9 | 375 |
| | 376 | | 351, 375 | | 315, 320, | 18.9-19 | 323 |
| 13.11 | 181 | 14.19 | 298 | | 321, 335 | 18.10 | 321 |
| 13.11-15 | 358 | 14.19-20 | 301 | 17–18 | 125, 167 | 18.11 | 323 |
| 13.11-18 | 87, 262, | 14.20 | 332 | 17.1 | 80 | 18.12-13 | 323 |
| | 344 | 15–16 | 300, 307 | 17.1–21.8 | 78, 194, | 18.14 | 375 |
| 13.12 | 277 | 15.1 | 55, 257, | | 308 | 18.16 | 324 |
| 13.12-15 | 292, 294, | | 301 | 17.2 | 311 | 18.23 | 243, 301, |
| | 324 | 15.2 | 301 | 17.3 | 56, 59, | | 321, 325 |
| 13.13-14 | 281, 300 | 15.2-4 | 302 | | 60, 69, | 18.24 | 324, 375 |
| 13.14 | 243, 277, | 15.3 | 304, 327, | | 230, 267, | 19 | 167 |
| | 301 | | 351, 375 | | 350, 375 | 19.1 | 327 |
| 13.15 | 83, 84, | 15.3-4 | 302, 365 | 17.4 | 308, 324, | 19.1-3 | 326 |
| | 282, 358 | 15.4 | 375 | | 325, 375 | 19.1-10 | 326 |
| 13.15-18 | 375 | 16 | 167, 320 | 17.5 | 89, 125, | 19.2 | 327, 351, |
| 13.16 | 89, 125 | 16.1-8 | 303 | | 126, 265, | | 375 |
| 13.16-17 | 180 | 16.2 | 375 | | 314 | 19.3 | 186 |
| 13.17 | 292 | 16.5-7 | 66 | 17.6 | 375 | 19.4 | 375 |
| 13.18 | 67, 68, | 16.6 | 303, 375 | 17.6-7 | 377 | 19.5 | 375 |
| | 87, 243, | 16.7 | 327, 351 | 17.7 | 125, 313, | 19.6 | 375 |
| | 284, 286, | 16.8-16 | 304 | | 315 | 19.6-8 | 362 |
| | 287, 288, | 16.9 | 307, 375 | 17.7-18 | 362 | 19.7d-8 | 344 |
| | 293, 322 | 16.11 | 307, 375 | 17.8 | 143, 181, | 19.8 | 375 |
| 14 | 295, 296, | 16.12 | 319 | | 314 | 19.9 | 327, 334, |
| | 303 | 16.13 | 86, 181, | 17.9 | 68, 243, | | 342, 348 |
| 14.1 | 107, 283, | | 262, 267, | | 267, 284, | 19.9-10 | 362, 377 |
| | 295, 339 | | 339 | | 315, 322 | 19.10 | 57, 58, |
| 14.2-3 | 301 | | | 17.9-11 | 127 | | 66, 72, |

|  |  |  |  |  |  |  |
|---|---|---|---|---|---|---|
|  | 75, 79, | 20.7 | 257, 380 |  | 342, 345, | **OTHER** |
|  | 83, 84, | 20.7-20 | 332 |  | 348, 362 | **ANCIENT** |
|  | 92, 262, | 20.10 | 262, 267 | 22.6-21 | 78, 194, | **REFERENCES** |
|  | 328, 334, | 21.1 | 234 |  | 342 | **Early Jewish and** |
|  | 344, 362, | 21.2 | 344 | 22.7 | 195 | **Christian** |
|  | 375, 376 | 21.3 | 337 | 22.8 | 362, 377 | **Authors** |
| 19.10d | 72 | 21.5 | 327, 342, | 22.8-9 | 58, 80, 84 | *Ascension of Isaiah* |
| 19.11 | 217, 327, |  | 348 | 22.9 | 362, 375 | |
|  | 330, 376 | 21.5-7 | 339 | 22.10 | 195 | 3.10      97 |
| 19.11-21 | 332 | 21.7 | 339 | 22.10d | 58 | *Didache* |
| 19.11–21.8 | 330, | 21.8 | 375 | 22.11 | 375 | 11           377 |
|  | 334 | 21.9–22.5 | 194, | 22.14 | 345, 375 | 11.7-8     358 |
| 19.12 | 394, 395 |  | 336, 342 | 22.15 | 375 | 11.7-12   263 |
| 19.13 | 330 | 21.9–22.9 | 78 | 22.16a | 58 | 12.1        358 |
| 19.14 | 309 | 21.10 | 56, 59, | 22.17 | 57, 60, | Irenaeus |
| 19.15 | 236, 261 |  | 60, 69, |  | 62, 65, | *Against Heresies* |
| 19.19 | 380 |  | 230, 350 |  | 75, 98, | 5.30.2     291 |
| 19.20 | 160, 181, | 21.17 | 109, 110, |  | 121, 351 | |
|  | 262, 281, |  | 285 | 22.18 | 121, 195 | *Shep. of Herm.* |
|  | 300, 344 | 21.22 | 375 | 22.18-19 | 345, 362 | 11.12-13 358 |
| 19.21 | 236, 261 | 21.27 | 355 | 22.19 | 195 | 11.16      358 |
| 20.3 | 257 | 22.1 | 338 | 22.20 | 58, 66 | |
| 20.4 | 125, 265, | 22.6 | 63, 66, | 22.21 | 58 | *Wis* |
|  | 332, 376 |  | 83, 327, |  |  | 19.14-17  97 |
| 20.5 | 257 |  |  |  |  | |

# INDEX OF AUTHORS

Achtemeier, P.J. 234
Alexander, K.E. 2, 25, 27, 101, 102, 130, 146, 157
Alexander, P. 384
Alkier, S. 5, 9, 38
Allen, G.V. 5
Allo, E.B. 291
Althouse, P. 17
Anderson, A. 11, 12, 13, 14, 15, 16
Andrew of Caesarea 223, 289, 334
Apringius of Beja 198
Archer, K.J. 6, 11, 15, 16, 17, 20, 22, 23, 25, 27, 28, 41, 43, 44, 45, 46, 47, 370, 386
Archer, M.L. 21, 25, 27, 33, 42, 101, 157, 194, 196, 200, 201, 213, 214, 216, 220, 223, 225, 226, 227, 234, 250, 254, 277, 283, 298, 300, 302, 303, 314, 326, 328, 344, 345, 359, 362, 265, 373, 386
Arrington, F.L. 22, 44, 45
Augustine, D.C. 362, 368, 379, 383
Aune, D.E. 38, 39, 50, 75, 197, 201, 202, 203, 207, 213, 218, 219, 220, 222, 226, 231, 234, 235, 245, 247, 249, 250, 258, 259, 261, 262, 265, 268, 269, 280, 281,

282, 284, 285, 303, 309, 310, 311, 316, 320, 332, 337, 342
Bacchiocchi, S. 200
Baines, M.C. 311, 317, 320, 323, 341
Bandstra, A.J. 242
Barker, M. 237
Barr, D.L. 201, 214, 245, 246, 247, 314, 329
Bauckham, R. 29, 50, 59-63, 70, 72, 79, 80, 82, 85, 86, 94, 98, 194, 197, 199, 200, 201, 205, 206, 207, 209, 213, 217, 218, 224, 228, 231, 232, 233, 234, 235, 236, 239, 240, 241, 242, 243, 247, 248, 249, 250, 251, 253, 254, 255, 257, 261, 263, 265, 266, 268, 269, 271, 273, 277, 279, 288, 292, 293, 294, 298, 302, 306, 308, 311, 315, 317, 318, 323, 324, 325, 326, 328, 329, 330, 331, 337, 341, 342
Baynes, L. 235
Beale, G.K. 38, 39, 80, 94, 95, 195, 196, 197, 202, 204, 205, 208, 212, 217, 219, 222, 226, 228, 233, 235, 236, 237, 240, 241, 242, 243, 247, 250, 251, 253, 254, 255, 260, 263, 264,

265, 267, 269, 273, 274, 280, 282, 284, 285, 289, 292, 297, 298, 305, 306, 309, 310, 311, 312, 313, 314, 316, 317, 327, 337, 344
Beasley-Murray, G.R. 197, 202, 206, 221, 232, 241, 242, 265, 269, 282, 291, 312, 317, 323, 335, 343, 344
Beckwith, I. 50, 53, 55, 75, 197, 202, 233
Bede 29, 285
Benham, P. 33, 50, 83-84, 198, 201, 209, 211, 216, 219, 220, 225, 227, 234, 241, 261, 332, 339, 343, 391
Biguzzi, G. 344
Billerbeck, P. 203
Blount, B.K. 198, 205, 219, 232, 233, 239, 246, 249, 259, 261, 262, 273, 274, 282, 303, 313, 330, 331
Boesak, A.A. 246, 290, 342
Boring, M.E. 197, 206, 207, 216, 230, 232, 233, 248, 261, 281, 282, 295, 308, 333
Boxall, I. 32, 221, 223, 227, 231, 233, 247, 250, 256, 279, 281, 293, 295, 299, 301, 304, 307, 308, 312,

315, 317, 322, 326, 331, 332, 336
Braumann, G. 286
Bridges Johns, C. 21, 22, 35, 44, 370
Brownlee, W.H. 203, 204
Bruce, F.F. 50, 55-57, 60, 61, 62, 75, 197, 198, 239, 240, 330
Brueggemann, W. 286, 365, 366
Bryant, H.O. 25, 27
Caird, G.B. 197, 202, 231, 239, 242, 246, 252, 265, 268, 273, 274, 280, 289, 302, 304, 307, 314, 316, 324, 329, 332, 335, 344
Campbell, G. 279
Cartledge, M.J. 45, 348, 360
Charles, J.D. 237, 239
Charles, R.H. 50, 53, 55, 72, 75, 197
Cheung, P.W. 312, 316
Coleman, R.L. 386
Collins, J.J. 194
Colson, F.H. 287
Corell, A. 292, 293
Cox, H. 11, 13
Cruz, V.P. 343
Culpepper, R.A. 287
Dalrymple, R. 258
Davies, A. 35
Day, J. 305
de Smidt, K. 51, 70-72, 75, 197, 329
Decock, P.B. 321, 322
Deissmann, A. 288
Dempster, M.W. 381, 382
deSilva, D.A. 201, 205, 218, 278, 283, 296, 297, 303, 304, 322

Dix, G.H. 52, 53
Doyle, T. 247
du Rand, J.A. 336
Duff, P.B. 226, 273, 313
Dunn, J.D.G. 349, 358, 360, 362, 364, 372
Ellington, S.A. 22, 34, 35, 36, 45, 47, 365, 370, 374
Elliott, S.M. 322
Ellul, J. 276, 284, 291, 308, 310, 338
Emmerson, R.K. 32
Enroth, A.-M. 209, 228
Ervin, H. 17, 23, 29, 30, 34, 44
Farmer, R. 231, 234, 238
Faupel, D.W. 11, 12, 13, 14, 15
Fee, G.D. 33, 198, 207, 216, 220, 224, 238, 239, 268
Fekkes, J. 51, 52, 223, 234, 236, 250
Felix-Jager, S. 368, 373, 385
Ferguson, E. 202, 203
Filho, J.A. 194
Fish, S. 4, 7
Foerster, W. 277, 281
Ford, J.M. 50, 57-59, 72, 238, 302, 310
Fowl, S.E. 6, 358, 361, 368, 373
Friesen, S.J. 272
Fuller, J.W. 221
Gallusz, L. 231, 232, 234, 237, 248
Gause, R.H. 33, 77, 78, 197, 206, 207, 216, 220, 225, 231, 232, 236, 238, 239, 240, 279, 281, 307, 310, 313, 314

Giblin, C.H. 258, 260, 265, 268, 269
Gilbertson, M. 341
Glancy, J.A. 308
Goldingay, J. 34, 36, 37, 204
González, C.G. 218, 227, 299, 310
González, J.L. 218, 227, 299, 310
Gorman, M.J. 322
Gorringe, T.J. 363, 389
Grabiner, S. 233, 243, 300
Green, C.E.W. 11, 17, 21, 25, 27, 28, 44, 47, 353, 354, 355, 359, 363, 367, 368, 369, 371, 372
Green, J.B. 6, 23
Gregory, P.F. 296
Gulley, N. 236
Gumerlock, F.X. 288
Gundry, R.H. 337
Gwyther, A. 223, 277, 294, 295, 321, 323
Hays, R.B. 6, 23, 29, 30
Hemer, C.J. 206, 225
Herms, R. 33, 48, 51, 94-97, 194, 265, 341, 357, 391
Hill, D. 195, 257, 342
Hillers, D.R. 289
Hillyer, N. 238
Hollenweger, W.J. 2, 9, 11, 15, 23, 101
Horton, S.M. 77
Howard-Brook, W. 223, 277, 294, 295, 321, 323
Hurtado, L.W. 231, 232
Irenaeus 291
Jackson, A.R. 25, 332
Jauhiainen, M. 198, 239, 258, 260, 305

Jenson, R.W.  6, 23, 31
Jeske, R.L.  50, 63-65,
  66, 78
Johns, J.D.  16, 21, 35,
  44
Johns, L.L.  235, 238,
  239, 242
Johnson, A.F.  291
Johnson, D.R.  25, 381
Johnson, L.T.  348, 350,
  356, 358, 359, 362,
  363, 366, 367, 368,
  369, 371, 372, 379
Kay, W.K.  378
Keener, C.S.  32, 33,
  197, 200, 201, 208,
  212, 217, 219, 233,
  234, 239, 266, 273,
  305, 316, 325, 330
Kempson, W.R.  194
Kiddle, M.  251, 331
King, F.  312
Kirk, J.R.D.  43
Klauck, H.-J.  280
Koester, C.R.  32, 197,
  199, 206, 208, 210,
  213, 214, 216, 218,
  219, 221, 225, 226,
  231, 232, 233, 234,
  235, 240, 243, 245,
  246, 251, 253, 256,
  257, 258, 260, 261,
  262, 264, 265, 268,
  271, 272, 273, 275,
  276, 277, 278, 279,
  280, 282, 283, 288,
  291, 294, 298, 299,
  300, 301, 303, 310,
  311, 314, 315, 316,
  317, 319, 320, 321,
  322, 324, 325, 326,
  327, 328, 329, 330,
  331, 337, 339, 343,
  344, 345
Koester, H.  273
Kovacs, J.  32, 253

Kretschmar, G.  32
Kristeva, J.  4, 5
Ladd, G.E.  194, 197,
  201, 202, 207, 208,
  221, 241, 255, 257,
  265, 298, 323, 330,
  335, 343
Lambrecht, J.  249, 285
Lamp, J.S.  25
Land, S.J.  9, 16, 17, 23,
  30, 32, 44, 46, 349,
  353, 360, 361, 363,
  364, 369, 373
Landrus, H.L.  24, 29
Laws, S.  240, 331
Lenski, R.C.H.  319,
  328
Levison, J.R.  96, 354,
  358, 364, 382
Lichtenwalter, L.L.
  245, 247, 332
Lieb, M.  24
Linton, G.  195
Longenecker, B.W.  53
Luan, E.P.C.  322, 324,
  326
Lupieri, E.F.  288, 316
Luz, U.  24, 25, 26
Macchia, F.  33, 50, 51,
  87, 97-99, 198, 200,
  210, 224, 225, 228,
  243, 351, 352, 356,
  358, 359, 366, 371,
  377, 391
Maier, H.O.  223, 278
Mangina, J.L.  197, 198,
  203, 204, 207, 219,
  221, 227, 233, 242,
  282, 301, 307, 317,
  318, 321, 327, 332,
  338, 340
Martin, F.  77, 78, 358
Martin, L.R.  21, 25, 29,
  30, 36, 37, 47, 196
Mason, E.  24

Mathewson, D.  332,
  341
Mayo, P.L.  211
Mazzaferri, F.D.  65-66,
  79, 83, 194, 195,
  209, 254, 257, 261,
  329, 343
McIlraith, D.A.  327
McGinn, B.  32
McKay, J.  18, 46, 47
McLean, M.D.  17
McQueen, L.R.  16, 20,
  24, 25, 35, 45, 46,
  47, 108, 146, 169,
  172, 370, 374, 382
Metzger, B.M.  222,
  225, 233, 234, 237,
  240, 288
Michaels, J.R.  194, 196,
  202, 205, 206, 237,
  261, 275, 276, 278,
  301, 303, 314, 318,
  324, 329, 342, 343,
  345
Miller, K.E.  330, 332
Minear, P.S.  82, 96, 97,
  260, 264, 266, 272,
  280, 289, 305, 309
Mittelstadt, M.W.  11,
  15, 385
Moore, R.D.  17, 18,
  21, 361
Moore, S.D.  42, 308
Morris, L.  197, 209,
  232, 253
Mounce, R.H.  197,
  202, 216, 234, 238,
  247, 257, 261, 265,
  288, 299, 306, 309,
  313, 315, 318, 319,
  345
Moyise, S.  38, 39, 40,
  42, 43, 52, 91, 202,
  206, 238, 276, 282,
  302

Murphy, F.J. 208, 212, 218, 225, 230, 238, 245, 247, 248, 250, 257, 263, 276, 277, 293, 297, 303, 314, 316, 327, 329, 332, 337, 339, 342, 343

Murphy, R.E. 272

Newport, K. 32

Newton, J.K. 52, 195, 228, 281, 309, 331, 332, 339, 340, 348, 350, 352, 355, 356, 360, 365, 375, 377, 378, 385

O'Donovan, O. 281, 309

Oberweis, M. 288, 289

Oecumenius 197

Oropeza, B.J. 38

Osborne, G.R. 198, 201, 207, 213, 217, 224, 226, 233, 241, 243, 259, 265, 268, 274, 277, 284, 295, 297, 301, 316, 325, 331, 332, 338

Parker, S.E. 349, 354, 359, 360, 361, 363, 364, 368, 371, 372, 373

Pattemore, S. 245, 246, 247, 248, 249, 250, 261, 275, 279, 283, 293, 294, 295, 296, 337

Paul, I. 40, 195, 272, 290

Paulien, J. 39

Phillips, G.A. 5

Pinnock, C.H. 29, 30, 31, 34, 36, 37, 44, 45, 353, 354, 368

Powell, M.A. 41, 43

Powery, E.B. 24, 25

Powery, L.A. 242

Prigent, P. 197, 199, 204, 210, 212, 216, 225, 233, 240, 261, 284, 294, 314, 328, 331, 342

Provan, I. 21, 309, 322, 323, 324

Quash, B. 241

Rainbow, P.A. 198, 329

Ramírez Fernández, D. 326

Ramsay, W. 206

Reddish, M.G. 226, 238, 278, 293

Reed, D.A. 15

Rengstorf, K.H. 197, 294, 338

Resseguie, J.L. 41, 42, 43, 196, 198, 199, 201, 218, 221, 223, 226, 229, 231, 233, 237, 239, 242, 247, 253, 263, 269, 280, 304, 307, 310, 313, 314, 317, 325, 327, 331, 336

Richard, P. 226, 235, 281

Rico, S.L. 338

Robeck, C.M. 11, 13, 349, 354, 359, 361, 363, 368, 371, 372, 373

Roloff, J. 257, 266, 309, 312, 327

Rossing, B.R. 310, 338

Rotz, C. 285, 344

Rowland, C. 32, 216, 253, 276, 282, 283, 290, 293, 300, 311, 321, 334, 342, 345

Ruiz, J.-P. 38, 40, 51, 66-70, 196, 209, 210, 239, 279, 284, 309, 310, 312, 314, 316,

320, 321, 323, 324, 325, 328, 348

Schimanowski, G. 75-76, 242, 243

Schmidt, J. 316

Schneider, G. 196

Schreiner, T.R. 88-87, 197

Schüssler Fiorenza, E. 195, 200, 202, 206, 217, 242, 246, 258, 276, 278, 282, 283, 292, 293, 294, 296, 298, 303, 309, 313, 327, 330, 336, 337

Schweizer, E. 50, 54-55, 56, 58, 62, 82, 197, 329

Sheppard, G.T. 17

Shuman, J.J. 383, 384

Siitonen, K. 309

Skaggs, R. 33, 50, 83-84, 198, 201, 209, 211, 216, 219, 220, 225, 227, 234, 241, 247, 261, 332, 339, 343, 391

Smalley, S.S. 50, 51 73-75, 196, 198, 201, 202, 203, 207, 209, 211, 213, 216, 218, 219, 222, 226, 227, 233, 234, 247, 248, 250, 251, 255, 257, 258, 259, 261, 265, 267, 269, 273, 274, 280, 281, 284, 288, 289, 290, 292, 293, 298, 301, 303, 306, 307, 308, 310, 311, 312, 313, 316, 317, 320, 321, 326, 330, 332, 333, 338, 343, 344

Smith, C.R. 194, 247

Smith, J.K.A.    17, 34,
    35, 36, 45, 46, 47,
    48, 348, 366, 370,
    371, 373
Sorke, I.W.    50, 84-86,
    209, 298, 305
Spawn, K.L.    23, 44
Stefanović, R.    198,
    200, 201, 207, 216,
    219, 226, 235, 269,
    304, 312, 316
Stevens, G.L.    209, 309,
    321, 324
Strack, H.L.    203
Strand, K.A.    260, 261
Stronstad, R.    47
Stuckenbruck, L.T.
    232, 240, 241
Sweet, J.P.M.    197, 202,
    206, 210, 213, 219,
    221, 227, 230, 231,
    233, 234, 240, 241,
    242, 247, 250, 258,
    265, 273, 279, 281,
    282, 291, 301, 304,
    306, 308, 337
Swete, H.B.    50, 52-53,
    55, 57, 74, 197, 327,
    338
Synan, V.    11, 17
Tanner, C.    51, 93-94,
    260, 391
Tavo, F.    202, 206, 217,
    258, 259, 265, 272
Tenney, M.C.    194, 220
Thomas, J.C.    ix, 8, 17,
    19, 20, 21, 22, 23,
    24, 25, 29, 30, 31,
    32, 33, 41, 44, 45,

46, 47, 50, 51, 87-94,
    96, 97, 98, 99, 194,
    198, 199, 200, 201,
    205, 207, 209, 210,
    214, 215, 217, 225,
    227, 228, 229, 230,
    231, 233, 235, 240,
    241, 243, 245, 247,
    249, 250, 251, 255,
    256, 257, 258, 259,
    260, 262, 263, 265,
    265, 266, 269, 271,
    272, 279, 280, 281,
    284, 285, 287, 293,
    294, 297, 298, 301,
    302, 304, 305, 307,
    310, 311, 312, 314,
    316, 317, 319, 320,
    321, 327, 328, 329,
    330, 331, 332, 335,
    339, 343, 345, 350,
    351, 352, 356, 359,
    360, 363, 366, 377,
    382, 385, 386, 391
Thompson, L.L.    76-77,
    197, 208, 210, 233,
    269, 290, 316, 337
Tõniste, K.L.    337
Torr, S.C.    370
Trafton, J.L.    194, 199,
    212, 221, 240, 249,
    261, 264, 277, 293,
    296, 299, 306, 315,
    319, 323, 324, 325,
    332
Treacy-Cole, D.    272
Turner, M.    349
Twelftree, G.    357, 382
Vanni, U.    266, 334,
    344

Victorinus    198, 204
von der Osten-Sacken,
    P.    206
Waddell, R.C.    1, 4, 5, 6,
    7, 9, 10, 11, 16, 17,
    20, 23, 29, 32, 33,
    35, 37, 38, 39, 40,
    42, 43, 44, 46, 47,
    48, 50, 77-83, 96, 97,
    98, 100, 194, 198,
    232, 240, 253, 254,
    260, 261, 262, 263,
    264, 265, 266, 329,
    359, 391
Wall, R.W.    197, 207,
    222, 232, 240, 249,
    257, 268, 269, 280,
    281, 285, 316, 323,
    330, 331
Warner, W.E.    160
Waymeyer, M.    332
Weinrich, W.C.    32, 288
Wesley, J.    355
Westhelle, V.    278
Wilckens, U.    204, 240,
    248, 288
Wilcock, M.    213, 291
Williams, R.    368, 382
Williamson, P.S.    198,
    205, 216, 227
Wilson, M.M.    51, 72-
    73, 83, 209, 216,
    232, 328
Wright, A.T.    23
Yong, A.    22, 46, 356,
    361, 364, 365, 374,
    382, 385
Zimmermann, R.    336,
    344

Made in the USA
Las Vegas, NV
25 January 2021